SECOND EDITION

CRIMINAL COURTS

Structure, Process, and Issues

DEAN JOHN CHAMPION

Texas A & M International University

RICHARD D. HARTLEY

Texas A & M International University

GARY A. RABE

Minot State University

PEARSON

Prentice
Hall

Upper Saddle River, New Jersey 07458

Library of Congress Cataloging-in-Publication Data

Champion, Dean John
  Criminal courts : structure, process, and issues / by Dean John Champion, Richard D.
Hartley, and Gary A. Rabe. —2nd ed.
    p. cm.
  Gary A. Rabe's name appears first on earlier ed.
  Includes index.
  ISBN 0-13-118979-4
  1. Criminal justice, Administration of—United States.   2. Criminal courts—United
States.   I. Hartley, Richard D.   II. Rabe, Gary A.   III. Title.
  KF8700.Z9R33 2008
  345.73'01—dc22

2006038395

Editor-in-Chief: Vernon Anthony
Senior Acquisitions Editor: Tim Peyton
Associate Editor: Sarah Holle
Editorial Assistant: Jillian Allison
Marketing Manager: Adam Kloza
Production Editor: David Welsh, Carlisle Publishing Services
Production Liaison: Barbara Marttine Cappuccio
Managing Editor: Mary Carnis

Manufacturing Manager: Ilene Sanford
Manufacturing Buyer: Cathleen Petersen
Senior Design Coordinator: Miguel Ortiz
Cover Designer: Eva Ruutopold
Cover Image: Getty Images, Inc. Photodisc
Formatting: Carlisle Publishing Services
Printer/Binder: Courier Westford

Chapter-opening photo credits:
Chapter 1: Mark and Audrey Gibson, The Stock Connection; Chapter 2: Mark Wilson, Getty Images, Getty Images,
Inc.; Chapter 3: Corbis Royalty Free; Chapter 4: Marjorie Knoller (R), Lous Dematteis, Corbis/Reuters America
LLC; Chapter 5: Corbis Royalty Free, © Royalty-Free/CORBIS; Chapter 6: John Neubauer, PhotoEdit Inc.; Chapter 7: A. Lichtenstein, The Image Works; Chapter 8: Frank Siteman, PhotoEdit Inc.; Chapter 9: Tom Fox, AP Wide
World Photos; Chapter 10: Jose L. Pelaez, Corbis/Stock Market; Chapter 11: Douglas C. Pizac-Pool, Getty Images,
Getty Images, Inc.; Chapter 12: Ric Francis, AP Wide World Photos

Pearson Education Ltd.
Pearson Education Singapore, Pte. Ltd.
Pearson Education Canada, Ltd.
Pearson Education—Japan

Pearson Education Australia Pty. Limited
Pearson Education North Asia Ltd.
Pearson Educación de Mexico, S.A. de C.V.
Pearson Education Malaysia, Pte, Ltd.

10 9 8 7 VO13
ISBN: 0-13-118979-4

Dedication

For my three girls, Gerri, Chablis, and Lacey Jane.
Dean John Champion

For David and Donna Hartley, with love, and for numerous
debts that will never be able to be repaid.
Richard D. Hartley

Contents

Chapter 5   Judges   155

Chapter 6   Juries   213

Chapter 7   Pretrial Procedures: Initial Appearance, Bail Decision Making, and Alternative Dispute Resolution   257

Chapter 8   Pretrial Procedures: Plea Bargaining   297

Preface

Criminal Courts: Structure, Process, and Issues (second edition) is about process-ing criminal offenders from the point where they are arrested and charged with crimes. This book provides a comprehensive examination of the trial process whereby one's guilt or innocence is ascertained by either a judge or a jury.

The book begins with an examination of law and its social and political origins. Law is as ancient as time itself. Despite the different periods or eras into which world history has been divided by scholars, the pervasiveness and continuity of law is apparent. Laws have always existed in some form or an-other, but largely intended to fulfill the same general purposes regardless of the culture we choose to examine. The major functions of law are social control, dispute resolution, and social change. Over time, technological changes have occurred and social ideas have evolved that have contributed to how persons should orient themselves to others. Whether law has existed through verbal traditions passed from one generation to another in simple societies or in lengthy compendiums in more complex social systems, the primary objectives of law have remained constant over time.

Laws can be differentiated according to whether they pertain to civil or criminal matters. Statements about what the law says and how we should com-port ourselves when in the company of others have to do with substantive law. In less-complex social systems, substantive law tended to be espoused by the courts in the form of common law. Common law is traditional, dependent upon the particular needs and desires of groups of people living together in cities or towns. As our social systems have become increasingly complex, we have devised more elaborate legal schemes and more formal mechanisms to maintain the social order and regulate human conduct. How the law should be applied is the province of procedural law. In the United States, one of the most complex legal systems has been contrived. Today, there are all types of law pertaining to different aspects of our society. These laws are either civil or criminal, and a whole body of law focuses upon administrative law.

It is a legal reality that applications of the law from the beginning of time have favored particular interests over others. Some persons believe that our laws have been created to preserve the status quo for those who possess political and economic power. Thus, there are inherent disparities existing where applications of the law are implemented. Those suffering the most from legal disparities historically have been women, children, and minorities. In recent decades, sociolegal movements have prompted substantial social changes in response to disparate treatment of minorities and women in the courts. Derived from these movements have emerged different types of sociological jurisprudence, legal realism, critical legal studies, and feminist legal theories.

Understanding the laws of the United States begins with a critical examination and description of the dual court system this country possesses. The principal components of the dual court system are federal and state court apparatuses. Chapter 2 describes federal and state court organization, and various functions of these different types of courts. There are diverse court systems, and there is little continuity among the states concerning what these different courts should be called. We do not have a universal nomenclature that can be applied to all state and local courts at various levels. However, there is considerable continuity within the federal court system. Federal and state court jurisdictions are distinguished, and the processes and functions of different types of courts are described and discussed.

The court work group consists of the same types of actors, regardless of whether we are discussing federal or state jurisdictions. The government has created a prosecutorial system that enforces the laws passed by the different legislatures. Whenever one or more of these laws are violated, prosecutors at the state or federal level act against alleged offenders to bring them to justice. Thus, Chapters 3 and 4 examine prosecutors and defense counsels in some detail, identifying their principal functions and duties. The United States Constitution and the Bill of Rights have vested all citizens with particular rights to ensure that they will be treated equally under the law. All persons who are charged with a criminal offense are entitled to counsel if they are obligated to appear in court to answer criminal charges. Under particular circumstances, anyone may enjoy the right to a jury trial comprised of one's peers. The roles and functions of both prosecutors and defense counsels are examined and discussed.

The most important actor in the court system is the judge. Judges oversee all court proceedings and make important decisions. Several types of systems are used for judicial selection. These systems are described. While legal backgrounds are strongly recommended for those functioning as judges, it is not necessarily true that all judges have legal backgrounds or training. Thus, different methods for selecting judges are explained, together with the weaknesses and strengths of these methods. Merit selection of judges seems to be favored in many jurisdictions, although often the best judges do not gravitate into these important posts. There is a segment of the judiciary clearly lacking the qualifications and commitment to make good decisions. Some judges are corrupt and commit deliberate acts, which call their integrity into question. Judicial misconduct of various kinds will be described, and some of the remedies available to the public for recalling bad judges will be examined.

At the heart of our legal system is the jury process. Juries are comprised of persons from the general population. Methods of jury selection vary greatly among jurisdictions. In fact, juries account for only about 10 percent of all criminal cases that are pursued. Nevertheless, considerable time is devoted to examining the jury process and how jurors are selected to judge the conduct of others. Both prosecutors and defense counsel conduct *voir dires* or oral questioning of prospective juries from a list of veniremen or a *venire*. Sometimes experts are used to assist as consultants, since some persons believe that jury selection can enhance the chances of a conviction or an acquittal. Various methods for discharging prospective jurors are examined, including challenges for cause and peremptory challenges. Various standards among the states and the federal system are described to show that there are different criteria applied for determining the appropriate jury size and the process of jury decision making. The decision-making process of juries is examined in some detail, and the important topics of jury nullification and juror misconduct are explored.

Not all persons charged with crimes are ultimately processed by the criminal justice system. Some persons are diverted to civil courts or into civil dispute resolution programs where their cases can be concluded in noncriminal ways. Victims and offenders are often brought together in alternative dispute resolution actions, where victim compensation and restorative justice are sought as remedies for wrongdoing. For those who are eventually prosecuted criminally for violating the law, the arrest and booking process are described. The issue of bail is discussed. In some states, various laws are being scrutinized for the purpose of changing them and causing criminal acts to become decriminalized through legislative changes. Thus, the process of decriminalization will be examined.

Perhaps the most frequently used resolution strategy for criminal offenders is plea bargaining. Plea bargaining is a preconviction agreement between prosecutors, defense counsels, and their clients where guilty pleas are entered to criminal charges in exchange for some type of leniency. Plea bargaining results in a criminal conviction, but the penalties imposed are often less harsh compared with the penalties imposed through trial convictions. Different types of plea bargaining will be discussed. The pros and cons of plea bargaining are listed. Furthermore, some jurisdictions have abolished plea bargaining, and their reasons for doing so will be examined.

The actual trial process is illustrated. Those charged with crimes may undergo either bench or jury trials, where either a judge will decide their case or a jury will deliberate. The criminal trial process is described in some detail with various fictional scenarios that have paralleled some actual legal cases in the recent past. In any criminal trial, due process requires that we consider any defendant innocent of a crime until proved guilty beyond a reasonable doubt. This is a difficult standard to achieve in many cases. Prosecutors who pursue criminal cases against particular suspects believe that they can convince juries of the defendant's guilt. However, the defendant is represented by counsel who attempts to show that the defendant is innocent. Various witnesses are brought forth and testify, either for or against particular defendants. Some of these witnesses are eyewitnesses, while others are expert witnesses who testify about the quality and significance of collected evidence. Juries deliberate and decide one's guilt or innocence.

If the decision is a guilty verdict, then the offender undergoes a sentencing hearing. Sentencing hearings are conducted by trial judges and are to some extent replays of the court case originally presented against them. However, sentencing hearings permit victims or relatives of victims to make victim impact statements in either verbal or written form. Others testify on behalf of defendants. Judges are the final arbiters and impose different sentences, depending upon the seriousness of the crime, one's prior record, and other factors. Several different types of sentencing systems are used by U.S. courts today. These will be discussed in some detail, together with their implications for the early release of sentenced offenders. In the event that convicted offenders are dissatisfied with the verdict, they are entitled to appeal their cases to higher courts. The appellate process is discussed. Featured are death penalty cases, which are always automatically appealed. The appeals process is especially lengthy, and even those who are sentenced to death in states with capital punishment laws may not be executed for ten or more years.

A parallel system of justice exists for juvenile offenders. Thus, Chapter 11 examines the juvenile justice system in some detail, with particular emphasis upon how the juvenile court system is structured and operated. A different language applies to juvenile processing, and various comparisons are made between the juvenile and criminal justice systems. Several important landmark juvenile cases are cited where they have been granted certain constitutional rights by the U.S. Supreme Court. Over time, juvenile courts have taken on the characteristics of criminal courts. Some persons believe that in several years, the juvenile court may be abolished and that a unified court for both juveniles and adults will emerge.

Chapter 12 concludes with an examination of how the court process is influenced by the media. As our society has become increasingly complex in a technological sense, we have mastered ways of delivering information to more people through different mediums such as television and the Internet. At the same time that we have been increasingly exposed to what goes on in the courtroom, a major litigation explosion has occurred, where increasing numbers of lawsuits are filed. We have evolved into a very litigious society. One reason for the great increase in litigation is the great publicity derived from courtroom coverage by the media and the sensationalization of particular cases. Media in the courtroom will be explored, and the pros and cons of media coverage will be examined in terms of how public opinion is shaped.

Ancillaries and desirable features of this book include numerous questions at chapter ends for review. Key terms are boldfaced throughout the text and listed at the end of the chapter, and a comprehensive glossary of these and other terms is found in an appendix. Suggested readings accompany each chapter so that those interested in learning more about particular subjects can locate further reading for their edification and education. An up-to-date bibliography of both research publications and legal cases is provided in the end-of-book references to facilitate one's research and general study. A particularly interesting feature is the liberal use of box materials throughout each chapter. These boxes often contain interesting vignettes adapted from local newspapers and featuring stories and events that complement the text itself. These boxes are often criminal justice in action, and real people and events are described. They have been used to heighten student interest in learning more about our court system.

While this book is coauthored, it is acknowledged that the final result is the work of many persons. We wish to thank Tim Peyton, our Prentice-Hall editor, for his confidence in our ability to produce a useful text pertaining to the court system. We are also indebted to the following reviewers who made helpful suggestions and criticisms at critical points: Stephen Brodt, Ball State University, Muncie, Indiana; Kristine Mullendore, Grand Valley State University, Grand Rapids, Michigan; Timothy Garner, Ball State University, Muncie, Indiana.

Dean John Champion
Texas A & M International University

Richard D. Hartley
Texas A & M International University

Gary A. Rabe
Minot State University

About the Authors

Dean John Champion is Professor of Criminal Justice, Texas A & M International University, Laredo, Texas. Dr. Champion has taught at the University of Tennessee-Knoxville, California State University-Long Beach, and Minot State University. He received his Ph.D. from Purdue University and B.S. and M.A. degrees from Brigham Young University. He completed several years of law school at the Nashville School of Law.

Dr. Champion has written over 37 texts and/or edited works and maintains memberships in eleven professional organizations. He is a lifetime member of the American Society of Criminology, Academy of Criminal Justice Sciences, and the American Sociological Association. He is a former editor of the Academy of Criminal Justice Sciences/Anderson Publishing Company Series on *Issues in Crime and Justice* and the *Journal of Crime and Justice*. He is a contributing author for the *Encarta Encyclopedia 2000* for Microsoft. He has been a Visiting Scholar for the National Center for Juvenile Justice and is a former president of the Midwestern Criminal Justice Association. He has also designed and/or offered numerous online courses for the University of Phoenix, Excelsior University, the University of Alaska-Fairbanks, ITT Tech, and Texas A & M International University.

Some of his published books for Prentice-Hall include *Crime Prevention in America* (2007); *Research Methods for Criminal Justice and Criminology 3/e* (2006); *The Juvenile Justice System: Delinquency, Processing, and the Law 5/e* (2007); *Corrections in the United States: A Contemporary Perspective 4/e* (2005); *Probation, Parole, and Community Corrections 5/e* (2008). His specialty interests include juvenile justice, criminal justice administration, corrections, and statistics/methods.

Dean John Champion

Richard D. Hartley is assistant professor of criminal justice at Texas A&M International University. He holds a Ph.D. from the University of Nebraska at Omaha. His dissertation was entitled Attorney Type and its Effects on Criminal Court Outcomes in a Large Midwestern Jurisdiction. Do You Get What You Pay For? Some select publications include: Prosecutorial Discretion: An Examination of Substantial Assistance Departures in Federal Crack-Cocaine and Powder-Cocaine Cases, *Justice Quarterly*, in Press, coauthored with Sean Maddan, and Cassia Spohn, and Sentencing Practices Under the Arkansas Sentencing Guidelines Structure, *Journal of Criminal Justice*, coauthored with Sean Maddan, and Jefferey T. Walker. His research interests include disparities in sentencing practices, especially at the Federal level, prosecutorial and judicial discretion, sentencing for narcotics violations, and race/ethnicity and crime.

Richard D. Hartley

Gary A. Rabe is Vice President for Academic Affairs at Minot State University, North Dakota. He is an accomplished scholar and director of various federally funded projects investigating drug trafficking in North Dakota. He joined the Minot State University faculty in 1993, and he subsequently served respectively as Chair of the Department of Criminal Justice and as Dean of the College of Arts and Sciences. Dr. Rabe's interests include white-collar crime, criminological theory, and court process and functions. He has published several articles in his areas of interest.

Gary A. Rabe

Law
The Legal Battlefield

Chapter Objectives

As a result of reading this chapter, you will have accomplished the following objectives:

1. Understand what the law is and the role it plays in various facets of our daily lives.

2. Describe the different functions of law, including social control, dispute resolution, and social change.

3. Understand the evolution of disputes and the formal resolution of them.

4. Understand the difference between substantive law and procedural law.

5. Understand the different types of law, including common law, civil law, as well as criminal and administrative law.

6. Describe the different sociological perspectives on law such as sociological jurisprudence, legal realism, critical legal studies, and feminist legal theory.

■ The murder was especially heinous. The victim, William Forsythe, 41, had been struck over the head by his house guest, Gary Garibaldi, 38, and subsequently strangled to death with a cord from a nearby table lamp. Garibaldi disposed of Forsythe's body by dragging it to a bathroom tub, and cutting the arms, legs, and head from the torso with a large saw. He wrapped the different parts in large trash bags and placed them in the back of Forsythe's 2002 Ford SUV. He drove to a remote spot in a landfill where he dumped the trash bags containing the body parts. Thinking he had committed the perfect crime, he returned to his home in a Connecticut suburb. About an hour after he had dumped Forsythe's body in the landfill, a homeless person, Mark Isaiah Jones, was prowling through the landfill looking for items of value to sell for money at a local flea market. He discovered the trash bags and quickly determined their contents. He was spotted by a landfill security officer who alerted police. An investigation revealed Forsythe's identity and his connection with Garibaldi. The two men had been living together as lovers and Forsythe had taken out a large insurance policy naming Garibaldi as the beneficiary. Garibaldi was charged with capital murder and was tried for this crime. During the trial, numerous explicit photographs of Forsythe's remains were shown to the jurors over the objections of Garibaldi's attorney. Also introduced was a confession Garibaldi gave to investigators while he was being interrogated. Garibaldi was subsequently convicted and sentenced to death. Garibaldi appealed, alleging that the numerous photographs shown to the jury were procedurally unnecessary to illustrate what had happened, and the jury's exposure to them inflamed them sufficiently to recommend the death penalty. An appeals court subsequently overturned Garibaldi's capital murder conviction, remanding the case to the trial court for further proceedings. Should legal technicalities such as crime scene photographs be sufficient to overturn murder convictions where defendants have made confessions and where other substantial incriminating evidence exists that they committed the crime alleged?

Sam Riggs was very upset. He lived alone in a Nebraska farmhouse. Riggs was a hard worker. He was retired from his prior job, which was in law enforcement. Now he was a security guard for a small meatpacking house about 20 miles from his home in Omaha. During the past year, Riggs's home had been broken into four times, and several of his valuable possessions had been stolen. The thief or thieves had entered his home from a trapdoor in his attic. Although Riggs had put new locks on the trapdoor, these locks continued to be forced open, and seemingly the burglar(s) knew when he was away from the home working. Frustrated, Riggs decided to rig a device in his attic, which would prevent future burglaries. Riggs loaded a shotgun, affixed it to an apparatus in his attic, aimed it at the trapdoor, and adjusted a string to the trigger of the shotgun to activate if the trapdoor were opened. One evening a burglar, Marcus Washington, forced open the trapdoor on Riggs's roof and activated the shotgun, which wounded him in the shoulder. When Riggs returned home, he found that his shotgun had gone off, and that a substantial amount of blood was present in his attic and on the roof of his house. He notified authorities who contacted local hospitals. It seems that Washington had immediately sought medical attention for his wounds. Police arrested Washington on suspicion of burglary, and a subsequent search of his apartment yielded much of the property that had been stolen from Riggs's home. Washington was later convicted of burglarizing Riggs's home, but Washington filed a civil suit seeking damages from Riggs, because of the serious shotgun wound he had received. A jury later awarded Washington $500,000 in punitive damages, and Riggs was chided by the court for using potentially deadly force to secure his property. Eventually Riggs lost his appeals of the jury award and was forced to sell his home and farm to make a partial financial settlement to Washington. Riggs now lives in a modest apartment. Was the court decision correct to award a burglar a substantial amount of money from the person he had been victimizing? Was Riggs justified in setting a deadly trap to catch a burglar? How should courts decide these matters?

INTRODUCTION

Murder or attempted murder, criminally convicted or civilly liable: The preceding scenarios are real examples of different types of crimes. For each crime alleged, there are elements that must be proved beyond a reasonable doubt in a subsequent trial. To be held liable in civil court, there are also facts that have to be shown by a preponderance of the evidence. Being convicted will most likely result in some type of punishment in jail or prison whereas being held liable will result in the payment of damages (usually monetary) to the injured party. Criminal and civil court are two separate realms and one can be tried in both for the same crime. The fact is, there are several different kinds of laws or rules that attempt to govern our behavior and the way the citizenry conduct their lives. There are laws against many violations we may or may not know exist but are in place to protect us from things that may harm or injure us. Law is dynamic and has many definitions. What is against the law in one place or at one time may not be a violation in another place or at another time. What elements of a crime need to be proved to meet the different evidentiary standards? Different states and the federal government define crimes in particular ways. There is much variation among the states about the nature and seriousness of different types of offenses. There is also variation among different jurisdictions in the application of laws, even if they have the same or similar laws. This is referred to as interdistrict disparity. For example, if two persons commit the same federal narcotics violation and have similar backgrounds, but one is being convicted in district court in Texas and the other in district court in North Dakota, their sentences may be very different because of local court contexts (plea bargaining, departure rates, prison overcrowding) even though they violated the same federal law.

There are also many definitions of criminal law in various places and also at various times. While these definitions are important to learn, it is also important to understand the different functions of law for a society as well as the consistency and inconsistency with which the law is applied. This chapter examines various perspectives regarding the purposes and functions of law. Law can be used as a means to regulate the behavior of society, it can be used to settle disputes between grieving parties, and it can be used to elicit change in current practices or ideas. This chapter also provides a framework for the evolution of disputes and their formal resolution. There are different stages in the evolution of disputes. Persons investigating this evolution are concerned with developing a conceptual framework in order to better understand which disputes will reach the courts for formal resolution. Different types of law are also described—substantive versus procedural law, common law, civil law, administrative law, and criminal law. The final section describes some of the more important contributions of sociolegal scholars like Oliver Wendell Holmes, Roscoe Pound, Karl Llewellyn, Roberto Unger, as well as some feminist legal theorists who have investigated the interplay between law and society.

WHAT IS LAW?

Law is the body of rules of specific conduct, prescribed by existing, legitimate authority, in a particular jurisdiction, and at a particular point in time. Law is an expression of the needs of the ruling class. Depending on our particular view of the legal system, law might be perceived as either liberating or oppressive, preserving the *status quo*, or providing the means and opportunity to challenge the existing social order. Law has been used both to perpetuate and eliminate slavery, to dominate and liberate women, and to convict and acquit the innocent. Law is related closely with all of these different definitions (Vago 2006).

The Dred Scott Case and the Law

The role of law was very apparent in the Dred Scott case in which the slavery issue was raised. This case was more about citizenship than slavery. Dred Scott was the slave of an army officer. The officer took Scott from Missouri, and then to Wisconsin, and eventually to Illinois. When Scott returned to Missouri, he claimed that he was no longer a slave because slavery was not recognized in either Wisconsin or Illinois. Therefore, an important constitutional question arose as to whether citizenship and freedom were vested in former slaves as the result of their relocating in states where slavery was prohibited. The U.S. Supreme Court heard and decided the case in 1857. Recognizing the rights of individual states, the U.S. Supreme Court held that citizenship was not a federal issue. Rather, the issue of slavery was to be determined by the individual states. Thus, according to this decision, Dred Scott was still considered a slave, since the U.S. Supreme Court chose not to interfere in states' rights. This decision encouraged antislave activists to make federal citizenship take priority over state citizenship. Subsequently, the efforts of these antislave activists resulted in the ratification of the Fourteenth Amendment. The Fourteenth Amendment became the instrument that insured the citizenship and freedom of blacks wherever they might choose to reside (Vago 2006).

Women and the Law

The status and role of women in society have been continually restructured through the law. The law plays a powerful but not an exclusive role in shaping and maintaining women's subordination. The law has operated directly and explicitly to prevent women from attaining independence in the public sphere, thereby reinforcing their dependence upon men. Simultaneously, the law's continued absence from the private sphere where women have been relegated not only has deprived women of formal legal remedies, but they have also been devalued and discredited as a class.

The Law and Women

The law has also been used to control women's reproduction (*Webster v. Reproductive Services*, 1989), access to professional credentials (*Bradwell v. Illinois*, 1873), as well as the role of women in the workforce (*Muller v. Oregon*, 1908).

The law has been used to redress these inequalities through affirmative action, which provides in part for fair and equitable hiring or promotion practices. Recently (*Stenburg v. Carhart*, 2000) the Eighth Circuit struck down a Nebraska statute banning partial birth abortions because the statute didn't include an exception for when the woman's health is at stake. The government however has appealed this decision and the Supreme Court in March of 2006 has decided to hear the appeal in the case of *Gonzales v. Carhart*.

Determining precisely what the law should and should not be has proved to be elusive. Legislators, prosecutors, defense attorneys, judges, defendants, businesspersons, consumers, parents, students, priests, the wealthy, and the poor all have different perspectives about what the law is and how it should be applied. Despite these diverse views of the law, there are several fundamental assumptions about the functions of law.

THE FUNCTIONS OF LAW

Various legal scholars have studied the functions of law in different social systems and at different points in time. Their many observations about the functions of law can be classified according to: (1) social control, (2) dispute resolution, and (3) social change.

Social Control

Social control consists of efforts by society to regulate the behavior of its members. The most visible form of social control is the application of the law (e.g., being arrested, prosecuted, and sentenced). For most citizens, this method of control is often the subject matter of the evening news and only happens to other people who we believe deserve to be controlled by the state. We seldom realize that we are subject to these same social controls in our daily lives.

Legal scholars distinguish between informal and formal social controls. Informal social controls are an integral feature of the socialization process. From early childhood, we are constantly taught the norms of behavior that our parents and the social world expect of us. These norms are a product of cultural expectations regarding dress, language, and behavior and our biological capacity to comprehend and adapt to these expectations. These informal social controls are effective because we are rewarded or punished by people who are important to us. Such persons are known as significant others in our lives.

For example, if we do things that offend our parents, close friends, or significant others, the sanctions administered by these people that we have grown to love and respect are very powerful, and we often refrain from engaging in these offensive behaviors. If our grandparents learn that we have been engaging in underage drinking, they issue stern words to us, and their glances have great influence on our personal conduct. The usual impact of this informal social pressure is that we frequently refrain from those behaviors that tend to elicit harsh words, warnings, or glares. Gossip is another form of informal social control. Gossip flourishes in offices around the watercooler or during smoking breaks from our office buildings. Gossip also flourishes at weekly bridge games, conversations with our friends over the telephone, and/or through computer e-mail. The effects of gossip are fairly consistent. Our behaviors are influenced significantly by the verbal and nonverbal cues we receive from others, either directly or indirectly. Through these different informal sanctions, we conform with what we believe are social expectations of us.

Dispute Resolution

A second function of law is **dispute resolution.** Persons frequently engage in disputes with others. Spouses might disagree about the division of labor in their household. Employees may disagree with their employers about their work effectiveness and quality. Sometimes disagreements occur among total strangers about how to drive on the interstate highways or how we or our children should behave in shopping centers or stores. Historically, persons involved in disputes have relied on informal methods for dispute resolution. In colonial times, families or individuals relied on their village elders to settle disputes. Not so long ago, disputes about many issues were considered private matters settled in nonlegal ways. In more recent decades, informal nonlegal resolutions of disputes have changed considerably. Increasingly, **disputants** rely on the legal system to resolve issues that once were settled privately. A major change in our social dynamics is largely responsible for this shift. Informal methods for dispute resolution used to be more effective in small, closely knit homogeneous societies. Often, the members of these communities were more closely related either through family ties or economically. Therefore, disputes were quite disruptive to the stability of the community and had to be resolved quickly. It was not deemed necessary to use legal means for resolving disputes because these disputes rarely rose to such formal levels.

One additional benefit of nonlegal methods to resolve disputes is that agreements are usually reached that are satisfactory to both parties. In traditional courtroom litigation, legal dispute resolution resulted in winners and losers. One side was dissatisfied with whatever decision was rendered, but tradition called for accepting that decision without further argument. However, as social systems became increasingly complex and heterogeneous, informal dispute resolution methods were less effective. There was no clear interdependence among the disputants, and the authority attempting to resolve the dispute was unclear. This social evolution generated more formal methods for dispute resolution, which gradually replaced less formal methods. Although formal, legal methods may settle the disputes to the satisfaction of the legal system, this doesn't necessarily mean that the dispute will never recur. It has been claimed, for instance, that a legal resolution of a conflict does not necessarily result in a reduction of tension or antagonism between the aggrieved parties (Vago 2006, 20). However, it is unlikely that most disputes are ever fully resolved; rather, they are temporarily quelled but eventually are resurrected into new conflicts and disputes.

Social Change

Social change is another important function of law. Social change is the process whereby ideas and practices are modified, either actively or passively through natural forces or deliberate social actions. Law is the principal avenue through which social ills and biases are resolved. History is replete with examples of law used to effect social changes of various kinds. State legislatures continually implement new laws to change the existing social order. Legislative actions are diverse and change our lives in various ways. For instance, new laws passed by legislatures may require us to wear seat belts, pay increased taxes, raise or lower the speed limit, or declare new national holidays. Judges also create social change through their own interpretations of the law and how it should be applied. Because of greater attention given to police methods by the media, most Americans are aware of their Miranda rights during custodial interrogations. Most citizens are aware of their right to counsel if they cannot afford an attorney (*Gideon v. Wainright*, 1963). The judiciary has been most influential in social change through issuing their decisions in legal cases. Thus, precedents established by judges have formed the bases of changes in various social policies. These changes are the functional equivalent of law-making. Legislators regard this activity as **judicial activism** and are opposed to it, since they believe that legislatures, not the judiciary, should have the exclusive authority to make law. Beyond this, law is also a method by which to initiate broader societal changes.

THE EVOLUTION OF DISPUTES

Disputes occur frequently among citizens. We may have disputes with our spouses and bosses; however, we rarely rely on the legal system to resolve or settle these types of disputes. It is important to realize that many disputes follow particular patterns, and that there is a system for seeking legal remedies only when several important factors converge. Some investigators have conceptualized the dispute process as consisting of various stages.

Naming, Blaming, and Claiming

Felstiner, Abel, and Sarat (1980) identify three stages in the evolution of disputes: (1) naming, (2) blaming, and (3) claiming. These investigators are concerned with developing a conceptual framework to understand the evolution of disputes before they reach the courts for formalized resolution. Their view of disputes starts with classifying injuries into either perceived or unperceived. For instance, sometimes we are victimized or injured but aren't aware of being victimized or suffering any injuries. If we don't understand that we have been victimized, then we do not consider the viability of a dispute. Have you ever wondered why all of the gasoline prices are the same in your neighborhood? Perhaps this reflects a free and open market where competition has driven gas prices down as far as they can go. Or maybe all of the gas station owners have secretly conspired to set fuel prices at fixed levels so that they can all benefit from higher prices. The point is that you never know when this situation actually occurs and whether you are being victimized. Each time you refuel your vehicle, you may be benefitting from the free-market system, or you may be being victimized through price-fixing. Thus, you may be the unwitting victim of a crime. When this occurs, even though you are a victim, no dispute arises. However, when you are able to identify yourself as a victim through **naming,** this is the first stage in formulating a legitimate dispute. The second stage in the dispute process is **blaming.** This stage involves translating your victimization into a formal grievance. In order for this event to occur, you must blame someone else for your victimization. Smokers move from naming to blaming when they allege that the tobacco companies have failed to inform them about the hazards of smoking. The final stage in the formulation of disputes is **claiming.** This occurs whenever victims believe that they have been injured, have identified a particular victimizer, and formally express a grievance against the person or organization responsible for their victimization. In most cases, victims seek monetary remedies. These claims ultimately evolve into disputes when the claim is initially rejected by another person or an organization. Not surprisingly, most disputes do not result into formal lawsuits. Most injuries are never perceived, and if they are, it is difficult to identify a particular victimizer. Therefore, the courts are faced with and address only a small fraction of the disputes that evolve into formal complaints and where those involved seek legal remedies.

A similar typology of disputes has been developed by Nader and Todd (1978) and Nader (1979). Like Felstiner, Abel, and Sarat (1980), Nader and Todd describe three stages in the dispute process: (1) the grievance or pre-conflict stage, (2) the conflict stage, and (3) the dispute stage. The **grievance** or **pre-conflict stage** requires that individuals or groups must perceive that they have been involved in an unfair or unjust situation. If the grievance is not resolved at this stage, then it progresses to a **conflict stage** where the victims confront the party they believe is the cause of their victimization. The dispute fully evolves when it reaches the **dispute stage** and the dispute is made public.

TYPES OF LAW

Substantive Law

Typologies of law are both important and necessary. Law varies according to who prosecutes, the nature and types of existing penalties, and its particular historical origins. A broadly applicable typology is difficult to develop that includes all types of law. A common distinction is made between **substantive law** and **procedural law.** Substantive law is the **law in books.** Substantive law is what the law says. Basically this is the compilation of local, state, and federal laws created by legislatures. A law exists that defines when someone is under the influence of alcohol when operating a motor vehicle. All states now have .08 BAC as the intoxication standard. Thus, if a motorist has a BAC of .08 or higher, then the motorist is legally intoxicated. If the motorist has a BAC level of .07 or lower, then the motorist is not legally intoxicated. Persons who take money from others by force commit robbery. If they use a dangerous weapon in order to take money from others by force, they commit armed robbery. Laws exist that define these and other criminal acts. Many additional laws combine to form the substance of substantive law.

Procedural Law

Procedural law or the **process of law** pertains to how the law is applied. Procedural law is also called the **law in action.** Procedural law specifies how police officers must obtain and execute a search warrant. It also details how jurors should be selected, how witnesses should be sworn when testifying in court, and how evidence should be admitted in the courtroom. Procedural law also includes how persons should be sentenced when convicted of one or more crimes. For example, in North Dakota judges are required to consider the following factors to determine the desirability of sentencing an offender to imprisonment:

1. The defendant's criminal conduct neither caused nor threatened serious harm to another person or his property.
2. The defendant did not plan or expect that his criminal conduct would cause or threaten serious harm to another person or his property.
3. The defendant acted under strong provocation.
4. There were substantial grounds that, though insufficient to establish a legal defense, tend to excuse or justify the defendant's conduct.
5. The victim of the defendant's conduct induced to facilitate its commission.

6. The defendant has or will make restitution or reparation to the victim of his conduct for the damage or injury that was sustained.

7. The defendant has no history of prior delinquency or criminal activity, or has led a law-abiding life for a substantial period of time before the commission of the present offense.

8. The defendant's conduct was a result of circumstances unlikely to recur.

9. The character, history, and attitudes of the defendant indicate that he is unlikely to commit another crime.

10. The defendant is particularly likely to respond affirmatively to probationary treatment.

11. The imprisonment of the defendant would entail undue hardship to himself or his dependents.

12. The defendant is elderly or in poor health.

13. The defendant did not abuse a public position of responsibility or trust.

14. The defendant cooperated with law enforcement authorities by bringing other offenders to justice, or otherwise cooperated (North Dakota Century Code, 12.1-32-04).

Common Law

Another type of law is **common law.** Common law is whatever is prevalent, traditional, or customary in a given jurisdiction. It is the law of precedent. There are no specific statutes that govern particular situations. Judges decide cases by common law on the basis of whatever is customary or traditional, not what is written down or codified.

Common law originated in England. Common law is judicially created law compared with law made by legislatures. English judges would travel to different cities and towns and decide cases on their circuits. Their decisions and the sentences they imposed were a combination of existing precedent and local custom. Because customs vary, common law varies among jurisdictions. For example, a judge in one jurisdiction may find that local residents are very tolerant of political dissent. If a defendant is arrested and charged with political dissent in this jurisdiction, it may be customary for the judge to impose a lenient sentence. The judge will probably not impose a harsh sentence because the citizenry would oppose it. However, in another jurisdiction where political dissension is unpopular, a judge might impose a harsh sentence upon a political dissident and have substantial community approval.

Although American society has become formalized and the laws at all jurisdictional levels are largely codified, it is not the case that common law has ceased to exist. In the United States, more than a few jurisdictions have common law and utilize it. Also, they might supplement their common law with

BOX 1.1 TWO EXAMPLES OF COMMON LAW

■ The Case of Ghen, the Whale Hunter

It happened in Massachusetts Bay. A whale hunter, Ghen, shot a whale with a bomb lance off the coast and the whale swam away and died about 25 miles from where it had been shot. Rich, a wandering beachcomber, came upon the dead whale lying on the beach. He stripped the blubber from the beached whale and converted the fat to oil, which he later sold at a nearby market. Subsequently, he bragged about his luck to others, and eventually, word reached Ghen about where his whale had gone. Ghen tracked down Rich and accused him of converting the whale remains for profit, thus denying Ghen any revenue from the whale he had shot. Rich refused to turn over the money he had received from the whale remains, arguing that he had found the whale, didn't know it was someone else's property, and did a lot of work converting the remains to fat. Ghen sued Rich, seeking to recover damages.

An interesting case was presented to the presiding judge. In the Cape Cod area, there were *no laws* governing whale rights. However, it was customary for those finding whales to alert the whale hunters where the whale had washed ashore so that the whale hunters could obtain the blubber and make valuable oil from the remains. The bomb lances used by different whalers were thus marked distinctively, so that anyone familiar with whaling knew whose lance it was and thus, who owned the whale. In Massachusetts, the custom was that the original whale hunter who shot a whale possessed it through a type of ownership, regardless of where the whale eventually swam or washed ashore. When Rich found the beached whale, he either knew or should have known the proper procedure to follow regarding turning the whale remains over to the rightful owner. In his case, he ignored custom and precedent and converted the whale remains for his own benefit. Thus, the judge ruled against Rich and in favor of Ghen, who was subsequently reimbursed for his loss by Rich.

■ The Case of the Bradbury's Dead Sister

Bradbury lived in a large two-story building with his sister, Harriet, in a Maine community. During a particularly severe winter, his sister became ill and died in the apartment. Bradbury had little money and could not afford to pay for a funeral for his sister. Therefore, he concluded, he could dispose of his sister in the large apartment house furnace in the basement. He dragged her body to the basement, where he cremated it in the large furnace. Neighbors detected a foul odor and called police, who investigated. They determined what Bradbury had done and arrested him. At the time, there was no law or written statute prohibiting anyone from disposing of a dead body in an apartment furnace. However, the court determined that Bradbury had violated the common law, which spoke against indecent burials of dead bodies. The fact that Bradbury had indecently disposed of his sister's body and had not given her a decent Christian burial was sufficient to find him in violation of the prevailing common law.

In both the *Ghen* and *Bradbury* cases, no statutes existed during those times that prohibited the specific conduct described. In both cases, judges decided these matters strictly on the basis of prevailing precedent established by common agreement through common law. Today in the United States, many states continue to have common laws, although statutory law has replaced much of it. At the federal level, there is no common law anymore, replaced entirely by statutory law. [Sources: *Ghen v. Rich,* 8 F. 159 (1881) and *State v. Bradbury,* 136 Me. 347 (1939).]

codified statutory law. For example, many urban areas do not condone prostitution, although some prostitution exists and is accepted informally. There is a certain area of town where prostitution exists. If prostitutes are arrested, they are fined a nominal amount and are soon back on the street engaging in more prostitution. In many rural areas of the United States, prostitution might be treated quite differently. If police arrested a prostitute, the prosecutor would be expected by the community to pursue the case against the prostitute as a serious crime. Therefore, certain crimes vary in their seriousness according to jurisdictional variations and prevailing customs and definitions of criminal conduct.

Civil Law

Civil law originated in ancient Roman law. Contrasted with common law, civil law stresses codification. Early civil law existed as compilations of rules and laws that were made under the emperor Justinian. Rather than rely on local custom to resolve disputes, common-law judges would refer to the written law when deciding cases. Civil law in America is used to resolve disputes between private parties. Unlike criminal law, the private party originates a case against another person or an organization rather than the prosecutor. The penalties sought are typically monetary. If one party is found to be at fault, damages are assessed. These damages are largely financial. Another feature of civil law is the standard of proof. In a civil case, the plaintiff must prove that the defendant was negligent by a **preponderance of the evidence,** which means more than 50 percent. Most Americans were made aware of this difference in the case of O. J. Simpson. While O. J. Simpson was acquitted of murder charges in a criminal case in California in 1995, subsequently he was found at fault in the wrongful deaths of his former wife, Nicole Brown Simpson, and a friend, Ronald Goldman, in the civil case that followed. The media attributed the different outcomes in the two trials to the different standards of proof required for criminal and civil cases. In O. J. Simpson's criminal case, the more difficult standard of **beyond a reasonable doubt** caused jurors to question the evidence against him and find him not guilty of the crimes. However, in the civil case that followed, another jury believed the plaintiffs who asserted that Simpson was responsible for the two deaths. In the latter case, Simpson's culpability was demonstrated according to the civil standard of the preponderance of evidence or weight of the evidence, not the criminal standard of beyond a reasonable doubt.

Criminal Law

For many citizens, the evening news on television is their primary source of information about how the criminal justice system operates. Television dramas such as *Law and Order, CSI,* and *N.Y.P.D. Blue* feature stories about the legal system and do much to shape our views about criminal law. We might see a story where an offender is sentenced in California to life in prison because he stole a pizza, or a story where a serial sex offender released by a parole board subsequently commits a new sex crime. For most people, the efficacy of the justice system is measured by the sound application of criminal laws or the poor application of these laws.

   Criminal law is differentiated from civil law according to the following criteria:

	Criminal Law	Civil Law
Who Is the Victim	State	Individual
Who Prosecutes	State	Individual
Possible Punishments	Fine, probation, or imprisonment	Monetary awards

In both civil and criminal law, the victim is a person or class of persons, such as an aggregate of smokers, inmates in a jail or prison facility, or persons who use marijuana. However, in criminal law the offense is regarded as so disruptive to the social order that society as a whole is the nebulous victim. This is because under criminal law, society is considered harmed by someone's illegal actions. In civil law, someone is the victim and brings suit against the victimizer. Punishments under criminal law are more severe than the punishments prescribed under civil law. Persons convicted of crimes may be fined and/or incarcerated. The most severe form of criminal punishment is the death penalty. In civil cases, however, victimizers who are found liable are not imprisoned or put to death. In most instances, however, they are obligated to

BOX 1.2 CAREER SNAPSHOT

Samantha J. O'Hara
Senior U.S. Probation Officer
U.S. Probation Office for the Southern District of Iowa

Statistics: B.A. (Criminology), University of Northern Iowa; M.A. (Sociology), University of Northern Iowa; PhD (Criminal Justice), University of Nebraska at Omaha

Background and Interests: After completing several internships and undergraduate and graduate degrees at the University of Northern Iowa, I was hired first in the criminal justice system as a residential officer and then as a counselor at a State of Iowa Department of Correctional Services residential facility located in Marshalltown, Iowa. There, I first truly became aware of my size and gender. For about six months, I worked the weekend overnight shifts as the only employee among about 40 male work release and probation offenders. We also had a small wing of female offenders, and typically they numbered between zero and six. I relearned at the halfway house to treat every person with respect. When you are a 22-year-old, 5'6", 125-pound female working nights with a bunch of male offenders, with convictions ranging from domestic abuse, burglary, sexual assaults, theft, and drug offenses, it became clear that diplomacy and good interpersonal skills were key. Bullying, false bravado, and ego have no place in the toolbox of a residential officer. Most of all, I learned that if you treat someone with respect, most of the time, it will be reciprocated. Although I was never in a situation that warranted it, I knew that if I pressed the "panic button" (an electronic warning signal routed to the police), help would arrive several minutes later. A lot of damage can be done in several minutes, and I had no desire for that damage to happen to me. (By the way, shortly after I left Marshalltown, due to safety concerns, management required two overnight staff persons per shift.)

While still in my master's program, I had set my goal for employment in the criminal justice system as a U.S. Probation Officer (USPO). After less than a year at the state halfway house, I was fortunate to be appointed as a U.S. Probation Officer for the U.S. District Court in the Southern District of Iowa, headquartered in Des Moines. At the U.S. Probation Office, officers comprise groups in the pretrial, presentence, and supervision units. Some officers monitor defendants awaiting trial or sentencing, while others provide supervision of those placed on probation or who are coming out of a penal institution on supervised release. For my first eight years of employment, my work in the presentence unit included interviewing the defendant, conducting a thorough criminal and

(continued)

BOX 1.2 (continued)

social history investigation, reviewing offense conduct materials provided by the U.S. Attorney's Office and case agents, calculating and applying the now-advisory U.S. Sentencing Guidelines, working with both counsels, and conveying the finished product (the Presentence Report) to the federal district court judge.

I enjoyed my work as a presentence report writer for several reasons: I liked learning of people's stories and how they became involved in their offenses. The contact with a variety of people, including offenders, their families, assistant U.S. attorneys, defense counsel, case agents, and the federal judges, makes for an extremely diverse mix. It was personally rewarding to me to see that the final product is helpful to the U.S. District Court judges, the Federal Bureau of Prisons, and eventually my colleagues in the U.S. Probation Office supervision units across the country. It has been very interesting getting the "big cases," ones that grab public attention, too. I have conducted presentence investigations on violent individuals, from individuals ranging from a man who planted pipe bombs on bike trails in the Des Moines metro area, young men who robbed banks by shotguns, older motorcycle gang members involved in gun and drug running to money-laundering, young gang members illegally selling firearms that were used in home invasions, and the like. I have written presentence reports on a large number of marijuana, cocaine, and methamphetamine drug traffickers and methamphetamine manufacturers and marijuana growers. I have investigated fraud cases ranging from simple thefts from U.S. postal facilities, to identity theft, credit card fraud, and bank fraud and embezzlement in the millions. I have been assigned illegal reentry and fraudulent immigration cases—people who are in the United States without legal permission. I have conducted presentence investigations on defendants who possess child pornography and misdemeanants (prior convictions of domestic abuse) in possession of firearms. I have authored reports that detailed huge methamphetamine conspiracies involving the distribution of hundreds of pounds of drugs into this state. As part of my investigation, I speak with the defendants, with family members, and with case agents (federal agents such as those with the FBI, ATF, DEA, Secret Service, or other agencies, or local police departments or sheriff's offices). I also have conducted home visits on some of these individuals, which goes toward verification of residency. In retrospect, I have had some cases that will forever be in my memory.

One of my first large drug conspiracy cases involved an individual from Des Moines who was his high school prom king and attended the University of Iowa in hopes of medical school, prior to his first involvement in the federal system. At the time I wrote his report, he was facing his third federal felony drug trafficking conviction. By all accounts, he was subject to the "three strikes" legislation and could have been sentenced to life imprisonment, but he was sentenced to more than 20 years instead. This man used juveniles to distribute and sell his drugs for him, as he believed that they would not implicate him nor be subject to the harsh adult drug sanctions. Clearly, his plan did not work out, as he was prosecuted and convicted. However, the most troubling aspect of the case was the physical and sexual abuse that he allegedly perpetrated on one juvenile, with whom he was living. The juvenile was later taken into state custody, and his mother, who allowed the defendant to live with her and her son for small amounts of methamphetamine, committed suicide. To me, everything seemed wrong in this case. The mother was dead, the defendant was in federal prison, and the son was in state care. I think this case stays with me because of the child abuse, and how it seemed that nobody cared about that child, until it was too late.

When defendants are detained prior to sentencing, we interview them at the jail (or whatever location they may be). Even though the people I interview are "law-breakers," they still tend to follow the rules most of the time. Mostly, the defendants are very agreeable and seem to like to be able to tell me their personal stories. Not all do, however. One individual, who was convicted of methamphetamine trafficking, and was a long-time user, actually became so agitated during an interview that he began shaking the typewriter at me (as if to pick it up) that was in the interview room at the jail. Others have told me, although not this kindly, to take a flying leap. Primarily, I have learned again the importance of treating everyone with respect. If not for good manners, then for safety. Almost everyone who is imprisoned will be released and will be returning to our communities.

Although there is danger anytime members of the criminal justice system come into contact with offenders, we train for officer safety especially when we are in the field. Police officers know that the most dangerous time for them is when they are in the homes of suspects—the residents know where weapons may be stashed, or if anybody is hiding in the residence who is wanted, and so forth. Research tells us that domestic disturbances are especially dangerous for police officers. For my work in the presentence unit, I have partnered with pretrial staff or supervision staff to make home visits in pairs. Recently, my partner and I had a successful home visit with an offender in southwest Iowa. I came back to my office, and a few weeks later went about the process to learn about the offense conduct from the government's discovery materials. My stomach became a little queasy when I learned that this individual, who distributed more than ten pounds of "ice" or "crystal" methamphetamine (which is much more pure than methamphetamine), was known to carry firearms, and the police allegedly missed several pounds' worth in his garage at the time of his arrest. By their nature, home visits are generally brief. One was especially so last summer, when I partnered with an officer in the pretrial unit, to verify residency for a bond client.

(continued)

BOX 1.2 *(continued)*

The defendant's home was isolated, off a gravel road, nearly hidden from the road, near a river, and with no neighbors in sight. The defendant's wife and "friend" (who was not identified and appeared nervous) were present, and after a short visit, we left. In a word—it was creepy—due to various factors, such as the lack of cell phone coverage, and the distance from possible help. Mainly, it was that feeling in our stomachs, a hunch, whatever you want to call it. Using our observations, our brains, and our feelings are needed in this work, too.

Recently, I have been fortunate to be promoted to the position of a Senior U.S. Probation Officer tasked with the Drug Abuse Treatment Specialist responsibilities. As we all know, both the state criminal justice systems and the federal system are inundated with drug offenses and other types of offenses committed by those who abuse drugs. Drug treatment expenditures rank as the single largest expense in our office, evidence again of how widespread substance abuse is in our society. I am looking forward to learning and researching how best we are able to serve our offenders in their struggle to abstain from drug use. In our state, methamphetamine is the current drug of choice. I have a 22-year-old female in my caseload currently undergoing the process of pulling her remaining teeth (10) to be fitted for dentures. She weighed as little as 85 pounds and was up for almost 30 days straight during one period of methamphetamine use. Unfortunately, such heavy methamphetamine abuse is not isolated. Another thing that I have truly learned here is that criminal offending does not affect just the criminal—it impacts his or her family members, work life, friendships, and so much more. It affects us, the law-abiding public. Sometimes I think that if only people would understand, prior to committing the act rather than at their sentencing hearings, of how their conduct impacts so, so, so many others. But I digress into the "if-onlys . . ."

A desire to constantly learn and change has been a theme in my life, so much so that in the fall of 1999, while working full-time as a USPO, I began part-time as a doctoral student at the University of Nebraska at Omaha's criminal justice department. I wished to obtain the tools in which to more critically look at our criminal justice system. With the encouragement and office hour flexibility of my then-chief probation officer, I traveled to Omaha bi-weekly for three years. I graduated in 2006 with a Ph.D. in Criminal Justice. With the assistance of the wonderful faculty and challenging courses, I have been able to put my schooling and correctional experience to work. I feel that I am better able to critically examine specific issues as a Ph.D. who wrote federal presentence reports, and will be able to bring research and policy ideas into the position of Drug Abuse Treatment Specialist. When judges ask for my opinion on an issue or have questions, I have an improved base with which to hold a discussion.

Advice to Students: I strongly suggest that students interested in the criminal justice system learn about criminology—the study of law-makers, law-breakers, and reactions to law-breakers. Also, because of the diversity of our offenders and their offenses, I also recommend students study languages (fluency in Spanish is quite an asset, especially in certain parts of this country), mathematics, and business or public administration (leadership courses; helpful to learn how organizations work; how complex financial crimes are perpetrated, investigated, and discouraged). Communication skills (such as public speaking or English degrees) and law degrees are also very much needed in the federal probation system. I suppose I am biased on the topic of advanced education—I believe that, generally speaking, more education is better than less and we need to continue to learn. I believe that my two internships (one at a police department and one at a state halfway house) were crucial in two aspects: (1) I learned what adventures I was getting myself into; and (2) it opened up the doors of state and federal community corrections. If you have a high level of enthusiasm, passion, integrity, and enjoy hard work, state or local courts and community corrections could be just for you!

compensate victims for their losses and suffering. These penalties are monetary judgments or awards for damages.

Again, the O. J. Simpson case demonstrates this difference. If Simpson had been convicted in that criminal case, he would have been sentenced to prison. In the subsequent civil case against him, Simpson was found liable and ordered to pay damages. He was ordered by the court to pay $25 million in punitive damages, which were intended to punish him for his conduct, and he was further ordered to pay $8.5 million in compensatory damages, which were intended to compensate the families of his victims for their pain and suffering.

Administrative Law

Administrative law is the body of laws, rules, orders, and regulations created by administrative agencies. While the other forms of law may not directly affect us in our daily lives, administrative law is pervasive and affects all of us in various ways. There are over fifty federal regulatory agencies that promulgate and enforce a diverse array of regulations. Other administrative agencies exist at the state and local levels. The result is an overwhelming amount of bureaucratic control. When we travel on an airline, for example, we are subject to the administrative rules developed by the Federal Aviation Administration. The food and drugs we consume are approved and regulated by the Food and Drug Administration. When we telephone others, this communication is regulated by the Federal Communications Commission. If we purchase a house, our actions are influenced by interest rates, which are indirectly related to the actions of the Federal Reserve.

An interesting example of the high degree of governmental regulation and control is given by Vago (2006). Vago indicates that a couple may be awakened by the buzz of an electronic clock or perhaps by a clock radio. This signals the beginning of a highly regulated existence for them. The clock or radio that wakes them is run by electricity provided by a utility company, regulated by the Federal Energy Regulatory Commission and by the state utility agencies. They listen to the weather report generated by the National Weather Service, part of the Commerce Department. When they go to the bathroom, they use products, such as mouthwash and toothpaste, made by companies regulated by the Food and Drug Administration (FDA). The husband might lose his temper trying to open bottle of aspirin with a childproof cap required by the Consumer Product Safety Commission (CPSC). In the kitchen the wife reaches for a box of cereal containing food processed by a firm subject to the regulations of the United States Department of Agriculture (USDA) and required to label its products under regulations of the Federal Trade Commission (FTC). When they get into their car to go to work, they are reminded by a buzzer to fasten their seat belts, compliments of the National Highway Traffic Safety Administration. They paid slightly more for their car than they wanted to, because it contains a catalytic converter and other devices stipulated by the Environmental Protection Agency (EPA) (Vago 2006, 123–124).

SOCIOLEGAL PERSPECTIVES AND THE LAW

Just as there are various types of law, there are also many perspectives about the interaction between society and law. The analysis of the interaction of law and society has its early American roots in the writings of Oliver Wendell Holmes Jr., Louis Brandeis, and Roscoe Pound. These authorities were among the first to criticize classical jurisprudence. Classical jurisprudence was concerned with applying a strict interpretation and application of the law. This formal and mechanical method of jurisprudence did not permit the courts to effect changes in social policy. Holmes, Brandeis, and Pound believed that law should be active and dynamic and useful for changing the social order. The perspective on law proposed by these authorities is **sociological jurisprudence.**

Sociological Jurisprudence

Sociological jurisprudence indicates that a part of law should concern itself with making social or public policy. Today this legal agenda is called judicial activism. Oliver Wendell Holmes believed that law should be responsive to and incorporate changing social conditions, although the legislature should remain the primary method of social change. Holmes said that "for the rational study of the

BOX 1.3 ON THE POSSIBLE LEGALIZATION OF MARIJUANA

■ Decriminalization in California

In the November 1996 elections, a California citizen-initiated proposal was put before residents for a vote. Should marijuana for medical purposes be legalized? This is not the first time that states have considered decriminalizing the use of previously controlled or illegal substances. Under federal law (Controlled Substance Act of 1970), marijuana use for any purpose is illegal. Since California first proposed this issue, many states have or are considering putting this issue to a vote, and several states have voted to legalize marijuana for medicinal purposes. The Ninth Circuit Court of Appeals in San Francisco is again set to hear arguments in 2006. They are going to decide the right-to-life issue: Should medical marijuana be allowed in cases where it is needed to keep the patient alive or reduce excruciating pain? As a public policy issue, do you think marijuana should be legalized? How much crime would be eliminated through the legalization of marijuana? Should the same decriminalization be applied to substances such as heroin and cocaine? [Source: Adapted from Associated Press, "Medical Marijuana Issue Returns to Court," *Omaha World Herald*, March 26, 2006.]

law the black letter man may be seen as the man of the present, but the man of the future is the man of statistics and the master of economics" (Holmes 1897, 457). This statement suggests that law and/or judges should acknowledge and utilize social science to further develop and answer legally relevant questions.

The first person to use social science in litigation was Louis Brandeis. Brandeis embraced sociological jurisprudence and utilized social science to win cases. He often incorporated social science results into briefs to the court to bolster his arguments. One noteworthy case was *Muller v. Oregon* (1907), which involved a dispute about the working hours of women. Two years earlier, the case of *Lochner v. New York* (1905) was decided by the U.S. Supreme Court. The Court declared a statute unconstitutional that limited working hours to sixty per week. Aware of this case and holding, Brandeis believed that he had to show that it was harmful for women to work more than sixty hours per week. To substantiate his claim, Brandeis wrote a brief that included statements arguing that women were deleteriously affected by long hours of work. Brandeis used a variety of sources from labor statistics and statements from international conferences about labor legislation as his scientific sources. Dr. Theodore Wely has added that women bear the following generation whose health is essentially influenced by that of the mothers, and the State has a vital interest in securing itself for future generations capable of living and maintaining it (Wely 1904).

Breckenridge supported this sentiment by suggesting that the assumption of control over the conditions under which industrial women are employed is one of the most significant features of legislative policy. In many advanced industrial countries, the state not only prescribes minimum standards of decency, safety, and healthfulness, but they also specify minimal limits for wage earners. The state also takes cognizance of several ways for distinguishing sex differences and sex relationships. Furthermore, the state sometimes takes cognizance of the peculiarly close relationship that exists between the health of its women citizens and the physical vigor of future generations. It has been declared a matter of public concern that no group of its women workers should be allowed to unfit themselves by excessive hours of work, by standing, or other physical strain, for the burden of motherhood, which each of them should be able to assume. He adds that the object of such control is the protection of the physical well-being of the community by setting a limit to the exploitation of the improvident, unworkmanlike, unorganized women who are yet to be mothers, actual or prospective of the coming generation (Breckenridge 1906).

The U.S. Supreme Court was persuaded by this argument and held that the adverse effects of women working long hours were detrimental to the public interest. There is no doubt that the justices of the U.S. Supreme Court were influenced by the social science evidence provided by Brandeis in his brief. The Court reasoned in *Muller* that a woman's physical structure and the performance of maternal functions place her at a disadvantage in the struggle for subsistence is obvious. This is especially true when the burdens of motherhood are upon her. Even when they are not, by abundant testimony of the medical fraternity, continuance for a long time on her feet at work, repeating this from day to day, tends to injurious effects on the body, and as healthy mothers are essential to vigorous offspring, the physical well-being of women becomes an object of public care in order to preserve the strength and vigor of the race (*Muller v. Oregon*, 1908).

Roscoe Pound elaborated on the purpose and goal of sociological jurisprudence in several of his essays. He recognized that law was not and could not be autonomous or influenced by social conditions. He wrote that the important part of our system is not the trial judge who dispenses justice to litigants, but rather the judge of the appellate court who uses the litigation as a means of developing the law (Pound 1912, 489). Pound developed five strategies by which sociolegal jurists could distinguish themselves from more traditional jurists. These strategies include:

1. They are looking more to the working of the law than to its abstract content.
2. They regard law as a social institution, which may be improved by intelligent human effort, and hold it their duty to discover the best means of furthering and directing such effort.

3. They stress upon the social purposes which law subserves rather than upon sanction.

4. They urge that legal precepts are to be regarded more as guides to results, which are socially just ills less as flexible molds.

5. Their philosophical views are very diverse (Pound 1912, 489–490).

These three legal scholars and practitioners represented a dramatic change in thinking about the law. They believed that classical jurisprudence and jurists should be the only ones to strictly apply existing law. These jurists believed that law and society were inextricably linked. One influenced the other. One was necessary for the other. Judges cognizant of or trained in sociological jurisprudence realized that one of the major functions of law was social change. Lawyers and jurists should apply law with the idea of fostering social change.

Legal Realism

Sociological jurisprudence provided the foundation for **legal realism.** This perspective is described in the early work of Karl Llewellyn (1931). Llewellyn had a broader agenda than his predecessors. He argued that law was dynamic and often inconsistent. Interestingly, the development of the National Reporter system published by West Publishing Company is believed to have contributed to this perspective. This is because the Reporter system disclosed that similar cases or existing legal precedents were actually applied or interpreted differently, depending upon the jurisdiction. Thus, it was that an appellate judge in California applied a particular legal precedent differently compared with how another appellate court judge in Texas applied the same legal precedent.

Karl Llewelyn also believed that the existing understanding of law was inadequate. He believed that law and society were constantly evolving. Realists also believed that law should be the means to a social end rather than an end in itself. Realists were distrustful of legal rules and the perspectives of rule formation. Rather, they were interested in determining the effects of law (Llewellyn 1931).

Critical Legal Studies

Critical legal studies is one of the most dynamic and controversial perspectives on law. This movement began with a group of junior faculty members and law students at Yale in the late 1960s. In 1977, the group organized itself into the Conference of Critical Legal Studies, which presently has over 400 members and holds annual conferences that attract 1,000 or more participants (Vago 2006, 67).

BOX 1.4 CHANGING THE LAW: LAWSUITS AGAINST DRUG DEALERS?

■ Suing the Dealers?

It happened in Wilmington, North Carolina. Blaire Thompson, daughter of Keith Thompson, was a drug addict. She had struggled with heroin addiction for years, attempting to stop using several times but without success. Blaire was a kindergarten teacher and hid her addiction from her peers and students. Nevertheless, the heroin use affected her work. One last attempt to break free of the drug habit led to a 60-day period of abstinence from heroin. In her moments of clarity, Blaire decided to write a book about the dangers of illegal drugs, including heroin. But Blaire's drug dealer called her one morning and offered her another fix. She succumbed and overdosed and died later that night. She was 26.

In the days following her death, Keith Thompson found Blaire's drug connection and confronted him. But Thompson found that he couldn't persuade authorities to prosecute the man for lack of evidence of his drug dealings. Frustrated, Thompson contacted State Senator Julia Boseman of Wilmington, advising her of his concerns and what had happened to his daughter. Subsequently, Boseman proposed a bill that provided, among other things, that drug dealers can be held responsible for the damages inflicted on their clients, whether it be death or physical or mental impairment. Thompson said, "Drug dealers are parasites in our community. They suck the quality of life from our citizens. We must use any and all means we can to continue this war on drugs."

According to the bill, a dealer does not have to be responsible for the damages. Virtually any person or group, even the state, can sue any convicted drug dealer. Dealers could be forced to pay for injuries, treatment, emotional distress, or loss of employment or companionship suffered by drug users or those in their community. The American Civil Liberties Union of North Carolina opposes the bill, saying that the measure is unconstitutional because the dealer sued doesn't have to be the one who causes the injury. Furthermore, the ACLU claims that lawsuits wouldn't be effective deterrents and it would be difficult to determine any particular dealer's assets. But doing something is better than doing nothing. What do you think? Should drug dealers be liable for the harm they cause to their clients through the use of illicit drugs?

In 2001 Steven Steiner, Jr. overdosed and died in New York. He was in his early 20s. His father, Steven Steiner, Sr., subsequently organized New York-based Dads and Moms Against Drug Dealers (DMADD). DMADD wants to raise drug awareness, pay cash rewards for information leading to the arrest and conviction of drug dealers, and solicit tips from informants about those who deal drugs of any kind.

Similar initiatives are underway in other states, including Hawaii. In Kalihi, Hawaii, for instance, a particular home has been a drug center for years. Illicit drug sales have transpired on a continuing basis under the noses of law enforcement on Stanley Street. The home is owned by a convicted drug dealer who is serving a prison sentence in Oklahoma on drug-related charges. But his sons are continuing the illicit drug trade. Authorities in Hawaii say that as long as there's a demand for these drugs, there is little they can do to prevent their spread and use. But those who live next door to these drug dealers feel differently. Not only do they feel threatened as unwitting observers of constant illegal activity, but they must also suffer the round-the-clock noise and antisocial activities that are a part of this seedy underground industry.

In recent years, Hawaii has launched several bills aimed at combating the drug trade. Among other provisions, several bills proposed would allow families, individuals, companies, government agencies, and anyone else who can show an injury or financial harm resulting from a person's drug addiction to file lawsuits seeking compensation from drug pushers. Citizens who file complaints would also be protected from drug dealer retaliation in the same way that witnesses are protected who testify against persons in criminal proceedings. Do you believe that lawsuits against drug dealers are an effective way of combatting the dissemination of illegal drugs? [Sources: Adapted from Mike Baker and the Associated Press, "Proposed Bill Would Allow Lawsuits Against Drug Dealers," June 2, 2006; Editorial, "We Can Organize to Ostracize Drug Dealers," *Honolulu Advertiser*, June 20, 2006.]

The critical legal studies movement involves a thorough examination of the entire legal system. The theoretical underpinnings of critical legal studies is most often attributed to Roberto Unger. The critical legal studies movement had its origins in legal realism. Similarly, critical legal studies takes issue with formal rational law. Critical legal studies contends that we must recognize that the law is subjective rather than objective.

Critical legal scholars believe that law is not value-free. Essentially these scholars believe that the law serves to preserve existing power relations in society. Law schools are structured to train students for hierarchy. In the classroom students learn their social position during lectures. Law school teachers rely heavily on the Socratic method, whereby teachers ask students about different points of the law. The students, regardless of their responses, are always incorrect. The teacher relies on either lower or higher levels of abstraction to fit particular situations. Law schools justify this method because many law professors believe that it makes students think like lawyers. However, for many law school students, this process is a humiliating experience and serves to reinforce the hierarchy of law.

BOX 1.5 ON THE LEGALITY OF ASSISTED SUICIDE

■ The Case of Dr. Jack Kevorkian

His name was Jack Kevorkian. He was a physician. He assisted people who wished to end their lives. He enabled them to commit suicide. Was he a monster? Was he a savior? According to police, prosecutors, and his victims, he was both. Kevorkian was a long-time advocate for euthanasia, a practice of ending one's life when one has a terminal illness and is suffering from intense pain. If there is no hope for survival or a prolonged useful life, many patients in this condition want to end their pain and suffering in the most painless way possible. Kevorkian supplied many terminally ill people with "suicide kits," enabling them to use their own automobiles as their personal death chambers through death by carbon monoxide poisoning.

Kevorkian was in several courtrooms defending himself against various types of murder charges over the years. Testifying in his behalf were many family relatives of those who have terminated their lives with his assistance. Living wills recorded on videotape from victims themselves have absolved Kevorkian from beyond the grave. Yet, prosecutors and state legislators continued to bring Kevorkian into court, attempting to secure a murder conviction.

One dilemma was that Kevorkian took an oath when he became a physician. The oath required him to prolong a person's life, not terminate it. Yet, Kevorkian insisted that in all cases where he assisted the terminally ill, he merely provided the means whereby persons can die with dignity, instead of screaming to death in a lonely hospital bed from unbearable pain from cancer and other diseases.

Kevorkian almost always delivered the bodies of victims to hospitals where they could be properly examined. He insisted that although he was referred to in the media as "Dr. Death," he didn't deserve such an appellation. Rather, he saw his role as alleviating the suffering and pain of terminally ill patients. Other doctors rejected his philosophy and claimed that doctors should do everything they can to prolong life. Kevorkian was indicted and eventually convicted of murder in 1999 in a Michigan court for his role in the assisted suicide of one victim. In 2006 he was serving a 10- to 25-year sentence in a Michigan prison. Do you believe that persons should be allowed to choose whether they live or die, if they are suffering from a terminally ill condition and are suffering and in great pain? How should Dr. Jack Kevorkian have been treated by the criminal justice system? Was he guilty of multiple murders under the guise of assisted suicide? Is this a moral issue? What values are evident in this debate over medically assisted suicide? How should it be resolved? What do you think? [Sources: Adapted from Associated Press, "Kevorkian Assists Suicide No. 33," July 11, 1996; Adapted from the Associated Press, "Kevorkian Denied Parole in Bid for Freedom," May 20, 2006.]

In order to remedy certain problems associated with acquiring a legal education, a radical restructuring of law school curricula and how law is taught is needed. In an ideal legal education, there would be few legal skills classes (e.g., learning legal rules and the categorization of cases), and the major focus in law school would be upon mastering social and political theory and an analysis of the existing social system (e.g., housing, welfare, and criminal justice).

Feminist Legal Theory

Another perspective on the law has its origins in feminism. The diverse experiences of women and the law have evolved into various perspectives on the relationship between law and gender. The feminist's perspective of the law or **feminist legal studies** ranges from the radical to the pragmatic. Some feminists have examined how the law protects male interests. Some persons have argued that the law treats women as objects of men (Abrams 1995). Other feminists have examined how women have had an impact on the legal system. These investigations include research on the impact of women in law school and as attorneys (Chambers 1989) and as judges. The rationale for this view is that women reason differently from men, and therefore as lawyers and judges, women will use a different type of logic when applying the law. Women may be less adversarial and confrontational compared with men. This is quite possibly a positive result. The confrontational adversarial process has a winner and a loser. Women often express dissatisfaction with the win-lose nature of litigation because the real needs of the litigants are never addressed or accommodated. Rather, female lawyers might advocate a process involving less litigation and more mediation and fewer winner-take-all results (Menkel-Meadow 1986).

SUMMARY

Law has a variety of functions. Law is often used as a method of social control or to regulate our behavior. For instance the law regulates whether or not females have the right to have an abortion, whether patients can use marijuana for medicinal purposes, and whether physicians can legally assist persons in ending their lives. When someone violates the law, the law is used as a method to punish them for their past behavior and to control their future behavior. Another function of the law is dispute resolution. The law serves as a guide for resolving disputes. When there is a dispute between two parties, the law is often used to resolve that dispute. The law provides for rules of evidence and procedure that are employed to hear and process disputes. For example, the law resolves whether or not a person has violated a property law if their tree grows too far into a neighbor's yard; the law resolves whether or not a toy company has produced a faulty toy that has led to child injury and whether they are responsible to pay damages. Another function of the law is social change. In the United States that law is often used as an agent of social change. State legislatures are constantly passing laws to change the existing social order. For example, the legislature passes a law allowing narcotics users to sue their dealers, the legislators in various states amend their drinking and driving laws and lower the legal blood alcohol limit to .08, or the Supreme Court decides that the death penalty as administered is unconstitutional. Legislative action or law has changed how we perceive and react to various criminal offenses as a society.

The law can be categorized as either substantive or procedural. Substantive law is the law on the books, the laws created by the legislature of federal and state governments and also by local authorities as well. Therefore, substantive law is what the law says. It tells us what the legal drinking age is, what the legal blood alcohol content is, and which type of establishments can and cannot serve alcohol to their patrons. It also gives the definitional guidelines of what a particular crime is. For instance, what elements of a crime are necessary for someone to be convicted of rape? What is the difference between first degree, second degree, and negligent murder? Finally, it can tell us in some instances what the penalties for being convicted of certain behaviors are. What length of time is appropriate for someone convicted of armed robbery? What is the sentence length for someone convicted of possessing ten grams of crack cocaine? Truth in sentencing statutes mandate that offenders serve at least 85 percent of their sentence. Habitual offender statutes mandate that those convicted of a third felony be sentenced to 25 years to life in prison. Procedural law on the other hand is the process of the law, how the law is applied. Procedural law is sometimes referred to as the law in action. It gives, for instance, officers guidelines on how to get a search warrant. It gives judges guidelines on evidence that is and is not admissible in court. It gives prosecutors and defense attorneys rules for selecting jurors for particular cases. Both substantive and procedural law are typologies or classifications of the law that tell us what the laws are, as well as how they are to be implemented.

Four types of law were identified. Common law originated in England and was made by judges who traveled in circuits and dispensed justice according to the customs common to the region. For this reason, common laws vary in different jurisdictions. Although in recent years we have tried to make what violates law, and the punishments for those violations more uniform, common law still exists. For example, in certain jurisdictions in the country the punishment for prostitution may amount to what is thought of as a slap on the wrist, where a prostitute is basically arrested, required to pay a fine, and be released back to the street to again engage in prostitution. However, the punishment for a conviction of prostitution in another area of the country may involve aggressive prosecution of prostitutes to send a message and act as a deterrent to going back on the streets. It may depend on the prosecutor's agenda; it may depend on the sentiment from the community. How vigorously certain violations of law will be pursued depends on a number of things; the fact is that this is a form of common law that differs across jurisdictions. Civil law is codified or written and documented. Civil law originated in ancient Roman law. Unlike common law, judges refer to the written law when deciding cases; these decisions then become law. Civil law is used for dispute resolution amongst private parties. The penalties are typically monetary, and are not crimes against the state. In civil law there is also a different standard of proof to be held liable for your actions; it is by a preponderance of the evidence. Criminal law is differentiated from other types of law in that the society as a whole is a victim, and the government brings charges against the accused when a criminal law is violated. Punishments under criminal law are more severe than those under civil law, and could include imprisonment. Those convicted have to be found guilty beyond a reasonable doubt as opposed to the preponderance of evidence standard in civil court. Administrative law is the body of law, rules, orders, and regulations created by administrative agencies. Although we may not think about it too often, administrative law affects our lives almost daily. A number of regulatory agencies at both the federal and state level exist and impose a lot of bureaucratic control on our lives. Every time you drive down the street, pick up prescriptions from the pharmacy, or take a flight to visit friends and relatives, there are various regulations that you, and others, are adhering to in order to ensure everyone's safety. When you drive your car, rules from the Highway Traffic Safety Commission stipulate that you should fasten your seat belt, and be sure your car has had a safety inspection. When you go to the pharmacy, rules from the Food and Drug Administration provide guidelines for how many pills to take and other drugs to avoid because of possible interaction effects. When you go to the airport, the Federal Aviation Administration mandates that certain items will not be allowed on aircraft. All in all, our daily lives are greatly affected by rules put forth by administrative agencies.

Another important aspect of law is how it is dynamic in that it interacts with society. Four perspectives were presented exploring this interaction. Sociological jurisprudence believes law should be concerned with making social or public policy. Oliver Wendell Holmes and Roscoe Pound were avid proponents of this perspective and believed that the law cannot be uninfluenced by, and must be responsive to, existing social conditions. Legal realism believes that law should be the means to a social end. Karl Llewellyn believed that law and society were constantly evolving, and that we should be mindful of the effects of law. Critical legal studies is a rather controversial perspective in that it believes that the law is subjective not objective, and therefore is not value-free. In other words, Roberto Unger and other proponents believed that the law was used as an instrument to preserve the existing power relations in society. Finally, feminist legal theory purports that the law is used to protect male interests, or treats women as the objects of men. Feminist theorists believe that women apply a different logic to law, and that the law may better serve society if it was less adversarial and confrontational. Each of these offer different perspectives on the interaction between law and society.

KEY TERMS

Administrative law
Beyond a reasonable doubt
Blaming
Civil law
Claiming
Common law
Conflict stage
Criminal law
Critical legal studies
Disputant
Dispute resolution
Dispute stage
Feminist legal studies
Grievance

Judicial activism
Law
Law in action
Law in books
Legal realism
Naming
Pre-conflict stage
Preponderance of the evidence
Procedural law
Process of law
Social change
Social control
Sociological jurisprudence
Substantive law

QUESTIONS FOR REVIEW

1. What is law? What are two different types of law? Differentiate between each.
2. What was the significance of the Dred Scott case?
3. What are four functions of law?
4. What is the significance of the view containing naming, blaming, and claiming?
5. How does substantive law differ from procedural law? What do these different types of law govern? Explain.

6. What is common law? How do judges decide cases on the basis of common law?

7. What is meant by administrative law? Why is it important for social change?

8. What is sociological jurisprudence? How is sociological jurisprudence related to social change?

9. What is meant by legal realism? How does critical legal studies compare with legal realism?

10. How has feminism affected the development of law in the United States?

SUGGESTED READINGS

1. D. E. Altus et al. (2004). "The Birth of a New World: Utopian Visions of Justice in Theory, Practice, and Literature." *Contemporary Justice Review: Issues in Criminal, Social, and Restorative Justice* **7**:267–333.

2. Robert Boyle, Donna R. Newman, and Sam A. Schmidt (2003). "Center for Professional Values and Practice Symposium: Criminal Defense in the Age of Terrorism." *New York Law School Law Review* **48**:3–384.

3. C. S. Cooper (2002). "Drug Courts: Current Issues and Future Perspectives." *Substance Abuse and Misuse* **38**:1671–1711.

4. A. Henneth (2004). "Recognition and Justice: Outline of a Plural Theory of Justice." *Acta Socioloica* **47**:351–364.

5. C. W. Mullins, K. Kauzlarich, and D. Rothe (2004). "The International Criminal Court and the Control of State Crime: Prospects and Problems." *Critical Criminology* **12**:285–308.

6. N. Pithy (2004). "Do New Crimes Need New Laws? Legal Provisions Available for Prosecuting Human Trafficking." *SA Crime Quarterly* **9**:7–10.

7. V. Toscano (2005). "Misguided Retribution: Criminalization of Pregnant Women Who Take Drugs." *Social and Legal Studies* **14**:359–386.

8. Steven Vago (2006). *Law and Society*, 8th ed. Upper Saddle River, NJ: Prentice Hall.

Chapter 2

The Structure of American Courts

Getty Images, Inc.

Chapter Objectives

As a result of reading this chapter, you will have accomplished the following objectives:

1. Understand the different ways to classify American courts by jurisdiction, by its dual nature, and by type of court.

2. Describe the different types of jurisdiction like subject matter, geographic, and hierarchical.

3. Understand that the United States has two court structures, a federal structure and a state structure.

4. Describe the difference between trial and appellate courts.

5. Describe the federal court structure including U.S. Magistrate Courts, U.S. District Courts, U.S. Circuit Courts of Appeal, and the U.S. Supreme Court.

6. Describe the state court structure including, Courts of Limited Jurisdiction, Courts of General Jurisdiction, Intermediate Courts of Appeal, and Courts of Last Resort.

■ Rodney Deevers, 16, was driving the family car. He and his family were vacationing in a national park. His father asked Rodney, who had just obtained his driver's license, if he would run an errand and pick up some groceries for the family at a market in a nearby town. While out on the open highway still in the national park, Deevers sped along the road at 70 mph. The speed limit was 40 mph. An alert national park officer stopped Deevers for speeding and gave him a ticket. The ticket also included a charge of reckless driving, since Deevers had passed several cars in a double-lined no-pass zone. Deevers was ordered to appear before the U.S. Magistrate in a city 200 miles away from the public park. Anthony Deevers, the father, called the court and asked if he could mail in the cost of the ticket, whatever the fine(s) might be. The clerk simply stated that Rodney Deevers must appear in person on the appointed date; otherwise, a warrant would be issued for his immediate arrest. The Deevers family finished their vacation and on the appointed date, appeared in the court of the U.S. Magistrate, some 800 miles from their home state. The U.S. Magistrate fined Deevers $500, as well as $350 in court costs, and ordered him to perform 100 hours of public service. He then placed Deevers on probation for 6 months, with orders to report to the U.S. Probation Office in Deevers's home city. U.S. Magistrates have jurisdiction over national parks and most violations of the law, at least misdemeanors, that occur on federal land.

■ Ethan Morgan, 32, Mohammed Rhabil, 28, and Tony LaFranco, 39, are trial defendants. Morgan is charged with breaking and entering, burglary, and vehicular theft. Rhabil is being sued for 6 months of back rent, which he has allegedly failed to pay to his landlord. He claims that they failed to fix leaky faucets and other household items in the apartment he is renting. LaFranco is charged with aggravated assault and attempted murder resulting from a bar/restaurant brawl. The cases of all three men are being heard by Judge Grady O'Murphy. O'Murphy is a circuit court judge. His court is a court of general jurisdiction. O'Murphy's court hears both criminal and civil cases. Juries can be selected in O'Murphy's court and can hear landlord-tenant disputes, property crime charges, and even capital murder cases.

INTRODUCTION

The American court system is one of the most confusing systems in the world. In many countries, the court structure is a centralized system that is very uniform and easy to understand. For persons from other parts of the world, the American public, and even students studying the American court system, it is difficult to understand the structure and operations of U.S. courts. There are 51 different court structures in the United States. Each state and the federal government has its own structure and process for resolving disputes and prosecuting criminals. Some states have indeterminate sentencing; others and the federal system have determinate sentencing systems and sentencing guidelines. There are mandatory minimums, habitual offender statutes, and truth in sentencing laws in various jurisdictions that further complicate the U.S. system of courts and sentencing. Also, acquiring an awareness of only the state and federal court systems ignores other court systems, such as military tribunals, juvenile and family courts, probate courts, tribal courts, chancery courts, drug courts, and housing and land courts.

This chapter examines the structure of the American court system. It is beyond the scope of this book to list and describe all of the subtle differences of every type of court structure. Rather, this chapter will classify these court structures according to different jurisdictions with the hope of providing students a better understanding of the American court system. It will discuss three types of jurisdiction, geographic, subject matter, and hierarchical. The chapter also discusses the dual court system, meaning that in the United States there is both a federal court structure and a state court structure. Finally, it will discuss the difference between trial courts and appellate courts, and the functions of each. The federal system is made up of U.S. Magistrate Courts, U.S. District Courts, U.S. Circuit Courts of Appeal, and the U.S. Supreme Court. The state court system is characterized by Courts of Limited

Jurisdiction, Courts of General Jurisdiction, Intermediate Courts of Appeal, and Courts of Last Resort. We should not focus strictly on court names, however, since the meaning associated with a particular court name varies among counties and states. The opening scenario is an example of such confusion. Correctly, it may be assumed that the Supreme Court is an appellate court of last resort at the state and federal levels. Most trial courts are called circuit courts or district courts. However, in New York, felony trials are within the purview of the Supreme Court. New York Supreme Courts are the functional equivalent of criminal courts in other states. They simply use the term, "Supreme Court," for this type of court. Thus, this conceptual Tower of Babel needs to be understood in order to compare and contrast the different courts and their functions.

CLASSIFYING AMERICA'S COURTS

One way of classifying American courts is by **jurisdiction.** Jurisdiction is the legal authority or power of a court to hear specific kinds of cases. Jurisdiction varies most often according to where the offense occurred, the seriousness of the offense, or whether the case is being heard for the first time or on appeal. There are three types of jurisdiction: (1) subject matter jurisdiction, (2) geographic jurisdiction, and (3) hierarchical jurisdiction.

Subject Matter Jurisdiction

Subject matter jurisdiction refers to the type of case the court has authority to hear. Usually misdemeanors and preliminary hearings are processed or conducted by courts of **limited jurisdiction.** For example, if a person burglarizes a house and steals $499 worth of goods, the case typically will be heard by a court of limited jurisdiction (e.g., municipal court, city court, county court). However, if the same person burglarizes the same house and steals $500 or more worth of goods, this case will likely be heard in a court of **general jurisdiction** (e.g., district court, circuit court, superior court). Thus, the actual dollar value of property stolen determines whether the jurisdiction is limited or general. The greater the dollar value of property stolen, the more likely the case will be heard in a court of general jurisdiction. Courts of limited jurisdiction most often decide petty offenses where minor monetary sums are involved.

In many areas of the country, courts of limited jurisdiction are responsible for processing the initial stages of felony cases. These courts usually issue warrants, conduct initial appearances, establish bail, and advise felony defendants of their rights and the charges they are facing, together with a date for a preliminary hearing to determine whether probable cause exists.

Geographic Jurisdiction

Geographic jurisdiction is determined by the political boundaries where the crime was committed. Geographic jurisdiction is the clearest type of jurisdiction to understand. A defendant's case will be heard by a court within the political boundary in which the offense occurred. If a crime is committed in a county outside of the city limits, a county court will preside if there is a later trial. However, if the crime occurs in the city, then a city criminal court will preside. In Knoxville, Tennessee, for instance, there are courts of general jurisdiction known as **general sessions courts.** Anyone who commits a crime within the city limits of Knoxville will be tried in one of these courts. However, if the crime is committed in Knox County where Knoxville is also located, then a different court will hear the case. In this instance, the case will be heard in circuit courts. Tennessee is one of a few states that has retained the circuit court concept. In the early 1800s, circuit court judges would ride the circuit or ride on horseback or in buggies to remote, sparsely populated areas of Tennessee to conduct trials for those charged with crimes. These circuit judges would hold court, probably once a month. Both civil and criminal cases were heard by these circuit judges. In recent times, circuit courts in urban areas of Tennessee hear criminal and civil matters that occur outside of the Knoxville city limits but within Knox County boundaries. Furthermore, Tennessee cities also have **criminal courts** that hear more serious criminal cases that are beyond the jurisdiction of general sessions courts. Thus, Tennessee has a relatively complex and overlapping court system compared with other states.

There are other types of geographic jurisdiction besides the political boundaries of cities and counties. For instance, almost every Native American reservation and military base, fort, or installation is located within a particular state or territory. Thus, if someone commits a crime in Sequoia National Park in California, geography itself would seem to indicate that California would have jurisdiction. However, since Sequoia National Park is a federally protected area, the federal court has jurisdiction. Many offenses occurring in federally protected areas are heard by U.S. magistrates. Also, if a crime is committed on the premises of Minot Air Force Base in North Dakota, it is not relevant that the crime has occurred within the geographic boundaries of North Dakota. Minot Air Force Base is a federal military installation, and military police and courts will arrest, prosecute, and try criminal defendants. North Dakota state courts do not have jurisdiction in these cases, even though the land upon which Minot Air Force Base rests is centered within the geographical boundaries of North Dakota. Politically, the jurisdiction of North Dakota courts ends at the Minot Air Force Base gates.

Geographic jurisdiction may also be influenced by the perpetrator and victim (e.g., federal agent or federal property). For instance, in the case of *Morrissette v. United States* (1952), Morrissette, a civilian, was hunting deer one afternoon on a U.S. Army artillery range in Michigan. Although there were signs stating "Danger—Keep Out—Bombing Range," the area was known as good deer country and Morrissette hunted there anyway. In the course of his hunting, he came across a number of spent copper bomb casings that appeared to be discarded. After a frustrating day of hunting, Morrissette decided if he couldn't find a deer, he would offset some of his trip expenses by taking some of these casings and selling them for their copper value. He was arrested and charged with stealing United States government property. He was tried in federal district court and convicted, sentenced to imprisonment for two months, and fined $200. The U.S. Supreme Court reversed Morrissette's conviction, holding that Morrissette had no intention of committing a crime. Furthermore, he did not know that what he was doing was unlawful, and through his good character and openness in the taking of the casings, he demonstrated that his action was not deliberately criminal. It is significant here that Morrissette's case was not heard in a military tribunal. This is because Morrissette was a civilian and not subject to military law and sanctions. If the perpetrator had been a soldier in the U.S. Army, however, the soldier would have been tried by a military court for the criminal trespass offense.

Hierarchical Jurisdiction

Hierarchical jurisdiction is basically the difference between appellate and trial courts. Trial courts are often referred to as courts of fact, while appellate courts are referred to as courts of law. **Trial courts** are courts of fact because they are the forum where a judge or jury listens to the facts presented in the case and determines whether the defendant is guilty or not guilty. Trial courts are also responsible for sentencing the defendant. In contrast, **appellate courts** do not hear testimony or impose sentences. Appellate courts determine if the law was applied correctly. For example, a trial court judge during the course of a trial may make many decisions regarding the admissibility of evidence and testimony. For each of these decisions, the judge relies on their understanding of constitutional and procedural law. When a case is appealed, appellate court judges review whether the trial court judge followed constitutional law when they made their decisions.

FEDERAL COURT ORGANIZATION

Most courts in the United States trace their roots to the actions of colonists during the Constitutional Convention in the 1780s. Prior to the final vote on the Bill of Rights, convention delegates passed the **Judiciary Act of 1789.** Under the provisions of the Judiciary Act of 1789, three "tiers" of courts were created: (1) thirteen **federal district courts,** each presided over by a district judge; (2) three higher-level **circuit courts,** each comprising two justices of the

Supreme Court and one district judge; and (3) a **Supreme Court,** consisting of a chief justice and five associate justices.

The federal district courts were given jurisdiction in all civil and criminal cases. The circuit courts reviewed decisions of federal district courts, although they had some limited original jurisdiction. And finally, the Supreme Court was given jurisdiction that included the interpretation of federal legislation and balancing the interests between the state and the nation through the maintenance of the rights and duties of citizens. Figure 2.1 shows the structure of the federal and state court systems.

The court system in the United States can be divided into two separate entities. One court system is at the federal level and consists of the U.S. Supreme Court, the U.S. Circuit Courts of Appeal, U.S. District Courts, and the U.S. Magistrate. The other court system is established through the authority of the states and consists of state and local courts. These court structures at the state and federal levels are referred to as a **dual court system.** The

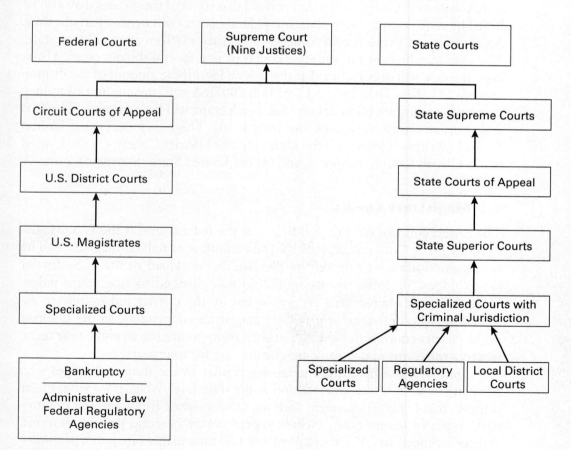

FIGURE 2.1
The Federal and State Court Systems

federal court system has the authority to hear cases identified by the Constitution. Article III, Section 2 of the Constitution identifies disputes that may be heard by federal courts. This includes cases in which the United States government or one of its officers is being sued. The Constitution also grants authority to the federal courts to hear cases, in the language of the Constitution, "Controversies between two or more states; between Citizens of the same State claiming land under grants from other states." For example, one state might sue another state for importing hazardous waste. The case is heard at the federal level because the impartiality of the state courts in either state jurisdiction might be questioned.

The Constitution also extends federal court authority to hear cases involving counsels, ambassadors, and other public ministers. The federal courts are also authorized to hear cases involving laws enacted by Congress, treaties and laws related to maritime jurisdiction, and commerce on the high seas. Because of this authority, the federal courts often decide disputes involving interstate commerce. Congress has determined that some of these cases may also be heard by state courts, giving state and federal courts **concurrent jurisdiction.** An example is when a citizen from one state sues a citizen from another state. The case may be heard in the state courts or in a federal district court. However, the case will only be heard at the federal level if the amount of the dispute exceeds $75,000 (Title 28 U.S.C. §1332, 2007). Again, the amount of money involved in a dispute often determines which court will hear the case. The federal court structure consists of four basic levels. These include: (1) the United States Magistrate Courts, (2) the United States District Courts, (3) the United States Circuit Courts of Appeal, and (4) the United States Supreme Court.

U.S. Magistrate Courts

The lowest court of limited jurisdiction at the federal level is the U.S. Magistrate. In 1968, Congress created the judicial office of federal magistrate. The magistrate's office was created to alleviate the workload of the U.S. district court judges. In 1990, the position title was changed to magistrate judge. **United States magistrates** are appointed by the district judge and are assigned as either full-time or part-time magistrates depending on the caseload of the district court. Full-time magistrates are appointed to an eight-year term, whereas the terms of part-time magistrates are for four years.

Duties of the magistrate judge are similar to the duties of judges who serve in courts of limited jurisdiction at the state level. Magistrate judges hear disputes involving civil consent matters, misdemeanor trials, and the preliminary stages of felony cases, including preliminary hearing, pretrial motions, and conferences. In 2002, there were 486 full-time magistrate judge positions. There were also 51 part-time magistrates and 3 additional clerks of court/magistrate judges (Maguire and Pastore 2005).

U.S. District Courts

At the federal level, **United States District courts** are courts of general jurisdiction. Most civil and criminal cases are tried and disposed of in the U.S. District courts. Approximately 85 percent of all federal court cases are civil, while 15 percent are criminal. There are 94 district courts in the United States. Each state has at least one federal district court and these courts can also be found in the U.S. territories of Guam, Puerto Rico, the U.S. Virgin Islands, and the Northern Mariana Islands. Thirty-one states and the U.S. Territories have only one U.S. District court with the jurisdiction to hear federal cases. The remaining states have two or more federal district courts.

In 2007, there were 603 federal district judges in practice in the United States within the various circuits (Title 28, U.S.C. Sec. 133, 2007). Federal district judges are also appointed by the president of the United States. They also serve life terms. Federal district judges who serve ten or more years with good behavior are entitled to retire at their option anytime thereafter and receive their annual salary for life. Although judicial appointments are ideally made without regard to one's race, color, sex, religion, or national origin, these appointments are primarily political and reflect the interests and views of the president. The advise and consent of Congress is required for all such appointments.

The Jurisdiction of U.S. District Courts

The jurisdiction of federal district courts is considerable. The federal district court is the major trial court for the United States. All violations of federal criminal laws are tried in the district court. Besides hearing criminal cases, federal district courts have the following jurisdictional authority:

1. To hear all civil actions where the matter exceeds $10,000 and arises under the laws, Constitution, or treaties of the United States;
2. To try diversity of citizenship matters, determine amounts in controversy, and costs;
3. To entertain bankruptcy matters and proceedings;
4. To hear interpleaders or third-party complaints;
5. To enforce ICC orders;
6. To hear commerce and antitrust suits;
7. To hear cases involving patents, copyrights, trademarks, and charges of unfair commercial competition;
8. To hear internal revenue cases and customs duty matters;
9. To judge tax matters by states;
10. To hear civil rights cases; and
11. To hear matters where the United States is a plaintiff or defendant.

Criminal cases heard in these district courts are commenced in the same way as cases are commenced in local and state courts. Federal law enforcement officers arrest suspects directly, or federal grand juries or federal prosecutors may issue indictments, presentments, or criminal informations against defendants. These defendants appear before magistrates where their bonds are established or where they are released on their own recognizance. Arraignment proceedings at the federal level are conducted in district courts by federal judges. Since arraignments include the entry of a plea by criminal defendants and the determination of a trial date, federal judges and their staffs can best determine an appropriate trial date because of the schedule of events on the federal court docket or calendar.

Federal judgeships are lifetime appointments. There is no mandatory retirement age, and federal district court judges may serve as long as they desire. In the language of the Constitution, they "hold their office during good behavior, and shall at stated Times, receive for their services a compensation, which shall not be diminished during their Continuance in Office." This provision provides for an independent judiciary and allows judges to make decisions without the threat of being removed from office or having their salary reduced.

BOX 2.1 CAREER SNAPSHOT

Micaela Alvarez
U.S. District Judge Southern District of Texas

Statistics: B.S.W., University of Texas (1980); J.D., University of Texas (1989)

Background and Interests: I grew up in a small town on the Texas–Mexico border. Most of the people in our community were Hispanic, poor and uneducated. Most were also very hard working, in particular doing field work both locally and out of state. Like our neighbors, my family and I worked the fields locally and also migrated out of state. I realized early on that I did not want to spend my life doing field work and that education would provide the door to a different world. While I did not know anybody in the legal profession, at an early age, I decided to become a lawyer.

After graduating from high school in 1976, I attended the University of Texas at Austin where I obtained a bachelor's degree in social work. For about three years, I worked as a social worker. I then attended the University of Texas School of Law and graduated in 1989. I returned to South

Texas and began working for a law firm. In 1995, I was appointed by then Governor Bush to serve as the District Judge for the 139th Judicial District Court in Hidalgo County, Texas. I was the first woman to sit as a District Judge in Hidalgo County. In 1997, I returned to private practice and was a founding partner in a new law firm.

In 1997, I was appointed by Governor Bush to serve as a board member of the State Office of Risk Management. In 2002, I was also appointed by President Bush to serve as a commissioner of the Presidential Commission on Educational Excellence for Hispanic Americans. In mid 2004, I was nominated by President Bush to serve as a United States District Judge for the Southern District of Texas. I was confirmed by the Senate in November 2004 and now serve as a United States District Judge in Laredo, Texas.

Work Experience: As a District Judge in South Texas, I handle a large volume of criminal cases on a daily basis. My daily routine includes handling pretrial matters, taking pleas, conducting trials, and sentencing those adjudged guilty. I also deal with individuals on supervised release who violate the terms of that release. Many of these cases involve either drug or immigration violations. Some of the defendants that I deal with have a long history of similar offenses. However, many are first-time offenders who are lured by the offer of easy money. A large percentage of these defendants also have some sort of drug and/or alcohol problems.

One of the hardest parts of my job is sentencing. I read a report for each defendant, which provides me with information regarding criminal history and personal background. Also quite often, I receive letters from the defendants, their families, neighbors, and coworkers. These letters paint a partial picture of the individual to be sentenced. Many tell heartwrenching stories of dire circumstances either leading to the instant offense or as a result of the incarceration. While I cannot respond individually to these letters, at the sentencing I try to convey to the defendant my sympathies for his/her particular situation but also the societal interests that must be considered. The saddest cases that I deal with are those involving young offenders who have made a bad choice and are now facing a lengthy prison sentence. In all of these cases, I try to remember that while I may do this for a living, I am dealing with the life of an individual.

Advice to Students: I am a firm believer in the American Dream and that education opens the door to that dream. However, regardless of what you choose to do in life, you should make sure it is something that provides you with personal satisfaction. Once you have chosen your career, then you should strive to do the best job possible. If you are considering a legal career, do not do it for the money or glamor; do it for the pursuit of justice.

U.S. Circuit Courts of Appeal

In the early years of the United States, there were only three circuit courts of the United States without any permanent personnel. Two Supreme Court justices and a federal district judge comprised the transient judiciary of the circuit courts. These judges were called **circuit riders.** These judges were obligated to hold 28 courts per year. This created considerable hardship because transportation was poor and it was difficult to travel great distances. Furthermore, since federal district judges were a part of the original circuit judiciary, this placed them in the prejudicial position of reviewing their own decisions.

Over the next two centuries, numerous changes occurred in circuit court structure. Several reforms such as the Judiciary Act of 1891 or **Evarts Act** were introduced to create what is the current scheme for federal appellate review. In 2007, there were 13 **United States Circuit Courts of Appeal** at the federal level (these include the District of Columbia and Federal Circuits) with 179 circuit court judges in practice (U.S. Code, Title 28, Section 41, 2007). These

TABLE 2.1   THE THIRTEEN JUDICIAL CIRCUITS, COMPOSITION, AND NUMBER OF CIRCUIT JUDGES, 2007

Circuits	Composition	Number of Circuit Judges
District of Columbia	District of Columbia	12
First	Maine, Massachusetts, New Hampshire, Puerto Rico, Rhode Island	6
Second	Connecticut, New York, Vermont	13
Third	Delaware, New Jersey, Pennsylvania, Virgin Islands	14
Fourth	Maryland, North Carolina, South Carolina, Virginia, West Virginia	15
Fifth	Canal Zone, Louisiana, Mississippi, Texas	17
Sixth	Kentucky, Michigan, Ohio, Tennessee	16
Seventh	Illinois, Indiana, Wisconsin	11
Eighth	Arkansas, Iowa, Minnesota, Missouri, Nebraska, North Dakota, South Dakota	11
Ninth	Alaska, Arizona, California, Idaho, Montana, Nevada, Guam, Oregon, Washington, Hawaii	28
Tenth	Colorado, Kansas, New Mexico, Oklahoma, Utah, Wyoming	12
Eleventh	Alabama, Florida, Georgia	12
Federal	All Federal Judicial Districts	12
Total		179

(*Source:* Title 28, U.S. Code, Sec. 44, 2007.)

are shown in Table 2.1. These circuit court geographical boundaries are also shown in Figure 2.2.

Typically, circuit courts hear cases with three-judge panels. In certain circuits, the volume of cases may be such that several three-judge panels may be convened simultaneously. These three-judge panels hear appeals from decisions in U.S. District courts. On rare occasions, a case may be heard *en banc.* This is where the entire aggregate of judges in the circuit hears and decides the case appeal. Usually, appeals heard *en banc* involve important constitutional issues, and input from a larger number of judges is deemed important.

Like district court judges, appellate judges are appointed for life by the president and confirmed by the Senate. One of these judges is designated as the chief judge. Usually the chief judge is the one with the greatest seniority and who is also under 65 years of age. Chief judges perform additional duties apart from hearing cases, and their maximum terms are seven years.

Each of the circuit courts of appeal has appellate jurisdiction for all federal district courts in the particular circuit. For instance, the Eleventh Circuit Court of Appeals includes Alabama, Florida, and Georgia. These states are divided into several divisions, each containing one or more federal district courts. When a defendant wishes to appeal a decision of any federal district court

FIGURE 2.2

District and Appellate Court Boundaries (*Source:* Administrative Office of the United States Courts.) *Note:* The large numerals indicate the Court of Appeals, and the broken lines represent jurisdiction boundaries of district courts.

within Alabama, Florida, or Georgia, the appeal is directed to the Eleventh United States Circuit Court of Appeals.

While all circuit courts of appeal have appellate jurisdiction from all final decisions from district courts, there are occasions where a direct review may be made by the United States Supreme Court. Panels of three circuit judges must convene at regular intervals to hear appeals from federal district courts. Of course, if a defendant disagrees with the decision of a circuit court, the United States Supreme Court is the court of last resort for appeals.

The U.S. Supreme Court

The court of last resort at the federal level is the **United States Supreme Court.** It is the only court specifically mentioned in Article III, Section 1 of the Constitution. The Constitution states that "the judicial power of the United States, shall be vested in one supreme court, and in such inferior courts as the Congress may from time to time ordain and establish." Like all of the other federal courts, U.S. Supreme Court justices hold their positions for life. They are nominated and appointed by the president, with Senate confirmation. The Supreme Court consists of eight associate justices and one chief justice. The chief justice has the additional responsibility of conducting conferences, supervising the federal judiciary, and assigning the task of writing various case opinions to a member of the judicial majority. Each of the associate justices is assigned to one of the appellate circuits for emergencies, such as death penalty appeals. In 2006, the annual salary of U.S. Supreme Court chief justice was about $212,100 and for the associate justices it was about $203,000 (*New York Times*, January 1, 2006, 1.13).

The U.S. Supreme Court has both **original jurisdiction** and **exclusive jurisdiction** over (1) all actions or proceedings against ambassadors or public ministers of foreign states; and (2) all controversies between two or more states. Original jurisdiction means the court may recognize a case at its inception, hear that case, and try it without consultation with other courts or authorities. Exclusive jurisdiction means that no other court can decide certain kinds of cases except the court having exclusive jurisdiction. A juvenile court has exclusive jurisdiction over juvenile matters, for example. The adult criminal courts have no juvenile jurisdiction.

The *Case of* Marbury v. Madison *(1803)*

One of the most important decisions that established review powers for the U.S. Supreme Court was the case of *Marbury v. Madison* (1803). This case was a political conflict between the Federalists and anti-Federalists. Outgoing president John Adams made several new circuit court appointments and signed commissions for their appointment on the his last day of office. However, Secretary of State James Madison withheld the processing of these commissions, anticipating a new president (and a change in political party) where party appointments could be made instead of the old administration appointees. This was an obvious attempt to create additional judicial appointments from party members favorable to the incoming president. One of these appointments was William Marbury who petitioned the U.S. Supreme Court to force Secretary of State Madison to issue his new appointment. Chief Justice John Marshall ruled in Marbury's favor and issued a *writ of mandamus* to compel the Secretary of State to issue the commissions authorized by ex-president John Adams. Thus, the right of **judicial review** established the power of the U.S. Supreme Court to review and determine the constitutionality of acts of Congress and the executive branch.

The Supreme Court is the ultimate reviewing body regarding decisions made by lower appellate courts or state supreme courts. The Supreme Court is primarily an appellate court, since most of its time is devoted to reviewing decisions of lower courts. It is the final arbiter of lower court decisions unless Congress declares otherwise. Congress may change existing Constitutional Amendments or other Acts. The United States Supreme Court meets 36 weeks annually from the first Monday in October until the end of June (U.S. Code, Title 28, Sec. 5, 2007).

The U.S. Supreme Court is in session from the first Monday of October until the preceding day the next year. The year of the annual session is the year when the session is commenced. When the U.S. Supreme Court convenes in October 2006, all cases decided during that term are considered as cases decided during the 2006 term, even though a particular case might not be heard until May or June, 2007.

Annually, the court receives approximately 7,000 case appeals. Most appeals are disposed of when the U.S. Supreme Court decides not to hear the case because of the subject matter, or if it is not significant enough to merit court review. The decision to hear a case is made when the justices meet to review all cases. In order for all of the justices to hear a particular appeal, the case must pass a screening, which is known as the **Rule of Four.** This means that at least four of the nine justices must agree that the case has constitutional merit or national importance and that it should be heard by the entire court. If a case receives four or more votes from the justices, it is placed on the docket and scheduled to be heard. Only about 150 cases annually pass the Rule of Four and are placed on the docket for an opinion.

The primary method that cases reach the Court is through a petition known as a **writ of** *certiorari.* This is an order issued by the Supreme Court to the lower court to send the record for review. When the Court decides to hear a case, it is scheduled for written and oral arguments by the opposing lawyers. The written arguments are filed with the Court and made available to the public. In some cases other interested parties may file briefs for the Court to hear, on behalf of other parties. These types of filings are called ***amicus curiae*** briefs. *Amicus curiae* means "a friend of the court," and refers to a broad class of briefs that may be filed by one party on behalf of one or more other parties. For instance, an *amicus curiae* brief was filed on behalf of Gary Gilmore, a convicted murderer in Utah, by Amnesty International, an organization opposed to capital punishment. The brief was on behalf of Gilmore who was scheduled to be executed. The brief sought relief in the form of a stay of Gilmore's execution, until the U.S. Supreme Court had time to hear and consider new arguments for why the death penalty should not be imposed in Gilmore's case. Although the brief was successful, in that it gave Gilmore several additional weeks, Gilmore did not wish to pursue further appeals. He declared that he wanted to die, and that the state should be allowed to execute him, despite the objections of Gilmore's family and Amnesty International. Gilmore was subsequently executed by a Utah firing squad.

Appearances by attorneys before the U.S. Supreme Court are highly regimented by prevailing protocol. The attorneys for the opposing sides are permitted 30 minutes each to present oral arguments. Green, yellow, and red lights similar to those that regulate automobile traffic flash for the different litigants. A green light means oral argument may proceed. A yellow light flashes when the 30-minute oral argument time limit is approaching. And a red light means that the oral argument terminates. During this time justices are allowed to ask questions of the attorneys presenting the oral arguments. After oral arguments, the justices schedule a meeting, which is called a case conference. In this meeting the justices take an initial position.

Traditionally, if the chief justice is in the majority, this justice assigns the writing of the majority opinion to one of the other majority justices. The senior justice for the minority or dissenting opinion assigns the writing of this opinion to one of the dissenting justices. The writing of the opinion may be quite complicated, especially when the justices on both sides have conflicting opinions about the case. For instance, not all of the majority justices may believe the case should be decided in a given way for the same reasons. Thus, each majority justice may write an independent opinion about why the justice voted a certain way. Accordingly, dissenting justices do not have to agree about why they dissent. Thus, several dissenting justices may write independent opinions about why they dissented. These opinions make for interesting reading for Supreme Court historians and others, since often the personal views of justices are made evident in their opinions.

When the topic of the opinion is controversial, such as a case involving abortion or the death penalty, each justice expresses different views about the issue. For example, in *Furman v. Georgia* (1972), all justices wrote separate opinions. In most cases, the opinion goes through several drafts before it is approved by the majority or dissenting justices, and before it is subsequently made available to the public. Unlike cases heard at the appellate level, the U.S. Supreme Court hears all cases *en banc*. All nine justices hear the case.

There are exceptions. Sometimes, a death or resignation from the U.S. Supreme Court may leave the court with seven or eight members temporarily, until a new justice or justices can be appointed. During the time interval when the Court does not have nine justices, it may still convene and hear and decide appeals. A majority of justices is still required, although a majority is more difficult to achieve. Eight justices may divide equally on a given issue, with a 4–4 vote. Such a vote results in no decision rendered about that particular appeal. Five or more justices are required to support any appeal. When a 4–4 vote occurs, the case is simply discarded and not scheduled for rehearing. The litigants may bring the case before the U.S. Supreme Court again, provided that they raise a different and meaningful issue as the basis for challenging a lower court decision. And the Rule of Four exists for all new case filings, regardless of whether a particular case has been previously heard. Four or more justices must agree to hear the case before it will be docketed.

STATE COURT ORGANIZATION

Studying the American courts would be relatively easy if we didn't have to consider state court organization. But as we have seen, states such as Tennessee provide numerous different court structures and jurisdictions to create some complexity. And each state is different from the others in state court organization and function. Thus, we must add to the federal system the different court systems found in all 50 states. Figure 2.3 shows the federal court system.

The organization and functions of the 50 different state court structures are diverse and complex. For example, Massachusetts has a supreme judicial court, appeals court, superior court, district court, probate/family court, juvenile court, housing court, municipal court, and land court. In contrast, South Dakota has only a two-tiered system with a circuit court and a supreme court. State courts often have overlapping and conflicting jurisdictions. The state courts are also very busy with variable caseloads. Millions of cases are filed and disposed of each year. In 2003, over 100 million disputes were heard by state courts (Schauffler, Lafountain, Kauder, and Strickland 2004). Most of these cases (about 40 percent) were traffic offenses. Caseloads in all five categories (criminal, civil, domestic relations, juvenile, and traffic) have continued to increase over the past several years (Schauffler et al. 2004). Figure 2.4 shows a basic state court system. Not all states follow this particular diagram, with some states having separate criminal and civil appellate levels. But generally, this model is representative of most state court systems.

A more elaborate type of state court system is referred to as the traditional court model or the Texas Model. This type of court system is illustrated in Figure 2.5. It provides more extensive detail than the state court organization depicted in Figure 2.4.

BOX 2.2 THE POWER OF THE U.S. SUPREME COURT

The 2004–2005 Term

The U.S. Supreme Court decides many important cases annually. Most of the cases involve constitutional issues. Compared with Congress, the country's law-making body, the U.S. Supreme Court interprets the law and how the law should be applied. For instance during the 2004–2005 term, they made decisions on many important matters. At issue was whether or not the monument of the Ten Commandments at the state capitol in Austin, Texas, violates the Establishment Clause; whether or not companies that produce file-sharing services allowing the illegal downloading of music are in violation of copyright infringement laws; and whether or not executing individuals who commit crimes before their eighteenth birthday is in violation of the Eighth Amendment against cruel and unusual punishment. What did the Supreme Court decide?

First, the monument of the Ten Commandments can remain on the ground of the capitol in Austin, Texas. The monument has been there for about 40 years and simply having religious content does not violate the Establishment Clause. Second, the Court ruled, in a unanimous decision, that companies making software enabling illegal downloads are in violation of copyright infringement because they acted with a purpose to cause copyright violations. Third, the Court decided that execution of those who committed crimes before their eighteenth birthday does constitute cruel and unusual punishment because the United States is the only country that allows the execution of juveniles.

In other decisions, the U.S. Supreme Court ruled the federal sentencing guidelines unconstitutional and discretionary instead of mandatory. The Court also expanded the criteria for age discrimination lawsuits, ruled in favor of religion in prisons, and overturned the conviction against the accounting firm of Arthur Andersen. Do you think these powers are within the scope of authority originally vested in the U.S. Supreme Court? Should the U.S. Supreme Court be subject to the scrutiny of other bodies, such as the executive branch or Congress? What do you think? [Source: Adapted from the Associated Press, "New Order in the Court," *Los Angeles Times*, July 3, 2005.]

Other types of court organizational systems have been proposed in past years. For instance, Ezra Pound advocated a simple model, consisting of a supreme court as the highest court, a major trial court, and a minor trial court. The American Bar Association has proposed its own simplified court organizational structure, modifying the Pound model by adding an intermediate appellate court. A later version of court organization devised by the American Bar Association envisioned a three-tiered system, with a supreme court at the top,

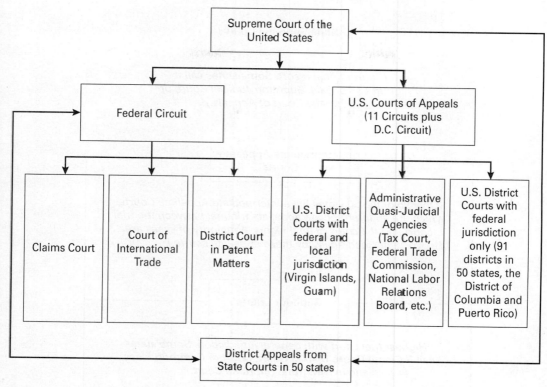

FIGURE 2.3
The Federal Court System

an intermediate appellate court in the middle, and a trial court at the bottom. Figure 2.6 shows these three models.

Many jurisdictions do not require that judicial officers have a law degree. In fact, 36 states do not require that judges in a court of limited jurisdiction must be educated in the law. One reason is that many judges are elected rather than appointed or through some other form of merit selection. In short, these judges need to convince the electorate that they have the ability to serve rather than be legal practitioners with professional credentials. The lack of education and knowledge of the judicial process among many state court judges has caused a number of problems. Most of these courts are not courts of record, and so it is difficult to monitor their activities formally. Because many elected judges do not know the limits of their authority or are unfamiliar with the processes of the judicial system, many states have established a legal training requirement for newly elected judges. Most of these judges are required to attend a legal training seminar sponsored by the state judicial conference or a committee or program sponsored by the Administrative Office of the U.S. Courts.

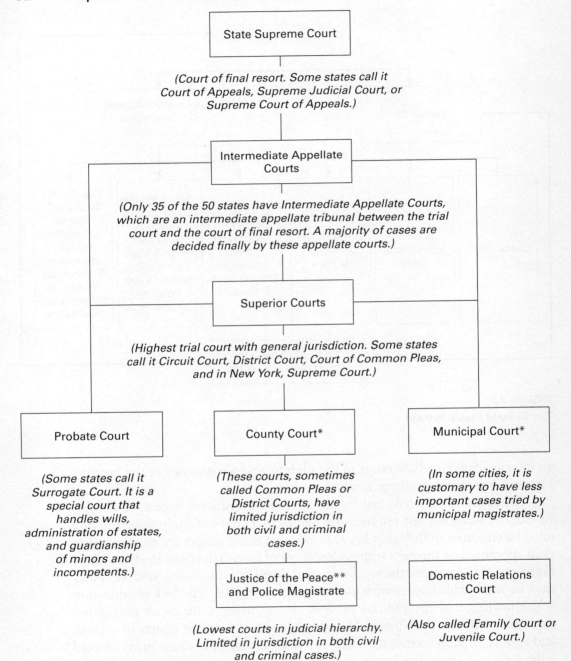

FIGURE 2.4

The State Judicial System

*Courts of special jurisdiction, such as probate, family, or juvenile courts, and the so-called inferior courts, such as common pleas or municipal courts, may be separate courts or part of the trial court of general jurisdiction.

**Justices of the peace do not exist in all states. Where they do exist, their jurisdictions vary greatly from state to state.

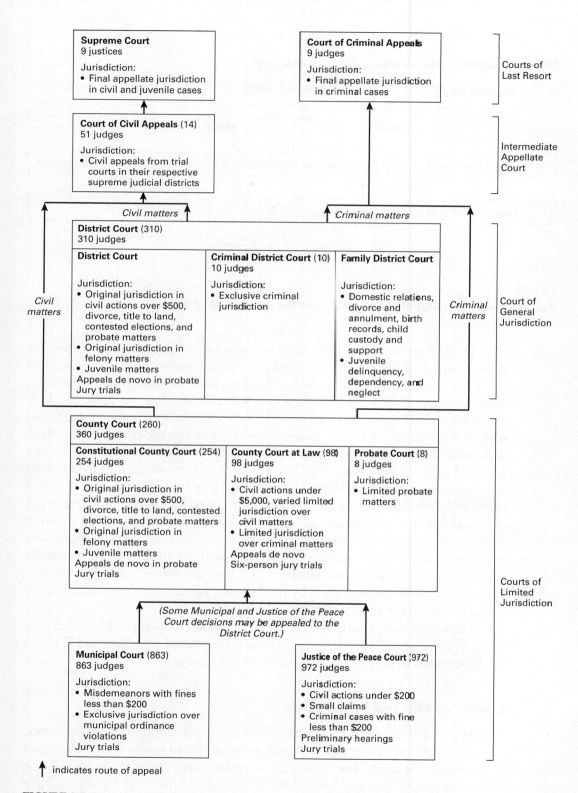

Supreme Court
9 justices

Jurisdiction:
• Final appellate jurisdiction in civil and juvenile cases

Court of Criminal Appeals
9 judges

Jurisdiction:
• Final appellate jurisdiction in criminal cases

Courts of Last Resort

Court of Civil Appeals (14)
51 judges

Jurisdiction:
• Civil appeals from trial courts in their respective supreme judicial districts

Intermediate Appellate Court

Civil matters   *Criminal matters*

District Court (310)
310 judges

District Court

Jurisdiction:
• Original jurisdiction in civil actions over $500, divorce, title to land, contested elections, and probate matters
• Original jurisdiction in felony matters
• Juvenile matters
Appeals de novo in probate
Jury trials

Criminal District Court (10)
10 judges

Jurisdiction:
• Exclusive criminal jurisdiction

Family District Court

Jurisdiction:
• Domestic relations, divorce and annulment, birth records, child custody and support
• Juvenile delinquency, dependency, and neglect

Civil matters   *Criminal matters*

Court of General Jurisdiction

County Court (260)
360 judges

Constitutional County Court (254)
254 judges

Jurisdiction:
• Original jurisdiction in civil actions over $500, divorce, title to land, contested elections, and probate matters
• Original jurisdiction in felony matters
• Juvenile matters
Appeals de novo in probate
Jury trials

County Court at Law (98)
98 judges

Jurisdiction:
• Civil actions under $5,000, varied limited jurisdiction over civil matters
• Limited jurisdiction over criminal matters
Appeals de novo
Six-person jury trials

Probate Court (8)
8 judges

Jurisdiction:
• Limited probate matters

(Some Municipal and Justice of the Peace Court decisions may be appealed to the District Court.)

Municipal Court (863)
863 judges

Jurisdiction:
• Misdemeanors with fines less than $200
• Exclusive jurisdiction over municipal ordinance violations
Jury trials

Justice of the Peace Court (972)
972 judges

Jurisdiction:
• Civil actions under $200
• Small claims
• Criminal cases with fine less than $200
Preliminary hearings
Jury trials

Courts of Limited Jurisdiction

↑ indicates route of appeal

FIGURE 2.5
The Traditional Court Model (Texas Model)

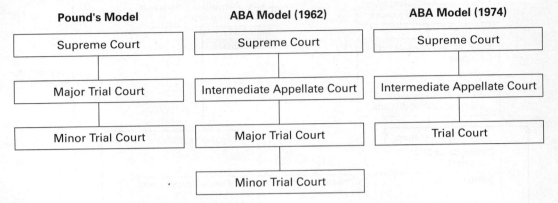

FIGURE 2.6
Pound's Model, the ABA Model of 1962, and the ABA Model of 1974

Despite provisions for the legal training of new judges in most jurisdictions, research about courts of limited jurisdiction has revealed that more than few inequities exist. Some of these injustices, such as judicial incompetence, have been highlighted in U.S. Supreme Court cases. For example, the U.S. Supreme Court was confronted with the matter of judicial competence in the case of *North v. Russell* (1976). Judge Russell worked in the coal mines of Kentucky after he dropped out of high school. Later he was elected as a judge and presided over the case of Lonnie North who had been accused of drunk driving. Judge Russell denied North's request for a jury trial, did not inform North of his right to counsel, and denied North's right to appeal the subsequent decision. Judge Russell listened only to the arresting officer's version of the incident and did not permit North testify in his own behalf and provide his version of events. Judge Russell sentenced Lonnie North to 30 days in jail when the statute provided a maximum sentence of a fine and no jail time. In this case, North's conviction was set aside by the U.S. Supreme Court and Judge Russell was criticized for his incompetence.

Generally state courts have a four-tiered court structure. These tiers are (1) courts of limited jurisdiction, (2) courts of general jurisdiction, (3) intermediate courts of appeal, and (4) courts of last resort.

Courts of Limited Jurisdiction

Courts of limited jurisdiction have the greatest variability among the states. These courts hear minor offenses such as violations of traffic laws, minor civil cases, and infractions. They also perform other administrative duties. Courts of limited jurisdiction comprise about 80 percent of the total number of state courts. They are the courts with the greatest caseloads in the nation (Ostrom, Cheesman, and Jones 1999). On the average, they dispose of over 50 percent

BOX 2.3 TECHNOLOGY AND ACCESS TO THE FEDERAL JUDICIARY

Technological advances have affected all of us in some way. The federal judiciary is not immune to this trend. Since the 1990s the federal court has made available to the public a number of resources to access information about the cases before the Court and the decisions reached by the Court. The service offered allows the public to obtain information about the actions of the Court without ever stepping foot inside the courthouse. Some of the services offered by the Court are:

The U.S. Supreme Court Electronic Bulletin Board System The U.S. Supreme Court Electronic Bulletin Board System (EBBS) service provides online access to the court docket, opinions, argument calendar, rules, and bar information forms. Additional information includes general and tour information and special notices.

U.S. Supreme Court Clerk's Automated Response Systems (CARS) The U.S. Supreme Court Clerk's Automated Response System (CARS) provides callers with information about the status of cases by instructing callers to respond to telephone prompts.

Appellate Bulletin Board System (ABBS) The Appellate Bulletin Board System (ABBS) is a source of information about judicial opinions offered to the public by federal circuit courts of appeal. These courts offer the public access to court decisions, argument calendars, case dockets, reports, notices, and press releases. Information can be downloaded and viewed online by computer users. Currently, there is a $.60 per minute fee for this service.

Public Access to Court Electronic Records (PACER) The Public Access to Court Electronic Records (PACER) is a service that allows users to dial into the bankruptcy court computer to access information about cases and decisions. Again there is a $.60 per minute charge. Users must first register with the PACER service center before they can use this service. Many district and circuit courts have established toll-free numbers to users where additional costs of long-distance telephone calls are not incurred.

Party/Case Index In 1977, the courts started a new service that would allow users to conduct searches of the bankruptcy court by party name or Social Security number. Searches can also be conducted to locate civil or criminal cases or cases beginning to be appealed. The search will retrieve the case filing date and filing location.

Electronic Filing and Attorney Docketing Service The Electronic Filing and Attorney Docketing Service (EFADS) is another service that is being tested in selected district courts. This service allows attorneys to submit pleadings and other docket entries through the Internet. The case file and official docket can be viewed online or downloaded electronically.

of all cases brought before the state courts. The District of Columbia, Iowa, South Dakota, Idaho, and Illinois are the only states without courts of limited jurisdiction.

State courts of limited jurisdiction have many different names. Most of these courts are called municipal courts, county courts, city courts, or justice of the peace courts. Other courts are specialized courts of limited jurisdiction. Some of these courts might be called juvenile court or family court, probate court, and courts of workers compensation. Recent caseload estimates indicate that traffic cases between 1994 and 2003 in municipal courts comprised the largest percentage of incoming cases. These courts continue to be busy with heavy caseloads because of increases in all other types of cases, not just those involving traffic violations (Schauffler et al. 2004).

Courts of General Jurisdiction

Courts of general jurisdiction have jurisdiction over all major civil and criminal cases. These courts also differ from courts of limited jurisdiction because they are **courts of record** and **general trial courts.** They are courts of record because a record is made of all of the proceedings. Various methods are used to make records of these proceedings. Court reporters use tape recorders and several other devices to record whatever is said. With a few exceptions, courts of general jurisdiction are called circuit courts, district courts, superior courts, courts of common pleas, and supreme courts. A list of names of these courts for the different states is provided in Table 2.2.

In 2002, state courts processed and sentenced over 1,051,000 adults for felony offenses. This figure does not include civil filings (Bureau of Justice Statistics 2005). Contrary to what is reported and portrayed by the media, criminal jury trials are relatively rare events. This is because over 90 percent of all criminals who are prosecuted are convicted in criminal courts through plea bargaining, where guilty pleas are entered in exchange for some form of leniency from prosecutors and judges. Thus, criminal trials are conducted only for about 10 percent of all criminal cases.

In recent years, the criminal courts have been processing cases more rapidly than in past years. For instance, in 1988, state courts processed 667,366 cases and the average case processing time from arrest to conviction was about seven months. In 1994 the courts processed 872,217 cases and the average time between arrest and conviction was six and a half months (Maguire and Pastore 2005). In 2000, the court processed 924,700 cases with a median time between arrest and sentencing of 5.1 months (Maguire and Pastore 2005). Many factors account for this decrease in processing time. One reason is that courts, faced with increasing caseloads, have learned and incorporated more efficient caseload management processes to reduce court delays. Or courts may realize the increased caseload and deliberately limit the number of delays and continu-

TABLE 2.2 COURTS OF GENERAL JURISDICTION FOR EACH STATE.*

Circuit Court

Alabama, Arkansas, Florida, Hawaii, Illinois, Indiana,[1] Kentucky, Maryland, Michigan, Mississippi, Missouri, Oregon, South Carolina, South Dakota, Tennessee, Virginia, West Virginia, Wisconsin

Superior Court

Alaska, Arizona, California, Connecticut, Delaware, District of Colombia, Georgia, Maine, Massachusetts, New Hampshire, New Jersey, North Carolina, Puerto Rico, Rhode Island, Vermont,[2] Washington

District Court

Colorado, Idaho, Iowa, Kansas, Louisiana, Minnesota, Montana, Nebraska, Nevada, New Mexico, North Dakota, Oklahoma, Texas, Utah, Wyoming

Court of Common Pleas

Ohio, Pennsylvania

Supreme Court

New York[3]

*Compiled by authors.

1. Indiana has both circuit courts and superior courts.
2. Vermont has superior courts and district courts.
3. New York also has county courts.

ances that have been allowed in past years. The workload of the court is strongly associated with where the court is located. Typically, urban courts have more cases to process than rural courts. For example, Los Angeles, the busiest court system in the nation, processed 50,197 felony cases in 1994 (Maguire and Pastore 2005). This figure is greater than all of the felony cases processed in the entire federal system during that same year.

The demand for court services fluctuates greatly depending upon certain areas of the country. In 2003, for example, South Dakota processed only 26,384 cases in courts of general jurisdiction; this amounts to about 3,452 cases per 100,000 persons. In that same year, however, Wisconsin processed 248,960 cases in courts of general jurisdiction; this amounts to about 4,549 cases per 100,000 persons (Schauffler et al. 2004).

Judges in the courts of general jurisdiction usually have practiced law either as prosecutors or working in a law firm before becoming a judge. However, in Maine and Massachusetts, judges at this level are not required to have a law degree. The only requirement is that they are learned in the law (Rottman, Flango, Cantrell, Hansen, and LaFountain 2000). Surprisingly, Maine requires that judges who preside over courts of limited jurisdiction have law degrees, while their counterparts in the trial courts have no such requirement. Most states require some combination of a law degree, being a member of the state bar for 5 to 10 years, as well as local and/or state residency requirements. Some states have age limitations for judges at this level. Usually, the minimum age is 25–30 years and the maximum age is 70–75. The median salary for judges in trial courts is $112,724. Judges in the District of Columbia's general courts were the highest paid in the nation with a salary of $154,700. The lowest-paid trial judges were in New Mexico with a salary of $86,896 (Maguire and Pastore 2005).

Intermediate Courts of Appeal

Eleven states and the District of Columbia do not have intermediate courts of appeal. Most states have developed an intermediate court of appeal to review and screen the caseload on the state supreme court. These intermediate courts of appeal became necessary shortly after 1900. A few states such as Alabama, Tennessee, and Texas have separate appellate courts for civil and criminal cases. North Dakota has a statutory provision providing for an appellate court at this level, although these judges must be called to action by the state's supreme court. Such an event rarely occurs in North Dakota. Most cases are heard with a panel of three judges. Unlike the courts of last resort, they do not have discretionary appellate review. Thus, they are required to hear all cases that are properly filed.

Most of the judges at this level are appointed by the governor after being selected by a nominating commission. Appellate court judges make slightly more than their colleagues in the general trial courts. The median salary was $121,697. Appellate court judges in California are paid the most at $164,604 and appellate court judges in New Mexico were paid the least making $91,469 (Maguire and Pastore 2005). Table 2.3 shows the intermediate courts of appeal for different states.

Courts of Last Resort

The highest court structures at the state level are called **courts of last resort.** Usually these are also called supreme courts. In states with an intermediate court of appeals, these courts have discretionary appellate review. This means that they decide which cases they will hear. By refusing to hear a case, they are allowing the decision of the lower court to stand. In states where there is no intermediate court of appeal, the state supreme court has no discretionary authority. Alabama, Oklahoma, and Texas are unique in this regard because they have two courts of last resort. One is designated to hear civil cases, while the other hears only criminal cases. Judges who preside in state supreme courts are usually selected by a nominating commission and appointed by the governor.

TABLE 2.3   INTERMEDIATE COURTS OF APPEAL FOR DIFFERENT STATES.*

Appeals Court

Massachusetts

Appellate Court

Connecticut, Illinois

Appellate Division of Superior Court

New Jersey

Appellate Division of Supreme Court

New York, West Virginia

Commonwealth Court

Pennsylvania

Courts of Appeal

California, Louisiana, Texas

Court of Civil Appeal

Alabama

Court of Appeals

Alaska, Arizona, Arkansas, Colorado, District of Columbia, Georgia, Idaho, Indiana, Iowa, Kansas, Kentucky, Maryland, Michigan, Minnesota, Mississippi, Missouri, Nebraska,

New Mexico, New York, North Carolina, North Dakota, Ohio, Oklahoma, Oregon, Puerto Rico, South Carolina, Tennessee, Utah, Virginia, Washington, Wisconsin

District Courts of Appeal

Florida

Intermediate Court of Appeals

Hawaii

Superior Court

Pennsylvania

Courts of Appeals

Texas

Court of Civil Appeal

Alabama, Oklahoma

Court of Criminal Appeal

Alabama, Oklahoma, Tennessee, Texas

Court of Special Appeals

Maryland

District Court of Appeals

Florida

(*Source:* Compiled by authors.)

In order to remain in their position, they must receive a majority vote in a retention election. The median salary for the state's highest court is $125,292. The highest-paid supreme court justices reside in California and make $175,575. The lowest-paid supreme court justices are in West Virginia where they receive annual salaries of $95,000 (Maguire and Pastore 2005).

SUMMARY

The American court system is one of the most confusing in the world. Each state has its own court structure, and in many cases courts that perform the same functions are referred to by different names. Therefore,

in order to understand the American court structure, we must understand how each court functions as well as the kind of matters they can
hear. We must also compare these courts among the different states.
The best and easiest way to understand the American court structure is
to classify these courts according to their particular jurisdiction. One of
these is subject matter jurisdiction, which refers to the type of case a
court can hear. Courts of limited jurisdiction are granted the legal authority to hear misdemeanor cases or the preliminary stages of felony
cases. Courts of general jurisdiction are basically felony trial courts.
They are also referred to as courts of fact. However, appellate courts are
called courts of law because they do not determine the facts of the case.
Rather, they are charged with determining whether the law has been applied correctly. This is a classification known as hierarchical jurisdiction,
basically that trial courts decide the case and appellate courts decide if
the law was applied correctly in a case. Geography also defines the limits of a court's authority. A court's legal authority is limited by political
boundaries. For example, a state court in Arizona does not have the legal authority to hear a criminal case from Nevada. Many municipalities
have their own court systems, and their jurisdiction is limited to cases
that occur within the city limits.

With court systems at both the state and federal levels, this scenario is often referred to as the dual court system. The basic trial courts
in the federal system are the U.S. District courts. Most civil and criminal cases of federal interest are tried and disposed of in these courts.
There are 94 district courts in the United States. Federal district court
judgeships are lifetime appointments and there is no mandatory retirement age. The court below the U.S. Disrtict court is the U.S. Magistrate courts. These courts were created to alleviate the caseload of
district court judges. These magistrate judges are appointed by the district judge, and depending on the caseload, work either full- or part-
time. Full-time magistrate judges have an 8-year appointment,
whereas part-time magistrate judges have a 4-year appointment. Magistrate judges typically will hear misdemeanor cases, or the preliminary
hearings, pretrial motions, and conferences of felony cases. The federal system also has 13 appellate jurisdictions or Circuit Courts of Appeal. These are the intermediate appellate courts at the federal level.
Again these were created to alleviate the rising caseload of the
Supreme Court. These courts then hear the appeals from the decisions
made by the U.S. District courts. Like their district court counterparts
they are appointed for life by the president. Finally, the U.S. Supreme
Court is the court of last resort or the highest court in the land. Nine
justices hear an average of 7,000 cases per year and write opinions in
about 200 of them. Unlike trial courts, which have no control over

what cases are presented to them, most state courts of last resort and the U.S. Supreme Court decide which case appeals they will or will not hear. They do not however have the time to hear every case; rather, they marshal their time and use their discretion to hear the most important matters of the time, or matters that involve important federal questions.

The state court structure is a little more confusing. The state court structure is more difficult to understand because the functions and organization of the 50 different state court structures are diverse. The same or similar courts often have different names in different states, and state courts often have overlapping and conflicting jurisdictions. Many of the state jurisdictions do not require that judges have a law degree, 36 states do not even require education in the law for their limited jurisdiction court judgeships. One of the most likely reasons for this is that these judges are elected rather than appointed. Therefore, they need only convince the electorate that they can serve in the position well. This has caused a number of problems in the past regarding judicial incompetence and knowledge of the law.

The courts in most states have a four-tiered structure. The tiers include: courts of limited jurisdiction, courts of general jurisdiction, intermediate courts of appeal, and courts of last resort, or state supreme courts. The courts of limited jurisdiction are the courts that are the least consistent among the states. These courts hear the most minor of offenses, minor civil cases, traffic violations, and also perform administrative duties. They are the courts with the highest caseloads in the country. Courts of general jurisdiction hear all major civil and criminal cases. These courts are the general trial courts in the state system and are courts of record. Again, these courts have a fairly high caseload, however, contrary to popular media perceptions, more than 90 percent of these cases are disposed of through a plea bargain. A court's activity, however, varies in different areas of the country. The courts in large urban jurisdictions are obviously busier than those in rural areas. The judges in courts of general jurisdiction are usually more learned in the law than their limited jurisdiction judicial counterparts and have probably practiced law either as a prosecutor or defense attorney. The intermediate courts of appeal screen the caseload of the supreme court. Eleven states and the District of Columbia, however, do not have intermediate courts of appeal. States with high appellate caseloads probably have an intermediate court of appeal. Most of these judges, like their state supreme court counterparts, are appointed by the governor. These courts do not, however, have discretionary appellate review, which means that they have to hear all cases that have been properly filed. Courts of last resort, also called state supreme courts, do have discretionary appellate review in the states that do not have intermediate courts of appeal. These judges are usually selected by a nominating commission, then appointed by the governor.

The court structure in the United States can be confusing due to the fact that each state has its own structure and many courts performing the same or similar functions are known by different names. In order to make it easier to understand these courts we must classify them according to their functions and hierarchy.

KEY TERMS

Amicus curiae
Appellate courts
Circuit courts
Circuit riders
Concurrent jurisdiction
Courts of last resort
Courts of record
Criminal courts
Dual court system
En banc
Evarts Act
Exclusive jurisdiction
Federal district courts
General jurisdiction
General sessions courts
General trial courts
Geographic jurisdiction

Hierarchical jurisdiction
Judicial review
Judiciary Act of 1789
Jurisdiction
Limited jurisdiction
Original jurisdiction
Rule of four
Subject matter jurisdiction
Supreme court
Trial courts
United States Circuit Courts of Appeal
United States District courts
United States magistrates
United States Supreme Court
Writ of *certiorari*

QUESTIONS FOR REVIEW

1. Differentiate between courts of limited and general jurisdiction.

2. What is meant by geographic jurisdiction? What is the power of courts with geographic jurisdiction?

3. Describe the U.S. magistrate and the duties of this particular type of court.

4. What is the basic trial court for the federal system?

5. When a defendant in a U.S. District court case is found guilty of a crime, where is the appeal directed? What are the jurisdictional limits of the appellate court you have indicated?

6. What is the court of last resort? Why is it called the court of last resort?

7. What are courts of limited jurisdiction? What are some of the functions of courts of limited jurisdiction?

8. Describe intermediate courts of appeal. Are these courts the same in all states? Why or why not?

9. What is meant by *en banc*?

10. What is the function of an *amicus curiae*?

SUGGESTED READINGS

1. Annalise Acorn (2004). *Compulsory Compassion: A Critique of Restorative Justice.* Vancouver, CAN: UBC Press.
2. Monica R. Cowart (2004). "Understanding Acts of Consent: Using Speech Act Theory to Help Resolve Moral Dilemmas and Legal Disputes." *Law and Philosophy* **23**:495–525.
3. Paula Hannaford-Agor and Nicole Mott (2003). "Research on Self-Represented Litigation: Preliminary Results and Methodological Considerations." *Justice System Journal* **24**:163–181.
4. Gordon Hughes (2004). "The Community Governance of Crime, Justice and Safety: Challenges and Lesson-Drawing." *British Journal of Community Service* **2**:7–20.

Chapter 3

The Prosecution

Chapter Objectives

As a result of reading this chapter, you will have accomplished the following objectives:

1. Understand the criminal court as an adversarial system seeking to determine the guilt or innocence of defendants charged with crimes.

2. Understand the many dimensions of the role of prosecutors in pursuing cases against criminal suspects.

3. Depict both exculpatory and inculpatory evidence that may be presented in criminal cases.

4. Describe the process of screening and prioritizing cases for criminal prosecutions.

5. Describe the interrelatedness of law enforcement with government prosecutors.

6. Assess the potential for prosecutorial misconduct or discretionary abuses arising from the extensive powers of prosecutors.

■ John Forbes is the district attorney of a large rural county in a midwestern state. He has $300,000 allocated to his office per year for criminal prosecutions. While the county has its share of crime annually, most of it is property crime. Violent crimes make up only about 20 percent of all criminal activity. One of Forbes's responsibilities is to manage the $300,000 budget wisely, pursuing those cases most likely to result in convictions. This year, however, there have already been four murders and several rapes. Two cases of child sexual abuse have been presented to him by police. Almost all of these violent crimes have resulted in arrests of likely suspects, where probable cause exists. Criminal trials are expensive, and one alternative available to Forbes is to encourage various defendants to enter "guilty" pleas and accept more lenient sentences than if they were to insist on a criminal trial. Unfortunately for Forbes, the rape cases have involved youthful defendants from a few wealthy families, and they are insisting on formal trial proceedings. Furthermore, one child sexual abuse case involves a high-profile television reporter in his 40s who has denied sexually molesting his 12-year-old daughter. Two murders involve the parents of a 17-year-old female, who is the principal suspect. The deceased parents were the owners of a major grocery chain in the state, and thus, the case has received considerable media attention. The public is outraged over all of this violence, and the county wants to see justice served with the convictions of these and other persons charged with such violent offenses. Forbes has two assistant district attorneys to assist him, and his resources will be quickly expended if protracted criminal trials are held in ten or more of these cases. With Forbes's limited resources, he cannot afford to have all of these cases reach the trial stage. Therefore, he must attempt to strike plea deals with some of these defendants. What criteria should govern his choices? Who most deserves to be prosecuted fully in a formal criminal trial?

■ Jean Langley is the chief prosecutor in Lennox County, Georgia. She has performed her job for eight years, but not without criticism from the media, particularly the *Lennox Daily*, a paper noted for its scathing editorials. One reporter, Mary Williams, has been especially critical of Langley and how Langley conducts her cases and the seemingly low conviction rate for those charged with serious offenses. Williams has openly advocated that a new prosecutor should be selected to replace Langley. One evening, Williams is pulled over by police for "weaving." She is given a breathalyzer test and it is evident that she has been drinking. She admits being at a local bar, and her blood–alcohol (BAC) level is .07, slightly under the legal intoxication limit of .08. Nevertheless, the officers charge her with driving under the influence (DUI) of alcohol and resisting arrest, and she is locked up overnight in the county jail following a brief physical struggle to prevent police officers from handcuffing her. Langley becomes aware of Williams's arrest and studies the police report, which details Williams's driving and responses to police, who considered her insulting and uncooperative. Ordinarily, Langley considers DUI arrests, even resisting arrest, to be relatively minor offenses, and she often assigns these cases to her assistant prosecutors. But in the Williams matter, Langley decides to handle this case personally. She files a criminal information against Williams based on the police report. She charges Williams with driving while intoxicated, reckless endangerment because of her erratic driving, and assault on a police officer, because of her struggle to avoid being handcuffed. Williams's lawyer attempts to reach a plea agreement with Langley, with downgraded charges, but Langley rejects any plea offer. The case will go to trial. Eventually, Williams is tried on these charges, and because of their seriousness, a jury hears the case. Subsequently, she is acquitted of assault on a police officer and reckless endangerment. Since her BAC was less than the legal intoxication limit, she is acquitted of drunk driving charges as well. Williams has spent over $20,000 in legal fees in the matter. Has Langley engaged in a malicious prosecution of Williams in this case?

INTRODUCTION

Criminal courts in the United States are exclusively adversarial proceedings. Adversarial proceedings mean that opposing sides present evidence and arguments favoring their position, either to a judge or a jury, in order to convince them that a particular action should be taken. Depending upon the compelling arguments presented favoring these opposing positions, judges or juries are persuaded to find for or against criminal defendants.

Persons charged with one or more crimes, defendants, are prosecuted by the government. The interests of defendants are represented by defense counsels, whose job it is to convince judges or juries that insufficient evidence exists to conclude that the defendants are guilty of committing a crime. Criminal proceedings against defendants may be conducted at local, state, or federal levels, and in each case, one or more prosecutors represent the government's interests in pursuing prosecutions.

This chapter opens with a description of the adversarial system of American courts, which is characterized by opposing sides who want to win. In some respects, this adversarial system is like an athletic contest or sporting event, complete with rules of conduct and different strategies calculated to advantage one side or the other in winning the contest. The outcome of a criminal trial is far different from the outcome of an athletic event, however. One or more lives are at stake, and one's freedom within the community may be in jeopardy. Prosecutors present inculpatory evidence to judges and juries. Such evidence shows defendant guilt. In contrast, defense counsels present exculpatory evidence that shows defendant innocence. Usually both sides have such evidence and present it to bolster their arguments for why judges or juries should decide in their favor. The conduct of any criminal case in court, as well as the introduction of both exculpatory and inculpatory evidence, is governed by rules of criminal procedure and evidence. Both state and local court systems have codified these procedures so that trials are uniformly conducted and everyone understands what is and is not permitted.

The following section describes the prosecutorial role. The role of prosecutors at all levels—local, state, or federal—are very similar. One consistent feature of all prosecutors is that they have many duties and responsibilities. Prosecutors must screen cases for prosecution and decide whether to bring criminal charges against particular suspects. As the opening chapter scenarios suggest, prosecutors must prioritize the cases they prosecute. Not everyone who deserves to be prosecuted can be prosecuted, given present system economic constraints. Beyond screening cases to be prosecuted, prosecutors must devise effective strategies that they believe will enable them to obtain convictions against criminal defendants. In many cases, the inculpatory evidence against many suspects is overwhelming and the prosecutor's role is greatly simplified. The prosecutor often drafts a plea agreement wherein a defendant enters a guilty plea to one or more criminal charges in exchange for some form of sentencing leniency, which is usually initiated by the prosecutor and approved by the judge. The plea bargaining process is discussed at length in Chapter 8.

Although fewer than 10 percent of all criminal cases proceed to trial, this does not mean that there are few criminal trials. There are many thousands of criminal trials annually. In fact, the incidence of criminal trials is such that there are serious case backlogs in more than a few jurisdictions. Interestingly, because there are so many criminal trials to conduct and a limited time period within which to conduct them, this is a major reason why prosecutors must screen their cases and prioritize them for prosecution. It is simply not possible to prosecute everyone who deserves to be prosecuted for a crime. The screening process used by prosecutors to prioritize their cases will be examined and explained.

In larger cities where a much larger volume of criminal cases is generated, government prosecutors, sometimes known as state's attorneys, district attorneys, or U.S. attorneys, will have several assistant prosecutors to handle larger caseloads. Thus, the prosecutor has the responsibility of assigning cases to various assistant state's attorneys or assistant district attorneys, or assistant U.S. attorneys, and these persons become responsible for prosecuting the cases they are assigned. Among the different responsibilities of prosecutors is interviewing witnesses and conducting depositions that will enable them to build compelling cases against criminal defendants. Prosecutors also work closely with law enforcement officers who made arrests and/or collected important incriminating evidence. These persons will eventually testify in court or provide information about a defendant's guilt. These interactions between witnesses, law enforcement officers, and prosecutors will be described and explained.

All attorneys, regardless of whether they are prosecutors or defense counsels, are expected to abide by a code of ethics that prescribes a particular conduct that places these persons above reproach. However, more than a few attorneys have and continue to violate one or more of these ethical codes by engaging in prosecutorial misconduct. Like any type of misconduct in any profession, there are degrees of misconduct that may occur. Like misdemeanors and felonies, there are less serious and more serious forms of misconduct. Several types of prosecutorial misconduct are examined.

One type of misconduct is encouraging deceit from witnesses who testify against criminal defendants. Most prosecutors do not ask witnesses to lie under oath or commit perjury. But many prosecutors encourage witnesses to slant their testimony in ways that make criminal defendants look like they might be guilty. In many jurisdictions, prosecutors rehearse their witnesses prior to trial, reviewing the types of questions the prosecutors will ask, as well as the kinds of questions defense attorneys might ask. Suggestions are given by prosecutors as to what witnesses might say or how they might respond. While rehearsing witnesses before trial is not unethical, it may raise questions about how such testimony might be interpreted by jurors. Some witnesses may exaggerate the significance of their testimony, and prosecutors may allow juries to draw their own conclusions about these exaggerated remarks. Of course, it is expected that good defense attorneys will clarify for jurors what certain witnesses say and how such information should be interpreted.

Another type of prosecutorial misconduct occurs behind closed doors in confidential grand jury proceedings. About half of all states use grand juries to determine whether sufficient evidence exists against particular defendants in order for the case to proceed to trial. Grand jury proceedings are one-sided affairs, where prosecutors present only evidence that they want grand jurors to see. Thus, prosecutors are in absolute control concerning the particular evidence a grand jury will see against a criminal suspect. If the prosecutor knows of any exculpatory evidence that favors the defendant, he/she may withhold such evidence from the grand jury. This is the prosecutor's decision. If the prosecutor has strong feelings about the case and wants the grand jury to indict the defendant, excluding exculpatory evidence from the grand jury will improve the prosecutor's chances of securing an indictment. Ultimately the exculpatory evidence will come to light in court when the trial is conducted. In the meantime, however, the defendant, who may be innocent, remains charged with a crime through the indictment. Although indictments do not mean that indicted defendants are guilty of anything, many citizens interpret "being indicted" as tantamount to guilt anyway. The trial process will result in a finding of guilt or acquittal in any event.

The process of prosecutorial bluffing will be described. Prosecutors may attempt to bluff their way through a case prior to trial, leading some defendants to believe that they have inculpatory evidence against them when they have no such evidence. Many guilty pleas have been entered by innocent defendants because of prosecutorial bluffing. If defendants believe that the jury will likely convict them of a crime and their sentence will be severe, these defendants may decide to accept a plea agreement offered by the prosecutor, which usually involves considerable leniency in punishment compared with what a judge may have imposed through a jury verdict of guilt. Several types of prosecutorial bluffing will be described, and the implications of prosecutorial bluffing for defendants will be indicated.

More serious forms of prosecutorial misconduct include deliberately withholding exculpatory evidence from defense counsels prior to trial. Another form of misconduct is pursuing a case against a criminal defendant where no basis exists for the criminal charges that have been filed. As one of the opening scenarios of this chapter suggests, sometimes prosecutors may file frivolous charges against defendants where such charges have little or no basis in truth. These malicious prosecutions against innocent defendants are clearly inexcusable, although proving malicious intent on the part of the prosecutor is often difficult.

Although it is not technically a form of misconduct, prosecutors almost always attempt to select jurors who are most likely to convict the defendant. Some prosecutors hire professional jury consultants to assist them in making such juror selections (Clark 2004b). Both prosecutors and defense counsels have several peremptory challenges and an unlimited number of challenges for cause, whereby they can strike any particular prospective juror from sitting on the jury. Defense counsels also attempt to select jurors who will react favorably toward their clients. They also hire jury consultants to assist them in juror selection. Since the jury selection process is not an exact science, it is questionable whether accurate forecasts can ever be made about how particular jurors will vote once the evidence from both sides has been presented. Another form of prosecutorial misconduct involves backdooring hearsay evidence. Prosecutors and defense counsel are both barred from making certain kinds of statements in front of jurors. But both sides may make occasional improper utterances or statements anyway, only to have the judge instruct the jury to disregard these statements. But once jurors have heard statements they shouldn't hear, it is difficult, if not impossible, for them to forget that they heard these statements. It is impossible to determine how much these improper statements influence juror opinions and voting during juror deliberations. Different types of backdooring hearsay will be described. The chapter concludes with an examination of the ethical norms and guidelines presently in place to regulate prosecutors and their conduct. Only during the last few decades have prosecutors been more carefully scrutinized by the legal profession and others. Prosecutorial codes of conduct or ethics will be described.

THE ADVERSARY SYSTEM

When a crime is committed, law enforcement officers frequently arrest a suspect who is believed to have committed the crime. Criminal suspects become defendants charged with one or more crimes. While all criminal defendants in the United States are entitled to the presumption of innocence before their guilt is established in court beyond a reasonable doubt, they are also entitled to counter the charges against them. Therefore, defendants are represented by defense counsel, whose job it is to defend their clients against these criminal charges. Presumably, defense counsel who represent clients in court are more or less effective according to their training, expertise, and practical trial experience. The system of alleging criminal charges against defendants and defending them against such charges is known as the **adversary system** (Emmelman 2003). This adversarial system is not exclusively a U.S. creation. It is found and used frequently in other countries, such as England, Yugoslavia, Italy, and Australia (Ambos 2003). Also, it is found in both adult and juvenile proceedings (Schmidt, Reppucci, and Wollard 2003).

The adversarial nature of the criminal court is evident by paying attention to the different roles of the **prosecutor** and **defense attorney**. The prosecutor's aim is to prove that the defendant committed a crime, and that the level of such proof should rise to beyond a reasonable doubt. The defense attorney contests any criminal allegations made against his/her client and seeks to dissuade the court or a jury from thinking that the defendant is guilty of a criminal offense.

In 2004 for instance, Scott Peterson, a California resident, was tried on charges of murdering his pregnant wife, Laci, 27, and dumping her body in the ocean. Portions of her body washed ashore some months following her disappearance ten days before Christmas in December 2002. Subsequent circumstantial evidence led to Scott Peterson's conviction in December 2004. Peterson was sentenced to death in early 2005. Between the time of Laci Peterson's disappearance and Scott Peterson's conviction, Scott Peterson retained the services of several high-profile criminal defense attorneys. His trial lasted for several months during 2004, while both sides presented evidence to an impartial jury. Scott Peterson claimed he was out of town fishing at the time of his wife's disappearance. Coincidentally, her body washed ashore just a few miles from where Peterson claimed he had been fishing when she had disappeared. Although there was no direct evidence of Scott Peterson's guilt, there was substantial circumstantial evidence, including his prolonged involvement with another woman. The jury was ultimately convinced that he had committed the murder of his wife in order to seek a future life with the other woman. Both sides in this adversarial proceeding provided compelling arguments for and against Peterson's guilt. Following the trial, Peterson's attorney said that the jury was persuaded by the location of Laci Peterson's body in close proximity to where Scott Peterson claimed to have been fishing when she disappeared (Associated Press 2005).

Comparing the criminal court to a game being played out from beginning to end is not new. The gamelike nature of the courtroom is reinforced by using court-relevant terminology, such as **sides** and prosecutorial or **defense strategy**. Prosecutors are on one side and use a particular strategy that they believe will enable them to win the game. For prosecutors, a win is a conviction against the accused. For the defense side, a win is the defendant's acquittal. Prosecutors and defense counsel are often labeled as players by different writers who seek to characterize courtroom procedures in certain ways. The more skillful player using the better strategy will win the game by defeating the other player (van Koppen and Penrod 2003).

The adversarial system of justice in the United States is rooted in the tradition of English jurisprudence dating back several centuries (Ambos 2003). In U.S. courts, the key players, prosecutors, defense attorneys, and judges, are the courtroom work group (Hoskins, Ruth, and Ruback 2004). They are bound to observe standardized **Rules of Criminal Procedure** as well as a well-defined **ethical code** (Birzer and Tannehill 2003; Boyle, Newman, and Schmidt 2003). Thus, there are specific rules governing the order in which a case is presented against a defendant and the response from defense counsel (DiCristina 2004). Besides following a predetermined pattern or protocol for presenting a case against and for a defendant, other rules exist that govern the nature and types of evidence and witnesses who may be called for either side. Each side attempts to manipulate the evidence presented in ways that enhance their respective arguments. **Witnesses** are examined and cross-examined by the different sides in an effort to bolster their arguments. Ideally, the side with the most persuasive and compelling argument, either against or for the accused, wins. Juries decide the facts in the case before them, and their deliberations most often favor either guilt or acquittal. On rare occasions, juries may not be able to reach agreement as to which side, the prosecution or defense, has the more persuasive argument. In these instances, juries are deadlocked or hung, and mistrials are declared. Subsequently, the adversarial process begins anew with another trial. In each trial proceeding, it is expected that both sides will adhere to an accepted ethical code and conduct themselves accordingly.

Throughout the criminal trial, evidence is presented by both sides for its persuasive effect. Prosecutors usually present **inculpatory evidence**, or testimony or other forms of evidence that tends to show the guilt of the defendant. For instance, the defendant's fingerprints might have been found on the murder weapon, or eyewitnesses may have seen the defendant pull the trigger of the gun that killed the defendant. This evidence would be considered inculpatory, because it shows the guilt of the accused. In contrast, defense counsel introduces **exculpatory evidence**, or testimony and other forms of evidence that show the innocence of the defendant. For example, one or more persons may testify that the defendant was with them at the time the murder was committed. Theater ticket stubs in the defendant's possession may indicate that the defendant was watching a movie when the crime occurred. Thus, alibis and other relevant information may show that the defendant couldn't have been the one who committed the crime when it occurred (Cossins 2003).

THE PROSECUTION

Besides the judge who makes important rulings in criminal cases and oversees trial proceedings, the prosecutor is perhaps the most powerful position in the criminal justice system (Schoenfeld 2005). Prosecutors are either elected or appointed officials who pursue criminal cases against those charged with crimes. Prosecutors are held to the same standards of ethical conduct as defense counsel (Connell 2004). Depending upon the jurisdiction, prosecutors are known by different names. In Tennessee, for example, prosecutors are known as **district attorneys**. Their assistants are called assistant district attorneys. In North Dakota, prosecutors are called **state's attorneys** or **assistant state's attorneys**. Many other jurisdictions use such designations for their prosecutors.

In the federal system, each U.S. district court has a **United States attorney's office**. The **United States attorney** in each federal district is appointed by the president of the United States with the advice and consent of Congress. The **attorney general** of the United States, also a presidential appointee, appoints one or more **assistant U.S. attorneys (AUSAs)** to serve in each of these district offices. The number of AUSAs varies from district to district, depending upon the civil and criminal caseload (Houston 2005; U.S. General Accounting Office 1999).

The Roles of Prosecutors

The primary roles of all prosecutors in criminal courts are to represent the government's interests and pursue criminal charges against those alleged to have committed crimes. For state's attorneys or district attorneys, their roles are similar throughout the different U.S. jurisdictions. A summary of these roles is as follows:

1. To screen cases for prosecution
2. To determine the best strategy for prosecuting cases
3. To make case assignments to assistant district attorneys
4. To interview prospective witnesses against the accused
5. To work closely with law enforcement officers to determine the nature of inculpatory evidence against the accused

In the federal system, the U.S. attorney's offices in the various federal districts are charged with the following broad roles:

1. Prosecute all offenses against the United States
2. Prosecute or defend, for the government, all civil actions, suits, or proceedings in which the United States is concerned
3. Appears on behalf of the defendants in civil actions and suits or proceedings pending in the district against collectors or other officers of the revenue or customs for things they have done or for the recovery of any money exacted by or paid to them
4. Institutes and prosecutes proceedings for the collection of fines, penalties, and forfeitures incurred for violation of any revenue law
5. Reports as the attorney general directs

Screening Cases

Screening cases means to assign priority to different cases on the basis of which ones are most deserving of prosecution. The screening function of prosecutors is very important as it relates to obtaining guilty pleas from criminal defendants. Most convictions are obtained through plea negotiations between prosecutors and defense counsel, where some form of leniency from the prosecution is extended in exchange for a defendant's guilty plea. Thus, prosecutors have broad discretionary powers concerning which cases to pursue and what types of offers to extend those charged with crimes as inducements for guilty pleas (Forst 2004).

Prosecutors have the power to determine the types of cases that will be prosecuted more vigorously than others. Drunk-driving cases may receive high priority in certain jurisdictions, since strong interest groups, such as Mothers Against Drunk Driving (MADD), may wish to decrease alcohol-related driving accidents and deaths in their communities. Prosecutors can assist them in their prevention and deterrence efforts by pursuing DWI cases and seeking maximum penalties. Organized crime may have high priority for prosecutions in certain jurisdictions.

Prosecutors seek convictions, and prosecutorial effectiveness is often gauged by the number of convictions they obtain (Keller 2005). The greater the number of convictions, the more effective are the prosecutors. Therefore, it is in the prosecutor's interest to select cases for prosecution that are the easiest to prosecute. Where clear and convincing evidence exists against an accused, prosecutors are in a stronger position to succeed in obtaining a conviction. More than a few cases have little incriminating evidence and are based purely on circumstantial evidence. Their vigor, persistence, and demeanor are often sufficiently convincing for jurors in courtrooms (Rockwell and Hubbard 2004). Prosecutors must decide whether these cases are worth pursuing, where the conviction of the accused is less of a certainty compared with a case with considerable inculpatory evidence.

Determining Court Strategy

Prosecutors must devise their theory of how and why the crime was committed. They must attempt to link the defendant to the crime in such a way so that the jury will be convinced beyond a reasonable doubt of the accused's guilt. There are many potential explanations for a defendant's conduct relative to the crime. It is not necessary that the prosecutor selects the true explanation, only a plausible one. The theory of the crime and its commission is often suggested by the nature and quality of the evidence against the defendant. For example, if one's spouse was violently killed and the surviving spouse stands to collect on a $1 million insurance policy, then this fact provides a motive for why the surviving spouse probably committed murder. However, if there is another person with whom the surviving spouse has had an affair, then the motive for the murder may be love and not money. It is fairly easy to see how different spins can be given to any criminal scenario.

In the Scott Peterson murder case mentioned earlier in this chapter, following Peterson's conviction, the family of Laci Peterson sought to sue Scott Peterson in a civil action for damages. Earlier during Peterson's trial, Peterson and his defense counsels claimed that Laci Peterson had been kidnapped by others, and that somehow her body was deposited in the ocean near where Scott Peterson had claimed to be fishing when she disappeared. This was a deliberate act to incriminate Peterson, the defense claimed, since it became known where Scott Peterson was or alleged to be at the time of his wife's disappearance. The prosecution countered that Scott Peterson had taken his wife's body to a marina where he launched his boat, took the boat far out in a bay, and dropped his wife's body, weighted down with cement blocks, into the ocean. The prosecution surmised that Scott Peterson never imagined that his wife's body would somehow reappear later and be discovered by police. In a subsequent civil action, Laci Peterson's family would argue that Scott Peterson benefitted from killing his wife because of his affair with another woman, and that he deliberately killed and disposed of his wife in order to facilitate this romantic relationship. While the complete truth about Laci Peterson's murder will never be known, this fact gives fuel to all types of speculation about what happened to her and why. Even today, it cannot be conclusively demonstrated by investigators that Laci Peterson was killed in a specific place with a specific instrument and that her body was conveyed by Peterson to the ocean where it was dumped. No eyewitnesses were ever produced linking Scott Peterson directly with his wife's disappearance. A civil jury will have to weigh the circumstantial evidence and decide whether to award Laci Peterson's family any damages against Scott Peterson in a separate civil proceeding.

Assigning Cases

Prosecutors in most jurisdictions usually have assistant prosecutors who can handle some of the case workload (Champion 2005a). In fact, most large-city district attorney's offices are bureaucratized to the extent that there are various specialty areas for different types of legal cases. A general civil-criminal distinction exists, where some of the assistant district attorneys may be assigned civil cases, while other assistants are assigned criminal ones. Further subdivisions may be made, depending upon case volume. Criminal cases may be divided according to sex crimes, property crimes, and other logical divisions. Certain prosecutors acquire considerable expertise in selected legal areas, and this expertise enables them to prosecute certain cases involving their expertise more effectively than other prosecutors without this expertise. For instance, prosecutors with substantial experience with forensic evidence, such as DNA testing, may be more skillful at eliciting more compelling testimony from expert witnesses, and they may also do a better job of cross-examining defense experts on the same subject matter. Other prosecutors may have considerable experience and facility with child eyewitnesses. Each case poses certain types of problems for prosecutors, and thus, it is prudent for prosecutors to make strategic case assignments on the basis of which assistant district attorneys can do the best job of prosecuting under the circumstances.

Interviewing Witnesses

Prosecutors and their assistants must interview persons who have knowledge about the crime. Often, witnesses for both the prosecution and defense are **deposed**. A deposition is a sworn written record of oral testimony. Persons who are deposed are **deponents.** The purpose of a deposition is to have a written record of what one's testimony is as well as an indication of its relevance to the case. When witnesses testify in court later, their depositions can be used to refresh their recollections. Sometimes depositions can be used to impeach witnesses if they are lying or say things that are inconsistent with their earlier depositions (Carey 2001).

Information provided prosecutors by witnesses can be interpreted various ways. Witness interviews can help prosecutors to formulate their strategy for prosecuting a case. The state may use expert witnesses to verify whether a defendant is sane or insane, competent or incompetent. If certain defendants are sufficiently incompetent to stand trial, then prosecutors can use this information to seek their commitment indefinitely in a mental hospital (Bullock 2002).

Prosecutors can determine in which order they will present their witnesses against the accused later in court. Thus, they can use witnesses to build their case against defendants. In complex serious criminal cases, there will probably be numerous witnesses called by both sides. It is important, therefore, that some effort should be made to organize the witnesses into an orderly presentation that will create the most convincing case against the accused. Observations of actual criminal trials reveal such orderly presentations of witnesses for both sides.

Working Closely with Law Enforcement Officers

It is important for prosecutors to develop a working rapport with law enforcement officers. Law enforcement officers have direct crime scene experience and can testify about their conversations with the defendant. If a confession has been obtained, or if the defendant has provided police officers with incriminating information, this information can be developed in court to the defendant's disadvantage.

Law enforcement officers are subject to cross-examination by defense counsel. Experienced defense attorneys can seriously impair the state's case against a defendant by evoking responses from officers that show their ineptness. Prosecutors and their assistants can assist officers in learning how to give testimony that will minimize any weaknesses in the state's case.

Police officers also testify about the evidence they collected at the crime scene that incriminates the defendant. Their testimony is quite important in this respect, and it is vital that prosecutors have the trust of these officers when they are questioned under direct examination in court (Leo 1994). In federal district courts, AUSAs work closely with FBI agents and other federal authorities in presenting evidence against those charged with federal crimes. FBI agents learn to permit AUSAs the latitude of presenting the case against the defendant in a particular way. FBI agents also learn to give testimony in certain ways that will heighten the inculpatory or incriminating effect of it. In a criminal case in the U.S. district court in Knoxville, Tennessee, an FBI agent advised the AUSA that he would not get on the stand and lie. The AUSA advised him that he [the prosecutor] didn't want the agent to lie; rather, the prosecutor wanted the FBI agent to "tell the story *our way*." This implies that there was more than one way to relate the testimony, and that the prosecutor wanted the FBI agent to put a spin on the story, which would place the defendant in the most incriminating light. It would be up to the defense counsel, therefore, to attempt to get the FBI agent to admit that other less-sinister interpretations of his testimony might be made by the jury.

Changing the Venue for Trials

The **venue** is the jurisdiction where the case originates. If a crime is committed in Los Angeles, California, the venue is Los Angeles. Los Angeles judges will likely hear the case. The jury will be selected from Los Angeles County. If the case is an especially high-profile one, either the defense or the prosecution may attempt to change the venue where the case is heard. This is because of the substantial publicity given the case and the possibility that an impartial jury cannot be impaneled to hear it. Jurors in any criminal case are expected to hear all evidence impartially and to render an objective decision as to the guilt or innocence of a defendant. If pretrial publicity is adverse to defendants, defense counsels may make a motion to change the venue for hearing the case to another county. Prosecutors may oppose such motions.

But changes of venue, which are rarely granted, may also be initiated by prosecutors. If the crime occurs in a locality where the defendant is well known and liked by the community, it may be difficult to find an impartial jury that would convict the defendant, despite the compelling evidence favoring a conviction. In these cases, prosecutors may attempt to change the venue to a jurisdiction where the defendant is less well known. Thus, both prosecutors and defense counsels have a stake in determining the best location for where the ensuing trial will be held. Many circumstances, including pretrial publicity and media coverage, influence such decision making and which side will request a change in venue (Posey and Dahl 2002). Neither prosecutors nor defense counsels can mandate changes of venue for their cases, but they can make motions for such changes. They must present compelling arguments to judges for venue changes. Unless there are overwhelming circumstances suggesting that defendants would not receive a fair trial in the original venue, motions for changing the venue of the trial are typically not granted.

Obtaining Indictments or Filing Criminal Informations

In about half of all states, grand juries are convened to hear evidence against particular defendants. This evidence is presented by prosecutors in most circumstances, and based on the evidence presented, grand juries issue **true bills** or **indictments**. These true bills or indictments are merely declarations by grand juries that sufficient probable cause exists to believe that one or more crimes were committed and that the defendant may have committed the crime(s). Grand juries do not decide one's guilt or innocence, therefore. Prosecutors work to persuade grand juries to indict defendants so that their cases may proceed to trial (Schmid 2002).

For less-serious offenses, such as misdemeanors, prosecutors may act on their own and file charges against criminal defendants by filing **criminal informations** or simply **informations**. Informations are similar to indictments, except that prosecutors initiate them on their own. Prosecutors believe that probable cause exists that a crime was committed and that a particular defendant committed the crime. Therefore, prosecutors can file an information against any criminal suspect. The result is the same as an indictment. The defendant will face a criminal trial where their guilt can be decided by the judge or jury.

Prosecutorial Misconduct

Whether prosecutors in various jurisdictions are elected or appointed, there are many pressures on them from different sources. First, there is the immediate pressure to win cases and obtain convictions against defendants. Second, there is pressure to make a weak case look like a strong case. This means that the evidence may have to be manipulated or collected in ways that are inconsistent with proper police procedure (White 2002).

Just like there are varying degrees of attorney competence, there are also varying degrees of prosecutorial misconduct (Schoenfeld 2005). Not all forms of misconduct have the same weight or importance. Some misconduct may be trivial, although the cumulative effect of minor or trivial misconduct may arouse juror suspicions to the degree that a guilty verdict is subsequently rendered. Prosecutors may encourage experts to exaggerate their claims or evidence to enhance their case against a defendant; prosecutors may overwhelm grand juries with purely inculpatory evidence and deliberately exclude any exculpatory evidence; prosecutors may bluff with defendants and threaten or intimidate them; prosecutors may suppress certain types of exculpatory evidence from the defense; prosecutors may exclude prospective jurors who have views favorable to defendants; prosecutors may offer inadmissible evidence in court; and prosecutors may engage in malicious prosecutions. While it is presently unknown precisely how much prosecutorial misconduct occurs nationally, it has been reported by the Center for Public Integrity that since 1970, 20 percent of 11,452 appellate-reviewed cases where the defendants claimed prosecutorial misconduct were dismissed, reversed, or reduced from the original sentence partly or wholly because of prosecutorial misconduct (Weinberg, Gordon, and Williams 2005).

BOX 3.1 CASES OF PROSECUTORIAL MISCONDUCT

■ *Chapman v. California*, 386 U.S. 18 (1967)

Chapman and a confederate, Teale, were charged with robbing, kidnapping, and murdering a bartender. During the trial, Chapman did not testify. At that time, California had a statute permitting the judge and prosecutor to comment on the fact that the defendant did not testify in his or her own defense and that inferences about guilt could be drawn from that failure to testify. The trial judge told the jury that they could draw adverse inferences from the defendant's failure to testify, and Chapman was convicted. Before she appealed, the U.S. Supreme Court decided another case, *Griffin v. California* (1965), which held that commentary by a judge or prosecutor about a defendant's refusal to testify in a criminal case must not infringe on his or her right not to be compelled to be a witness against him- or herself guaranteed by the Fifth Amendment. The California Supreme Court, therefore, admitted that Chapman had been denied a federal constitutional right because of the judge's instructions to the jury about that silence, but it held that the error was *harmless*. Chapman appealed. The U.S. Supreme Court reversed Chapman's conviction, holding that the error was *not harmless* when the state prosecutor's argument and the trial judge's jury instructions continuously and repeatedly impressed the jury that the refusal of the defendant to testify required inferences to be drawn in the state's favor. Chapman was granted a new trial, in which judicial and prosecutorial commentary on her refusal to testify in her own case were prohibited.

■ *Fletcher v. Weir*, 455 U.S. 603 (1982)

Weir was in a fight with Buchanan outside a nightclub and stabbed Buchanan, who died. Weir fled the scene. Later, when apprehended by the police, he said nothing about the incident. However, during the trial, he took the stand in his own defense and for the first time alleged self-defense as the reason for stabbing Buchanan. The prosecutor sought to discredit him by referring to his prearrest silence. When Weir was convicted, he appealed, alleging a violation of his Fifth Amendment rights against self-incrimination by the prosecutor's effort to impeach his testimony in court. The Supreme Court ruled that for impeachment purposes, it is proper for prosecutors to make such comments about the defendant's prearrest silence, particularly if the defendant raises self-defense as his defense. Thus, Weir's right against self-incrimination had not been jeopardized by the prosecutor who cross-examined him regarding his prearrest silence.

■ *Caldwell v. Mississippi*, 472 U.S. 320 (1985)

Caldwell had shot and killed the owner of a small grocery store while robbing it. After he was apprehended and tried, the defense and prosecution gave their summations. The prosecution told the jury not to view it-self as finally determining whether Caldwell would die, because a death sentence would be reviewed for correctness by the Mississippi Supreme Court. Caldwell was convicted and sentenced to death. He appealed, ar-guing that the prosecutor's remarks during summation had been im-proper and had misled the jury into believing that they would not be responsible for the death of Caldwell. The U.S. Supreme Court reversed his conviction, holding that the prosecutor's remarks had been improper because they were inaccurate and misleading in a manner that dimin-ished the jury's sense of responsibility. Thus, the U.S. Supreme Court concluded, these prosecutorial remarks and the jury's subsequent rec-ommendation for the death penalty had violated Caldwell's Eighth Amendment right to due process.

■ *Darden v. Wainwright*, 477 U.S. 168 (1986)

Darden was a convicted murderer under sentence of death. He filed a *habeas corpus* petition challenging the exclusion of a juror from his ear-lier trial, allegedly improper remarks made by the prosecutor during his summation to the jury, and ineffective assistance of counsel. One prospective juror had been excused by the judge when the juror declared a moral and religious opposition to the death penalty, which was one op-tion in Darden's case. The prosecutor had referred to him as an "animal." Darden thought the one-half hour preparation by his attorney between the trial's guilt phase and the penalty phase insufficient to prepare an ad-equate mitigation statement. The U.S. Supreme Court rejected all of Dar-den's arguments. It held that jurors may be excused from death-penalty cases if their religious views or moral feelings would render them unable to vote for such a penalty. Further, the emotional rhetoric from the pros-ecutor was insufficient to deprive Darden of a fair trial. Finally, evidence showed that the defense counsel had spent considerable preparatory time for both the trial and mitigation statement during the penalty phase.

■ *Brecht v. Abrahamson*, 507 U.S. 619 (1993)

At a murder trial in a Wisconsin court, Brecht admitted shooting the victim but claimed it was accidental. State prosecutors in their jury arguments cited Brecht's pre-*Miranda* statements that he failed to tell anyone of the acci-dental nature of the shooting. More important, a prosecutor commented on his silence following the *Miranda* warning. The jury convicted Brecht and he appealed, arguing that the errors committed by the prosecutor were preju-dicial. The U.S. Supreme Court upheld Brecht's conviction, holding that the prosecution statements did not have a substantial or injurious effect or in-fluence in determining the jury's verdict.

(continued)

BOX 3.1 (continued)

■ *Buckley v. Fitzsimmons*, 509 U.S. 259 (1993)

Buckley was charged with murder. Prosecutors made various statements surrounding the indictment of Buckley for the murder, including several untrue statements. Subsequently, the charges against Buckley were dropped, and he sued the prosecutors under Title 42 U.S.C. Section 1983, alleging that his civil rights had been violated by this prosecutorial misconduct. The prosecutors sought absolute immunity from this suit and the U.S. Supreme Court heard the case. The U.S. Supreme Court upheld Buckley's right to sue the prosecutor, who only enjoyed qualified immunity from such suits. Prosecutors are liable for statements they make publicly if such statements are false and they result in harm to defendants who are innocent of criminal wrongdoing.

■ *Old Chief v. United States*, 519 U.S. 172 (1997)

Old Chief was convicted in federal court of being a felon in possession of a firearm, and he appealed. His appeal alleged that he had offered to stipulate to the federal court that he had previously been convicted of a crime punishable by a term exceeding one year, but that the court disallowed this stipulation. Rather, the prosecution admitted into evidence the specific prior conviction by name, which was assault causing serious bodily injury. Old Chief believed that the actual name of his crime would prejudice the jury in his case. The trial court and appellate court rejected his appeal, and the U.S. Supreme Court heard his case. The U.S. Supreme Court reversed Old Chief's conviction, holding that it is an abuse of judicial discretion when the court spurns a defendant's offer to admit evidence of the prior conviction element of an offense and instead admits the full record of prior judgment of conviction when the name and nature of the prior offense raise the risk of a verdict, and that the evidence of the name and nature of the defendant's conviction was not admissible to show the prior felony conviction element of the offense of possession of a firearm by a felon.

■ *Portuondo v. Agard*, 529 U.S. 61 (2000)

Agard was convicted of anal sodomy and several weapons charges in a New York state court. During the summation, the prosecutor commented about Agard's opportunity to sit in the courtroom and listen to witnesses, and then to easily fabricate stories to fit his own version of events when he testified in his own behalf. Agard filed a writ of *habeas corpus* with the federal district court, contending that the prosecutor's comments were unconstitutional and in violation of his Fifth and Sixth Amendment rights to be present at trial and confront his accusers, and his Fourteenth Amendment right to due process. The federal district court denied Agard's motion, but the Second Circuit Court reversed his conviction. The government appealed, and the U.S. Supreme Court heard the case. The Supreme Court reversed the Second Circuit, reinstating Agard's conviction, holding that the prosecutor's comments did not violate Agard's Fifth and Sixth Amendment rights. The Supreme Court noted that the prosecutor's comments were intended to challenge Agard's credibility. The Supreme Court added that no promise of impunity is implicit in a statute requiring a defendant to be present at trial, and there is no authority whatever for the proposition that the impairment of credibility, if any, caused by mandatory presence at trial violates due process.

■ *Williams v. Taylor*, 529 U.S. 420 (2000)

Williams was convicted of two capital murders in Virginia and sentenced to death. During his trial, Williams sought to discover the results of a psychiatric examination of Jeffrey Cruse, his accomplice and the main witness against him. The court refused to permit him access to these psychiatric records, and he was convicted. The Virginia Supreme Court subsequently dismissed Williams's *habeas corpus* petition requesting an evidentiary hearing on three claims: (1) that Williams and his counsel were denied access to a psychiatric evaluation of Cruse, (2) that a juror was possibly biased, and (3) that the prosecutor knew about the biased juror and the nature of the bias and permitted the juror to be seated anyway. The Virginia Supreme Court dismissed Williams's *habeas corpus* claims. Williams appealed to the U.S. Supreme Court, where the case was heard. The U.S. Supreme Court upheld the lower court denial of access to Cruse's psychiatric reports, because Williams had failed to develop a factual basis for the claim that the prosecutor's nondisclosure of the report violated the *Brady* discovery rule. However, the U.S. Supreme Court overruled the lower courts and held that Williams had been wrongfully denied an evidentiary hearing on the biased juror and the prosecutor's misconduct resulting from a knowledge of the biased juror. The juror issue was that the seating of one juror, Ms. Stinnett, was unfair because during *voir dire*, Stinnett denied knowing Deputy Sheriff Meinhard, who had investigated the crime, interrogated Cruse, and later became the prosecution's first witness. Stinnett had a previous 17-year marriage to Sheriff Meinhard and four children with him. Further, Stinnett denied knowing the prosecutor, Woodson, when in fact Stinnett had retained Woodson as her attorney to represent her in her divorce from Meinhard. Later, Woodson admitted that he knew that Stinnett and Meinhard had been married and divorced, but stated that he did not consider divorced people to be related and that he had no recollection of having been hired by Stinnett as her private attorney in the divorce action. Stinnett's reticence to admit that she knew either Meinhard or Woodson, and Woodson's failure to divulge this same information, disclose the need for an evidentiary hearing, according to the U.S. Supreme Court.

(continued)

BOX 3.1 *(continued)*

■ *Banks v. Dretke*, ___U.S.___, 124 S.Ct. 1256 (2004)

Delma Banks was convicted of capital murder in the death of 16-year-old Richard Whitehead, which occurred in mid-April 1980. Banks was originally implicated in the murder by two associates, Jefferson and Farr, who were working with the county sheriff, Willie Huff, as informants. Unknown to Banks before and during the trial was the allegation that Jefferson and Farr were testifying against Banks in order to avoid drug charges, which were threatened by the sheriff and prosecutor. At the same time, a confidential informant, Cook, also furnished the prosecution with incriminating circumstantial evidence against Banks. This information was also withheld from Banks pursuant to a motion for discovery. Although Banks had no prior criminal record, testimony from Farr and Jefferson provided the jury with innuendo that Banks had an unsavory and criminal past, which was untrue. Banks's efforts to impeach Farr and Jefferson were undermined because of his own witnesses, who were themselves impeached on cross-examination. Banks was sentenced to death and sought postconviction relief, alleging that the prosecution failed to disclose exculpatory evidence as required by *Brady v. Maryland* (1963), including the threats made to Farr and Jefferson as well as the confidential informant, Cook. In its answer, the state claimed that nothing had been kept secret from Banks and no deals had been made with government witnesses, including Cook. In 1993 Banks's postconviction claims were denied outright by an appellate court. Following this loss, Banks filed for *habeas corpus* relief in a U.S. district court, which granted relief on Banks's death sentence. In 1999 Banks filed discovery and evidentiary hearing motions, both supported by affidavits sworn to by Farr and Jefferson that the prosecution had wrongly withheld crucial exculpatory and impeaching evidence. The federal court determined that the state, indeed, had failed to disclose Farr's informant status during the original discovery phase of Banks's trial. Therefore, a writ of *habeas corpus* was granted Banks with respect to his death sentence, but not to his conviction. Banks petitioned the U.S. Supreme Court, who heard the case. The U.S. Supreme Court reiterated that under *Brady*, a prosecutorial misconduct claim must establish three things: (1) the evidence at issue must be favorable to the accused, either because it is exculpatory, or because it is impeaching; (2) that evidence must have been suppressed by the state, either willfully or inadvertently; and (3) prejudice must have ensued. In its response, the state contended that "it can lie and conceal and the prisoner still has the burden to discover the evidence." The U.S. Supreme Court ruled this assertion to be untenable and a violation of Banks's due process rights. Banks presented sufficient evidence to support his *Brady* claim and was thus entitled to a full evidentiary hearing and a certification of appealability.

Encouraging Deceit from Experts and Other Types of Witnesses

When prosecutors construct their case presentation, they arrange the testimony of various expert witnesses and others who have relevant evidence to present. Often, expert witnesses may be able to provide too much information in court, and prosecutors must work with them to ensure that only selected pieces of information are disclosed about the case (McKimmie et al. 2004). Thus, experts have their testimony shaped and tailored by prosecutors so that it fits more closely with the scenario of the crime and its commission as envisioned by the state. In a federal case involving two coconspirators on interstate transportation of stolen property charges, one of the coconspirators pleaded guilty and accepted a lenient sentence in exchange for his testimony against the other coconspirator. The other coconspirator went to trial after entering a plea of not guilty to the stolen property charges. While the guilty conspirator was being coached by AUSAs, he said at one point, "I'm not going to go into court and lie." And the lead AUSA said to him, "No, no, no. We don't want you to lie either. But we *do* want you to tell the story [about the other coconspirator] *our way*." [Emphasis mine]

Therefore, much of the prosecutorial melodrama in court is carefully orchestrated in advance. If certain witnesses are considered weak and have little direct inculpatory information against the accused, they may be brought to the witness stand to testify early in the trial, so that the jury can forget about their weaknesses toward the end of the trial.

Seemingly innocent expert witness statements can appear very incriminating. The prosecutor may ask, "Was the blood found on the defendant's shirt consistent with the blood of the victim?" The expert witness says, "Yes, I can say definitely that there was such a consistency." The jury is transfixed by such riveting testimony. However, the defense breaks this bubble by asking the expert witness on cross-examination, "Can you say positively that the blood on the defendant's shirt is the victim's blood?" And the expert witness lowers his head and says, "No, I can't say positively that the blood found is that of the victim's. I can only say that it is consistent with the victim's blood." The defense probes further. "In what respect is the blood found consistent with the victim's blood?" The expert witness says, "It is Type O positive." And the defense asks, "And is it not so that the defendant also has Type O blood?" And the expert says, "Yes, that is true." And the defense asks, "And is it not possible that the blood on the defendant's shirt is the defendant's own blood from a cut on the defendant's arm?" And the expert witness says, "Yes, that is true."

While DNA matching is increasingly important to show precisely whose blood it is that is found at crime scenes, the fact remains that much contamination of blood can occur to make blood typing and identification somewhat unreliable. This does not prevent prosecutors from using this evidence, regardless of its potential unreliability, to the disadvantage of the defendant. Only a skillful defense counsel can undo damage done by a prosecutor who twists the facts to fit the state's case against the defendant (Swedlow, 2004).

Overwhelming Grand Juries

When grand juries are convened, prosecutors are interested in obtaining indictments against defendants. Grand juries consider evidence presented by the prosecutor and determine whether there is sufficient probable cause to believe that a crime was committed and that the defendant probably committed it. Grand juries do not determine the guilt or innocence of the accused. They merely determine whether probable cause exists and that a case should go forward to trial for a legal resolution.

Prosecutors are in a unique position relative to grand juries. Prosecutors direct which evidence and testimony will be presented to the grand jury. Thus, if a prosecutor has considerable evidence and numerous witnesses, he/she may decide to present only the most damaging evidence and the most incriminating testimony. Some witnesses interviewed by the prosecutor may actually provide an alibi for the defendant, showing that the defendant may not have been at the place where the crime was committed at the time when it occurred. Prosecutors exercise their discretion here and determine to present only the evidence and witnesses that show the defendant's guilt.

Since grand juries see only one side of the case against an accused person, they may think only the worst about that defendant. Indictments are issued, therefore, when grand juries are convinced that there is sufficient probable cause to believe that the defendant committed the crime. They are not permitted the luxury of a presentation by the defense counsel to rebut whatever was presented by the prosecutor.

Several attempts have been made by different court systems to monitor prosecutorial conduct before grand juries. For instance, in federal grand jury proceedings, tape recordings have been made and reviewed later by federal district court judges. Misconduct before the grand jury has been referred to as pre-indictment impropriety, and it is often detected only by chance. However, recordings of grand jury proceedings can help to uncover any prosecutorial misconduct that is disclosed. Some of these federal judges have recommended that a full disclosure of grand jury proceedings be made available later to defense counsel and others. Presumably, these recommendations are intended to cause prosecutors to engage in more ethical conduct. It is doubtful that such recordings of grand jury proceedings and subsequent disclosures have curbed prosecutorial abuses of discretion in grand jury proceedings, however.

Prosecutorial Bluffing with Criminal Defendants: Threats or Intimidation?

When criminal defendants are not represented by counsel or are represented by weak defense lawyers, and/or when the cases against criminal defendants are weak, prosecutors may engage in **prosecutorial bluffing** (White 2002). Prosecutorial bluffing means to threaten defendants with a lengthy list of charges, each of which carries serious penalties of fines and lengthy incarcerative terms.

BOX 3.2 PROBLEMS WITH PROSECUTORS

The Center for Public Integrity and other organizations have conducted various polls and surveys of prosecutorial misconduct in recent years with some fascinating results. For instance, it has been found that within the 2,341 jurisdictions in the United States, local prosecutors in most of these jurisdictions have stretched, bent, or broken the rules to win convictions since 1970. Individual judges and appellate court judges have cited numerous instances of prosecutorial misconduct as a major factor in dismissing many cases, reversing convictions, or reducing sentences in over 2,000 cases. Prosecutorial misconduct has been found to warrant reversals of jury verdicts in another 500 cases. In thousands more of these cases, judges have labeled prosecutorial behavior as inappropriate, but they have upheld convictions nevertheless under the doctrine of "harmless error." Misconduct by prosecutors has led to the convictions of many innocent individuals who were later exonerated. Even guilty defendants have had their convictions overturned and released back out on the streets because of prosecutorial misconduct. Some prosecutors violate the rules more than others. More than a few are cited multiple times for misconduct. These prosecutors give recidivism a new meaning.

An Idaho Falls, Idaho prosecutor, Kimball W. Mason, pleaded guilty on March 20, 2006 to three felony counts stemming from misconduct involving the theft of 16 firearms in uncharged felonies. He admitted through a plea bargain in open court that he stole 16 guns from the city of Idaho Falls that had been seized in criminal cases. Mason was required to truthfully disclose the disposition of the stolen firearms and other property he obtained. He is required to pay restitution for the stolen property to the city of Idaho Falls. Mason has also surrendered his license to practice law. The Idaho State Bar Association has moved to revoke his license and membership. Mason agreed not to oppose the suspension of three prison sentences of 1–5 years in the Idaho State Penitentiary in exchange for a 12-month confinement in the county jail. Attorney General Lawrence Wasden said that "This is a serious case involving a serious breach of the public trust. In resolving this case, the primary concerns of this office were to assure that Mason was convicted of multiple felonies, that judgment was not withheld, that the value of the public property taken would be paid back, and that the defendant would lose his license to practice law so that this conduct could never be repeated."

Robert Stevens, a former Louisville, Kentucky prosecutor, was caught on videotape having sex with a female defendant in a criminal case. The woman, Erica French, was being prosecuted for various property offenses when the sexual encounters occurred. Despite the damning evidence of the videotaped sexual encounters with Ms. French, Stevens was subsequently acquitted of official misconduct. It is unclear why he was

(continued)

BOX 3.2 *(continued)*

acquitted, although blackmail was mentioned during the testimony in his trial. Also, Stevens said that he was not the prosecutor in the woman's case. Following the verdict, Stevens, married with children, held his head in his hands and sobbed. He turned toward his wife and children, who sat near him during the trial. Parts of the videotaped sexual encounters had been shown to the jury during the trial.

Assistant District Attorney Birgitta Tolvanen of Lawrence County, Pennsylvania, was accused of committing fraud by helping to convict a man of robbery in 2003. The president of the Pennsylvania Bar Association, Jonathan Solomon, has filed a complaint with the Disciplinary Board of the State Supreme Court, contending that Tolvanen improperly cross-examined a key witness in the trial that resulted in Justin Kirkwood's armed robbery conviction. Kirkwood, who has appealed his conviction, remains imprisoned. During Kirkwood's trial, several alibi witnesses, including Bill Fitts, owner of a local Ford dealership, testified that he had spoken with Kirkwood by telephone on the day and at the very time the robbery was to have occurred. Tolvanen produced Fitts's telephone records and asked whether he saw any telephone calls to Kirkwood. Fitts replied that he would be very surprised that such calls did not appear on his telephone records. But he insisted that he did make a phone call to Kirkwood at the time of the robbery. A subsequent examination of the telephone records showed that not all local calls are necessarily recorded on the dealership's statements, and that Tolvanen knew that at the time of her cross-examination of Fitts. Fitts's testimony was a crucial alibi for Kirkwood, who was convicted of stealing $170 from a Family Craft Center in another city. A female clerk in the store identified him as the robber, claiming that he had brown eyes even though his eyes are blue. Furthermore, Kirkwood had numerous tattoos on his arms and legs. None of these body markings were mentioned by prosecution witnesses to implicate Kirkwood. Tolvanen could not be reached for comment.

What sanctioning mechanisms should be in place to punish prosecutors who bend the law to fit their own purposes and ensure convictions of innocent defendants? How much prosecutorial misconduct occurs, in your estimation? Should those who engage in prosecutorial misconduct be allowed to continue prosecuting cases? What do you think?

[*Sources:* Adapted from the Associated Press, "Breaking the Rules," June 26, 2003; adapted from the Associated Press, "Mason Admits Gun Thefts, Surrenders His Law License," April 19, 2006; adapted from the Associated Press, "Former Prosecutor Acquitted of Misconduct," October 13, 2005; adapted from Bill Moushey and the *Pittsburgh Post-Gazette,* "Lawrence County Prosecutor Accused of Trial Misconduct," May 24, 2005.]

The intent of prosecutorial bluffing is to cause a defendant to enter a guilty plea to one of the more minor charges in exchange for prosecutorial leniency. For instance, if the defendant pleads guilty to one felony charge, the other 20 felony charges will be dropped. Or maybe the prosecutor will accept the defendant's guilty plea to a misdemeanor, in exchange for a sentence of probation and dropping more serious felony changes.

This overcharging tactic is successful in many cases, even where more competent defense counsel are involved. In one case, a 21-year-old restaurant waiter ran over and killed two drunk men who were wrestling in the middle of a poorly lit street late at night. The waiter had completed his 11:00 p.m. shift at the restaurant, had a few beers, and drove home at 1:00 a.m. He obeyed all traffic laws and was not legally intoxicated. Nevertheless, when he turned a corner near his apartment on a secondary road near a major highway, he suddenly saw two men wrestling on the road in front of him. Although he was only traveling about 20 miles per hour, he could not stop his vehicle in time to avoid running over them. The prosecutor charged the waiter with vehicular homicide. Vehicular homicide includes the elements of intent to commit homicide with one's automobile. Since it was never the waiter's intent to drink some beer and then drive his car until he could run over two drunk men fighting in the middle of the road, it was doubtful that the vehicular homicide charge could be sustained. Subsequently, the prosecutor said that if the waiter would plead guilty to involuntary manslaughter, he would drop the vehicular homicide charge. The defense counsel rejected the offer and insisted on a trial for his client. Later, the prosecutor offered to drop the vehicular homicide charge if the waiter pleaded guilty to reckless driving. Again, the waiter's defense attorney rejected the offer. A few months later, the prosecutor advised that the case against the waiter had been dropped. There was no criminal conduct on the part of the waiter. The prosecutor attempted to bluff, but the defense counsel called his bluff and insisted on a trial to clear the waiter's name.

Prosecutorial bluffing is not limited to criminal defendants. Prosecutors may also threaten or intimidate prospective witnesses. In 1998, for example, independent counsel and special prosecutor Kenneth Starr was investigating alleged illegal campaign contributions by the Democratic Party and President Bill Clinton. Starr cast a wide net in an effort to implicate Bill Clinton in any type of wrongdoing. At one point, one of Clinton's former White House interns, Monica Lewinsky, 24, had disclosed to a friend that she and Clinton had been sexually intimate. However, in a sworn affidavit in another matter, Lewinsky said that she had never had any sexual encounters with Clinton. Starr engaged in various tactics designed to threaten and intimidate Ms. Lewinsky into giving testimony that would implicate Clinton. The intimidation included surrounding her with FBI agents and various prosecutors at a hotel and interrogating her for two days about her presidential encounters and statements made to her friend. Various informed sources said in newscasts that Starr had engaged in misconduct when interrogating Lewinsky, and that this misconduct was grounds to have him removed as a special independent counsel in the case. Starr countered these allegations of misconduct by saying that he was merely seeking the truth in matters involving Bill Clinton.

Suppressing Evidence from the Defense

Prosecutors are able to view all evidence collected from the police and material witnesses in criminal cases. While some of this evidence may tend to show the guilt of the defendant, other evidence may show the defendant's innocence. If a prosecutor has such exculpatory evidence, he/she is obligated to disclose this evidence to the defense for its use. However, evidence suggests that much of the time, exculpatory evidence is deliberately suppressed by prosecutors, even in capital cases (Harmon 2000, 2001).

During the trial of O. J. Simpson on double-murder charges in Los Angeles in 1995, for instance, a Los Angeles detective, Mark Fuhrman, gave substantial incriminating testimony about evidence he had found that linked Simpson to the crime. Other testimony was given by Fuhrman about his feelings toward blacks. Fuhrman denied being prejudiced against blacks. Furthermore, he denied under oath that he had made derogatory racial slurs or statements for more than a decade. Later, defense attorneys produced a witness with tape-recorded interviews with Fuhrman. These tape recordings clearly revealed that Fuhrman had made numerous racially derogatory statements against blacks, sharply contradicting what he had previously said on the witness stand under oath. Subsequently, Fuhrman entered a guilty plea to perjury charges. However, the damage of his earlier testimony incriminating Simpson had already been done. And there was the strong implication made by defense counsel that the prosecutors knew about Fuhrman's racism in advance of his testimony about it. Further, defense counsel alleged, prosecutors caused Fuhrman to let them tell the story their way, and they deliberately withheld from the jury any reference to Fuhrman's racism, although the prosecutors knew about it. This is an example of suppressing evidence. An adversary's ability to demonstrate the opposition's racial or ethnic bias often makes a significant difference in case outcomes (Ball 2005).

Excluding Prospective Jurors Who Are Favorable to Defendants

When prospective jurors are being questioned concerning their qualifications and beliefs or prejudices, both the prosecution and defense have an opportunity to challenge them. Particularly in high-profile trials involving well-known persons, a concerted attempt is made by both sides to configure the best jury most favorable to either side. While jury voting cannot be predicted by either side in advance, prosecutors and their associates attempt to select jurors who will be pro-prosecution in their views.

In a capital murder case, for instance, prospective jurors with strong feelings against the death penalty may be excluded because these prospective jurors believe that their own feelings might not permit them to impose the death penalty if they find the defendant is guilty of the capital crime. When prosecutors dismiss these jurors, they narrow the pool of prospective jurors who might be favorably disposed toward the defendant. Frequently, prospective jurors are dismissed by prosecutors since these jurors exhibit other views that are associated with anti-death penalty sentiments. Defense counsel can engage in similar behavior by excluding those who are in favor of capital punishment (Martin and Roberts 2005). Always the number of jurors who can be dismissed by either the prosecution or defense because of the juror's sentiments is limited. Despite these limitations, prosecutors can skillfully maneuver and create a jury composition that they believe is unfavorable to a defendant (Nadeau, Burek, and Williams 2005). Because of the diffuse grounds used to dismiss particular prospective jurors, it is not easy to determine when prosecutors are engaging in this type of misconduct.

Offering Inadmissible Evidence in Court

A prosecutorial tactic sometimes used in a weak criminal case is to backdoor hearsay evidence. **Backdooring hearsay evidence** means to mention or comment about evidence against the accused that is not admissible evidence. Perhaps the defendant, charged with trafficking in heroin, has been arrested five times in the past for heroin and cocaine possession. However, these arrests have resulted in case dismissals. Insufficient evidence existed to move forward with criminal prosecutions in each of these five arrest situations. In many jurisdictions, prosecutors may only introduce evidence about one's prior criminal convictions. It is not permissible for prosecutors to mention any arrests that never resulted in convictions. But the prosecutor might make a statement in court while questioning the defendant or a witness. "Were you with the defendant when he was arrested for cocaine and heroin possession on five different occasions during the last three years?" the prosecutor might ask. Before the witness can speak, an objection is made by the defense and the judge sustains the objection, admonishing the jury to disregard the prosecutor's question. But the damage has already been done. The question has been raised and heard by the jurors. They now know that the defendant has been arrested in the past for heroin and cocaine possession. More important, the jurors have no way of knowing that these arrests never resulted in prosecutions or convictions on the drug charges. Inadmissible evidence has been admitted through the back door, although the judge has declared that the jury should ignore it. Jurors cannot ignore whatever they have heard.

It is difficult for the court to determine whether the utterances of prosecutors are deliberate or wilful, intentional or unintentional. Prosecutors may claim that they had no intention of violating court rules by mentioning inadmissible evidence, although they may have done so deliberately. Most courts interpret such utterances as harmless error. In some jurisdictions, federal rules may be applied in ways that fit particular cultures. Native American law, for instance, is articulated under Title 18, Section 1152 of the U.S. Code (2005) and known as the Indian General Crimes Act. Thus, in the United States today, many Native American tribes have their own legal apparatuses that govern the admissibility of evidence, how crimes are defined, and how cases are prosecuted (Clark 2005).

Malicious Prosecutions

The pressure on prosecutors to obtain convictions may induce them to file charges against certain defendants who are innocent of any crime. When prosecutors bring charges against the accused with the full knowledge that the accused is innocent of the crimes alleged, this is a **malicious prosecution**.

Misconduct Risks and Sanctions

When prosecutors commit **prosecutorial misconduct**, particularly in the courtroom, there is always the chance that the misconduct will be detected and sanctioned in some way. Prejudicial commentary by the prosecutor will cause defense counsel to object. Judges will sustain these objections, but the harm has already been done. The jury has heard the prejudicial commentary, and despite an admonition from the judge to disregard such prejudicial commentary, the jury cannot forget about it entirely. For instance, a prosecutor may be barred from mentioning a defendant's sexual preferences in a murder trial occurring in a small religious community. However, the prosecutor may allude to a homosexual defendant's gay rights activism, even though this commentary has nothing to do with the case before the court. Defense counsel will object strenuously, and the judge will sustain this objection. But the jury cannot erase from their memories the prosecutor's statement about the defendant's gay rights activities. Jurors may assume that the defendant is gay, and this assumption may be sufficient to prejudice some of them. Because some of the jurors may dislike gays, they may punish the defendant by voting for his guilt, despite the fact that the defendant's guilt has not been established beyond a reasonable doubt. The prosecutor is successful, therefore, in prejudicing jurors against the defendant by alluding to one or more extralegal factors.

Ethical Norms

Prosecutors can get away with their courtroom misconduct largely because of an absence of ethical norms as standards against which to gauge their conduct. In case after case where prosecutorial misconduct is alleged, the U.S. Supreme Court has failed to articulate clear and consistent ethical norms to guide prosecutors.

Interestingly, juries are more inclined to consider inadmissible evidence favorable to defendants than inadmissible evidence unfavorable to defendants. Despite this factor of defense favoritism, prosecutors might be tempted to sway the jury by introducing highly prejudicial inadmissible evidence. By doing so, they risk jeopardizing any resulting conviction. However, the likelihood of having one's conviction overturned in these instances is extremely remote. The most significant reason for the continued presence of prosecutorial misconduct is the **harmless error doctrine**. Under this doctrine, an appellate court can affirm one's conviction despite the presence of serious prosecutorial misconduct during the trial. Thus, the desirability of the doctrine is undermined when the prosecutor is able to commit misconduct himself without fear of sanction (Carter 2001). The harmless error doctrine also can pertain to serious cases where the death penalty can be invoked.

BOX 3.3 CAREER SNAPSHOT

Joseph C. Skibek
Sergeant, Connecticut State Police

Statistics: B.A. (forensic studies, telecommunications) Indiana University

Background and Experiences: After completing high school in Fairfield, Connecticut, I attended Indiana University. In 1980 after receiving a B.A. in forensic studies and telecommunications, I accepted a commission as a lieutenant in the U.S. Marine Corps and was assigned to the Basic School in Quantico, Virginia. For the next four years, I served in various assignments and locations within the United States as a HAWK Missile Battery platoon commander, executive officer, and battalion legal officer. After completing active duty, I briefly served as a trooper in the New Hampshire State Police and as an officer in the Fairfield, Connecticut Police Department. Since 1985 I have served as a trooper with the Connecticut State Police and currently am assigned as a duty supervisor at the Bradley International Airport in Windsor Locks, Connecticut.

During the past 19 years with the Connecticut State Police, I have served in a variety of positions including patrol trooper, resident trooper,

(continued)

BOX 3.3 *(continued)*

polygraphist, major crime unit detective, and patrol sergeant. My current duties especially since 9/11 involve facility security, dignitary protection, and incident investigation. The airport is a unique assignment due to the variety of individuals and situations that you encounter during a duty shift.

Work Events: What really comes to mind when reflecting on the past years of service are some of the individual incidents that had a profound effect on my life. There are the major incidents such as Hurricane Gloria that had a devastating effect on our state during the fall 1985. As members of the recruit trooper training class, we were assigned to ride with patrol troopers who staffed several of the shoreline communities. During the height of the storm, the barracks dispatched troopers to a man kicking in cottage doors along the beach in Old Lyme. The winds were over 100 mph and most of the beach access streets were flooded. The individual was taken into custody after a brief foot pursuit. Even though I knew that troopers rode alone, that situation emphasized the camaraderie and team spirit that existed between not-so-ordinary persons doing extraordinary tasks. During 1989 an F-3 tornado destroyed several homes, businesses, and vehicles throughout a wide area in western and central Connecticut. A tornado is a very infrequent and unusual event in our state. I will never forget the look on the faces of residents as they were literally crawling out of their basement windows and destroyed homes. Our assignment was to climb over the hundreds of trees that had fallen onto homes and blocked the streets, in order to locate and bring the survivors to area shelters. It was unbelievable to see the wide path of destruction and hear the personal stories of terror that the residents experienced during that evening. As a law enforcement officer you will be involved in both good and bad situations that test your physical stamina, logical reasoning ability, devotion to duty, moral fiber, and ethics during almost every duty shift. Be prepared for that challenge.

During 1992–1996 I served with our criminal investigative unit, including the Central District Major Crime Squad. Part of our unit's mission was to investigate misdemeanor and felony crimes, including homicides, within our state police towns and all state buildings and facilities within our jurisdiction. During one Sunday afternoon, patrol troopers and local police officers had responded to a reported shooting within an office building of a small state community college. The investigation determined that the victim was the spouse of a professor at the college that had recently died due to cancer. She was in his office to pick up her husband's personal effects following his death. An unarmed security officer contacted the local police department and reported that our victim had been shot while she was inside the ladies' restroom. Since the building was locked during nonbusiness hours, the only authorized occupants were the security guard and the victim. After a few hours of crime scene processing and interviews, the security guard became an identified suspect. A search warrant was obtained for his clothing, personal vehicle, and family residence. I recall that two senior detectives from our unit interviewed this suspect and he wouldn't admit any involvement in the crime. What sealed his fate was a variety of physical evidence including positive gunshot residue on his hands and clothing, a ballistics match with one of his personal handguns, and an expended shell casing that was lodged within one leg of his cuffed security uniform trousers. He eventually pleaded guilty and was sentenced to several years in prison. Sometimes good luck cements good police work.

Advice to Students:

1. Don't be afraid to shop around and explore your options in the criminal justice arena. There are many different academic and professional careers available within the criminal justice field. I personally completed three police academy programs before I found the right agency. Doing your homework and checking out the individual agency is a good start. Most agencies have some type of intern or ride-along program, to give you a small taste of working within their system. Don't be afraid to change gears if you discover that the career path or your specific agency isn't personally rewarding and satisfying. As the old saying goes, the grass always seems to look greener somewhere else. Being unhappy in a law enforcement career field just to achieve better pay and get retirement benefits will lead to serious problems including poor job performance and burnout.

2. Never compromise your personal values, your moral values, and your integrity. As you progress through a career in criminal justice, there will be many situations, including possible peer and supervisory pressures, that place you in difficult moral dilemmas. Reflect back upon your solid ethical standards and do the right thing. It's not easy to be involved in a touchy situation where you stand out from the crowd, but your personal reputation is worth so much more than a short-term reward for being "one of the boys or girls." Remember, you chose the criminal justice profession to assist people within our communities. Don't destroy your moral integrity for short-term personal or financial gain.

3. Have fun! Unfortunately during your career you will become well acquainted with some very unusual situations, including all types of untimely deaths and very bizarre incidents. If you can maintain a decent and appropriate sense of humor during the process, it will help you deal with the unavoidable horrors of police work. Not one of us will ever forget our first child death or an especially grisly crime or accident scene. Remember that cops and other criminal justice professionals aren't immune to serious family issues including divorce, substance abuse, and being victims of brutal assaults. Keeping the job in perspective with the rest of your ordinary life, getting some counseling if its appropriate, and keeping it real will help you survive several years in the criminal justice system. Good luck with your education and career path. Please take advantage of opportunities to attend additional training within your agency and from outside sources such as academies, colleges, and community programs. Stay prepared and be safe.

Also, the standards currently used in ruling on motions for retrial based on false testimony fail to strike an acceptable balance between the right of the accused to a fair and impartial trial and the demand for efficient administration of the criminal justice system in court. Ideally, motions for retrial based on false testimony presented by prosecution witnesses should be governed by a standard drawn from newly discovered evidence and prosecutorial misconduct. The proper test for a new trial based on newly discovered evidence of false testimony is whether there is a significant chance that a jury with a knowledge of the false testimony would avoid convicting the defendant.

SUMMARY

The courtroom work group consists of a number of individuals, including the judge, prosecutor, bailiff, court reporter, defense counsel, and other parties who oversee trials and ensure that protocol for the trial process is precisely observed. Next to the judge who presides over trials, the prosecutor, also known as the state's attorney, the district attorney, or the U.S. attorney or assistant U.S. attorney, depending on whether the jurisdiction is state or federal, is one of the most powerful members of this work group.

Prosecutors represent the state's or federal government's interests whenever one or more crimes are alleged against defendants. Prosecutors are often political appointees or elected persons, all of whom have law degrees or other equivalent entitlements that enable them to practice law. Many prosecutors started out as public defenders or private attorneys working for law firms. As attorneys, all prosecutors are bound by codes of ethics, depending upon the professional organizations to which they belong. Most attorneys in the United States belong to the American Bar Association (ABA), which has articulated ethical codes and standards over the years for its membership to follow. The ABA Code of Professional Responsibility and Canons of Professional Ethics are examples of the ethical behaviors espoused by this organization. Prosecutors may also belong to local bar associations, which consist largely of state and local attorneys. State bar associations have articulated similar ethical codes to the ABA, and their respective memberships are expected to abide by them.

Canons of ethics include exhibiting integrity and competence, assisting the legal profession in various ways to bring distinction upon it, assisting in preventing the unauthorized practice of law, preserving confidences of clients and others, representing the government and/or clients competently, representing the government and/or clients zealously within the boundaries of the law, assisting in improving the legal system, and avoiding the appearance of impropriety. Prosecutors have

evolved their own organizations as well, and these and other ethical behaviors have been articulated to provide guides for their own conduct
prior to, during, and after trial proceedings.

The criminal court is an adversarial system. The adversaries are
the prosecutor and defense counsel. These persons are regarded as
sides in a form of competition to win. The general goal of the prosecutor is to convict those accused of crimes, while the goal of the defense
counsel is to secure an acquittal for his/her client. Deciding which side
is right are either the judge or jury in a bench or jury trial proceeding.
Both sides abide by rules, including state or federal rules of criminal
procedure and rules of evidence. These rules regulate virtually all permissible conduct from the beginning of a prosecution to the end of it.
Evidentiary matters are also a part of this process, and various rules
have been established to govern whether certain types of evidence are
admissible by either the prosecutor or the defense or both. Judges decide on questions of whether these rules are violated by either side
when motions are made by prosecutors or defense counsel objecting to
particular behaviors or evidence. Evidence introduced by either side is
either inculpatory or exculpatory. Inculpatory evidence shows the defendant's guilt, while exculpatory evidence shows defendant innocence.

Depending upon the jurisdiction, the roles of prosecutors are relatively simple. All prosecutors function to screen which cases to prosecute and which ones not to prosecute. This means that they must
prioritize their cases. One reason for such case prioritizing is that there
are almost always case backlogs in state and federal courts, and it is simply not possible to prosecute all cases presented to prosecutors for
prosecutorial merit. Thus, prosecutors decide on their own or in
groups whether to pursue particular cases. These decisions are often
made according to how much evidence exists against particular defendants, the likelihood of winning the case and securing a conviction, the
media visibility of the case, and case seriousness. Prosecutors are responsible for devising the best strategies for winning cases. They must
interview witnesses, including victims of crime and those who saw the
crime occur. They must work closely with law enforcement officers
who made arrests and conducted criminal investigations. They must
also work with forensic teams who analyze evidence collected from
crime scenes. The lead prosecutors in any jurisdiction may also assign
cases for prosecution to their assistant district attorneys or state's attorneys. At the federal level, U.S. attorneys assign different criminal
cases to their group of assistant U.S. attorneys.

Prosecutors have an immense amount of power. In jurisdictions
with grand jury systems, prosecutors attempt to secure indictments or
charges against those accused of crimes. They make their cases before

grand juries and present inculpatory evidence to them. These are largely one-sided proceedings, since defense counsels are not permitted to present exculpatory evidence in favor of their clients. Thus, prosecutors may elect to present only the most incriminating evidence, and they may refrain from introducing evidence to grand juries that may be exculpatory or in a defendant's favor. Almost any prosecutor can secure an indictment against almost any criminal defendant under the grand jury system, which is used in about half of all states. Therefore, there is the potential for prosecutorial abuse of discretion or misconduct.

Prosecutorial misconduct does not typify most prosecutors, although it exists throughout state and federal systems to an uncomfortable degree. Several forms of prosecutorial misconduct have been described. Prosecutors may coach their witnesses by encouraging them to relate what evidentiary information they have in ways that favor the prosecutor's argument that the defendant is guilty of a crime. These spins on witness revelations about what they saw or heard often convince jurors of defendant guilt. Defense counsels must counter by pointing out inconsistencies in witness statements through cross-examination, or they must give their own spin of events to these statements. Jurors must decide, therefore, what to make of any evidence presented. In some instances, prosecutors may encourage defendants to commit perjury on the witness stand and say things about the defendant that are not true. This is subornation of perjury and a crime. Prosecutors themselves may be charged with subornation of perjury and be prosecuted for such an offense if it is detected. There is often a diffuse line between the spins sought by prosecutors from witnesses and their statements and subornation of perjury. It is difficult to determine whenever this line is crossed.

Another form of prosecutorial misconduct is malicious prosecution. Malicious prosecution is the prosecution of someone who is innocent of the crime alleged, and this innocence is known or believed by the prosecutor. Nevertheless, the prosecutor moves forward against these defendants anyway. Grand juries are easily overwhelmed by one-sided presentations of events by prosecutors, and indictments or charges against defendants are not difficult to obtain. Once a defendant has been indicted, a dark cloud of suspicion overwhelms the defendant in the eyes of a critical public who often have a poor understanding of what indictments mean or how easily they may be obtained. More than a few innocent defendants have been pressured into pleading guilty to crimes they have not committed in an effort to escape the possibility of a conviction through trial, where the punishment may be severe. Prosecutors usually obtain over 90 percent of their convictions against criminal defendants through plea bargaining. While judges must approve all plea bargain agreements, they do not always detect when innocent defendants enter pleas of guilty to crimes they have not committed.

Prosecutors may also engage in prosecutorial bluffing. Prosecutorial bluffing is intended to frighten criminal defendants and their defense counsels into thinking that prosecutors have more inculpatory evidence than they really have. Often prosecutorial bluffing encourages defendants to enter into guilty pleas through plea bargain agreements, especially if defendants are offered light sentences of probation in exchange for guilty pleas to minor charges. Again, defendants do not wish to gamble and expose themselves to possible lengthy incarcerative sentences that may accrue through the trial process.

Another form of prosecutorial misconduct is to deliberately withhold exculpatory evidence from defense counsels prior to or during trials. Under discovery rules, certain materials and evidence must be made available to defense counsels. These materials, known as Brady or Jencks materials after their respective U.S. Supreme Court cases that declared certain materials as discoverable, must be disclosed to defense counsels and are often crucial in showing the innocence of their clients. If prosecutors fail to disclose some of this information to defense counsels, they are violating the rules of discovery and may jeopardize any subsequent conviction they may obtain.

Less obvious prosecutorial behaviors that border misconduct in various ways include attempts to configure juries most likely to convict defendants. Some prosecutors have used professional jury consultants, especially in high-profile trials such as the 2004–2005 trial of Scott Peterson in California who was convicted of murdering his wife and unborn child. Both prosecutors and defense counsels are given designated numbers of peremptory challenges they can use to excuse prospective jurors in criminal cases. These challenges may be used by either side to excuse prospective jurors without giving a reason for doing so. Sometimes this use of peremptory challenges is unethical and illegal. For instance, until the 1980s, it was somewhat customary, especially in southern states, for prosecutors to use their peremptory challenges to excuse all black prospective jurors in cases involving black defendants. This practice was subsequently declared unconstitutional, but it is an indication of how an abuse of prosecutorial discretion can occur.

Finally, prosecutors may backdoor hearsay testimony before juries during trial proceedings. This is clearly an unethical and unwarranted practice, where prosecutors will ask questions of witnesses or make statements during their opening or closing arguments that violate either the rules of criminal procedure or the rules of evidence or both. These statements, which often tend to incriminate defendants or disclose past behaviors that are clearly inadmissible in court, often result in sustained objections from the opposing side, but the jury has heard these statements. Despite the judge's admonition to ignore these statements, jurors do not easily forget statements they have heard, especially if they incriminate defendants or reveal adverse facts about them. By the same token, defense counsels cannot make such statements either, where their intent is to introduce inadmissible but favorable evidence of an exculpatory nature for their clients. No trial proceeding is perfect, and almost always, both prosecutors and defense counsel make inadmissible statements, either deliberately or unintentionally, that jurors should not hear. When such statements are made deliberately, this is backdooring hearsay evidence and not permitted. Judges must determine whether one or more statements made in the jury's presence by either side are substantial or harmless, and they may declare any statements they hear as harmless error whenever they are made. Such statements and the judicial rulings about them may be bases for appeals later if a defendant is convicted.

KEY TERMS

Adversary system
Assistant state's attorneys
Assistant U.S. attorneys (AUSAs)
Attorney general
Backdooring hearsay evidence
Criminal informations
Defense attorney
Defense strategy
Deponents
Deposed
District attorneys
Ethical code
Exculpatory evidence
Harmless error doctrine
Inculpatory evidence

Indictments
Informations
Malicious prosecution
Prosecutor
Prosecutorial bluffing
Prosecutorial misconduct
Rules of Criminal Procedure
Screening cases
Sides
State's attorneys
True bills
United States attorney
United States Attorney's Office
Venue
Witnesses

QUESTIONS FOR REVIEW

1. What is meant by the adversary system? Which actors make up the adversary system? What rules govern the adversary system in courts?

2. At the federal and state levels, who are the prosecutors?

3. What are the functions of prosecutors?

4. Under what circumstances might prosecutors engage in misconduct? What are four types of prosecutorial misconduct?

5. How do prosecutors overwhelm grand juries?

6. How do prosecutors perform screening functions in criminal cases?

7. What is meant by prosecutorial bluffing? What are some examples of prosecutorial bluffing?

8. How can prosecutors bias a case in favor of the prosecution? Give some examples.

9. What is meant by backdooring hearsay evidence?

10. What is a malicious prosecution? What are some sanctions the court might use to reprimand district attorneys who engage in malicious prosecutions of suspects?

11. What is meant by the harmless error doctrine?

SUGGESTED READINGS

1. Anthony V. Alfieri (2002). "Community Prosecutors." *California Law Review* **90**:1465–1511.
2. D. Beichner and C. Spohn (2005). "Prosecutorial Charging Decisions in Sexual Assault Cases: Examining the Impact of a Specialized Prosecution Unit." *Criminal Justice Policy Review* **16**:461–498.
3. A. Farrell (2004). "Measuring Judicial and Prosecutorial Discretion: Sex and Race Disparities in Departures from the Federal Sentencing Guidelines." *Justice Research and Policy* **6**:45–78.
4. R. E. Geiselman and B. A. Mendez (2005). "Assistance to the Fact Finder: Eyewitness Expert Testimony Versus Attorneys' Closing Arguments." *American Journal of Forensic Psychology* **23**:5–15.
5. B. A. McPhail and D. Dinitto (2005). "Prosecutorial Perspectives on Gender-Bias Hate Crimes." *Violence Against Women* **11**:1162–1185.
6. B. K. Payne, V. Time, and S. Raper (2004). "Regulating Legal Misconduct in the Commonwealth of Virginia: The Gender Influence." *Women and Criminal Justice* **15**:81–95.
7. Welsh White (2002). "Curbing Prosecutorial Misconduct in Capital Cases: Imposing Prohibitions on Improper Penalty Trial Arguments." *American Criminal Law Review* **39**:1147–1185.

Chapter **4**

The Defense

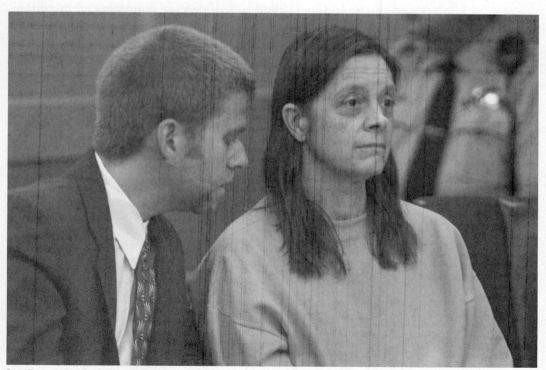

Lou Dematteis, Corbis/Reuters America LLC

Chapter Objectives

As a result of reading this chapter, you will have accomplished the following objectives:

1. Understand the legal ethics and responsibilities of defense counsels who represent criminal clients.

2. Understand the Sixth Amendment and one's right to counsel regardless of whether the defendant is indigent.

3. Describe the process of self-representation or acting *pro se*.

4. Understand the attorney–client privilege and the confidentiality associated with that relationship.

5. Describe what is meant by ineffective assistance of counsel and learn the criteria used by courts to assess attorney competence.

6. Assess the circumstances under which defendants may request and receive a jury trial.

7. Understand the multidimensional role of defense counsels and the different functions they perform.

8. Describe different types of public defender systems, including the assigned counsel system and the contract system.

9. Understand what is meant by defense misconduct and describe its various forms.

10. Understand the relation between prosecutors and defense counsel and the discovery process.

11. Describe the various affirmative defenses attorneys may raise when representing persons charged with crimes.

■ George Gray is a public defender. He finished law school two years ago and has decided to enter criminal law. He has been employed by the Quinn County, Virginia Public Defender's Office for the past year. His job is to assist indigent defendants charged with crimes. The office is overworked and understaffed. Regular staff meetings are held where the office manager declares that the staff should seek quick resolutions of criminal cases where possible. "Get the district attorney's office to downgrade the charges against your defendants if they plead guilty to lesser charges," instructs the office manager. "Do whatever you can to speed these cases along." Gray meets with a homeless person, Jose Garcia, who appears to be mentally retarded. Garcia is charged with robbery, since he was seen by witnesses loitering near a convenience store one night shortly before it was robbed by masked persons. Garcia is from Albuquerque, New Mexico, and has a poor command of the English language. He claims to have been in Operation Desert Storm in the 1990s and a military veteran with a Purple Heart. Gray doesn't bother checking on this information, primarily because he has neither the time nor the interest. Garcia also claims that he was drinking some cheap wine that night and was drunk, having no idea why he was arrested for robbery. He claims to have been in the convenience store earlier that night to get a plastic cup for his wine. But he was ejected from the store by one of the employees. Gray decides that it would be in Garcia's best interests to plead guilty to simple robbery, since no one was injured in the crime and little money was taken. Gray advises that if the case goes to trial, Garcia could end up doing 25 years to life for robbery, but there is a good chance Garcia might only get 5 years or less if he enters a "guilty" plea to the charges. After considerable argument and badgering from Gray, Garcia agrees to plead guilty. Gray telephones one of the prosecutors and advises what Garcia is willing to do. The prosecutor agrees to accept Garcia's guilty plea in exchange for a sentence recommendation of from 2–5 years in prison. Did Gray act in Garcia's best interests? Was justice served?

Timothy Dalton is a private criminal attorney who has been practicing law for 25 years. He knows all of the judges and prosecutors in his county. He has an established reputation as being a high-paid, successful defense counsel who wins most of the cases he takes to trial. He is also known for his courtroom antics, including outrageous displays that sway or shock jurors. Dalton has just agreed to defend Jeff Greer, a career criminal with numerous convictions for violent offenses. Greer is charged with sexually assaulting a local woman he had picked up at a local bar. The woman, a local prostitute, claims that Greer forced her to have sex with him at knife point in a motel room where they had gone for "a few more drinks." Greer tells Dalton that "the bitch wanted to charge me $100 for sex, and I told her I'd give her $25. She scratched my face, and I hit her. Sure, I had sex with her afterwards. And I flashed a knife at her to show I meant business. But she didn't have any complaints afterwards. I thought everything was fine. She got her money and left. Next thing I know, police are breaking down my door arresting me for sexual assault." Dalton calls John Persons, the local district attorney, and says, "Listen John, this thing against Greer shouldn't go to trial. The complainant is a known whore, she got paid for sex, and now she's complaining about the price. Sexual assault? I don't think so. This woman has at least 15 arrests for soliciting, and I don't know how many prostitution convictions she has. She's just got a bad case of sour grapes. My client will agree to simple assault and we can make this whole thing go away with one year of probation and counseling for Greer. What do you say?" Persons gets back to Dalton the next day and consents to the simple assault plea with a recommendation for probation and counseling. Is there anything wrong with this agreement?

INTRODUCTION

All persons charged with crimes are entitled to counsel. This chapter examines the role of defense counsel in great detail. The first section describes one's right to counsel and how it is exercised. Some criminal defendants are indigent and cannot afford to hire counsel. In these cases of indigence, public defenders will be appointed by the court to furnish indigent defendants with legal representation to ensure that their rights are observed. Some defendants wish to represent themselves and reject counsel appointed by the court. These persons proceed on a *pro se* basis, but they are warned by the court that self-representation is a dangerous step and a potentially devastating one. The process of self-representation will be described.

The chapter next examines the attorney–client relation and the confidentiality associated with such interaction. Whatever conversations pass between an attorney and his/her client cannot be compelled for disclosure to the prosecutor and others. This confidentiality privilege is quite important in preserving the integrity of the criminal justice system, and it protects defendants against self-incrimination. Also examined in this section is the issue of ineffective assistance of counsel. Not all defense counsels are equally gifted in the ways of the law, and from time to time, some defense counsels will fail to act in ways that best represent their clients' interests. When this situation occurs, convicted offenders may challenge their convictions by alleging ineffective assistance of counsel. Subsequently the U.S. Supreme Court has ruled decisively and determined the criteria used to evaluate whether or not a defense counsel is competent.

For the small percentage of cases that proceed to the trial phase of one's criminal processing, defense attorneys must present convincing cases to judges or juries, whether bench or jury trials are conducted (Zalman 2004). The standards for jury trials have been articulated by the U.S. Supreme Court and will be examined here. For petty offenses and for offenses where the maximum incarceration is six months or less, defendants are not entitled to a jury trial as a matter of right. This situation will be discussed.

The chapter next examines the process whereby indigent defendants have attorneys appointed for them. Different states use one of several types of public defender systems. Some states use several systems simultaneously, but in different counties. These systems include the public defender system, the contract system, and the assigned counsel system. Each system is described, and the advantages and disadvantages of each system for indigent defendants are discussed. The general question of whether private counsel or publicly appointed counsel are more effective in representing clients will also be examined. In one of the chapter opening scenarios, an indigent client is convinced by his public defender to enter a guilty plea to a crime he swears he didn't commit. This practice, which occurs more often than the criminal justice system would care to admit, will be explored.

The following section examines the various functions of defense counsels. These functions include faithfully representing clients, attacking vigorously the prosecutor's case against the defendant, counseling with defendants to determine the best defense strategy, negotiating with prosecutors in plea agreement proceedings to configure a plea most favorable for the defendant, vigorously cross-examining prosecution witnesses during trials to undermine their credibility or impeach their veracity, and using any and all legal means at their disposal to defeat the government's case against their defendant. In one of the chapter opening scenarios, a defense counsel suggests to a prosecutor that a complainant has an unsavory past and a prior record that would be adverse to the state's case against his client. The implied threat of using this information to support his client's actions raises certain ethical issues about appropriate defense counsel conduct. These issues will be examined.

One important function of defense counsels is to interact with prosecutors and seek discovery of relevant evidentiary information. The discovery process is described as well as its significance for the trial outcome. Discovery has been influenced by several important U.S. Supreme Court cases, which will be described. Materials subject to discovery rules have been variously labeled as Brady materials or Jencks materials, after the major cases where high court rulings were rendered. Much of the discoverable evidence provided to defense counsels is important to the defense's case. Several types of evidence are distinguished and examined, including conclusive evidence, direct evidence, circumstantial evidence, and demonstrative evidence. Defense counsels must decide how and when to use different types of evidence they possess most effectively.

The chapter concludes with an examination about what several of the defense attorneys might use to explain away the conduct of their clients. These are mostly affirmative defenses, and they include automatism or insanity, intoxication, coercion or duress, necessity, alibi, entrapment, defense of property, ignorance or mistake, and self-defense. While this list of defenses is not exhaustive, most affirmative defenses used by defense counsels are presented here. Several examples of these defenses are also discussed.

ON LEGAL ETHICS AND PROFESSIONAL RESPONSIBILITY

Lawyers have been the butt of more than a few jokes. For instance, there's the one about a lawyer who was fishing with his lawyer friends in the Atlantic Ocean. Suddenly a big wave washed over the boat, spilling one of the lawyers into the shark-infested waters. A 20-foot great white shark came along and grabbed the flailing lawyer between its teeth. But instead of heading to the depths of the ocean with the lawyer, the shark swam alongside the boat and placed the lawyer back on the deck. The shark started to swim off, but the lawyer called out, "Hey, why didn't you eat me?" The shark turned around, smiled, and said, "Professional courtesy."

There are several reasons for such jokes. First, some lawyers have engaged in disreputable or dishonest activities. When they have been caught, they often make headlines in their local newspapers. There are hundreds of disbarment proceedings against lawyers every year, where different forms of misconduct have been alleged. The U.S. Supreme Court has rejected most of their appeals for reconsideration. A third reason is that some lawyers have bad reputations for taking advantage of their clients and exploiting them. The public seems to reflect a general mistrust of lawyers as well. Public opinion polls have been taken regarding the honesty of lawyers and other professional persons. In 1997, for instance, lawyers were ranked nineteenth in honesty behind funeral directors, newspaper reporters, dentists, police, and real estate agents (Maguire and Pastore 2005). Between 1976 and 1997, the public's low or very low rating of the honesty and ethical standards of lawyers rose from 26 percent to 40 percent (Maguire and Pastore 2005). In 1997 a national poll showed that 15 percent of the public surveyed rated the ethical standards and honesty of lawyers as very high or high, while 41 percent rated them as low or very low regarding their standards and honesty.

In an effort to improve the image of lawyers throughout the United States, various professional associations and organizations have evolved codes of ethics or standards by which lawyers can conduct themselves. For instance, the American Bar Association (ABA) first published its **Canons of Professional Ethics** in 1908. Intended as a means of self-regulation, the Canons of Ethics are a part of the **ABA Model Code of Professional Responsibility.** Attorneys in all U.S. jurisdictions ideally are expected to adhere to this code on a voluntary basis. Whenever violations of this code occur or are alleged, disciplinary rules are invoked to sanction those who are believed to have engaged in unethical conduct. There are nine Canons of Ethics. These are:

1. A lawyer should assist in maintaining the integrity and competence of the legal profession.
2. A lawyer should assist the legal profession in fulfilling its duty to make legal counsel available.
3. A lawyer should assist in preventing the unauthorized practice of law.
4. A lawyer should preserve the confidences and secrets of a client.
5. A lawyer should exercise independent professional judgment on behalf of a client.
6. A lawyer should represent a client competently.
7. A lawyer should represent a client zealously within the bounds of law.
8. A lawyer should assist in improving the legal system.
9. A lawyer should avoid even the appearance of professional impropriety (Morgan 1983, 3).

Besides the ABA and its rules and Canons of Ethics, all states have **state bar associations.** These associations are powerful enough to require that all persons who practice law in these states must be approved by these bars in advance. Thus, attorneys who attend law school and graduate with a law degree must first pass one or more state bar examinations in order to qualify as practicing lawyers in those states.

Defense counsels are practicing lawyers and must pass state bar examinations in order to demonstrate their familiarity with local and state laws. Besides passing tests and taking other types of examinations, all lawyers are expected to adhere to codes of ethics and to conduct themselves in a way that will not compromise their integrity. Thus, it is expected that the ABA Canons of Ethics and the ABA Model Code of Professional Responsibility is applicable to virtually all practicing attorneys in the United States. Although not all attorneys in the United States belong to the ABA, the ethical and professional responsibility provisions promulgated by the ABA are generally and implicitly applicable to them anyway.

THE RIGHT TO COUNSEL

The Sixth Amendment says that all defendants shall have the right to a speedy trial by an impartial jury, the right to be informed of the nature of the charges against them, the right to confront their accusers in court, and the right to have assistance of counsel for their defense. While the Sixth Amendment does not declare that counsel must be competent, we have the *Strickland* guidelines by which to gauge attorney effectiveness and competence.

The right to counsel as guaranteed under the Sixth Amendment has not always been clearly defined among the states. It was assumed for many decades, for instance, that the right to counsel meant that persons charged with crimes were free to hire their own attorneys to represent them (Smith 2004). However, for **indigent defendants,** defendants without the money or means to hire their own counsel, they were often tried and convicted without benefit of any defense counsel (Cunningham and Vigen 1999). States, such as Florida, had their own legislative provisions for providing attorneys in criminal cases. Until the 1960s, indigent defendants in Florida courts were not entitled to a court-appointed attorney unless they were charged with a capital crime, such as murder. If indigents were charged with noncapital offenses, then they were unable to compel courts to furnish them with an attorney. Without an attorney to defend them, therefore, many indigents were convicted, whether or not they were guilty of the crime(s) alleged. In some instances, indigent defendants suffered from mental illnesses and were unaware of their right to counsel (Arrigo and Bardwell 2000).

In 1942, the U.S. Supreme Court condoned these state practices. In the case of *Betts v. Brady* (316 U.S. 455 [1942]), Betts, a robbery suspect, claimed that he was indigent and demanded a court-appointed attorney to defend him on the robbery charge. The court said that Betts could only be appointed counsel in rape or murder cases, and his request for an attorney was denied. In felony cases in which life or death was not an issue, the U.S. Supreme Court ruled that the states were not required to furnish counsel to indigent defendants in every case. It should be noted, however, that many states *did* provide counsel for indigent defendants during this period because it was required by the state legislatures.

The U.S. Supreme Court Changes Its Mind

In 1963, the U.S. Supreme Court reviewed and decided the case of *Gideon v. Wainwright* (372 U.S. 335 [1963]). Clarence Gideon broke into a Florida poolroom with the intent to commit larceny. This act was a felony in Florida. Gideon was indigent and asked for a lawyer to represent him. He was advised by the judge that counsel could only be appointed to indigents if they were charged with a capital crime. Since he was denied an attorney, Gideon represented himself. Subsequently, he was convicted and appealed. The U.S. Supreme Court overturned Gideon's conviction, holding that all indigent defendants are entitled to court-appointed counsel in any serious case. The Florida courts interpreted serious case to mean any felony. Thus, the *Gideon* case established that court-appointed counsel would be provided any indigent defendant who was charged with a felony.

Nine years later, the case of *Argersinger v. Hamlin* (407 U.S. 25 [1972]) was decided by the U.S. Supreme Court. This also occurred in Florida. Argersinger was an indigent charged with carrying a concealed weapon. This charge was a misdemeanor in Florida and punishable by a fine and six months' imprisonment. Argersinger claimed to be indigent and demanded that the court appoint counsel to represent him. Argersinger's request was denied, because, according to *Gideon*, only felony charges entitled indigent defendants to court-appointed counsel. Argersinger was convicted of the misdemeanor and sentenced to 90 days in jail. He appealed, and the U.S. Supreme Court overturned his misdemeanor conviction. Essentially, the U.S. Supreme Court said that anyone facing possible imprisonment is entitled to court-appointed counsel if they are indigent and cannot afford to hire private counsel.

Self-Representation

Under certain circumstances, defendants may wish to represent themselves in court and not use the services of a defense attorney (Sabelli and Leyton 2000). Any criminal defendant may elect to defend himself/herself and reject court-appointed counsel. When defendants engage in **self-representation,** they are said to be proceeding *pro se,* which means "on his or her own behalf" (Arrigo and Bardwell 2000). Defendants who defend themselves do not have to be trained lawyers, nor do they have to be skilled in criminal law or trial techniques. However, in most instances where persons have elected to represent themselves in court, judges have appointed lawyers to assist or advise them anyway, although the roles of these counsels are somewhat passive (Cunningham and Vigen 1999). Self-representation in criminal proceedings is not exclusively an American phenomenon. Other countries, such as England, permit defendants to represent themselves if they request to do so (Tague 1999).

One of the most sensational cases of self-representation is the case of Colin Ferguson, who was a Jamaican immigrant living in New York in 1993. Ferguson was unemployed and divorced. He had recently been rejected for public assistance by New York officials, and one afternoon, he boarded a Long Island commuter train armed with a semiautomatic pistol. After the train was underway, he arose from his seat and methodically began shooting passengers at point-blank range. He paused only long enough during the shooting to change clips in his pistol. At some point while he was reloading his weapon, some of the passengers rushed him and wrestled him to the floor of the car. They disarmed him and at the next train stop, they turned him over to waiting police. Ferguson had killed six persons and seriously wounded 19 others. There were numerous eyewitnesses who saw Ferguson shoot them or others. Ferguson left behind a note that explained his actions to those finding his body. It was clear that he did not expect to be taken alive.

At Ferguson's trial later, Ferguson was appointed counsel. Two prominent criminal defense attorneys were assigned to represent him. They were William Kunstler and Ron Kuby. Kunstler believed that with the overwhelming direct and conclusive evidence against Ferguson, Ferguson's best and only chance to escape punishment was to claim temporary insanity. Kunstler also briefly entertained the "black rage" defense, which suggested that Ferguson had gunned down oppressive white persons who he felt were against him. Early during the trial proceedings, Ferguson dismissed Kunstler and Kuby, requesting that the judge permit him to defend himself. He advised the judge that he considered himself to be a "formidable opponent." The judge appointed a psychiatrist to examine Ferguson, and the psychiatrist pronounced Ferguson sane. Therefore, the judge permitted Ferguson to represent himself.

The trial itself was a sham, since Ferguson was attempting to refute irrefutable evidence against him. At one point, Ferguson told the jury, "There are 93 counts against me. Ninety-three counts. That is because the year was 1993. If it had been 1925, there would have been 25 counts." He cross-examined several persons he had wounded on the commuter train. All of this action was futile, although Ferguson had acquired considerable sophistication and experience during the trial. Toward the end of the proceedings, Ferguson attempted to call President Bill Clinton as a witness, since Clinton had given a pair of cuff links to one of the train survivors who had visited the White House.

Ferguson contemplated calling another witness who purportedly was on the train when Ferguson began to shoot the other passengers. The potential witness claimed to see an Oriental man who placed a computer chip in the back of Ferguson's neck. Then the Oriental man took out a black box and moved some dials, activating Ferguson to shoot passengers. The man did not testify. Subsequently, at the sentencing hearing, Ferguson's victims testified against him. When Ferguson rose to rebut these persons and tell the court why he should not receive the full measure of the law against him, the entire courtroom cleared as spectators simply walked out. They were expressing their contempt for Ferguson. Ferguson was convicted and sentenced to life imprisonment for the train murders. Ron Kuby said in retrospect that Ferguson should never have been permitted to defend himself, since he was clearly mentally ill.

Relatively few persons defend themselves in court. An old adage says that one who represents himself has a fool for a client. At one point in our history, however, indigent defendants were compelled to defend themselves. As we saw earlier in the case of *Gideon v. Wainwright* (1963) [see Box 4.1], Clarence Gideon was on trial in Florida for burglary. At the time of Gideon's trial, it was the law in Florida that indigent defendants were not entitled to court-appointed counsel unless they were charged with a capital offense. Gideon defended himself and was subsequently convicted. He appealed, contending that he was entitled to counsel and was denied counsel. The U.S. Supreme Court heard his appeal and overturned his conviction, holding that all indigent criminal defendants are entitled to court-appointed counsel in serious cases or felonies. Subsequently, court-appointed counsel were extended to any person charged with either a misdemeanor or felony (*Argersinger v. Hamlin*, 1972) (See Box 4.1).

Attorney–Client Privilege and Confidentiality

Other rules have evolved as well to cover the relation between attorneys and their clients (Canon 4). **Attorney–client confidentiality and privilege** is intended to protect clients from having their attorneys disclose incriminating details of their lives to others, such as prosecutors. If a defense attorney hears a confession from a client, the attorney is vested with considerable legal protection. Prosecutors cannot compel defense counsels to provide them with incriminating information about their clients. The attorney–client privilege is as inviolate as the relation between parishioners and their priests.

Attorney Competence and Effective Assistance of Counsel

Probably all attorneys think that they are competent. However, a troubling number of allegations are arising from convicted offenders who believe that their defense counsels are incompetent and ineffective. There is considerable variation among lawyers regarding **attorney competence**, both defense counsel and

BOX 4.1 ABOUT SELF-REPRESENTATION AND ASSISTANCE OF COUNSEL

■ *Hamilton v. Alabama,* 368 U.S. 52 (1961)

Hamilton, an indigent, was indicted for murder by a grand jury. At his arraignment following the indictment, he was not represented by counsel and he was subsequently convicted of murder. He appealed, contending that he had been disadvantaged by not having counsel present during the arraignment. The U.S. Supreme Court overturned his conviction, saying that arraignments are critical stages requiring the presence of a court-appointed attorney in indigent cases. In Alabama at the time, defendants were required to show that they were in need of counsel. Hamilton had not requested counsel at the time, but counsel had not been offered either.

■ *Gideon v. Wainwright,* 372 U.S. 335 (1963)

Gideon broke into a poolroom allegedly with the intent to commit larceny. This act was regarded as a felony in Florida. Gideon was indigent and asked for a lawyer to represent him. He was advised by the judge that counsel could only be appointed to persons if the offense involved the death penalty. Therefore, Gideon represented himself and was convicted. He appealed. The U.S. Supreme Court overturned his conviction, saying that all indigent defendants are entitled to court-appointed counsel in felony cases. (See *Argersinger v. Hamlin* [1972] for a narrowing of this provision to minor crimes or misdemeanor cases).

■ *Illinois v. Allen,* 397 U.S. 337 (1970)

Allen was charged with robbery. He waived his right to counsel and elected to represent himself. During the jury selection and trial, he was abusive and argued constantly with the trial judge until eventually he was ordered removed from the courtroom. The trial was held anyway and he was convicted. Later, Allen appealed to the U.S. Supreme Court, arguing that his Sixth Amendment right had been violated because he was not present at his own trial when convicted. The U.S. Supreme Court upheld his conviction, saying that repeated warnings to Allen from the judge had had no effect on his conduct, which was so disruptive as to prevent the jurors from properly considering the evidence. Thus, there was nothing unconstitutional about the judge's removing Allen from the courtroom.

■ *Argersinger v. Hamlin,* 407 U.S. 25 (1972)

Argersinger was an indigent charged with carrying a concealed weapon. In Florida, this crime is a misdemeanor punishable by imprisonment of up to six months and a $1,000 fine. Argersinger was not allowed to have court-appointed counsel, as required for a *felony,* because his crime was

(continued)

BOX 4.1 *(continued)*

not a felony (see *Gideon v. Wainwright* [1963]). He was convicted of the misdemeanor and sentenced to 90 days in jail. He appealed, and the U.S. Supreme Court overturned his misdemeanor conviction. The U.S. Supreme Court said that any indigent defendant is entitled to counsel for *any* offense involving imprisonment, regardless of the shortness of the length of incarceration. Thus, it extended the *Gideon* decision to include misdemeanor offenses, holding that no sentence involving the loss of liberty (incarceration) can be imposed where there has been a denial of counsel; defendants have a right to counsel when imprisonment might result.

■ *Faretta v. California*, 422 U.S. 806 (1975)

Faretta, who was charged with grand theft, desired to represent himself. The judge ruled that he had no constitutional right to represent himself in the case and appointed a public defender to defend him. Faretta was convicted. He appealed, arguing that he had a right to represent himself. The U.S. Supreme Court overturned his conviction, holding that Faretta indeed had a right knowingly and intelligently to waive his right to counsel and represent himself in the criminal proceeding. Thus, he had been denied his constitutional right to act as his own counsel.

■ *Baldasar v. Illinois*, 446 U.S. 222 (1980)

Baldasar was convicted in a theft of property not exceeding $150 in value. Although this offense was a misdemeanor, it was Baldasar's second offense, and therefore, it became a felony. He was sentenced to 1–3 years in prison. He appealed, claiming that he had not been represented by counsel at the time of his first conviction. Therefore, the enhanced penalty from the second conviction was not constitutional. The U.S. Supreme Court agreed with Baldasar and overturned his conviction, holding that no indigent criminal defendant shall be sentenced to a term of imprisonment unless the state has afforded him the right to assistance of counsel. Baldasar had requested but had been denied counsel in the trial for his original misdemeanor, which became a crucial step in enhancing the penalty resulting from his second conviction.

■ *Godinez v. Moran*, 509 U.S. 389 (1993)

Moran was charged with several murders, although he had entered a plea of not guilty by reason of insanity. Several doctors reported test results that indicated Moran was competent to stand trial. Following these psychiatric reports, Moran advised the Nevada court that he wished to dismiss his attorneys and plead guilty to the multiple murders. The court determined that Moran made these guilty pleas knowingly, intelligently, and voluntarily. Further, Moran waived his right to assistance of counsel and other rights associated with guilty pleas. Subsequently, after he was convicted and sentenced to death, he filed a *habeas corpus* petition alleging that even though he had earlier requested to represent himself, he was incompetent to do so. The U.S. Supreme Court upheld the conviction and death sentence, holding that the competency standard for pleading guilty or waiving the right to counsel is the same as the competency standard for standing trial. Moran had been found competent in both instances and had knowingly and intelligently waived the rights he was now alleging had been violated.

■ *Becker v. Montgomery, 532 U.S. 757 (2001)*

Becker was an Ohio state prisoner who instituted a *pro se* civil rights action in federal court contesting the conditions of his confinement under Title 42 U.S.C. Section 1983. The federal district court dismissed the complaint because of Becker's failure to state a claim for relief. In a timely manner, within 30 days of the federal court action, Becker appealed, filing a *pro se* notice of appeal with the Sixth Circuit Court of Appeals. However, Becker failed to sign the appeal form. The form contained no requirement indicating that it should be signed. The Sixth Circuit dismissed Becker's appeal because it was unsigned. The Sixth Circuit further declared that Becker's notice of appeal was fatally defective and deemed this defect jurisdictional and therefore not curable outside the time allowed to file the notice of appeal. No court officer had earlier called Becker's attention to the need for a signature. Becker appealed to the U.S. Supreme Court. The Court reversed the Sixth Circuit, holding that when a party files a timely notice of appeal, the failure to sign the appeal does not require the court of appeals to dismiss the appeal. The Court stated further that imperfections in noticing an appeal should not be fatal where no genuine doubt exists about who is appealing, from what judgment, and to which appellate court.

■ *Dodd v. United States, 125 S.Ct. 2478 (2005)*

Michael Dodd was convicted of engaging in a continuing criminal enterprise of conspiring with others to possess and distribute marijuana and 16 counts of using and possessing a passport obtained by false statement. He was sentenced in 1993 on most counts and sentenced to 360 months in prison, followed by 5 years of supervised release. Dodd appealed, but his conviction became final in 1997. In 1999 the case of *Richardson v. United States* was decided, which held that a jury must agree unanimously that a defendant is guilty of each of the specific violations that together constitute a continuing criminal enterprise. In April 2001, Dodd filed a *pro se* motion asking that his conviction be set aside, since his jury had not been instructed that they had to agree unanimously on each predicate violation. A one-year statute of limitation existed for filing an appeal based on the subsequent U.S. Supreme Court ruling in the *Richardson* case. The U.S. District court and the appellate court affirmed Dodd's conviction and rejected

(continued)

BOX 4.1 *(continued)*

his appeal, and he thus sought relief by appealing to the U.S. Supreme Court who heard his case. The Court affirmed, holding that the one-year statute of limitation for filing motions to vacate sentences based on newly recognized rights by the Court runs from the date on which the Court initially recognized the right asserted. Since Dodd had waited beyond one year to file his appeal, the statute of limitation barred him from having his sentence vacated.

■ *Halbert v. Michigan,* 125 S.Ct. 2582 (2005)

Antonio Halbert, an indigent defendant, pleaded *nolo contendere* to two counts of second-degree sexual assault involving his stepdaughter and another young girl. When the judge imposed two consecutive sentences, Halbert sought to withdraw his plea, but the court denied his motion. Halbert then filed a *pro se* application for leave to appeal, asserting sentencing error and ineffective assistance of counsel, seeking among other things court-appointed counsel for his appeal. Michigan denied his request for an appellate counsel and rejected his claims. Subsequently the U.S. Supreme Court heard Halbert's case. Michigan viewed Halbert's initial *nolo* plea as a knowing and intelligent waiver of his right to appeal the convictions and sentences. Michigan also contended that the appointment of counsel for indigents seeking appellate reviews of their sentences is discretionary with trial judges. The U.S. Supreme Court rejected Michigan's views, holding that the due process and equal protection clauses of the Constitution require the appointment of counsel for defendants who are convicted on their pleas, and who seek access to first-tier review in the Michigan Court of Appeals. At the time Halbert entered his *nolo* plea, he had no recognized right to relinquish his entitlement to appellate counsel. Furthermore, the Michigan trial court did not tell Halbert, simply and directly, that in his case, there would be no access to appointed counsel. Halbert's denial of relief by the Michigan Supreme Court was vacated and remanded.

■ *Johnson v. United States,* 125 S.Ct. 1571 (2005)

Johnson was convicted in 1994 on federal drug charges and enhanced his sentence because of two previous Georgia drug convictions. In 1998 Johnson succeeded in having his Georgia state drug convictions overturned, which had been used earlier to enhance his federal sentence. Johnson waited almost 3 years before bringing a *habeas corpus* petition challenging his federal sentence enhancement. Johnson claimed that the delay was attributable to his *pro se* status while filing his appeal and his lack of education. A district court and appellate court affirmed his federal drug conviction and enhanced sentence and the U.S. Supreme Court heard Johnson's appeal. The Court upheld Johnson's conviction and enhanced sentence, holding that Johnson had failed to act in a timely manner in at-

tacking his prior state convictions as the bases for federal sentence enhancements. The U.S. Supreme Court rejected Johnson's *pro se* and "lack
of education" arguments.

■ *Kane v. Garcia Espitia*, 126 S.Ct. 407 (2006)

Joe Garcia Espitia was convicted in California of carjacking and other offenses. Garcia Espitia rejected court-appointed counsel and elected to represent himself. He requested access to a law library while confined in jail
prior to his trial. His repeated requests for law library access were denied.
Garcia Espitia proceeded *pro se*. During the trial, he was permitted 4 hours
of law library time just before closing arguments. Following his conviction,
he petitioned a federal court with a *habeas corpus* motion, declaring that
his Sixth Amendment rights had been violated since he had been denied
access to a law library. The district court rejected Garcia Espitia's appeal but
the court of appeals reversed. The government appealed and the U.S.
Supreme Court heard the case. The U.S. Supreme Court reversed the court
of appeals, holding that defendants do not have a clearly established right
under federal law to access law libraries while they are in jail awaiting trial
as required for federal *habeas corpus* relief. This case is significant because
had Garcia Espitia allowed himself to be represented by court-appointed
counsel, the defense attorney would have had unlimited access to law libraries and all other legal materials. By knowingly and intelligently waiving
his right to counsel, a defendant also relinquishes his right under prevailing
federal law to a law library while proceeding *pro se*. This decision does not
rule out the possibility that individual states might grant or deny *pro se* defendants access to law libraries and other forms of legal assistance.

prosecutors, concerning their quality and effectiveness. Attorneys of all types
vary considerably according to their expertise, years on the job, personal and professional experience, and enthusiasm for defending or prosecuting. However, attorneys are tacitly expected to zealously perform their defense tasks, and in a
competent manner (Canons 5, 6, and 7).

Ideally at least, attorneys are expected to do their best, whether they are
prosecuting or defending someone on a criminal charge. Counsel competence
is difficult to assess objectively. It is more frequently the case that the effectiveness and competence of counsel are assessed subjectively. It is precisely because of the diffuseness of the concepts of effectiveness and competence that
more than few challenges are made by convicted offenders where the performance of their attorneys is called into question. These questions pertain to the
ineffective assistance of counsel.

The leading case concerning attorney competence is *Strickland v. Washington* (466 U.S. 668 [1984]). Conduct in Strickland's case of whether ineffective

assistance of counsel as rendered was measured according to the following standards: Was the counsel's conduct such that it undermined the functioning of the adversarial process that a trial cannot be relied upon to render a just result? and Did the counsel's behavior fall below the objective standard of reasonableness? There must be a reasonable probability that, but for counsel's unprofessional errors, the result of the proceedings would be different.

Thus, *Strickland* established the standards of (1) whether counsel's behavior undermined the adversarial process to the degree that the trial outcome is unreliable; and (2) whether counsel's conduct was unreasonable to the degree that the jury verdict would have been different otherwise. This does not mean that all attorney conduct must be flawless and that every stone, large or small, has been overturned in all cases. Most attorneys make one or more mistakes and exercise bad judgment occasionally when defending a client. But many of these mistakes or instances of bad judgment are inconsequential and would not ordinarily affect the trial outcome. There is no obligation on the part of any attorney to raise every nonfrivolous issue in a criminal case (*Jones v. Barnes*, 463 U.S. 745 [1983]; *Murray v. Carrier*, 477 U.S. 478 [1986]).

Ineffective Assistance of Counsel

The U.S. Supreme Court has decided instances of **ineffective assistance of counsel** on occasion. For instance, in the case of *Lozada v. Deeds* (498 U.S. 430 [1991]), Jose Lozada was convicted of four crimes relating to narcotics. He was earlier convicted in Nevada on four counts of possession and sale of controlled substances. Following the trial proceedings, Lozada's attorney failed to notify him of his right to appeal, of the procedures and time limitations of an appeal, and of his right to court-appointed counsel. Further, Lozada alleged that his attorney failed to file a notice of appeal or to ensure that Lozada received court-appointed counsel on appeal. Finally, it was alleged that the attorney misled Lozada's sister, and hence, Lozada, when he told her that the case had been forwarded to the public defender's office, which it hadn't. Lower appellate courts dismissed Lozada's subsequent *habeas corpus* **petition** on the grounds that he had ineffective assistance of counsel as the result of these alleged events. The U.S. Supreme Court found otherwise, however, and reversed his convictions, holding that Lozada had made a substantial showing that he was denied the right to effective assistance of counsel.

Defendants should have a reasonable expectation, therefore, that the counsel representing them is competent and effective. But this expectation should not be that the defense counsel is necessarily the best defense available. The standard of reasonableness is very important, since there are varying degrees of counsel competence and effectiveness that are within the reasonable parameters articulated in *Strickland*. Furthermore, defendants may assume with some confidence that defense counsel will adhere to the ethical codes and manner of professional responsibility articulated by their state bar associations and other professional organizations established to regulate attorney quality and performance.

BOX 4.2 ON DEFENSE COUNSELS AND MISCONDUCT

■ The Case of Luis Antonio Figueroa

It happened in Laredo, Texas, and began with an FBI investigation in 1998 of Juan A. Rodriguez, who was suspected of committing extortion and conspiracy. Rodriguez was represented by Luis Antonio Figueroa, a prominent defense attorney in the area. Rodriguez was subsequently convicted of these crimes in a six-week trial and sentenced to serve several years in prison. In an appeal later, Rodriguez sought to overturn his conviction by alleging that his attorney was approached by a member of the U.S. Attorney's Office and offered a plea bargain that may have resulted in probation for Rodriguez instead of incarceration. Furthermore, Rodriguez alleged, Figueroa did not pass along this information about the plea bargain offer to Rodriguez for him to consider. Thus, Rodriguez was denied an opportunity to cooperate with the federal government in exchange for leniency, all because of his attorney's failure to advise him of the plea bargain offer.

Regarding plea bargaining in federal cases, it is routinely practiced. In fact, most federal criminal cases are plea bargained rather than brought to trial. This is usually because the government offers one or more concessions, such as a reduced sentence or probation, in exchange for information from the defendant, which may implicate others. However, Figueroa denied ever being approached with a plea bargain offer from the U.S. Attorney's Office. However, several witnesses on behalf of Rodriguez came forward to claim that they had overheard an assistant U.S. attorney make such a plea bargain offer to Figueroa prior to Rodriguez's trial. In fact, one of these witnesses was assistant U.S. attorney Marina Marjolejo, who advised in a sworn statement that she did, in fact, make a plea offer to Figueroa prior to trial. According to Marjolejo, the conversation between her and Figueroa occurred on an elevator in the federal building, and that she asked Figueroa what he planned to do about Rodriguez's case. Figueroa claimed that he understood by that question that she was asking about the case itself and not about any plea offer, and that he answered simply, "I'm ready for trial." Figueroa vigorously maintained that at no time did he understand that a plea bargain was being made, or that the possibility of negotiations existed.

(continued)

BOX 4.2 (continued)

In most criminal cases throughout the United States, it is unusual *not* to engage in plea bargaining prior to trial proceedings. Generally the concessions derived from plea bargaining are such that accepting a plea agreement is in the client's best interests. In this case, however, Figueroa flatly denied that a plea bargain offer had been made. The case was subsequently referred to the Commission for Lawyer Discipline, where it was alleged by Rodriguez and others that Figueroa had engaged in defense misconduct by failing to inform his client of the plea offer in accordance with the Texas Disciplinary Rules of Professional Conduct and the Texas Rules of Disciplinary Procedure. Defending Figueroa was Jerry Zunker, who called several witnesses to testify about Figueroa's reputation, competence, and ethics. Attorney Paul Homburg III represented Texas in its case against Figueroa.

With testimony from an assistant U.S. attorney and several others who heard her make a plea offer to Figueroa, Homburg concluded that Figueroa had indeed violated the rules of professional responsibility by withholding that plea offer from Rodriguez. He said that Figueroa's lack of action constituted professional misconduct and the Commission for Lawyer Discipline should sanction him accordingly. However, Zunker countered by saying that there were discrepancies between the witnesses' statements. Four witnesses could not agree about what the plea offer consisted of—just generalities. Furthermore, he said that the interaction between Figueroa and the assistant U.S. attorney on the elevator was nothing more than general conversation. Zunker also said that he was disturbed by the testimony because it could affect the life and livelihood of his client, whose career up to this point had been unblemished. Zunker said that if Figueroa had heard the plea offer, it would defy imagination for him not to extend the offer to Rodriguez when he was facing a lengthy jury trial. Zunker concluded by saying that there was no professional misconduct, and that in the event there was a finding of misconduct, that there should be no sanctions.

After deliberating for several hours, Judge Mickey Pennington who presided in the matter declared that the commission had failed to meet its burden of proof to substantiate the claims of professional misconduct. Figueroa hugged his family and said, "I'm pleased it's over and the truth has come out—that I didn't do anything wrong." Homburg refrained from commenting in the case. At least in this instance, it shows how difficult it is to find an attorney incompetent or guilty of misconduct, even where credible witnesses such as an assistant U.S. attorney provide first-hand testimony that underscores such misconduct.

[*Source:* Adapted from the Associated Press, " Local Attorney Accused of Misconduct Exonerated," April 21, 2004.]

BOX 4.3 INCOMPETENCE OF COUNSEL

■ *Strickland v. Washington*, 466 U.S. 668 (1984)

Conduct in Washington's case of whether ineffective assistance of counsel was rendered was measured according to the following standards: Was the counsel's conduct such that it undermined the functioning of the adversarial process so much that a trial could not be relied on to render a just result? Did the counsel's behavior fall below the objective standard of reasonableness? There must be a reasonable probability that, but for counsel's unprofessional errors, the result of the proceedings would have been different.

■ *Rompilla v. Beard*, 125 S.Ct. 2456 (2005)

Ronald Rompilla was convicted in a Pennsylvania court of first-degree murder and other offenses. During the penalty phase, the jury found several aggravating factors that were presented by the prosecution. Rompilla's family provided several mitigating factors. Rompilla's attorney relied upon these mitigating factors and made no effort to discover other mitigating evidence, such as Rompilla's troubled childhood, alcoholism, and mental illness. Rompilla was sentenced to death, therefore, and appealed, arguing that his counsel was ineffective because he failed to make a reasonable effort to obtain and review both evidence of aggravation and mitigation. The state courts rejected Rompilla's appeals, and ultimately the U.S. Supreme Court heard his case. The U.S. Supreme Court reversed, holding that (1) defense counsel's failure to examine the file on Rompilla's prior convictions for rape and assault at the sentencing phase of his capital murder trial fell below the level of reasonable performance, and (2) such failure was prejudicial to Rompilla, warranting *habeas corpus* relief on the grounds of ineffective assistance of counsel.

THE RIGHT TO A TRIAL BY JURY

One of the most significant cases challenging the court's authority to grant or deny a defendant the right to a **jury trial** was *Duncan v. Louisiana* (391 U.S. 145 [1968]). Duncan was convicted in a bench trial of simple battery in a Louisiana court. The crime was a misdemeanor, punishable by a maximum prison term of two years and a fine of $300. However, Duncan was sentenced to only 60 days and fined $150. He appealed, contending that he was denied his constitutional right to a jury trial under the Sixth Amendment. The U.S. Supreme Court agreed with Duncan, saying that any crime carrying a maximum punishment of two years is a serious crime, despite the fact a jail sentence of only 60 days was imposed. Thus, for serious crimes, under the Sixth Amendment, Duncan was entitled to a jury trial as a matter of right.

Eventually the standard was established whereby criminal defendants are entitled to a jury trial as a matter of right. The standard was set in the case of *Baldwin v. New York*, 399 U.S. 66 (1970). Baldwin was arrested and prosecuted for jostling or **pickpocketing,** a Class A misdemeanor punishable by a maximum term of imprisonment of one year in New York. Baldwin asked for a jury trial, but he was denied one. At the time, New York law defined jostling as a petty offense, one that did not require a jury trial. Baldwin was subsequently convicted and sentenced to 90 days in jail. He appealed. The U.S. Supreme Court heard Baldwin's appeal and declared that **petty offenses** carrying a one-year incarcerative term are *serious* in that jury trials must be provided if requested by defendants. Specifically, the wording of *Baldwin* gives substantial significance to the *months* of imprisonment that define a serious crime. The U.S. Supreme Court said that a potential sentence in excess of six-months of imprisonment is sufficiently severe by itself to take offense out of the category of petty as respects one's right to jury trial (at 1886, 1891). Therefore, the U.S. Supreme Court overturned Baldwin's conviction on these grounds. Presently, jury trials must be granted to any defendant where the possible punishment involves incarceration of beyond six months.

No Jury Trials for Defendants Charged with Petty Offenses

The U.S. Supreme Court has made clear its position about jury trials and when defendants are entitled to them. According to *Baldwin*, jury trials are available as a matter of right only to defendants charged with serious crimes, where their loss of liberty is beyond six months. Jury trials are not available as a matter of right in other nonserious cases. For instance, in *United States v. Nachtigal* (507 U.S. 1 [1993]), Nachtigal was convicted of drunk driving while operating a motor vehicle in a national park. When he appeared before the U.S. Magistrate, Nachtigal asked for a jury trial but was denied one. His offense carried a maximum incarcerative penalty of six months in jail, and thus it did not qualify for a jury trial. Nachtigal appealed his conviction on the Sixth Amendment grounds that he was denied a jury trial, but the U.S. Supreme Court upheld his conviction, saying that jury trials may not be granted in petty offense cases.

Another drunken-driving case was *Blanton v. North Las Vegas* (489 U.S. 538 [1989]). Blanton was convicted in Nevada for operating a motor vehicle while under the influence of alcohol. Blanton demanded a jury trial but was denied one because the charge was considered a petty offense. Blanton was convicted under Nevada law, where the maximum prison term for drunk driving is six months. However, the court also required Blanton to pay a fine and perform 48 hours of community service. Blanton's driver's license was also revoked for 90 days. The court also required Blanton to attend a victim-impact panel and a course on alcohol abuse. Blanton appealed to the U.S. Supreme Court, arguing that the cumulative effect of all of these sanctions and conditions elevated his case to the level of a serious one, thus entitling him to a jury trial. However, the U.S. Supreme Court was not persuaded by Blanton's argument and rejected his appeal. Thus, the other conditions of one's sentence, including attending courses and panels and performing community service, are not considered as relevant factors in determining a crime's seriousness.

One exception to *Baldwin* is as follows. Sometimes judges will conduct bench trials without juries when a defendant is charged with a serious crime. But these judges will advise the defendant in advance that if the defendant is found guilty, the incarcerative punishment will be six months or less. Judges must keep this promise. Thus, if a defendant is found guilty by the judge later following court proceedings in a bench trial, then the judge cannot impose an incarcerative sentence longer than six months. If a judge were to violate his/her promise to a defendant and sentence them to a term of imprisonment of beyond six months, then the convicted offender would have solid grounds to have a higher court review the judge's action and overturn the conviction. Judicial promises made must be kept.

THE DEFENSE

Defense counsel are attorneys who represent those individuals charged with crimes. Defense attorneys adhere to the ABA code of professional responsibility and are obligated to do all that is ethically possible to defend their clients. All criminal defendants are entitled to an attorney as a matter of right. Many defense counsel are retained privately by persons able to afford them. Yet other defense counsels are appointed by the courts in their jurisdictions to represent clients without money to hire their own attorneys. Thus, both indigents and others are entitled to counsel. Defense counsel who are hired by the state or are appointed to represent indigent defendants are called public defenders (Maxwell, Dow, and Maxwell 2004).

Forms of Legal Aid for Indigents

By 1992 about 80 percent of all criminal defendants charged with felonies were represented by court-appointed counsel. Court-appointed legal representation for indigent criminal defendants plays a critical role in the criminal justice system. About $357,000 was spent on court-appointed counsel for indigents in 1979; $1,336,000 in 1990; and $2.6 million in 1999 (Maguire and Pastore 2005). Table 4.1 shows various types of public defender systems in the United States from a National Prosecutors Survey conducted in 1992.

Not every state has the same type of public legal aid for indigent defendants (Smith and DeFrances 1996, 1). Each state is at liberty to establish its own particular form of legal aid services. Thus, different states have evolved different public defense systems. The most common public defender system

TABLE 4.1   INDIGENT DEFENSE DELIVERY SYSTEMS USED BY LOCAL JURISDICTIONS

Type of System	Percentage of Prosecutors' Offices Indicating the Type of Counsel Provided by Their Jurisdiction
Total	100
Public defender program only	28
Assigned counsel system only	23
Assigned counsel and public defender	23
Contract attorney system only	8
Public defender and contract	8
Assigned counsel, public defender, and contract system	6
Assigned counsel and contract system	3
Other	1

Source: Steven K. Smith and Carol J. DeFrances. *Indigent Defense.* Washington, DC: U.S. Department of Justice, 1996, 2.

used in 28 percent of all U.S. counties is called simply the **public defender system.** This system is state- and county-funded and serves the needs of numerous persons unable to afford legal aid. The public defender system began in 1914 in Los Angeles, California (Klein and Spangenberg 1993). Public defenders are hired by the state and county to represent indigent clients who are in need of a defense. They draw salaries and are expected to mount the best defense possible, under the limited resources of their agencies. Quite often, their funds for legal defense are limited, and they do not enjoy investigative luxuries and other expenditures that might be available to privately acquired counsel by more affluent defendants.

Two other types of systems are known as the **assigned counsel system** and the **contract system.** The assigned counsel system, used in 23 percent of all local jurisdictions, is used in cities and towns where there aren't many attorneys. Small towns and sparsely populated counties may not have a great many practicing lawyers. Local bar associations function as liaisons between association members and the courts to provide legal services for indigent clients on a voluntary basis. Ordinarily the local bar association submits a list of attorneys' names to judges who select defense counsel to represent indigent defendants on a case-by-case basis. In most jurisdictions where assigned counsel systems are operative, assigned counsel are paid a fixed rate per day for compensation. Compensation may range from $50 to $125 per day for these attorneys, and thus, this is a small sum compared with what an attorney might charge a private client. Actually these per diem rates are more like

BOX 4.4 INDIGENT DEFENDANTS AND THE RIGHT TO COUNSEL

■ *Betts v. Brady*, 316 U.S. 455 (1942)

Betts claimed that he was indigent and thus demanded a court-appointed attorney to defend him on a robbery charge. The court said that Betts could be appointed counsel only in rape or murder cases, and denied his request. He appealed. The Supreme Court ruled that in felony cases in which life or death is not an issue, the states are not required to furnish counsel in every case; many states at this time, however, provide counsel because it is required by their own constitutions or by court rulings in state courts. This decision was overturned as the result of the ruling in *Gideon v. Wainwright* (1963), in which the U.S. Supreme Court concluded that in all felony cases, state or federal, indigent defendants are entitled to counsel.

■ *White v. Maryland*, 373 U.S. 59 (1963)

White, an indigent, was suspected of murder. At his arraignment, he entered a not-guilty plea, but later at a preliminary hearing, he pleaded guilty. He was not represented by counsel at the preliminary hearing, and his guilty plea was introduced later in the trial as evidence against him. He was convicted. White appealed, contending that the preliminary hearing was a critical stage requiring appointment of counsel to represent him. Thus, the guilty plea he entered should have been inadmissible in court later. The U.S. Supreme Court agreed with White and overturned his conviction, saying that preliminary hearings are critical stages in which indigent defendants must be represented by counsel.

■ *Coleman v. Alabama*, 399 U.S. 1 (1970)

Several defendants, including Coleman, were accused of assault with intent to commit murder. As indigents, they were denied counsel at their preliminary hearing, with the Alabama judge declaring that nothing that happened at the preliminary hearing would influence the trial later. Coleman was convicted, and appealed. The U.S. Supreme Court ruled that preliminary hearings are critical stages. Because indigent defendants are entitled to counsel at critical stages, which Coleman had been denied, his conviction was overturned.

hourly rates attorneys may charge who are affiliated with small law firms. Some more experienced attorneys in large law firms may bill their clients at the rate of $500 per hour or more. About 23 percent of all local jurisdictions use a combination of the assigned counsel and public defender systems (Weiss 2004).

Because the compensation for indigent client legal services is inadequate, those who furnish their legal services to indigent clients under such a system are not particularly enthusiastic about defending their clients. For many of these attorneys, they merely want to go through the motions of negotiating the best deals for their clients with prosecutors. They often encourage their clients, though innocent, to plead guilty to a lesser criminal charge in exchange for a short jail term or probation. They may persuade their clients to waive their right to a jury trial and opt for a quick plea bargain. The saying, "You get what you pay for," is often applicable to attorneys who work as either public defenders or assigned counsel for indigents. The lack of incentives (e.g., monetary remuneration for legal services) causes them to lack the motivation and zeal they should have, in view of the Canons of Ethics and professional responsibility codes they should abide by through the ABA and other state professional legal affiliates.

The contract system involves competitive bidding among different law firms in various jurisdictions for providing legal services to indigent clients. A law firm may submit a bid to represent indigent clients on the basis of a fixed amount of money per hour or per day. The state or county will accept the most attractive bid in order to hold down defense costs. About 8 percent of all U.S. counties use the contract system (Smith and DeFrances 1996, 2). Another 8 percent of all local jurisdictions use a combination of the contract and public defender systems, while another 10 percent use various combinations of all three systems.

One drawback is that the low bidders under the contract system may not be the most competent counsel. A law firm may assign its new and least experienced lawyers to defend indigent clients charged with serious crimes. When the least trained attorneys are expected to defend indigent clients in serious and complex cases, they may not be qualified to perform an adequate defense job. In fact, their defense of indigent clients may be downright incompetent, such that ineffective assistance of counsel charges may be alleged by convicted indigents.

Despite the flaws of these and other defense systems for indigents and others, the fact remains that all criminal defendants are entitled to counsel. The U.S. Supreme Court has never made explicit the exact nature of attorney competence other than what has previously been articulated in *Strickland v. Washington* (1984). In the *Strickland* case, the U.S. Supreme Court declared that an attorney's performance should be such that the adversarial process should not be undermined, or that but for the attorney's conduct, the trial verdict may have been different. The *reasonableness* of attorney conduct was stressed by the Court, although it failed to give precise definition to reasonableness. Therefore, the U.S. Supreme Court has left this determination up to individual state supreme courts and lower courts whenever allegations of attorney incompetence are lodged by convicted offenders.

Are Public Defenders as Effective as Privately Retained Counsel?

Under assigned counsel, public defender, and contract systems, states and the federal government set fixed hourly rates for remunerating attorneys who defend indigent clients. These hourly rates, which may range from $25 to $50, are well-below the $250 to $500 hourly rates (or higher) charged by private counsel who are hired by more affluent criminals. Many public defenders who work in public defender's offices are fresh out of law school and are interested in acquiring courtroom experience. They are willing to work for low pay in exchange for this experience. Other public defenders and court-appointed counsel who work on an assigned-counsel basis may be apathetic or hostile toward their clients and the general job of defending criminals. In many of these cases, public defenders will attempt to rush their clients into plea agreements and conclude these low-paying cases quickly, without testing adequately the strength of the case (Weiss 2004). This rapidity of case processing is particularly prevalent in those jurisdictions with contract systems. A primary consideration in contracting is economizing resources and expediting case processing for maximum efficiency. Such rapid resolution of criminal cases may deprive some defendants of an adequate defense and seriously jeopardize their chances of obtaining equity (Maxwell, Dow, and Maxwell 2004).

At the federal level, the Federal Defender Services program exists, which provides legal counsel for those who cannot afford attorneys. The cost of operating this program has tripled during the 1990–1995 period, and projections are that costs will go much higher in future years. In some jurisdictions, budget cutbacks have occurred. These cutbacks have directly influenced the numbers of court-appointed counsel available for indigent defendants as well as the amount of time allocated to each of these cases. In Fulton County, Georgia, for instance, the indigent defense system is at best fragmented and disjointed (Spangenberg 1990). There is a substantial lack of communication, coordination, and cooperation among the various agencies providing indigent defense services. There is an insufficient number of staff in every category to handle the current caseload and a lack of early representation in the public defender's office. There is virtually no training for public defenders in the office, and little supervision. Salaries are low as well as the morale. Greater use of technology has enabled many jurisdictions to cut their operating costs while maintaining fairly high-quality attorney representation for indigents, however (Spangenberg et al. 1999).

Thus, the general question arises, are court-appointed counsel as effective compared with their privately retained counterparts? Some early research suggests that defense services for indigents in certain jurisdictions such as Hamilton County, Ohio, have been substandard, especially in homicide cases (Steelman and Conti 1987). More extensive continuing education requirements were recommended in order for many of these defense attorneys to improve their criminal law skills. More recent research suggests that inadequate compensation of attorneys for indigents in capital cases produces an increasing number of appeals from convicted offenders who allege ineffective assistance of counsel (Champion 2005a). Despite these criticisms, public defender programs have been defended as being on par with private counsel who defend indigent clients. In short, public defenders have been found to be equally effective at defending indigent clients compared with private counsel, thus contradicting long-standing criticisms portraying indigent defenders as incompetent, ill-equipped, and poorly trained.

In sum, there is perhaps an element of truth in both views of public defender or assigned-counsel systems. Particularly in larger urban jurisdictions, it is true that public defender's offices are often staffed with new attorneys with little or no criminal trial experience. This fact operates to their disadvantage when relating with prosecutors and configuring plea agreements beneficial to criminal defendants. But in assigned-counsel and contract systems, there are also many seasoned attorneys with considerable criminal law experience. Presently there is great diversity in quality concerning court-appointed legal representation for indigent criminal defendants. At least 80 percent or more of all criminal defendants continue to have court-appointed counsel, and it is likely that this figure will not change substantially in future years (Weiss 2004).

Functions of the Defense

The functions of defense counsel are to (1) represent their clients faithfully, (2) attack the prosecution's case vigorously, (3) counsel with the defendant as to the best course of action in the case, (4) negotiate with prosecutors for a case resolution most favorable to their client, (6) vigorously cross-examine prosecution witnesses to attack and undermine their credibility in front of jurors, and (6) use all legal means to defeat the government's case.

Representing Clients Faithfully

It is expected that defense counsel will represent their clients faithfully. This means that they will take an active interest in the case rather than a detached passive interest. They will strive to collect relevant exculpatory evidence, interview crucial witnesses, and engage in proper trial preparations. They will consider the defendants' needs and give them every consideration. They will assume that their clients are innocent, even though incriminating evidence might exist to the contrary.

Attacking the Prosecution's Case Vigorously

Defense counsel are expected to attack the government's case in a vigorous manner. They should take steps to point out all aspects of the prosecutor's case that are weak or raise reasonable doubt about the defendant's guilt. They should be aggressive and promote their clients' interests to the best of their ability.

Counseling with Defendants Concerning the Best Course of Action in a Case

It is sometimes the case that defense counsel will be assigned cases where overwhelming direct and conclusive evidence exists about the defendant's guilt. In these types of cases, a vigorous defense should be implemented, designed to provide a plausible explanation for why the crime was committed. One part of the counseling process involves determining the client's view of the case and a disclosure of crime details. This shared information and subsequent defendant disclosures are confidential through attorney–client confidentiality and privilege. Whatever the defendant tells his/her attorney will remain private and confidential. If the defendant admits guilt to his/her attorney, the defense counsel must continue to represent the client with enthusiasm. Defense counsels are in crucial positions to understand the consequences of a trial. In some cases, it may be more prudent to work out deals for clients with prosecutors instead of proceeding with a trial. These bargains often involve some measure of leniency for their clients. The prosecutor may be amenable to reducing more serious charges to less serious ones in exchange for a defendant's guilty plea. If a counsel's client were to reject the bargain offered by the prosecutor and proceed with a trial, a conviction would almost guarantee an increase in the harshness or severity of the penalty imposed by the judge. Therefore, good defense counsels should explain all viable options to their clients and work out what is best for them through close collaboration. Good advice to a client might be to plead guilty to a lesser charge and accept a less severe punishment rather than take a chance in court where a conviction and more severe sentence are imminent.

Negotiating with Prosecutors for a Case Resolution Most Favorable to Clients

Prosecutors determine which charges should be filed against defendants. Defense counsels are expected to negotiate with prosecutors in an effort to reach a compromise with them favorable to their clients. Sometimes, defense counsels may request diversion for their clients, where their cases are temporarily removed from the criminal justice system. Under diversion, clients would be expected to be law-abiding, pay monthly maintenance fees, and perhaps pay restitution to victims or engage in community service. The result of a successful diversion might be that the prosecutor would drop all criminal charges against the defendant or downgrade the charges eventually filed from felonies to misdemeanors. Defense attorneys are key players in facilitating such negotiations between prosecutors and defendants.

Vigorously Cross-Examining Prosecution Witnesses and Undermining Their Credibility

Good defense attorneys engage in vigorous cross-examinations of prosecution witnesses in an effort to undermine their credibility. Often, eyewitness testimony is damaging to defendants, and defense counsels can sometimes cause eyewitnesses to express doubt about what they observed. If defense counsels can encourage prosecution witnesses to admit to uncertainty about what was seen, this strategy undermines the prosecution's case considerably (Bradfield and McQuiston 2004).

Using All Legal Means to Defeat the Government's Case

Within the limits of propriety and the code of ethics that binds together defense counsels throughout the United States, defense attorneys are encouraged to use any and all legal means at their disposal to defeat the government's case against their client. Some of the means may be considered unsavory, although they may be entirely legal. For instance, if a man is suspected of killing his wife and if there are older children or relatives who did not get along with the deceased, it is proper for the defense counsel to suggest to the jury that others might have been motivated to kill. Thus, certain relatives might be named as possible suspects, even though the defense attorney may not believe that they were involved in the woman's death. Rather, the intent of such a strategy is to plant a seed of doubt in the minds of jurors. Someone else may have committed the crime. Others may have had strong motives to kill besides the defendant. If sufficient doubt can be raised by deflecting possible guilt to others, then the jury may acquit the defendant later following their deliberations (Roberts, Gau, and Brody 2004).

One fact that operates to the disadvantage of defense counsels everywhere is that other types of attorneys do not hold criminal defense lawyers in particularly high regard. Defending criminals is viewed by more than a few citizens as an unsavory profession. Defending criminals means having to interact with them. For many attorneys, interacting with criminals is undesirable. Therefore, criminal defense counsels often engage in thankless tasks. They may even be viewed with disdain by their own criminal clients. If they win their cases, they are accused of "getting guilty defendants off" and escaping punishment. If they lose, their clients may appeal and allege that their defense counsels are incompetent or ineffective. Even criminal court judges regard defense counsels with a certain amount of contempt. Thus, for many criminal defense attorneys, considerable stress is generated.

Defense Misconduct

Much of the misconduct that occurs in court is the result of prosecutorial actions or abuses of judicial discretion. However, some misconduct is committed by the defense counsel. While prosecutors are barred from mentioning or admitting into evidence certain types of incriminating information, defense counsels are likewise admonished to avoid saying anything that might prejudice the jury in favor of their client. Certain scientific advancements are such, for instance, that they may not be sufficiently reliable for introduction as evidence in courtrooms (Cook, Arndt, and Lieberman 2004).

For instance, it is widely accepted that testimony about **polygraph tests (lie detectors)** is inadmissible. This is because lie detector results are unreliable and cannot be interpreted with the same degree of precision as fingerprint evidence or other tangible direct evidence. But suppose the defendant submitted to a lie detector test administered by the local police department. Further assume that the defendant passed the lie detector test. The test results would be interpreted to mean that the defendant was telling the truth and that this fact might be considered exculpatory evidence. However, the prosecutor decides to move forward with the prosecution anyway, feeling that the polygraph test results were unreliable. What if the defense counsel asked a police officer who was testifying for the state, "My client took a lie detector test about this crime and passed, didn't he?" The prosecutor would object and the judge would sustain the objection. Just as prosecutors would be guilty of committing harmless errors by backdooring inadmissible evidence, the defense counsel would be equally guilty of backdooring another type of inadmissible evidence, such as the lie detector test results. The judge can order the jury to disregard the defense counsel's question, but can the jury ever forget the question/statement by the defense? No. This is one example of defense misconduct.

Another type of defense misconduct occurs whenever the defense attorney knows that the defendant is guilty. The defendant has confessed his crime to the defense counsel, and it is expected that this confession will remain confidential. The privilege of confidentiality exists between an attorney and his/her client, and it is unethical for an attorney to violate this privilege. While the defense counsel is obligated to defend his client despite the confession, the defense counsel is prohibited from advising his client to take the stand and lie about his role in the crime. Advising one's client, or advising the client's witnesses to lie, is the **subornation of perjury.** Suborning perjury means to encourage someone to lie under oath. If a defense attorney were to suborn perjury, this would constitute defense misconduct. Further, it would be a crime.

INTERACTIONS BETWEEN PROSECUTORS AND DEFENSE ATTORNEYS

Most of us are quite familiar with courtroom drama. We see programs on television such as *Law and Order*. These shows focus on the courtroom as the major contact point between prosecutors and defense counsels. But these programs give us only one dimension of a much larger picture of interaction between the defense and the prosecution. Both prosecutors and defense attorneys are integral parts of the courtroom work group. Actually, their interactions with one another and other members of the courtroom work group are more frequent outside rather than inside the courtroom. For instance, defense attorneys who maintain good relations with various court officers can benefit by being assigned more cases. Defense attorneys, especially recent law graduates, need to earn a living. Being assigned more cases will enable these attorneys to earn more money to support themselves and help to establish their law practices. Defense attorneys with poor attitudes may lose out on various case assignments who are given to more compliant defense counsels.

Defense attorneys consult frequently with prosecutors concerning defendants. Prosecutors work closely with the police and detectives who gather incriminating evidence of crimes, interviews with suspects, and conversations with various experts and eyewitnesses. Some of this information is made available to defense attorneys so that they may advise their clients concerning which course of action is best.

Although the interactions between defense counsels and prosecutors are often characterized as adversarial and antagonistic, the fact is that most of these persons have amicable relations with one another both on and off the job. Most prosecutors are known by defense counsels on a first-name basis. Their relationships are almost always friendly, even though in the courtroom, their respective demeanors might suggest otherwise.

Another consequence of close interactions between prosecutors and defense attorneys is that they both learn about each other's interests and objectives. They are able to assess each other's skills and strategies. Thus, some prosecutors know that they can expect a serious challenge from some defense attorneys who have been successful in garnering acquittals for their clients. This mutual understanding between prosecutors and defense attorneys facilitates the process of whether defendants will enter guilty pleas to certain charges in exchange for leniency.

Also, it is important for both prosecutors and defense counsels to maintain good relations with one another, since they are both interested in ensuring that justice is served when processing defendants. The wheels of justice turn more smoothly to the extent that relations between prosecutors and defense counsels are cordial and cooperative. However, some prosecutors resent having to share case information with defense attorneys. Some defense attorneys are openly antagonistic toward prosecutors. Information exchanges from both sides are slowed and hampered by formality. Under a cooperative scenario, for example, prosecutors would willingly share case information with defense attorneys since it is important for these attorneys to know what they are facing regarding inculpatory evidence against their clients. Under less-cooperative conditions, defense counsels would be obligated to write detailed letters requesting case information to which they are entitled. Prosecutors might drag their feet and delay turning over case materials in a timely manner. Ultimately, however, both sides will exchange information in the process known as discovery.

THE DISCOVERY PROCESS

Discovery is the procedure or mechanism whereby the prosecution shares information with the defense attorney and the defendant. More than a few countries permit discovery of relevant evidence and materials related to crimes (Gubanski 2004). Specific types of information are made available to the defendant and his/her counsel before trial, including results of any tests conducted, psychiatric reports, transcripts, or tape-recorded statements made by the defendant. Also shared between prosecution and defense are the list of witnesses both sides plan to call to testify at the trial (Gubanski 2004).

If the defendant confessed to the crime, and if the confession was videotaped and transcribed, then the defense is entitled to see a copy of the videotape and have a transcription of it for use in the subsequent trial. Accordingly, if the defense has certain types of information, it is also discoverable by the prosecution. Thus, discovery involves an exchange between the prosecution and the defense of relevant information in the case. Both sides must allow each other to see certain types of information they plan to introduce as evidence at the subsequent trial.

BOX 4.5 ON DISCOVERY

■ *Campbell v. United States*, 365 U.S. 85 (1961)

Campbell was charged with bank robbery. During the testimony of a government witness, it became known that a previous statement had been made by that witness. The defense sought to obtain that statement, but the court denied them access to it. The government also denied the *existence* of the statement, when, in fact, it actually existed. Campbell was convicted. He appealed, arguing that under the Jencks Act, he was entitled to discovery of the prior statement given by the government witness in order to impeach the witness. The U.S. Supreme Court overturned his conviction and held that under the Jencks Act, such information is discoverable and should be turned over to the defense by government attorneys. Thus, Campbell had been deprived of the right to a fair trial.

■ *United States v. Agurs*, 427 U.S. 97 (1976)

Agurs was charged with first-degree murder in the killing of her boyfriend, Sewell. Sewell was known to carry knives. Agurs took one away from him and stabbed him repeatedly. During her trial, information about Sewell's prior criminal record of assault and carrying a deadly weapon and his bad character were excluded from the prosecution's case against Agurs. Agurs was convicted. She appealed, arguing that this information about the victim

(continued)

BOX 4.5 *(continued)*

would have helped her own case. The U.S. Supreme Court upheld Agurs's conviction, holding that the prosecutor was under no constitutional duty to disclose or volunteer any exculpatory information in the case against Agurs. The U.S. Supreme Court adopted a standard for evaluating the materiality of evidence. If such evidence would have been persuasive and produced reasonable doubt about the guilt of the defendant, then it would have been material. Under the circumstances, however, such disclosures would have been irrelevant.

■ *Gardner v. Florida*, 430 U.S. 349 (1977)

Gardner was convicted of first-degree murder. Following the conviction, a sentencing hearing was held in which the jury recommended life imprisonment. However, the judge cited aggravating factors and imposed the death penalty. It was important that portions of the presentence investigation relied on by the judge for his knowledge of aggravating factors were not given to the defense under discovery. Apparently, several mitigating factors were cited in the report favorable to Gardner but ignored by the judge. Gardner appealed. The U.S. Supreme Court overturned his conviction, acknowledging that the government had not complied with the discovery law by failing to give Gardner a complete presentence investigation report. The report contained information to support a life sentence rather than the death penalty. The U.S. Supreme Court declared that the failure of the Florida Supreme Court to consider or even read the confidential portion of the report violated Gardner's right to due process under the Fourteenth Amendment.

■ *Arizona v. Washington*, 434 U.S. 497 (1978)

Washington was convicted of murder, but an Arizona court granted him a new trial because the prosecution had withheld exculpatory evidence. At the beginning of the second trial, the defense counsel made various remarks about "hidden" information from the first trial. The prosecutor moved for a mistrial, which was granted. Washington was subsequently convicted in a third trial. Later, as a prison inmate, he filed a *habeas corpus* petition seeking to have his conviction overturned because the second judge's decision to declare a mistrial had been erroneous and had led to his being placed in double jeopardy by a third trial. The U.S. Supreme Court rejected Washington's arguments, holding that the mistrial had been proper. Thus, no previous trial had been concluded with an acquittal and so Washington was not being tried again for the same offense.

■ *Kyles v. Whitley*, 514 U.S. 419 (1995)

Kyles was accused in Louisiana of first-degree murder. During the trial, the prosecution failed to disclose to Kyles favorable and exculpatory evidence under discovery. For instance, eyewitness testimony and statements favorable to Kyles were withheld, as were statements made to police by an informant, Beanie. A computer printout of all car license numbers at or near the murder scene, which did not include Kyles's car license number, was in the possession of the prosecution but was not made available to Kyles or his attorney when they demanded discovery. Kyles was convicted and sentenced to death. Appeals by Kyles to higher state courts resulted in affirmation of his original conviction and sentence. Then he sought relief by an appeal to the U.S. Supreme Court. The Court overturned Kyles's conviction, holding that the prosecution had violated Kyles's *Brady* rights (see *Brady v. Maryland* [1963]) to have relevant exculpatory information made available to him by the prosecution. The significance of this case is that it is the constitutional duty of prosecutors to disclose favorable evidence to defendants in criminal prosecutions.

■ *Bracy v. Gramley,* 520 U.S. 899 (1997)

Bracy was tried, convicted, and sentenced to death in an Illinois court presided over by Judge Thomas J. Maloney. Maloney was subsequently convicted of taking bribes for fixing other murder cases in Operation Greylord, a federal sting operation intended to detect and prosecute judicial corruption. Bracy appealed his conviction and filed a *habeas corpus* action, arguing that Judge Maloney had a vested interest in Bracy's conviction in order to deflect suspicion that he was taking bribes in other cases. Further, Bracy alleged that Maloney had deliberately suppressed exculpatory evidence that may have mitigated Bracy's sentence. His *habeas corpus* appeals were denied and he appealed directly to the U.S. Supreme Court, where the case was heard. The U.S. Supreme Court reversed Bracy's conviction, holding that Bracy, who was convicted before a judge who was himself later convicted of taking bribes from defendants in criminal cases, showed "good cause" for discovery on his due process claim of actual judicial bias in his own case.

■ *Strickler v. Greene,* 527 U.S. 263 (1999)

Strickler was convicted of capital murder in Virginia and sentenced to death. During his trial, Strickler's attorney was permitted to examine prosecutors' files for exculpatory evidence. However, the prosecutor did not advise defense counsel that police files may have contained exculpatory information favorable to Strickler, which may have impeached the veracity of one of the witnesses against Strickler. Strickler filed a *habeas corpus* petition, alleging that the prosecutor had a duty to reveal police documents that may have impeached witnesses against him. Presently, there are three components of a true *Brady* violation: (1) the evidence at issue must be favorable to the accused, either because it is exculpatory, or because it is impeaching; (2) the evidence must have been suppressed by the state, either

(continued)

BOX 4.5 *(continued)*

willfully or inadvertently; and (3) prejudice must have ensued. The U.S. Supreme Court heard Strickler's case and decided that although the *Brady* rule had been violated in part, the materiality of the evidence would not have affected the trial outcome. The U.S. Supreme Court held that (1) undisclosed documents impeaching eyewitness testimony as to circumstances about the abduction of the victim were favorable to Strickler for purposes of *Brady*, and (2) Strickler reasonably relied on prosecution's open-file policy and established cause for procedural default in raising a *Brady* claim, but (3) Strickler could not show either materiality under *Brady* or prejudice that would excuse Strickler's procedural default.

■ *Banks v. Dretke*, 124 S.Ct. 1256 (2004)

Delma Banks was convicted of capital murder in the death of 16-year-old Richard Whitehead, which occurred in mid-April 1980. Banks was originally implicated in the murder by two associates, Jefferson and Farr, who were working with the county sheriff, Willie Huff, as informants. Unknown to Banks before and during the trial was the allegation that Jefferson and Farr were testifying against Banks in order to avoid drug charges, which were threatened by the sheriff and prosecutor. At the same time, a confidential informant, Cook, also furnished the prosecution with incriminating circumstantial evidence against Banks. This information was also withheld from Banks pursuant to a motion for discovery. Although Banks had no prior criminal record, testimony from Farr and Jefferson provided the jury with innuendo that Banks had an unsavory and criminal past, which was untrue. Banks's efforts to impeach Farr and Jefferson were undermined because of his own witnesses, who were themselves impeached on cross-examination. Banks was sentenced to death and sought postconviction relief, alleging that the prosecution failed to disclose exculpatory evidence as required by *Brady v. Maryland* (1963), including the threats made to Farr and Jefferson as well as the confidential informant, Cook. In its answer, the state claimed that nothing had been kept secret from Banks and no deals had been made with government witnesses, including Cook. In 1993 Banks's postconviction claims were denied outright by an appellate court. Following this loss, Banks filed for *habeas corpus* relief in a U.S. district court, which granted relief on Banks's death sentence. In 1999 Banks filed discovery and evidentiary hearing motions, both supported by affidavits sworn to by Farr and Jefferson that the prosecution had wrongly withheld crucial exculpatory and impeaching evidence. The federal court determined that the state, indeed, had failed to disclose Farr's informant status during the original discovery phase of Banks's trial. Therefore, a writ of *habeas corpus* was granted Banks with respect to his death sentence, but not to his conviction. Banks petitioned the U.S. Supreme Court, who heard the case. The U.S. Supreme Court reiterated that under *Brady*, a prosecutorial misconduct claim must establish three things: (1) that the evidence at issue must be favorable to the accused, either because it is exculpatory, or because it is impeaching; (2) that evidence must have been suppressed by the state, either willfully or inadvertently; and (3) that prejudice must have ensued. In its response, the state contended that "it can lie and conceal and the prisoner still has the burden to discover the evidence." The U.S. Supreme Court ruled this assertion to be untenable and a violation of Banks's due process rights. Banks presented sufficient evidence to support his *Brady* claim and was thus entitled to a full evidentiary hearing and a certification of appealability.

■ *Illinois v. Fisher,* 124 S.Ct. 1200 (2004)

Gregory Fisher was arrested for and charged with cocaine possession following a routine traffic stop by police officers in Chicago, Illinois, in September 1988. In October 1988, Fisher filed a motion for discovery, requesting all physical evidence seized by police officers when he was arrested. Prosecutors stated that all evidence would be made available to Fisher at a reasonable date and time upon request and a trial date was set for July 1989. When the trial date occurred, it was discovered that Fisher had fled the jurisdiction, ultimately residing in Tennessee for the next 11 years. An outstanding arrest warrant for Fisher was subsequently executed in September 1999, and Chicago authorities reinstated the 1988 cocaine charges. Fisher renewed his demand to have access to the original evidence seized, but the prosecutor stated that according to established procedures, the substance seized from him had been destroyed after several years of preservation. Fisher moved to have the charges against him dismissed, as the evidence against him no longer existed. The trial court denied his motion and Fisher was convicted by a jury for cocaine possession, based in large part upon police testimony and the admission of four laboratory tests that confirmed the substance seized at the time of Fisher's 1988 arrest was cocaine. Fisher was sentenced to one year in prison. Fisher appealed, alleging a violation of his right to due process, since the substance he was accused of possessing had been destroyed by police years earlier, and thus they had framed him for the crime. The appellate court reversed Fisher's conviction, holding that the due process clause required the dismissal of the original charge in the absence of incriminating evidence. The government appealed and the U.S. Supreme Court heard the case. The Supreme Court reversed the Illinois Appellate Court, holding that due process did not require dismissal of cocaine possession charges on the ground that police, nearly 11 years after Fisher was charged, destroyed the cocaine seized. The Supreme Court held that unless a criminal defendant can show bad faith on the part of police, their failure to preserve potentially useful evidence does not constitute a denial of due process of law. Fisher failed to demonstrate bad faith on the part of police; thus, his claim of a violation of his due process rights was dismissed. There is nothing in the record to indicate that the alleged cocaine was destroyed in bad faith.

The premise upon which discovery is based is that all defendants are entitled to a fair and impartial trial. If the government with its immense resources were to restrict access to various test results and tangible evidence, even oral testimony and reports of experts, this restriction would jeopardize a defendant's right to a fair trial (Schmid 2002). Fundamental fairness is that the defense shall not be deprived of a fair trial. This means that the disclosure of certain types of evidence by the prosecution is mandatory (O'Sullivan 2001).

In several jurisdictions, defense counsel must make a motion for discovery, itemizing the testimony and other evidence it wants. If the defense does not ask for specific items in the possession of the government, the government is not obligated to volunteer them to the defense. This fact is underscored in the case of *Kimmelman v. Morrison* (477 U.S. 365, 1986). In this case, Neil Morrison was convicted of rape in a bench trial in New Jersey. During the trial, a police officer testified about some evidence, a bedsheet found at the crime scene, which had been seized without a proper search warrant. The defense attorney objected and moved to suppress statements about the bedsheet. The judge, however, ruled that it was too late to register such an objection, that the proper time would have been during discovery, when the items seized and to be used as evidence against Morrison were disclosed to him. Following his conviction, Morrison filed a *habeas corpus* petition, alleging ineffective assistance of counsel relating to the bedsheet issue and the motion to suppress it. Because of the defense attorney's incompetence by not raising a motion at an earlier and more proper time, Morrison argued, he was deprived of the effective assistance of counsel, and this problem led to his conviction. An appellate court reversed his conviction on these grounds, and the state appealed to the U.S. Supreme Court. The U.S. Supreme Court heard the case and affirmed the lower appellate court, concluding that Morrison's counsel was ineffective due to his failure to conduct any pretrial discovery and determine what the state had planned to present as incriminating evidence. Further, the counsel clearly failed to make a timely motion to suppress such evidence. On these grounds, Morrison's conviction must be reversed.

It is beyond the scope of this book to list all types of discoverable information. One reason is that there is considerable interstate variation concerning what is or is not discoverable material or statements. Confession statements are always discoverable in all jurisdictions. However, the statements of material witnesses may or may not be immediately discoverable. Usually, when lists of witnesses are exchanged by the prosecution and defense, each side seeks to interview the witnesses to be called. This is to avoid a trial by ambush, where a witness will give testimony unknown to the other side, and the testimony given will influence the trial outcome. Neither side wishes to be surprised by the other.

A leading case about discovery is *Brady v. Maryland* (373 U.S. 83 [1963]). Brady was convicted of murder and sentenced to death. He appealed on the grounds that he was denied access to various statements made by a confeder-ate, Boblit. Actually, Brady took the stand in his own defense and admitted to participating in the crime, but Brady declared that Boblit was the one who ac-tually killed the victim. Various statements had been made to police and pros-ecution by Boblit. The prosecutor denied the defense access to these statements, alleging confidentiality. Following Brady's conviction, some of this evidence came to light and proved favorable and exculpatory to Brady. He sought an appeal, claiming that he was denied due process by having these im-portant statements withheld during his trial. The U.S. Supreme Court agreed with Brady and overturned his murder conviction, saying that "suppression by prosecution of evidence favorable to an accused upon request violates due process where evidence is material either to guilt or to punishment, irrespec-tive of good faith or bad faith of prosecution." Subsequently, both prosecutors and defense attorneys have referred to discoverable materials and evidence as **Brady materials.** When the prosecutor or defense counsel withholds certain discoverable information, this is called a **Brady violation.**

Actually an earlier case involving a similar issue was *Jencks v. United States* (353 U.S. 651, 1957). The *Jencks* case involved the withholding by prosecutors from the defense of prior inconsistent statements by a key government witness against Jencks. In the *Jencks* case, the U.S. Supreme Court ruled that the gov-ernment must disclose such inconsistent statements to the defense prior to a criminal trial. In Brady's case, the U.S. Supreme Court overturned his convic-tion and held that according to ruling in the *Jencks* case, such information is discoverable and should be turned over to the defense by government attor-neys. In a way similar to the case of *Brady v. Maryland* (1963), the *Jencks* case has led to discoverable evidence being called **Jencks materials.**

DEFENSE ATTORNEYS AND THEIR DEFENSES FOR CRIMINAL CONDUCT

Who Bears the Burden of Proof in Criminal Prosecutions?

In any criminal prosecution, it is the responsibility of the state to prove beyond a reasonable doubt that the defendant committed the crime(s) charged. This means that prosecutors must prove beyond a reasonable doubt that (1) a crime was committed and (2) the defendant committed the crime. Thus, the prose-cutor bears the **burden of proof** in asserting a criminal charge (Haynes 2000; Schmid 2002). This burden is meant by providing the jury with **evidence** of the crime.

The burden of proof standard, also known as the **evidentiary** standard, in all criminal cases does *not* mean that prosecutors must produce witnesses or victims who can furnish **conclusive evidence** of a defendant's guilt. Conclu-sive evidence might suffice if several persons watched a defendant commit the crime in plain view. Such evidence is so compelling and strong that it cannot be disputed or contradicted. For instance, a man might shoot his wife, killing her. Then he turns the gun on himself, intending to commit suicide. But somehow he survives the bullet wound and is subsequently tried for his wife's murder. He might have left a highly incriminating suicide note indicating the reasons for why he killed his wife. The suicide note is a type of **derivative evidence,** or written evidence. The weapon he used has his fingerprints on it, his hands have powder residue from firing the weapon, and he is found holding the weapon after his neighbors report the sound of gunshots to police. In this instance, the facts are generally not disputed. District attorneys sometimes prosecute cases with this sort of conclusive evidence (Fisher 1999).

Also, the burden of proof standard does *not* mean that prosecutors must produce any **direct evidence** of the crime. As in the case of conclusive evidence, direct evidence involves incriminating information such as fingerprints or eyewitness testimony (Prentice 2001). Rather, prosecutors may be able to convince a jury that a defendant is guilty of the crime based on **circumstantial evidence** alone. In one New York murder case, for example, a physician, Robert Bierenbaum, was suspected of killing his wife, Gail Katz Bierenbaum, in the summer of 1985. Prosecutors believed that he loaded her body aboard a rented airplane, flew out over the ocean, and dumped her body into the sea. No trace of his wife was ever found. Furthermore, police investigators never found any traces of Bierenbaum's wife's blood in Bierenbaum's automobile trunk or inside the airplane. If such evidence would have been found, this would have been **demonstrative evidence** or derivative evidence, since it is tangible and does not relate to eyewitness testimony. Neighbors reported that they often heard Bierenbaum arguing with his wife. On the day his wife disappeared, Bierenbaum was seen taking off from the airport and flying in the direction of the ocean in a rented airplane, although the police didn't know Bierenbaum had rented the airplane until a year had elapsed. The case was dormant for 15 years, because police didn't have sufficient evidence to charge Bierenbaum with a crime. Subsequently, a check of airport records showed that Bierenbaum had altered his flight log to show that his flight occurred on a different day and time. Also, on the day his wife disappeared, she had spoken with a friend that morning and said that she was leaving Bierenbaum and moving in with a new boyfriend. When the person called her back 40 minutes later, Bierenbaum answered the telephone and told the caller that his wife had just left and he didn't know when she was returning. All of these circumstances and **corroboration** didn't prove that Bierenbaum killed his wife. But prosecutors eventually decided to indict Bierenbaum for his wife's murder in December 1999. He was tried and convicted of murder in New York on October 24, 2000. Despite the fact that the case against Bierenbaum was entirely circumstantial, the jury drew inferences from all of this information and found him guilty of second-degree murder (Rogers, Cotliar, and Erwin 2000, 91).

In another murder case, this time in Atlanta, Georgia, a man was accused of killing his wife and setting his own home on fire to cover up any incriminating evidence. He managed to crawl out of a second-story window of his home while it went up in flames. He told passersby that his wife was inside and had been overcome with smoke. He said that the fire seemed to come from the kitchen in a downstairs area, and that he and his wife were sleeping. He claimed that his wife was too overcome with smoke to assist in her own flight to safety, and that he was too weak to carry her to a window. Thus, he was only able to save himself. Again as in the New York murder, this man had taken out a large life insurance policy on his wife a few months earlier, and he had named himself as the primary beneficiary. It was also found that he was deeply in debt and that his business was failing. Prosecutors surmised that he killed his wife in an effort to save his company from bankruptcy by using the insurance money from her death. The case was purely circumstantial, but the jury was convinced that the man did, indeed, murder his wife and he was convicted of her murder.

Usually, prosecutors must convince a jury that the accused had the means, motive, and opportunity to commit the crime(s) alleged. Since many criminals perform their criminal acts in secret and do not brag about what they have done because they don't want to get caught and convicted, the prosecutor's burden is a somewhat difficult one. Judges will eventually instruct jurors about how they should regard the evidence presented during the trial, and how to weigh that evidence.

The defense is under no obligation to prove anything to the jury. It is not their place to prove their client's innocence. Rather, they may simply offer alternative explanations for how the crime may have occurred. When television and movie personality O. J. Simpson was accused of murdering his ex-wife, Nicole Brown Simpson, and her friend, Ron Goldman, in 1994, his attorneys suggested alternative scenarios that may have accounted for the murders. Because Nicole Brown Simpson had been known to use cocaine and other drugs, Simpson's defense team suggested that she was the victim of drug dealers. Furthermore, they offered a reward leading to the arrest and conviction of these drug dealers whom they believed had executed Simpson's ex-wife. They also suggested that other persons who knew Ms. Simpson had motives to murder her. All of their alternative scenarios about how Ms. Simpson and Ron Goldman were murdered were intended to dissuade jurors from considering O. J. Simpson as the guilty party. He was subsequently acquitted of these crimes. One factor that contributed to his acquittal was that one of the investigating detectives committed perjury during his trial, and the detective's perjury was detected and brought to the attention of jurors. Another factor was that some of the inculpatory evidence against Simpson, blood evidence, had allegedly been planted in Simpson's home by investigating detectives. All of this information was weighed by the jury. The fact that the case was largely circumstantial did not help prosecutors either.

Defense counsels often recommend that their clients should not testify. The fact that defendants do not often testify in their own criminal trials is greatly misunderstood by the public, even many defendants. One of the first things an innocent defendant wants to do is get up on the witness stand and proclaim his/her innocence to the jurors. But prosecutors have many clever ways of distracting and upsetting innocent defendants and twisting their own words to prosecutorial advantage. The defendant's demeanor and self-control are important factors that jurors can observe. On more than one occasion, prosecutors have disturbed defendants so much on the witness stand that they lose their tempers and act guilty, even though they are innocent. It is a fundamental right of defendants, therefore, to remain silent while the prosecution attempts to prove their guilt. This is due process, and all defendants are entitled to it. Some jurors might believe that if the defendant doesn't take the stand and testify, that this is some sort of guilt by omission. That is, if defendants do not declare their innocence on the witness stand, an inference may be drawn that they have something to hide. This is absolutely untrue. While all defendants have the right against self-incrimination, they also have the right to due process, which means in part that if they do not testify, this is *not* a form of incrimination. Ordinarily judges read jury instructions to jurors and highlight this fact so that jurors must not and cannot consider a defendant's refusal to testify as evidence of their guilt. In fact, *no* inferences may be drawn by jurors about the defendant's guilt or innocence when the defendant does not testify.

However, defense attorneys are seldom content to allow the prosecutors' allegations to go unchallenged. A vigorous defense is expected from any competent defense attorney. But most frequently these defenses are designed to explain away the case prosecutors have crafted against the accused. As we have seen, defense attorneys may provide jurors with alternative explanations for why the crime occurred and who might have committed the crime. But when there is direct evidence that a defendant committed the crime, the defense must act aggressively here as well. Under these circumstances when criminal conduct is alleged, the defense attempts to counter the criminal charges with one or more **defenses to criminal conduct.** Defenses to criminal conduct also are called **affirmative defenses.** These defenses include automatism, intoxication, coercion or duress, necessity, alibi, entrapment, defense of property, ignorance or mistake, and self-defense (Fisher 1999).

Automatism and/or Insanity

The defense of **automatism** is that the defendant was incapable of formulating criminal intent because he/she blacked out or was acting unconsciously. For example, someone may sleepwalk and commit the crime of breaking or entering, entering the home of another when they think they are entering their own home. The *mens rea* or guilty mind is eliminated as a criminal element (Jordan and Meyers 2003).

Insanity is occasionally raised in criminal cases. Insanity is defined in different ways among U.S. jurisdictions (Arpey 2003). Usually, it means acting under an irresistible impulse, an inability to conform one's conduct to the requirements of the law, a mental disease or defect, and not knowing the difference between right and wrong (Arpey 2003). If the defendant was not sane when the crime was committed, then the *mens rea* component of a crime can be overcome (Litwack 2003). Therefore, a crime is not committed.

When John Hinckley shot and wounded President Ronald Reagan and James Brady in 1981, for example, he was charged with attempted murder. His defense counsel raised the defense of insanity, claiming that Hinckley was not sane at the time he attempted to kill President Reagan. The act itself was never denied. Hinckley was acquitted, largely because of the great burden on the prosecution to prove Hinckley was sane when he committed these crimes. The public and various state legislatures were incensed over Hinckley's acquittal and sought to reform existing insanity provisions in courts. Currently, most states and the federal government have adopted the guilty, but mentally ill plea, where it is no longer the burden of the prosecution to show that one is sane (Mulford et al. 2004). The insanity defense is used in other countries besides the United States. In England, for instance, insanity is used to indicate diminished capacity in criminal cases (Mitchell 2003).

Intoxication

Intoxication is often raised in criminal cases to show that the defendant was not fully capable when the crime was committed. However, intoxication rarely excuses criminal conduct. Intoxication may be used to show that certain elements of the crime may not be present (Brocke et al. 2004). For instance, in premeditated murder cases, the intoxication of the defendant may help the defense to show that the defendant was not capable of premeditating the crime. States differ in the weight given to intoxication as a way of negating criminal intent.

In Tennessee, for instance, Wayne Adkins was charged with and convicted of first-degree murder in the death of Junior Adams (*State v. Adkins*, 1983). Witnesses testifying about what they saw said that Adkins had consumed a case of beer shortly before the shooting and was drunk when he killed Adams. The jury recommended the death penalty nevertheless. The Tennessee State Supreme Court set aside the death penalty, however, and ruled that Adkins was not capable of premeditating the murder as the result of intoxication. This holding is not necessarily indicative of how other state supreme courts might rule on similar issues. Canada and other countries have revised their laws regarding intoxication and whether it can be used as an affirmative defense against criminal conduct (Champion 2005b).

Coercion or Duress

When persons act under **coercion** or **duress,** they feel compelled to act in certain ways in order to avoid harm from others. In youth gang activities, for instance, the gang may pressure younger members of the gang to commit various crimes. The older gang members may threaten younger gang members by threatening them with bodily harm. "We will beat you up, maybe even kill you, if you don't steal these things from the store," the gang might say to younger gang members. Thus, when the younger gang members commit theft and are caught, they may claim duress. They will allege that the gang made them do it or else (Gilbertson 2005).

In another case involving duress, two female inmates held in a California minimum-security prison were charged with escape when they walked away from the prison. They fled the prison when they were threatened by other inmates, lesbians, with physical harm if they did not submit to sexual advances. Later when the women were free of the prison and the circumstances that might have caused them physical harm, they surrendered themselves to local law enforcement authorities. They claimed duress resulting from the threats of lesbian inmates. They were convicted of escape in a lower California court, but an appellate court set their conviction aside, accepting their defense of duress as valid (*California v. Lovercamp*, 1974). This doesn't mean that prisoners are always entitled to flee from their prison confines if they feel threatened by other prisoners. Each case must be resolved on an individual basis. However, in this California case, duress was successfully used. Thus, if a defendant is made to perform conduct that is criminal, duress or coercion may be an affirmative defense to remove it from criminal conduct.

Necessity

In 1996, a man was arrested in Minot, North Dakota, for breaking and entering a car dealership. However, his case was dismissed during trial when he cited necessity as the reason for his actions. In his case, he was driving a car toward Minot from Bismarck when a storm struck. The powerful snow and winds caused a whiteout, where he could not see the road in front of him. During this blizzard, his car slid off the road and he was stranded. He knew that he must seek shelter or die. He walked in the blizzard for about a mile, finally coming to a large automobile dealership on the outskirts of Minot. He broke a window to gain entry into the facility and climbed into an automobile on the showroom floor to keep warm. Employees found him asleep in one of the showroom cars a day later when the storm subsided. They called police and he was arrested. His defense of **necessity** was accepted as valid by the court. He was merely trying to save his life.

Alibi

Whenever a defendant claims an alibi, he/she intends to show that he/she was somewhere else when the crime was committed. Thus, if a crime is committed in St. Louis, Missouri, at 10:00 p.m. on a Monday night, and if the defendant can show that he/she was in New York City at 10:00 p.m. on that same Monday evening, the witnesses who testify in his behalf provide him/her with an alibi. Depending upon the veracity or truthfulness of these other witnesses, an **alibi** defense is a strong defense to criminal conduct.

Entrapment

Entrapment occurs whenever a defendant is lulled into criminal conduct by another. Usually, the conduct is something that is extraordinary for the defendant, and not conduct that is normally a routine or practice (Gubanski 2004). Law enforcement officers often seek to induce people to commit a crime so that they can make an arrest. Female officers pose as prostitutes in an effort to arrest those seeking to buy sexual favors. Many prospective customers of prostitutes are thus snared in police stings. However, sometimes the police go out of their way to encourage others to violate the law. They may knock on motel doors until they find someone willing to invite the officer/prostitute in for sex. This aggressive policing often leads to charges of entrapment, where customer/defendants are lured into committing acts that are not ordinarily contemplated by them.

A high-profile example of entrapment was the case of John DeLorean, an automobile manufacturer. DeLorean was becoming financially destitute after his attempt to market a particular type of automobile was unsuccessful. Desperately in need of operating capital, DeLorean was susceptible to undercover police suggestions that he purchase a large quantity of cocaine for resale. The profits from the resale of cocaine, according to undercover police officers, would be sufficient to bail out DeLorean and save his failing automobile company. Thus, DeLorean succumbed to their suggestions and arranged for the purchase of a large quantity of cocaine. DeLorean was videotaped purchasing cocaine from these undercover officers and charged with possession of cocaine for resale. However, his attorney raised the defense of entrapment. The jury agreed with DeLorean and acquitted him of the criminal charges. They believed that he had been illegally entrapped by police in the cocaine sale. If one is entrapped, then one is not guilty of criminal conduct.

Defense of Property

Defense of property can sometimes be cited as an excuse for criminal conduct. If someone attempts to steal one's car, for example, a defendant is entitled to use reasonable force to deter criminals from committing this crime.

While deadly force is never an acceptable defense of property, it is plausible that a defendant might engage in aggravated assault to discourage criminals from stealing his/her valuables. Thus, more than a few persons have been acquitted of criminal charges when they have been able to demonstrate that they were merely defending their property when they attacked their attackers.

Ignorance or Mistake

The old adage, ignorance is no excuse, is applicable here to a degree. If someone doesn't know what the law is regarding a certain type of conduct, this fact should reduce the seriousness of whatever they do. Persons who visit foreign countries, for instance, may not know what the laws of the foreign country are. They may unwittingly violate a criminal law by engaging in conduct that might be acceptable in their own country.

In certain cultures, for example, it is customary to perform an operation on all female children to remove their clitoris. This is a ritual that is condoned and socially and religiously approved. However, it is against the law in the United States for such a procedure to be performed. In California and other states, however, some persons have been prosecuted for performing these religious rituals. Thus, the courts have had to weigh the religious and cultural significance of these illegal rituals and their legality in other countries (Tonry 2004). In the United States, however, these rituals are considered illegal and are therefore prohibited.

Mistake or ignorance may be acceptable under other conditions. For example, Morrissette was a hunter who routinely hunted on an army artillery range. It seems that this particular artillery range, although enclosed by a perimeter wire fence, was considered a good deer-hunting area by local hunters. Furthermore, a section of the army post wire fence perimeter had been cut away where private citizens could drive their trucks through and make it easier to hunt deer. One afternoon, Morrissette drove his truck into the military artillery range and hunted deer. After a long unsuccessful afternoon of deer hunting, Morrissette was about to leave when he spied a pile of copper artillery shell casings. Weeds had grown up around the pile of copper shell casings, and it appeared to Morrissette that these casings, some of which were rusting away, had been abandoned. Thus, Morrissette loaded the shell casings into his truck and sold them subsequently at a local flea market for their metal value. With the money, he went to a bar and treated his friends to several rounds of drinks. Nearby enlisted men from the military post overheard Morrissette brag about the copper shell casings he had found and he was reported to police who arrested him for theft of military property. He was convicted, but he appealed, arguing that he didn't know that he was stealing government property when he took the copper shell casings. In this instance, the appellate court believed Morrissette and overturned his conviction. However, this is a relatively rare instance where courts will accept ignorance or mistake as an excuse for otherwise criminal conduct.

Self-Defense

If someone commits a crime and raises the affirmative defense of **self-defense,** it must be shown that the conduct was justified because the defendant believed his/her life was in jeopardy (Hemenway 2004). Self-defense is often raised in homicide cases where one person kills another. If the facts are unclear, a murder charge may be filed against the defendant. Later in court, the defendant raises self-defense as the explanation for the conduct (Hollander 2004). The trial provides the factual forum, where witnesses and others testify about what happened. If the defendant believed that his/her life was in jeopardy and that the only course of action available was to kill the aggressor and eliminate the threat, then the jury will acquit the defendant of the murder charge. Self-defense is always a good defense to this type of criminal conduct if there is sufficient factual information to back up that particular defense (Kaufman 2004).

SUMMARY

All criminal defendants have the right to counsel. When any person is charged with a crime, he/she has the right to counsel, even if indigent. Whenever persons are charged with one or more crimes, they have counsel appointed for them or hire their own private counsel. Under certain circumstances, persons may act as their own counsel and represent themselves. This self-representation is called acting *pro se*, and almost every judge advises defendants against it. Most defendants lack the legal expertise and knowledge to know when to object and when not to object, what types of evidence are admissible or inadmissible, and a host of other topics that are well known to trained counsels. Frequently attorneys are appointed to sit with these defendants anyway, and legal assistance may be offered even if it is not desired.

Most defense counsels are members of the American Bar Association, and many of them belong to local bar associations. These associations have established Canons of Professional Ethics. The ABA has evolved the Model Code of Professional Responsibility. These professional ethical codes have been reviewed previously, although it is incumbent upon defense counsels to represent their clients vigorously and competently, within the bounds of the law. Also, all defense counsels are under an obligation to avoid the appearance of impropriety. Attorneys who violate one or more of these ethical codes are subject to varying degrees of sanctions, including possible loss of membership and disbarment proceedings, depending upon the seriousness and nature of the ethical code violation.

There exists an attorney–client confidentiality privilege between the defendant and his/her counsel, and prosecutors may not seek to violate this confidentiality by any means. Some convicted offenders may challenge their convictions and allege ineffective assistance of counsel. The U.S. Supreme Court has articulated standards governing what conduct rises to the level of incompetence and what conduct doesn't. Under *Strickland v. Washington* (1984), ineffective assistance of counsel occurs whenever counsel's behavior undermines the adversarial process to the extent that the trial outcome is unreliable, and/or if the counsel's conduct is unreasonable to the extent that the jury verdict would have been different otherwise. Both actions and inactions on the part of defense counsel may rise to the level of ineffective assistance of counsel. These counsels may say or do something to jeopardize one's case, or they may fail to do important tasks with the same result. Most defendants alleging ineffective assistance of counsel find that it is difficult to sustain such charges against their attorneys if convicted of a crime.

The standards governing whether defendants are entitled to a jury trial have been clarified by the U.S. Supreme Court. If defendants are in jeopardy of being incarcerated for a period of beyond six months, they are entitled to a jury trial with one exception. This exception is if the judge assures the defendant that he/she will not suffer loss of liberty of beyond six months if a bench trial is conducted and finds the defendant guilty.

For indigent defendants who cannot afford counsel, each state and the federal government has established methods for assigning defense counsel to such defendants. States such as Texas use several different methods for assigning defense counsel to indigents. The most common types of systems include the public defender system, the assigned counsel system, and the contract system. Under the public defender system, state- or county-funded public defender agencies are established and staffed with defense counsels who are assigned to indigent criminal cases. Public defenders are salaried employees of the county or state where they reside. They are expected to provide the best defense possible, under their prevailing circumstances. More than a few persons working in public defender offices are new attorneys with little or no trial experience. Working as a public defender is like an apprenticeship to gain experience in working within the legal system.

The assigned counsel system is used in about one-fourth of all states. Often the jurisdictions where the assigned counsel system is operative are sparsely populated and there are few attorneys. The local bar association rotates defense counsel duties among its membership, and the payment for one's services as defense counsel for indigents is modest. Under the contract system, different law firms in more urban jurisdictions will submit bids to the state or county specifying how much they will charge per client per day to represent indigents. County or state agencies will award contracts to these firms according to varying criteria, most often associated with the lowest cost to the government. One commonality is that all forms of defense for indigents lack financial sources equivalent to those of private law firms who are retained by more affluent clients. Lacking financial resources greatly restricts public defenders from conducting their own thorough investigations, and thus, the generalization is frequently made that indigent representation by public defenders or assigned counsel is not as effective as representation by private counsel. The literature suggests that there is often a factual basis for this generalization, given the outcomes of many indigent criminal cases.

Criminal defense attorneys perform various duties and have several important functions. Several of these duties and functions relate closely to the ethical codes of conduct or canons of professional responsibility of their professional organizations. Defense counsels must represent their clients faithfully and vigorously, within the boundaries of the law. They must attack the prosecution's case and do their best to show the innocence of their defendants. In this respect, they must meet with their clients and determine the best strategies to use in winning the case and securing an acquittal for their defendants. When defending their clients during a trial, defense counsels must attack prosecution witnesses and attempt to impeach them or challenge their credibility.

In cases where there is overwhelming evidence of defendant guilt, it is the defense counsel's responsibility to secure the minimum punishment for their clients through plea bargaining (Fisher 2000). This means that defense counsels must consult with prosecutors and agree on a plea and a punishment. Judges approve all plea agreements contemplated between the defense and the prosecution.

Some defense counsels may engage in unethical or illegal practices when defending their clients. While it is permissible to coach clients who will testify in court in their own behalf, it is illegal to suggest to clients that they commit perjury on the witness stand. This is subornation of perjury, and if it is detected, defense counsels may be charged with a crime and prosecuted. Such proceedings will result in organizational sanctions and possible disbarment. Also, like prosecutors, defense counsels are forbidden from making certain statements in court that are inadmissible and may prejudice the jury (Cook, Arndt, and Lieberman 2004). For instance, it is improper for defense counsels to mention the results of lie detector or polygraph tests administered to their clients by law enforcement personnel, even if those results are exculpatory. This is because polygraph test results are inadmissible in court as evidence. This prohibition also applies to prosecutors who must refrain from mentioning to the jury that the defendant failed the polygraph test. If such statements are made, possible mistrials may be declared, since the harmless nature of such utterances is questionable.

Defense attorneys must be responsible and seek discovery of any and all information about the crime and the defendant in the possession of prosecutors and police. Some of this information is not discoverable, but much of it is. Obtaining this information usually benefits criminal clients in different ways. Materials subject to discovery include confessions, transcripts of interviews between police interrogators and the defendant, psychological test results, and other materials. These discoverable materials are called Brady materials or Jencks materials after the U.S. Supreme Court cases where such materials were declared discoverable. It is improper, unethical, and illegal for prosecutors to withhold discoverable materials from the defense when a timely request is made for such materials.

Different types of evidence may be presented during a criminal trial. The prosecution bears the burden of proof and must show one's guilt beyond a reasonable doubt. This task is accomplished usually by introducing different types of evidence for the jury to consider. Some of this evidence is conclusive, where one or more witnesses watched the defendant commit the crime. Other evidence is derivative. This may be written notes, fingerprints, powder residue from a firearm, hair fibers, and other tangible items that link the defendant with the crime. Evidence may be direct or circumstantial. Direct evidence is usually the most damaging, and it is either eyewitness testimony or incriminating fingerprint evidence (Schram, Koons-Witt, and Morash 2004). Circumstantial evidence is less compelling, but it is nevertheless important. In murder cases, for instance, bodies of victims are sometimes never discovered. Nevertheless there may be substantial circumstantial evidence showing defendant guilt. Evidence may also be corroborated by other persons as well. This assists prosecutors in building their cases against defendants (Matthews, Pease, and Pease 2001).

Defendants and their attorneys have available to them a variety of defenses to criminal conduct. These defenses are often known as affirmative defenses. One type of affirmative defense is automatism or insanity. The argument is that the defendant was incapable of formulating criminal intent or lacked the *mens rea* to understand what he/she was doing was wrong. The insanity defense isn't used often, and when it is used, it is often not used successfully. Legislatures have modified the insanity defense standard so that today, many jurisdictions allow defendants to plead guilty but mentally ill. This type of plea usually lessens the harshness of their punishment (McSherry 2004).

Other affirmative defenses include intoxication, coercion or duress, necessity, and alibi. Some defendants claim that they were intoxicated at the time the crime was committed. This is sometimes considered a mitigating circumstance, although most jurisdictions consider intoxication to be a voluntary condition and merely consider it as a minor contributing factor. Coercion or duress means that the defendant was made to commit the crime by means of a threat. The defense of necessity means that the crime was committed because it was necessary to do so. Someone who breaks into a neighbor's home late at night to put out a fire may claim necessity later if charged with breaking and entering. Alibi as a defense means that the defendant alleges he/she was elsewhere when the crime was committed. Usually one or more persons will testify as to one's alibi if it is used as an affirmative defense.

Other affirmative defenses include entrapment, defense of property, ignorance or mistake, and self-defense. Entrapment occurs when someone is encouraged to break the law, usually by some law enforcement officer acting in an undercover capacity, and it is not customary for the defendant to engage in such criminal behavior. Defense of property may be a defense if it can be shown that the defendant was merely defending his/her property from damage, intrusion, or theft by another. Some trespassers have been shot by home owners who later claim defense of property. Under some circumstances, this affirmative defense is successful.

The defense of ignorance or mistake is sometimes used. While ignorance of the law may be claimed, it is usually insufficient to excuse a violation of the law. But sometimes defendants make an honest mistake and violate the law. On income tax returns, for instance, some persons may avoid criminal prosecution for income tax evasion if they are ignorant of the tax laws in some way or if they make a genuine mistake. This situation is almost always a judgment call by either the judge or jury. Finally, some defendants allege that they were acting in self-defense. Self-defense is usually a good affirmative defense if it can be shown that the victim's behavior was menacing, potentially lethal, and could not be avoided. The use of one or more of these defenses is available to any defense attorney when representing a client in criminal court. In jury trials, juries must decide whether to believe the defendant when such defenses are alleged to account for their criminal conduct.

KEY TERMS

ABA Model Code of Professional
Responsibility
Affirmative defenses
Alibi
Assigned counsel system
Attorney competence
Attorney–client confidentiality and
privilege
Automatism
Brady materials
Brady violation
Burden of proof
Canons of Professional Ethics
Circumstantial evidence
Coercion
Conclusive evidence
Contract system
Corroboration
Defense of property
Defenses to criminal conduct
Demonstrative evidence
Derivative evidence
Direct evidence

Discovery
Duress
Entrapment
Evidence
Evidentiary
Habeas corpus petition
Indigent defendants
Ineffective assistance of counsel
Intoxication
Jencks materials
Jury trial
Lie detectors
Mistake
Necessity
Petty offenses
Pickpocketing
Polygraph tests
Pro se
Public defender system
Self-defense
Self-representation
State bar associations
Subornation of perjury

QUESTIONS FOR REVIEW

1. What are five defenses to criminal conduct? Explain in each case how each might be used.

2. What are the general rules governing discovery? What is discovery and what are its purposes?

3. Under what circumstances are criminal defendants entitled to an attorney? Under what circumstances are defendants entitled to a jury trial? What are some leading legal cases having to do with the right to counsel and to jury trials?

4. What is meant by ineffective assistance of counsel? What are some leading cases where ineffectiveness of counsel is defined?

5. What are some major canons of ethics that are a part of the ABA Model Code of Professional Responsibility? Why are they important?

6. What is meant by the courtroom work group and who makes up its key components? Why is it important for defense attorneys to work closely with the courtroom work group?

7. What are several forms of legal aid for indigent defendants?

8. Are court-appointed counsels as effective as privately retained counsel when representing criminal defendants? Why or why not? Explain.

9. Compare the assigned counsel system with the contract system. What are the different benefits of each?

10. What is meant by defense misconduct? What are some different forms of defense misconduct?

11. What is meant by subornation of perjury?

12. What is meant by a Brady violation?

13. Who bears the burden of proof in criminal prosecutions? Under due process, what can be assumed about the guilt or innocence of the accused?

14. Can defendants be convicted of crimes solely on the basis of circumstantial evidence? Why or why not? Explain. Give an example.

▒▒ SUGGESTED READINGS ▒▒

1. Jay S. Albanese (2004). *Organized Crime in Our Times*, 4/e. Cincinnati: Anderson Publishing Company.
2. Robert Boyle, Donna R. Newman, and Sam A. Schmidt (2003). "Center for Professional Values and Practice Symposium: Criminal Defense in the Age of Terrorism." *New York Law School Law Review* **48**:3–384.
3. Stephen H. Dinwiddie and William Briska (2004). "Prosecution of Women Psychiatric Inpatients: Theoretical and Practical Issues." *International Journal of Law and Psychiatry* **27**:17–29.
4. Saul M. Kassin and Rebecca J. Norwick (2004). "Why People Waive Their Miranda Rights: The Power of Innocence." *Law and Human Behavior* **28**:211–221.
5. Whitley Kaufman (2004). "Is There a 'Right' to Self-Defense?" *Criminal Justice Ethics* **23**:20–32.
6. Stuart M. Kirschner and Gary J. Galperin (2002). "The Defense of Extreme Emotional Disturbance in New York County: Pleas and Outcomes." *Behavioral Sciences and the Law* **20**:47–50.
7. Daniel A. Krauss and Bruce D. Sales (2001). "The Effects of Clinical and Scientific Expert Testimony on Juror Decision Making in Capital Sentencing." *Psychology, Public Policy and the Law* **7**:267–310.
8. N. L. Piquero and J. L. Davis (2004). "Extralegal Factors and the Sentencing of Organizational Defendants: An Examination of the Federal Sentencing Guidelines." *Journal of Criminal Justice* **32**:643–654.
9. Alison Dundes Rentelm (2004). *The Cultural Defense*. New York: Oxford University Press.
10. Cynthia Siemsen (2004). *Emotional Trials: The Moral Dilemmas of Women Criminal Defense Attorneys*. Boston: Northeastern University Press.
11. John Wooldredge and Amy Thistlewaite (2004). "Bilevel Disparities in Court Dispositions for Intimate Assault." *Criminology* **42**:417–456.

Chapter 5

Judges

© Royalty-Free/Corbis

Chapter Objectives

As a result of reading this chapter, you will have accomplished the following objectives:

1. Understand the different kinds of judges and the diversity of their powers.

2. Understand the qualifications a judge must have in order to sit on the bench.

3. Describe the different judicial selection methods including partisan and nonpartisan elections, gubernatorial appointment, merit selection, and legislative appointment.

4. Describe the advantages and disadvantages with each type of judicial selection method.

5. Understand which method of selection is best for selection of judges.

6. Describe the different methods of judicial training, and standardization of qualifications.

7. Describe the different types of judicial misconduct and abuses of discretion.

8. Understand some of the current criticisms of judges, and the ways in which judges can be removed from office.

■ It happened in Los Angeles. Ms. Doe, a rape victim, was testifying in the case against her rapist, Mercedes Porfidio Lopez. Lopez was charged with multiple counts of rape, oral copulation, and attempted murder. Following a jury trial where Lopez was found guilty, Los Angeles County Superior Court Judge John D. Harris sentenced Lopez to two life sentences plus 155 years to life for the various rape and attempted murder counts. Then something strange happened. Following the conviction and sentencing, Judge Harris, 66, who has been married for 31 years and has two grown children, invited the prosecutor, Karla Kerlin, and the victim, Ms. Doe, to his office. He complimented the victim on her trial testimony and invited her to join him and his family for an upcoming Jewish holiday at a local restaurant. When Ms. Doe called Judge Harris's office to accept the invitation, Judge Harris said that his wife was ill and said that he and Ms. Doe should meet alone together at a restaurant. He referred to the meeting as a "date." Subsequently, Ms. Doe began to have doubts about the dinner and the meeting with the judge without his family present. She called and cancelled the dinner plans. Later she brought the matter to the attention of the prosecutor's office where an investigation of Judge Harris's actions was commenced. The prosecutor's office alleged that Judge John Harris had violated judicial ethics by suggesting that the victim meet him at a West Los Angeles restaurant for a date, according to Assistant District Attorney Michael Tranbarger. Tranbarger said in a letter that "it is our opinion that Judge Harris's conduct might have created an appearance of impropriety and might constitute a violation of the judicial ethics code. Judicial ethics rules ban a judge from using the prestige of his office to advance personal interests." In response to these allegations, Judge Harris's lawyer, Ed George, said that his client had done nothing wrong. "Judge Harris denies everything, absolutely and adamantly, that there is an impropriety or an ethical violation. I think he was trying to comfort her," George said. Since the allegations have been made, Judge Harris has been transferred from the Criminal Courts Building in Downtown Los Angeles to a civil court in Van Nuys. Defense lawyer, Sean Erenstoft, who represented the convicted rapist, Lopez, said he would ask the appellate court for a new trial for his client based on Harris's conduct. Should judges ask victims to dinner following rape and attempted murder trials, even if it is with their own families? Was the judge wrong to invite Ms. Doe to dinner by himself at a West Los Angeles restaurant? What sanctions would you impose on the judge, if indeed this is a case of an ethical violation? What do you think? [Source: Adapted from the Associated Press, "Judge Asks Victim to Dinner After Sentencing Rapist to Life," November 18, 2000.]

■ Laurie Show was slashed to death with a butcher knife on December 20, 1991 by Lisa Michelle Lambert. According to police reports and a confession by Lambert, 19, Lambert was living with her boyfriend, Lawrence Yunkin, when she learned that Yunkin had previously dated Laurie Show. The liaison enraged Lambert. She lured Show's mother away from the condominium they shared in East Lampeter Township near Lancaster, Pennsylvania. Then she and a friend, Tabitha Buck, entered Show's home while Yunkin waited in a getaway car. Show was stabbed several times and her throat was slashed. Subsequently, police investigators obtained a confession from Lambert, indicating that she accompanied Buck into the apartment. She said she only intended to play a prank on Show by tying her up and cutting off her hair. Later, Hazel Show, Laurie Show's mother, returned to her apartment and found her daughter dying. Laurie Show's last words to her mother were, "Michelle did it." Despite Michelle's confession, which she later recanted, Michelle was tried for Laurie Show's murder and convicted. However, a federal judge, Stewart Dalzell, subsequently ruled on two different occasions when the case was appealed that Michelle was an innocent victim of misconduct by both the police and prosecutors. The dying declaration of Laurie Show to her mother was admitted during Lambert's murder trial, and this evidence was considered hearsay and inadmissible by the federal judge on appeal. Lambert remained in prison while the government appealed the judge's ruling. As the tenth anniversary of Laurie Show's murder approached, her father, John Show, sought an investigation of the federal judge who has twice ruled favorably for Michelle Lambert. John Show wrote a letter to Congress seeking an investigation of Judge Dalzell. "If she (Michelle) gets out, it'll be a nightmare. It will be an outrage to us, to this community." Police Chief Dale Jerchau, East Lampeter Township, said "It's the case that won't go away." Apparently there were irregularities on the part of police and prosecutors during the murder investigation that called into question the validity of Lambert's confession. Should families of victims be able to have federal judges replaced whenever they make rulings that might set convicted criminals free? If the case were to result in a retrial for Lambert, should the dying declaration of Laurie Show to her mother be allowed into evidence against Lambert? [Source: Adapted from Timothy D. May and the Associated Press, "Family Wants Federal Judge Thrown Off Girl's Murder Case," December 10, 2001.]

■ Clarence Dickson, 52, is a successful grocer in Franklin, Maryland. He has always been in the grocery business. He is a high school dropout. Gerald Ruffington, 56, is a successful trial attorney and civil arbiter. He obtained his law degree from Yale University and has practiced law for 29 years. Both men are running for election as the Fourth Circuit Court county judge, which is vacant because of the recent death of the incumbent judge, Mary Lambeth. Dickson is immensely popular in the community, belongs to several fraternal organizations, and has learned to become an effective public speaker. He makes frequent sizeable donations to worthy causes and has contributed a lot of money to local schools. Ruffington has a winning record of defending criminal defendants, and he worked for a number of years early in his career for the prosecutor's office as an assistant district attorney. The judicial position is an elected one, and no special qualifications are required. Elected judges spend six weeks at a judicial training school, where trial procedures and other judicial functions are covered by lecturers and practicing judges who teach as adjuncts. Who would make the better judge if elected, Dickson or Ruffington? Should there be stringent qualifications for county judges?

INTRODUCTION

There are many different kinds of judges with diverse amounts of **judicial powers.** The public has several general conceptions about judges and what they are supposed to do. But many of these conceptions are actually misconceptions. For instance, we usually think of a judge as being an ultimate arbiter, a ruler over courtroom proceedings and the person responsible for meting out punishments. Although a judge is all of these things, in some instances the judge does not have as much education, training, or discretion as we may think.

This chapter examines judges and their qualifications. There is great variation among judges in the United States in their backgrounds, the legal expertise, and how they became judges. Not all judges have the same degree of legal expertise, nor are all judges lawyers or possess law degrees. They differ greatly in their personalities and idiosyncrasies. They have many prejudices and limitations. More than a few persons are interested in how certain persons in our society become judges, and how they come to make decisions. Spohn (2002) speaks of judges sometimes playing a leading role and at others only a supportive role. Spohn points out that in the sentencing process, for instance, a number of persons are involved. For example, the legislature enacts legislation regarding sentencing, the prosecutor decides which charges to file, a jury may be involved in conviction or acquittal, a probation officer may recommend a sentence to a judge through a presentence investigation report, and then the judge has the responsibility for deciding a sentence. This chapter will describe the judicial selection process in different jurisdictions. Some judges are elected, others are appointed, and still others reach the bench through a merit selection process. This chapter will also discuss the advantages and disadvantages of each of these methods for judicial selection.

The next section of the chapter discusses judicial training. All judges are bound by certain rules that are integral to a court's efficiency and effectiveness. Judges sometimes, however, make decisions that are reversed by a higher court, or sometimes judges allow evidence that should have been inadmissible. The judge decides what is or is not relevant testimony. The judge uses these rules and these decisions to control the trials that come into the courtroom. Some judges are not learned in law; as such, there have been criticisms of some of their decisions, as well as blaming them for court delays. Most jurisdictions now have special training that most judges must go through to make them better able to manage their court caseload.

Because there is great variation in the quality of the judiciary throughout all U.S. jurisdictions, the nature of judicial appointments will be examined. In recent years, the judiciary has come under close scrutiny by various interests and agencies, and some evidence of judicial misconduct has surfaced. This misconduct has led some jurisdictions to fetter the discretion that some judges enjoy by implementing determinate sentencing and guideline sentencing structures. Some of these abuses of discretionary powers will be presented. Selected criticisms of judges will be provided, together with an examination of several relevant judicial issues.

JUDGES AND THEIR QUALIFICATIONS

In any courtroom, the key figure is the **judge.** Judges make decisions that affect the lives of defendants. All judges have certain rules to follow that are an integral feature of **judicial process.** Sometimes judges make decisions that are reversed by higher courts. A judge may allow the introduction of incriminating evidence against a defendant, or the judge may decide to exclude such evidence. The judge decides what is or is not relevant testimony. The judge controls the conduct of all trials.

It is a common misconception among citizens that all judges are lawyers and have legal expertise. However, in numerous jurisdictions throughout the United States, many judges have no legal training and are not former lawyers. One implication is that in many jurisdictions, judicial selection is more a matter of politics than judicial expertise. The political nature of judicial selection has its roots in seventeenth-century England. Table 5.1 shows selected qualification

TABLE 5.1 SELECTED QUALIFICATION REQUIREMENTS OF JUDGES OF APPELLATE AND TRIAL COURTS OF GENERAL JURISDICTION, BY TYPE OF COURT AND JURISDICTION, AS OF JANUARY 1, 1998

Jurisdiction	U.S. Citizenship — Appellate	U.S. Citizenship — Trial	Years of Minimum Residence: In State — Appellate	In State — Trial	In District — Appellate	In District — Trial	Minimum Age — Appellate	Minimum Age — Trial	Member of State Bar (years) — Appellate	Bar — Trial	Other — Appellate	Other — Trial
Alabama	(a)	(a)	5[b]	5[b]		1	25	25				
Alaska	Y	Y	5[b]	5[b]					Y[c]	Y[c]		
Arizona			10[d]	5	(e, f)	1	30	30	10[d]	5	(g, h)	(g, h)
Arkansas		Y	2	2			30	28	(i, j)	(i, j)	(g)	(g)
California			(f)	(f)					10[i]	10[i]		
Colorado			(f)	(f)		(f)			5	5	(h)	(h)
Connecticut							18	18	10	10		
Delaware			(b)	(b)					(i)	(i)		
Florida			(f)	(f)	Y[k]	Y[k]			10	5	(h)	(h)
Georgia	(a)	(a)	Y[k]	Y[b,k]	Y[k]	Y[b,k]		30	7	7		
Hawaii	Y	Y	Y[b,k]	Y[b,k]					10	10		
Idaho	Y	Y	2	1	(f)	(f)	30	30	10	10		
Illinois	Y	Y	Y[k]	Y[k]	Y[k]	Y[k]			Y[k]	Y[k]		
Indiana	Y	Y	Y[k]	Y[k]	Y[k]	Y[k]			10[i]	Y[k]		
Iowa									Y[k]	Y[k]		
Kansas			2	2		Y[k]	30	30	Y[k,j]	Y[k,j]		
Kentucky	Y	Y	2	2	2	2			8	8		
Louisiana			2	2	2	2			5	5		
Maine									(i)	(i)		
Maryland			5[b,f]	5[b,f]	(l)	(l)	30	30	Y[k]	Y[k]	(g)	(g)
Michigan			(f)	(f)	(f)	(f)			Y[k]	Y[k]	(g)	(g)
Minnesota									Y[i,k]	Y[i,k]		
Mississippi			5[b]	5[b]			30	26	5	5	(h)	(h)

State										
Missouri	(a)	(a)	(f)	(f)	Y[k]	1	30	30	Y[k]	Y[k]
Montana	Y	Y	2	2					5	5
Nebraska	Y	Y	3	3	Y[f,k]	Y[k]	30	30	5i	5i
Nevada			2[f]	2[f]		Y[k]	25	25	Y[k]	Y[k]
New Hampshire										
New Jersey			(n)	(n)		(n)	35	35	10	10
New Mexico			3	3	Y[k]	Y[k]	18		10i,j	6i,j
New York	Y[k]	Y[k]	Y[k]	Y[k]					10	10
North Carolina		Y	Y[k]	Y[k]	Y[k]	Y[k]			Y[k]	Y[k]
North Dakota		Y[k]	Y[k]	Y[k]	Y[k]	Y[k]			Y[j,k]	Y[j,k]
Ohio			(f)	(f)	(f)	(f)	30		6i	6i
Oklahoma			3	3	(f)	1			5i	4i
Oregon	Y	Y	1[b]	1[b]	Y[k]	Y[k]			Y[k]	Y[k]
Pennsylvania	Y	Y	5[b]	5[b]			21		Y[k]	Y[k]
Rhode Island							26	26		
South Carolina	Y	Y	Y[k]	Y[k]	Y[f,k]	Y[f,k]	35[o]	30	5	5
South Dakota	Y	Y	5	5	(e)	1	35		Y[k]	Y[k]
Tennessee	Y	Y	(b)	(b)		2	30[q]	25	Y[j,k]	Y[j,k]
Texas	Y	Y	5[p]	3		Y[k]			Y[j,k]	Y[j,k]
Utah			5	5	Y[k]	Y[k]			Y[k]	Y[k]
Vermont	Y[k]	Y[k]	Y[k]	Y[k]			30	30	Y[j,k]	Y[j,k]
Virginia			1	1	1	Y[k]			5	5
Washington			5	5		1	30	30	Y[k,r]	Y[k]
West Virginia			Y[k]	Y[k]	(s)	(s)			10i	Y[j,k]
Wisconsin	Y	Y	(s)	(s)	(t)	(t)			5	5
Wyoming	Y	Y	3	2			30	28	9i,j	(i)
District of Columbia									5i	5i
Northern Mariana Islands	Y						30	30	(i)	(i)

(continued)

TABLE 5.1 SELECTED QUALIFICATION REQUIREMENTS OF JUDGES OF APPELLATE AND TRIAL COURTS OF GENERAL JURISDICTION, BY TYPE OF COURT AND JURISDICTION, AS OF JANUARY 1, 1998. (continued)

	U.S. Citizenship		In State		In District		Minimum Age		Member of State Bar (years)		Other	
Jurisdiction	Appellate	Trial	Appellate	Trial	Appellate	Trial	Appellate	Trial	Appellate	Trial	Appellate	Trial
Puerto Rico	Y	Y	5				25		10		Yj, k	

Years of Minimum Residence

"Appellate" refers to judges of courts of last resort and intermediate appellate courts. "Trial" refers to judges of courts of general trial jurisdiction. In some instances, information on the length of time for residency and legal experience requirements was not supplied. There are no qualification requirements for judges in Massachusetts. In the table, "y" indicates that the requirement applies.

a Citizen of the United States. Alabama—5 years, Georgia—3 years, Missouri—15 years for appellate court, 10 years for trial courts.

b Citizen of the state.

c Length of time as member of state bar not specified but must have been engaged in active practice of law for a specific number of years: 8 years for appellate court, 5 years for trial court.

d For court of appeals, 5 years.

e For court of appeals judges only.

f Qualified elector. For Arizona court of appeals, must be elector of county of residence. For Michigan Supreme Court, elector in state; court of appeals, elector of appellate circuit. For Missouri supreme and appellate courts, elector for 9 years; for circuit courts, elector for 3 years. For Oklahoma Supreme Court and Court of Criminal Appeals, elector for 1 year; court of appeals and district courts, elector for 6 months. For Oregon court of appeals, qualified elector in county.

g Specific personal characteristics. Arizona, Arkansas—good moral character. Maine—sobriety of manners. Maryland—integrity, wisdom, and sound legal knowledge.

h Nominee must be under certain age to be eligible. Arizona—under 70 years. Colorado—under 72 years, except when name is submitted for vacancy. Florida—under 70 years, except upon temporary assignment or to complete a term. Michigan, Ohio—under 70 years.

i Learned in law.

j Years as a practicing lawyer and/or service on bench of court of record in state may satisfy requirement. Arkansas—appellate: 8 years; trial: 6 years. Indiana—10 years admitted to practice or must have served as a circuit, superior, or criminal court judge in the state for at least 5 years Kansas—appellate: 10 years; trial: 5 years. Texas—appellate: 10 years; trial: 4 years. Vermont—5 of 10 years preceding appointment. West Virginia—appellate: 10 years; trial: 5 years. Puerto Rico—appellate: 10 years; trial: 5 years.

k Length of time not specified.

l 6 months.

m Record of birth is required.

n There are 260 restricted superior court judgeships that require residence within the county at time of appointment and reappointment. There are 144 unrestricted judgeships for which assignment of county is made by the chief justice.

o 30 years for judges of court of appeals and court of criminal appeals.

p Supreme court is 5 years; court of appeals is 3 years.

q Supreme court is 30 years; court of appeals is 25 years.

r For court of appeals, admitted to practice for 5 years.

s 10 days.

t 90 days.

u Superior court judges must also have 5 years of legal government practice or serve as law school faculty.

Source: Maquire and Pastore 2000, 66–67.

requirements for judges in state appellate and trial courts of general jurisdiction. Table 5.1 shows that in 1998, the minimum age for appellate and trial court judgeships ranged from 18 to 30 (Maguire and Pastore 2005). These minimum-age requirements are somewhat deceptive, since it might appear that an 18-year-old might qualify as an appellate or trial court judge. States with these minimum-age provisions eliminate this possibility by requiring their prospective judges to be members of the state bar association for five or ten years or longer. Thus, it is inconceivable that any 18-year-old would ever hold a judicial post in these states where 18 is the minimum age. Almost every state requires judicial candidates for these posts to be members of the state bar association for specified periods.

About half of the states in 1998 did not require U.S. citizenship for persons to hold appellate or trial judge posts. Furthermore, the years of residence within the state to qualify for a judicial post varied from one year to ten years. More than a few states had no provisions for minimum residence times for either appellate or trial court judges (Maguire and Pastore 2005). Some states specified certain personal characteristics as qualifications, including good moral character, sobriety of manners, integrity, wisdom, and sound legal knowledge. Thus, there is considerable variation among the states about the qualifications of judicial candidates.

The Politicalization of Judicial Selection

The politicalization of the judicial selection process cannot be overstated. When politics is the dominating factor in judicial appointments, one's qualifications for a judgeship are practically irrelevant. Whether a partisan election, or a gubernatorial or a presidential appointment leads to one's becoming a judge, the result is often a judicial appointment that reflects party politics rather than one's professional qualities for deciding cases fairly. This doesn't mean that political judicial appointees are incapable of being fair in judging cases, but rather, they are expected to adhere to a fixed political agenda associated with the party placing them in power (Pinello 1995).

Political influence also works to the detriment of women in judicial appointments. Gender bias has been found in more than a few systems whereby judges are appointed by politicians and women are routinely excluded from judicial consideration. Several critics argue that political appointments of judges place too much power in the hands of the appointer, such as the governor or president (Tomasi and Velona 1987). Politically appointed judges have considerably lower levels of accountability, and weak sanctioning mechanisms are in place for the discipline or removal. Those who oppose elections of judges say that voter apathy and disinterest, political influence, and a general lack of information about candidates and their qualifications make this process meaningless.

President Jimmy Carter created nominating commissions for federal circuit courts and district courts. Under Carter's administration, judicial appointees were more likely to have professional experience, age and years at the bar, a legal education, and higher American Bar Association ratings compared with subsequent Reagan appointees. Subsequently, President Reagan discontinued the nominating commission method of judicial appointments.

President Clinton appointed the highest percentage of females to the bench; 28.5 percent were female. Clinton also appointed an increased number of racial and ethnic minorities; 17.4 percent were African American and 5.9 percent were Hispanic (Maguire and Pastore 2005, 75). Roughly 20 percent of President George W. Bush's appointees have been female, and about 7 percent were African American and Hispanic (Maguire and Pastore 2005, 76).

Early research about the qualities of judicial applicants has shown that nominating commissions have identified the following criteria for their judicial selections: age, health, impartiality, integrity, judicial temperament, industry, professional skills, community contacts, social awareness, collegiality, writing ability, and decisiveness and speaking ability (Greenstein and Sampson 2004). However, no precise guidelines have been established to indicate how these qualities should be measured or assessed. There is historical precedent for these ambiguities relevant to the judicial selection process. In early England, for example, much secrecy was involved in the process of selecting judges (Pickles 1987). Judicial selection criteria were purposely diffuse and ambiguous, so that only conservative types of persons could hold judicial posts. These persons were often manipulated by politically influential constituencies (Pickles 1987).

In selected jurisdictions, model guidelines have been generated to assist judges in learning about courtroom protocol and the diverse functions of courtroom personnel. For instance, the National Center for State Courts in Williamsburg, Virginia has produced a resource manual that is designed to enhance the performance of trial judges (Hewitt 1995). The manual includes a discussion of terminology interpretation, judicial training issues, and general court interpreter services.

Reforms relating to judicial selection are not new. Aggressive court reforms have been undertaken for many decades, as different waves of state and federal judges have manifested characteristics that suggest inexperience and ineffectiveness. Many formal recruitment and judicial selection systems have been proposed, but relatively few have come up with any conclusive data indicating the kinds of qualitative differences that might result from alternative selection systems. Interviews with judges themselves suggest mixed reactions to any type of selection system, whether it is through appointment or election (Johnson 2004).

BOX 5.1 ON BAD JUDGES

■ Judge Robert Taylor of Palm Springs, California is responsible for allow-ing hundreds of child-abuse case victims being allowed to continue living with the abusive parents. Taylor admits in official court documents that he knows little or nothing about family court law. He relies mostly on infor-mation provided by divorce lawyers and court-appointed psychologists to help him do his job. His appointment to his present position was a politi-cal one. He professes ignorance about the Parental Alienation Syndrome inculcated in children by alienating and emotionally abusive parents. Should he be allowed to continue judging child-abuse cases? What can be done about judges like him?

■ Judge Cornelia Shuford-Hartman, Indio, California, is a former commis-sioner of the Indio California Family Court. During the performance of her judgeship, she engaged in serious, substantiated judicial and personal mis-conduct while discharging her duties. She has been reprimanded numer-ous times by higher courts on appeals, and she receives more complaints than any other judge in Riverside County. She has been married three times, has a history of alcohol abuse, and has several children who have histories of trouble with the law. Her numerous family court decisions have left abused children in the custody of their abusive parents and has re-jected pleas and suggestions from other courts about how to improve her decision making in this regard. She consistently discriminates against fa-thers in child custody cases. She refuses to accept any of these suggestions for improving her judicial behavior, including abolishing the current ad-versarial system in child custody cases and introducing mandatory media-tion and education programs of dispute resolution. She appears to have little or no regard for the welfare of children at risk in her court. Court an-alysts claim that her court is one of the worst family court systems in the United States.

Judge Watch is a grassroots organization comprised of citizens whose sole objective is to remove unethical and incompetent judges from Amer-ica's courtrooms. Theoretically, by exposing these judges to millions of cit-izens, pressure may be brought to bear on public officials who are in the position of removing these incompetent and dangerous judges from their posts. Judge Watch says that while most judges in America know the law and interpret it fairly, it only takes one bad decision by one bad judge to destroy a life or family. Judge Watch encourages any citizen who feels vic-timized by a judge to write to them about it. All claims against judges must be documented. Is Judge Watch an overreaction to the actions of a few bad judges? Or is there a more pervasive problem in the United States that is indicative of incompetent and untrained judges making bad decisions that impact citizens' lives adversely? [Source: Alliance for Non-Custodial Parents Rights, "The Worst Family Court Judges in America," Los Angeles, CA: June 20, 2006.]

State Judicial Selection Methods

Judges are either appointed or elected. Alfini (1981, 253) has identified five methods of judicial selection as basic variations on appointments or elections: (1) partisan election, (2) nonpartisan election, (3) gubernatorial appointment, (4) selection through the merit plan, and (5) legislative appointments.

Partisan Elections

Partisan elections of judges are the same as elections for other public offices. Democrats, Republicans, and others advance their own slate of candidates for various offices, including judicial vacancies. The public votes for their choice by secret ballot. Persons who win these elections become judges for a fixed term, such as four years. In 2004, the following six states used partisan elections for selecting the highest appellate judges: Alabama, Illinois, Louisiana, Pennsylvania, Texas, and West Virginia (Maguire and Pastore 2005, 83).

Nonpartisan Elections

In **nonpartisan elections,** candidates are simply listed to fill judicial vacancies regardless of their political affiliation. In 2004, 15 states used nonpartisan elections to fill the highest appellate court posts. These states included Arkansas, Georgia, Idaho, Kentucky, Michigan, Minnesota, Mississippi, Montana, Nevada, North Carolina, North Dakota, Ohio, Oregon, Washington, and Wisconsin (Maguire and Pastore 2005, 83).

Problems with Partisan and Nonpartisan Elections of Judges

There are several problems with electing judges by popular vote. One criticism is whether either partisan or nonpartisan elections actually reflect the people's choices. Usually, some amount of private financing is behind each judicial candidate. The slate of candidates is generated by different political parties and special-interest groups, regardless of whether elections are partisan or nonpartisan. Thus, those persons who are placed on the ballot may not be the persons most likely to represent the interests of the general public.

But despite the partisan nature of judicial voting, there is evidence to indicate that an attentive public is out there who makes informed selections of judges in their voting booths. Interestingly, investigations of voter knowledge of the judicial selection process show that while voters may not understand fully the nature of voting reforms, they are informed about the opinions and views of the respective judicial candidates (Pinello 1995).

In contrast, research has shown that depending upon the section of the country where judicial selections are made, there is significant partisanship in public voting. For instance, in the South, the Democratic Party has been successful most of the time in the promotion of partisan judicial candidates. Many incumbents in southern criminal courts have been re-elected repeatedly, reflecting the public's interest in maintaining the status quo for both major and minor judgeships. Other areas of the country exhibit strong differences from the South, such as the moralistic and individualistic political culture of the West. Less money is spent on campaign financing for judicial elections in the West compared with the South. Despite the differential impact of money spent, the overriding variable influencing the outcomes of judicial elections in almost every jurisdiction was the party affiliation.

Perhaps the most significant criticism of using elections for filling judicial vacancies is that the most popular judges may not be the most qualified judges. One's political influence may take precedence over one's competence to be a judge. There are no objective criteria used to evaluate one's judicial qualifications. Most jurisdictions do not require judges to pass tests or engage in any sort of qualifying competition for these important posts. Those elected to judicial positions but who lack judging experience are often sent to schools offering crash courses on how to act like judges. These schools attempt to familiarize judges with the rules of criminal procedure and the rules of evidence associated with their jurisdictions. But it is doubtful that any short course on judge-making can bring an unlearned judge to the point where he/she possesses the competence and experience to make the best decisions in important criminal cases. But for better or worse, partisan and nonpartisan elections are prevalent in most states, and it is unlikely that these states will change their methods of judicial selection in the near future. Other methods for judicial selection, judicial appointments by executives, are equally flawed.

Appointments of Judges by Governors

In 2004, governors made the highest appellate **judicial appointments** in four states: California, Maine, New Hampshire, and New Jersey (Maguire and Pastore 2005, 83). Governors may or may not make use of state and local bar association recommendations for judgeships. Gubernatorial appointments are not necessarily made on the basis of which judges are best qualified to serve. Rather, these judgeships are political appointments. Thus, major contributors to a governor's election campaign make recommendations to the governor for particular judgeships, and quite often, these recommendations result in particular judges being appointed (Pinello 1995).

In many other jurisdictions, persons campaign for judgeships much as candidates run for political offices. In fact, politics is the primary contributing factor that accounts for large numbers of nonlawyers in posts such as municipal judges, justices of the peace, and county court judges. There has been considerable debate about whether judges should be appointed or elected, although no judicial selection method has been found superior to others.

Some researchers have observed that gubernatorial judicial appointments in certain jurisdictions result in racial or gender bias in judicial decision making (Pinello 1995).

A study was conducted in 1980–1981 of state supreme court judicial selection according to gubernatorial appointments or merit plans. Questionnaires were mailed to political science professors, judges, and court administrators in each state, with a resulting response of 135 (Glick and Emmert 1987). On the basis of responses, researchers were able to describe and compare judges selected by different methods. Most judges selected by governors rather than the merit system tended to be born out of state, although these judges were from similar regions (e.g., southern governors tended to appoint southern judges, northern governors tended to appoint northern judges). The merit system, however, resulted in selecting judges who graduated from more prestigious law schools (e.g., Harvard, Yale, Columbia) compared with those who were governor-appointed. Protestant judges were more abundant in southern courts, while Catholic and Jewish judges were more prevalent in northern and eastern courts (Glick and Emmert 1987). One interesting outcome of this study was that merit selection tended to result in fewer appointments of women and minorities as judges. Thus, gubernatorial appointments are more likely to yield selections from women and minorities as political considerations. Tables 5.2, 5.3, and 5.4 show the method of selection and length and retention terms of the highest state appellate court justices, intermediate appellate court judges, and judges in courts of general jurisdiction.

Table 5.2 shows that of June 2004, six states used partisan elections for selecting judges, while 14 states used nonpartisan elections. Twenty-five states used nominating commissions, while governors appointed judges in four states. Only one state used a legislative appointment (Maguire and Pastore 2005, 83–87). Judicial terms for state supreme court justices range from 6 to 15 years, although in three states (Massachusetts, New Hampshire, and Rhode Island), these selections are for life or until age 70 is reached. Most of these states have retention elections following the different judicial terms.

Table 5.3 shows the method of selection, length of term, and retention process for state intermediate appellate court judges. For the most part, the selection methods for intermediate judiciary are the same as for state supreme court justices. However, the terms of intermediate appellate judges are somewhat shorter, ranging from 6 to 12 years with a median. Most of these states also have retention elections following the different judicial terms similar to those held for supreme court justices (Maguire and Pastore 2005, 85).

Table 5.4 shows the method of selection and the length of initial and retention terms for state general jurisdiction judges. Over 30 of these states used partisan or nonpartisan elections for these judges in 1999. The terms of these general jurisdiction judges ranged from 4 to 15 years (Maguire and Pastore 2005, 86–87).

Problems with Politically Appointed Judges

Politically appointed judges raise several important issues, however. Some of these issues are the same as those raised in jurisdictions where partisan and nonpartisan elections are used to fill judicial vacancies. Are the most qualified persons selected for the judgeship? An investigation of elected and appointed judges for the California Superior Court from 1959 to 1977 compared their demographic characteristics, educational backgrounds, and pre-judicial career experiences (Dubois 1990). Of the 739 judges investigated, 662 of them had been appointed. Most of these had earlier careers as attorneys or had some previous legal experience. When their decisions were examined for technical accuracy and legal justification, however, no significant differences between elected or appointed judges were found (Dubois 1990). No conclusions could be made about which selection method was best when the quality of their judicial decision making was compared.

Another issue is whether political appointments contribute to corruption among the judiciary. Judges, because of their powerful positions, may influence trial outcomes, dismiss cases, or find innocent defendants guilty. They can also regulate the harshness of penalties imposed whenever a jury verdict of guilty is rendered. All states have judicial sanctioning boards. These are usually operated through state bar associations, and provisions exist for officially questioning judicial behavior. Studies comparing the qualities of judges elected versus those appointed tend to show little difference in placing high-quality judges on the bench. Judicial accountability versus judicial independence models don't seem to differ significantly as means for improving the quality of judges generally (Blankenship, Sparger, and Janikowski 1994).

Some jurisdictions, such as Pennsylvania, have attempted to hold the governor primarily accountable in instances where political judicial appointments have resulted in the selection of either incompetent or corrupt judges (*Villanova Law Review* 1982). Particularly with respect to gubernatorial appointments of appellate judges, insufficient monitoring methods have historically been used that have resulted in occasional selections of poor judges. Suggested alternative judicial selection methods include a gubernatorial appointment system whereby the records of prospective judicial appointees can be carefully scrutinized by the press and state bar associations. Further, all gubernatorial candidates would have to be approved by the state legislature through some type of confirmation process (*Villanova Law Review* 1982). Perhaps the best method of judicial selection is on the basis of merit.

Merit Selection of Judges

Prior to 1933, no state had any type of **merit selection** plan for filling vacant judgeships. By far the most popular methods of selecting judges involved partisan and nonpartisan elections. Other systems used included gubernatorial or

TABLE 5.2 METHOD OF SELECTION AND LENGTH OF INITIAL AND RETENTION TERMS OF THE HIGHEST APPELLATE COURT JUSTICES

By State, as of June 2004

State	Initial selection		Retention	
	Method[a]	Term	Method	Term (in years)
Alabama	Partisan election	6 years	Partisan election	6
Alaska	Nominating commission	Until next general election but not less than 3 years	Retention election	10
Arizona	Nominating commission	Until next general election but not less than 2 years	Retention election	6
Arkansas	Nonpartisan election	8 years	Nonpartisan election	8
California	Appointed by governor	12 years	Retention election	12
Colorado	Nominating commission	Until next general election but not less than 2 years	Retention election	10
Connecticut	Nominating commission	8 years	Commission reviews, governor renominates, legislature confirms	8
Delaware	Nominating commission	12 years	Competitive reapplication to commission, reappointment by governor, senate confirms	12
District of Columbia[b]	Nominating commission	15 years	Reappointment by judicial tenure commission or President	15
Florida	Nominating commission	Until next general election but not less than 1 year	Retention election	6
Georgia	Nonpartisan election	6 years	Nonpartisan election	6
Hawaii	Nominating commission	10 years	Reappointment by commission	10
Idaho	Nonpartisan election	6 years	Nonpartisan election	6

State	Initial selection method	Initial term	Subsequent selection method	Term (years)
Illinois	Partisan election	10 years	Retention election	10
Indiana	Nominating commission	Until next general election but not less than 2 years	Retention election	10
Iowa	Nominating commission	Until next general election but not less than 1 year	Retention election	8
Kansas	Nominating commission	Until next general election but not less than 1 year	Retention election	6
Kentucky	Nonpartisan election	8 years	Nonpartisan election	8
Louisiana[c]	Partisan election	10 years	Partisan election	10
Maine	Appointed by governor	7 years	Reappointment by governor, legislature confirms	7
Maryland[d]	Nominating commission	Until next general election but not less than 1 year	Retention election	10
Massachusetts	Nominating commission	To age 70	X	X
Michigan[e]	Nonpartisan election	8 years	Nonpartisan election	8
Minnesota	Nonpartisan election	6 years	Nonpartisan election	6
Mississippi	Nonpartisan election	8 years	Nonpartisan election	8
Missouri	Nominating commission	Until next general election but not less than 1 year	Retention election	12
Montana	Nonpartisan election	8 years	Nonpartisan election, but if unopposed, retention election	8
Nebraska	Nominating commission	Until next general election but not less than 3 years	Retention election	6
Nevada	Nonpartisan election	6 years	Nonpartisan election	6
New Hampshire	Appointed by governor[f]	To age 70	X	X
New Jersey	Appointed by governor	7 years	Reappointment by governor, with senate consent	To age 70
New Mexico	Nominating commission	Until next general election	Partisan election the first time; after that, winner runs in retention election	8

(continued)

TABLE 5.2 METHOD OF SELECTION AND LENGTH OF INITIAL AND RETENTION TERMS OF THE HIGHEST APPELLATE COURT JUSTICES, *(continued)*

By State, as of June 2004

State	Initial selection		Retention	
	Method[a]	Term	Method	Term (in years)
New York[d]	Nominating commission	14 years	Competitive reapplication to commission, reappointment by governor, senate confirms	14
North Carolina	Nonpartisan election	8 years	Nonpartisan election	8
North Dakota	Nonpartisan election	10 years	Nonpartisan election	10
Ohio[g]	Nonpartisan election	6 years	Nonpartisan election	6
Oklahoma[h]	Nominating commission	Until next general election but not less than 1 year	Retention election	6
Oregon	Nonpartisan election	6 years	Nonpartisan election	6
Pennsylvania	Partisan election	10 years	Retention election	10
Rhode Island	Nominating commission	Life tenure	X	X
South Carolina	Nominating commission[j]	10 years	Reappointed by legislature	10
South Dakota	Nominating commission	Until next general election but not less than 3 years	Retention election	8
Tennessee	Nominating commission	Until the biennial general election but not less than 30 days	Retention election	8
Texas[h]	Partisan election	6 years	Partisan election	6
Utah	Nominating commission	Until next general election but not less than 3 years	Retention election	10
Vermont	Nominating commission	6 years	Retained by vote in general assembly	6
Virginia	Appointed by legislature	12 years	Reappointed by legislature	12
Washington	Nonpartisan election	6 years	Nonpartisan election	6

West Virginia	Partisan election	12 years	Partisan election	12
Wisconsin	Nonpartisan election	10 years	Nonpartisan election	10
Wyoming	Nominating commission	Until next general election but not less than 1 year	Retention election	8

Note: These data were compiled through a survey of State statutes; they were then verified by personnel of the American Judicature Society.

"Initial selection" is defined as the constitutional or statutory method by which judges are selected for a full term of office. "Retention" refers to the method used to select judges for subsequent terms of office. "Partisan election" refers to elections in which the judicial candidates' names on the ballot with their respective party labels; "nonpartisan election" refers to elections in which no party labels are attached to judicial candidates' names appearing on the ballot. Caution should be used when interpreting partisan and nonpartisan designations as definitions may vary. "Retention election" refers to an election in which a judge runs unopposed on the ballot and the electorate votes solely on the question of the judge's continuation in office. In a retention election, the judge must win a majority of the vote in order to serve a full term, except in Illinois which requires 60% and New Mexico which requires 57%. "Nominating commission" is a merit selection procedure that refers to the nonpartisan body, composed of lawyers and nonlawyers, which actively recruits, screens, and nominates prospective judicial candidates to the executive for appointment. The nominating commission method of selection was established by executive order in Delaware, Maryland, and Massachusetts and by constitutional or statutory authority in all other jurisdictions. Readers should consult State Constitutions for special provisions and procedures related to issues of premature vacancy (e.g., death, resignation) and other circumstances.

[a]In States that use nominating commissions, selection requirements may vary. The governor may make the appointment solely, with senate confirmation, or with legislative confirmation.

[b]Initial appointment is made by the President of the United States and confirmed by the Senate. At expiration of term, judge's performance is reviewed by the commission. Those found "well qualified" are automatically reappointed. For those found "qualified," the President may nominate for an additional term, subject to Senate confirmation. If the President does not wish to reappoint the judge, the District of Columbia Nomination Commission compiles a new list of candidates.

[c]Although party affiliation of judicial candidates appears on ballots, judicial primaries are open and candidates generally do not solicit party support. This gives judicial elections a nonpartisan character.

[d]The highest State court is named the Court of Appeals.

[e]Party affiliation of judicial candidates are not listed on the general election ballot, so the election is technically nonpartisan. However, candidates are nominated at party conventions.

[f]Subject to approval of an elected five-member executive council.

[g]Party affiliations of judicial candidates are not listed on the general election ballot, so the election is technically nonpartisan. However, candidates run in partisan primary elections.

[h]Oklahoma and Texas have two courts of final jurisdiction: the supreme court, which has final civil jurisdiction; and the court of criminal appeals, which has final criminal jurisdiction. The selection process is the same for both.

[i]The Judicial Merit Selection Commission screens and then recommends a list of judicial candidates to the legislature. The legislature votes only on the list submitted by the commission. If all candidates on the list are rejected, the process begins again with the commission.

Source: American Judicature Society, *Judicial Selection in the United States: A Compendium of Provisions*, 2nd edition (Chicago: American Judicature Society, 1993); http://www.ajs.org/js/judicialselectioncharts.pdf [Jan. 25, 2005]; and data provided by the American Judicature Society. Reprinted by permission.

TABLE 5.3 METHOD OF SELECTION AND LENGTH OF INITIAL AND RETENTION TERMS OF INTERMEDIATE APPELLATE COURT JUDGES IN 39 STATES

As of June 2004

State	Initial selection		Retention	
	Method[a]	Term	Method	Term (in years)
Alabama[b]	Partisan election	6 years	Partisan election	6
Alaska	Nominating commission	Until next general election but not less than 3 years	Retention election	8
Arizona	Nominating commission	Until next general election but not less than 2 years	Retention election	6
Arkansas	Nonpartisan election	8 years	Nonpartisan election	8
California	Appointed governor	12 years	Retention election	12
Colorado	Nominating commission	Until next general election but not less than 2 years	Retention election	8
Connecticut	Nominating commission	8 years	Commission reviews, governor renominates, legislature confirms	8
Florida	Nominating commission	Until next general election but not less than 1 year	Retention election	6
Georgia	Nonpartisan election	6 years	Nonpartisan election	6
Hawaii	Nominating commission	10 years	Reappointment by commission	10
Idaho	Nonpartisan election	6 years	Nonpartisan election	6
Illinois	Partisan election	10 years	Retention election	10
Indiana	Nominating commission	Until next general election but not less than 2 years	Retention election	10
Iowa	Nominating commission	Until next general election but not less than 1 year	Retention election	6
Kansas	Nominating commission	Until next general election but not less than 1 year	Retention election	4
Kentucky	Nonpartisan election	8 years	Nonpartisan election	8
Louisiana[c]	Partisan election	10 years	Partisan election	10
Maryland	Nominating commission	Until next general election but not less than 1 year	Retention election	10
Massachusetts	Nominating commission	To age 70	X	X
Michigan	Nonpartisan election	6 years	Nonpartisan election	6
Minnesota	Nonpartisan election	6 years	Nonpartisan election	6

State	Initial selection	Term	Subsequent selection	Years
Mississippi	Nonpartisan election	8 years	Nonpartisan election	8
Missouri	Nominating commission	Until next general election but not less than 1 year	Retention election	12
Nebraska	Nominating commission	Until next general election but not less than 3 years	Retention election	6
New Jersey	Appointed by governor	7 years	Reappointment by governor with senate consent	To age 70
New Mexico	Nominating commission	Until next general election	Partisan election the first time: after that, winner runs in retention election	8
New York	Nominating commission	5 years	Commission reviews, makes recommendation to governor, governor reappoints	5
North Carolina	Nonpartisan election	8 years	Nonpartisan election	8
Ohio[d]	Nonpartisan election	6 years	Nonpartisan election	6
Oklahoma	Nominating commission	Until next general election but not less than 1 year	Retention election	6
Oregon	Nonpartisan election	6 years	Nonpartisan election	6
Pennsylvania[e]	Partisan election	10 years	Retention election	10
South Carolina	Nominating commission[f]	6 years	Reappointed by legislature	6
Tennessee[b]	Nominating commission	Until the biennial general election but not less than 30 days	Retention election	8
Texas	Partisan election	6 years	Partisan election	6
Utah	Nominating commission	Until next general election but not less than 3 years	Retention election	6
Virginia	Appointed by legislature	8 years	Reappointed by legislature	8
Washington	Nonpartisan election	6 years	Nonpartisan election	6
Wisconsin	Nonpartisan election	6 years	Nonpartisan election	6

Note: See Note, table 1.91. States not listed do not have intermediate appellate courts.

[a] In States that use nominating commissions, selection requirements may vary. The governor makes the appointment solely, with senate confirmation, or with legislative confirmation.

[b] Alabama and Tennessee have two intermediate appellate courts: the court of civil appeals, which has civil jurisdiction, and the court of criminal appeals, which has criminal jurisdiction. The selection process is the same for both.

[c] Although party affiliation of judicial candidates appears on ballots, judicial primaries are open and candidates generally do not solicit party support. This gives judicial elections a nonpartisan character.

[d] Party affiliations of judicial candidates are not listed on the general election ballots, so the election is technically nonpartisan. However, candidates run in partisan primary elections.

[e] Pennsylvania has two intermediate appellate courts; the superior court and the commonwealth court. The selection process is the same for both.

[f] The Judicial Merit Selection Commission screens and then recommends a list of judicial candidates to the legislature. The legislature votes only on the list submitted by the commission. If all candidates on the list are rejected, the process begins again with the commission.

Source: American Judicature Society. Judicial Selection in the United States: A Compendium of Provisions, 2nd edition (Chicago: American Judicature Society, 1993); http://www.ajs.org/js/judicialselectioncharts.pdf (Jan. 25, 2005); and data provided by the American Judicature Society. Reprinted by permission.

TABLE 5.4   METHOD OF SELECTION AND LENGTH OF INITIAL AND RETENTION TERMS OF GENERAL JURISDICTION COURT JUDGES

By State and name of court, as of June 2004

State/name of court(s)	Initial selection		Retention	
	Method[a]	Term	Method	Term (in years)
Alabama Circuit court	Partisan election	6 years	Partisan election	6
Alaska Superior court	Nominating commission	Until next general election but not less than 3 years	Retention election	6
Arizona Superior court[b]	Nominating commission	Until next general election but not less than 2 years	Retention election	4
Arkansas Circuit court	Nonpartisan election	6 years	Nonpartisan election	6
California Superior court	Nonpartisan election or gubernatorial appointment[c]	6 years	Nonpartisan election[d]	6
Colorado District court	Nominating commission	Until next general election but not less than 2 years	Retention election	6
Connecticut Superior court	Nominating commission	8 years	Commission reviews, governor renominates, legislature confirms	8
Delaware Superior court	Nominating commission	12 years	Competitive reapplication to commission, reappointment by governor, senate confirms	12
District of Columbia Superior court[e]	Nominating commission	15 years	Reappointment by judicial tenure commission or President	15

State / Court	Initial selection	Term	Retention	
Florida				
Circuit court[f]	Nonpartisan election	6 years	Nonpartisan election	6
Georgia				
Superior court	Nonpartisan election	4 years	Nonpartisan election	4
Hawaii				
Circuit court	Nominating commission	10 years	Reappointment by commission	10
Idaho				
District court	Nonpartisan election	4 years	Nonpartisan election	4
Illinois				
Circuit court	Partisan election[g]	6 years	Retention election	6
Indiana				
Circuit court	Partisan election[h]	6 years	Partisan election[h]	6
Superior court	Partisan election[i]	6 years[j]	Partisan election[k]	6
Iowa				
District court	Nominating commission	Until next general election but not less than 1 year	Retention election	6
Kansas				
District court	Nominating commission, partisan election[l]	Until next general election	Retention election[m]	4
Kentucky				
Circuit court	Nonpartisan election	8 years	Nonpartisan election	8
Louisiana[n]				
District court	Partisan election	6 years	Partisan election	6
Maine				
Superior court	Appointed by governor	7 years	Reappointment by governor, legislature confirms	7
Maryland				
Circuit court	Nominating commission	Until next general election but not less than 1 year	Nonpartisan election	15
Massachusetts				
Trial Court of the Commonwealth	Nominating commission	To age 70	X	X
Michigan				
Circuit court	Nonpartisan election	6 years	Nonpartisan election	6

(continued)

TABLE 5.4 METHOD OF SELECTION AND LENGTH OF INITIAL AND RETENTION TERMS OF GENERAL JURISDICTION COURT JUDGES, *(continued)*

By State and name of court, as of June 2004

State/name of court(s)	Initial selection		Retention	
	Method[a]	Term	Method	Term (in years)
Minnesota				
District court	Nonpartisan election	6 years	Nonpartisan election	6
Mississippi				
Circuit court	Nonpartisan election	4 years	Nonpartisan election	4
Chancery court	Nonpartisan election	4 years	Nonpartisan election	4
Missouri				
Circuit court	Partisan election[o]	6 years[p]	Partisan election[q]	6
Montana				
District court	Nonpartisan election	6 years	Nonpartisan election, but if unopposed, retention election	6
Nebraska				
District court	Nominating commission	Until next general election but not less than 3 years	Retention election	6
Nevada				
District court	Nonpartisan election	6 years	Nonpartisan election	6
New Hampshire				
Superior court	Appointed by governor[r]	To age 70	X	X
New Jersey				
Superior court	Appointed by governor	7 years	Reappointment by governor with senate consent	To age 70
New Mexico				
District court	Nominating commission	Until next general election	Partisan election the first time: after that, winner runs in retention election	6
New York				
Supreme court	Partisan election	14 years	Partisan election	14
County court	Partisan election	10 years	Partisan election	10

State / Court		Term		
North Carolina				
Superior court	Nonpartisan election	8 years	Nonpartisan election	8
North Dakota				
District court	Nonpartisan election	6 years	Nonpartisan election	6
Ohio[s]				
Common Pleas court	Nonpartisan election	6 years	Nonpartisan election	6
Oklahoma				
District court	Nonpartisan election	4 years	Nonpartisan election	4
Oregon				
Circuit court	Nonpartisan election	6 years	Nonpartisan election	6
Pennsylvania				
Common Pleas court	Partisan election	10 years	Retention election	10
Rhode Island				
Superior court	Nominating commission	Life tenure	X	X
South Carolina				
Circuit court	Nominating commission[t]	6 years	Reappointed by legislature	6
South Dakota				
Circuit court	Nonpartisan election	8 years	Nonpartisan election	8
Tennessee				
Circuit court	Nominating commission	8 years	Partisan election	8
Texas				
District court	Partisan election	4 years	Partisan election	4
Utah				
District court	Nominating commission	Until next general election but not less than 3 years	Retention election	6
Vermont				
Superior court	Nominating commission	6 years	Retained by vote in general assembly	6
Virginia				
Circuit court	Appointed by legislature	8 years	Reappointed by legislature	8
Washington				
Superior court	Nonpartisan election	4 years	Nonpartisan election	4

(continued)

TABLE 5.4 METHOD OF SELECTION AND LENGTH OF INITIAL AND RETENTION TERMS OF GENERAL JURISDICTION COURT JUDGES, *(continued)*

By State and name of court, as of June 2004

State/name of court(s)	Initial selection		Retention	
	Method[a]	Term	Method	Term (in years)
West Virginia				
Circuit court	Partisan election	8 years	Partisan election	8
Wisconsin				
Circuit court	Nonpartisan election	6 years	Nonpartisan election	6
Wyoming				
District court	Nominating commission	Until next general election but not less than 1 year	Retention election	6

Note: See Note, table 1.91. Courts of general jurisdiction are defined as having unlimited civil and criminal jurisdiction (Larry C. Berkson, "Judicial Selection in the United States: A Special Report," *Judicature* 64 (October 1980) p. 178).

[a] In States that use nominating commissions, appointment procedures may vary. The governor may make the appointment solely, with senate confirmation, or with legislative confirmation.

[b] Counties with populations less than 250,000 select and retain superior court judges in nonpartisan elections for 4-year terms.

[c] Local electors can choose either nonpartisan elections or gubernatorial appointment.

[d] Judge must be elected to a full term on a nonpartisan ballot at the next general election. If the election is not contested, the incumbent's name does not appear on the ballot.

[e] Initial appointment is made by the President of the United States and confirmed by the Senate. At expiration of term, judge's performance is reviewed by the commission. Those found "well qualified" are automatically reappointed. For those found "qualified," the President may nominate for an additional term, subject to Senate confirmation. If the President does not wish to reappoint the judge, the District of Columbia Nomination Commission compiles a new list of candidates.

[f] Voters in each circuit may opt for merit selection and retention of circuit court judges.

[g] Circuit court associate judges are appointed by the circuit judges in each circuit for 4-year terms, as provided by supreme court rule.

[h] In Vanderburgh County initial selection and retention are by nonpartisan election.

[i] A nominating commission is used for the superior court judges of Lake and St. Joseph Counties. In Allen and Vanderburgh Counties the election is nonpartisan.

[j] In Lake and St. Joseph Counties each appointed judge serves until the next general election but not less than 2 years.

[k] Nonpartisan elections are used in Allen and Vanderburgh Counties. Retention elections are used in Lake and St. Joseph Counties.

[l] Seventeen of 31 districts use a nominating commission for district judge selection; the remaining 14 select district judges in partisan elections.

[m] Fourteen of 31 districts use partisan elections.

[n] Although party affiliation of judicial candidates appears on ballots, judicial primaries are open and candidates generally do not solicit party support. This gives judicial elections a nonpartisan character.

[o] Nominating commissions are used for selecting circuit court judges in Jackson, Clay, Platte, and St. Louis Counties.

[p] An associate circuit court judge's term is 4 years; also in counties that use nominating commissions, the appointed judge serves until the next general election but not less that 1 year.

[q] Retention elections are used in Jackson, Clay, Platte, and St. Louis Counties.

[r] Subject to approval by an elected five-member executive council.

[s] Party affiliations of judicial candidates are not listed on the general election ballot, so the election is technically nonpartisan. However, candidates run in partisan primary elections.

[t] The Judicial Merit Selection Commission screens and then recommends a list of judicial candidates to the legislature. The legislature votes on the list submitted by the commission. If all candidates on the list are rejected, the process begins again with the commission.

Source: American Judicature Society. *Judicial Selection in the United States: A Compendium of Provisions*, 2nd edition (Chicago: American Judicature Society, 1993); http://www.ajs.org/js/judicialselectioncharts.pdf [Jan. 25, 2005]; and data provided by the American Judicature Society. Reprinted by permission.

legislative appointments. One reason for the slow adoption of merit systems for judicial appointments is the strong sentiment in predominantly rural communities for the elective process. By the early 1990s, 15 states and the District of Columbia had evolved merit systems for filling judicial vacancies. These included Alaska, Arizona, Colorado, Connecticut, Delaware, District of Columbia, Hawaii, Iowa, Kansas, Maryland, Massachusetts, Nebraska, New Mexico, Utah, Vermont, and Wyoming. By 2004, 25 states had nominating commissions to select judges to fill the highest appellate vacancies (Maguire and Pastore 2005, 83).

The Missouri Plan

A popular method of judicial selection adopted by several states is the **Missouri plan.** The Missouri plan was introduced in 1940 and is a method of judicial selection using the merit system for appointments to judgeships (President's Commission on Law Enforcement 1967, 66–67). The essential features of the Missouri plan are:

1. A nominating committee consisting of lawyers and nonlawyers appointed by the governor and chaired by a judge.
2. A listing of qualified candidates who are nominated by the committee for each judicial vacancy.
3. Each judicial vacancy is filled by the governor by referring to the list of candidates nominated by the committee.
4. Any appointed judge seeking reelection will run only on the issue of whether or not he/she should be retained on the basis of merit.

The Missouri plan is a version of the 1914 **Kales plan** (Kales 1914). The Kales plan has survived in various forms in several states over the years, and its influence on the Missouri plan is evident. The Kales plan requires a nonpartisan committee of lawyers, judges, and nonjudicial personnel to draft a list of the most qualified judicial candidates on the basis of their records and expertise. This list is then submitted to the governor to make judicial appointments. Judicial vacancies occur because of death, retirement, or removal because of incompetence. Any choice a governor makes from the approved list would by definition be a good choice. Ideally, politics is removed from such gubernatorial appointments.

But some critics question whether *any* merit plan including both the Kales and Missouri versions can eliminate politics from judicial selection (Blankenship, Sparger, and Janikowski 1994). However, other analysts find the merit plan useful for promoting greater accountability and fairness among judges (Scheb 1988).

One way of making the merit selection plan more palatable to the public is to ensure that the qualification procedures for judicial applicants should be made more rigorous (Dubois 1990). In effect, a thorough screening procedure should be operative as a standard against which to compare different judicial candidates. Thus, when the matter of selecting a judge to fill a judgeship arises, the public knows that all judicial nominees have been thoroughly screened and tested concerning their competency and abilities.

One troubling aspect of merit selection occurs in those states where governors have the power to appoint **interim judges** to fill unexpected vacancies. When a judge dies, becomes infirm, or unable to perform his/her duties in midterm, governors make temporary judicial appointments without consulting any merit selection committee. Interim judges generally have an easier time as **incumbents** when it comes time to appoint a new judge for a subsequent term. The politicalization of the interim judicial appointment process is furthered by gubernatorial appointments of nominating committee members who convene later to review the credentials of applications for new judicial vacancies.

In some instances, governors have removed themselves entirely from the judicial selection process, even from the process of appointing interim judges to fill temporary vacancies. In New Mexico, for instance, a judicial nominating commission is in place and acts to screen and fill temporary judicial vacancies. The nominating commission submits their recommendations to the governor, and the governor appoints particular persons to vacant judgeships. Thus, the governor is not directly involved in candidate screenings or selecting judges on the basis of his/her own preferences, independent of some nominating commission. Several other states that have nominating commissions include Delaware, Georgia, Maryland, Massachusetts, Minnesota, New York, North Carolina, Pennsylvania, Rhode Island, and West Virginia (Vago 2006).

Under President Jimmy Carter, Executive Order 11972 was issued, establishing the U.S. Circuit Judge Nominating Commission. This commission radically altered the method of selecting federal judges. Carter wanted to devise a system whereby judges would be appointed on the basis of their professional merit and potential for quality service on the bench. Further, he wanted to develop a mechanism that would allow him to place larger numbers of women and minorities in judgeships. One criticism of this method of judicial selection is that Carter may have undermined the merit system in favor of affirmative action considerations. During his presidency, Carter selected 86 percent of the judges from his own Democratic party. However, he dramatically increased the presence of women and minorities on the federal bench, with 25 percent being women and 29 percent being racial or ethnic minorities. Subsequently, other U.S. presidents have made partisan judicial appointments (Goldman et al. 2003).

Legislative Appointments of Judges

In 2004 only Virginia appointed judges to the highest appellate bench through legislative elections. Nominating committees advance a list of judicial candidates for legislative approval. Legislative voting results in the appointment of judges to benches in various state jurisdictions. Although legislative appointments of judges affect only a small portion of the total federal and state judiciary, the impact of legislatively selected judges has been studied by several researchers. Daniel Pinello (1995) has indicated that where judges have been selected by legislatures compared with those selected by partisan/nonpartisan elections or by gubernatorial appointments, their subsequent performance as judges has been characterized as acquiescent and inactive. Governor-appointed judges tend to choose the interests of individuals over state interests more often than legislatively appointed judges.

Legislative appointments are extremely political and reflect the political leanings of legislators who have been voted into office by the citizens of the state. Thus, a legislature controlled by Democrats might be disposed to appoint Democrat judges, while Republican-dominated legislatures would be expected to appoint Republican judges. Relatively little depends upon the qualifications of those considered to hold judgeships in these jurisdictions. There is a great propensity on the part of state legislators to appoint former legislators to judicial vacancies. Also, any person in the state who has formerly held a political office stands a much greater chance of receiving a judicial appointment from the legislature compared with someone without political experience. Does the legislature appoint the most qualified persons to vacant judgeships? Not if these appointments are based on former political ties to the legislature or other political offices within the state. Virtually the same thing can be said of gubernatorial appointments, which are most often made on the basis that an appointed judge has held one or more state political offices.

Are Merit Systems for Judicial Selection Better Than Election Methods?

The debate over which judge selection plan is best is largely dependent upon the assumption that it makes some kind of measurable difference which plan is used—that one plan results in better-qualified judges. However, there are few discernible differences among the various plans in terms of the quality of judges. Partisan elections may not produce better judges than other means of selection, but neither, apparently, do they produce worse ones (Swain 1985). According to one view, the legal profession tends to ignore research findings and blindly and steadfastly adheres to the Missouri merit selection method. One proposed but unlikely modification would be to democratize the Missouri plan by rectifying some of its major weaknesses (Swain 1985).

For many decades, it has been assumed by the public that judicial selection systems that emphasize merit rather than political interests create greater judicial accountability and independence. Elections are perceived as popularity contests, often rigged to accommodate one vested interest group or another. Gubernatorial selection methods result in the appointment of political hacks as judges who cater to the interests of the governor and the governor's friends. Merit selection, it is argued, results in the most qualified persons per-forming judicial roles. However, several researchers have raised questions about whether any of these methods is better than the rest. Michael Blanken-ship, Jerry Sparger, and Richard Janikowski (1994) suggest that the election-merit selection dichotomy is more a myth than fact. They contend that appointive methods for selecting judges are no more effective than the elective process in placing qualified judges on the bench. They add that neither elec-tions nor appointments of judicial candidates succeed in fulfilling the long-range philosophical expectations of judicial accountability and independence.

Federal Judicial Selection Methods

The Nature of U.S. Supreme Court Appointments

The president of the United States exerts direct influence on the nature of U.S. Supreme Court appointments and judicial appointments to lower federal courts. The president recommends persons for district, circuit, and supreme court judgeships, with the advice and consent of Congress. U.S. Supreme Court appointments have not necessarily depended upon previous judicial ex-perience, however. From 1930 to 1967, there were 23 U.S. Supreme Court jus-tices appointed. Of these, only seven had previous federal judge experience with all but one serving five or fewer years on the federal bench. And only four of these 23 appointments had experience as state judges. Only former Justice Cardozo, appointed in 1932, had more than eight years' experience, having served 18 years in state courts.

U.S. Supreme Court Justiceships are appointments by the president of the United States, subject to Congressional approval. These are lifetime ap-pointments. In 2004, the salary of U.S. Supreme Court Justices was $194,300. Because these judgeships are presidential appointments, they often reflect a president's vested interests. Therefore, judges with judicial philosophies con-sistent with those of the president are appointed instead of other, sometimes more qualified, judges who hold contrary philosophies. When former Presi-dent George Bush, a Republican, nominated Clarence Thomas, also a Repub-lican, to fill a U.S. Supreme Court vacancy, the nomination was hotly debated by the U.S. Senate Judiciary Committee after examining Thomas's views on various issues. Those most critical of Thomas were Senate Democrats. Politi-cal differences were influential in Judge Thomas's eventual acceptance as a Supreme Court justice. Considerable time and attention focused upon sexual harassment allegations against Judge Thomas by Anita Hill, a University of Oklahoma professor who had worked for him. Conflicting testimony before the Judiciary Committee left many persons doubting Hill's accusations and Judge Thomas's appointment to the U.S. Supreme Court was approved.

During the 1990s, two U.S. Supreme Court justices were appointed by President Bill Clinton, a Democrat. His most significant appointment was Ruth Bader Ginsburg in 1993. She was the first Democrat to serve on the U.S. Supreme Court in 26 years as well as the second woman appointed since Sandra Day O'Connor. Although there have been Jewish U.S. Supreme Court Justices in past years, Justice Ginsburg's appointment marked another turning point in the composition of the U.S. Supreme Court as well as the religious composition of it became more diverse.

In 2006, George W. Bush's nomination of Harriet Miers, former White House counsel and longtime advisor to the president, sparked intense debate from both Democrats and Republicans who argued that she didn't have the constitutional or judicial experience necessary for appointment to the bench. Miers subsequently withdrew her nomination after the likelihood of a confirmation seemed slim.

Presidential appointments to the U.S. Supreme Court are also characterized according to whether the appointees are conservative, liberal, or moderate. U.S. Supreme Court justices under Republican administrations have tended to be very conservative or conservative, while justices appointed under Democratic administrations have tended to be moderate or liberal. These philosophical orientations have been very crucial in determining various social policies during the last 50 years. For instance, in the 1960s, the chief justice of the U.S. Supreme Court was Earl Warren, who had been appointed to the high court in 1953 by President Dwight Eisenhower. When Warren became chief justice, the Court became known as the "Warren court." Under Warren's guidance, the U.S. Supreme Court made a number of rulings that regulated police tactics relative to custodial interrogations and searches and seizures. During Warren's tenure as chief justice, the U.S. Supreme Court seemed to be anti-police, since many of its rulings were viewed by critics as tying the hands of law enforcement officers when investigating crimes. The most notable rulings included *Mapp v. Ohio* (1961), which required police officers to have search warrants before conducting searches of one's premises, and *Miranda v. Arizona* (1966), which required police officers to advise suspects of their right to an attorney prior to being interrogated.

Later U.S. Supreme Courts issued rulings that created various exceptions to warrantless searches and effectively untied the hands of police. Under Warren E. Burger, the chief justice of the U.S. Supreme Court who was appointed by President Richard M. Nixon in 1969, the "Berger court" established the "totality of circumstances" and "good faith" exceptions to the exclusionary rule, which permitted law enforcement officers considerable latitude when conducting warrantless searches of one's premises, person, and automobile. During the 1990s, the newly configured U.S. Supreme Court presided over by Chief Justice William H. Rehnquist, the "Rehnquist court," has issued more conservative rulings relating to searches and seizures. These rulings resemble those of the Warren court 40 years earlier.

Will the newly appointed chief justice, John Roberts, follow in Rehnquist's footsteps? Roberts was once a clerk for Rehnquist, and Rehnquist's teaching has had an impact on Robert's life and legal career. It is likely that the Court will continue to steer to the right with Roberts at the helm.

Thus, the influence of presidential appointments on the composition of the U.S. Supreme Court cannot be ignored. These appointments, which are highly political, are intended to increase the likelihood of particular social agendas contemplated by those presidents making such appointments. During any election year, a key factor governing one's decision to vote for one presidential candidate or another is what types of Supreme Court justices will be appointed and what will be the nature of their decision making in future years? Since these appointments are lifetime appointments, the long-term social policy implications are quite clear.

Circuit Court Judgeships

Judges who serve in Circuit Courts of Appeal are appointed by the president of the United States. Their nomination by the president must be approved by the advice and consent of Congress. The salary of United States circuit judges was $165,500 in 2003. The Senate Judiciary Committee hears arguments both for and against these presidential appointees and either approves or rejects them. Not all nominated judges are acceptable to the Senate Judiciary Committee. One example of a rejection is the case of Miami U.S. District Court Judge Kenneth L. Ryskamp, who had been appointed as a federal district judge by then-president Ronald Reagan in 1986. At that time, the Senate Judiciary Committee recommended his nomination and his appointment was eventually confirmed. However, during the next five years on the federal bench, Judge Ryskamp made numerous disparaging remarks of racial and ethnic minorities. When the Senate Judiciary Committee conducted a subsequent hearing of Ryskamp's qualifications for the Circuit Court of Appeals judgeship in April 1991, committee members called to Ryskamp's attention remarks that he had made once to four blacks who filed suit after being mauled by police dogs. Ryskamp told the four blacks that "It might not be inappropriate to carry around a few scars to remind you of your wrongdoing," even though two of the four were never actually charged with a crime. He also complained from the federal bench that some people were thin-skinned if they took offense at calling a black area "colored town." Judge Ryskamp also belonged to a Miami country club that excluded blacks and Jews. Also while in Washington, Ryskamp failed to follow recommendations from Washington politicians or adhere to advice given him from his aides. When President George Bush nominated Ryskamp to the Circuit Court of Appeals encompassing Florida, Georgia, and Alabama, there would have been a conservative majority among the judges. While President George Bush had 76 previous confirmation victories and the Senate Judiciary Committee hadn't rejected any Republican president nomination since 1988, they did reject Ryskamp.

Tables 5.5 shows the characteristics of appellate judicial appointees by presidential administration for the years 1963–1998. It is observed that presidential appointments in most cases involve persons who are members of the president's political party.

Table 5.5 shows, for instance, that 95 percent of Democratic President Lyndon Johnson's circuit court judicial appointments were Democrats; 93 percent of Republican President Richard Nixon's appointments were Republicans; 92 percent of Republican President Gerald Ford's appointments were Republicans; 82 percent of Democratic President Jimmy Carter's appointments were Democrats; 96 percent of Republican President Ronald Reagan's appointments were Republicans; 89 percent of Republican President George H. W. Bush's appointments were Republicans; 85 percent of Democratic President Bill Clinton's appointments were Democrats; and 81 percent of George W. Bush's appointments were Republican. President Lyndon Johnson's and President Bill Clinton's appointments were regarded by the American Bar Association as exceptionally well qualified as circuit court judges, while President Ford and President Reagan had the lowest ratings of their circuit judgeship appointments, with ratings of 58–59 percent as exceptionally well qualified.

Table 5.5 also shows an interesting pattern of circuit judicial appointments over time according to gender of appointees. Presidents Johnson, Nixon, and Ford made male appointments to circuit judgeships almost exclusively during their administrations. President Carter was the first to appoint nearly 20 percent women to these posts. President Reagan's appointments returned the pattern to the Johnson-Nixon-Ford years, with over 95 percent of all circuit judgeship appointments being male. But presidents Bush, Clinton, and now George W. Bush have appointed more women to these positions. President Clinton, in fact, nominated women in about a third of all appointments. This percentage was unprecedented during all previous presidential administrations.

President George W. Bush appointed the greatest percentage of blacks (18.8 percent) to circuit court posts, followed by President Clinton (10.4 percent), however President Clinton appointed the largest percentage of Hispanic judges to these positions (11.5 percent).

U.S. District Court Judges

There were 678 federal district judges in 2003 (Maguire and Pastore 2005). Federal district judges are also appointed by the president of the United States. They also serve life terms. Annual salaries of federal district court judges in 2004 were $158,100. Federal district judges who serve ten or more

TABLE 5.5 CHARACTERISTICS OF PRESIDENTIAL APPOINTEES TO U.S. COURTS OF APPEALS JUDGESHIPS

By Presidential administration, 1963–2002[a]

	President Johnson's appointees 1963–68[b] (N=40)	President Nixon's appointees 1969–74 (N=45)	President Ford's appointees 1974–76 (N=12)	President Carter's appointees 1977–80 (N=56)	President Reagan's appointees 1981–88 (N=78)	President George H.W.Bush's appointees 1989–92 (N=37)	President Clinton's appointees 1993–2000 (N=61)	President George W. Bush's appointees 2001–2002 (N=16)
Sex								
Male	97.5%	100%	100%	80.4%	94.9%	81.1%	67.2%	81.2%
Female	2.5	0	0	19.6	5.1	18.9	32.8	18.8
Race, ethnicity								
White	95.0	97.8	100	78.6	97.4	89.2	73.8	81.2
Black	5.0	0	0	16.1	1.3	5.4	13.1	18.8
Hispanic	0	0	0	3.6	1.3	5.4	11.5	0
Asian	0	2.2	0	1.8	0	0	1.6	0
Education, undergraduate								
Public-supported	32.5	40.0	50.0	30.4	24.4	29.7	44.3	43.8
Private (not Ivy League)	40.0	35.6	41.7	51.8	51.3	59.5	34.4	37.5
Ivy League	17.5	20.0	8.3	17.9	24.4	10.8	21.3	18.8
None indicated	10.0	4.4	0	0	0	0	0	0
Education, law school								
Public-supported	40.0	37.8	50.0	39.3	41.0	32.4	39.3	50.0
Private (not Ivy League)	32.5	26.7	25.0	19.6	35.9	37.8	31.1	25.0
Ivy League	27.5	35.6	25.0	41.1	23.1	29.7	29.5	25.0
Occupation at nomination or appointment								
Politics or government	10.0	4.4	8.3	5.4	6.4	10.8	6.6	6.2
Judiciary	57.5	53.3	75.0	46.4	55.1	59.5	52.5	50.0
Law firm, large	5.0	4.4	8.3	10.7	14.1	16.2	18.0	6.2

Law firm, medium	17.5	22.2	8.3	16.1	9.0	10.8	13.1	12.5
Law firm, small	7.5	6.7	0	5.4	1.3	0	1.6	6.2
Professor of law	2.5	2.2	0	14.3	12.8	2.7	8.2	12.5
Other	0	6.7	0	1.8	1.3	0	0	6.2
Occupational experience								
Judicial	65.0	57.8	75.0	53.6	60.3	62.2	59.0	68.8
Prosecutorial	47.5	46.7	25.0	30.4	28.2	29.7	37.7	25.0
Other	20.0	17.8	25.0	39.3	34.6	32.4	29.5	25.0
Political party								
Democrat	95.0	6.7	8.3	82.1	0	2.7	85.2	12.5
Republican	5.0	93.3	91.7	7.1	96.2	89.2	6.6	81.2
Independent	0	0	0	10.7	2.6	8.1	8.2	6.2
Other	0	0	0	0	1.3	0	0	0
American Bar Association rating								
Exceptionally well/well qualified	75.0	73.3	58.3	75.0	59.0	64.9	78.7	68.8
Qualified	20.0	26.7	33.3	25.0	41.0	35.1	21.3	31.2
Not qualified	2.5	0	8.3	0	0	0	0	0

Note: These data were compiled from a variety of sources. Primarily used were questionnaires completed by judicial nominees for the U.S. Senate Judiciary Committee, transcripts of the confirmation hearings conducted by the Committee, and personal interviews. In addition, an investigation was made of various biographical directories including *The American Bench* (Sacramento: R.B. Forster). *Martindale-Hubbell Law Directory* (Summit, NJ: Martindale-Hubbell, Inc.), national and regional editions of *Who's Who*, *The Judicial Staff Directory*, and local newspaper articles.

Law firms are categorized according to the number of partners/associates: 25 or more associates for a large firm, 5 to 24 associates for a medium firm, and 4 or less for a small firm. Percent subtotals for occupational experience sum to more than 100 because some appointees have had both judicial and prosecutorial experience.

The American Bar Association's (ABA) ratings are assigned to candidates after investigation and evaluation by the ABA's Standing Committee on Federal Judiciary, which considers prospective Federal judicial nominees only upon referral by the U.S. Attorney General or at the request of the U.S. Senate. The ABA's Committee evaluation is directed primarily to professional qualifications—competence, integrity, and judicial temperament. Factors including intellectual capacity, judgment, writing and analytical ability, industry, knowledge of the law, and professional experience are assessed. Prior to President George H. W. Bush's administration, the ABA's Standing Committee on Federal Judiciary utilized four ratings: exceptionally well qualified, well qualified, qualified, and not qualified. Starting with that administration, the ABA Standing Committee on Federal Judiciary dropped its "exceptionally well qualified" rating and "well qualified" became the highest rating. Nominees who previously would have been rated "exceptionally well qualified" and nominees who would have been rated "well qualified" now receive the same rating. The "exceptionally well qualified" and "well qualified" categories have been combined for all administrations' appointees, and therefore figures prior to President George H.W. Bush's administration may differ from previous editions of SOURCEBOOK. Some data have been revised by the Source and may differ from previous editions of SOURCEBOOK.

[a]Percents may not add to 100 because of rounding.
[b]No ABA rating was requested for one Johnson appointee.

Source: Sheldon Goldman, "Reagan's Judicial Legacy: Completing the Puzzle and Summing Up," *Judicature* 72 (April–May 1989), pp. 323, 324, Table 3; and Sheldon Goldman et al., "W. Bush Remaking the Judiciary: Like Father Like Son?," *Judicature* 86 (May–June 2003), p.308. Table adapted by SOURCEBOOK staff. Reprinted by permission.

BOX 5.2 CAREER SNAPSHOT

Richard Lowell Nygaard
Senior Judge, United States Court of Appeals for the Third Circuit

Statistics: B.S., University of Southern California, 1969; J.D., University of Michigan, 1971; D.L., *Honoris Causa,* Edinboro University

Background and Interests: After being admitted to the Supreme Court Bar of Pennsylvania, I went into private practice with one other attorney in a small Pennsylvania town. As with most law practices in small towns, our practice was general, and we performed nearly every legal service required by the families and businesses we represented. In 1981, I was appointed by the governor of Pennsylvania to a position on the Pennsylvania Court of Common Pleas, a court of general jurisdiction. Pennsylvania has a modified "Missouri system" for judicial selection, and in 1983 I was required to stand for election to maintain my position. After receiving the nomination of both political parties, I was sworn in to a ten-year term on the Court. During my eight-year tenure on the Court, I presided over criminal and civil trials, both jury and non-jury. The most exciting and frustrating part of my job as a trial judge was sentencing criminal offenders. It was exciting because I felt I was able to effect positive change in some who came before me. It was frustrating because I knew with some change in the law, I could do more. In 1988, President Ronald Reagan appointed me to the United States Court of Appeals for the Third Circuit. I was unanimously confirmed by the Senate.

Work Experiences: "Good morning, Judge." That is how Jim S. began each one of his letters to me. Jim was in prison. By the time he was released, my file of his letters was over two-inches thick. Jim had been in and out of prison for many years. Indeed, he spent most of his life in prison. I put him there twice. I am not quite sure why, but over the course of years, Jim's dislike (perhaps hatred) of me, was transmuted into respect and he began to write to me as one who he knew would listen and respond. Indeed, throughout my 25 years on the bench, I have considered it my obligation, not only to read, but to answer all letters and communication I receive from people in prison. I also have felt it my obligation to visit the prisons to which I have sentenced criminal defendants.

Jim was gruff, tough, and was educated in the streets, not in the academy. His letters were filled with "I ain't" and "he don't" grammar. In one letter he proudly informed me that he had "taken a black eye" on my behalf because some had "dissed" me. I learned a lot from Jim. I learned what prison was like. Indeed, I learned what *prisons* were like because he had served time in several. It was he who awakened me to the fact that our criminal justice system was not working well and the aging concept of prison was in serious need of overhaul.

In his last letter to me, he said he was through with prison. "I ain't going back," he said. "Prison ain't what it used to be. I'm going straight." Jim is doing fine now. He is out of prison. He has a job and I am happy for him.

"Well, goodbye old friend." This is how Carmen M. now closes his letters to me. Carmen is doing life for murder. He is in his twenty-fifth year behind bars. Carmen entered prison uneducated, but while there earned a bachelor's degree through the Pell grant program, which unfortunately has now been discontinued. He is literate, articulate, and speaks several languages. I enjoy hearing from him. Indeed, I consider him my equal. I learned a lot about prison from Carmen also; the sex—voluntary and otherwise; the anger and bitterness; the feelings of despair and hopelessness; abandonment by family and friends; and the violence—prisoner on prisoner and officer on prisoner. But what grieved me most about my friend is when I hear how arbitrarily and unfairly he has been dealt with by the correction officers, many of whom are less educated and less intelligent than he. In one of my personal visits to the prison where he is now housed, I asked him what was the hardest adjustment he had to make. He thought for a long time before answering, then he said, "the despair and the fact that I can trust no one—not fellow inmates, not correctional officers, and not even my counselor." I cannot imagine a life without relationships built on trust, and told him so. He replied, "It leads to despair." Carmen knows that he will die in prison. It bothered him to think that he would likely be buried in the prison cemetery. As his friend, I would not have let that happen. But, he has solved this problem in his same understated and intellectual way—by donating his body to a university medical center for research. I enjoy receiving letters from him. I enjoy writing to him. I begin my letters to him, "Dear Friend." Indeed, he is my friend.

I recently wrote a book entitled, *Sentencing As I See It,* in which I proposed significant changes to the way we treat those who have violated our laws. Therein I stated, and I continue to believe, that sentencing must change—both in concept and in practice. It must, because it is unproductive. With over two million persons now warehoused behind bars, the system "graduates" roughly 500,000 ex-convicts a year. That number, educated in the antisocial ways of prison, are changing the societies into which they reenter because of their sheer numbers. This will eventually have a devastating effect on American culture unless we recognize it and change. It must change because it is too expensive: In Pennsylvania approximately $30,000 is spent per inmate per year. It must change because it is too inhumane. If society is measured by how it treats its inmates, we come up very short. I am not so naive as to believe that there are not those in prison who should never get out. But for those who will, we must provide a better, more effective system and a practice of behavior

(continued)

BOX 5.2 (continued)

modification so that one reenters society better behaved and better pre-pared than he left it. This is not now happening.

Advice to Students: The criminal justice system is generally thought of as a pyramid. At the top we place the Supreme Court, beneath which we have the various courts of appeal and trial courts, beneath them lie the prosecu-tors and defenders, below that are police and law enforcement, and at the bottom are the correctional officers and those who actually deal with the prisoners. I disagree totally with this concept. It is upside down. I believe the most important people in the system are those who deal with people. Indeed, in this group I would say that the correctional officers are the most important of all. They can make the system work if they are diligent, con-scientious, fair, and use their power and authority wisely. They can make the system fail if they are arbitrary, cruel, or unjust. The correctional officers, the probation and parole officers, and those who deal one-on-one on a daily basis with those who violated our laws are the only heroes in this hor-ror story we euphemistically call the criminal justice system. It is not a sys-tem. It is more like a jigsaw puzzle in which none of the pieces really match, but when placed together they form a mosaic that is nonetheless recog-nizable. You, the student, will inherit this system. You the student, you the graduate, you the practitioner, can make it better. You must make it better. I am counting on you. Your culture is counting on you.

years with *good behavior* are entitled to retire at their option anytime thereafter and receive their annual salary for life. Although judicial appointments are ide-ally made without regard to one's race, color, sex, religion, or national origin, these appointments are primarily political and reflect the interests and views of the president. The advice and consent of Congress is required for all such appointments.

President Jimmy Carter made various appointments that were considered liberal. Investigators examined Carter's appointments to federal circuit courts of appeal and found that he had appointed 56 judges during his tenure as pres-ident. Interestingly, of these 56 judicial appointees, 22 were either female or a member of a racial minority. The liberal influence of these judges was tracked over time to see whether there was corresponding liberal decision making on appeals from convicted minority offenders. A study was made of 301 criminal and prisoner's rights cases, 169 sex discrimination cases, and 295 racial dis-crimination cases. Minority appointees by Carter cast 79 percent of their votes to favor the rights of accused minorities and women compared with only 53 percent of the white male judges he had appointed. Race and gender discrim-ination cases disclosed more liberal rulings from these judges compared with prisoner's rights cases. Thus, presidential influence in appointing judges at various levels of appeal is not to be underestimated insofar as it influences judicial decision making and social policy relevant to women and minorities.

The pattern of partisanship indicated by presidential appointments to circuit court judgeships was also found for presidential appointees to benches of federal district courts in 2002. Presidential appointments of these judges were very much along party lines, with over 80 percent of all federal district court judges being of the same political party of their appointing president. These appointments are shown in Table 5.6. The ratings of federal district court judges by the American Bar Association were fairly consistent across the different presidencies, regardless of whether the president was a Republican or Democrat. For these different administrations, the ABA ratings ranged from 45 to 69 percent of the federal district judges as exceptionally well qualified (Maguire and Pastore 2005,76).

Regarding the gender and race/ethnicity of U.S. district court judge appointments, President Bill Clinton had the largest percentage of females (28.2 percent) appointed, followed by President George W. Bush (20.5 percent) and President George Bush (19.6 percent). President Clinton also had the largest percentage of black appointees (17.4 percent) while President Carter was second (14 percent). All other U.S. presidents have appointed fewer than 8 percent black judges to these district court judgeships. Both President Bush and President Clinton appointed the largest numbers of Hispanic federal district court judges (7.2 percent and 5.9 percent, respectively).

U.S. Magistrates

U.S. magistrates have jurisdiction over petty federal crimes. They may conduct preliminary stages of felony cases and set bail for criminal defendants. They decide numerous civil cases. They are appointed by U.S. district court judges and serve terms of either eight years or four years, depending upon whether they are full-time or part-time magistrates). The salary of U.S. magistrates in 2004 was $145,452. The various duties of U.S. magistrates are shown in Table 5.7. Besides having jurisdiction over cases involving federal misdemeanors and petty offenses, these magistrates also issue search warrants, arrest warrants/summonses, hold detention hearings, review bail for arrestees, issue seizure warrants, and conduct preliminary examinations. These magistrates also have civil duties as well as criminal ones, although their criminal responsibilities outweigh their civil responsibilities 2 to 1. They hold pretrial conferences, rule on motions, conduct evidentiary hearings, appoint special masterships, and hear some prisoner litigation involving *habeas corpus* petitions and civil rights submissions.

By far the bulk of a U.S. magistrate's duties consist of preliminary proceedings, such as issuing search warrants, arrest warrants and summonses,

TABLE 5.6   CHARACTERISTICS OF PRESIDENTIAL APPOINTEES TO U.S. DISTRICT COURT JUDGESHIPS

By Presidential administration, 1963–2002[a]

	President Johnson's appointees 1963–68 (N=122)	President Nixon's appointees 1969–74 (N=179)	President Ford's appointees 1974–76 (N=52)	President Carter's appointees 1977–80 (N=202)	President Reagan's appointees 1981–88 (N=290)	President George H.W. Bush's appointees 1989–92 (N=148)	President Clinton's appointees 1993–2000 (N=305)	President George W. Bush's appointees 2001–2002 (N=83)
Sex								
Male	98.4%	99.4%	98.1%	85.6%	91.7%	80.4%	71.5%	79.5%
Female	1.6	0.6	1.9	14.4	8.3	19.6	28.5	20.5
Race, ethnicity								
White	93.4	95.5	88.5	78.7	92.4	89.2	75.1	85.5
Black	4.1	3.4	5.8	13.9	2.1	6.8	17.4	7.2
Hispanic	2.5	1.1	1.9	6.9	4.8	4.0	5.9	7.2
Asian	0	0	3.9	0.5	0.7	0	1.3	0
Native American	NA	NA	NA	0	0	0	0.3	0
Education, undergraduate								
Public-supported	38.5	41.3	48.1	55.9	37.9	46.0	44.3	42.2
Private (not Ivy League)	31.1	38.5	34.6	34.2	48.6	39.9	42.0	51.8
Ivy League	16.4	19.6	17.3	9.9	13.4	14.2	13.8	6.0
None indicated	13.9	0.6	0	0	0	0	0	0
Education, law school								
Public-supported	40.2	41.9	44.2	52.0	44.8	52.7	39.7	53.0
Private (not Ivy League)	36.9	36.9	38.5	31.2	43.4	33.1	40.7	39.8
Ivy League	21.3	21.2	17.3	16.8	11.7	14.2	19.7	7.2
Occupation at nomination or appointment								
Politics or government	21.3	10.6	21.2	5.0	13.4	10.8	11.5	8.4

Judiciary	31.1	28.5	34.6	44.6	36.9	41.9	48.2	48.2
Law firm, large	2.4	11.2	9.6	13.9	17.9	25.7	16.1	24.1
Law firm, medium	18.9	27.9	25.0	19.3	19.0	14.9	13.4	9.6
Law firm, small	23.0	19.0	9.6	13.9	10.0	4.7	8.2	4.8
Professor of law	3.3	2.8	0	3.0	2.1	0.7	1.6	2.4
Other	0	0	0	0.5	0.7	1.4	1.0	2.4
Occupational experience								
Judicial	34.4	35.2	42.3	54.0	46.2	46.6	52.1	53.0
Prosecutorial	45.9	41.9	50.0	38.1	44.1	39.2	41.3	50.6
Other	33.6	36.3	30.8	31.2	28.6	31.8	28.9	22.9
Political party								
Democrat	94.3	7.3	21.2	91.1	4.8	6.1	87.5	7.2
Republican	5.7	92.7	78.8	4.5	91.7	88.5	6.2	83.1
Independent or none	0	0	0	4.5	3.4	5.4	5.9	9.6
Other	NA	NA	NA	0	0	0	0.3	0
American Bar Association rating								
Exceptionally well/well qualified	48.4	45.3	46.1	51.0	53.5	57.4	59.0	69.9
Qualified	49.2	54.8	53.8	47.5	46.6	42.6	40.0	28.9
Not qualified	2.5	0	0	1.5	0	0	1.0	1.2

Note: See Note, table 1.81. Percent subtotals for occupational experience sum to more than 100 because some appointees have had both judicial and prosecutorial experience. Some data have been revised by the Source and may differ from previous editions of SOURCEBOOK.

[a]Percents may not add to 100 because of rounding.

Source: Sheldon Goldman, "Reagan's Judicial Legacy: Completing the Puzzle and Summing Up," *Judicature 72* (April–May 1989), pp. 320, 321, Table 1; and Sheldon Goldman et al., "W. Bush Remaking the Judiciary: Like Father Like Son?," *Judicature* 86 (May–June 2003). p. 304. Table adapted by SOURCEBOOK staff. Reprinted by permission.

**TABLE 5.7 DUTIES PERFORMED BY MAGISTRATE JUDGES IN U.S. DISTRICT COURTS
1990, 1997–2003**

Activity	1990	1997	1998	1999	2000	2001	2002	2003
Total	448,107	579,771	612,688	648,097	807,401	873,948	880,129	948,570
Trial jurisdiction cases	100,930	85,257	96,832	109,101	88,449	84,067	72,109	83,247
Class A misdemeanors	13,248	10,177	10,633	10,773	8,990	8,687	8,816	9,616
Petty offenses	87,682	75,080	86,199	98,328	79,459	75,380	63,293	73,631
Preliminary proceedings	157,987	217,616	241,031	259,153	264,997	286,299	293,002	315,455
Search warrants	20,672	29,563	30,371	32,607	29,824	31,571	29,929	32,539
Arrest warrants/summonses	18,972	23,116	26,252	28,749	26,880	29,891	30,541	31,291
Initial appearances	49,624	60,419	68,982	74,875	77,752	83,582	86,324	93,991
Preliminary examinations	7,145	13,049	14,436	16,059	16,589	18,067	19,279	20,062
Arraignments	34,311	41,559	45,524	48,132	49,740	54,687	54,339	57,977
Detention hearings	17,191	28,996	32,948	36,381	37,490	39,468	43,198	47,860
Bail reviews	7,858	10,018	10,250	10,833	10,741	11,557	11,052	11,397
Other[a]	2,214	10,896	12,268	11,517	15,981	17,476	18,340	20,338
Additional duties	171,127	236,964	234,974	235,803	405,661	450,639	461,848	490,617
Criminal	35,576	52,382	49,587	51,182	108,823	126,813	138,504	156,115
Motions[b]	26,509	27,329	24,071	24,623	67,099	78,450	85,693	98,299
Evidentiary hearings	2,256	1,788	1,998	2,302	1,990	1,985	1,899	2,041
Pretrial conferences[c]	3,488	5,737	5,763	5,793	10,965	12,024	13,532	14,620
Probation/supervised release	529	2,600	2,960	3,007	3,109	3,570	3,948	4,570
Guilty pleas	NA	NA	NA	NA	10,614	13,150	15,275	17,018
Other[d]	2,794	14,928	14,795	15,457	15,046	17,634	18,157	19,567
Civil	114,968	155,158	158,003	158,830	271,025	296,921	298,109	309,720
Settlement conferences	12,656	23,549	23,113	24,666	24,255	24,997	24,420	26,506
Other pretrial conferences[c]	32,545	40,999	40,107	39,265	49,724	50,776	55,371	55,632
Motions[b]	61,594	66,535	69,517	68,043	171,659	194,918	192,075	200,068

Evidentiary hearings	1,964	981	988	771	650	639	851	646
Social Security	5,112	4,553	5,261	6,132	5,516	5,514	6,654	6,472
Special masterships	1,097	963	886	753	734	677	504	550
Other[e]	NA	17,578	18,131	19,200	18,487	19,400	18,234	19,846
Prisoner litigation	20,583	29,424	27,384	25,791	25,813	26,905	25,235	24,782
State *habeas corpus*	6,078	8,046	9,261	9,692	10,125	10,180	9,503	9,482
Federal *habeas corpus*	2,339	3,778	4,024	3,406	3,469	4,256	4,441	3,837
Civil rights	12,166	16,480	13,151	11,922	11,419	11,403	10,531	10,766
Evidentiary hearings	NA	1,120	948	771	800	1,066	760	697
Civil consent	4,958	10,081	10,339	11,320	11,481	12,024	12,710	13,811
Without trial	3,950	8,318	8,791	9,822	10,181	10,945	11,751	13,044
Jury trial	495	964	892	850	750	590	472	479
Non-jury trial	513	799	656	648	550	489	487	288
Miscellaneous matters[f]	13,105	29,853	29,512	32,720	36,813	40,919	40,460	45,440

Note: The Federal Magistrates Act (28 U.S.C. 636(b)) provides the authority under which magistrate judges assist courts in the performance of "additional duties." This authority was both broadened and clarified by Public Law 94-577, Oct. 21, 1976, and by new procedural rules governing most *habeas corpus* proceedings in the district courts, effective Feb. 1, 1977. The changes make clear the ability of the parties of a civil case to consent to have the case referred to a magistrate for trial as a special matter: the changes also empower magistrates to conduct evidentiary hearings in prisoner petition cases. Additionally, the role of magistrates in providing pretrial assistance to district judges in both dispositive and non-dispositive matters has been clarified. A magistrate's authority to conduct arraignments following indictment in a criminal case is provided under Rule 10 of the Federal Rules of Criminal Procedure in 86 Districts. Data for 1990 are reported for the 12-month period ending June 30. Beginning in 1997, data are reported for the Federal fiscal year, which is the 12-month period ending September 30. Some data have been revised by the Source and will differ from previous editions of SOURCEBOOK.

[a]Data for 1990 include material witness hearings only; data for 1997–2003 include material witness hearings and attorney appointment hearings.

[b]Prior to 2000, data include contested motions only; beginning in 2000, data include both contested and uncontested motions.

[c]Prior to 2000, data do not include status conferences; beginning in 2000, data include status conferences.

[d]Data for 1990 include writs only; data for 1997–2003 include writs, mental competency hearings, and motion hearings.

[e]Beginning in 1997, data include fee applications, summary jury trials, and motion hearings.

[f]Prior to 2000, this category included seizure/inspection warrants and orders of entry, judgment debtor exams, extradition hearings, contempt proceedings, Criminal Justice Act fee applications, naturalization proceedings, grand jury returns, civil and criminal IRS enforcement proceedings, calendar calls, and *voir dire*. Beginning in 2000, civil and criminal other jury matters, and international prisoner transfer proceedings were added.

Source: Administrative Office of the United States Courts, Judicial Business of the United States Courts: 2000 Annual Report of the Director, pp. 66, 67; 2001 Annual Report of the Director, pp. 62, 63; 2002 Annual Report of the Director, pp. 61, 62; 2003 Annual Report of the Director, pp. 58, 59 (Washington, DC: USGPO). Table adapted by SOURCEBOOK staff.

conducting initial appearances, and setting bail. Much of their civil work relates to conducting pretrial conferences, ruling on motions, and screening prisoner litigation (Maguire and Pastore 2005,79).

What Do Judges Think About Different Judicial Selection Methods?

If judges are surveyed, they seem to favor merit plans over elections (Scheb 1988). In 1987, for instance, a national survey of 562 state appellate judges was conducted and their attitudes toward alternative judicial selection methods were solicited. When asked to compare the Missouri plan of merit selection with the judicial selection methods of political appointment and partisan elections, the judges responded overwhelmingly that the merit plan was the more professional selection method. By this the judges meant that the Missouri merit plan tended to professionalize the courts. Judges selected under the merit system were far less likely to become involved in political causes or debates compared with those judges who were either gubernatorial appointees or elected (Scheb 1988).

In some jurisdictions, such as Texas, judges believe that performance evaluations are made unfairly, since the judicial selection methods used in their state have not been changed since 1891 (Champion 2005a). Thus, creating new jurisdictional divisions among Texas's existing courts could do much to improve case processing efficiency. The performance of judges would be enhanced accordingly with specific organizational reforms. One reform would be to empower presiding judges in different jurisdictions to move other judges to courts on an as-needed basis, and to control court dockets. Restricting the monetary jurisdiction of various criminal and civil courts to $5,000 would also improve court efficiency (Champion 2005a).

JUDICIAL TRAINING

Theories of management and organizations have sometimes been applied in the judicial selection and training process. For instance, **bureaucracy** and its derivative bureaucratic theory emphasizes **centralization** of authority in decision making, thus creating a degree of standardization in judicial selection. However, strict adherence to bureaucratic principles may not always result in selections of the most qualified judges in local jurisdictions. A departure from bureaucratic theory would be to decentralize the judicial selection process, to place greater decision-making power in the hands of local commissions for judicial appointments, with some authority given to state supreme courts to oversee the selection process. The legislative electoral process is one way of rationalizing and objectifying the selection process. This would enable local bar elements to recommend those most qualified for judgeships, while the legislature would make the best judicial selections with state supreme court approval.

In the late 1970s, a survey by the American Judicature Society disclosed that there was no uniformity or pattern of organization among different lower courts among state jurisdictions (Knab 1977). The qualifications for state judges were diverse and inconsistent from one jurisdiction to the next. Different standards existed for selecting judges, determining their qualifications to serve in judicial positions, compensation, and retirement or removal of judges.

Several recommendations have been made to improve the quality and accountability of judges in different jurisdictions. For instance, the U.S. Advisory Commission on Intergovernmental Relations (1971) suggested that a set of uniform rules should be established to govern the conduct of judges. Further, procedures for judicial retirement, removal, and discipline should be established with a high degree of uniformity. Finally, a term limit should be established to eliminate the possibility of certain judges serving for long periods. Mandatory retirement ages should be implemented. In order to upgrade and improve the quality of judicial selection, codes of judicial ethics ought to be established, together with explicit judicial compensation and qualification criteria.

Other recommendations for standardizing the qualifications, training, and selection of judges are that judicial elections should be publicly financed and not dependent upon private contributions. A standard amount of money should be available to all judicial candidates for their election campaigns. No private contributions of any kind should be allowed. Further, filing fees should not be required of anyone seeking a judgeship (Beechen 1974). In some county elections, more affluent judges may spend considerably more of their own money on judicial campaigning compared with less affluent candidates. The relative difference in campaign money spent by the different candidates may create the potential for the appearance of improper influence. Further, those candidates of modest means are disadvantaged and may be deterred from seeking public office.

Whether a judicial candidate is an incumbent or one seeking a judgeship for the first time makes a substantial difference in the amount of financial support generated for the campaign. In the 1984 Cook County Circuit Court elections, for instance, judicial incumbents were able to raise substantially more money for their campaigns from lawyer contributions compared with fresh candidates. Even sitting judges who were sure losers were able to generate substantially greater funding compared with more desirable candidates (Nicholson and Weiss 1986).

Subsequent studies of the judicial selection process through partisan elections have revealed that private contributions and frivolous candidate expenditures have raised more than a few questions about judicial ethics and fairness

(Kiel et al. 1994). Further, the bars of various states have disclosed that they have little influence on the nature of voting for one judicial candidate or another in terms of their comparative qualifications (Kiel et al. 1994).

Evidence suggests that voters are more attentive to the judicial policy preferences and ideological inclinations of judges than researchers have predicted. Based on a random sample of 1,012 ballots cast in the November 1988, Marion County, Oregon, judicial race, which occurred simultaneously with the Bush–Dukakis presidential campaign, voters were very much aware of the political philosophies and personal ideologies of those competing for judicial vacancies. In nearby Washington State, a survey of voters in a 1986 judicial election indicated that voter knowledge about judicial candidates and their views was critical in their voting participation (Lovrich and Sheldon 1994). In other states such as California, however, voters in judicial elections did not appear to be as informed or educated about the issues involved in other judicial selections (Champion 2005b).

JUDICIAL MISCONDUCT AND ABUSES OF DISCRETION

Judicial conduct is monitored by different persons and organizations among jurisdictions. For instance, in New York, judicial conduct is monitored by the Commission on Judicial Conduct. The commission receives or initiates complaints with respect to the conduct, qualifications, fitness to perform, or performance of official duties of any judge in New York State. After investigation and a hearing, the commission may admonish, censure, remove, or retire a judge. Decisions by the commission may be appealed to the court of appeals.

Forms of Judicial Misconduct

There are several forms of judicial misconduct. However, most misconduct relates to the performance of one's job as judge. A judge is a powerful entity. The courtroom is dominated by the judge. Judges make rulings that have immense influence over trial outcomes.

Judges Can Influence Trial Outcomes by Exhibiting Prejudice in Evidentiary Rulings

One of the most frequent types of judicial misconduct is to prejudice the court proceedings in such a way that the trial outcome is favorable to either one side or the other. Such behavior on a judge's part is difficult to detect, however. Simply ruling unfavorably against one side or the other may be explained by numerous frivolous motions filed by that side. Further, most judges can rationalize their conduct if pressed to do so.

Judges Can Deliberately Aggravate or Mitigate One's Sentence Following Conviction

When offenders are convicted, judges can deliberately increase or decrease the severity of the sentence imposed. Again, it is difficult for court watchers to detect whenever judicial intervention is the result of objective decision making or personal vindictiveness.

Judges Can Accept Bribes from Various Parties in Court Actions

Judges may also accept bribes from politicians or others where their rulings are influential. Especially in bench trials where judges decide the outcomes of cases, it is easy to decide in favor of someone where a financial bribe has been received. Again, this form of misconduct is difficult to detect. It is not completely undetectable, however. Bribery and judicial corruption were targeted in Operation Greylord in the late 1970s.

Corrupt Judges and Operation Greylord

In 1978 one of the largest and most successful investigations of judicial misconduct was launched. The investigation was called **Operation Greylord.** It was an FBI undercover sting operation and targeted the judges of Cook County, Illinois (Bensinger 1988). The history of judicial corruption in and around Chicago was notorious and well known throughout the United States. Politically corrupt judges would accept bribes for favorable bench decisions. Organized crime was able to flourish because of judicial participation in illicit activities.

The FBI organized a task force that fabricated a variety of court cases to be heard in Cook County courts. Tape-recorded conversations were made between undercover FBI agents posing as attorneys and defendants and judges. Electronic surveillance and telephonic wiretaps were installed in different judges' offices in an effort to acquire incriminating information. The results of Operation Greylord were shocking. Over 60 judges and judicial adjuncts were prosecuted and convicted of various forms of judicial misconduct and corruption, including accepting bribes and prejudicing judgments in favor of certain undercover clients. The immediate public reaction to Operation Greylord was a general loss of confidence in the Illinois judiciary, despite the fact that only Chicago and Cook County were targeted. But in later years, public confidence in the judiciary was restored through implementing a series of judicial selection reforms. The Illinois Bar Association and judicial organizations adopted new ethical standards and modes of professional conduct. Merit selections of judges throughout Illinois were the rule rather than the exception. The administration of justice in Cook County was drastically overhauled and revised. While judicial corruption and misconduct have not been entirely eliminated, Operation Greylord did much to reduce its existence (Illinois Supreme Court 1993).

BOX 5.3 JUDGES CONVICTED OF CRIMES

■ District Judge Alan Green was convicted in New Orleans, Louisiana, on two of six counts of mail fraud involving two $5,000 cash payments he took from a bail bonding company. A mistrial was declared on the remaining counts and it is likely that Green will be retried. Green is a former Jefferson Parish prosecutor who became a judge in 1992. He faced up to 20 years of prison on his conviction offenses. Green was accused of taking $20,000 in cash from Louis Marcotte, III, a New Orleans bail bondsman. Bail Bonds Unlimited, operated by Marcotte, enables those charged with crimes to remain jail-free while awaiting their subsequent trials. Marcotte claimed that Green extorted monies from him as a bribe for his court business. Marcotte sent Judge Green two $5,000 checks by mail. Green's attorney claimed that these checks were considered campaign contributions and were later returned to Marcotte. But the prosecution proved otherwise. Green is the first state district judge convicted at trial since 1983, when Judge Roy Price, also of the Jefferson Parish state court, was found guilty in federal court of bank larceny and other crimes. He served 18 months and died in 1989. Under Louisiana law, Green has been convicted of two felonies, sufficient to put him on interim disqualification pending sanctions, including removal from the bench. He was currently suspended without pay.

■ New Jersey Superior Court Judge Stephen W. Thompson, 59, traveled to Russia in September 2002 where he had several sexual encounters with a young teenage boy in a St. Petersburg hotel room. Thompson had his sexual sessions with the boy videotaped by a local pimp. In one of the videotapes showing Thompson having sex with the boy, Thompson is heard telling an unidentified man to ask the child to take off his clothes. Then Thompson is seen climbing into bed nude with the boy and engaging in sexual acts with him. About 40 minutes of sexual footage were recorded. The judge then transported the videotape back to the United States.

Judge Thompson's sexual activities relating to the Russian boy came to light as a result of his affiliation with a group known as the North American Man Boy Love Association (NAMBLA), a group that promotes sexual relations between adult men and children. Apparently an informant tipped off police officers to Thompson's illicit activities, including his possession of an extensive array of child pornography at his home and judicial office. Search warrants were issued subsequently and 17 VHS tapes were found containing child pornography, children engaged in explicit sexual acts, magazines containing child pornography and child erotica, and materials associated with NAMBLA. More than 300 printed images of child pornography were found; also 57 floppy disks contained over 6,000 images of child pornography. Thompson was charged with multiple counts of having sex with a teenage boy and sexual exploitation of children in a federal district court. He was subsequently convicted of traveling in interstate and foreign commerce with the intent of engaging in sexual conduct with a minor for the purpose of producing a visual depiction of the sexual conduct. His conviction carries a mandatory minimum sentence of ten years in prison. NAMBLA is currently represented by the American Civil Liberties Union.

How much illegal activity is there among judges throughout the United States? While these incidents represent only two cases, how many other undiscovered cases are there involving judges who preside in criminal and civil court matters? What types of investigations are necessary or warranted as the result of various judges convicted of different crimes? What do you think? [Sources: Adapted from the Associated Press, "La. Judge Convicted of Mail Fraud," June 30, 2005; adapted from Jim Douri and the Associated Press, "Superior Court Judge Convicted of Sex Crimes with Boy," October 12, 2005.]

CRITICISMS OF JUDGES

Some Judges Are Incompetent and Inexperienced

Judicial incompetence is often associated with one's inexperience as a judge. When inexperienced judges rule on motions from the prosecution or defense, these judges may not understand fully the rules of evidence and whether the motion should be granted or denied. Often, inexperienced judges make these decisions on the basis of their emotional sentiment during the trial. Whenever judges make mistakes of judgment in ruling on motions, these are errors. They vary in their importance. Many errors are harmless, meaning that the outcome of the trial would not have been affected if the judge had ruled differently. Other types of errors are **harmful errors** or **reversible errors.**

Harmful errors or reversible errors may result in judicial decisions being overturned by higher appellate courts. But (1) not all errors are detected in a trial; (2) not all *guilty* verdicts are appealed; and (3) not all appeals are heard on their merits by higher courts. The United States Supreme Court hears only about 4 percent of the appeals it schedules annually.

For instance, in a murder case, a judge admitted into evidence photographs of the murder victim. These photographs showed the mutilated corpse of the victim, and the photographs had absolutely no bearing on the guilt or innocence of the accused. There were eyewitnesses to the murder, and the defendant's guilt had been proven beyond a reasonable doubt without the photographs. But the photographs obviously inflamed the jury and influenced their decision to impose the death penalty. The murder conviction was appealed, but the verdict was affirmed by the higher court. In that case, the court said there was so much evidence against the accused that the admission of these inflammatory materials into evidence resulted in harmless error. Under other circumstances, however, the admission of inflammatory photographs might be the final element necessary to persuade a jury to render a guilty verdict in an otherwise weak case against the defendant. Again, the trial judge controls the courtroom and influences the general course of the trial as well as the defendant's chances for conviction or acquittal.

It is assumed by all appellate courts that the original judgment or verdict rendered by a lower trial court was the correct one. Therefore, clear and convincing evidence must be presented by the defendant supporting a reversal of a verdict by the trial judge or jury. It is insufficient simply to prove that errors were committed. Even harmful errors are insufficient under certain conditions when attempting to overturn a judge's decision.

Some Judges Contribute to Court Delays and Clogged Court Calendars

Serious court delays are commonplace in most jurisdictions. A study of case processing in New York City, for instance, has revealed that a significant obstacle contributing to court delays is inadequate judicial training. Technology presently exists that facilitates case processing in many modern court systems. However, some New York City judiciary are slow to acquire new technology. Further, courses offered for judges on case management training have relatively low enrollment. Realistic timetables are not adhered to, and more than a few judges inadvertently impede one's right to a speedy trial because of their inefficient case management practices (Correctional Association of New York 1993).

Other factors besides judicial inexperience contribute to case processing delays as well. In some cases, there are attorney appearance conflicts, witness unavailability, attorney unpreparedness, vacations, and illness-precipitated court appearances. Court delays in various jurisdictions are also due to a lack of resources and judicial support staff and equipment. Increasing judicial education through mandatory education programs is one means of facilitating case processing (Clark, 2004a).

Many Judges Impose Disparate Sentences

Judicial discretion in sentencing is often criticized in that judges make decisions primarily on extralegal factors rather than legal ones. Legal factors include one's prior record, seriousness of the current offense, age, and acceptance of responsibility. Extralegal factors refer to race or ethnicity, gender, socioeconomic status, and attitude (Champion 2005b). Sentencing disparities attributable to race, gender, socioeconomic status, and other extralegal factors have plagued judges for years (Champion 2005b). Attempts have been made by commissions and state legislatures to create greater sentencing consistency and bind judges to nonarbitrary standards. Sentencing guidelines have been created in most jurisdictions to make uniform the punishments for various offenses. Some observers question whether structured sentencing guidelines will eliminate disparities in judicial decision making, however. Experiments on various types of sentencing reforms have evidenced some success in improving judicial fairness (Kramer and Ulmer 1996). Other research, however, shows that despite the fact that sentencing guidelines were designed to reduce unwarranted disparity in sentencing, the results of recent research suggests that minorities and the poor may continue to receive harsher treatment because judges find ways to manipulate the reforms, or circumvent them altogether. Additionally, there is evidence of unwarranted disparity in departures from the guidelines (Stith and Cabranes 1998); whites and females more often receive non-prison sentences, and downward departures (Kramer and Ulmer 1996).

The recent Supreme Court case of *Blakely v. Washington* (2004) seriously called into question the constitutionality of the federal sentencing guidelines as well as those of nearly a dozen states. Following *Blakely*, the case of *United States v. Booker* (2005) ruled that the Sixth Amendment necessitates that the federal sentencing guidelines be advisory in nature rather than mandatory. This now means that judges are to consult the guidelines when meting out sentences but do not necessarily have to follow them.

REMOVING JUDGES FROM OFFICE

Whenever corrupt or incompetent judges are identified, there are relatively few mechanisms available to remove them from office. In New York, judicial conduct is monitored by the Commission on Judicial Conduct. The commission receives or initiates complaints with respect to the conduct, qualifications, fitness to perform, or performance of official duties of any judge in New York State. After investigation and a hearing, the commission may admonish, censure, remove, or retire a judge. However, decisions made by the commission are directly appealable to the New York Court of Appeals.

The creation of independent commissions to oversee judicial misconduct is not new. The first state to implement a commission to deal with judicial misconduct was California. In 1960 California created a **judicial conduct commission,** which was charged with investigating complaints against judges. Comprised of attorneys, other judges, and politically prestigious others, these commission members function as a part of the California Supreme Court. They meet in secret and their findings are confidential. They investigate misconduct reports against various California state trial judges and make recommendations to the California Supreme Court. Their array of sanctions includes recommendations for private censure, removal from the bench, or retirement.

The California Supreme Court has the final authority concerning recommendations made by the judicial conduct commission.

Unfortunately, the United States has one of the poorest records for sanctioning the behaviors of bad judges. Compared with other nations, such as France, Italy, and England, judicial conduct organizations in the United States institute relatively few cases of judicial sanctioning (Volcansek, DeFranciscis, and Lafron 1996). One reason for this lack of commitment to sanction bad judges is that American judges enjoy near-absolute judicial independence. There is relatively little accountability for judicial misconduct. However, bad judges can be removed either through impeachment or recall elections.

In order to provide some idea about the effectiveness of processing complaints that allege judicial misconduct, during the period for 1999, 12,068 misconduct complaints were received by various state judicial conduct organizations. In the various states anywhere from 71 percent to 100 percent of these complaints were dismissed outright, while most of the remaining cases were informally disposed of with reprimands, short-term suspensions, and fines. Only 48 cases resulted in judges vacating their offices during the investigation, and only 11 judges were suspended as a final sanction (Maguire and Pastore 2005). Thus, the system is weighed heavily in favor of judges, even bad ones. The likelihood that a complaint against any given judge will be sustained is less than 5 percent. It is even more alarming that there are few provisions for issuing severe sanctions against the worst judges. Thus, while the existence of judicial conduct organizations is commendable, it is also clear that these organizations have relatively little power in administering judicial sanctions.

Impeachment

Impeachment means to allege wrongdoing against a judge or other public official before a legislative or judicial body vested with the authority to remove that judge or public official from office. In order for impeachment to be successful, the allegations must be well founded and upheld by compelling evidence against the accused. In many jurisdictions, the state supreme court is the sanctioning body that hears impeachment allegations against judges and has the power to act to either remove the judge or dismiss the allegations.

For instance, suppose a judge continually fails to safeguard the rights of indigents in criminal cases. A judge might require a defendant to plead without representation by court-appointed counsel. A judge may tell a jury that he believes a defendant is guilty. A judge might set a particularly high and arbitrary bail amount for someone who is not dangerous or likely to flee the jurisdiction. The judge may coerce defendants out of the appeal rights. These forms of disrespect for the law occur from time to time in U.S. courts. However, few mechanisms have existed to remove these persons from office.

In more recent years, procedures have been suggested to systematize the judicial sanctioning process. Certain rules have been promulgated by the Federal Judicial Center, such as rules governing how complaints are filed; the review of complaints by chief judges; the review of the chief judge's disposition of the complaint; an investigation and recommendation by a special committee; rules dealing with **confidentiality;** public availability of decisions rendered; disqualification; and withdrawal of complaints and petitions for review.

Recall Elections

Another mechanism is through a **recall election.** A petition is circulated by interested citizens or by a city council in response to one or more complaints against a judicial official. A special election is held, with alternative candidates presented to fill the judicial post. A popular vote results in the bad judge being removed from office. The election also results in the support of a new judge who replaces the bad one. Recall elections depend heavily on citizen involvement and concern.

One other option is for a bad judge to simply resign. For instance, in Lakewood, Washington, a suburb of Seattle, Lakewood municipal judge Ralph H. Baldwin admitted to drinking beer with a defense lawyer and the prosecutor while the jury deliberated the fate of a defendant facing drunk-driving charges. Even after the case was over and the jury had rendered a verdict of guilty, the judge invited the jury members into his chambers and served them alcoholic beverages. Some jurors were clearly offended by the judge's actions, and his conduct was immediately reported to the Lakewood City Council. The city council confronted Baldwin with the allegations and he admitted them, stating that "I want you to know that none of my words or actions on that evening arose from malice but rather from a misguided sense of congeniality and extremely poor judgment. To each of you, I extend my sincere apologies." Baldwin had only served for three months as municipal judge, a $65,000 a year job, when the incident occurred (Associated Press 1998, A2). Baldwin was not available for comment about his resignation when reporters attempted to contact him.

SUMMARY

In any court proceeding, the key official is the judge. Although, as we have seen some of the judicial duties such as sentencing can be thought of as a collaborative process. The judge makes decisions about admissibility of evidence, whether or not bail will be set, courtroom administration, in some cases guilt or innocence, and finally punishment. At the local, state, and federal levels, judges are either elected or appointed. Among state courts, partisan and nonpartisan elections account for about two-thirds of all judicial positions. State governors and the U.S. president make other judicial appointments. The president selects U.S. district court judges, U.S. circuit court appellate judges, and U.S. Supreme Court justices, subject to congressional approval. An increasingly popular judicial selection method is judicial appointments on the basis of merit. One of these merit plans is known as the Missouri plan.

Both partisan and nonpartisan elections are criticized that those on the ballot are not the most qualified, and that voter apathy makes the process meaningless. Gubernatorial and legislative appointments are criticized that the nominations are too political and again the best candidate is not being appointed. Merit selection attempts to overcome these criticisms by requiring that a list be drafted of the most qualified judicial candidates based on their expertise or qualifications and then the governor can use this list to make appointments. Judges themselves, when surveyed, seem to favor merit selection over election as a more professional method. Research, however, has shown that really there are few differences in the type of judicial selection method used and the quality of judges on the bench. If you look at the characteristics of presidential appointees to district, appellate, and Supreme Court positions, they overwhelmingly come from the same political party as the president, indicating that the selection process is highly political.

The backgrounds of judges are varied. Many persons performing the judicial role have limited legal experience or expertise, and a large portion lack law degrees. Demographic qualifications vary as well; for instance, minimum age ranges vary from 18 to 30, some states do not require citizenship, and years of residence in a state also vary. In order to ensure better judicial performance among those less skilled in the law, many judges are required to undergo judicial training. This training familiarizes judges with procedural and evidentiary law, and it socializes them concerning different motions that may be made by prosecutors or defense counsel, as well as how to rule on such motions. Surveys by the American Judicature Society have shown that there is no uniformity or model of organization in the lower state courts. In virtually every U.S. jurisdiction, there have been instances of judicial misconduct. There is great variation among judges concerning their judicial effectiveness and how their courts are administered or managed.

More than a few judges deliberately engage in various forms of misconduct, which may include influencing trial outcomes because of bribery, or deliberately aggravating or mitigating one's sentence upon conviction. Judges are supposed to be impartial and base their decisions with reference to the facts of the case and the law; however, prejudicing a case can be sometimes difficult to detect and most judges can rationalize their decisions if confronted. Some judges are simply incompetent and make poor decisions that cause appellate courts to reverse their verdicts or sentences. Other judges sentence particular offenders according to extralegal criteria, such as race/ethnicity, socioeconomic status, and/or gender. Again justice is supposed to be blind, but research shows that extralegal factors can and do influence judicial decisions in some instances. Again, in some cases it is difficult to uncover whether the decision was objectively made or was based on some sort of bias. These variations in sentencing are called sentencing disparities and reflect bias or prejudice. There have been many criticisms of judges, not only on the basis of harmful errors; other criticisms have been levied that judges are the reason for court delays and clogged court calendars. This could be due to inefficient case management practices, where again proper training may help alleviate these issues, or factors out of their control like attorney time conflicts, unavailable witnesses, and attorney unpreparedness. In some instances technology could help facilitate case processing; however, judiciary in some states have been reluctant to use this.

Appellate courts can usually more easily manage their caseloads. When appeals are filed by either side following a judgment, appellate courts assume that the original trial judge's decision was the correct one, regardless of whether it was. This presumption is quite difficult to overcome by appellants who must prove by a preponderance of the evidence that the ruling was wrong. Errors are cited by appellants, which may be harmless, harmful, or reversible. Harmless or harmful errors may be insufficient to change the original trial outcome. Reversible errors often result in convictions being set aside or simply overturned. Under these circumstances, prosecutors must decide whether to retry the case and expend scarce resources for a new trial.

For judges who engage in misconduct, it is difficult to recall them and have them removed from office. Various states have judicial conduct commissions, where complaints are heard from different persons, usually convicted offenders, about their treatment in court and how judicial misconduct or abuse of office caused their convictions. While commissions investigate all of these complaints, most complaints are rejected. Hard evidence must be presented in order for particular judges to be sanctioned, and even harder evidence is necessary for judges to be removed from office. In some jurisdictions, judges may be removed from their positions through recall elections. Usually, in response to complaints about an elected official, a special election is held to fill the position. A popular vote will result in removal of the judge from office. Another strategy for removing judges from office is impeachment. Under the rules of impeachment, evidence must be presented to a legislative body of a judge's wrongful conduct. Usually, it is the state supreme court that oversees the impeachment proceedings. Again, a high standard of proof is required in order for particular charges of misconduct against judges to be sustained and to justify the type of sanction taken.

KEY TERMS

Bureaucracy
Centralization
Confidentiality
Harmful errors
Impeachment
Incumbents
Interim judges
Judge
Judicial appointments
Judicial conduct commission

Judicial powers
Judicial process
Kales plan
Merit selection
Missouri plan
Nonpartisan elections
Operation Greylord
Partisan elections
Recall election
Reversible errors

QUESTIONS FOR REVIEW

1. Are there any national qualifications for judges in state courts? What kinds of qualifications would you propose if you could do so?

2. Distinguish between partisan and nonpartisan elections of judges. Is one type of election better than the other? Why or why not?

3. In some states, judges are appointed by governors. What are some criticisms of gubernatorial appointees?

4. How are U.S. Supreme Court justices appointed? Who must approve these appointments?

5. Describe how federal circuit court judges, U.S. district court judges, and U.S. magistrates are appointed.

6. What is a popular merit method for selecting judges? Why is it favored in various states?

7. Is the merit plan for judicial selection superior to legislative or gubernatorial appointment methods? Why or why not?

8. Differentiate between the Kales and the Missouri plan.

9. What sort of training do judges typically receive before becoming judges?

10. Identify four types of judicial misconduct.

11. How can we sanction judges who engage in misconduct?

12. What are two mechanisms for removing bad judges from the bench? Describe each process briefly.

SUGGESTED READINGS

1. A. Borowski and M. Ajzenstadt (2005). "A Solution without a Problem: Judges' Perspectives on the Impacts of the Introduction of Public Defenders on Israel's Juvenile Courts." *British Journal of Criminology* **45:**183–200.

2. B. Greg, J. Feinblatt, and S. Glazer (eds.) (2005). *Good Courts: The Case for Problem–Solving Justice.* London, UK: New Press.

3. D. A. Krauss (2004). "Adjusting the Risk of Recidivism: Do Judicial Departures Worsen or Improve Recidivism Prediction Under the Federal Sentencing Guidelines?" *Behavioral Sciences and the Law* **22:** 731–750.

4. G. S. Yacoubian, Jr. (2003). "Should the Subject Matter Jurisdiction of the International Criminal Court Include Drug Trafficking?" *International Journal of Comparative Criminology* **3:**1201–1207.

5. D. L. Yearwood (2005). "Judicial Dispositions of Ex-Parte and Domestic Violence Protection Order Hearings: A Comparative Analysis of Victim Requests and Court-Authorized Relief." *Journal of Family Violence* **20:**161–170.

Chapter 6

Juries

Chapter Objectives

As a result of reading this chapter, you will have accomplished the following objectives:

1. Understand the history of juries as well as the development of the grand jury and the petit jury.

2. Understand the jury selection process including what the *venire* is as well as the purpose of the *voir dire*.

3. Understand the different ways in which jurors can be excluded including challenges for cause and peremptory challenges.

4. Describe what jury consultants are, and understand the science behind jury selection.

5. Understand the meaning of jury size and whether a verdict has to be unanimous.

6. Understand jury sequestration and other methods of minimizing exposure of the jury to trial publicity.

7. Describe the process of jury decision making and voting.

8. Understand some of the current controversies surrounding jury verdicts.

9. Understand jury nullification.

10. Describe what constitutes jury or juror misconduct.

■ William Sullivan is on trial and accused of killing Jeanne Dominico of Nashua, New Hampshire. Prosecutors contend that Sullivan and Dominico's daughter plotted to kill Jeanne Dominico because Mrs. Dominico would not permit them to live together. The trial, which has lasted several weeks, has not been without incident. One of the jurors, Henry McElroy, a former state legislator, openly slept during some of the trial proceedings, where critical evidence was being presented against Sullivan by the prosecutor. McElroy also attempted to pass several notes to the judge during the trial, but these notes were intercepted by court officers and McElroy was advised not to attempt to contact the trial judge. Once both sides in the case rested, the jury began deliberating. One day McElroy brought a copy of a popular law dictionary into the jury room, supposedly to look up some legal terms he didn't understand. A court officer was advised by another juror about what McElroy had done, and his actions were reported to the judge. In the meantime, prosecutors discovered that McElroy had served on a previous jury and was investigated for attempting to tamper with the jury in a civil case in another county. This information was not disclosed to either the prosecutor or defense during jury selection and when McElroy was interviewed by both sides during *voir dire*. The judge therefore removed McElroy from the jury and he was sent home. An alternate juror took his place. The defense immediately complained, arguing for a mistrial and that their defendant's constitutional rights were violated when McElroy was removed from the jury by the judge. Should a mistrial be declared? Was the judge correct in removing McElroy from the jury? Can Sullivan receive a fair trial with the alternative juror who replaced McElroy? [Source: Adapted from the Associated Press, "Juror Booted: Deliberations Start Over in Murder Trial," July 15, 2005.]

■ It happened in Anchorage, Alaska. Frank W. Turney was convicted of jury tampering in 1994 because he approached prospective jurors at the state courthouse and passed to them information about their rights as jurors. He was the chairman of the Alaska chapter of the Fully Informed Jury Association. Turney attempted to convey information to prospective jurors about their powers in listening to cases and deciding one's guilt or innocence, despite judicial instructions. Turney maintained that he did nothing wrong by attempting to inform prospective jurors about their juror rights under the law. Specifically he gave prospective jurors information about jury nullification, where the term was explained and suggestions for its use were given. Eventually one of the persons Turney contacted became a juror in a case involving a man accused of weapons misconduct. The jury deadlocked when the juror called an 800 number given to him by Turney and the juror decided to vote as he wanted rather than with the other jurors. Subsequently, Turney was charged with and convicted of jury tampering, given a 60-day jail sentence and a $500 fine. He appealed and ultimately exhausted his state remedies. Next he sought relief through the federal court system. He contended that he was merely exercising his right to free speech and did nothing wrong to interfere with the jury process. A three-judge panel with the Nineth Circuit Court of Appeals rejected his most recent appeal in March 2005. Should any person be allowed to distribute information about juror rights to prospective jurors in court houses or any other public place where trials are held? [Source: Adapted from Amanda Bohman and the Associated Press, "Turney's Jury Tampering Conviction Upheld," March 18, 2005.]

INTRODUCTION

Many persons assume that the right to a jury trial has always been an important part of most societies. However, history suggests that using juries to make judgments in disputes is relatively rare. In ancient times, disputes or conflicts were resolved through direct interpersonal violence. The disputants engaged in some form of physical confrontation (e.g., duel or battle), and the winner of the confrontation was also the winner of the dispute. Jurors like judges are supposed to be impartial and hear the facts of the case, and base a decision of guilt or innocence on those facts only.

The next part of the chapter will discuss the history of the jury, and relate anecdotes on the development of the grand and petit jury. Being selected for jury duty is an involved process that begins with a list of potential jurors called a *venire*, potential jurors are asked questions relating to their appropriateness to serve, if they answer in the affirmative they will be asked to further proceed with a process called a *voir dire*. The process is to ensure the appropriateness of persons to sit on a jury but also to ensure a defendant's right to a "speedy and public trial, by an impartial jury in the state and district wherein the crime shall have been committed" (Sixth Amendment). This means trial by a fair jury composed of an adequate cross section of the community. Constructing an adequate cross section of one's peers who are impartial can sometimes be difficult and there have been many defendants who have appealed their cases based upon a violation of their Sixth Amendment rights. There have been calls that jurors have been removed for no other reason than their gender or their skin color. The Supreme Court has made several rulings relating to the process of jury selection. These decisions will be detailed in this chapter. A number of these have been related to the use of peremptory challenges. These challenges are used by prosecution and defense to remove a juror for no particular reason; these challenges, however, are limited. Another way to remove a juror, which are unlimited, is a challenge for cause. This type of challenge removes the juror for a particular reason—the person is biased in some way or does not meet the requirements to serve.

The role of the jury has been constantly challenged and revised. A number of cases in the last few decades have caused more than a few critics to question the integrity of the jury system, and have spurred calls for reform. It seems that we are constantly confronted with cases where we believe the defendant is guilty only to have the jury announce a verdict of not guilty and the defendant is freed. Often, we are outraged by reports of juries awarding multimillion dollar damages to plaintiffs where the allegations against defendants have been questionable. It is the idea of excessive jury verdicts, and even calls for jury nullification of the law that have led to calls for reform. Many legal scholars argue that juries should be replaced with panels of experts who would be more likely to see the merits of a case, understand the law, and not be swayed by emotion (Adler 1995). In fact, we have a system now that is quite the opposite, where experts in the law, law enforcement, professors of law, and members of the medical community are readily excused from sitting on a jury.

THE HISTORY OF JURIES

The jury system in America has not had a direct, linear evolution. The ancient Greeks were the first to rely on certain persons in their community to pass judgment in a variety of cases. At one point the entire population of Athens was required to hear appeals from the magistrates. Thus, it is not surprising that this process became difficult to administer. This process was subsequently replaced with a procedure designed to select jury members drawn from a cross section of the community to work with the magistrate and render decisions in criminal cases. This new jury was called a dicastery.

The ancient Romans also relied on an early form of the jury. In 190 B.C., for instance, magistrates could assemble a jury for certain criminal acts, including forgery, counterfeiting, and embezzlement. The jury was comprised of 35 to 75 people who decided the guilt of the accused. No provisions for appeals of verdicts were made.

In earlier times, common-law juries had a dual function. They had the responsibility of investigating crimes and conducting trials of accused persons. However, subsequent to the Norman invasion, these two responsibilities were divided into separate functioning units. The grand jury was created to investigate and report crimes, while the petit jury was used to determine a defendant's guilt or innocence. Today, these different jury systems continue to perform the same functions.

THE DEVELOPMENT OF THE GRAND JURY

The earliest forms of the **grand jury** can be traced back to Germanic tribal law and Anglo-Saxon dooms. The earliest versions of the grand jury had its origins in the Assize of Clarendon in 1166. An assize is essentially an order by the king and is binding throughout the kingdom. On this occasion, King Henry II ordered that 12 of every 100 family heads be placed under oath and report offenses or known criminals to the authorities. The most commonly reported offenses were robberies, murders, and theft. This practice was very similar to our contemporary neighborhood watch programs.

In colonial times, since judges traveled in circuits and were only scheduled to visit certain cities or towns every few months, members of the grand jury were responsible for gathering information about known criminal activity and present their information to the authorities whenever they were in town. Most often, when judges heard the cases presented to them by the grand jury, they ordered the defendant banished from the community. In essence, all trials during these early years were bench trials. The judge decided the guilt or innocence of defendants and determined the nature of the punishment. The petit jury or trial jury as we know it did not descend directly from the grand jury. Rather, it gradually replaced trials by ordeal.

THE DEVELOPMENT OF THE PETIT JURY

In medieval England, trials by ordeal were used to determine a defendant's guilt or innocence. The prevailing practice was to have the process blessed by a priest. The belief was that because the proceeding was endorsed by the church and ultimately God, it was also just. The trial participants believed that if a defendant was innocent, God would intervene and protect them from harm. For example, the trial by hot water required that defendants place their hands into a pot of boiling water and remove a rock placed at the bottom. Once the accused placed their hands into the water and removed the rock, their hands were wrapped in bandages. After a specified time, the bandages were removed and if the hands were burned, the defendants were believed to be guilty because God did not intervene and protect the accused from harm. This practice went unchallenged for centuries.

During the Fourth Lateran Council in 1215, the church withdrew its support for the trial by ordeal. This meant that priests would no longer be present to bless the trial. Without the benefit of blessings from priests and the presence of the church, it was also believed that God would not intervene on behalf of innocent defendants. The trial by ordeal was gradually replaced by the **petit jury** or trial jury. Initially, those accused of crimes were reluctant to accept a jury trial because if they were found guilty, they would lose their property and their descendants would lose their inheritance. The same fate would not befall those who opted for the bench trial. Consequently, the initial structure of the jury trial had an additional penalty that was not included in the bench trial.

Another significant event occurred in 1215. King John was forced to sign the Magna Carta. This document provided the foundations for the provisions of due process and the right to a jury trial of one's peers. The section of the Magna Carta that established this concept reads, "No Freeman shall be taken, or imprisoned or be disseized of his Freehold, or Liberties, or Free Customs, or be outlawed, or exiled, or otherwise destroyed; nor will we not pass upon him nor condemn him, but by lawful judgement of his peers, of by (a) the Law of the land. (2) We will sell to no man, (b) we will not deny or defer to any man either Justice or Right" (McCart 1964, 5).

Originally, these rights only extended to freemen or nobility. This meant that most people were still denied justice and the due process of law. The rights of a jury trial and due process were addressed in the Statute of Westminister of 1275. The relevant portions of this statute mandated that "no City, Borough, nor town nor any maybe amerced [fined or punished arbitrarily] without reasonable cause, and according to the Quality of his Trespass, that is to say, every Freeman saving his Freehold, a Merchant saving his Merchandise, a Villain saving his Gaynage [his rights in agricultural land, his tools and the product thereof] and that by his or their peers" (McCart 1964, 6).

During this same time period, there were no lawyers to act as advocates. To address this deficiency, Parliament authorized forty men to practice law throughout England. This number was believed adequate to fulfill the needs of the entire country. The trial jury during this period differed in one significant respect from the jury system in America today. The medieval jury was expected to have some knowledge of the case. It was believed that juror knowledge of the case would assist them in determining the guilt or innocence of the accused. Today, our notions of an impartial jury have been used to exclude those who have knowledge of the case. Historically, jurors were considered qualified if they were familiar with the facts of the case. Now jurors are considered more qualified if they have little of no knowledge of the facts of the case.

THE JURY SELECTION PROCESS

Venire

In medieval England jurors were selected by the king and only from the wealthy landowners. Throughout history those who were allowed to serve on juries were few in number. The selection of the *venire* or the **venireman list** of those qualified to serve as jurors has changed dramatically over time. For example, during most of American history, women were excluded from jury service. Some of the most prominent legal scholars of the eighteenth century argued that women should not be allowed to serve on juries. For example, it was believed that women should be excluded from jury service because of the defect of sex. This defect made it impossible for women to engage in intelligent decision making required for jury service. This perspective also existed in the United States. Women were excluded from jury service until 1919 when Utah became the first state to allow women to serve as jurors. The national sentiment against women as prospective jurors changed dramatically after the passage of the Nineteenth Amendment, which gave women the right to vote. When the Nineteenth Amendment was passed, most states allowed women to serve on juries. However, in many jurisdictions, women were not automatically included in the *venire*. As recently as 1966, three states did not permit women to serve on juries. In many other jurisdictions, women had to go to the courthouse and ask to be included in the list of potential jurors. This process was known as **affirmative registration.** In 1966, the U.S. Supreme Court upheld the practice of excluding women from the jury pool when it reasoned, "The legislature has a right to exclude women so they may contribute their services as mothers, wives, homemakers, and also to protect them . . . from the filth, obscenity, and noxious atmosphere . . . of the courtroom" (*Hoyt v. Florida*, 1961:57). It wasn't until 1975 in the case of *Taylor v. Louisiana* that the U.S. Supreme Court changed its mind and ruled that the affirmative registration process was unconstitutional.

Currently, most jurisdictions use voter registration lists to obtain prospective jurors for the jury pool. Once persons have been drawn from the list, the court sends them a short questionnaire summoning them for jury service and asking then to complete a short questionnaire to determine if they are qualified for jury service. The short questionnaire includes questions that might automatically exclude them from jury service. The standard questions include but are not limited to the following:

1. Are you a U.S. citizen?
2. Are you at least 18 years old?
3. Do you have any mental or physical disability?
4. Have you ever been convicted of a felony?

Answering "yes" or "no" to any of these questions may be sufficient grounds to exclude certain persons from the jury pool. If these persons pass the initial screening, they are sent a letter advising them to appear for jury service at the courthouse on a particular date and time.

Some persons have argued that relying solely on voter registration lists systematically excludes segments of the population. Levin (1988) has estimated that voter registration lists excluded 60 percent of the population. Who does this process exclude? The poor, undereducated, minorities, and women are less likely to register to vote than men, more educated persons, and nonminorities. Most defendants in the criminal court share most of the same characteristics as those who are excluded from jury service. Ultimately, voter registration lists are ineffective for obtaining a cross section of the community. Levin suggests that states must draw upon voter registration lists, tax rolls, public utility records, driver's license records, and the telephone directory to make better prospective juror selections from those groups who are typically bypassed whenever states rely on voter registration lists. In particular, the undereducated, poor, and minorities will most likely drive a car, have a telephone, and use electricity. Relying on these records will increase the representativeness of those who are called to jury service.

Voir Dire

We have the expectation that jurors should be unbiased or impartial when they hear the facts of a case. The process of determining a person's appropriateness or worthiness to serve as a juror is called *voir dire*. *Voir dire* is the opportunity to learn about the existing prejudices of prospective jurors. *Voir dire* means to "speak the truth." *Voir dire* is the crucial process through which attorneys attempt to uncover prospective juror biases, which might prevent certain jurors from providing defendants with a fair and impartial trial. Some persons have argued that while *voir dire* has frequently been called jury selection, this term really is inappropriate. This is because we don't actually select those who sit on a jury as much as we eliminate those who are unsuitable.

The *voir dire* process is described as follows. During *voir dire*, the trial judge and/or attorneys may ask questions of prospective jurors to determine their qualifications for jury service, their knowledge of the defendant and the

BOX 6.1 A CASE OF JURY TAMPERING

Justice takes a while to be concluded. In Frank W. Turney's case, it has taken at least 10 years. Turney, a Fairbanks, Alaska resident, was convicted of jury tampering in 1994. A case was being heard involving a man charged with illegal weapons possession. Turney's method was to approach jurors as they entered and exited the courthouse each day while the trial was in progress and give them information about juror's rights and an 800 number for the Fully Informed Jury Association. Turney was the chairman of the Alaska chapter. Turney also advised several of the jurors in the case that juries have the right to judge the law as well as the facts of a controversy. He told them that jury nullification is one of the checks and balances in our governmental laws, and he advocated that they consider jury nullification as a possible action in the case before them. One of the jurors Turney approached called the 800 number and told them he would vote how he wanted. But the jury deadlocked in the case. Subsequently, Turney's actions came to the attention of the presiding judge, and law enforcement authorities arrested Turney and charged him with jury tampering. He was convicted and sentenced to 60 days in prison and a $500 fine. Turney appealed, and eventually, the Alaska Supreme Court heard the case in 2005. The three-judge panel upheld Turney's conviction. Subsequently Turney was asked if he was going to appeal to the U.S. Supreme Court. "No," he said. "If there had been one dissenting judge, I would have. But it was a 3–0 slam dunk against me." Turney's attorney argued that Turney had the right of free speech in the case, and that he was only trying to educate the jurors about their rights and responsibilities. The court saw things differently. Should persons have the right to approach jurors in criminal cases and attempt to persuade them to vote in particular ways? Is free speech at issue here? Is "educating" juries about their rights jury tampering? What do you think? [Source: Adapted from Amanda Bohman and the Associated Press, "Turner's Jury Tampering Conviction Upheld," March 18, 2005.]

case, and attitudes toward issues or individuals on the case that bias their views of the trial evidence. For example, questions may be wide-ranging or more specifically related to the case, depending on what the trial judge allows.

Despite the purpose of the *voir dire* process to remove prospective jurors with biases, many persons have argued that the process actually achieves the opposite result. Both prosecutors and defense attorneys attempt to select jurors who might be sympathetic to their particular position. If one side is successful in soliciting crucial information during *voir dire*, they can use this information to remove unsympathetic jurors and increase jury bias either against or in favor of the defendant. Typically, prosecutors seek prospective jurors who are middle-aged, white, and middle class. It is believed that these persons are more likely to be supportive of the prosecution. However, defense counsels seek to remove prospective jurors with extreme views.

THE ELIMINATION OF JURORS

Challenges for Cause

During the *voir dire* process, the trial judge and attorneys attempt to uncover any biases that might hinder prospective jurors from serving in an impartial manner. There are two methods used to eliminate biased jurors or those considered undesirable by either side for whatever reason. One type of challenge is known as a **challenge for cause** (also a strike for cause). The other type of challenge is called a peremptory challenge. Prospective jurors may be challenged for cause and removed from the jury if they do not meet certain state mandatory requirements (e.g., being underage or not being a U.S. citizen), as well as for a specific bias (e.g., being related by blood or marriage to the accused), or for a nonspecific bias (e.g., expressing prejudice toward the defendant). Either the judge or the attorney may ask these questions. However, when the defense or prosecution wants to have a juror removed through the use of a challenge for cause, they must provide the judge with a compelling reason for doing so. When challenges for cause are used to strike certain prospective jurors, the judge is the final arbiter of whether the juror stays or goes.

For instance, a prominent black Tennessee defense attorney from Nashville, Avon Williams, was noted for his ability to dismiss prospective white jurors for cause whenever he represented black defendants. He would ask these prospective jurors if they were prejudiced toward blacks. Most would answer "No." Then Williams would ask them where they lived and if they belonged to any country clubs. Many of these white jurors lived in all-white neighborhoods, and some belonged to country clubs. He would then ask if these country clubs barred or admitted blacks. These white prospective jurors would become agitated and say that their country clubs and neighborhoods did not include blacks. Williams would then ask the judge to strike these white prospective jurors for cause. The judge usually granted Williams's request, based on the nature of his *voir dire* questioning.

Peremptory Challenges

The second method for removing prospective jurors is by using a **peremptory challenge.** Unlike challenges for cause, peremptory challenges do not require any explanations from attorneys for either side. Both prosecutors and defense counsel are given a limited number of these peremptory challenges. The number of peremptory challenges varies according to the seriousness of the case. In the most serious cases or cases with a significant amount of pretrial publicity, attorneys are given a larger number of challenges. Attorneys involved in less serious cases have fewer peremptory challenges. For instance, in most misdemeanor and less serious felony cases, each side is given six peremptory challenges. For more serious cases such as murder trials, each side is given a dozen or more peremptory challenges. In some jurisdictions, as many as 20 peremptory challenges may be given to each side for their use in striking prospective jurors they don't like, for whatever reason.

How do prosecutors and defense counsels know which prospective jurors to remove? During the *voir dire* process, attorneys usually ask members of the jury pool about their occupation, their attitudes toward law enforcement, and their general perceptions about the offense. For example, it is not uncommon for a defense attorney in a drunk-driving case to ask prospective jurors if it is a crime to drink and drive. Some of the members of the jury pool will say that drinking and driving is a crime. Some defense counsels will use this opportunity to educate the jury pool that drinking and driving is not a crime, and that it only rises to the level of a criminal offense when someone becomes legally intoxicated and drives a vehicle. Attorneys for both sides also use the information gathered from the *voir dire* together with juror demographics (e.g., age, gender, race) to develop a profile of how prospective jurors with similar characteristics feel about certain issues that might arise during the trial.

BOX 6.2 SELECTED JURY CASES

■ *Batson v. Kentucky*, 476 U.S. 79, 106 S.Ct. 1712 (1986)

In Kentucky, a black man, Batson, was convicted by an all-white jury of second-degree burglary. The prosecutor had used all of his peremptory challenges to exclude the few black prospective jurors from the jury pool. Ordinarily, peremptory challenges may be used to strike particular jurors without the prosecutor's having to provide a reason for doing so. In this case, the use of peremptory challenges was rather transparent, and Batson appealed. In a landmark case, the U.S. Supreme Court decided that peremptory challenges may not be used for a racially discriminatory purpose. Thus, creating an all-white jury by deliberately eliminating all prospective black candidates was discriminatory. The U.S. Supreme Court ruled in favor of Batson.

■ *Georgia v. McCollum*, 505 U.S. 42, 112 S.Ct. 2348 (1992)

McCollum was indicted on charges of aggravated assault and simple battery. During jury selection, his attorney used his peremptory challenges to strike certain prospective jurors from jury duty because of their race.

(continued)

BOX 6.2 *(continued)*

McCollum was acquitted. The state challenged the use of these peremptory challenges, arguing that they had created a biased jury as in *Batson v. Kentucky* (1986), in which the prosecutor used peremptory challenges for racial-bias purposes. The U.S. Supreme Court agreed with the state and rejected the defendant's attorney's use of peremptory challenges for racial purposes. Thus, according to *Batson* and *McCollum,* neither prosecutors nor defense attorneys may deliberately use their peremptory challenges to excuse jurors on the basis of their race.

■ *Griffith v. Kentucky,* 479 U.S. 314, 107 S.Ct. 708 (1987)

Griffith, a black man, was arrested for conspiracy to distribute marijuana. During his 1982 trial in Jefferson County, the prosecutor used four out of five peremptory challenges to strike from jury duty four out of five prospective black jurors. Griffith was convicted. He later appealed, saying that the prosecutor had violated his right to due process by striking from jury duty most of the black candidates. He said the case of *Batson v. Kentucky* (1986) should be retroactively applied to his case. The U.S. Supreme Court overturned his conviction, holding that the *Batson* case, prohibiting prosecutors from using their peremptory challenges to give racial bias to a jury pool, should be retroactively applied where a showing exists that such conduct has occurred. Thus, Griffith's case qualified for a retroactive application of *Batson.* The U.S. Supreme Court held that a new rule for the conduct of criminal prosecutions is to be applied retroactively to all cases, state or federal, pending on direct review or not yet final, with no exception for cases in which the new rule constitutes a "clear break" with the past.

■ *Teague v. Lane,* 489 U.S. 288, 109 S.Ct. 1060 (1989)

Teague, a black man, was accused of attempted murder. During jury selection, the prosecutor used all of his ten peremptory challenges to exclude blacks from the jury. He was eventually convicted by an all-white jury. In the meantime, *Batson v. Kentucky* (1986) had recently been decided, which established that blacks could not be excluded from jury duty by use of peremptory challenges. Teague sought to make this rule retroactive in his case, thus causing his conviction to be overturned and a new trial conducted. The U.S. Supreme Court rejected the retroactive principle relating to *Batson,* holding that convicted offenders are barred from making retroactive claims involving racial discrimination in jury selection. Further, Teague had failed to make a convincing case that the peremptory challenges had been used in a discriminatory fashion.

■ *Hernandez v. New York*, 500 U.S. 352, 111 S.Ct. 1859 (1991)

Hernandez was convicted of various crimes. During the selection of his jury, the prosecutor used several peremptory challenges to strike from potential jury duty four Latinos. Following his conviction, Hernandez filed an appeal, alleging that the prosecutor had deliberately deprived him of a fair trial by eliminating persons like Hernandez. The argument was similar to the one made in *Batson v. Kentucky* (1986), in which it was held that peremptory challenges cannot be used to create racially pure juries or to strike off members of a particular race. At the time, objections had been raised by defense counsel, but the prosecutor cited various valid reasons for using these challenges. The U.S. Supreme Court upheld his conviction, holding that an acceptable race-neutral explanation had been provided by the prosecutor for striking the Latino jurors in that case. No evidence to the contrary had been presented.

■ *Powers v. Ohio*, 499 U.S. 400, 111 S.Ct. 1364 (1991)

Powers was charged with murder, aggravated murder, and attempted aggravated murder, all with firearm specifications (calling for mandatory minimum sentences). A white man, he objected to the government's use of peremptory challenges to strike seven black prospective jurors from the jury. Subsequently, Powers was convicted. He appealed, alleging that his Fourteenth Amendment right had been violated under the equal-protection clause because of the alleged discriminatory use of peremptory challenges. The matter of excluding prospective black jurors by the use of peremptory challenges had already been decided in *Batson v. Kentucky* (1986), in which it was declared unconstitutional to use peremptory challenges to achieve a racially pure jury. In the *Batson* case, however, the defendant was black, and government prejudice was obvious in the use of these peremptory challenges. In the *Powers* case, the defendant was white, and prospective black jurors had been excluded. The U.S. Supreme Court heard Powers's appeal and overturned his conviction on the same grounds as *Batson,* holding that criminal defendants may object to race-based exclusions of jurors effected through peremptory challenges whether or not defendants and excluded jurors share the same race.

■ *Purkett v. Elem*, 514 U.S. 765, 115 S.Ct. 1769 (1995)

Elem, a black man, was accused of second-degree robbery. During the selection of jurors, the prosecutor used one of his peremptory challenges to strike from the jury pool a prospective black juror. Elem appealed, alleging that this use of a peremptory challenge was in violation of a policy set forth in *Batson v. Kentucky* (1986) prohibiting the use of peremptory challenges for racial purposes. The U.S. Supreme Court heard Elem's *habeas corpus* petition and argument. It upheld Elem's conviction when it determined

(continued)

BOX 6.2 *(continued)*

that the prosecutor had used the peremptory challenge in a racially neutral fashion. The reason given for striking this black prospective juror was that the man had long, unkempt hair and a mustache and beard. The U.S. Supreme Court accepted this explanation as being race-neutral. It held that opponents of peremptory challenges must carry the burden of proving that purposeful discrimination has occurred. The explanation given by those exercising their peremptory challenges need not be persuasive or even plausible; rather, these explanations are considered only in determining whether opponents have carried their burden of proof by showing that the peremptory strikes were discriminatory. In this case, the peremptory challenge was satisfactorily explained and Elem's conviction was upheld.

■ *Miller-El v. Cockrell,* 537 U.S. 322, 123 S.Ct. 1029 (2003)

Thomas Miller-El, his wife Dorothy, and Kenneth Flowers robbed a Holiday Inn in Dallas, Texas, in 1985. They bound and gagged two employees and then shot them. One employee died, but the other recovered and was able to identify Miller-El and his associates as his assailants. Subsequently, Miller-El was indicted and tried for capital murder in a Dallas criminal court in February and March 1986. During jury selection, the prosecutor used his peremptory challenges to exclude ten of the eleven African American prospective jurors, thus creating a largely white jury. Following the jury selection, Miller-El moved to strike the jury on the grounds that the prosecution had violated the equal-protection clause of the Fourteenth Amendment by excluding African Americans through the use of peremptory challenges. Miller-El's motion was denied. Upon his subsequent conviction for murder, Miller-El, a black, was sentenced to death. He began a lengthy series of appeals, contending that blacks had been systematically excluded from the jury. During his appeals, the case of *Batson v. Kentucky* (1986) was decided and established a three-part process for evaluating claims that a prosecutor used peremptory challenges in violation of the equal-protection clause. First, a defendant must make a *prima facie* showing that a peremptory challenge has been exercised on the basis of race. Second, if that showing has been made, the prosecution must offer a race-neutral basis for striking the juror in question. Third, in light of the parties' submissions, the trial court must determine whether the defendant has shown purposeful discrimination. Both Texas appellate courts and the federal Fifth Circuit Court of Appeals denied Miller-El's petitions, citing that insufficient evidence existed to show bias on the part of the prosecutor. The U.S. Supreme Court heard the case and disagreed. The U.S. Supreme Court overturned the circuit court, holding that Miller-El was entitled to appeal the issue of biased jury selection in his original trial, as there was evident unreasonableness associated with how the original jury was selected.

Miller-El was entitled to appeal this issue in a Texas court in light of the holding in *Batson v. Kentucky.*

■ *Johnson v. California,* ___ U.S. ___, 125 S.Ct. 2410 (2005)

Jay Johnson, a black man, was convicted of second-degree murder in the death of a 19-month-old white child. During jury selection, several prospective jurors were excused for cause. The prosecutor used three peremptory challenges to strike all of the prospective black jurors, thus leaving Johnson to be tried by an all-white jury. These peremptory challenges were opposed by Johnson, but the judge rejected his arguments. The prosecutor failed to explain why he had excused these black prospective jurors, but the judge declared that he (the judge) had reviewed the record and was convinced that the prosecutor's strikes could be justified by race-neutral reasons. Johnson appealed through the California courts, alleging that the exclusion of blacks from the jury deprived him of a fair trial. An appellate court set aside Johnson's conviction but the California Supreme Court reinstated it, acknowledging that although the exclusion of all three black prospective jurors looked suspicious, the court deferred to the judge's ruling and explanation. Johnson therefore appealed to the U.S. Supreme Court who heard the case. The U.S. Supreme Court reversed Johnson's conviction, holding that California's standard is an inappropriate yardstick to measure the sufficiency of a *prima facie* case of purposeful discrimination in jury selection. The fact that the trial judge said that the case was close and the California Supreme Court said that it was suspicious that all three black prospective jurors were removed were sufficient bases for a *prima facie* case of discrimination in Johnson's case.

■ *Miller v. Dretke,* ___ U.S. ___, 125 S.Ct. 2317 (2005)

Thomas Miller-El, a black man, and Kennard Flowers robbed a Dallas, Texas Holiday Inn in November 1985. During the robbery they bound and gagged two employees and then shot each twice in the back, killing one and seriously injuring the other. Subsequently, Miller-El was charged with capital murder. His trial lasted five weeks. At the beginning of Miller-El's trial during jury selection, 108 persons were selected as the *venire.* Of these, there were 20 blacks. Subsequently, 19 out of 20 blacks were rejected as jurors. Three were dismissed for cause; six were dismissed by parties' agreement; and ten were struck by the prosecutor through the use of peremptory challenges. Miller-El objected to these strikes but his objections were overruled. Miller-El was convicted and sentenced to death. He filed numerous appeals over the years on different grounds. His most recent appeal was a *habeas corpus* action alleging that the prosecutor engaged in purposeful discrimination by striking ten out of eleven black venirepersons. A U.S. district court denied the petition and this decision

(continued)

BOX 6.2 *(continued)*

was affirmed by the Fifth Circuit Court of Appeals. Miller-El appealed to the U.S. Supreme Court who heard the case. The U.S. Supreme Court reversed and remanded, holding that the Texas court's factual findings as to the nonpretextual nature of the state's race-neutral explanations for its use of peremptory challenges to excuse ten of eleven black venirepersons were shown to be wrong by clear and convincing evidence. Based on the totality of relevant facts in Miller-El's case, discriminatory jury selection had been demonstrated. The prosecutors used peremptory challenges to exclude 91 percent of the eligible black venire panelists, a disparity unlikely to have been produced by happenstance.

■ *Rice v. Collins,* ___ U.S. ___, 126 S.Ct. 969 (2006)

Steven Collins, an African American, was convicted of cocaine possession, in violation of California's three-strike rule, which would subject him to a harsher sentence. Collins sought postconviction relief on *habeas corpus* grounds, in particular objecting to the peremptory challenge of an African American prospective juror on allegedly race-based grounds (see *Batson v. Kentucky*). The dismissal of this juror, according to Collins, meant that his right to a fair trial by an impartial jury of his peers was violated. A *Batson* challenge, where peremptory challenges of jurors are used to strike prospective jurors on the basis of race, involves a showing that the prosecutor (1) exercised the peremptory challenge on the basis of race; (2) obligated the prosecutor to provide a race-neutral explanation for striking the juror in question; and (3) determining whether the defendant carried the burden of proof in demonstrating that the peremptory challenge was indeed race-based. The prosecutor defended his actions as race-neutral, contending that the prospective juror was struck because (1) she was young and might be too tolerant of drug offenders; (2) she was single and lacked community ties; and (3) she had rolled her eyes when asked certain questions by the court. State appellate courts, including the California Supreme Court, upheld Collins's conviction, but the Ninth Circuit Court of Appeals set aside Collins's conviction on the grounds of an unreasonable factual determination by the prosecutor based on trial information presented. The government appealed and the U.S. Supreme Court heard the case. The U.S. Supreme Court reversed the Ninth Circuit, reinstating Collins's conviction, holding that the Ninth Circuit's grounds for reversal were themselves based on a set of debatable inferences about prosecutorial conduct in jury selection. The U.S. Supreme Court said that while reasonable minds reviewing the record might disagree about the prosecutor's credibility, nothing on the record suffices to supersede the trial court's credibility determination of the prosecutor's actions regarding the peremptory strike of the African American juror and the race-neutral explanation provided.

Social scientists have discovered that often demographic characteristics are quite important and influence one's perceptions and attitudes. For example, Winston and Winston (1980) found that jurors who were opposed to the death penalty were usually under 45 years old, had a high school education, were employed, and did not watch the news on television. However, those favoring the death penalty tended to be males age 60 and older who had less than a high school education, were unemployed or retired, and watched the news on television. If either the prosecution or defense wish to strike particular prospective jurors, they may simply excuse them by using a peremptory challenge.

Several serious allegations made about prosecutors who systematically remove minorities from juries where the criminal defendants are also minorities. Some persons have alleged that this has occurred even in the most high-profile cases. For example, Suggs and Sales (1981) describe how prosecutors have used most of their peremptory challenges to remove most blacks from the jury panel where a black defendant is on trial for a serious offense. Defense attorneys have also been accused of using peremptory challenges to remove certain types of persons who they believe would be unsympathetic to their position. For example, in the trial of the Harrisburg Seven, the defense used its 28 challenges to remove those who were wealthy and exhibited conservative views (O'Rouke 1972).

For many decades, the use of peremptory challenges was inviolate. But in 1986, the U.S. Supreme Court decided to review the issue of using peremptory challenges to systematically remove black jurors in the case of *Batson v. Kentucky*. The U.S. Supreme Court found that the peremptory challenges used by the prosecutor were race-based and therefore unconstitutional. In 1991 the Court applied the equal-protection argument to defense counsels (*Georgia v. McCollum*) and in civil cases such as *Edmonson v. Leesville Concrete Co.* (1991). In 2000 the Court in *United States v. Martinez-Salazar* ruled that the use of a peremptory challenge to exclude a juror based solely on their gender, race, or ethnic group is unconstitutional. Lastly, the Third Circuit Court of Appeals in 2003 in the case of *Rico v. Leftridge-Byrd* applied the ruling in *Batson* to Italian American members of the jury because they had been excluded due to their Italian last names.

JURY CONSULTANTS AND SCIENTIFIC JURY SELECTION

F. Lee Bailey and Melvin Belli have been credited as being the first defense attorneys to hire experts to assist them in the jury selection process. However, it wasn't until the Berrigan brothers trial that **scientific jury selection** became an important trial tactic. Daniel and Philip Berrigan were Catholic priests who had been charged with conspiracy to kidnap then-secretary of state Henry Kissinger, raid draft boards, and bomb tunnels in Washington, D.C. Jay Schulman, a social scientist who sympathized with the defendants, decided to use his skill in social research methods to assist the defendants. He wanted to determine how several demographic characteristics (e.g., age, political philosophy, gender) influenced prospective jurors' perceptions of the issues surrounding the case and their attitudes toward the defendants. He and his colleagues conducted a telephone interview of 840 randomly selected registered voters. These interviews were followed by personal interviews of 262 people. During the face-to-face interviews, the respondents were asked questions in the following areas:

(a) Media contact—Respondents were asked of their choice of newspapers, magazines, radio, and television stations and their amount of contact with each.

(b) Knowledge of the defendants and their case—The names of the defendants were embedded with the names of other people in the news and respondents were asked if they had heard of the person and what they had heard about them.

(c) Greatest American of the past 10 or 15 years (to seek respondent's values).

(d) Trust in government—Three questions were asked relating to the governments' decisions and attempts to do what is right.

(1) "How much time do you think you can trust the Government in Washington to do what is right?"

(2) "Do you feel that the people who are running the Government are smart people who usually know what they are doing?"

(3) "Would you say that the Government is pretty much run for a few big interests looking out for themselves, or is it run for the benefit of the people?"

(e) Ages and activities of respondents children.

(f) Religious attitudes and commitment.

(g) Spare time activities.

(h) Organizational memberships.

(i) Attitudes that were potentially related to the trial. The interviewers sought the extent of agreement with eight statements concerning issues, such as right to private property, support for the government, police use of force, and the like.

(j) Scale of acceptable antiwar activities. (Wanamaker 1978, 348)

BOX 6.3 CAN JURY CONSULTANTS SELECT PREDICTABLE JURIES?

The job of jury consultants is to assist both defense and prosecuting attorneys in figuring out the types of people who will be most likely inclined to find in favor or against particular defendants. Several jury consultant firms have bragged that they have a nearly perfect batting average in picking juries favorable to defendants. However, the job of being a jury consultant is becoming increasingly difficult. This is primarily because of media coverage, particularly in high-profile trials such as those involving key officials at

Enron and Adelphia. New stereotypes have formed in the public's mind about company executives and their involvement in company scandals involving possible embezzlement and fraud.

A spokesperson for the jury-consulting firm, Zagnoli, McEvoy, and Foley of Chicago, has said that it is a rare jury that you talk to now where the majority of people have not lost money in the last couple of years. "Everybody's lost money. That's bad for defendants in trials involving corporate scandals, like Enron." Patricia McEvoy, with Zagnoli, McEvoy, and Foley, has indicated that when allowed by judges, jury-consulting firms can develop questionnaires that seek to draw out potential biases among jurors through a blend of psychology and educated guesswork, but their work to shape a favorable jury panel for a particular defendant is limited. She's not suggesting that corporate executives cannot get a fair trial in America, but it is extremely difficult to select jurors in such cases who will act in predictable ways and vote favorably for certain defendants.

In the case of Credit Suisse First Boston banker Frank P. Quattrone who was indicted on several counts of fraud, for instance, McEvoy said that the views of prospective jurors about stock market losses and who should be blamed are critical in jury selection. One type of juror targeted by jury consultant firms is the risk-taker, the person who understands that rules are flexible and appreciates that executives sometimes have to break them. Therefore, one of the questions McEvoy asks judges to ask prospective jurors is how much of a stickler they are for details and rules. "I don't want someone who thinks they would never do what these guys did," says McElvoy. Sometimes, a hung jury, as was the result in Quattrone's trial, is considered a "victory" of sorts for jury-consulting firms. While it isn't an acquittal, it does give the defense an opportunity to revise its strategy if charges against their clients are brought again. Also, it enables them to see prosecution strategy and hear incriminating evidence. In a subsequent trial, defensive strategy can be tailored to defeat such incriminating evidence.

How good are jury consultants at what they are supposed to do? There are mixed opinions. Phoebe Ellsworth, a professor of law and psychology at the University of Michigan, has conducted a number of studies about jury consultants. She says, "Whether they are any good is a tricky question. Because you never know how the case would have turned out without them." Another expert, Susan Macpherson, the vice president of the midwestern office of the National Jury Project, a consulting group, says that "I think it was all uncharged water pre-Enron. We didn't have a national stereotype in our heads about the types of people who get charged with these kinds of crime."

Can prospective jurors' behaviors be predicted with precision? Will certain types of jurors vote particular ways? How predictable are their behaviors? What do you think?

[*Source:* Adapted from Barry Meier and Jonathan D. Glater, Associated Press, "Picking a Jury for a Case in the Headlines," April 30, 2004.]

Using the results of this survey, the researchers were able to determine that conservatives with higher education and who received their news from metropolitan news sources held opinions that were unfavorable to the defendants. Surprisingly, the researchers found that religious affiliation was an important factor that the defense counsel should consider. Protestant denominations such as Methodists, Presbyterians, and Episcopalians were more likely to condemn the defendants for their actions. The research revealed that from the defendants perspective, the most favorable type of juror was a female Democrat with no religious preference and employed as a white-collar professional or possibly a skilled blue-collar job (Wanamaker 1978, 349). It is impossible to determine if the information collected was useful in selecting a sympathetic jury for these defendants, but the jury in the actual case voted 10–2 to acquit the defendants. Had the jury voted to convict them, then the scientific jury selection process engaged in by Schulman and his colleagues would probably have never received much attention. But since the outcome of the trial favored the defendants, the legal community took special notice, and scientific jury selection subsequently became an important component in the jury selection process.

The process of scientific jury selection has evolved into an entirely new professional enterprise. In most of the high-profile criminal cases (e.g., O. J. Simpson, William Kennedy Smith, and Rodney King), jury consultants have been used to assist both prosecutors and defense counsels in their selection of jury members. For example, in the O. J. Simpson criminal trial, the defense team hired Jo-Ellan Dimitrius from Trial Logistics, while the prosecution hired Don Vinson from DecisionQuest to aid in jury selection. Dimitrius and

BOX 6.4 CAN THE PERFECT JURY BE HANDPICKED?

■ Jury Selection in North Dakota

How are jurors chosen from criminal trials? How do lawyers choose prospective jurors and what criteria do they use for rejecting certain jurors? Answers to these and other questions have been provided by a jury selection psychologist, Jim Rasicot, a Minneapolis resident. Rasicot was a jury consultant who worked as a defense jury consultant for the Mike Tyson trial in Indiana. He also assisted in the jury selection for the trial on which the movie, *Paradise Lost,* was based. In addition, he also was in the movie as an "extra."

Rasicot has advised lawyers on how to handle jury selection in a way to make the jurors selected be the most favorable to their case. He said there are several steps in choosing the right jurors. First, the objective is to get rid of those jurors who pose the most danger to the defense. Second, it is important for lawyers to gain rapport with potential jurors, and having done that, to drop the seeds of the case into their minds. This is accomplished while questioning potential jurors about past experiences in an attempt to gain access to their biases that they don't like to talk about. Rasicot said that these things are important because they can cause problems for the defense later on during the trial.

One step in preparing to challenge jurors is to develop the right type of questionnaire and to keep questions short and concise. He said, "Get the information you need (about the potential juror) and get out." Questionnaires for jury trials can be 60 pages or longer. It might take someone several weeks to go through all of the answers. Another important factor in choosing a juror or having one removed for cause is attitude. A lawyer has to consider how the juror's past experiences can affect attitude. He urged lawyers to confirm an attitude the juror might already have, such as, "If someone breaks a window, they should have to pay for it, right?"

An important tactic is to get a potential juror to change an attitude. For instance, a juror might have the attitude that the defendant must have done something wrong if he was charged with a crime. "You have to try to change that attitude and create a new one," he said. He added, "Jurors don't want to talk to you, and so your job is to get them to talk. Let them know that there are no right or wrong answers during the jury selection, and to put them at ease." Other tips Rasicot passes along are to include talking to jurors about their occupations and be sure to ask them about any past occupations. One time, he said a potential juror told the lawyer that he was in the sheet metal business and managed the company. Later, during questioning, he said he knew about trial proceedings because he had been a chief of police, and possibly pro-prosecution, before going to work for the sheet metal company. The juror was dismissed from further consideration after that. "It's important to find out about things like that," Rasicot said. "Remember, people might change occupations several times," he added.

Another tip included not insulting any juror. He gave an example of a lawyer who was questioning a female juror who said that she was a housewife. The lawyer said, "Oh, you don't work then." The woman replied curtly, "I work very hard." She didn't serve on that jury. Rasicot said that you need to let the jury know where you are going with the case. Start off with the easy questions about the things they like to talk about, such as occupations and education. Then ease into more controversial subjects that might show juror bias. Can the perfect jury be selected? Do you think jury consultants are effective at selecting the best juries for their clients? Should lawyers be allowed to question prospective jurors at length concerning their qualifications for jury service? Should police officers or former law enforcement officers automatically be excluded as jurors? What do you think?

[Source: Adapted from Ken Crites, "Psychologist Discusses Jury Selection Process," June 16, 2000.]

Vinson conducted extensive surveys and relayed this information to their clients during trial strategy sessions. It is interesting to note that Dimitrius assisted during the entire trial. However, Vinson was dismissed by the prosecution after two court appearances (Lafferty, 1994).

Jury consultation has become a big business. This year the American Society of Trial Consultants will celebrate their twenty-fifth anniversary. Despite this rapid growth, much skepticism exists about the quality of scientific jury selection. Litigation Sciences boast a 95 percent success rate, although these success rates may not be attributable to scientific techniques.

Most of the jury consultants were hired in high-profile cases or political trials. In these cases, the defense attorneys are often in the best position to prepare their cases such that acquittal of their clients is more a matter of good lawyering rather than a matter of the advice received from professional jury consultants. Some persons have equated scientific jury selection with jury tampering, and they suggest that the integrity of the jury is undermined or compromised (Enriquez and Clark 2005).

JURY SIZE

Anyone unfamiliar with the court process and who is charged with a felony may be surprised to see only six people sitting as jurors to decide their guilt or innocence. Doesn't the Constitution guarantee them the right to a twelve-member jury? What effect will smaller jury sizes have on jury deliberations? Are smaller juries more likely to convict defendants rather than larger juries? These are just some of the questions defendants have raised about smaller jury sizes. These same questions have been asked and researched by legal scholars.

For instance, what is the special significance associated with the number, 12? Why is this number given such importance in our common-law legal history? Are twelve jurors better able to understand the evidence and reach a decision? One reason the number "12" is so deeply ingrained in our perception of the trial process has nothing to do with any scientific or legalistic reasoning. Rather, it has everything to do with historical tradition. Throughout most of the last several centuries, juries were comprised of 12 members.

Several legal scholars have studied the origins of the 12-member jury. Despite their intensive investigative efforts, there is still no definitive conclusion as to the origin of the number "12." Some scholars have traced the 12-member jury to ancient Greek mythology, while others have found antecedents of the 12-member jury in biblical writings (McConville and Mirsky 2005). The most direct lineage of the 12-member jury in America is traced to the Constitution of Clarendon, the Assize of Clarendon, and the Magna Carta.

The Constitution of Clarendon was signed by King Henry II in 1164. This constitution provided that the sheriff was to administer an oath to 12 men of the neighborhood that they would declare the truth and render verdicts in cases brought to them. The Assize of Clarendon was a court created by Henry II to give litigants a legal option to a resolve a dispute rather than resolve it in the traditional manner, which was often a duel to the death. If a disputant chose the court rather than the duel, the court would issue a writ to the king to have four knights from the region select 12 jurors. The litigants were allowed to challenge the knights' decisions. This process continued until 12 acceptable jurors were selected. Finally, the Magna Carta, signed by King John, established the constitutional importance of the jury. The right to a 12-member jury remained essentially the same for almost 800 years. This tradition was changed by the U.S. Supreme Court in *Williams v. Florida* (1970).

At the time Johnny Williams was charged with robbery, Florida permitted six-member juries to hear all non-capital criminal cases. Williams argued that his case should be heard by a 12-member jury. His motion was denied and he was tried and convicted by a six-person jury. He was ultimately sentenced to life in prison. He appealed his conviction on the grounds that the Sixth Amendment guaranteed him a right to a 12-member jury. The U.S. Supreme Court held that the Sixth Amendment does not require a 12-person jury. The U.S. Supreme Court majority reasoned that the 12-member jury is a historical accident and unnecessary for the proper functioning of a jury. Justice White said that the essential feature of the jury obviously lies in the interposition between the accused and his accuser of the commonsense judgment of a group of laymen, and in the community participation and shared responsibility that results for the group's determination of guilt or innocence. The performance of this role is not a function of the particular number of the body that makes up the jury (*Williams v. Florida*, 1970).

With authority from the U.S. Supreme Court, many states began to challenge other aspects of the Sixth Amendment. For instance, the use of non-unanimous verdicts was upheld by the U.S. Supreme Court in *Apodaca v. Oregon* (1972) and *Johnson v. Louisiana* (1972) (see Box 6.5).

In the Apodaca case the U.S. Supreme Court upheld the Oregon statute, which allowed a 10–2 vote for either conviction or acquittal. In Louisiana, the law allowed jury verdicts with a 9–3 vote. The U.S. Supreme Court also accepted this practice as not violating the Sixth Amendment or the Fourteenth Amendment. One year later in *Colgrove v. Battin* (1973), the Court ruled that six-member juries were acceptable in civil cases. In the majority opinion, the Court cited social science evidence they believed indicated that there was no substantial difference between twelve-member and six-member juries. The *Colgrove* court cited four studies they believed provided "convincing empirical evidence of the correctness of the *Williams* conclusion that there is no discernable difference between the results reached by the two different-sized juries" (*Colgrove v. Battin*, 1973:47). With the *Colgrove* decision, the Court seemed to give states the license to decrease their jury sizes. Georgia attempted this. A

BOX 6.5 ON JURY VOTING AND UNANIMITY

■ *Apodaca v. Oregon*, 406 U.S. 404, 92 S.Ct. 1628 (1972)

Apodaca and others were found guilty of various serious crimes by less than unanimous jury verdicts. Oregon has a statute mandating a conviction or acquittal on the basis of a 10-to-2 vote, or what is referred to by the Oregon legislature as a 10-of-12 vote. In Apodaca's case, the vote favoring conviction was 11 to 1. Apodaca challenged this vote as not being unanimous, and the U.S. Supreme Court heard the case contemporaneously with the case of *Johnson v. Louisiana* (1972) on an identical issue. In Apodaca's case, the U.S. Supreme Court upheld the constitutionality of the Oregon jury voting provision, declaring that votes of these kinds do not violate one's right to due process under either the Sixth or the Fourteenth Amendment. The significance of this case is that less than unanimous jury votes among the states are constitutional and do not violate one's right to due process.

■ *Johnson v. Louisiana*, 406 U.S. 356, 92 S.Ct. 1620 (1972)

Johnson was arrested without a warrant at his home based on a photograph identification by a robbery victim. He was later subjected to a lineup, where he was identified again. Johnson was represented by counsel. He was subjected to trial by jury for the robbery offense and convicted in a jury vote of 9 to 3. Johnson appealed, contending that the jury verdict should be unanimous. The U.S. Supreme Court affirmed his conviction, saying, in effect, that states have the right to determine whether conviction requires unanimity of jury votes or only a majority vote. The U.S. Supreme Court concluded by saying that the verdicts rendered by 9 out of 12 jurors are not automatically invalidated by the disagreement of the dissenting 3. Johnson was not deprived of due process or a fair trial because of the 9–3 vote. This U.S. Supreme Court decision applies to states only and does not affect federal juries, who must be unanimous in their verdicts. Federal criminal jury sizes of 12 may be reduced to 11 under special conditions with judicial approval; either size must be unanimous.

■ *Early v. Packer*, 537 U.S. 3, 123 S.Ct. 362 (2002)

William Packer was found guilty in a California court of second-degree murder, two counts of attempted murder, two counts of robbery, two counts of assault with a deadly weapon, and one count of assault with a firearm. He was acquitted on ten other counts. The jury had a difficult time in certain of its deliberations, with one juror in particular claiming illness, indecisiveness, and fatigue. At various points during jury deliberations, the trial judge requested information from the jury foreman about the status of jury voting, and he questioned the particular female juror at some length. The judge repeated various instructions to the jury as to their deliberations, including that they should follow the law, determine whether or not the elements of the offense were present, and find unanimously whether Packer was guilty or not guilty of each of those offenses. Subsequently, the jury rendered its verdicts as noted above and Packer appealed, filing a *habeas corpus* petition. The petition alleged that the trial judge coerced the female juror into agreeing with the majority of other jurors in reaching their guilty verdicts on the above counts. Thus, he claimed, he was denied his due process right to a fair and impartial jury. The Ninth Circuit Court of Appeals granted Packer's petition and reversed his convictions. California appealed and the U.S. Supreme Court heard the case. The U.S. Supreme Court reinstated Packer's convictions, holding that the trial judge's remarks and instructions to jurors were not coercive, nor were they unreasonable or contrary to established federal law. Thus, it is not unconstitutional for a trial judge to urge a jury to continue deliberating as long as the judge does not attempt to coerce a particular type of jury verdict. In this instance, all of the judge's remarks clearly admonished jurors to follow and apply the law objectively and to make their decisions about Packer's guilt or innocence consistent with that objectivity.

Georgia statute was passed allowing convictions based on deliberations by five-member juries. This practice was challenged in *Ballew v. Georgia* (1978). Ballew was a theater manager in Atlanta who was charged with violating a Georgia ordinance prohibiting the distribution of obscene material by showing a pornographic and sexually explicit movie starring Marilyn Chambers, *Behind the Green Door*. Ballew appealed his conviction by a five-member jury contending that it violated his Sixth and Fourteenth Amendment rights. Ballew's conviction was set aside after the U.S. Supreme Court declared that five-member juries are too small to constitute a representative cross section of the community. Thus, the minimum jury size was established as six.

In all previous U.S. Supreme Court decisions, the justices were reluctant to specify a minimum jury size. But with the *Williams* decision, the Court was faced with a potentially serious dilemma. Again relying on social science, the U.S. Supreme Court argued that their conclusion rested on the assumption there was no difference between twelve- and six-member juries. The Court believed that the deliberative ability, representativeness, verdict reliability, likelihood of conviction, and the minority ability to resist majority pressure was not hindered by decreasing jury size. However, the Court's reading of the literature was seriously flawed. Most of the studies they relied upon evidenced several empirical flaws or limitations. Additionally, where studies were cited that had credibility and were empirically sound, the U.S. Supreme Court misinterpreted some of the results. The U.S. Supreme Court cited a study conducted by Asch (1966), which examined the minority's ability to resist group pressure. Asch found that when the minority position has an ally, it is better

BOX 6.6 CAREER SNAPSHOT

Jill A. Caldwell
Senior Court Officer, Glynn County Juvenile Court
Brunswick, GA

Statistics: (criminal justice) South Georgia College

Background: I was born and raised in Claxton, Georgia. My grandfather was chief of police in Claxton and I had several uncles who were police officers. Law enforcement was instilled in me at an early age. I graduated from Claxton High School in 1972. In the fall of 1972, I moved to Douglas, Georgia and attended South Georgia College. I made the decision to major in criminal justice. There were a couple of things that helped me make this decision. The first and most important was my interest and compassion for troubled children. The second was the fact that few women in my area were working in the criminal justice field. I was one of two women in my criminal justice class. Prior to graduating from college, I was offered a job at the Glynn County Juvenile Court in Brunswick, Georgia. I took the job and never received my degree. For the past 29 years I have been working as a court officer with the Glynn County Juvenile Court.

My main job function is to provide supervision for children who are placed on probation by the court. I work closely with school administrators, mental health professionals, and other agencies to assist children in their rehabilitation. I am also the court coordinator for the Judicial Citizen's Review Panel. This is a program that operates under the Permanent Homes for Children in Georgia Program. The Judicial Citizen's Review Panel consists of a cross section of volunteers from the community, appointed by the local juvenile court judge. The volunteers receive 15 hours of specialized training from the Council of Juvenile Court judges' staff. Once their training is completed, they are sworn in as officers of the court. Their goal is to ensure every child in foster care is safe, stable, and in a permanent home. I've been working with deprived children for many years, and it never gets any easier.

Perhaps the most difficult part of my job is being a member of the Child Fatality Review Committee. In the State of Georgia, all child deaths must be reviewed if the child is 17 or younger. I have reviewed many heart breaking cases. For many years I was on call for one week out of every month. I provided intake and made detention decisions involving juveniles who were taken into custody by the police. If the child was detained, it was my responsibility to transport the child to the Regional Youth Detention Center, which was 65 miles away. I also served subpoenas for the juvenile court.

I look back on some of my responsibilities and see the danger in what I did. Subpoenas are now served by the Sheriff's Department, and children are transported by transport officers. In 1979 I was contacted by a 16-year-old male. He was a runaway, but he agreed to turn himself in if I would pick him up. Once I made contact with the child, he held me against my will. Approximately two hours later, when the ordeal was over, the police found a loaded gun on him. Fortunately, I came out of this incident unharmed. That was the last time I picked up a runaway. In 2002 I made a school visit involving one of my probationers who was disrupting class. The situation escalated to the point where the child picked up a pair of scissors and threatened to stab her teacher, the principal, and me. This child was later charged with aggravated assault and sentenced under the designated felony act. Her release date was May 2005. During the last two years, I've been supervising a 16-year-old male. This young man was one of the most pleasant children I have ever worked with. He had a heart of gold and a winning smile. I never would admit it, but he was my favorite probationer. The offenses he committed were never very serious until December 23, 2004. He was killed at 12:20 a.m. while driving a stolen vehicle. Needless to say, it was a sad Christmas.

Advice to Students: Criminal justice is an exciting profession. I promise you will never be bored but you will be frustrated, disappointed, and even heartbroken. Some people may tell you not to get too close to or involved with your clients. I believe just the opposite. So many children I have dealt with have few people, if any, who truly care about them. In order to be effective, you must take a sincere interest in the children. They will know if you really care or if it's just a job for you. The most important thing you need to know is that you can't save all of the children. There are those who don't want to be saved. Concentrate on the ones who want your help.

able to resist pressure from the majority position. In the context of jury deliberations, this means that in a jury vote of 10–2, the minority jury voters are better able to withstand group pressure more than minority jury voters where the jury vote is 5–1. However, the Court erred in its interpretation and understanding of the social research and concluded that there was no functional difference between the two juries. In any case, a 5–1 jury vote is unconstitutional, inasmuch as all six-member jury voting must be unanimous.

JURY SEQUESTRATION

Historically, **jury sequestration** has been used to isolate jurors from the potential biasing influences of the press and community sentiment. Preventing outside information from reaching jurors allows jurors to be influenced only by the information and evidence presented to them at trial, the instructions of judges, and their fellow jurors. While jury sequestration has many critics, some persons have discovered that sequestration may have some positive effects. Apart from the obvious benefit of not having jurors influenced by outside forces, sequestration, on many occasions, has fostered a group bonding process among the jurors. Following trials, jurors have often referred to themselves as becoming a family who plan to see each other after the trial. Thus, the emotional connection developed as a result of sequestration may have a positive effect on deliberations. Researchers have learned that group communication is enhanced when individuals have formed an interpersonal connection among themselves. Therefore, jurors who have developed relationships with one another are more willing to listen to each other and discuss their differences. When this event occurs, sequestration has enhanced the deliberative process. While these are a few of the positive effects of jury sequestration, these are far outnumbered by criticisms of it.

During sequestration, if the jury develops intergroup rivalries among and animosity toward each other, the deliberative process suffers. People are more likely to gravitate toward people like themselves. This highlights the differences between group members and they begin to resent one other. Alliances are formed between certain jurors, and they form coalitions that become fairly powerful during jury deliberations. Sequestration also puts pressure on jurors who disagree with the majority. The jurors in the minority position see themselves as prolonging the sequestration. If they would only capitulate and agree with the majority, they could all go home and get back to their lives. Jury sequestration is also expensive.

In the O. J. Simpson criminal trial the jury was sequestered for 266 days at a cost to the taxpayers of almost $1 million. Cost was one of the primary reasons the New York courts system eliminated its practice of mandatory sequestration. The cost savings by eliminating mandatory sequestration in criminal trials was almost $4 million each year. Sequestration may also be a primary reason people are trying to get out of jury service. For many jurors, being confined to a hotel and treated like a prisoner in a potentially hostile environment may be one reason why many persons who are called for jury service refuse to answer their calls for such service.

JURY DECISION MAKING AND VOTING

Considerable research has examined jury decision making and voting behavior. For instance, it has been found that women approach jury duty differently, perceive things differently, and often vote differently from men (Fischer 1997). Not only do gender differences influence decision making, but also the type of occupation, ethnicity, and socioeconomic status exert a profound influence on how people perceive things and process large amounts of evidence and other important information. The differences in juror decision making and final jury verdicts is highlighted the most in civil cases where damages are sought. For example, in the case of *Sterling v. Bechenheimer's Inc.* (1987), a jury awarded Debra Sterling $25,000 in compensatory damages and $1,501,000 in punitive damages after she had been handcuffed and thrown to the ground by a security guard who believed she had stolen a soda worth $1.49. Consider the jury actions in this case with the jury actions in the case of Patricia James. In *James v. K-Mart* (1987), a jury awarded $2 to Mrs. James and $502 to each of her teenage daughters after a security guard had twisted the daughters' arms behind their back and strip-searched them believing the daughters had been shoplifting. Why are there such different jury decisions and monetary awards?

It has been found that several important trial and victim factors influence jury voting behavior. Factors associated with guilty verdicts are physical evidence, a defendant's prior criminal record, and victim attractiveness. Male jurors seem more likely to vote not guilty when the victim puts up some resistance against the offender. Guilty verdicts are also more likely when jurors have had prior jury service. Not guilty verdicts have been associated with offenders being employed, offenders being attractive, and where there has been some degree of victim facilitation (e.g., the victim allows a stranger to take them home from a bar). Jurors who have a tendency to blame the victim are also more likely to vote not guilty (Enriquez and Clark 2005).

Another factor is whether jurors are verdict-driven or evidence-driven. Research indicates that once juries reach the jury room, they commence the decision-making process by following one of two patterns or methods (Champion 2005b). The first pattern is called an **evidence-driven jury.** In evidence-driven cases, juries come together and begin discussing how to proceed. Most jurors or at least a vocal few decide that they should review the evidence as a group before they can contemplate a verdict. With this method, all the evidence is discussed, not simply the evidence individual jurors believe is relevant. However, a **verdict-driven jury** believes that discussing the evidence before a vote is unnecessary. Why debate the evidence when all jurors might vote the same way without a review of the evidence? Using this method, the jury votes first to see how many jurors favor guilt or acquittal. When discussed, evidence is used to support one position or another. Verdict-driven deliberations often take less time than evidence-driven deliberations since there is little or no time taken to review the evidence before jury votes are cast.

Some research shows that the jury deliberation process may not have much impact on the final verdict. In Kalven and Ziesel's (1966) classic study of the jury system, they compared the initial jury vote to the final verdict. They revealed that in the vast majority of cases, the first vote was most often the same as the final verdict. For example, on a 12-person jury, if seven of the jurors initially voted not guilty, the subsequent verdict tended to be not guilty. However, if the majority of jurors voted guilty, the final verdict would almost always be guilty. Only on rare occasions does the minority succeed in convincing the majority to change their vote. Kalven and Ziesel have said that the real decision is often made before the deliberation begins. The deliberation process might well be likened to what the developer does for an exposed film: A picture is developed, but the outcome is predetermined (1966, 488–489).

JURY VERDICTS

The media always seem willing to report about how the justice system has failed in one respect or another to convict guilty defendants. This most often occurs when we perceive that an obviously guilty person is found not guilty or the jury delivers an excessive damage award to a plaintiff in a civil case. Armed with this anecdotal evidence, more than a few critics have called for reforming the jury system. When we advocate changing the jury system, we have to make two assumptions. First, we have to assume that the jury made a mistake. Second, we have to assume that there is a better alternative. In most cases, advocates for jury reform believe that juries composed of laypersons from the community are often not able to understand or comprehend the complex information presented at trial. This has also been referred to as the complexity exception. Stephen Adler has argued that if a judge doesn't think the jury will understand a particular civil case, he can decide it without a jury (Adler 1995, 143). Adler (1995) argues that jury reform should include a return to the **blue-ribbon jury.** During the 1960s and 1970s, blue ribbon juries were comprised from members of the best-educated or socially placed members of society because it was believed a jury should be composed of such persons. In fact, most persons who serve on juries today would not have been placed on these blue-ribbon juries in past years. In fact, the reverse of the blue-ribbon jury is often practiced in many jurisdictions. New York's judicial rules allow for the automatic exemption of lawyers, doctors, clergy, dentists, optometrists, psychologists, podiatrists, registered and practical nurses, embalmers, police officers, correctional officers, firefighters, sole business owners, and many other professional groups.

In many instances, if we agree with the idea that juries cannot understand the information presented to them and therefore are unable to arrive at a competent verdict, who will replace them? Most critics would shift the responsibility for determining guilt or innocence to the judges themselves. Are juries unable to understand the material presented to them? In an effort to answer this question, Kalven and Ziesel (1966) investigated how juries arrived at verdicts and how these jury verdicts differed from judicial decisions about the same cases. Kalven and Ziesel gathered data from 3,576 trials. In order to compare the differences between judges and juries, the researchers asked that judges say how they would have ruled in the particular case. The research showed that the verdicts of judges and juries were essentially the same in 78 percent of the cases. Conversely, judges and juries disagreed on the outcome in

22 percent of the cases. The data indicate the largest disagreement came where judges said they would have convicted the defendant and the juries said they would acquit the defendant. In essence, judges were more likely to convict than juries. Thus, juries seem to be more lenient than judges in decision making about criminal defendants.

Those critical of the jury system might argue that juries are not more lenient, but rather, the differences in judge and jury case outcomes can be attributed to jury incompetence. They would argue that juries disagreed with judges and acquitted defendants when they should have convicted them, largely because the jurors did not understand the law and the evidence presented to them at trial. In order to address this criticism, Kalven and Ziesel (1966) had the judges rate whether the evidence was difficult or easy to comprehend. If jury incompetence was the reason for the differences, we might expect a higher rate of disagreement in those cases where the judge indicated that the evidence was too difficult to understand. However, the results indicate that judges and juries disagreed equally in both complex and simple cases.

BOX 6.7 PLAIN ENGLISH FOR JURY INSTRUCTIONS?

The judicial counsel of California spent eight years rewriting some of its instructions to juries. They have now approved over 2000 pages of "plain language" jury instruction in the hopes of helping juries in the future better understand legal terminology so they can make better informed decisions about guilt or innocence. The instructions also did away with many old and rarely used terms, and introduced terms with the cultural sensibilities of today. Many of the legal terms included in California's jury instructions were complicated or up to speed with California lifestyle. For example, "willfully false" is more simply referred to as "lied," "innocent misrecollection" is now "honestly forgot," and the instructions now include information that not discussing the trial with anyone includes "spiritual advisors and therapists," as well, and that "confidential relationships" are not excluded. These revisions are part of an effort to ease the burden of the jury trial experience in California. California's judicial system, according to officials, is the second largest after the federal system. Do you think that these new instructions will better enable jurors to understand instructions given to them, thereby facilitating less-complex decision making? Should other states consider revising some of their complex legalese to help jurors understand? Does this decrease the seriousness of a court trial, or diminish the authority of the legal system?

[*Source:* Adapted from the Associated Press, "The New Language for Jurors in California: Plain English," *New York Times*, August 28, 2005:A12.]

JURY NULLIFICATION

Jury nullification is the refusal of juries to apply the law when they believe following the letter of the law would be a miscarriage of justice. In a criminal trial, the jury is the finder of fact and has the absolute authority to acquit the defendant regardless of the evidence. The jury is also our protection from the oppressive powers of the state. The constitutional protection against double jeopardy makes the jury's acquittal irreversible and the prosecution has no right to appeal the jury verdict. One exception is if there has been jury tampering or some other irregularity that has caused the jury to disregard the evidence against the accused. In a system designed with checks and balances to control state power, the jury system provides ordinary citizens with more power than our highest elected and appointed government officials.

Although we have observed jury nullification in some recent spectacular cases (e.g., Marion Barry, Lorena Bobbit, and John DeLorean), it is not something that is particularly unique to our time. Juries have nullified the law or, more accurately, the actions of the state, for as long as juries have functioned in American and English courts. Jury nullification was common in England during the Bloody Code of the eighteenth and nineteenth centuries. The Bloody Code prescribed over 200 offenses that were punishable by death, including such minor offenses as stealing bread and pickpocketing. Because of the severity of the punishment relative to the offense, juries were reluctant to find defendants guilty of these offenses. The authority of the jury to engage in the practice of nullification was not challenged in England until 1670 in the Bushell case, and later in America in the John Peter Zenger case.

In 1670, William Penn and William Mead were being tried at the Old Bailey, the Central Criminal Court of England. Penn, subsequently the founder of the Colony of Pennsylvania and a leading proponent of correctional reform, was a Quaker like Mead, and the authorities saw both of them as radicals and extremists. Consequently, they were banned from preaching in the streets. However, this was their only forum because the authorities had barred

---

BOX 6.8 ARE JURIES PRO-POLICE?

The Death of Amadou Diallo. It was a tragic event that occurred in New York City in 1999. An unarmed black man, Amadou Diallo, was shot and killed by four police officers in a small alcove of a dark building, in the aftermath of 41 shots being fired. In February 2000, the four officers went on trial for his murder. The trial was held in Albany, a middle-class, 90 percent white community with a strong Irish Catholic heritage. An Albany defense attorney, Terence Kindlon, said, "If there's a better place to defend a police officer, I haven't heard of it." Another observer, *New York Post* columnist Bob McManus, agreed. He said, "Irish Catholic conservative Albany has a civil service view of the world. They like their cops."

The murder trial of the four police officers charged in Diallo's death was moved to Albany from the Bronx in New York City because, according to authorities, it has a reputation for being hostile to police. It is two-thirds black and Hispanic, and the police have become outsiders. Does it really make a difference where the trial is held?

In January 2000, a jury in Albany was convinced that a well-respected detective actually forged a confession in the murder of an 82-year-old former minister and that police were overzealous in arresting a man who helped an alleged cop shooter to escape. In fact, in that particular case, camouflage-clad police officers were caught on videotape roughing up some store clerks while searching for the alleged shooter. The videotape led to internal disciplinary action against the police officers that once would have been unheard of.

Some criminal justice experts around the country believe that the location of trials is becoming less important in recent years. More jurors are able to make more sound and fair judgments, according to these observers. One observer, Boston College law professor Robert M. Bloom, said that "Confidence in police around the country is weakening because of such things as the Rodney King beating in Los Angeles and the Abner Louima case in New York City, where a black defendant was sodomized with a broomstick in a police station bathroom."

Amid allegations of pro-police officer bias, there have been numerous incidents around the United States to undermine public confidence in police officers. For example, police officers on highways throughout America have been routinely pulling over blacks in what is known as racial profiling. *Albany Times Union* columnist Fred LeBrun said, "Even in a place like Albany, conservative with an almost Midwestern feel, there is the general feeling that you just can't take a police officer's word anymore."

Echoing these comments and opinions is a law professor from Fordham University, James Cohen. Cohen says "The feeling is people in power—the white people—tend to treat people without power differently." But there is some concern among those prosecuting the case against the four officers in Albany. In 1999 in Albany, a black basketball player at the College of Saint Rose claimed he was beaten by two off-duty police officers in a police garage following a bar fight. The officers were acquitted. Is it a strong likelihood that juries in one part of the state may be more pro-police than juries in other parts of a state? What about your own state? Is it likely that two different juries in different parts of the state would arrive at different verdicts if police officers were accused of crimes? How can juries be selected in ways that minimize their possible bias and unfair attitudes toward either the prosecutor or defense? What do you think?

[*Source:* Adapted from the Associated Press, "Albany Is a Pro-Police Setting for Murder Trial of N.Y. City Cops," February 8, 2000.]

them from their churches. On one occasion while they were preaching in the street, they were arrested and charged with unlawful assembly. Their fate ultimately rested in the hands of the jurors selected to hear the case. The witnesses included those who testified that Penn and Mead had preached on Gracechurch Street.

At the conclusion of the testimony, the jury was instructed to retire to the jury room and reach a verdict. When they returned with a verdict of not guilty, they were instructed to return to the jury room and deliberate until they reached a correct verdict. When they returned a second time, they found Penn guilty of speaking at Gracechurch Street but refused to convict him on unlawful assembly charges. The court reacted to this verdict by threatening Edward Bushell, who was identified as the leader of the jury revolt. They were sent back to deliberate once again, and when they returned, they announced that they had again found Penn guilty of speaking at Gracechurch Street, although they persisted and did not find him guilty of unlawful assembly. Additionally, they declared Mead innocent of any wrongdoing. The court was in turmoil. The court announced that Bushell and the rest of the jury would not be dismissed until they reached a verdict acceptable to the court. The judge ordered them locked up without "meat, drink, fire, and tobacco" until they reached an acceptable verdict. Facing this demand, the jury retired to deliberate and returned with an acquittal for Penn. They were ordered to go back and deliberate again, but this time they refused. The judge was outraged. Bushell and the rest of the jurors were fined forty marks each and sent to jail until they could pay the fine. The jurors filed a *habeas corpus* appeal requesting their release from prison. The appellate court ordered that they be released and declared that the jury had the right to render a verdict according to its belief about the fairness of the law and not act consistent with what the court deemed appropriate.

BOX 6.9 WHAT HAPPENS WHEN JURIES CAN'T AGREE ON A VERDICT?

Victor David, 60, of Marysville, Washington, was married for years to his wife, Linda David, 52. Victor and his wife lived on a sailboat, docked at Everett Marina. The sailboat was filthy, and they shared the boat with seven German Sheperd dogs, some cats, and a wild goose. Eyewitnesses alerted authorities that Linda David had not been seen in several weeks, although they knew that she was aboard the sailboat. Subsequently a search by law enforcement officers led to the discovery of Linda David laying in a near-comatose condition on the vessel, having suffered brain damage, nearly blinded, and covered with scars. Victor David was charged with felony assault and was placed on trial.

During the trial, evidence of physical abuse came to light through the testimony of physicians who examined Linda and her body. It was also acknowledged that Victor David had obtained money from the state at one point to provide chore services and in-home care for his wife. Several persons who looked after Linda testified about her condition. Prosecutors alleged that Victor David had beaten his wife repeatedly over many years, causing her scars and brain injuries, largely between 1993 and 1997. A state social worker visited Linda in 1997 and reported her case to authorities. She expressed an opinion that Linda had been the victim of Victor David's assault.

But a strong defense was mounted. Victor David proclaimed his innocence and offered other explanations for his wife's injuries, including that she fell repeatedly and struck her head multiple times. He claimed she had a drinking problem and often had difficulty maintaining her balance around the boat.

When the evidence portion of the trial was concluded and prosecutors and defense counsel made closing arguments after three weeks, the jurors began deliberating. Several days of deliberations led to a **hung jury.** After four days, jurors were divided 6–6 on David's guilt. On the fifth day, the vote was 7–5 in favor of acquittal. One juror, John Nichols, was one of the five jurors who had voted for conviction. He said the evidence, including the traumas Linda David had received, swayed him. Linda David had testified against her husband, although her testimony was very difficult to understand. Much of the time it was incoherent and didn't make sense. One juror who voted for acquittal said that the way the prosecution handled her testimony, it sounded like she had been coached, or spoon-fed things to make her remember events that never happened. Some jurors were troubled that there were no witnesses to the alleged assaults.

Rebecca Roby, regional director of the Pathways for Women, said "I think the case is a tragedy." She was surprised and saddened by the lack of a verdict. "The emotional scars take a lot longer to heal than a bruise," Roby said. She was not surprised that jurors had trouble with the evidence presented, during the period of the statute of limitations. She sees women every day who don't report abuse until after it's too late for authorities to do anything about it. As far as Victor David is concerned, he considers himself totally innocent of all charges. Juror Kami Cramer said, "There was no verdict because we just couldn't get there with what we had to work with." It was uncertain whether prosecutors would seek a second trial against Victor David.

Can juries be made to agree by presiding judges? How many times should a defendant be tried for a crime before a unanimous decision by a jury can be reached? What inferences should be drawn, if any, from hung juries and the innocence or guilt of defendants? What do you think?

[*Source:* Adapted from Scott North and Jim Haley, "David Jurors Can't Agree," *The Daily Herald,* June 15, 2006.]

JURY AND JUROR MISCONDUCT

Juror misconduct falls into categories. The first is engaging in delinquency or lying to avoid jury service. The second is engaging in improper or prohibited behavior while serving as a juror. The first type of behavior is perceived as misconduct largely by those who believe that jury service is a civic duty and that all U.S. citizens are obligated to serve on juries when called to do so. Juror misconduct prior to trials most often involves jurors who lie to avoid jury service. Another problem involves jurors who lie and fail to disclose important information during *voir dire* so that they can remain on the jury. Those who are called to jury service often want to avoid it because of certain hardships jury service would pose. While jurors are compensated for their service, serving on a jury is still regarded by many persons as a financial hardship.

The types of financial hardships for jurors today are quite different from the financial burden on jurors in the 1700s. Jurors were usually compensated one to two dollars per day. However, many jurors had to travel long distances on foot or horseback to the courthouse. Because they could not return home each day, they had to pay for food and lodging. Often, these expenses were considerably more than the amount of their compensation received from the court for their jury service. Today, jurors continue to have the hardship of traveling to the courthouse, although in most instances, they are able to return to their homes each evening. In past centuries, judges routinely refused to feed jurors while they were deliberating in order to starve out a verdict. This is another hazard that contemporary jurors do not endure. The reasons for avoiding jury service have changed over time, although some persons still consider serving on a jury to be a hardship and that jury service is an activity to be avoided.

Another form of juror misconduct is lying. Most often jurors lie to avoid jury duty. In the early 1900s in Cleveland, for example, residents from the wealthiest neighborhoods claimed illnesses more often than those from poorer neighborhoods. Still other persons would fabricate stories about how they were related to defendants in criminal cases simply to be dismissed as jurors. It was later revealed that they had no particular relationship with the accused and that their lies were ruses to avoid jury service (Stalmaster 1931, 74)

Engaging in inappropriate or prohibited behavior while serving as a juror is the most serious form of juror misconduct. While juror misconduct has always plagued the jury system, it is more of a problem today than in the past. Over time, the definition of misconduct has not changed substantially, although what is different today is that jurors of the past had fewer opportunities to engage in inappropriate behavior. For instance, in past decades, it was not uncommon for a felony trial to have only one or two witnesses, and the trial lasted only a few hours. During this time, jurors were closely watched by the bailiff who prevented any misconduct from occurring. Today, trials are much longer and jurors have more unsupervised time. This provides jurors with

BOX 6.10 JUROR ACCEPTS BRIBES FROM DEFENDANT

■ **Juror Miguel Moya**

It happened in Miami. Defendants Augusto "Willie" Falcon and Salvador Magluta were on trial for drug smuggling and large-scale drug dealing. There was overwhelming and persuasive evidence of their guilt presented at trial. But the trial took a peculiar turn when the jury deliberated and came back with an acquittal. Later, jurors said that they had deliberated for three days when they sent a note to the judge that they were "hopelessly deadlocked." The judge ordered them to continue deliberating and "reach a verdict." That's when they decided to throw in the towel and acquit the alleged drug smugglers.

Following the trial, one of the jurors, Miguel Moya, suddenly became wealthy. He bought a $200,000 home in the Florida Keys, jewelry, furniture, vacations, season tickets to the Florida Marlins games, and a sports car. Moya explained that he had recently come into some money from his cousin, Ramon "Ray" Perez, who was also a convicted drug smuggler and former Miami policeman. Perez said that he had given Moya approximately $485,000 as a gift. At about the same time, Moya's parents retired, bought a new home in the Florida Keys, and took a Hawaiian vacation.

Prosecutors were more than a little suspicious about Moya's newfound wealth and they investigated. They discovered that Moya had received nearly $500,000 from Falcon and Magluta following the trial in exchange for his persuasiveness with other jurors in arriving at an acquittal. Prosecutors charged Moya with money laundering, witness tampering, conspiracy, bribery, obstruction of justice, and filing a false tax return. Moya was convicted in July 1999 of the different crimes alleged. He faced 138 years in prison, including substantial fines. His father, Jose, pleaded guilty to witness tampering and was sentenced in October 1999. Falcon and Magluta, reportedly the top drug traffickers in the United States during the 1980s, were charged with smuggling 75 tons of cocaine into the United States and making $2 billion. Their 1996 acquittal was a sound defeat for federal prosecutors, although both men were imprisoned later on lesser unrelated charges. What safeguards should exist to protect juror integrity and insulate jurors from potential bribes from criminal defendants? What policies would you put in place to ensure that jury tampering can be prevented? What do you think?

[*Source:* Adapted from the Associated Press, "Jury: Juror Guilty of Accepting Bribes," July 25, 2000.]

more opportunities to be exposed to external influences and bribes from a defendant's friends, visiting the crime scene, discussing the evidence and the case prior to final deliberations, drinking alcohol, and reading, listening to, or watching prohibited media.

BOX 6.11 LAPD IN TROUBLE AGAIN

■ A Case of Jury Bias?

Three Los Angeles Police Department officers were convicted of conspiracy and other crimes on Wednesday, November 15, 2000, following a lengthy trial. The police officers were part of a police department scandal involving an anti-gang unit at the police department's Rampart station. It began when former police officer Rafael Perez was caught stealing cocaine from an evidence locker and agreed to become an informant and government witness. Perez told the investigators that other officers framed people, planted evidence, committed perjury, and even shot innocent victims. More than 100 convictions of innocent suspects have been thrown out as the result of the scandal.

When the officers were convicted on November 15, an alternate juror came forward and disclosed to authorities that the jury foreman had decided that the defendants were guilty before any testimony had been presented. Another juror agreed and supported the alternate juror's assertions. Furthermore, the alternate juror said that other jurors often discussed the case outside of court before deliberations began, and that this was in direct violation of the instructions received from the judge. Alternate juror, Wendy Christiansen, 30, who did not participate in deliberations, told the judge that on the day the jurors were selected, she had lunch with another alternate and the jury foreman, Victor Flores. A comment was made that he believed the defendants were guilty. Christiansen said also that throughout the trial, other jurors openly said they thought the prosecution's witnesses were lying when they claimed they didn't remember things. They didn't like the defense attorneys.

When Flores was interviewed by KNBC-TV in Los Angeles, he denied the assertion that he had made up his mind about the defendants before trial and that he absolutely stood by the guilty verdicts. Flores said, "No I did not say that, that wouldn't be something I'd even utter, because the law says they're innocent until proven guilty." In support of Flores, another voting juror, Ingrid Utke, said that Flores had acted appropriately and had not uttered what had been alleged by Christiansen. Utke said, "We pointedly made sure that we never talked about the case. If someone veered toward that, we'd say, 'Anyone see a movie lately?' so we wouldn't talk about it. Also, every time we came back from being out here (in the courtroom), there were lots of comments being made about the defense attorneys. They didn't like the defense attorneys. The person they did like was Joel Isaacson," Utke said.

Defense attorneys for the convicted police officers were quick to say that this new evidence warranted a new trial. The district attorney's office refused to comment in the case. Sgt. Brian Liddy, Sgt. Edward Ortiz, and Officer Michael Buchanan were convicted of conspiracy and other crimes involving gang members four years earlier in 1996. Barry Levin, one of the officer's attorneys, said, "Whether they like me or not, I could care less. But whether you like an attorney or not, you can't take it out on the client. The crux of the judicial system is you're entitled to 12 unbiased jurors." Should these officers be granted a new trial based on the assertions of juror misconduct made by Christiansen? What safeguards should be in place to prevent jurors from discussing the case before jury deliberations? What do you think?

[*Source:* Adapted from the Associated Press, "Jury Bias Alleged in LAPD Trial," *San Francisco Chronicle,* November 18, 2000:A3.]

What are the implications of juror misconduct? For jurors themselves, they are most often held in contempt and are ordered to pay a fine or serve a short jail term. In rare instances they are charged with criminal behavior by the prosecutor. Interestingly, jurors most often charged with misconduct by the prosecutor were members of juries where the result was an acquittal or a mistrial. One of the most common forms of juror misconduct is drinking alcohol during the trial or deliberations. Judges have been reluctant to declare a mistrial when they learn that jurors have been drinking. However, most judges consider drinking during deliberations more serious than drinking during the trial (Stacey and Dayton 1988). In short, it appears that judges believe that jurors must have a clearer head when deliberating the evidence than when hearing the evidence.

Jurors who engage in misconduct are rarely punished. One of the primary reasons for this is because jurors are short-term actors in the criminal justice process. Jurors who engage in misconduct are punished after the trial, and so their fellow jurors are unaware of any punishment. Similarly, new jurors are entering the system everyday. They would typically not have any knowledge of prior punishment of deviant jurors. Therefore, when judges do punish jurors, it has little or no potential deterrent value. Thus, new jurors who elect to engage in misconduct have no knowledge of prior punishments imposed on other jurors. When jurors engage in misconduct, there is always the possibility that the judge will declare a mistrial. In fact, some defendants prefer mistrials, since the likelihood of a successive prosecution is minimized. One way to minimize the adverse effects of juror misconduct is the use of alternative jurors. Judges can replace offending jurors and continue with the trial.

SUMMARY

The role of the jury in the common-law legal system has changed over time. Initially, juries were used very little as disputes were settled using other methods. The ancient Greeks were premiere in using persons from the community to decide on cases, at one time using the entire city of Athens to hear appeals from magistrates. Obviously this became a very difficult task to manage. The ancient Romans also used what would be an early form of the jury. In early English times, common-law juries both investigated crimes and decided the trials of accused. Eventually it was decided that two separate units were needed for these tasks and the grand and petit juries were born. The grand jury's sole purpose was to investigate and report on crimes, whereas the petit jury was charged with determining the guilt or innocence of the accused. Over time, juries were granted more power and autonomy, and they have become an essential component of the American court process. Although the role the jury should play has been challenged, critics contending that they do not have the background or knowledge to hear complicated and expert testimony and decide a case, juries today are made up of cross sections of the community in which the crime has occurred. Indeed juries are an integral part of our court system; as stated in the Sixth Amendment, the accused enjoys the right to a public trial by an impartial jury.

Most attorneys would agree that one of the most important stages in the criminal court process is the selection of the jury. It is during the jury selection process (*voir dire*) that lawyers decide who will hear the case. Both sides in the adversarial process attempt to select jurors who will be impartial. It starts with a list of potential jurors called the *venire*. Traditionally in medieval England the king would choose wealthy landowners to sit as jurors. Obviously this limited the number of persons eligible to become a juror. Historically, in the United States, females were excluded from jury service as well. This has changed over time so that today persons chosen to form the venire are chosen from voter registration lists in an attempt to draw from a cross section of the community. Once names have been taken from this list of potential jurors, the court will send them a summons to appear for jury service. Questions relating to their citizenship status, their age, if they suffer from any physical or mental disabilities, and also whether they have been convicted of a felony are asked to ensure they are qualified. Those who pass this initial screening are sent another letter asking them to again appear for jury service. This starts a process known as the *voir dire*. This stage further determines the appropriateness of the person to serve as a juror. *Voir dire* literally means to speak the truth, and it is an opportunity for the prosecution and the defense to learn about any prejudices the potential jurors may have. This determination by both sides of impartiality is necessary to ensure a fair trial for the defendant. Although this has been referred to as jury selection, it is really the opposite where it eliminates those who are not appropriate to serve for jury duty. Some, however, argue that this process is really about the prosecution and defense determining which jurors will be sympathetic with their side. Jurors, who lawyers believe will not be sympathetic to their position, are removed.

Two methods for removing potential jurors from the jury pool include challenges for cause and peremptory challenges. Challenges for cause are used to excuse a person from jury duty for a specific reason. They may be used to eliminate a potential juror because the person does not meet the requirements to serve (underage), has a specific bias (related or an acquaintance of the accused), or for a nonspecific bias (having prejudice toward crimes or criminals). In order to use this type of challenge, the attorney has to provide a convincing reason to the judge for the removal of the juror. Peremptory challenges, unlike challenges for cause, do not require an explanation for the removal of a potential juror. Both sides are given a limited number of these types of challenges depending on the seriousness, or extent of pretrial publicity, of a case. In less serious cases, attorneys may receive six of these types of challenges, whereas in murder and other serious felony cases, attorneys may be given 12 or more. Attorneys can gauge the attitudes of a potential juror toward crime, criminals, and even law enforcement officials by asking them certain questions. Attorneys may even have a particular profile of jurors who share certain characteristics that will be more likely to be sympathetic to their position. They can then use this information and their peremptory challenges to eliminate those persons who do not fit this profile. In fact, social science has entered this process on occasion to assist attorneys in the jury selection process. Some question the use of scientific jury selection on ethical grounds that it is jury tampering and that it undermines or compromises the jury's integrity. Nonetheless, it has become big business, with associations boasting memberships in the hundreds, and success rates of 95 percent. There are, however, some who are skeptical about whether this success rate can be attributed to scientific techniques. It should also be noted that the Supreme Court has handed down several decisions regarding the jury selection process, specifically regarding where the pool of potential jurors comes from, the reasons for which a juror can be excluded from sitting on a jury, and jury size.

Jury sequestration is a method to isolate jurors from biases and influences from the media and the community. This is an attempt to prevent them from being subject to outside information that could possibly damage their impartiality. There have been other advantages to sequestration as well. Some believe it fosters a bonding process that better enables the jurors to come to a decision in deliberations. These advocates say that group communication is enhanced with sequestration because the jurors have formed an interpersonal connection with one another.

There have, however, been critics who point out that in the same ways that sequestration can foster bonding processes, it can also foster rivalries and animosities to be formed, which would hinder coming to a decision during deliberations. Although jury deliberations are protected from the public, there have been some studies on how juries make decisions. After the case is given to the jury for deliberations, they usually engage in one of two methods of reaching a decision about the guilt or innocence of the defendant. The first method is the evidence-driven jury where all evidence is examined and discussed before a jury vote is taken. The second form of decision making is the verdict-driven jury. In this scenario, the jury first conducts a vote and then, if needed, the evidence is examined and discussed. However, if all jurors agree on the verdict, their deliberations are concluded. Jury nullification is the process of returning a verdict contrary to the evidence presented in the case. In most cases a jury finds a defendant not guilty although the evidence suggests strongly the defendant's guilt. Finally, juror misconduct can be minor (lying to avoid jury service) or serious (engaging in improper conduct while serving on a jury), but is an ever-present concern, especially since today's trials are much longer, increasing the opportunity for engaging in inappropriate behavior.

KEY TERMS

Affirmative registration	Jury sequestration
Blue-ribbon jury	Peremptory challenge
Challenge for cause	Petit jury
Evidence-driven jury	Scientific jury selection
Grand jury	*Venire*
Hung jury	Venireman list
Juror misconduct	Verdict-driven jury
Jury nullification	*Voir dire*

QUESTIONS FOR REVIEW

1. Describe the history and development of the grand jury.
2. How has jury size changed over time?
3. What is jury nullification? Do you agree or disagree that juries should have this power?
4. Describe the difference between evidence-driven juries and verdict-driven juries.

5. Should defendants be allowed to spend money to hire scientific jury consultants? If so, does this give them an unfair advantage?

6. What is *voir dire*?

7. What is the relevant case law that has shaped our current constitutional requirement on jury size?

8. Differentiate between a verdict-driven jury and an evidence-driven jury.

9. What are some of the types of hardships cited by contemporary prospective jurors to avoid jury duty?

10. What are several different forms of juror misconduct?

SUGGESTED READINGS

1. T. Brewer (2004). "Race and Jurors' Receptivity to Mitigation in Capital Cases: The Effects of Jurors', Defendants', and Victims' Race in Combination." *Law and Human Behavior* **28**:529–545.

2. D. Graham Burnett (2001). *A Trial By Jury*. New York: Alfred A. Knopf.

3. John Clark (2000). "The Social Psychology of Jury Nullification." *Law and Psychology Review* **24**:39–57.

4. Clay S. Conrad (1998). *Jury Nullification: The Evolution of a Doctrine*. Durham, NC: Carolina Academic Press.

5. E. Finch and V. E. Munro (2005). "Juror Stereotypes and Blame Attribution in Rape Cases Involving Intoxicants." *British Journal of Criminology* **45**:25–38.

6. Norman J. Finkel (2000). "Commonsense Justice and Jury Instructions: Instructive and Reciprocating Connections." *Psychology, Public Policy and Law* **6**:591–628.

7. Shaun L. Gabbidon, Helen Taylor Greene, and Vernetta D. Young (eds.) (2002). *African-American Classics in Criminology and Criminal Justice*. Thousand Oaks, CA: Sage Publications.

8. Margaret Bull Kovera (ed.) (2004). "Psychology, Law, and the Workplace." *Law and Human Behavior* **28**:1–132.

9. Ana M. Martin, Martin F. Kaplan, and Jose M. Alama (2003). "Discussion Content and Perception of Deliberation in Western European Versus American Juries." *Psychology, Crime and the Law* **9**:247–263.

10. Robert D. Miller (2003). "Testimony By Proxy: The Use of Expert Testimony to Provide Defendant Testimony Without Cross-Examination." *Journal of Psychiatry and Law* **31**:21–41.

11. Judy Sheperd et al. (2002). "Reflections on a Rape Trial: The Role of Rape Myths and Jury Selection in the Outcome of a Trial." *Affilia Journal of Women and Social Work* **17**:69–92.

12. Donna Shestowsky and Leonard M. Horowitz (2004). "How the Need for Cognition Scale Predicts Behavior in Mock Jury Deliberations." *Law and Human Behavior* **28**:305–337.

13. Neil Vidmar (ed.) (2000). *World Jury Systems*. Oxford, UK: Oxford University Press.

14. S. Vollum, Rolando V. del Carmen, and Dennis R. Longmire (2004). "Should Jurors Be Informed about Parole Eligibility in Death Penalty Cases? An Analysis of *Kelly v. South Carolina*." *The Prison Journal* **84**:395–410.

Chapter 7

Pretrial Procedures
Initial Appearance, Bail
Decision Making, and Alternative
Dispute Resolution

257

Chapter Objectives

As a result of reading this chapter, you will have accomplished the following objectives:

1. Understand the arrest and booking process, and the initial appearance.

2. Describe bail-granting process and the conditions under which bail may be granted.

3. Understand the Bail Reform Act of 1984 and its implications for clients released on bail.

4. Describe the role of fugitive recovery agents or bounty hunters who track down those who fail to appear or abscond from the jurisdiction to avoid prosecution.

5. Understand the decriminalization process.

6. Examine alternative dispute resolution, including its applications, advantages, and disadvantages.

7. Understand the role and participation of victims in alternative dispute resolution and victim–offender reconciliation projects.

8. Describe pretrial diversion, its implications for divertees, and the advantages and disadvantages of diversion.

9. Describe several sanctioning options available to judges, including community service, fines, restitution to victims, and various types of victim compensation programs.

■ One early morning in Yuma, Arizona, four fugitive recovery agents or bounty hunters surrounded the house of a suspected fugitive who had jumped bail in Atlanta, Georgia, on armed robbery charges. The man had a violent past and a lengthy criminal record. He was known to carry a gun and considered very dangerous. These agents were armed with shotguns and pistols. They rammed their way through the front door of the house and quickly moved throughout the house. Soon gunfire erupted from one of the bedrooms. The agents returned fire. Another bedroom was entered and a man was standing in his underwear pointing a firearm at the entering agents. An exchange of gunfire resulted, and the man with the gun dropped to the bedroom floor mortally wounded. Another person in the home, a teenager, was wounded after firing a rifle at several intruders. Two of the fugitive recovery agents were also wounded in the shootout. Police officers and sheriff's deputies converged on the scene quickly and surveyed the damage. The fugitive recovery agents identified themselves and were taken into custody briefly for investigation. It was later determined that the fugitive recovery agents had received false information about the whereabouts of their fugitive, who was in another home across town at the time. They had entered the home of an innocent family and gunned down the father, who thought his home was being robbed. The wounded teen subsequently recovered. No criminal charges were ever brought against the fugitive recovery agents, because they were acting in good faith, despite the death of an innocent person and the wounding of another. They are still chasing fugitives. Was justice served in this case? Should criminal charges have been filed?

■ Mary Martin, an 82-year-old great grandmother, was asleep in her home one evening when she heard noise in another part of the house. She got up and looked at the clock. It was 2:30 a.m. Martin put on a robe and investigated the noise. All of a sudden, she was pushed hard to the floor and punched about the face. She lost consciousness. The next thing she remembered was being taken to the hospital in an ambulance. A neighbor had heard unusual noise and glass breaking at Martin's house that night and called police, who investigated. They apprehended Bobby Brown and Larry Ingram, two 16-year-olds, running down the street near Martin's home with a pillowcase full of jewelry and other valuables. Brown and Ingram were good friends and members of the local high school football team. They had been "hanging out" in a vacant house in the neighborhood earlier that night, drinking and smoking marijuana. They got the idea that it would be fun to break into someone's house and steal something. They picked Martin's house because they knew "an old lady lived there." Both boys were the sons of prominent businesspersons in the community. They had no prior record of such behavior. A defense attorney suggested that the case against them ought to be diverted to alternative dispute resolution, and that the boys deserved some leniency, given the fact that it was their first offense. Reluctantly the prosecutor agreed, and the boys met with Mrs. Martin in a victim–offender reconciliation meeting. They both apologized to Mrs. Martin, who suffered minor injuries. They agreed to perform 400 hours of community service by picking up trash in the city parks and to do other useful chores. They also agreed to make restitution to Mrs. Martin and repay her for her hospital bills and damages to her home. The local newspaper published an editorial about the prosecutor and how this decision was an example of being soft on crime. After six months, no more was heard about the incident. Was justice served in this case? Should the boys have been prosecuted for burglary, robbery, and aggravated assault?

INTRODUCTION

This chapter is an overview of several crucial pretrial procedures. It is important to note that how defendants are processed, from the time they are arrested for an alleged offense, until they are convicted, sentenced and are serving time for a crime, may be the basis for an appeal or legal challenge to a higher court. When a crime is committed, it is usually investigated. If one or more suspects are identified, they are arrested. Being arrested begins the criminal justice process. Persons arrested for crimes have allegedly committed either misdemeanors, felonies, or both. The use of the term, *alleged*, is critical because guilt is only established through a trial proceeding or plea bargaining. The chapter opens by discussing arrests and the booking process. Arrested persons are ordinarily taken to local lock-ups or jails, where they are processed and held. Early in a defendant's processing, he/she will have an initial appearance before a judicial official or magistrate. The initial appearance is important because it is usually during such a proceeding that the matter of bail is raised and settled.

Bail is a surety that guarantees a defendant's subsequent appearance in court for further proceedings, including a criminal trial. The right to bail is examined and discussed. Not everyone is entitled to bail as a matter of right. Normally persons who are likely to flee the jurisdiction or pose a significant danger or risk to others are denied bail. For others, bail is largely discretionary with the judicial official. Many persons are released on their own recognizance, or ROR, and the reasons for such a release are described. Bail bonds and the bonding process is described in some detail. The Bail Reform Act of 1984 is defined and discussed, and its implications for criminal defendants are described. Several bail experiments have been conducted in different jurisdictions, and the results of some of these studies will be presented and evaluated. Whenever persons placed on bail do not appear for additional criminal proceedings later, bounty hunters or fugitive recovery agents are sent after them. The practice of using bounty hunters is examined, and several examples of bounty hunter activities are discussed. In one of the opening chapter scenarios, bounty hunters entered the home of an innocent person and killed him in a shootout. They claimed it was simply a mistake and no prosecutions ever resulted. This and other issues associated with fugitive recovery agents will be examined.

The chapter next examines decriminalization as one way of removing an offense from the category of a crime. Some acts are decriminalized, such as the use of marijuana, where limited uses of this illegal drug have been prescribed for medical purposes. Some states have purportedly moved in the direction of legalizing marijuana generally, although no state has legalized it for the general public to date.

One civil option to a criminal proceeding is alternative dispute resolution. This pretrial option is discretionary with prosecutors who recommend its use under certain circumstances. Alternative dispute resolution (ADR) is a civil mechanism that occurs between the victim of a crime and the perpetrator, and a third neutral party presides. An agreement is reached among parties about how the matter is best resolved. Usually if victims sustain injuries or suffer losses or damaged property, some form of compensation from the perpetrator is designated. All parties must agree to the conditions of alternative dispute resolution. In one of the chapter opening scenarios, an older lady is assaulted by two teenagers and injured. Her home is burglarized and she is robbed. Later the case is resolved through ADR. Not everyone is favorable toward the use of ADR where crimes are committed. The most important implication for criminal defendants is that a civil resolution of a criminal matter eliminates the offense from the perpetrator's record. The alternative dispute resolution process is described. It is also compared with other forms of mediation, including restorative justice, an alternative method of victim–offender reconciliation program that is growing in popularity every year. The advantages and disadvantages of alternative dispute resolution are discussed.

Another pretrial option is pretrial diversion. Diversion programs permit prosecutors to defer prosecution of defendants for specific periods up to one year or longer, while offenders participate in various forms of rehabilitation or therapy. Once the conditions of their diversion program are satisfied, then at the prosecutor's discretion, the case may be dropped. The history, functions, and criticisms of diversion are defined and described.

The chapter concludes with an examination of several other noncriminal sanctions that may be ordered by judges on the recommendation of prosecutors. For instance, under victim–offender reconciliation, offenders may be required to complete a certain number of hours of community service. The nature of community service varies according to different jurisdictions. Sometimes restitution is ordered, especially where victims have been injured and/or suffered economic losses. Several types of victim compensation programs are described.

ARREST AND BOOKING

Arrest

An **arrest** means taking offenders into custody. Usually, arrests of criminal suspects are made by police officers. Figure 7.1 shows an arrest warrant. Figure 7.2 shows a summons on complaint, which orders defendants to be brought before the judge at a particular time and place.

Arrested persons are referred to as **arrestees.** Arrests of suspects may be made directly by police officers who observe law violations. Depending upon whether a **misdemeanor** or **felony** is alleged, officers must have at least reasonable suspicion to stop and detain for investigation anyone suspected of committing a felony. If subsequent developments provide the officers with **probable cause** to believe that the suspects they have detained probably committed the alleged offense, the officers can arrest the suspect(s) and take them to jail for further processing and identification. If a misdemeanor is committed and is not directly observed by the officer, the officer may stop suspects and

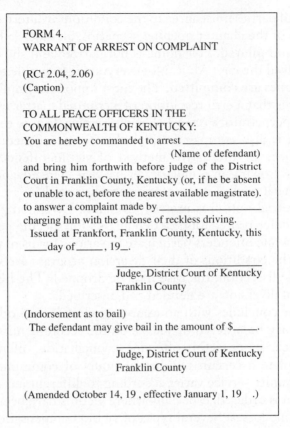

FIGURE 7.1
An Arrest Warrant

make inquiries. But without **reasonable suspicion** to inquire further, officers are not empowered to arrest possible misdemeanants if the officers lack probable cause (Beger 2003; Stalans et al. 2004).

In a felony case, for instance, officers in a cruiser sitting on the shoulder of Highway 55 may receive a report that a convenience store was just robbed by two men wielding shotguns. The men were described as two black males, one wearing a red cap and the other wearing a green cap. The men were last seen driving east on Highway 55 in a black 1966 Chevrolet van. Just then a black 1966 Chevrolet van driven by a black man in a red cap goes by. The officers give chase and eventually stop the van. The officers cautiously approach and order the suspects to exit from the van. When the suspects are out of the van, the officers observe that the passenger is also black but is wearing a green cap. The officers shine their flashlights into the van's interior and see some money bags on the back seat. These similarities are overwhelming, and thus the officers arrest the two men on suspicion of robbing the convenience store.

FORM 2.
SUMMONS ON COMPLAINT
(RCr 2.04, 2.06)

DISTRICT COURT OF KENTUCKY

Franklin County
COMMONWEALTH OF KENTUCKY
V.   SUMMONS

_____
                    Defendant.
TO THE ABOVE NAMED DEFENDANT:

You are hereby summoned to appear before the District Court, in the Franklin County Court House at Frankfort, Kentucky, at 9:00 a.m. (Eastern Standard Time) on Wednesday, October 31, 19 , to answer a complaint made by_____ charging you with the offense of reckless driving.

    Issued at Frankfort, Franklin County, Kentucky, this _____ day of _____, 19 __.

                        _____
                        Judge, District Court of Kentucky
                        Franklin County
(Amended October 14, 19 , effective January 1, 19 .)

FORM 3. SUMMONS IN INDICTMENT
               (RCr 6.52, 6.54)
(Caption)
TO THE ABOVE NAMED DEFENDANT:

    You are hereby summoned to appear before the Franklin Circuit Court in the Franklin County Court House at Frankfort, Kentucky, at 9:00 a.m. (Eastern Standard Time) on Wednesday, October 31, 19 , to answer an indictment charging you with the offenses of (1) malicious shooting and wounding with intent to kill and (2) carrying concealed a deadly weapon.

    Issued at Frankfort, Franklin County, Kentucky, this _____ day of _____, 19 __.

                        _____
                        Clerk, Franklin Circuit Court
                        By_____
                        Deputy Clerk

FIGURE 7.2
A Summons on Complaint

BOX 7.1 CAREER SNAPSHOT

Gary Schofield
Captain, Las Vegas Metropolitan Police Department

Statistics: A.A. (criminal justice) Community College of USAF; B.A. (criminal justice) Thomas Edison State College

Background and Interests: Well, my 24-year career in law enforcement began at the age of 17 when I enlisted in the U.S. Air Force after getting into an argument with my father about going in or out of state for college. As it turns out, I ended up going out of state in multiple places to get the necessary credits for my degree. My current assignment is as the commander assigned to the Special Operations Division of the Las Vegas Metropolitan Police Department. I oversee the Gang Crimes Section, Gang Enforcement Section, Special Investigations Section, and Organized Labor Detail. During my career, I have worked as a patrol officer, training officer, academy staff, S.W.A.T. team member and leader, military tactical unit leader, gang sergeant, undercover narcotics detective, patrol station commander, and training commander. I spent time both on active duty and reserve duty and was recalled to active duty during Desert Storm. Then I was put in charge of the training tactical units, and so in short, I cannot seem to hold down a job.

Formal education has always been a major component of my life. If you were to look at my transcript, you would find that I have taken classes from numerous schools. This is because of my work assignments and duty postings. But it is one thing that has allowed me to succeed. The professors in the courses over the years have always added a new dimension to the knowledge that I have applied to my daily jobs.

Experiences: One of the problems that I have seen over the years is the lack of a true connection between the academic world and the law enforcement world. In other professions, such as medicine, it is an intimate give-and-take between the two fields. It is rare to find that same level of connection in the study of law enforcement. I have attended numerous International Association of Chiefs of Police (IACP) conferences. The IACP annual conference is considered the largest gathering of law enforcement leadership in the world. Yet I note that there are few formal presentations by professors of criminal justice who have done research.

An example is that in our city, there are certain areas that are plagued with gang and drug problems. Yet in the middle of these problem areas, there are certain apartment complexes that have no such problems. They are like islands of peace in the middle of a storm. Having applied community policing and problem-oriented policing methods to the problem areas, I see that the problems always seem to pop back up. Yet the islands of peace continue to exist with no intervention on the part of the police or government. It would be interesting to apply true research methods to find out why. This is where the academic community has great strengths.

A career in law enforcement has exposed me both to the good and bad of society. The reality is that the daily work is at times extremely exciting and fun. I figure that this is the reason there is a television show called *Cops* that continues to be a hit, even after years of being on the air and in re-runs. In contrast, there is no show called *Plumber.*

One memory I have is my S.W.A.T. team and me making an overt entry into a house to rescue a mother and child who were being held hostage by an armed robber who broke into the house to escape from the police. As we made our approach, the suspect was holding the infant to his chest. He held a gun in one hand and the child in the other. In the corner was the terrified mother. The suspect had dozed off. There is no way to describe the tension of making an approach toward an armed suspect holding an infant. We grabbed the child, cuffed the suspect, and rescued the mother. That was a great day!

On another occasion, a suspect was holding an infant as a hostage. This time, the mother had escaped out a window. As we attempted to talk with the suspect, a shot rang out. We made an emergency entry into the home to try to rescue the eight-month-old infant, but we were too late. The child was shot by his father and was dying, and then the father shot himself. To my last days, the image of the baby will forever exist in my memory.

Advice to Students: My advice to students is that no matter what part of the criminal justice community you choose to serve in, remember that the goal is to attempt to make it safe for eight-month-old children to grow up.

While these officers didn't see the actual robbery, the descriptions of the fleeing suspects, their vehicle, and the money bags in the van have provided the officers with probable cause to make the arrests.

Booking

Once persons have been arrested, they are usually booked. **Booking** is an administrative procedure obtaining personal background information about arrestees for law enforcement officers (Palermo 2004). Booking includes compiling a file for defendants, including their name, address, telephone number, age, place of work, relatives, and other personal data. The extensiveness of the booking procedure varies among jurisdictions. Most jurisdictions photograph and fingerprint criminal suspects. Sometimes, arrestees are merely detained for several hours and released (Sacks and Pearson 2003). They are usually required to face charges in court later. For example, those arrested for drunk driving may be held temporarily in a local jail overnight. When they are sober in the morning, they are released but must appear before a judge to face DWI charges later. A growing number of jurisdictions are videotaping the entire booking process for individual offenders, in the event that irregular or improper actions are exhibited by jail or police officers as offenders are booked (Schulman 2005). Booking is also a phase of pretrial services. One reason for videotaping this phase is to ensure that discrimination does not occur based on racial, ethnic, gender, or socioeconomic factors (Lobo-Antunes 2004).

INITIAL APPEARANCE

The **initial appearance** of a defendant before a magistrate is a formal proceeding during which a magistrate or other judicial official advises the defendant of the charges. An initial appearance follows the booking process. The magistrate determines from a reading of the charges whether or not they are petty offenses. Petty or minor offenses vary in interpretation among states. Indicators of petty offenses are usually small fines (less than $500) and short sentences (six months or less) associated with the criminal offense. More serious offenses involve larger fines and longer sentences, usually one year or longer in duration (Champion 2005b).

Crime seriousness has been critical in determining whether or not defendants have a right to a jury trial. For instance, the case of *Duncan v. Louisiana* (1968) involved a nineteen-year-old man who was convicted and sentenced to serve 60 days in jail and pay a $150 fine for simple battery. Duncan requested a jury trial but was denied one. Louisiana claimed that Duncan's crime was a petty offense and thus the offense did not entitle him to a jury trial. The U.S. Supreme Court disagreed. The high court observed that Louisiana's law pertaining to battery, although a misdemeanor or petty offense, carried a two-year maximum sentence and a $300 fine. The U.S. Supreme Court observed that most states define petty offenses as punishable for terms less than one year, and in some jurisdictions, the maximum sentence is no more than six months and a $50 fine. Without defining precisely the meaning of a petty offense, the U.S. Supreme Court said that "We need not . . . settle in this case the exact location of the line between petty offenses and serious crimes. It is sufficient for our purposes to hold that a crime punishable by two years in prison is . . . a serious crime and not a petty offense." Duncan's conviction was overturned.

The Sixth Amendment says that all persons in criminal prosecutions are entitled to the right to a speedy and public trial, by an impartial jury of the state. But this amendment is interpreted differently depending upon the jurisdiction where the petty offenses are committed. Some jurisdictions discourage jury trials to resolve petty offense charges. In a New Jersey case, a defendant was indicted by a federal grand jury on federal misdemeanor charges, and the prosecutor for the government expressed strongly the opinion that the man ought to waive his jury trial rights. The man refused, and so the prosecutor brought new felony charges against the man in retaliation. In this case the court dismissed all charges against the man as the fair remedy, and the prosecutor was criticized for his misconduct (*United States v. Lippi*, 1977).

When any crime is alleged, it is important for defendants to be advised of the specific charges against them (Nunn 2003). They should also be advised of their rights under the circumstances (Vaughn, Topalli, and Pierre 2004). When persons are arrested by police, their initial appearance before a magistrate, therefore, is a formal proceeding where defendants are advised of the charges against them. At that time, the magistrate advises the defendants of their rights, and bail is considered. This is also the occasion where magistrates determine the date for a preliminary examination or a preliminary hearing to establish whether probable cause exists to move forward toward a trial. Between the time of a defendant's initial appearance and the preliminary hearing or examination, defendants can hire defense counsel to represent them (Nunn 2003). If a defendant is indigent, then an attorney will be appointed by the court to represent him or her. Before we examine preliminary examinations or hearings, the bail process will be described.

THE RIGHT TO BAIL

Bail has its roots in New England in the 1690s. Early English common law applicable during that period encompassed many of the guarantees later included in the Bill of Rights, including the right against unreasonable searches and seizures, double jeopardy, compulsory self-incrimination, grand jury indictment, trial by jury, and the right to bail (Hermida 2005; Kuckes 2004). Bail is not unique to the United States. Other countries, such as Australia, have done much to establish bail provisions for criminal defendants and conditions under which bail is granted (Demuth 2003). A bail bond form is shown in Figure 7.3.

Release on One's Own Recognizance (ROR)

Following one's arrest, a decision is made about whether the defendant will be brought to trial. If a trial is imminent because of case seriousness, most defendants can obtain their temporary release from jail. Many arrestees may not have to post bail, in that they be eligible for **release on their own recognizance (ROR).** If they have strong community ties and it is unlikely that they will flee from the jurisdiction, they may be freed on their own recognizance (ROR) by the magistrate or judicial officer (Harris and Dagadakis 2004).

BAIL BOND
(Caption)
_____ being in custody charged with
(Name of defendant)
the offense of _____ and being admitted to bail in
the sum of $ ____ , we undertake that he will appear and
be amendable to the orders and process of this and any
other court in which this proceeding may be pending
hereafter for any and all purposes and at all stages of the
proceeding (including, in event of indictment, proceedings thereafter) in accordance with
(Name of defendant)
   Executed this _____ day of _____ , 19 __.

_____   _____
(Name of defendant)   (Address)

_____   _____
(Name of surety)   (Address)
  Taken and subscribed before me this
_____ day of _____ , 19 __.
                                          _____
                                                 (Signature)

                                          _____
                                                   (Title)
   I, _____ , by entering into the (above) bond
obligation, do hereby submit to the jurisdiction of the
courts of   in which any forfeiture proceeding
arising out of my bail obligation may be pending, and do
further irrevocably appoint the clerk of such court as my
agent upon whom any process affecting my liability on
such bond may be served, such clerk to forthwith mail
copies to me at _____City
                           (Street address)
of _____ , County of _____ , State
of _____ , or at my last known address.
   Date this ___ day of _____ , 19 __.

                                          _____
                                                  (Name)

FIGURE 7.3
A Bail Bond Form

Bail Bonds

When the character of the defendant is unknown, or if the offenses alleged are
quite serious (e.g., aggravated assault, rape, armed robbery), the magistrate will
often set bail or specify a **bail bond.** Bail is a surety to procure the release of
those under arrest, to assure that they will appear to face charges in court at a
later date. A bail bond is a written guarantee, often accompanied by money or
other securities, that the person charged with an offense will remain in the
court's jurisdiction to face trial at a time in the future (Demuth 2003).

BOX 7.2 THE RIGHT TO BAIL

Schilb v. Kuebel, 404 U.S. 357 (1971). In a case in Illinois in which a defendant was ultimately acquitted, 1 percent of the bail amount was forfeited to the bail bond company, which by Illinois law is permitted to make a small amount of money as a commission for posting bail for criminal suspects. Schilb and others filed a class-action suit against the bail bond company as being discriminatory and unconstitutional in its procedures. They further challenged the release-on-own-recognizance scheme as discriminatory. The U.S. Supreme Court upheld the Illinois bail law, saying that its fee of 1 percent of bail was not excessive and that there had been no discrimination between the poor and the rich; in short, the Illinois law did not violate any constitutional amendment.

Stack v. Boyle, 342 U.S. 1 (1951). Stack was charged with conspiracy to commit a crime, and bail was set at $50,000. She protested, saying that the bail was excessive and that no hearing was ever held to determine how much bail should be set. The U.S. Supreme Court agreed with Stack and remanded the case back to the district court, where a hearing could be held on the bail issue. The Court held that bail had not been fixed by proper methods in this case. It did not try to determine or define "proper methods," however.

United States v. Salerno, 481 U.S. 739 (1987). Salerno and others were arrested for several serious crimes and held without bail as dangerous under the Bail Reform Act of 1984. Salerno was convicted and sentenced to 100 years in prison. He appealed, being among the first to challenge the constitutionality of the new Bail Reform Act and its provision that specifies that dangerous persons may be detained prior to trial until such time as their case may be decided. He objected that the new act violated the Eighth Amendment provision against "cruel and unusual" punishment. The Supreme Court upheld the constitutionality of pretrial detention and declared that it did not violate the defendant's rights under the Eighth Amendment if a specific defendant was found to be dangerous.

Motorists may be required to post a **cash bail bond** for minor traffic violations such as speeding or reckless driving. These cash bonds guarantee the motorist's appearance in court later to face charges of violating traffic laws. If the motorist fails to appear, the cash bond is forfeited. The bond set is often the exact amount of the fine for violating the traffic law anyway.

When arrestees do not have the money to post their bail, they may use **bail bond companies.** These companies are usually located near jails. For a fee, they provide the service of posting bail for various offenders. **Bail bondsmen or bondspersons** appear at the jail and post bond for defendants.

Defendants are usually required to pay the bonding company a fee for this service, which is 10 percent of the bail bond set by the magistrate. For instance, if the bond set by the magistrate for a particular offense is $25,000, the bonding company may post this bond for the defendant if the defendant is considered a good risk, and if the defendant or an associate of the defendant pays the bonding company a nonrefundable fee of $2500. If a defendant is unable to pay the fee and no one will pay it for him/her, the defendant must remain in jail until trial is held.

BAIL BONDSMEN AND BONDING COMPANIES

Bail bondsmen are persons who either own or work for bonding companies. Bonding companies are authorized to post bail for various criminal suspects up to a fixed amount. Bonding companies usually have property investments and other capital that they use as a type of insurance with a city or county government. For example, a bonding company may be authorized by a city to post bonds of up to $5 million for various persons charged with crimes. The bonding company owner may have stocks, securities, property, and other assets that he/she has assigned to the city or county as collateral. Thus, the city or county is protected from a potential loss of revenue if the bonding company guarantees the bond amount for the release of a defendant. If the defendant fails to appear later in court, the bonding company forfeits the bond it has posted unless it can produce the defendant later.

If the bonding company is authorized to write bonds of up to $5 million, once this ceiling has been reached, the bonding company can no longer write bonds for defendants. Bonding companies are released from their obligations to cities or counties once defendants have been convicted or acquitted of crimes or the bail bonds are cancelled. Bonding companies profit from the 10 percent nonrefundable fees they collect from persons who want to be released from jail before their trials are held. In most jurisdictions, there are several bonding companies who can provide bail for various arrestees.

COMPETING GOALS OF BAIL

Excessive Bail

Under the Eighth Amendment, citizens are advised that **excessive bail** shall not be required, nor excessive fines imposed. Some citizens believe that regardless of the offense alleged, bail will be set and defendants will be permitted to remain free until the date of trial. This is not true. Depending upon the circumstances of a particular criminal offense and the evidence obtained, some defendants may have a very high bail, while others may not be granted bail at all. They will be required to remain in jail until trial.

The Eighth Amendment provision against excessive bail means that bail shall not be excessive in those cases where it is proper to grant bail (*United States v. Giangrosso*, 1985). The right to bail is not an absolute one under the Eighth Amendment (*United States v. Bilanzich*, 1985; *United States v. Provenzano*, 1985). In some cases, suspects are detained for trial without bail (*United States v. Acevedo-Ramos*, 1984), while in others, defendants are subject to detention even if they are unable to pay high bail ranging from $25,000 to $1 million (*United States v. Szott*, 1985; *United States v. Jessup*, 1985). If a murder suspect is caught in the act or is a habitual offender, bail will probably be denied. This is because it is probable that such defendants will attempt to flee the jurisdiction to avoid prosecution. Are certain suspects dangerous to others? States vary in permitting judges the discretion for making this decision. In 31 states and the District of Columbia, however, this is a judicial consideration that often results in preventive pretrial detention (Gottlieb 1984).

Whether or not bail is granted is not exclusively determined by whether a crime is violent (Harris and Dagadakis 2004). More than a few defendants who are charged with nonviolent crimes are denied bail. Magistrates consider the **totality of circumstances** in setting bail on a case-by-case basis. A former bank president was denied bail in a case alleging fraudulent manipulation and theft of depositor's funds. While the former bank president had substantial community ties and property interests to protect, he also had a recently acquired passport and travel visas to several foreign countries where he also maintained property and business interests. In addition, $50 million in bank funds were missing as the result of a federal audit. The magistrate considered the bank president to be a poor risk for bail. There was a strong likelihood that the bank president would flee the jurisdiction and live on the embezzled $50 million in some remote location.

Bail provisions of the United States Constitution have been challenged by the American Civil Liberties Union and other civil rights organizations. Their efforts as well as the efforts of a variety of special-interest groups has prompted a number of bail reforms over the years. Some of the reasons given for such bail reforms have included the facts that (1) bail is inherently discriminatory against the poor or indigent defendant; (2) those who are unable to post a bail bond and must remain in jail cannot adequately prepare a defense or correspond effectively with their attorneys; (3) there is considerable variation from one jurisdiction to the next and from one case to the next within the same jurisdiction for establishing a bail bond for similar offenses; (4) withholding bail or prescribing prohibitively high bail offends our sense of one's presumption of innocence until guilt is proven in court; and (5) those who pose no risk to the community may suffer loss of job or other benefits from detention as the result of bail. It would seem, therefore, that to deny a defendant bail would be contrary to the presumption of innocence, which is an integral part of due process. Nevertheless, the right to bail is not absolute (Harris and Dagadakis 2004).

Race, gender, and socioeconomic status have been among the variables examined to determine their differential impact on bail decision making. These are extralegal variables and should have absolutely no bearing on whether a defendant is granted bail. However, minorities seem to be at a definite disadvantage in the criminal justice system regarding bail decision making. Racial or gender differences seem to make a difference to judges when making pretrial release and/or bail decisions about particular defendants. For instance, female defendants are granted more lenient pretrial release terms compared with men in many jurisdictions (Jordan 2004a).

Katz and Spohn (1995, 161–163) investigated whether these data might show a pattern of discrimination in bail decision making according to race or gender. The sample of 8,414 defendants was divided according to race and gender. Because of missing information, the sample consisted of 6,625 records for black defendants and 1,005 for white defendants. A small percent of the sample were females. These researchers asked whether it made any difference in the bail decision, as well as the amount of bail, whether defendants were black or white or male or female. When taking offense and prior record into account, race made no difference on the bail decision. However, gender did make a difference. For different types of offenses, female defendants faced significantly lower bail compared with their male counterparts. Regarding pretrial release decision making, however, white defendants were more likely to be released before trial compared with black defendants. Further, females tended to be granted pretrial release more than males. These findings are inclusive, but they suggest that while race and gender may help to explain bail and pretrial release decisions, these variables may not be as important in influencing these pretrial release and bail decisions as was previously thought by other investigators. Other researchers have found similar inconsistencies in bail decision making and race and gender variables (Gallinetti, Redpath, and Sloth-Nielsen 2004).

The Bail Reform Act of 1984

The bail reform movement assumes that bail is inherently discriminatory. The **Bail Reform Act** was passed in 1966 and provided that the purpose of this act is to revise the practices relating to bail to assure that all persons, regardless of their financial status, shall not needlessly be detained pending their appearance to answer charges. More recently the **Bail Reform Act of 1984** was passed that vested magistrates and judicial officers with greater autonomy in bail-setting and releasing persons on their own recognizance (Champion 2005b). Presently, bail is available only to those entitled to bail. These are usually persons who do not pose a threat to themselves or others and/or do not pose escape risks. There is nothing inherently unconstitutional about keeping persons jailed prior to their trials, however, under various forms of pretrial detention (*United States v. Salerno*, 1987). Sometimes, pretrial detention of suspects is abused and that lawmakers should keep its use within reasonable limits. One reason for this belief is that it is often difficult to forecast accurately who will or will not be dangerous or good candidates for bail (Champion 2007).

Several states have passed **sexual predator laws,** which are targeted at violent sex offenders (Levenson 2004). Washington State, for instance, passed a Sexual Predator Act in 1990 aimed at those likely to engage in future acts of sexual violence. However, the act was soundly criticized because of its failure to cite realistic predictive criteria, which would identify which sex offenders would actually commit future dangerous sexual acts following some type of sex therapy or treatment. Although such laws have drawn criticisms from various civil rights groups, the U.S. Supreme Court upheld the constitutionality of such laws in 1998.

Interestingly, Nebraska passed a sexual predator law concerning a sex offender's right to bail in 1978, 20 years before the U.S. Supreme Court upheld the constitutionality of the Washington State Sexual Predator Act. In 1978, Nebraska amended its constitution to require the denial of bail to defendants charged with forcible sex offenses when the proof is evident and the presumption of guilt is great. Other jurisdictions, such as Texas and California, have enacted similar provisions (Champion 2005b).

OTHER FORMS OF PRETRIAL RELEASE

Bail Experiments

The 1984 Bail Reform Act was innovative in that it contained provisions for judicial officers to release defendants subject to certain conditions, such as (1) complying with a curfew; (2) reporting on a regular basis to a designated law enforcement agency; (3) abiding by specific restrictions on one's personal associations, place of abode, and travel; (4) maintaining or commencing an educational program; and (5) maintaining employment or actively seeking employment if currently unemployed.

Before the Bail Reform Act of 1984 was passed, experiments were conducted to determine the effectiveness of ROR. A National Bail Study was conducted in 20 jurisdictions in the United States (Thomas 1976, 1977) between 1962 and 1971. There was a significant drop in both felony and misdemeanor defendants who were detained in jails during those years, and there was an accompanying increase in the numbers of defendants who were released on their own recognizance (ROR). More judges seemed to be relying on ROR for the pretrial release of defendants, and thus, this meant more limited use of cash bonds, a primary criticism of bail opponents.

Between January 1981 and March 1982, an experiment was conducted concerning bail guidelines in the Philadelphia Municipal Court. This was called the **Philadelphia Experiment** (Goldkamp and Gottfredson 1984).

Twenty-two judges were selected for experimentation. One objective of the study was to create visible guidelines for judges to follow in using ROR in lieu of bail in pretrial release decisions. When bail was established, median bail figures for judges not following prescribed guidelines was $2,000, whereas the median bail figure was $1,500 for those judges adhering to the guidelines provided.

Although the findings were inconsistent regarding the use of ROR, the researchers said that the experiment yielded significant improvements in the equity of bail decisions for defendants generally. The study also encouraged greater use of supervised or conditional release programs as outlined within the Bail Reform Act of 1984. As the Philadelphia Experiment suggested, this alternative would provide some degree of relief for jail overcrowding at the very least.

Subsequently, the New York City Department of Correction discharged 611 jail inmates in November 1983 (Gerwitz 1987). Of these, 75 percent were released on bail, while 25 percent were released on their own recognizance. Only four ROR defendants were charged with felonies, while about 75 percent of the bail defendants were similarly charged. Forty percent of the released defendants failed to appear for at least one pretrial hearing. ROR defendants were far more likely than bail-release defendants to fail to appear in court later. Over a third of the ROR defendants were rearrested prior to trial. **Failure to appear** means that persons scheduled for trial and are temporarily released on bail or ROR do not show up in court on their scheduled trial dates. Although obligating defendants to post bail does not necessarily guarantee their subsequent court appearances, but it does result in fewer failures to appear compared with those released on ROR.

BOUNTY HUNTERS

Bounty Hunters and Jumping Bail

It is advantageous for bonding companies if the defendant can post property assets as collateral for the bonding fee. Thus, if a defendant leaves the jurisdiction before trial and jumps bond, the bonding company forfeits the bond it has posted with the court, but it is entitled to seize the defendant's tangible assets or property to cover the cost of the forfeited bond. Defendants may bypass bonding companies altogether by pledging their own real property assets to the court as bond in lieu of confinement. Courts are permitted to accept other types of assets, such as bank deposits, securities, or valuable personal property. When defendants must post their own property as bail, there is a greater likelihood that they will appear later in court compared with those defendants who have bail posted for them by bonding companies. The bail options available to defendants vary among jurisdictions (Dabney, Collins, and Topalli 2004).

When bonding companies provide bond for defendants, they do so on the assumption that bailees will reappear later in court to face the criminal charges against them. Bonding companies avoid furnishing bail to those likely to jump bail and leave the jurisdiction to avoid a subsequent criminal prosecution. **Jumping bail** means to leave the jurisdiction while on bail to avoid prosecution. However, a certain number of defendants leave the jurisdiction and fail to appear later in court. When this happens, the bonding company forfeits its bond to the city or county court. The more bail jumpers a bonding company has, the less bonding funds it has available to use for other defendants. Sizeable profits are lost, at least temporarily, whenever someone jumps bail. For this reason, many bonding companies post **bounties** or monetary incentives to employ **bounty hunters** to track bail jumpers down for a fee and bring them to court. These persons are more recently known as **fugitive recovery agents** and **bail recovery agents** (Dabney, Collins, and Topalli 2004). Unfortunately, we have been unable to devise foolproof mechanisms for predicting which defendants will jump bail and which ones won't jump bail. However, some prediction models work better than others.

In recent years there have been several incidents involving acts of irresponsibility of bail bondsmen and bounty hunters. Specifically, the wrong persons have been targeted as bail jumpers. As a result, several innocent victims have suffered either serious injuries or deaths as the result of a bounty hunter's actions. Despite these inappropriate and indiscriminate actions by bounty hunters, bondsmen continue to enjoy a broad range of procedural safeguards in surety arrests under both federal and state statutes.

PRELIMINARY HEARINGS

Following an initial appearance and a bail hearing, defendants are entitled to a preliminary hearing. **Preliminary examinations** or **preliminary hearings** are held after defendants have been arrested and have had their initial appearance before a magistrate. Preliminary hearings are conducted by the magistrate or judicial official to determine whether defendants charged with a crime should be held for trial. It is an opportunity for magistrates to determine if probable cause exists that a crime has been committed and the person charged committed it. The preliminary hearing is the first screening of charges against defendants.

The preliminary hearing does not establish the defendant's guilt or innocence at a trial. The government is required to present evidence or proof that (1) a crime has been committed, and (2) the defendant committed the crime. If the government fails to present a convincing case to the magistrate, the charges against the defendant will be dismissed.

This option by the magistrate does not preclude the possibility that the prosecutor will take the case to the grand jury for their consideration. In those jurisdictions with grand juries, this is sometimes done. However, if the magistrate believes the case presented by the prosecutor is weak, grand juries probably will not issue indictments either. But there is an important difference in the two strategies. In preliminary hearings, defendants have the right to present facts and evidence supporting their innocence of the crimes alleged. Defendants may even cross-examine witnesses and bring in witnesses supportive of their own position. Again, this is an opportunity for magistrates to determine probable cause that a crime has been committed and the defendant committed it.

In a grand jury proceeding, however, prosecutors present only the government's side of the matter. If magistrates determine that the accused should be released for lack of probable cause, subsequent grand juries may issue indictments or presentments against defendants. In some jurisdictions, preliminary hearings are used instead of grand juries for the purpose of establishing probable cause. Defendants have the right to retain counsel, to be fully informed of the complaint against them, and of the general circumstances under which they may secure pretrial release. If the defendant cannot afford counsel, an attorney will be appointed to consult with and represent the defendant.

When the defendant appears before a magistrate, the magistrate will determine whether the defendant wishes to waive the preliminary hearing. With the exception of certain petty offenses, which may be tried by the magistrate directly, the defendant may either (1) waive the right to a preliminary hearing or (2) not waive the right to a preliminary hearing.

The Defendant Waives the Right to Preliminary Hearing

If the defendant waives his/her right to a preliminary hearing, the magistrate or judicial official will bind over the defendant to the grand jury. In those states without grand jury systems, prosecutors may file **informations** or **criminal informations** against defendants. Criminal informations are charges against defendants filed directly by prosecutors. The result of filing a criminal information against a defendant is a subsequent arraignment before a trial judge, one who will usually preside if a trial is forthcoming.

The Defendant Does Not Waive the Right to Preliminary Hearing

If the defendant does not waive the right to a preliminary hearing, then the preliminary hearing is held. The magistrate will determine whether probable cause exists or does not exist. If probable cause does not exist, in the opinion of the magistrate, the defendant is discharged. However, if probable cause exists, again in the opinion of the magistrate, then the defendant will face arraignment on the criminal charges.

Grand Jury Action

Grand juries are bodies of citizens convened to hear criminal charges against suspects. The grand jury will hear evidence from the prosecutor against the defendant and issue either a **true bill** or a **no bill.** If a no bill is issued, the defendant is discharged and the criminal charges are dismissed. If a true bill is issued, defendants face arraignment on the charges against them. About half of all states have grand jury systems.

Sometimes grand juries will be convened for special purposes. These may be **investigative grand juries.** Perhaps there is a car theft ring operating in several states. Grand juries are convened to hear evidence in these cases. On the basis of evidence collected and examined, these grand juries may issue **presentments,** which are the same thing as **indictments.** The difference is that presentments are not issued as the result of a request from a prosecutor. Rather, the grand jury, on its own, decides that probable cause exists that one or more persons have committed a crime and submit their own true bill. Thus, indictments are the result of requests from prosecutors to charge defendants with one or more crimes, while presentments are independent grand jury actions leading to the same result, but without prosecutor intervention. Prosecutors ordinarily present these charges before grand juries. Federal grand juries consist of 24 persons, while different states have variable numbers of grand jury members.

The result of a charge coming from the grand jury alleging certain criminal offenses on the part of defendants through indictment or presentment brings those defendants to the arraignment stage of the justice process. Thus, the arraignment stage is reached through (1) a finding of probable cause in a preliminary hearing (possibly resulting from a criminal information filed by the prosecutor), or (2) an indictment or presentment from grand jury action.

Arraignments

At the federal level and for many state and local jurisdictions, an **arraignment** is the official proceeding where defendants are informed of the formal criminal charges against them and they enter a plea of either (1) guilty, (2) not guilty, or (3) *nolo contendere.* An alternative set of pleas in the State of Kentucky includes (1) not guilty, (2) guilty, and (3) guilty, but mentally ill. Pleas of *nolo contendere* in Kentucky are prohibited, for instance.

If the arraignment stems from grand jury action rather than a preliminary hearing, a copy of the indictment or presentment is given to defendants. In many arraignments, indictments or presentments are read to defendants by either magistrates or clerks of the court. Figure 7.4 shows a summary of events leading to an arraignment stemming from preliminary hearings, informations, or through grand jury action. An example of a federal arraignment order is shown in Figure 7.5.

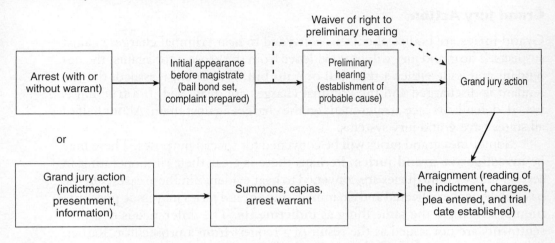

FIGURE 7.4
Alternative Procedures Leading to an Arraignment

DC 15
(Rev. 1/62)

NOTICE OF SETTING OF CASE FOR _____ ARRAIGNMENT _____

United States District Court
FOR THE

_____

THE UNITED STATES OF AMERICA

vs.

Criminal No.

To

☐¹ TAKE NOTICE that the above entitled case has been set for arraignment in said Court at Federal Courtroom   ,
on   , 19 , at

☐¹ As surety for the said defendant
you are required to produce   ² in said Court at said time, otherwise the bail may be forfeited.

_____ , 19___   _____

¹ Sentences allowing boxes which have been checked are applicable.

² Insert "him," "her," as appropriate.

FIGURE 7.5
Arraignment Order

Guilty Pleas

A guilty plea is the equivalent of a confession of guilt in open court. While the procedures vary among jurisdictions, judges usually are expected to inquire of defendants if their plea is voluntary, if they understand the nature of the charge or charges, the mandatory minimum penalty under the law, the possible maximum penalty under the law, and that they are still entitled to an attorney if they have not obtained one. Furthermore, the judge will likely inquire if the plea of guilty has been obtained through threats or coercion from anyone; that the plea can be withdrawn and a plea of not guilty entered, even at that late hour; that defendants are entitled to a trial if desired; that they have the right to confront witnesses against them and cross-examine them; that they have the right not to incriminate themselves; and that there is a factual basis for that plea. In short, the judge usually extends every opportunity to defendants to exercise all possible constitutional rights to which they are entitled.

Not Guilty Pleas

A plea of not guilty obligates the judge to fix a date for trial. The judge also determines whether bail will be continued, if the defendant is currently out of jail on bail. Or the judge may permit defendants to continue ROR if that is their current pretrial release status. Any number of options are available to the judge at this stage. The primary decision reached in an arraignment proceeding after a plea of *not guilty* has been entered is the establishment of a trial date, however.

Nolo Contendere Pleas

A plea of *nolo contendere* is considered the legal equivalent of a guilty plea. Technically, it is not a plea of guilty, but rather, a plea of no contest. The defendant is not contesting the facts as presented by the prosecution. However, the defendant may take issue with the legality or constitutionality of the law allegedly violated. For instance, the defendant may say, "Yes, your honor, I do not question the facts presented by the prosecution that I possessed two ounces of marijuana, but I also do not believe that the law prohibiting marijuana possession is constitutionally valid."

Sometimes, businesspersons enter pleas of *nolo contendere*. Even though these pleas are treated as the equivalent to guilty pleas in criminal proceedings, they are not considered admissions of guilt in possible future civil proceedings. If a businessman is charged with a criminal offense alleging fraud in the construction of a large building, a plea of *nolo contendere* or "no contest" will result in criminal penalties being invoked. The plea will be treated as though the businessman had actually plead guilty. However, if the building collapses and some persons are injured or killed as a result, they may sue the businessman for damages in a civil action later, but they are prevented from using the *nolo contendere* plea as evidence of an admission of guilt on fraud charges against the businessman. In the case of a guilty plea to the same fraud charges, the businessman could have the plea of guilty used against him in the subsequent civil action as evidence not only of his guilt in the fraud scheme, but also as evidence of his negligence. Therefore, a *nolo contendere* plea is sometimes a strategic option for a person wishing to avoid civil liability connected with criminal activities, traffic accidents, or some other law infraction where civil liability may be incurred.

Using a "worst case" scenario, if a defendant enters a not guilty plea, then the arraignment, usually conducted by the trial judge, will accomplish three objectives. As we have seen, arraignments involve entering a plea. They also involve a finalized listing of charges against the defendant. A third objective is to set a trial date. In sum, arraignments are for the purpose of (1) setting forth all charges against a defendant, (2) entering a plea, and (3) setting a trial date. This third feature is significant inasmuch as the trial judge presiding is usually the judge who will eventually hear the case. He/she knows the court docket and schedules the defendant's trial within a relatively short period of time following the arraignment.

DECRIMINALIZATION, ALTERNATIVE DISPUTE RESOLUTION (ADR), AND DIVERSION: EXPLORING ALTERNATIVES TO CRIMINAL PROSECUTION

It is important to understand that once a criminal case is placed into the criminal justice system, this doesn't necessarily mean that the case will proceed throughout the entire system and be processed fully. Several factors operate to determine whether specific cases will move further into the system or whether they will be removed from it. There is a great deal of pressure on prosecutors to resolve increasing numbers of cases expeditiously. Unfortunately, prosecutor's offices throughout the United States do not have sufficient person power or resources to prosecute all cases brought to their attention. Therefore, prosecutors must often prioritize cases and arrange them from the most to least serious. The most serious cases will likely receive the full attention of prosecutors and move forward. However, there is a massive number of less serious criminal cases that are relegated to lower priority for prosecution.

Several solutions have been devised or proposed to resolve these less serious cases and not consume valuable court time. For instance, a large number of cases involves possession of marijuana and/or recreational drug use. Some cases involve assault and battery or spousal abuse, where persons married or otherwise have physically injured one another. Subsequently, one or both parties have been arrested by police who have intervened. It is clear that while criminal laws have been violated, prosecutors do not always regard these types of offenses with the same degree of seriousness as armed robbery, rape, and murder.

In the case of illegal drug use, some persons have advocated legalizing certain drugs, thus rendering their possession as a noncriminal act. This doesn't mean that prosecutors don't think drug use is harmless. It is. But they might inquire as to whether the criminal justice system is the best place to deal with illicit drug use and punish it. Should drug users be treated rather than punished? No one knows the answer to this question. Certainly there are strong opinions favoring and opposing the legalization of certain drugs.

Accordingly, some types of assault and battery as well as spousal abuse may be regarded as less serious crimes. Again, this doesn't mean that prosecutors are insensitive to the needs of persons who have been assaulted, or that they condone spousal abuse. These are serious offenses deserving of some form of punishment. But should some of these crimes receive the same amount of attention and court time compared with murder, rape, and armed robbery? Again, there are no easy answers to this question. The following section, therefore, explores several strategies devised by legislators and others to reduce the caseloads of prosecutors and accelerate the justice process by focusing on the most serious cases. These strategies for reducing the sheer numbers of criminal cases confronting overworked prosecutor's offices include (1) decriminalization, (2) alternative dispute resolution, and (3) diversion.

Decriminalization

Decriminalization is removing an act from the category of crime (Sheehy 2004). Decriminalization might occur, for instance, in marijuana use (Jones 2003). Some states, such as Oregon and Washington, have entertained legislation that would legalize marijuana. California decriminalized marijuana use for medical purposes in the mid-1990s. When crimes are decriminalized, they may be shifted to civil courts for noncriminal resolution (Coomber, Oliver, and Morris 2003). Thus, a fight at a football game between overly enthusiastic fans may be shifted from criminal court to some type of civil resolution. At the same time that decriminalization is occurring with certain acts, however, criminalization is occurring with other acts, such as certain types of domestic violence and substance abuse (Sridharan et al. 2004).

Alternative Dispute Resolution

An increasingly used option to settle minor criminal cases is **alternative dispute resolution (ADR).** ADR is a community-based, informal dispute settlement between offenders and their victims. Most often targeted for participation in these programs are misdemeanants (Deukmedjian 2003). Some overly excited persons at a football game may get into a fight. One person may assault another, causing physical injuries and broken teeth. While criminal charges may be filed against the aggressor, these cases often consume considerable and valuable court time. However, if the offenders and victim agree, ADR may be used to conclude these cases quickly and informally to the mutual satisfaction of all parties involved. Victim–offender mediation or ADR programs originated in the midwestern United States (Schiff and Bazemore 2004). They are presently found in 100 U.S. jurisdictions, 54 in Norway, 40 in France, 26 in Canada, 25 in Germany, 18 in England, 20 in Finland, and eight in Belgium (Umbreit 1994, 25). Umbreit (1994, 25) notes that in most victim–offender programs, the process consists of four phases:

1. Case intake from referral sources.
2. Preparation for mediation, during which the mediator meets separately with the offender and the victim.
3. The mediation session, which consists of a discussion of what occurred and how people felt about it, followed by negotiation of a restitution agreement.
4. Follow-up activities such as monitoring restitution completion.

Umbreit found in a cross-site study that 79 percent of the victims were satisfied with the results of the mediation, 87 percent of the offenders were satisfied, and 83 percent of all parties believed that the mediation process was fair for both the victims and the offenders. Examples of the volume of referrals in specific mediation agencies are 591 mediations in 1991 in Albuquerque, New Mexico; 903 mediations in Minneapolis, Minnesota in 1991; 541 mediations in Oakland, California in 1991; and 1,107 mediations in Austin, Texas in 1991 (Umbreit 1994, 28).

Another name for alternative dispute resolution is **restorative justice** (Braithwaite 2002). Restorative justice seeks to produce a civil remedy between victims and their victimizers (Strang 2004). The roots of restorative justice can be traced to aboriginal courts in other countries, such as Australia and South Africa (Gallinetti, Redpath, and Sloth-Nielsen 2004; M. Harris 2004). The intent of restorative justice is not simply to restore to victims that which was lost or the value of services or lost wages due to injuries suffered. An additional objective is to heighten the accountability of the offender by requiring him/her to enter into a bilateral agreement with the victim in an effort to reach a compromise that will be mutually satisfying for both parties (Lemley 2004). Thus, although a criminal case has been transformed into a civil one, ADR involves the direct participation of the victim and offender, with the aim of mutual accommodation for both parties. The emphasis of ADR is upon restitution rather than punishment (Jones 2003). There are small costs associated with it compared with trials, and criminal **stigmatization** is avoided (Tishler et al. 2004; Tshehla 2004). Many criminal cases are being diverted from the criminal justice system through alternative dispute resolution (Hayes 2004). **Mediation** is increasingly used. ADR is recognized increasingly as a means by which differences between criminals and their victims can be resolved through civil means (Karp, Bazemore, and Chesire 2004).

Mediation in Action

Morrill and McKee (1993, 450) studied the Sunshine Mediation Center (SMC), the name for an urban mediation program founded in 1981 in a southwestern city. The SMC handled between 800 to 1,100 cases per year between 1985 and 1991. The problems and disputes handled by the SMC included barking dog nuisances, landlord-tenant disputes, spouse and child abuse, broken financial obligations, and unpaid private and small commercial debts, as well as various misdemeanor cases. The basic premises of the SMC included:

1. Delivery of dispute settlement services.
2. Personal growth.
3. Community improvement.

Mediation services provided by the SMC relieved congested criminal and civil courts. Volunteers were used as mediators. Often, they would resolve cases over the telephone between victims and offenders. Subsequently, a meeting was held between victims and offenders, where both parties worked out their differences and reached compromises or settlements. The SMC had a 90 percent success rate during the years investigated.

States vary in their use of ADR (Tifft 2004). For example, in North Carolina, there were 19 mediation programs operated in 1991 (Clarke, Valente, and Mace 1992). ADR is most frequently used to settle misdemeanor cases. In order to evaluate the effectiveness of mediation programs in North Carolina, an evaluation study was conducted comparing several counties with programs with several counties without programs. A sample of 1,421 clusters of cases filed in 1990 that matched eligibility criteria were followed in records of courts and mediation programs. Furthermore, interview data were collected from complainants and defendants. About 59 percent of the referred cases were mediated, with almost all reaching mutually satisfactory mediations between offenders and victims. These resolutions of differences are often called just solutions. ADR is another way of reallocating judicial business. ADR may or may not be operated by individual state courts (Lee-Tao and Kooi 2005).

Advantages and Disadvantages of ADR

Alternative dispute resolution has the following advantages:

1. Offenders do not acquire a criminal record following a successful resolution of the dispute.
2. Victims have the satisfaction of seeing punishment imposed for the criminal act committed.

3. Court dockets are eased because of the diversion of disputes to ADR.

4. Prosecutor caseloads are alleviated.

5. The community benefits where community service orders are issued to perpetrators.

6. Accountability is heightened, since victim compensation and restitution are required of offenders. (Palumbo, Musheno and Hallett, 1994)

The disadvantages of ADR include:

1. Offenders who have committed crimes escape criminal convictions. Some persons regard this as unjust and believe that if you commit a crime, you should receive a criminal conviction as a result.

2. ADR is insufficient as a punishment and causes some persons to flaunt the law, knowing that they will not be harshly treated if caught. ADR is perceived as too lenient.

3. Re-offending may occur if perpetrators believe that they can get away with crimes with only civil sanctions being imposed.

4. The criminal justice system image is tainted by excessive leniency from ADR programs.

5. The proportionate punishment is not the same as a criminal conviction and the record an offender would acquire as a result.

IMPARTIAL ARBITERS AND THEIR QUALIFICATIONS

Who Are the Impartial Arbiters?

Impartial arbiters in ADR programs may be retired judges, attorneys, or interested citizens. Depending on the jurisdiction, ADR arbiters are appointed on the basis of their fairness and integrity (Deukmedjian 2003). There are no special qualifications for arbiters. They do not have to have a precise and extensive knowledge of the law. Their actions are designed to be fair, and the resolutions they negotiate must be agreeable to both the offender and the victim. In the event that the arbiters cannot settle cases, then prosecutors can always reinstitute criminal charges against defendants and take these cases to court for resolution.

VICTIM PARTICIPATION AND INPUT

Victim involvement in offender sentencing and punishments has increased dramatically in recent years in both criminal and juvenile proceedings (Booth 2004; Carr, Logio, and Maier 2003). Testimony from victims can add much emotional appeal to formal proceedings. Victim feedback through direct participation in such proceedings is not always negative. In more than a few cases, victims have spoken on behalf of perpetrators and made requests for leniency (Hayes 2004). However, in ADR, victim participation ensures that all aspects of the offense and its results are brought to the attention of the arbiter. When prosecutors decide to divert cases to ADR, every effort is made to reconcile the dispute between victims and offenders. When victims have such input, often it is in the form of a **victim impact statement**, or a written and/or oral summary of the damages or injuries suffered from actions of the perpetrator (Roberts and Erez 2004). When the perpetrator and victim agree on the proposed punishment, under the supervision of an impartial arbiter, then **victim compensation** is discussed (Rojek, Coverdill, and Fors 2003). This is usually a monetary award to be paid by the perpetrator to the victim for the loss of property or work time. Many jurisdictions have **victim compensation programs** to provide guidelines about how much perpetrators should pay for the suffering and losses they have caused to victims (Myers et al. 2004).

Victim–Offender Reconciliation

Victim–offender reconciliation is another version of ADR (Lightfoot and Umbreit 2004; Presser, Hamilton, and Gaarder 2004). Roy, Sudipto, and Brown (1992) report that victim–offender reconciliation is a specific form of conflict resolution between the victim and the offender. Face-to-face encounter is the basic element in this process. Elkhart County, Indiana, has been the site of the **Victim–Offender Reconciliation Project (VORP)** since 1987. The primary aims of VORP are to: (1) make offenders accountable for their wrongs against victims, (2) reduce recidivism among participating offenders, and (3) heighten responsibility of offenders through victim compensation and repayment for damages inflicted (Roy, Sudipto, and Brown 1992).

VORP was established in Kitchener, Ontario, in 1974 and was subsequently replicated as PACT or Prisoner and Community Together in northern Indiana near Elkhart. Subsequent replications in various jurisdictions have created different varieties of ADR, each variety spawning embellishments, additions, or program deletions deemed more or less important by the particular jurisdiction (Lightfoot and Umbreit 2004). The Genessee County (Batavia), New York Sheriff's Department established a VORP in 1983, followed by programs in Valparaiso, Indiana; Quincy, Massachusetts; and Minneapolis, Minnesota in 1985. In Quincy, for instance, the program was named EARN-IT and was operated through the Probation Department (Lightfoot and Umbreit 2004). More than 25 different states have one or another version of VORP. ADR programs in other jurisdictions have been evaluated, and the results of these evaluations suggest that most victims and offenders are satisfied with the fairness of these proceedings. A high rate of restitution by offenders has been reported by many participating jurisdictions (Lightfoot and Umbreit 2004). But criticisms have been lodged against

VORPs that allege both victims and offenders do not benefit in ways originally conceived by this type of programming (Tifft 2004). VORPs are not unique to the United States. Other countries, such as Chile, England, Australia, and Italy, have experimented with such programs in recent years with positive results (Stanley 2004).

PRETRIAL DIVERSION

Pretrial diversion or simply **diversion** is the process where criminal defendants are diverted to either a community-based agency for treatment or assigned to a counselor for social and/or psychiatric assistance. Pretrial diversion may involve education, job training, counseling, or some type of psychological or physical therapy (Minor, Wells, and Jones 2004). Diversion officially halts or suspends criminal proceedings against a defendant (Ulrich 2002). The thrust of diversion is toward an informal administrative effort to determine (1) whether nonjudicial processing is warranted; (2) whether treatment is warranted; (3) if treatment is warranted, which one to use; and (4) whether charges against the defendant should be dropped or reinstated (Peters et al. 2004).

Most likely targeted for pretrial **diversion programs** are first-time petty offenders. If these programs are completed successfully, then the charges against these defendants are either downgraded or dismissed outright. The totality of circumstances of the offender's crime is ascertained by the prosecutor and the court, and a decision about diversion is made. Each case is evaluated and decided on its own merits. Persons charged with possessing marijuana may be diverted and required to attend counseling classes or sessions where drug abuse discussions are featured. Diverted defendants usually pay monthly fees during the period of their diversion in order to defray a portion of the expenses for their supervision (Maxwell and Morris 2002).

In a growing number of jurisdictions, **drug courts** are being used to process offenders charged with various types of drug offenses (Veneziano 2005b). Drug courts are specialized courts that hear and decide exclusively drug-related charges against defendants who may be either users or traffickers. There is a therapeutic milieu associated with drug courts (Maahs 2005). Often, judges will attempt to place drug abusers into programs where their drug problems can be remedied. These persons receive counseling and other forms of therapy, including drugs of use in assisting them to withdraw from highly addictive substances, such as heroin and methamphetamine (Atkins 2005; Veneziano 2005a). Thus, many drug offenders are more likely to be treated rather than punished, compared with more traditional offender processing in conventional criminal courts (Maahs 2005). These drug courts seem successful in assisting many offenders to overcome and deal with their addiction problems.

The History and Philosophy of Diversion

Diversion originated in the United States through the early juvenile courts in Chicago and New York in the late 1800s. Strong efforts were made by religious groups and reformers to keep children from imprisonment of any kind, since children over eight years of age were considered eligible for adult court processing. Cook County, Illinois, implemented a diversion program for youthful offenders in 1899 (National Association of Pretrial Services Agencies 1995).

The philosophy of diversion is community reintegration and rehabilitation (Proulx 2003). The objective is that offenders can avoid the stigma of incarceration and public notoriety. In most state courts where diversion is condoned, diversion does not entirely remove offenders from court processing, since the court usually must approve prosecutorial recommendations for diversion in each case. Since these approvals are often conducted in less publicized hearings, a divertee's crimes are less likely to be scrutinized publicly.

Functions of Diversion

The functions of diversion are:

1. To permit divertees the opportunity of remaining in their communities where they can receive needed assistance or treatment, depending upon the nature of the crimes charged.
2. To permit divertees the opportunity to make restitution to their victims where monetary damages were suffered and property destroyed.
3. To permit divertees the opportunity of remaining free in their communities to support themselves and their families, and to avoid the stigma of incarceration.
4. To help divertees avoid the stigma of a criminal conviction.
5. To assist corrections officials in reducing prison and jail overcrowding by diverting less serious cases to nonincarcerative alternatives.
6. To save the courts the time, trouble, and expense of formally processing less serious cases and streamlining case dispositions through informal case handling.
7. To make it possible for divertees to participate in self-help, educational, or vocational programs.
8. To preserve the dignity and integrity of divertees by helping them avoid further contact with the criminal justice system and assisting them to be more responsible adults capable of managing their own lives.
9. To preserve the family unit and enhance family solidarity and continuity.

Factors Influencing Pretrial Diversion

Excluded from diversion programs are recidivists with prior records of violent offending. Also, if offenders have drug or alcohol dependencies, they may be excluded from diversion programs. Probation and parole violators are also excluded. In view of these restrictive criteria, diversion is most often granted for low-risk, first-time property offenders. While recidivism rates among property offenders are not particularly different from those of violent offenders and drug traffickers, property offenders pose less public risk and are less dangerous compared with these other types of criminals. Relevant criteria operating in most jurisdictions where diversion exists as an option include the following:

1. The age of the offender.
2. The residency, employment, and familial status of the offender.
3. The prior record of the offender.
4. The seriousness of the offense.
5. Aggravating or mitigating circumstances associated with the commission of the offense.

One's residency, employment, and familial status are important considerations because they are indicators of one's stability. More stable persons are more likely to complete diversion programs successfully. Most diversion programs require at least some regular contact with probation agencies operated by state or local authorities. Unemployed and transient offenders are more likely to flee from the jurisdiction contrasted with those offenders who are gainfully employed and have families in the area.

Criticisms of Diversion

1. Diversion is the wrong punishment for criminals. Criminals ought to be convicted of crimes and sent to jail or prison. Diverting them to community programs is wrong.
2. Diversion assumes guilt without a trial. If prospective divertees accept diversion in lieu of a trial, this is regarded as their admission that they are guilty of the offenses alleged.
3. Diversion leads to net-widening. When diversion programs exist in communities, there is a tendency for prosecutors to assign persons to these programs who otherwise would not be prosecuted because of case backlogs and crowded court dockets.
4. Diversion excludes female offenders. In the 1990s this criticism is no longer a valid one, since many female offenders are diverted from criminal prosecutions.

5. Diversion ignores due process. When a case is diverted, the defendant is deprived of his/her right to a trial by jury, a mechanism where guilt must be established beyond a reasonable doubt. Diversion frustrates due process by avoiding a trial.

6. Diversion is too lenient with criminals. (Mackay and Moody 1996)

OTHER NONCRIMINAL OR CRIMINAL SANCTIONS

Community Service

Community service sentencing is one way of achieving offender accountability (Lo and Harris 2004). Community service is different from restitution in that usually, though not always, offenders perform services for the state or community. The nature of community service to be performed is discretionary with the sentencing judge or paroling authority (Teske and Zhang 2005). Judges may also impose **fines** as a part of an offender's sentence for almost any crime, but in many jurisdictions, fines are imposed only about a third of the time. Also, when fines are imposed, not all offenders pay them. The Victim and Witness Protection Act of 1982 made restitution to victims a mandatory part of one's sentence. Victim advocates strongly urge that restitution to victims be an integral feature of the sentencing process (Xenos 2003).

Is Community Service a Punishment?

Community service is considered a punishment and is court-imposed. Many types of projects are undertaken by offenders as community service. Usually, these projects are supervised by probation office staff, although supervisors may be recruited from the private sector. Some amount of offender earnings is allocated to victims as well as to the state or local public or private agencies that provide supervisory services (McCold 2003). Restitution to victims may be through periodic payments from offender earnings while on work release, probation, or parole. Sometimes, restitution takes nonmonetary forms, where offenders rebuild or restore property destroyed earlier by their crimes (Ruback 2002).

Is Community Service Effective?

Because many offenders are released into their communities for the purpose of performing community service raises a public risk issue for some people, although those offenders ordinarily selected for community service are low-risk and nonviolent (Ruback 2002). Other criticisms relate to the personal philosophies of judicial and correctional authorities, the offender eligibility and selection criteria used among jurisdictions, organizational arrangements, the nature of supervision over offenders performing community services, and how such services are evaluated. Most researchers regard community service and restitution as just and fitting punishments to accompany whatever incarcerative sentence is imposed by judges.

Restitution and Victim Compensation

Restitution is also a victim-initiated action. Restitution is the practice of requiring offenders to compensate crime victims for damages offenders may have inflicted. If the victim fails to notify the court of financial losses or medical expenses, the restitution order may be neglected. Currently, there are no reliable statistics concerning the proportion of convictions where restitution orders are imposed, nor are there statistics showing the extent to which probationers and parolees must make restitution as a part of their probation or parole programs (Ruback 2002). Several models of restitution have been described. These include:

The Financial/Community Service Model

The **financial/community service model** stresses the offender's financial accountability and community service to pay for damages inflicted upon victims and to defray a portion of the expenses of court prosecutions. It is becoming more commonplace for probationers and divertees to be ordered to pay some restitution to victims *and* to perform some type of community service. Community service may involve clean-up activities in municipal parks, painting projects involving graffiti removal, cutting courthouse lawns, or any other constructive project that can benefit the community. These community service sentences are imposed by judges. Probation officers are largely responsible for overseeing the efforts of convicted offenders in fulfilling their community service obligations. These sentencing provisions are commonly called **community service orders.**

Community service orders involve redress for victims, less severe sanctions for offenders, offender rehabilitation, reduction of demands on the criminal justice system, and a reduction of the need for vengeance in a society, or a combination of these factors (Lutz 1990). Community service orders are found in many different countries and benefit the community directly. Further, where convicted offenders are indigent or unemployed, community service is a way of paying their fines and court costs. Some of the chief benefits of community service are that: (1) the community benefits because some form of restitution is paid, (2) offenders benefit because they are given an opportunity to rejoin their communities in law-abiding responsible roles, and (3) the courts benefit because sentencing alternatives are provided (Jaffe and Crooks 2004).

The Victim–Offender Mediation Model

The **victim–offender mediation model** focuses upon victim–offender reconciliation. Alternative dispute resolution is used as a mediating ground for resolving differences or disputes between victims and perpetrators (Lightfoot and Umbreit 2004).

The Victim/Reparations Model

The **victim/reparations model** stresses that offenders should compensate their victims directly for their offenses. Many states have provisions that provide **reparations** or financial payments to victims under a U.S. Victims of Crime Act (VOCA). VOCA is a federally financed program of reparations to persons who suffer personal injury and to dependents of persons killed as the result of certain criminal conduct. In many jurisdictions, a specially constituted board determines, independent of court adjudication, the existence of a crime, the damages caused, and other elements necessary for reparation.

Repaying Victims and Society Through Restitution

President Ronald Reagan signed Public Law 98-473 on October 12, 1984, which established the Comprehensive Crime Control Act. Chapter 14 of this act is known as the **Victims of Crime Act of 1984** or the **Comprehensive Crime Control Act of 1984.** Currently, all states and the federal government have victim compensation programs. As a part of offender work release requirements, a certain amount of their earned wages may be allocated to restitution and to a general victim compensation fund. In fact, in the federal system, the Federal Victim/Witness Protection Act of 1982 created a statute whereby federal judges should order restitution to the victim in all cases in which the victim has suffered a financial loss, unless they state compelling reasons for a contrary ruling on the record. Thus, fines, restitution, and some form of community service have become common features of federal sentencing (18 U.S.C. Sec. 3563(a)(2), 2005; Keller and Spohn 2005).

SUMMARY

The criminal justice process commences with the commission of a crime. The crime is investigated, and in a proportion of the cases, one or more perpetrators are arrested. An arrest means to take someone into custody. Types of crimes for which persons are arrested include misdemeanors and felonies. Misdemeanors, or minor crimes, are distinguished by the fact that they are punishable by less than one year in a jail or prison, and a possible fine. A felony, or major crime, is punishable by confinement in a jail or prison for one year or longer, and a fine may also be assessed contemporaneous with one's incarceration. Persons are arrested based on probable cause that a crime was committed and the person arrested probably committed it. Subsequently a trial will decide whether the defendant is innocent or guilty of the crime(s) alleged.

Following an arrest, arrestees are booked, usually at a local jail or police station. Booking is a process whereby law enforcement officers collect detailed information about one's identity, formal criminal record if any, and other relevant information. Those charged with serious offenses are subject to an initial appearance before a magistrate or other judicial official. The purpose of an initial appearance is to advise the defendant of the charges against him/her and determine whether bail should be granted. Bail is a surety, sometimes known as a bail bond, which is usually posted for less serious offenses and permits defendants freedom in the community until they can be tried for the crime(s) alleged.

Bail is not an entitlement to everyone. Under the Eighth Amendment, excessive bail is prohibited, but this does not mean that all persons are eligible for bail. Those denied bail are usually deemed likely to flee the jurisdiction to avoid prosecution or they pose a serious risk to the community if released temporarily pending trial. Bail bondspersons usually are available to post bail for persons granted it. For many persons, bail is not necessary, and such persons may be released on their own recognizance (ROR). Under the Bail Reform Act of 1984, greater autonomy was given to magistrates and other judicial officials to determine the amount of bail or whether bail should be required to guarantee one's appearance in court later. Several bail experiments have been conducted over the years with many of these studies showing that persons released on their own recognizance subsequently appear in court. The Philadelphia Experiment was designed to determine bail fairness, and although the results were inconclusive, the equity of bail decision making was greatly improved in Philadelphia and other jurisdictions. ROR is increasingly used instead of cash bonds or other forms of sureties. A totality of circumstances test is usually used to determine which persons should be granted bail and which ones should not be granted it.

When some persons fail to appear in court to face the criminal charges against them or jump bail, fugitive recovery agents or bounty hunters usually are hired to track them down. Bonding companies in various cities usually have a fixed amount of money they may use for posting one's bond, and if someone flees, the bond is forfeited. Bonding companies cannot afford to lose these bonds and thus resort to bounty hunters to recover their funds.

Several states have sought to decriminalize various laws seeking to lessen the number of defendants charged with minor crimes. Decriminalization means to remove a particular act from the classification of misdemeanor and/or felony. Often when certain crimes are decriminalized, some of these acts, which were previously crimes, fall within civil jurisdiction and are resolved through civil courts. Another pretrial option is to use alternative dispute resolution or ADR. ADR is an informal process of dispute settlement between an offender and a victim, under the supervision of a third party. Sometimes known as restorative justice or victim–offender mediation or victim–offender reconciliation, ADR seeks to remove less serious offenses from the jurisdiction of criminal courts and decrease their case volumes. When ADR is used, offenders ordinarily do not acquire criminal records; victims are compensated for their losses or injuries; court dockets are eased; prosecutor caseloads are alleviated; the community benefits in various ways; and one's accountability is heightened through the restitution process. However, some disadvantages are that ADR permits many persons to escape prosecution as criminals; it may be an insufficient punishment and deterrent to future offending; reoffending may be encouraged if offenders think their crimes will only result in civil resolutions; excessive leniency may be alleged by an increasingly critical public; and the proportionality of punishment may be questioned. Several victim–offender reconciliation projects (VORPs) have been used as the basis for experiments designed to heighten offender accountability, reduce offender recidivism, and provide adequate compensation to victims for their losses.

Pretrial diversion is another option that prosecutors may use to divert cases from the criminal justice process, at least temporarily. Diversion is the temporary cessation of a prosecution against someone, usually a low-risk first offender, who may be required to participate in one or more community programs and complete different types of activities for periods of six months or longer. If persons, known as divertees, complete their periods of diversion successfully, they often have the charges against them dismissed and the records of the arrest expunged. At the very least, divertees are often eligible for a substantial reduction in the seriousness of the original charges against them.

There are many functions of diversion. These include permitting offenders to remain in their communities and continue earning a living and supporting their dependents; making restitution to victims if appropriate; avoiding the stigma of a criminal conviction; reducing jail and prison overcrowding; participating in self-help programs, and receiving possible individual or group counseling for certain problems they may have; and to preserve family unity. Factors influencing whether diversion is granted to particular persons include their age, residency, employment, prior record, seriousness of the instant offense, and any aggravating or mitigating circumstances associated with the present offense. Criticisms of diversion are that it sends a leniency message to offenders, that they can get away with violating the law and have their records expunged as a result; guilt is assumed without a trial; net-widening is encouraged; some gender bias results, as proportionately greater numbers of men are placed on diversion compared with women; due process is ignored; and the policy of diversion is too lenient. These arguments for and against diversion have never been resolved.

Other types of noncriminal or pretrial sanctions include community service, victim compensation, and restitution. The forms of community service vary from maintaining public parks, cutting courthouse lawns, and picking up highway litter, to participating in youth leagues or assisting the elderly in their residences or group homes. Restitution heightens offender accountability by obligating offenders to pay for the damages they have caused to property or for the loss of wages if victims are injured. Victim compensation is a way of offsetting the damages caused to victims. The nature of victim compensation may vary. Different victim compensation programs have been described. These include the financial/community service model, the victim–offender mediation model, the victim/reparations model, and repaying victims through restitution. Each of these models offers victims some form of compensation or restitution, and perpetrator involvement in such programs is mandatory. Offender accountability is heightened.

▨ KEY TERMS ▨

Alternative dispute resolution (ADR)
Arraignment
Arrest
Arrestees
Bail
Bail bond
Bail bond companies
Bail bondsmen or bondspersons
Bail recovery agents
Bail Reform Act
Bail Reform Act of 1984
Booking
Bounties, bounty hunters
Cash bail bond
Community service

Community service orders
Comprehensive Crime Control Act of 1984
Criminal informations
Decriminalization
Diversion
Diversion programs
Drug courts
Excessive bail
Failure to appear
Felony
Financial/community service model
Fines
Fugitive recovery agents
Grand juries

Impartial arbiters
Indictments
Informations
Initial appearance
Investigative grand juries
Jumping bail
Mediation
Misdemeanor
No bill
Philadelphia Experiment
Preliminary examinations
Preliminary hearings
Presentments
Pretrial diversion
Probable cause
Reasonable suspicion
Release on their own recognizance
(ROR)

Reparations
Restitution
Restorative justice
Sexual predator laws
Stigmatization
Totality of circumstances
True bill
Victim
Victim compensation
Victim compensation programs
Victim impact statement
Victim-offender mediation model
Victim-offender reconciliation
Victim-Offender Reconciliation
Project (VORP)
Victim/reparations model
Victims of Crime Act of 1984

QUESTIONS FOR REVIEW

1. What are four types of victim–offender mediation? Describe each briefly.
2. Distinguish between diversion and alternative dispute resolution.
3. What is a bail bondsman? Is a bail bondsman also a bounty hunter? Distinguish between each.
4. What is a bail bond? How can persons obtain bail?
5. Is everyone entitled to bail? Under what circumstances might one not be entitled to bail?
6. Describe the process of arrest, booking, and an initial appearance.
7. What is a preliminary examination or hearing?
8. What does it mean to release someone on their own recognizance?
9. How are failure-to-appear rates affected by whether one is granted bail or is released on his/her own recognizance?
10. What are the competing goals of bail?
11. What were some important provisions of the Bail Reform Act of 1984 in terms of how citizens were treated when arrested?
12. What are sexual predator laws? What is their significance regarding whether someone is granted bail?
13. What is meant by decriminalization?

▰▰▰ SUGGESTED READINGS ▰▰▰

1. O. O. Elechi (2005). "Repairing Harm and Transforming African-American Communities Through Restorative Justice." *Community Safety Journal* **4:**29–36.
2. John C. Goodman and Philip Porter (2002). "Is the Criminal Justice System Just?" *International Review of Law and Economics* **22:**25–39.
3. J. L. Herman (2005). "Justice from the Women's Perspective." *Violence Against Women* **11:**571–602.
4. Pamela K. Lattimore et al. (2003). "A Comparison of Prebooking and Post-booking Diversion Programs for Mentally Ill Substance-Using Individuals with Justice Involvement." *Journal of Contemporary Criminal Justice* **19:**30–64.
5. Ruth E. Masters (2004). *Counseling Criminal Justice Offenders.* Thousand Oaks, CA: Sage Publications.
6. Roger H. Peters and John Petrila (2004). "Co-Occurring Disorders and the Criminal Justice System." *Behavioral Sciences and the Law* **22:**427–610.
7. Thomas Trenczek (2002). "Victim-Offender Reconciliation: The Danger of Cooptation and a Useful Reconsideration of Law Theory." *Contemporary Justice Review: Issues in Criminal, Social, and Restorative Justice* **5:**23–34.

Chapter 8

Pretrial Procedures
Plea Bargaining

Chapter Objectives

As a result of reading this chapter, you will have accomplished the following objectives:

1. Understand what is meant by plea bargaining and the conditions under which it is applied.

2. Describe different forms of plea bargaining, including implicit plea bargaining, charge-reduction bargaining, sentence recommendation bargaining, and judicial plea bargaining.

3. Understand the advantages and disadvantages of plea bargaining both for the criminal justice system and criminal defendants.

4. Understand why plea bargaining has been banned in various U.S. jurisdictions and the reasons for this action.

5. Describe judicial actions when approving plea bargain agreements, including the information required by judges before they can accept guilty pleas from criminal defendants.

6. Understand different sentencing systems used by judges in various jurisdictions at both the state and federal levels, and how these sentencing schemes relate to plea bargaining.

■ It happened in Bentonville, Arkansas. Two men raped and killed a 13-year-old boy, Jesse Dirkhising, on September 26, 1999. Subsequently they were apprehended. The two men, Davis Don Carpenter, 39, and Joshua Brown, 23, his lover, were linked to the crime by various circumstances. Subsequently, they both gave confessions implicating the other. These are their stories. Brown says that he bound Jesse with duct tape and raped him with various objects, including food, but he never intended for the youth to die. Medical examiners concluded that Jesse died of positional asphyxia, which is being unable to breathe because of the way in which he was bound on Brown's bed. He was also given an antidepressant and was too drugged to be moved to a position where he could catch his breath. Brown claimed that Carpenter had directed the assault but did not take part in it. However, in a jailhouse interview later, Brown admitted that Carpenter was actively involved in Jesse's murder. According to Brown, Carpenter had diagrammed how the murder should occur. Carpenter's version of events was that for most of the sexual assault, he was asleep. He claimed that he was awakened by Brown when Brown took a break from the assault to eat a sandwich. However, a witness said that she saw Carpenter buy duct tape at her all-night grocery store in the middle of the night. The prosecutors have surmised that both men were equally culpable in the sexual assault and murder. The state sought the death penalty for both men. However,

Brown was subsequently sentenced to life without the possibility of parole for his role in Jesse's murder. Subsequently, Carpenter was allowed to plea bargain and receive the same sentence of life without parole to avoid the death penalty. Many citizens and family members of Jesse Dirkhising were outraged that Carpenter and Brown were not given the death penalty in the case. While the judge was the final arbiter in the case, the prosecutors were the ones who negotiated the life-without-parole sentences with Brown and Carpenter. Is plea bargaining a just way of concluding a heinous crime such as that committed by Brown and Carpenter? Should plea bargaining be permitted in death penalty cases? Do prosecutors have too much power? What do you think? [Source: Adapted from Brian Skoloff and the Associated Press, "Man Pleas to Get Life Sentence," April 19, 2001.]

■ It happened in Texas. On July 31, 2000, Reymundo Obregon, 25, was shot to death. Also shot in the ordeal was Jose Obregon. He was shot in the head but survived to identify his attacker. The shooter turned out to be Moises Villarreal, III, 20. It turned out that Villarreal had previously been convicted of another felony, in this case, cocaine possession. Thus, he was charged with the unlawful possession of a firearm by a felon as well as murder and attempted murder. He was facing the death penalty as a maximum punishment. Subsequently, Assistant District Attorney Roberto Balli configured a plea agreement and offered it to Villarreal and his attorney. The plea agreement called for Villarreal to serve 50 years in the state penitentiary. But Villarreal, and his attorney, Sergio Martinez, rejected the offer. Later, the state returned to the bargaining table with another offer. If Villarreal would accept a prison term of 22 years, then the state would drop the sentence enhancement and dismiss the charge of unlawful possession of a firearm by a felon. Villarreal accepted the new deal and faced the 22-year sentence by the presiding judge. The victim's family was pleased with the plea agreement, primarily because it will enable the victim's family an opportunity to get on with their lives and heal. Villarreal was subsequently sentenced to 22 years in prison and ordered to pay court costs. Should murderers be permitted to bargain down the terms of their possible sentences? To what extent is just deserts undermined by plea bargaining, if at all? Do you believe that a 22-year sentence is fair in this particular case? Why or why not? [Source: Adapted from Laurel Almada and the Associated Press, "Man Agrees to 22-Year Prison Plea Sentence," November 27, 2001.]

INTRODUCTION

It is difficult to imagine an efficient criminal justice system operating without plea bargaining. This chapter explores plea bargaining in great detail. Plea bargaining is a preconviction agreement or negotiated guilty plea between the government and defendant wherein the government offers some form of leniency, usually a lighter sentence, in exchange for a guilty plea to lesser charges. Thus, through plea bargaining, the state benefits because it avoids a protracted and expensive trial. The defendant benefits in that a sentence is accepted, which is often much shorter and less severe than a sentence that may have been imposed had the case proceeded to trial and the person had been convicted. All plea bargain agreements are subject to judicial approval.

The chapter opens with an examination of plea bargaining generally and the issue of why defendants should enter into plea bargain agreements. A brief history of plea bargaining in the United States is presented. Plea bargaining is not unique to the United States and occurs with some frequency in many other countries. Over 90 percent of all criminal cases are concluded annually through plea bargaining of some kind. This section examines the conditions under which plea bargaining may occur and when it may occur, which is at any time from the point when one is arrested through the jury deliberation process. The coercive aspects of plea bargaining are examined. Also discussed is the matter of promises made by prosecutors to induce defendants to enter guilty pleas. Under all circumstances, these promises from prosecutors must be honored; otherwise, plea agreements are invalidated.

The next section examines several types of plea bargaining. Implicit plea bargaining is examined, where it is generally understood by both prosecutors and defense counsels alike what the going rate is for a particular crime charged. Usually agreements are reached between these opposing parties about the type of plea the defendant will enter and the punishment recommended. Another type of plea bargaining is charge-reduction bargaining. Where many charges have been filed against criminal defendants, prosecutors may agree to drop most charges if defendants plead guilty to one or more of the lesser charges. A third type of plea bargaining is judicial plea bargaining, where the judge recommends a sentence to a defendant in exchange for a plea of guilty. The fourth type of plea bargaining is sentence recommendation bargaining. Under this type of plea bargaining, the prosecutor recommends a specific sentence to the defendant in exchange for a guilty plea. The weaknesses and strengths of each of these types of plea bargaining are examined.

The chapter next examines a wide array of arguments favoring plea bargaining as well as a lengthy list of arguments opposing it. Arguments in favor of plea bargaining include that it results in fewer trials and trial delays; more convictions are obtained; expensive trials are avoided; and defendants can anticipate some form of leniency in sentencing. Opponents of plea bargaining claim that plea bargaining violates one's right against self-incrimination, since one must admit guilt in order to receive a more lenient sentence or sentence recommendation. Other arguments include that judges lose control over cases that are plea bargained; defendants may be ignorant of the rights they are waiving when entering into plea agreements; guilty pleas may be rejected by the court; habitual offender statutes may be circumvented; some persons may receive more lenient sentences when their crimes deserve harsher penalties; some heinous aspects of crimes are not disclosed through plea agreements; plea agreements may appear to be too routine and rubber-stamped; the potential exists for gender bias in plea bargaining; the jury process may be invalidated; sentencing reforms may be hampered; negotiated guilty pleas are too bureaucratized; and lawyers may be vested with too much authority in the plea bargaining process. In some jurisdictions, plea bargaining has been banned. Despite the ban on plea bargaining, it still exists even in jurisdictions that have banned it. Some of the reasons for banning plea bargaining are listed and discussed.

The chapter next examines the important role of judges in the plea bargaining process. Judges must determine whether defendants wish to waive their right to a trial. They must also determine if there is a factual basis for the guilty plea. More than a few instances have occurred where defendants have been bullied into guilty pleas by aggressive prosecutors where no evidence of defendant guilt exists. Under these circumstances, judges have rejected such plea agreements and acquitted defendants, despite the fact that they entered guilty pleas to various crimes. Also, judges may or may not participate in the plea bargaining process. North Carolina is a state that allows judges to sit in while plea bargaining occurs between prosecutors, defendants, and their attorneys. In most jurisdictions, however, judicial participation in this process is banned. Furthermore, in some jurisdictions where sentencing guidelines have been established, plea bargaining may pose problems for enforcing these guidelines. Thus, different forms of sentencing may affect the plea bargaining process in a variety of ways (Wooldredge and Griffin 2004).

PLEA BARGAINING: NEGOTIATED GUILTY PLEAS

Why Should Any Defendant Plea Bargain?

Ideally, defendants who wish to enter guilty pleas to criminal charges know that they are guilty. There is substantial evidence against them. They have the right to compel the state to try them in a court of law. All criminals have a right to their day in court. However, in cases where one's guilt is not seriously contested, trials are perfunctory rituals with almost absolutely predictable results.

Unfortunately for criminal defendants, trial convictions usually result in more stringent applications of sanctions (Champion 2005a). Judges tend to deal more harshly with convicted offenders who have insisted on trials despite the existence of substantial evidence of their guilt beyond a reasonable doubt. However, pretrial agreements where guilty pleas are entered often result in less severe sanctions or sentences. Early research on the differences in sentences imposed through plea bargaining or trial has highlighted a pattern of judicial sentencing behavior. In more than a few jurisdictions, judges have advised defendants of the sentences judges plan to impose (Cummingham 2005). Judges further advise that if the plea bargain is rejected and the case proceeds to trial, convicted offenders are likely to incur a harsher sentence. Thus, those who contest their guilt compared with those who plead guilty are subjected to established practices whereby judges sentence them more harshly (Kirschner and Galperin 2001). The harsher sentence is imposed as a punishment for burdening the state with the responsibility of proving one's guilty beyond a reasonable doubt.

Plea bargaining usually results in reduced charges for criminal defendants. In some instances, criminal charges may be dropped altogether in exchange for valuable information about a crime. For instance, a man was engaged to a school teacher in a northeastern state during the 1980s. The woman broke off the engagement. Enraged, the man killed the woman and buried her body off an old logging trail about 10 miles from her home. The woman's disappearance was quickly noticed, although there was no evidence of foul play. The man was the key suspect in the case, but the prosecutor was helpless. There was no direct or circumstantial evidence of his culpability or anything to suggest that he had harmed her. The man subsequently moved to a western state where he found work and started a new life for himself. After over a decade of searching for the missing woman, the prosecutor contacted the man during the 1990s and said that if the man told him where the body could be found, no charges would be brought against him for the crime. The man entered into an agreement with the prosecutor to disclose details about how the woman came to be missing. The man said that he had killed her in a jealous rage when she had spurned him. And then he carefully concealed the body in a large shower curtain and buried the woman on the logging trail. He led police and the prosecutor to the exact spot where the woman was buried. Her body was recovered and she was given a proper burial by her family members. The man was not prosecuted for this murder and returned to his state to resume his life. The prosecutor was soundly criticized by the public and media for this agreement not to prosecute the man, but the prosecutor stated that unless he had made that agreement, the woman's body never would have been recovered. At least her family had the peace of mind of knowing what had happened.

In less dramatic cases played out in courtrooms throughout the United States, prosecutors and defense counsel attempt to arrive at the most favorable sentences for state interests and for defendant's interests. Depending upon whether offenses alleged are felonies or misdemeanors, negotiations between prosecutors and defense counsel are geared to arrive at an appropriate term of years or months for defendants who wish to enter guilty pleas. The prosecution seeks to maximize these years or months, while the defense seeks to minimize them (Tappan 2005).

For instance, suppose a defendant is charged with burglary and conversion of stolen property. The burglary and conversion of stolen property statutes provide a $5,000 fine and up to five years in prison on each charge. A worst case scenario would result in a jury trial and convictions on both charges, a $10,000 fine, and consecutive sentences of the maximum five years each for a total of ten years. Seeking to avoid both the fine and a ten-year term of imprisonment, the defendant may enter into a plea bargain agreement and plead guilty to one of the charges, such as the burglary. The prosecutor will drop the conversion of stolen property charge and recommend waiver of the $10,000 in fines. The prosecutor may suggest a two- or three-year prison term in exchange for a guilty plea to burglary. While the defendant wishes to avoid prison entirely, he is faced with either accepting the two- or three-year sentence or he can take his chances in court. There is a strong likelihood that he would be convicted of both offenses. Further, the judge would likely impose a harsher sentence, such as five or more years. Therefore, a powerful incentive exists for defendants to enter guilty pleas rather than face potentially harsher punishments in courts if they are subsequently convicted.

Fines attached to criminal statutes are imposed, but infrequently. One reason for not imposing fines is the state's inability to collect fines from convicted offenders, who are most frequently unemployed and indigent. Crime may be their only livelihood. When offenders are apprehended, convicted, and incarcerated, they have no means whereby to earn money to pay off fines imposed earlier by judges. An offender's inability to pay fines cannot be used to lengthen one's sentence. However, if certain defendants have assets, including property, automobiles, or expensive possessions, these items of value may be subject to seizure under asset forfeiture. An embezzler might have purchased property and other material possessions with money stolen from a business. One way of restoring the business's money is to seize the offender's assets and liquidate them. The proceeds from such liquidations are given to the business from which the money was stolen.

In typical property offense cases, however, convicted offenders may be drug- or alcohol-dependent. Their drug or alcohol habits may cause them to steal and obtain money to purchase more drugs or alcohol. Gambling addiction may drive offenders to steal another's property and convert it to money to satisfy their gambling addiction. Thus, many offenders have no assets and are deeply in debt when arrested by police. Because there are no assets to seize, the government can impose fines of any amount with little or no expectation of ever recovering even a fraction of the fines imposed.

Why Should Prosecutors Bargain with Criminals?

Are prosecutors obligated to collaborate with defense counsels and work out negotiated guilty pleas for each defendant? No. The U.S. Supreme Court has declared that prosecutors are under no obligation to enter into plea bargain agreements with any criminal defendant (*United States v. Benchimol*, 1985). Plea bargain agreements are sought by both prosecutors and defense counsels. It is to a prosecutor's advantage to resolve criminal cases without formal trial proceedings. Trials involve considerable preparation and state expense. Juries don't always convict guilty defendants, regardless of how much evidence exists against them. Plea bargains avoid trials and the often difficult burden of proving defendants guilty beyond a reasonable doubt. Most successfully concluded plea agreements result in convictions. Prosecutors are driven to convict defendants by one means or another. By far the cheapest and easiest convictions obtained by prosecutors are through plea bargain agreements (Thompson 2005).

The effectiveness of prosecutors is most often evaluated in terms of their record of successful prosecutions. Successful prosecutions are those resulting in convictions. Thus, the more convictions, the more a prosecutor's effectiveness. The fewer convictions, the less a prosecutor's effectiveness. If some prosecutors have political aspirations, aspire to judgeships, or seek promotions within their own district attorney's offices, their conviction records are direct evidence of their effectiveness as prosecutors (O'Sullivan 2001). Their reputations are enhanced and their careers are furthered to the extent that they are effective at whatever they do (Schram, Koons-Witt, and Morash 2004). It is in the prosecutor's best interests to seek quick convictions through plea bargaining.

Politics and Plea Bargaining

Thus, plea bargaining has subsequently emerged as a powerful political tool. It has become an increasingly visible and integral part of the criminal justice process. Politically it has shifted a great deal of power to prosecutors who have become the ultimate decision makers about a defendant's life chances (Boari and Fiorentini 2001; Rose-Ackerman 2002). Prosecutors now perform pivotal roles as they decide which cases should be prosecuted and which cases should be dropped. Prosecutors contemplate particular sentences for defendants charged with various crimes.

It is important also to understand that in most plea bargaining and the hearings that follow, ordinarily judges see only what prosecutors decide to reveal against criminal defendants. Judges may be unaware that other charges against specific defendants were not included in the plea agreement but simply ignored by the prosecutor in order to elicit a guilty plea. This is not the fault of judges. Usually there are so many plea agreements submitted to judges for their approval that most judges don't have the time to study each agreement in detail. Furthermore, many judges view plea bargaining as a fundamental feature of the criminal justice process, and they cooperate with prosecutors by approving plea agreements that are seen as a reasonable trade-off between crime control and due process (U.S. Sentencing Commission 2003). There are some important exceptions, however.

In an Alabama case, James Smith entered a guilty plea and was convicted of first-degree burglary and rape. Earlier a grand jury had indicted Smith for burglary, rape, sodomy, and assault. In exchange for a 30-year sentence, Smith entered a guilty plea to the burglary and rape charges, provided that the prosecutor dropped the sodomy charge. When the judge approved the plea agreement, he sentenced Smith to two concurrent 30-year sentences. However, a procedural technicality raised later by Smith resulted in a higher court vacating his original 30-year sentences. Subsequently, Smith went to trial on all four charges and was convicted by a jury. This time, the same judge sentenced Smith to life imprisonment on the burglary and sodomy convictions, and 150 years on the rape conviction. The judge explained the different sentences because he had not been fully aware of the circumstances under which these terrible crimes had occurred. The trial disclosed all of these details. Smith appealed unsuccessfully to the U.S. Supreme Court, contending that the judge was deliberately being vindictive with the imposition of these enhanced sentences. Rejecting his appeal, the U.S. Supreme Court said that in cases that go to trial, greater and more detailed information is available to sentencing judges compared with the information contained in a plea bargain agreement. This additional information justifies the court's harsher sentencing decision (*Alabama v. Smith*, 1989).

District attorneys and their assistants factor in one's criminal history, age, gender, and numerous other factors to arrive at what they consider to be the **going rate** for particular offenses (Wilmot 2002). Going rates are implicit sentence lengths and penalties associated with specific crimes. These going rates are influenced greatly by many factors, including the quality of one's defense counsel. Public defenders are at a disadvantage compared with private counsel, primarily because they often lack experience in negotiating plea bargains that are favorable to their clients. Further, because they don't receive much money for defending indigent clients, they are often involved in one's defense only perfunctorily, simply going through motions that will lead to a rapid conclusion of a case. Private counsels, however, are compensated well by a wealthier clientele. They also have a more intimate familiarity with the criminal justice system and the key actors who must be contacted in the right way to negotiate the best possible plea bargain for their clients (U.S. Sentencing Commission 2003).

Ultimately, however, the decision to charge any particular defendant with specific crimes lies with the district attorney's office. Whether prosecutors interact with private counsel or public defenders, these persons wield considerable power in deciding how rigorously certain cases should be pursued. Prosecutors have the greatest amount of power in cases where multiple offenses have been committed by a defendant. If a gun was used during the commission of a robbery, for example, prosecutors can decide whether or not to include this charge in a subsequent indictment or information. Usually, plea bargaining will result in some reduction in the number of charges filed. If prosecutors can be persuaded by defense counsel to leave out the fact that a weapon was used during the commission of a felony and charge simple robbery instead of armed robbery, the result will likely be a guilty plea to the lesser charge. This is because when weapons are used during felonies, they often involve mandatory incarcerative penalties. For example, Michigan has a use-a-gun-and-get-two-additional-years provision, meaning that an automatic addition of two years of **flat time** is added to a convicted offender's sentence where a weapon was used during the commission of a felony. It is to the defendant's advantage if the prosecutor decides not to file a weapons-related charge. Thus, this fact becomes a bargaining chip for the prosecutor and can be used strategically to elicit guilty pleas more easily from defendants who have committed weapons-related offenses (Cummingham 2005).

Another factor that affects the prosecutor's decision making about which cases to pursue vigorously is case pressure. In jurisdictions where the volume of cases processed is high, prosecutors may elect to *nolle prosequi* or decline to prosecute marginal cases that might have been pursued earlier for a guilty plea. Prosecutorial options under these conditions might include reducing more charges against defendants, recommending lighter sentences, or demanding more severe sentences after a trial.

How Long Has Plea Bargaining Been Used in the United States?

Historians have investigated the use of plea bargaining in the United States. Evidence suggests that plea bargaining occurred in the various states during the period following the Declaration of Independence in 1776. A study of plea bargaining in New York during the period 1800–1865 shows a pattern of plea bargaining usage that escalated during the second half of the nineteenth century (McConville and Mirsky 2005). The use of plea bargaining accompanied the rise in importance of district attorney's offices, the presence of elected judges, the judicialization of magistrates, the reorganization of the police, the marginalization of juries, and politicization of crime.

During the 1800s plea bargaining was simply referred to as a **guilty plea.** No formal classification of guilty pleas existed. In the early part of the nineteenth century, jury trials were proscribed for almost all criminal offenses. State reliance on jury trials was strong. However, by the mid to late 1800s, the growth of attorney organizations and increasing professionalization of police work modified greatly the art of criminal investigations. At the same time, court dockets became overcrowded and the glut of jury trials worsened. Thus, guilty pleas with one or more prosecutorial concessions gained in popularity as an alternative to formal courtroom trial procedure.

The professionalization of police meant that larger numbers of minor prosecutions were shifted to municipal and police courts, such as those in Boston during the period 1814–1850 (Ferdinand 1992). Data analyzed from over 30,000 cases from the Boston Police Court during the early to mid-1800s showed that between 1814 and 1850, the caseload for police courts doubled.

BOX 8.1 PLEA BARGAINING

There is no mention of plea bargaining in the U.S. Constitution. Although the Bill of Rights makes no mention of plea bargaining, this practice has consistently been upheld by different courts, including the U.S. Supreme Court. Over 90 percent of all criminal convictions are obtained through plea bargaining, even in jurisdictions where it has been banned. In most plea bargained cases, defendants enter guilty pleas to reduce charges in order to avoid more serious penalties. This strategy almost always works to the benefit of both prosecutors and defendants. Michael Kopper, an Enron accountant, and John Walker Lindh, an American Taliban and Afghan fighter against U.S. armed forces, both plea bargained with the government in order to avoid severe penalties during the early 2000s. Lindh entered a "guilty" plea in order to avoid an execution. Kopper entered a guilty plea to avoid exposing security sources.

In the eighteenth century public prosecutions of persons became more pervasive. Prosecutors generally dictated what sentences defendants would receive, although judges controlled and continue to control actual offender sentencing. In some ways, plea bargaining is an outgrowth of industrialization and has reduced substantially the courtroom workload. A brief history of plea bargaining is in order:

> 1633: Galileo gets house arrest during the Inquisition in exchange for his reciting penitential psalms weekly and recanting Copernican heresies.

> 1931: Al Capone brags about his light sentence for pleading guilty to income tax evasion and Prohibition violations. The judge then declares that he isn't bound by the bargain, and Capone does 7 1/2 years in Alcatraz.

> 1969: To avoid execution, James Earl Ray pleads guilty to assassinating Martin Luther King Jr. and gets 99 years.

> 1973: Spiro Agnew resigns as vice president and pleads no contest to the charge of failing to report income; he gets 3 years of probation and a $10,000 fine (roughly one-third of the amount at issue).

> 1990: Facing serious federal charges of insider trading, Michael Milken pleads to lesser charges of securities fraud; soon after, his 10-year sentence is reduced to 2 years.

Although other countries throughout the world have been slow to adopt it, plea bargaining now occurs virtually everywhere, including Japan where it is officially banned. Italy has legalized it formally; Germany says it is controversial; and Japan says the practice is horrible. Scandinavian countries largely maintain prohibitions against it.

A hypothetical case of why plea bargaining is so successful and widely used in the United States is the district attorney who has 100 cases a year

(continued)

BOX 8.1 *(continued)*

and a budget of $100,000. With only $1,000 to spend investigating and prosecuting each case, half the defendants will be acquitted. But if the prosecutor can get 90 percent of all defendants to enter guilty pleas and avoid expensive investigations and trials, then the prosecutor can concentrate office resources on the 10 who refuse, and spend $10,000 on each case and get a conviction rate of 90 percent.

Viewed from the defendant's perspective, plea bargaining makes a lot of sense. In the federal system, the conviction rate of criminal cases that go to trial is over 90 percent, depending on the nature of the offense. If there is a 90 percent chance of being convicted and receiving a severe sentence, most defendants will enter into plea bargains with U.S. attorneys to obtain less severe sentences. Conceivably all defendants would be better off if they rejected offers from prosecutors to plead guilty in exchange for leniency, forcing their cases to trials. But individual rationality does not always lead to group rationality. [Source: Adapted from Dirk Olin, "Plea Bargain," *The New York Times Magazine,* September 29, 2002.]

During the same time interval, the municipal court docket load increased by over 1,000 percent. Plea bargaining in Boston became increasingly commonplace as a means of resolving most cases. At the same time, court officers became more professional and formal courtroom procedures grew more intricate (Ferdinand 1992). It was in just such a milieu that the modern criminal court was born. Today's criminal courts are high-volume and multipurpose. The sheer numbers of cases crowding these court dockets made plea bargaining especially appealing, since valuable court time could be saved by out-of-court bargaining between prosecutors and defense attorneys.

The growth of formal legal education was apparent during this same period. More persons were acquiring formal legal training from newly established law schools, and the numbers of lawyers invading criminal courts to represent growing numbers of clients meant more protracted litigation. A relief valve was plea bargaining. A more educated lawyer contingent made plea bargaining more attractive to criminals as well as to judges, since criminals could bargain their way to lesser penalties without formal trial proceedings (Blackwell 2004). The trend toward greater use of plea bargaining continued into the 1900s. Since the 1960s, plea bargaining has escalated in use to the extent that over 90 percent of all criminal convictions are secured through plea negotiations. Because of the great savings in case processing time, most courts today are able to function with only moderate delays. It is difficult to contemplate what our courts would be like today if plea bargaining were banned outright.

Is Plea Bargaining Unique to the United States?

No. Many countries use some form of plea bargaining as a means of speeding up criminal case processing. Plea bargaining is used frequently in Australia, Canada (Kellough and Wortley 2002), France (Ma 2002), Germany (Ma 2002), Israel (Ajzenstadt and Steinberg 2001; Herzog 2003), Italy (Boari and Fiorentini 2001), and the United Kingdom (Ma 2002). Citizen discontent with plea bargaining in these countries is about the same as it is in the United States. In Canada, for example, a survey of 1,049 citizens revealed that most disapproved of plea bargaining. One primary complaint was that plea bargaining appeared to result in insufficient penalties for criminals. However, these citizen-respondents also indicated that if judges were to take a more proactive role in the plea bargaining process to ensure fairness to victims and the punishment process generally, then they would be inclined to be supportive of it (Goodman and Porter 2002). And in Germany, plea bargaining has been evaluated by prosecutors, judges, and defense counsels. They vary in their opinions toward plea bargaining depending upon the various costs and benefits of plea bargaining versus trial (Ma 2002).

How Much Plea Bargaining Is There Today?

In order to understand both the need for and use of plea bargaining, we must first appreciate the magnitude of federal and state litigation and rapid growth of criminal cases. In the federal system, for example, there were 44,144 criminal prosecutions in U.S. district courts in 1982. This figure had risen to 64,000 in 1994. There were approximately 49,000 convictions in federal courts in 1994. Judges dismissed or threw out nearly 9,000 cases that same year for various reasons, including insufficiency of evidence. About 92 percent of all federal criminal convictions were obtained through plea bargaining and without an expensive and lengthy trial. At the same time, there were over 500,000 prosecutions in state courts in 1982. By 1994 there were 1.2 million prosecutions in state courts, resulting in 872,217 convictions (Champion 2005b). Of these, 89 percent had entered guilty pleas while the remaining 11 percent were convicted through trials.

The rate of plea bargaining has remained fairly constant during the period 1970–2005 (U.S. Department of Justice 2005). In the 1970s, at least 90 percent of all convictions were obtained through plea bargaining. Even with 90 percent of all guilty pleas in either state or federal courts resulting from plea bargaining, the trial court delays in the criminal justice system today are notorious. Some cases, such as the California murder trials of the Menendez brothers and the O. J. Simpson murder trial, consume several months of court time before they are resolved. In the Menendez case, two brothers were accused of killing their parents. There was considerable incriminating evidence. Nevertheless, the brothers sought and got two juries to hear their cases, only to have both juries deadlocked at the conclusion of the first lengthy trial. A second trial, which resulted in guilty verdicts, took several months to conclude.

But these cases are high-profile and received considerable media attention. But less celebrated cases also consume large amounts of court time. What about the length of time taken to prosecute low-profile cases? In 1995, for instance, federal courts conducted 7,421 criminal trials. Of these, 4,400 were concluded in 1 or 2 days, while about 400 took 10 or more days. At least 110 of these trials took 20 days or longer. Most of these cases were low-profile and received little media attention (Maguire and Pastore 2005). Despite this inattention, these trials are sufficiently drawn out to underscore the necessity for plea bargaining. Without it, federal and state courts would probably come to a grinding halt. Or at the very least, case backlogs would be such that most scheduled criminal cases could not be heard for at least one or more years. In view of a defendant's right to a speedy trial, these courts would be hard-pressed to comply with this important constitutional provision. A real federal plea bargain agreement is shown in Figure 8.1 with the defendant's name deleted for purposes of anonymity.

Do All Jurisdictions Use Plea Bargaining?

No. Most jurisdictions use it. In some jurisdictions, plea bargaining has been banned. The most visible jurisdiction prohibiting plea bargaining is Alaska (Champion 2005b). The ban against plea bargaining was announced by the Alaska Judicial Council in 1975. Routine sentence agreements between prosecutors and defense attorneys were virtually eliminated after the ban and have not returned. Presently, most defendants are sentenced by a judge at an open hearing, with participation by the prosecutor, defense, and presentence reporter. Thus, the responsibility for sentencing rests primarily with the judge.

Some jurisdictions, such as Bronx County, New York, have sought to limit plea bargaining to specific phases of criminal processing. Whether a defendant has been indicted is significant here. A pre-indictment period is the time before criminal defendants are formally indicted for specific offenses. A post-indictment period occurs following their indictment. Once indictments have been issued in Bronx County, plea bargaining has been discouraged under a new policy. At the same time, pre-indictment plea bargaining has been openly encouraged.

In El Paso, Texas, a felony plea bargaining ban was implemented in 1975 (Holmes et al. 1992). Researchers investigated the effects of this ban on case processing and dispositions. While the conviction rate was generally unaffected, much greater numbers of cases went to trial. As a result, there was a gradual decrease in the disposition rate. Thus, it was concluded that the plea

United States Department of Justice

UNITED STATES ATTORNEY
EASTERN DISTRICT OF TENNESSEE
P.O. BOX 872
KNOXVILLE, TENNESSEE 37901
July 15,

IN REPLY, PLEASE
REFER TO FILE NO.

Dear

RE:

On May 2,   , Ed Wilson and I met with   regarding a proposed plea bargain for the captioned individual. Due to your absence from the office the original deadline for acceptance was informally extended "until you had time to discuss the situation with   ". To date, I have not heard anything relative to acceptance or rejection.

As we are now prepared to begin Grand Jury proceedings in the immediate future on this matter which will involve calling a number of witnesses from various parts of the country at significant expense to the Government, I want to clarify our offer and set a firm deadline for action.

We believe that Mr.   violated 18 U.S.C.   and   as the result of his purchasing, transporting and subsequently selling certain stolen   beginning in the summer of   . This office has proposed the following plea bargain which if accepted would be followed by the filing of an information and subsequent presentation of the plea bargain to Judge Taylor for approval. This offer is also contingent upon a proffer by you or your client's testimony regarding this matter and which, if acceptable to us, would be followed by the following plea bargain presentation to the Court:

1) $10,000 fine
2) Three year probation (payment of fine condition thereto)
3) Furnish detailed account of his dealings with the stolen   to FBI
4) No   prosecution
5) Immunity for any further violations arising from transactions from June,   , to date of information. (Please note as I have advised you earlier this is not as broad as the "transactional immunity" previously discussed with Mr.   on May 2nd.)

If in fact the case is going to be plea bargained, it must be done so before the Government incurs additional significant expense. Therefore, I am placing a deadline of July 31,   , on the offer. If the bargain is not accepted by the end of that date, it will be withdrawn and terminated. Please discuss this matter with Mr.   and advise us of your decision.

Very truly yours,

JOHN H. CARY
United States Attorney

J. Michael Haynes

BY: J. MICHAEL HAYNES
Assistant United States Attorney

JMH:sjv

FIGURE 8.1

A Federal Plea Bargain Agreement

bargaining ban in El Paso adversely impacted the ability of district courts to move felony case dockets along efficiently.

Later in 1981, the Superior Court of Merrimack County, New Hampshire, banned plea bargaining in response to criticisms of the practice and the perceived decline in public confidence in the judicial system's ability to effectively administer criminal sanctions. Unexpectedly, the quality of indictments against criminal defendants in Merrimack County did not improve. Actual sentence lengths imposed for various criminal offenses have remained unaffected by the ban. Court backlogs were increasing when researchers conducted a two-year follow-up and ban assessment (Champion 2005a).

When Can Plea Bargaining Occur?

In most jurisdictions unless otherwise prohibited by either policy or legislative statements, plea bargaining can occur at virtually any stage of a criminal proceeding prior to a finding of guilt. While most plea bargaining occurs before a trial is conducted, plea bargain negotiations may transpire throughout a trial.

In some cases, plea bargains have been struck while a case is in progress or while a jury is deliberating. In September 1997, for example, a television sportscaster, Marv Albert, was accused by a woman of sexual assault. The case went to trial in Virginia. During the trial, the alleged victim described to the jury how Albert attacked her. Later, the defense was able to impeach the woman's credibility with exculpatory evidence of their own. But the prosecution brought forth an additional witness who testified to similar treatment by Albert on another occasion and under different circumstances. Albert's attorney sought to introduce other evidence of an exculpatory nature, including testimony and records of past sexual behavior of the victim. But the judge ruled against the introduction of this evidence. Shortly thereafter, Albert's attorney announced that his client was going to plead guilty to a lesser included offense rather than sit through more disclosures by other witnesses. When the jurors were reconvened, the judge announced the decision of Albert to plead guilty and the jurors were dismissed.

Ironically, one of the jurors said that she didn't think the state had presented a sufficiently strong case to convict Albert, even with the additional witness and her damaging testimony about Albert's alleged actions. No doubt Albert was thinking that if the jurors were persuaded by this later testimony (which they apparently weren't), then he would be convicted and suffer a more severe sentence. In retrospect, Albert probably would have been acquitted of all charges.

Interrupting a criminal trial with a plea bargain has about the same effect of refusing to plea bargain in the pretrial and pre-indictment periods. Considerable expense has been incurred by the state in the defendant's prosecution. Judges are unhappy with events such as these. However, the prosecution bears some of the responsibility by entering into these late plea bargaining negotiations. Perhaps the prosecutor in the Albert trial believed that there was a good chance that Albert would be acquitted. Thus, the plea bargain was attractive since it would guarantee a conviction, even for a lesser included offense. In the Albert case, it seemed that neither side was willing to gamble on the jury outcome in view of the different types of evidence presented.

Is Plea Bargaining Coercive?

There is no question that plea bargaining is coercive. Almost no offender wants to admit guilt to any wrongdoing. Therefore, when an offer is made by the prosecutor to plead guilty to reduced charges or face prosecution on more serious charges, most defendants find this choice coercive. Even judges think plea bargaining is coercive (Champion 2005a). At the same time, however, judges concede that plea bargaining is a suitable trade-off between due process and crime control. Further, plea bargaining makes life much easier for these judges, prosecutors, defense counsel, and criminals.

The U.S. Supreme Court has ruled in several important cases where coercion relating to plea bargaining has been alleged. Three cases dealing with coercion in eliciting guilty pleas through plea bargaining are *McMann v. Richardson* (1970), *North Carolina v. Alford* (1970), and *Bordenkircher v. Hayes* (1978).

BOX 8.2 THE PLEA

■ The Case of Charles Gampero, Jr.

Charles Gampero, Jr., 20, was arrested and charged with second-degree murder in 1994. Gampero insisted that he was innocent of the crime. He admitted to having a fight with the victim outside of a bowling alley on the night the victim died, but he claimed that the victim was very much alive when he left him. There were numerous unanswered questions about the case. The victim's family, for instance, had told police that the victim had been the target of harassment and vandalism by unknown parties during several weeks before his death. Gampero believed that a jury would acquit him if the case went to trial.

During the process of jury selection, however, the judge advised Gampero that if the case went to trial and Gampero were found guilty, the punishment would be a sentence of 25 years to life. But if Gampero pleaded guilty to a lesser charge, then the judge would impose a sentence of only 7 to 21 years instead. The judge told Gampero's parents point blank, "I will give your son 25 years to life, so you better take the plea, or if you don't take the plea, he's getting it." Charles Gampero, Sr., Gampero's father, encouraged his son to take the plea, believing that his son would only serve 7 years. Gampero, Sr., said, "We took the plea agreement, thinking that my son would be home by the time he's 27. It didn't work out."

■ The Case of Erma Faye Stewart

Erma Faye Stewart was arrested in a major drug sweep based on information provided by a police informant who was later deemed not credible. Stewart, 30, maintained her innocence, but her court-appointed attorney didn't want to hear it. "He was like, pushing me to plead guilty and take

(continued)

BOX 8.2 *(continued)*

probation. He wasn't on my side at all." After spending 25 nights in a crowded jail, Stewart finally agreed to follow her attorney's advice and plead guilty. "Even though I wasn't guilty," she said, "I was willing to plead guilty because I had to get home to my kids. My son was sick." When she accepted the plea bargain and a 10-year probation, Stewart was freed. What she didn't know was that under the terms of her probation, she would be required to pay a monthly fee to the probation department. Her felony conviction also meant that the single mother was banned from the federal food stamps program. Within 3 years of falling behind in her probation payments, Stewart was evicted from her home. Steve Bright, a defense attorney and law professor with the Southern Center for Human Rights, says of plea bargaining that "One reason a lot of people plead guilty is because they're told that they can go home that day, because they will get probation. What they usually don't take into account is that they are being set up to fail."

■ The Case of Patsy Kelly Jarrett

In 1973, 23-year-old Patsy Jarrett, a North Carolina resident, drove to New York with a friend for a summer vacation. Three years later, police showed up at her door and she learned that sometime during their New York stay, her friend had robbed a gas station and murdered the attendant. The evidence against Jarrett's friend was strong. The only evidence against Jarrett was that an elderly witness said he saw a car at the time of the crime with someone inside. The man did not know, however, whether the person was a man or a woman. To avoid a trial, prosecutors offered Jarrett a plea bargain: If she would plead guilty to the robbery, they would drop the murder charge and give her a 5- to 15-year prison sentence. Jarrett said, "I told my attorney I can't do this." Her attorney said, "Well, my hands are tied. They want to drop the murder charge against you if you plead guilty to the robbery." And Jarrett said, "But I haven't robbed anybody." Convinced that the jury would believe her, Jarrett refused the plea bargain and went to trial. She was subsequently convicted and sentenced to 25 years to life. Jarrett commented after the trial and sentence, "I believed in the American system of justice. I believed that, you know, just tell the truth and the judge and jury will hear you and nothing will happen to you. But I was wrong." Interestingly, 12 years into her prison sentence, Jarrett's case was reversed, but the state appealed the reversal. The state offered her another plea bargain: admit to committing the crimes, and she would be sentenced to time served and released. Jarrett steadfastly maintained her innocence and refused the plea bargain. Her conviction and sentence were reinstated and she has now spent over 30 years in prison for crimes she claims she never committed. [Source: Adapted from "The Plea," *Frontline*, June 17, 2005.]

In the case of *McMann v. Richardson*, the defendant entered a guilty plea knowingly and voluntarily and pleaded guilty to murder. He was sentenced to 30 years in prison as the result of the plea bargain agreement. Later, he appealed, contending that his guilty plea had been coerced by the prosecutor. The U.S. Supreme Court heard his argument and ruled that no evidence existed to show that his guilty plea was coerced. Merely alleging coercion is insufficient to succeed on an appeal and have one's conviction overturned.

In the case of *North Carolina v. Alford* (1970), Alford was indicted for first-degree murder and faced the death penalty if convicted. Alford maintained his innocence and that he had murdered no one. Subsequently, he was permitted to enter a *nolo contendere* plea to second-degree murder in exchange for a 30-year sentence, which the judge imposed. *Nolo contendere* pleas are treated the same as guilty pleas, although they technically do not involve admissions of guilt by defendants. Rather, defendants enter such pleas and merely acknowledge the facts as set forth in indictments without actually admitting their guilt. Later, Alford contested the 30-year sentence, arguing that he was coerced into pleading guilty in order to avoid the death penalty, which may have resulted from a subsequent jury verdict. The U.S. Supreme Court was unsympathetic and held that when an accused, such as Alford, enters a plea voluntarily, the accused knowingly and understandingly consents to the imposition of a prison sentence even though he is unwilling to admit participation in the crime, or even if his guilty plea contains a protestation of innocence, when, as here, he intelligently concludes that his interests require a guilty plea and the record strongly evidences his guilt. Put more simply, plea bargaining is not considered coercive when a defendant chooses a lengthy prison sentence in order to escape the possible imposition of the death penalty (Foley 2003).

The leading case on this specific point is *Brady v. United States* (1970). Brady was a codefendant in a case involving kidnapping. The offense carried the maximum penalty of death. Brady initially pleaded not guilty to the kidnapping charge. However, Brady's codefendant decided to plead guilty to a lesser charge in exchange for his testimony against Brady in a later trial. Brady changed his mind and pleaded guilty to the kidnapping charge in exchange for a 50-year sentence, which was subsequently commuted to 30 years. However, Brady brooded about the lengthy prison term and eventually filed an appeal, alleging that his guilty plea had been coerced. The U.S. Supreme Court heard Brady's appeal and upheld his conviction. The Court held that a plea of guilty is not invalid merely because it is entered to avoid the possibility of the death penalty. The U.S. Supreme Court further noted that although Brady's plea of guilty may well have been motivated in part by a desire to avoid a possible death penalty, we are convinced that his plea was voluntary and intelligently made and we have no reason to doubt that his solemn admission of guilt was truthful.

In a noncapital Kentucky case, *Bordenkircher v. Hayes* (1978) involved a career criminal, Paul Hayes. Hayes was arrested for check forgery in Fayette

County, Kentucky. The possible punishment for check forgery was a prison sentence of from 2 to 10 years. Hayes had several prior felony convictions, and thus, he was eligible to be prosecuted under Kentucky's Habitual Offender Statute. Under this statute, Hayes faced a sentence of life imprisonment. The prosecutor offered Hayes a plea bargain, which included a guilty plea to a bad check charge in exchange for a 3-year sentence in prison. Hayes rejected the plea bargain and proceeded to trial. Hayes was prosecuted on the forgery charge as well as a habitual offender under the Habitual Offender Statute. He was convicted and sentenced to life imprisonment. Later he appealed to the U.S. Supreme Court and claimed that the prosecutor had attempted to coerce him into pleading guilty to one crime while threatening to prosecute him for another crime. The U.S. Supreme Court concluded that Hayes had not been coerced. If prosecutors have grounds for filing particular criminal charges, then their threats to file such charges if defendants don't plead guilty to lesser charges are not considered coercive. In sum, prosecutors may use additional charges against defendants as leverage to elicit guilty pleas to lesser charges whenever there is probable cause to believe that the additional crimes have been committed by the defendant. There must be a factual basis underlying any criminal charge.

If Promises Are Made by Prosecutors to Obtain Guilty Pleas from Defendants, Are Prosecutors Obligated to Fulfill These Promises?

Yes. If a prosecutor promises to recommend leniency or a specific sentence in a plea agreement, then the prosecutor is bound to observe that promise if it is used to elicit a guilty plea. A prosecutor cannot promise a specific form of leniency merely to elicit a guilty plea from a defendant. Prosecutors must follow through on their promises.

In the case of *Santobello v. New York* (1971), Santobello was charged with two felony counts and pleaded guilty to a lesser-included offense following a prosecutor's promise *not* to make a sentence recommendation at the plea bargain hearing. However, the plea bargain hearing did not occur for several months. When the proceeding was conducted, a new prosecutor had replaced the earlier one. The new prosecutor, unaware of the earlier prosecutor's promise to Santobello, recommended the maximum sentence under the law, which was imposed by the judge. Santobello appealed, arguing that his guilty plea resulted from a promise by the former prosecutor not to recommend a particular sentence. While the judge himself said that he was unaffected by the new prosecutor's statement to maximize Santobello's sentence, the U.S. Supreme Court saw things differently. Santobello's conviction and sentence were overturned, since a promise had been made to Santobello as a means of inducing him to plead guilty. The U.S. Supreme Court held that the second prosecutor was honor-bound to observe the earlier prosecutor's promise. Santobello was allowed to withdraw his guilty plea. A prosecutor may not make promises to defendants to obtain guilty pleas from them, unless the prosecutor fully intends to keep the promises.

This same idea works both ways. If a prosecutor offers a reduced sentence to a defendant in exchange for that defendant's testimony against another defendant, then the defendant must fulfill his/her promise to testify or the plea bargain and sentence imposed are withdrawn. In the case of *Ricketts v. Adamson* (1987), Adamson was one of several codefendants charged with first-degree murder. Before his conviction, however, Adamson entered into a plea agreement with prosecutors to testify against his codefendants. In exchange for his testimony against other codefendants in separate trials later, Adamson was permitted to plead guilty to second-degree murder and receive a prison term instead of the death penalty. Adamson was convicted of second-degree murder. Later, when the trials of his codefendants were scheduled, Adamson refused to testify, breaking his earlier promise to prosecutors. The prosecutors appealed Adamson's conviction and sentence and the Arizona Supreme Court overturned the conviction. New first-degree murder charges were filed against Adamson and he was later convicted of this offense, which carried the maximum penalty. Adamson appealed to the U.S. Supreme Court, alleging that his right against double jeopardy had been violated with the new trial following his earlier conviction. The U.S. Supreme Court upheld his second conviction saying that his breach of the original plea agreement removed the double jeopardy bar that otherwise would prevail, assuming that under state law, second-degree murder is a lesser-included offense of first-degree murder. Therefore, even criminal defendants are obligated to keep their promises in order to make the plea agreement enforceable.

TYPES OF PLEA BARGAINING

There are four types of plea bargaining. These include (1) implicit plea bargaining, (2) charge reduction bargaining, (3) judicial plea bargaining, and (4) sentence recommendation bargaining. These types of plea bargaining are ordinarily distinguished according to which party initiates the bargaining. In three types of plea bargaining discussed below, either judges or prosecutors initiate plea negotiations with defense counsels and their clients. A fourth type of plea bargaining actually occurs through a mutual understanding among parties of what charges will result and what penalties will be expected in exchange for guilty pleas entered (Champion 2005a).

Implicit Plea Bargaining

Implicit plea bargaining is an understanding between defense counsel and the prosecutor that a guilty plea will be entered to a specific offense, which carries a conventional punishment. The expected and contemplated punishment is usually somewhat less than the maximum sentence that could be imposed. The key word in this definition is *understanding*. Much hinges upon what sentences have been imposed for similar offenses in the past, depending upon the jurisdiction. Those who have entered guilty pleas to burglary charges in the past have sustained penalties ranging from straight probation to 48-month prison terms. There are also jurisdictional variations among cities and counties involving identical crimes, even within the same states (Myers and Reid 1995).

In view of one's prior record, age, mental state, and a host of other factors, defense attorneys are generally in a position to know the going rate for specific offenses. For first offenders, the going rate for burglary may be 18 months in prison. Depending upon the circumstances of the burglary (e.g., whether there were victim injuries, the amount of property loss/damage), a defendant may receive probation for a specified period, such as two or three years. In the case of chronic offenders who have multiple convictions for burglary and other crimes, courts are inclined to impose more severe sentences. Maximum sentences may be contemplated. Further, because the defendant is a habitual offender, there is an additional charge that could be filed by prosecutors. Most states have habitual offender statutes, meaning that for habitual offenders, a conviction on a habitual offender charge would lead to life imprisonment or life without parole.

Thus, when defense attorneys consult with their clients, they acquire an intimate familiarity with the defendant's prior record and other background factors. Defense counsels have a fairly good idea of what they can expect from the prosecutor's office regarding a plea bargain for their clients. A knowledge of the going rate for specific offenses enables these defense counsels to advise their clients accordingly and to let them know what they can likely expect from the prosecutor and court.

The practice of implicit plea bargaining begins when a defense counsel advises his/her client that if the client enters a guilty plea to a specific charge, the result will probably be a particular sentence. The defendant is induced to plead guilty based upon the expertise of the defense attorney and his/her familiarity with the legal system. Offers to enter guilty pleas in exchange for particular punishments are attractive to prosecutors, since it relieves them of having to prove the case against the defendant later in court. Because of the defense counsel's knowledge and agreeability of prosecutors, most plea agreement negotiations are completed rather quickly.

Exceptions are high-profile cases or cases that are particularly offensive, such as child sexual abuse, mutilation or torture, or some type of perversion. However, in some types of cases, court policy may dictate that no plea bargains will be struck with certain types of offenders. For instance, a large suburban county in the Midwest enacted a policy of no deals with dope pushers (Church 1976). Those who dealt in illicit drugs knew that they could not plea bargain their way into lenient punishments. Thus, a strong law-and-order stance taken

BOX 8.3 CAREER SNAPSHOT

Susan Stenson Waild
Manager, Probation Services, King County Superior Court

Statistics: BA, (Sociology), University of California, Santa Barbara; MSW (social work), University of Washington

Work History and Background: Social work can be an excellent choice of study for students who are interested in working in the field of probation and/or law. This is particularly true in Washington State where state law clearly defines three mandates when dealing with juvenile offenders: accountability, treatment, and community protection. To be successful in this field you must be able to balance these three distinct and different mandates. Skills taught in a university level social work curriculum can establish a solid basis for future success in the field. In the early 1970s, while obtaining my bachelor's degree majoring in sociology at the University of California (Santa Barbara), I came across an internship position at the Santa Barbara County Juvenile Probation Department. I have always found it fascinating how, given similar or dissimilar backgrounds, people live and why they make the choices they do. That, combined with my interest and love of kids, made juvenile probation a natural "draw" for me.

After becoming a familiar face around the Department, I was offered the chance to be an on-call worker at the local juvenile detention center. This meant working the unpopular shifts of swing, graveyard, or weekends. Even so, I jumped at this opportunity to learn the work of probation. Thus, I began my first "professional" job, supervising juvenile detainees. This was an invaluable experience and I learned a lot. While attending to their individual needs, I also had to monitor the group and its dynamics. This was my first experience learning how to balance competing needs, a necessary skill now used daily in my current work. The administration was pleased with my work. I was reliable and, to get my foot into the door, willing to take any shift. It was a very positive experience for me and I learned from some wonderful staff.

Subsequently I was hired as full-time staff to work at La Morada, the Probation Department's group home for teenage girls. The girls residing at La Morada had been ordered by the local juvenile court judge to live at the group home and participate in treatment. Again, I learned from some of the best. One night there was a potential riot brewing at the group home. Although there were only 20 girls, they came from different backgrounds, communities, and socioeconomic groups. This was the beginning of the "gang era" and the girls were quickly becoming part of that phenomenon. When events like this happened, protocol dictated calling in extra staff to

(continued)

BOX 8.3 (continued)

help diffuse the situation. Attempts at reasoning, intervention, and even trickery proved unsuccessful. We were unable to get the kids to disperse and go to bed. Finally, the director, Faith Ryan, was called. She walked in and immediately chastised the girls for having food on the new piano (a clear violation of a house rule) and sent them to bed. Being caught totally off guard they went to their rooms. I was furious! What was she doing? She hadn't gotten to the heart of the matter. She didn't attempt a treatment intervention. However, what I eventually realized was, in fact, what she did do was diffuse a potentially violent situation. She was wise and skilled enough to know that 2:00 a.m. was not the time or place to deal with these types of issues. The next day the situation was addressed and sanctions were meted out based on each girl's participation and culpability.

Desiring to pursue social work as a career, obtaining my masters in social work became a necessary next step for obtaining this goal. At the University of Washington, School of Social Work, my focus of study was on administration and direct services, primarily working in group home–type settings. Upon graduation I was hired by Lutheran Social Services to work in their group care facilities. Initially I worked with younger boys but always came back to the teenage population. It seemed to be my natural "fit." In the late 1970s and early 1980s Washington State embarked on a full-scale revision of its juvenile code. As part of the revisions, judges no longer had the authority to order youth into group care. This change, in addition to funding reductions, resulted in the closure of many group homes state-wide. Personally, I felt the strain and toll of being on call 24/7 especially having a young child of my own.

Still desiring to work with adolescents, in 1985 I started working for the King County Superior Court Conference Committee (diversion) Program. This nationally recognized program provides first-time juveniles involved in minor offenses with an alternative to court. The youth appears before a panel of community volunteers who review the matter and then enter into an agreement with the youth. The agreement identifies sanctions (e.g., community service hours) with which the youth must comply as a consequence for his/her offense. The volunteers were amazing. They cared about the kids in their community. They wanted to help rather than just punish and they wanted to be an active participant in addressing what they believed was a local neighborhood problem. Recruiting, training, and supervising this group was pure joy.

Up until 2000, with the agreement of the King County Superior Court, the Department of Youth Services, an executive branch department, administered juvenile probation and juvenile detention. In 2000, juvenile probation was returned to the administration of King County Superior Court. With the resulting change in leadership I was asked to take on the position of Probation Manager. It was a very difficult time of transition. In addition to changes in administration, due to budget constraints the department required downsizing. Programs were ending and others were beginning. There was a long list of labor grievances and labor contracts were up for renegotiation. There was a lot to do. Once again, a most amazing group of talented staff from all levels and branches of government came together and worked through these very difficult tasks. Each person provided a special area of skill and expertise, creating an incredible transition team. In a relatively short period of time it became clear we all shared the same goal: to bring about stability in the department and create an environment that allowed staff to do their best work with kids and families.

During these administrative changes in King County another significant change was taking place at the state level. Based on an extensive study by the Washington State Institute for Public Policy, the state became more strategic in targeting juvenile justice program funding. Programs backed by research showing them to be cost-effective at reducing juvenile recidivism received funding and funding was cut for other programs, including programs that we intuitively felt might work or believed intellectually should work. Additionally, the Washington State Risk Assessment tool was developed and instituted. This is a validated tool designed to assess a youth's risk to re-offend. In Washington State, every child who is formally charged with an offense receives an assessment. All staff are trained and certified in the use of the tool.

The focus on "proven programs" and implementation of the risk assessment tool significantly impacted my job as the probation manager. First, it provided focus on where to direct probation resources. With research showing that for low-risk youth probation contact actually increases a juvenile's risk level, a low-level supervision unit was created. Low-risk kids are assigned to this unit where caseloads are larger than for regular supervision JPCs and are contacted less frequently. Removing low-risk kids from the general supervision population allowed the shifting of resources (probation staff) for the moderate- and high-risk youth, resulting in reduced probation caseloads. These youth also are eligible for the "proven programs." The positive outcomes from these changes are several: As intra-agency refocusing occurred, to increase capacity in the community for serving these youth, we also expanded our efforts in collaboration with other county and private agencies; our staff are better trained on assessing and engaging families and youth and are no longer seen as the probation "officer," the enforcer of the court order; and our judges have better information upon which to make decisions.

In addition to these programs, we have instituted a specialized juvenile drug court and are now piloting a treatment court for kids with co-occurring disorders (substance abuse and mental health). Most recently a family treatment court became operational, working with families with children in foster care due to a parent's substance abuse. I am blessed to

(continued)

BOX 8.3 *(continued)*

work with such amazing people. They come from varied professional backgrounds, with lots of experience and a commitment to do good work.

This is an exciting time to be in the field of social work. More is being learned about youth and what works and what doesn't work. This is a significant change from the traditional making program decisions based on intuition and personal logic. We are more attentive to the cultural backgrounds of the families served and their personal family dynamics. We are developing advocacy teams to help families build their own support systems so they can continue to function successfully after probation ends.

Social work, research, and the law are mutual catalysts. Each drives the other to be better. Each has a role in assisting the youth and protecting the community. This is not easy work. It is constantly changing. Professionals who choose this field need to be open and understand that working with children and families who are in need of our services is a painful business. No one comes to court because they are happy and things are going well. Most if not all are in crisis. As social workers, our job is to assess, develop, and then implement plans for getting beyond these issues and making their lives better.

Advice to Students:

1. Get a degree.
2. Be humble. Do not expect to start at the top or to get where you want to be too quickly. You may need to start working the "graveyard." Volunteer, take beginning but related jobs. Use each opportunity as a chance to become a better professional.
3. Bad things can happen to good people. People come to court in pain. Often others will blame you or be angry with you because you can't make it right. They often don't agree with your position. They may lash out or want to walk away from their child. You can't let them. You have to treat them ALL with respect and dignity.
4. You have to have a big heart with a big brain. While understanding their struggle, you need to keep your boundaries straight and hold yourself to the highest professional standards. You are not their buddy. You are a role model, every day, so be a good one.
5. While doing all of that, you need to keep balance in your life. You will do no one any good if you do not take care of yourself.
6. Look around you. You will be presented with great teachers from which to learn. Sometimes they will be coworkers, sometimes families and kids, and sometimes even your superiors. You can learn what to do and you can learn what not to do.
7. This is important work. You will touch many lives and you will be touched by many others.

by the courts and prosecutors in this county was intended as a deterrent to drug dealing. Drug dealers knew that if they were arrested, their plea bargaining chances were nonexistent. However, while prosecutors were not permitted to plea bargain drug cases, this did not prevent judges from dispensing with such cases quickly, often without trial. In these instances, judges would dismiss more troublesome cases or make their own sentence recommendations to conclude cases. In short, one form of plea bargaining was replaced with another, as the responsibility for initiating bargains shifted from prosecutors to judges (McConville and Mirsky 2005).

An example and comparison of implicit plea bargaining is illustrated as follows. Suppose we have two criminals, Joe Jones and Phil Smith, both of whom are charged with burglary and larceny. Each has broken into homes and stolen jewelry and other valuables assessed at $2,000. Profiles of the two criminals are highlighted here:

	Joe Jones	Phil Smith
Age	25	24
Education	9th grade	completed high school
Family stability	stable	stable
Marital status	single, never married	divorced, two children
Prior record	three felony convictions for larceny, fraud	none
Employment	unemployed	employed as day laborer
Drug use	yes	no
Alcohol use	yes	yes

This information is often derived from arrest reports and booking documents. It is known both to the defense counsel and the prosecutor. Jones has a more serious record compared with Smith. The most important factor weighing against Jones is his prior record, consisting of three prior felony convictions for larceny and fraud. The most important factor weighing in favor of Smith is his lack of a criminal record. In other respects, compared with Smith, Jones has less education, less of a chance for holding a steady job, and is involved with both drugs and alcohol. The going rate for Jones in the present case may be 5 to 7 years in prison. The prosecutor may threaten to bring habitual offender charges against him, and these charges would be easily substantiated. In Smith's case, the going rate might be probation or a short jail sentence. The fact that Smith is a first-offender, employed, has two children from a prior marriage, and has a high school education make him an ideal candidate for some form of probation or leniency.

One point made by this comparison is that the going rate varies depending upon an offender's prior record and general background. The same crime committed is punished differently because of the difference in criminal histories for two otherwise similar offenders. Another feature of implicit plea bargaining is that no specific agreement or bargain is reached between the defendant and prosecutor. Guilty pleas are entered in the hope that leniency will be extended by both the prosecutor and the judge. In most situations, some form of leniency issues from judges in exchange for guilty pleas. However, there are no rules that obligate judges or prosecutors to extend leniency to anyone who enters a plea of guilty to any crime. Judges remind defendants of this very fact before the guilty plea is accepted (Pohlman 1995).

Charge Reduction Bargaining

Charge reduction bargaining or **charge bargaining** is an offer from the prosecutor to minimize the number and seriousness of charges against defendants in exchange for their pleas of guilty to lesser charges. When crimes are perpetrated, often there are multiple offenses arising from the original crime. For instance, Joe Jones and Phil Smith steal a car; enter a convenience store and rob it at gunpoint with automatic weapons; wound two customers who attempt to intervene; shoot and kill the convenience store clerk who attempts to telephone police; elude police who chase them through four counties; cause extensive damage to multiple vehicles during the hot pursuit; engage in a shootout with police and wound several innocent bystanders; and severely wound a police officer before they are subdued and taken into custody. The list of charges against Jones and Smith include murder, attempted murder, armed robbery, menacing, eluding police, firing upon law enforcement officers; resisting arrest, hit-and-run, aggravated assault on the police and bystanders, vehicular theft, and possession of illegal automatic weapons.

Charge reduction bargaining would involve the prosecutor, who would probably suggest a guilty plea to second-degree murder and armed robbery. The punishment sought would be life imprisonment. Without the plea bargain offer, the prosecutor would file all of these charges against these defendants. The death penalty would probably be sought as well. The result might well mean the imposition of the death penalty or consecutive life imprisonment terms. The offer to reduce the charges and the recommended punishment might sound attractive to Jones and Smith. After all, they avoid the death penalty and are parole-eligible. But plea bargaining of this sort is not always one-sided (Worden, 1995). Negotiations include counter offers from defense counsels. Thus, charge reduction bargaining and several other forms of plea bargaining are considered episodic, occurring over time and involving multiple defense counsel/prosecutor encounters. Further affecting the use of charge reduction bargaining is the bureaucratization of courts in different jurisdictions.

The greater the sheer volume of cases in particular jurisdictions, the greater the use of charge reduction bargaining as a technique to facilitate case processing and move more cases through the system more rapidly (Champion 2005b).

In another case, this time involving two real defendants, two young men were under police surveillance and suspected of dealing drugs. They happened to be members of a nationally recognized football team in a southern state and were quite popular. The city police, county detectives, and state bureau of criminal investigation were involved in a coordinated effort to investigate them and determine the extent of their alleged drug dealing. An informant, another football player, agreed to plant a bug in the telephone of their apartment. Other listening devices were planted throughout the apartment at the order of the local criminal court. Subsequently, the young men were videotaped and telephonically recorded engaging in at least 28 transactions. Each of these 28 transactions involved Class X felonies, which meant life-without-parole sentences on each count or charge. This is because the quantity of drugs (many kilos of cocaine, heroin, and marijuana) was substantial and qualified their crimes as Class X, the most serious felony category in the state.

The young men were eventually arrested. The most prominent criminal defense attorneys were hired for them by the football team's booster's club and other private supporters. With this formidable defense and the local popularity of these football players, the prosecution knew that despite their clear-cut evidence of criminal conduct and seized drugs, there was a possibility that these men would either be acquitted later or be convicted of some downgraded charge. Thus, the prosecutor approached their attorneys with the following deal: Have your clients plead guilty to simple possession of a controlled substance (cocaine), and get six months' jail time (with time off during days and weekends to play football), and do an additional two years on probation with 400 hours of community service. The plea agreement was concluded quickly and the young men were sentenced to six-month jail terms. Each was permitted to leave during the day for football practice and required to report back to the jail during evening hours at 9:00 p.m. Weekends were spent playing football with the rest of the team.

Many citizens in the community were upset by the excessive leniency extended to these football players by the court. It was believed that their status and popularity as football players overshadowed their otherwise criminal conduct, which under other circumstances would have qualified them for 28 consecutive terms of life without parole. But the prosecutor defended his action by arguing that a jury may have thrown out the case against these defendants, despite the mountain of evidence that had been compiled, the incriminating drug deals videotaped and telephonically recorded, and numerous statements of informants and undercover agents. The final irony of this case is that *both* players failed to comply even with the simplest of conditions associated with their jail terms. They failed to observe their 9:00 p.m. curfew on at least three occasions and the judge invited them back to his courtroom where four-year prison terms were imposed. The football players eventually were sent to the state penitentiary.

Cases such as this have been cited to underscore the ethics of plea bargaining and the morality of prosecutorial discretion in reflecting public interest in honest law enforcement (Connell 2004). Cases in which prosecutorial discretion is flagrantly abused, such as the football player scenario above, do little to foster public perceptions of prosecutorial integrity. In fact, such prosecutorial indiscretions have functioned as platforms for plea bargaining and sentencing reforms in most states (Wilmot and Spohn 2004). Also, plea bargaining may be unethical and counterproductive relative to the court's manifest goals of retribution, deterrence, incapacitation, and rehabilitation.

Charge Reduction Bargaining and Labeling Theory

Criminologists have investigated the nature and consequences of charge reduction bargaining for different types of clients. Downgrading the seriousness of charges against certain defendants may be accompanied by greater public acceptance. Thus, charge reduction bargaining is considered a socially acceptable punishment, especially for persons of higher socioeconomic statuses. In the context of **labeling theory,** when potential felony charges are reduced to misdemeanors, for instance, this modification of criminal charges is far less likely to result in unfavorable labeling by others. It is logical that less serious charges are more socially acceptable and considered less deviant compared with more serious charges. Thus, being labeled as deviant is more forgivable where charges have been downgraded to misdemeanors from felonies. Convicted offenders are more likely to suffer only short-term impacts and adverse reactions from others. Therefore, charge reduction bargaining often explains relations between allegations of deviance and societal reactions.

Judicial Plea Bargaining

Judicial plea bargaining occurs when judges make offers of sentences to defendants in open court in exchange for their guilty pleas. One of the most frequent uses of judicial plea bargaining involves petty offenses, such as public order offenses, such as public intoxication or disturbing the peace. Persons arrested for being drunk and disorderly appear before judges in the morning following their arrest. Very often, they are eager to leave the courtroom and get on about their business. The judge knows that the criminal punishment for their conduct is not especially severe.

In New Orleans, for instance, judges must face thousands of intoxicated arrestees every Mardi Gras. Bourbon Street and the French Quarter generate large numbers of targets inviting arrest by police for public intoxication. While

BOX 8.4 JUDGE REJECTS PLEA BARGAIN AGREEMENT

■ **Geraldo Montoya, 19**

On October 16, 2001, Daniel Herrera was shot and seriously wounded in Laredo, Texas. He was hit in his upper leg following an argument with another man, Geraldo Montoya, 19. A subsequent investigation by police and a search of Montoya's residence disclosed a sawed-off shotgun, a 9 mm handgun, and several other weapons. Montoya was arrested and charged with two counts of aggravated assault with a deadly weapon. The second charge arose from an earlier incident, where Montoya allegedly pistol-whipped a woman in the face.

Montoya's attorney met with the district attorney later and worked out a plea bargain. According to the terms of the plea bargain, Montoya would plead guilty in exchange for a two-year sentence in a Texas penitentiary. Montoya agreed and pleaded guilty to the charges. However, Judge Manual Flores examined the plea bargain and rejected it. The judge said, "This doesn't sound like a plea bargain I would accept." The implication was that the offer made by the state to Montoya was too lenient. The judge ordered the attorneys back to the bargaining table to craft a more suitable plea agreement, where more time served might be contemplated. The reason given by the judge was that there were deadly weapons involved in both incidents, and that these weapons constituted serious aggravating circumstances.

Should judges have the power to reject plea bargains wherein the state has offered a reduced sentence to a defendant in exchange for his guilty plea? Some people criticize plea bargain agreements as being too lenient on offenders. How does this judge's ruling regarding the original plea agreement counter these criticisms? What sentence do you think would be suitable for Montoya for shooting one man and pistol-whipping a woman? [Source: Adapted from Laurel Almada and the Associated Press, "Judge Denies Plea Bargain Agreement," November 17, 2001.]

their crime is not especially serious, they may do themselves harm by being out on city streets in their condition. Thus, the drunk tanks of local jails fill rapidly and empty the following morning. Judges bring in 20 or more persons charged with public intoxication and inform them as a group as to the punishment contemplated. They are usually given fines and suspended sentences. Many courts accept credit cards in lieu of cash payments. The proceedings are concluded quickly, as justice is rapidly dispensed through judicial plea bargaining. Anyone wishing to contest the matter can remain jailed and stand trial later, where the outcome will likely be the same (McDonald 1985). A guilty plea acceptance form for New Orleans, Louisiana is shown in Figure 8.2.

CRIMINAL DISTRICT COURT
PARISH OF ORLEAN
STATE OF LOUISIANA
SECTION "D"

STATE OF LOUISIANA

vs.

_____

JUDGE: <u>FRANK A. MARULLO, JR.</u>

NO. _____

VIO: _____

<u>PLEA OF GUILTY</u>

    I, _____ , defendant in the above case informed the Court that I wanted to plead guilty and do plead guilty to the crime of _____ and have been informed and understand the charge to which I am pleading guilty. (_____)

The acts which make up the crime to which I am pleading have been explained to me as well as the fact that for this crime I could possibly receive a sentence of _____ . (_____)

    I understand that in pleading guilty in this matter I waive the following rights:

        (1) To a trial by either a judge or a jury and that further the right to a trial by judge extends until the first witness is sworn, and the right to a trial by jury extends until the first juror is sworn, and if convicted the right to an appeal.
             Please specify: Judge trial or Jury trial.   (_____)

        (2) To face and cross-examine the witnesses who accuse me of the crime charged.   (_____)

        (3) The privilege against self-incrimination or having to take the stand myself and testify.   (_____)

        (4) To have the Court compel my witness to appear and testify.   (_____)

    I am entering a plea of guilty to this crime because I am, in fact, guilty of this crime. I have not been forced, threatened, or intimidated into making this plea, nor has anyone made me promises in order that I enter a plea. I am satisfied with the handling of my case by my attorney and the way in which he has represented me. I am satisfied with the way the Court has handled this matter. (_____)

_____
DEFENDANT

_____
JUDGE

_____
ATTORNEY FOR DEFENDANT

DATE: _____

    NOTE: Defendant is to place his initials in the blocks provided for same.
               Defendant is to block out Judge trial or Jury trial as it applies.

FIGURE 8.2

Guilty Plea Acceptance Form for New Orleans, Louisiana: Alternative Procedure for Accepting Guilty Pleas Used by Local Judges

    Judicial plea bargaining is the functional equivalent of a bench trial, but without much of the formality of prosecutorial involvement. In many cases, defense attorneys are not involved. Historically, bench trials such as those described above frequently involve a defendant's waiver of the right to a jury trial.

However, defendants who waive this right are rewarded, while those who demand a jury trial are punished (Cohen 2004). Known as the **jury waiver system,** this method of concluding cases is far less restrictive of one's Sixth Amendment rights than plea bargaining per se.

But the frequency with which judicial plea bargaining occurs has certain adverse consequences for defendants. Decisions to plead guilty are encouraged, and the circumstances under which judges offer specific sentences to defendants, even fines, are somewhat coercive and threatening. Many defendants do not take the time to consider their options and frivolously enter guilty pleas, even if there is the possibility that they are innocent. Being rushed into a guilty plea, therefore, compromises due process to an extent. This is especially true regarding indigent defendants. In New York, for instance, data were obtained from 236 indigent defendants involved in 150 felony cases from 1984–1985 (McConville and Mirsky 2005). Assignment of counsel to these indigent defendants included showing defendants that they will receive more severe penalties if they fail to plead guilty. Then these defendants are given exactly 15 seconds to accept or reject the pleas and sentences offered by these judges. Almost all defendants acceded to the judge's request for them to plead guilty to the recommended charge and accept the proposed sentences (McConville and Mirsky 2005).

One unfortunate consequence is that once a guilty plea has been entered, even to a minor charge, it cannot ordinarily be withdrawn later. If it is withdrawn successfully later, there is little to prevent prosecutors from using the initial plea of guilty to their advantage in the courtroom later if the case proceeds to trial. Thus, defendants lose in several different ways no matter what their decision might be.

Judicial plea bargaining also results whenever power is removed from prosecutors to strike deals or plea bargains with defendants. If charge reduction or sentence recommendation bargaining is minimized or prohibited, then the responsibility for deciding punishments and negotiating with defendants shifts to judges. When judges are given this additional responsibility, they become **concession givers,** roles previously performed by prosecutors. More than a few judges get bogged down in their docket loads when dealing with defense counsel who seek reassurances for their clients that probation or some minimal jail time will be imposed. Judges who are not prepared to grant probation in certain cases tend to develop docket problems.

Sentence Recommendation Bargaining

The fourth type of plea bargaining is **sentence recommendation bargaining.** Sentence recommendation bargaining occurs when the prosecutor proposes a specific sentence in exchange for the defendant's guilty plea. In one respect, sentence recommendation bargaining is an overt articulation of implicit plea bargaining. A prosecutor informs the defense counsel representing a client as to the contemplated sentence in exchange for a guilty plea. In a take-it-or-leave-it fashion, the defense counsel relays the information to the client, who decides whether the proposed punishment is worth the guilty plea. It usually is.

Sentence recommendation bargaining is not entirely discretionary with the prosecutor. In fact, judges must approve all plea bargain agreements in all jurisdictions (Worden 1995). Therefore, if the prosecutor proposes a punishment that will later be rejected by the judge, this is viewed as a waste of court time, and the prosecutor will be chastised accordingly. Thus, prosecutors must be knowledgeable about what the court will or will not accept. This means that all actors (e.g., prosecutor, defense counsel, and judge) must have a general understanding of the going rate for any crime, given contextual factors and defendant backgrounds, including their criminal histories.

Sentence recommendation bargaining is often finely tuned, depending upon a prosecutor's experience with the system and relationship with the judge. There is a clear relation between a judge's beliefs about the leniency and coerciveness of plea bargaining and the trade-off between crime control and due process, and their own willingness to cooperate with a prosecutor who attempts plea negotiations with defendants (Worden 1995). In the mid-1990s, however, efforts were underway in several jurisdictions to overhaul the architecture of plea bargaining to remove its extralegal properties. Various forms of sentencing classification have been proposed as guidelines in plea negotiations. Of course, this raises the informal nature of plea bargaining to a much more formal and predictable level. Thus, the clear intent of plea bargaining reformers is to structure plea bargaining and eliminate the often protracted interplay between prosecutors and defense attorneys. In many respects, the reform envisioned would be similar to guidelines-based sentencing schemes such as those used in Minnesota and other state jurisdictions, as well as the federal court. Offense-specific charts would be consulted, where one's crimes would be cross-tabulated with one's criminal history. Where the points intersect would define a range of months or years that would determine the latitude of the plea bargainers. Jurisdictions such as Massachusetts have been experimenting with sentencing commissions vested with such powers over plea bargaining and certain sentencing issues (Champion 2005a).

One troubling feature of sentence recommendation bargaining and other plea bargaining forms is gender disparity (Auerhahn 2004). Gender disparity occurs when one gender receives preferential treatment or consideration in plea negotiations and sentencing. Gender disparity studies indicate that females with no prior records are more likely than similar males to receive charge reductions and less severe sentence recommendations from prosecutors (Champion 2005a). The **typicality hypothesis** has been described, which proposes that women are treated with chivalry in criminal processing, but only when their charges are consistent with stereotypes of female offenders. **Selective chivalry** suggests that decision makers extend chivalry disproportionately toward white females. Finally, **differential discretion** suggests that disparity is most likely in informal charge reduction bargaining than in the final sentencing process and sentencing hearing (Champion 2005a). Records of 9,966 felony theft cases and 18,176 felony assault cases were investigated for the year 1988. Given the similarity of prior records, women were more likely than their male counterparts to receive charge reductions and have a greater chance of probation. Such chivalry has been described in other jurisdictions as well, as evidence of gender bias and preferential treatment by courts (Williams, Craig-Moreland, and Cauble 2004).

We have also seen how indigents seem to receive unfair treatment during plea bargaining, especially when they are assigned public defenders who are usually courtroom novices (Weiss 2004). Not only are they assigned less-competent counsel, they also are rushed into accepting reduced sentences from prosecutors and judges in exchange for their guilty pleas. The coerciveness for indigents is that they almost always face the prospect of harsher penalties from a jury trial on more serious charges. Plea bargaining is the symbolic poster child for socioeconomic unfairness in the criminal justice system. The phrase, "You get what you pay for," has special significance here.

Unfortunately, there is no easy way to eliminate socioeconomic status as a relevant extralegal variable in the complex plea bargaining equation. This is one reason plea bargaining was banned in Alaska in 1975. However, simply banning something does not mean its informal abandonment. In fact, plea bargaining did not disappear in Alaska following the ban, and it is alive and well now. Prosecutors and defense counsel have simply modified their strategies for circumventing the Alaska plea bargaining ban (Champion 2005b).

But because plea bargaining occurs at the front end of the criminal justice system and affects virtually every stage following it, the potential for disparities attributable to most any variable must be carefully monitored (Ball 2005). While the bureaucratic apparatus is in place to ensure strict compliance with sentences imposed through plea bargains, there is a glaring absence of controls to protect against the unwarranted intrusion of social status variables in any particular plea negotiation.

THE PROS AND CONS OF PLEA BARGAINING

Plea bargaining has its proponents and opponents (Herzog, 2004). Below is an extensive list of reasons why plea bargaining is both popular and unpopular with the public and justice experts.

Arguments for Plea Bargaining

Reducing the Uncertainties of Criminal Trials

There are several arguments favoring the use of plea bargaining in the United States. Plea bargaining reduces the uncertainties and risks inherent in a trial for willing participants (Herzog 2004). This means that offenders who decide to plead guilty to one or more criminal charges know with some degree of certainty the nature and extent of their punishment, including about how much time they will serve, either on probation or in jail, and any other conditions contemplated by the prosecutor and approved by the judge. If the case were to go to trial and the defendant were convicted, it is more difficult to predict with certainty what the judge will impose. Case processing time is more rapid through plea bargaining (Greenstein 1994). If cases are plea bargained, case processing time is much faster than if the case were to go to a lengthy trial.

Fewer Trials and Trial Delays

Plea bargaining also means fewer trials and **trial delays.** Prosecutors do not have to prove critical elements in state's cases against defendants. Trials obligate prosecutors to present arguments to the jury about the defendant's guilt beyond a reasonable doubt. Juries may not be easily convinced. This does not relieve prosecutors from proving one's guilt, however. In any plea agreement, the prosecutor must lay out for the judge in writing what evidence would have been presented to show the defendant's guilt beyond a reasonable doubt if the case had gone to trial. This is called the **factual basis for the plea.** This evidence is often minimal, but it may be sufficient to convince most judges of the soundness of the prosecutor's case against the defendant. It should not be assumed literally that prosecutors do not have to prove anything against the accused in a plea bargain agreement. The prosecutor is obligated to furnish the judge who oversees the plea agreement with sufficient evidence that would have been introduced to show the defendant's guilt, if the case had gone to trial. Some plea bargain agreements have been rejected by judges because of insufficient evidence presented by prosecutors.

Plea Bargaining Means More Convictions

Plea bargaining results in larger numbers of convictions. Usually the concessions arising from plea bargaining are sufficient to induce most defendants to plead guilty. Ninety percent or more of all convictions are obtained through plea bargaining. Without plea bargaining, trials would determine one's guilt or innocence. With juries deciding many cases, it is likely that there would be fewer convictions, even under conditions where evidence against the accused is strong. There are fewer jail backlogs and less jail and prison overcrowding as the result of plea bargaining. This is because the use of probation and nonincarcerative alternative sentencing options (e.g., **home confinement, electronic monitoring, intensive supervised probation**) are seriously considered and often imposed as enticements to elicit guilty pleas (Erez and Ibarra 2004).

Plea bargaining involves **negotiated guilty pleas.** Because these guilty pleas are negotiated, they are often better than trials in terms of the deals arranged for guilty defendants. Again, trials are often unpredictable in outcome. And if a defendant is found guilty through a trial, then the punishment is often harsher than if the case had been concluded through plea bargaining. Plea bargaining avoids potential jury bias and emotional influence of adverse evidence. More rational sentencing decision making through bargaining is achieved and the factual circumstances of terrible crimes, such as murder or aggravated rape, are less emotionally charged (Fearn 2004). Juries may be persuaded to find someone guilty of a serious crime because of sympathy generated by the prosecutor for the victim and the victim's survivors (Enriquez and Clark 2005). Emotional persuasion is often strong and overrides sound, cold deliberations that are expected of jurors when both sides have presented their case (Fryling 2005).

Offenders convicted through plea bargaining often avoid the taint of a formal criminal prosecution. They do not spend much time in court, except to participate in the plea agreement hearing. Little fanfare accompanies such hearings, which are not attended by many persons. As opposed to trials, plea agreement hearings are not usually announced to the public. Most plea agreement hearings, although open to the public, are held only with the judge, court reporter and other court officers, the prosecutor, defense counsel, and defendant. Thus, the specter of a lengthy courtroom drama is avoided. Judicial discretion is more limited because of the conditions and concessions outlined in plea agreements (Champion 2005a). Judges reserve the right to reject plea agreements if they feel that plea agreements are too lenient. However, judicial rejection of plea agreements is rare. Most plea agreements are rubber-stamped by most judges in most jurisdictions.

Plea Bargaining and Anticipated Leniency

Plea agreements may also soften the impact of sentencing guidelines in states that have them (Barrile and Stone 2005). Guidelines schemes tend to be excessively rigid. Prosecutors may downgrade the seriousness of one's offense or write the plea agreement in such a way so as to subvert the intended impact of guidelines to systematize the sentencing process and create greater uniformity in sentencing (U.S. Sentencing Commission 2003). However, each case is developed and rests on its own merits. Each plea bargain agreement is slightly different from others, even the same jurisdictions. Their uniqueness is about as varied as personality systems.

Reducing the Costs of Trials

Regarding its cost-effectiveness, plea bargaining is far less expensive than jury trials (Champion 2005b). In jury trials, witnesses must be subpoenaed. Experts must be obtained. Evidence must be examined in greater detail for use in court. The valuable time of judges, court officers, and other key participants is expensive. Thus, from a pure economic standpoint, plea bargaining is a cheap way of getting a guilty plea. In the federal system, for instance, the U.S. sentencing guidelines have severely limited the use of plea bargaining with extremely lenient sentences to less than 20 percent (U.S. Sentencing Commission 2003). Under the pre-guidelines indeterminate sentencing followed by the U.S. district courts, probation was granted to convicted offenders about 60 percent of the time. Under the **United States sentencing guidelines** which went into effect in October 1987, the use of probation as a sentence in federal courts decreased to about 12 percent. In fact, the U.S. sentencing guidelines table provides for probation in only the least serious misdemeanor or felony cases. U.S. probation officers are obligated to file more complete reports under the federal sentencing guidelines. The additional mandatory information to be included negates any attempt by federal prosecutors to leave out details that would intensify one's offense seriousness (Barrile and Stone 2005). Under previous indeterminate sentencing, prosecutors could leave out details, such as the use of a weapon during the commission of the crime, in an attempt to negotiate a more lenient sentence for a federal defendant in exchange for a guilty plea. The fact that federal judges used probation 60 percent of the time under pre-guidelines sentencing is strong evidence that presentence investigation reports were often modified to give judges the impression that they were sentencing less serious defendants.

Arguments Against Plea Bargaining

The Self-Incriminating Nature of Plea Bargaining

There is considerable opposition to the use of plea bargaining in negotiating guilty pleas. One argument is that defendants who plea bargain give up their constitutional right to a jury trial. Further, they give up the right to cross-examine their accusers. They also relinquish their right against **self-incrimination.** However, the greater leniency extended to defendants in exchange for giving up these rights is sufficient to justify their waivers of jury trials and insistence of observance of their constitutional rights to full due process. Many convicted offenders are thankful for plea bargaining, since a jury trial would almost certainly have involved harsher punishment for them. As a consequence, there are fewer trials with plea bargaining, and thus, fewer forums are convened where defendants can present the full body of exculpatory evidence showing their innocence (Holmes et al. 1992). More than few experts are bothered by this fact. Their belief is that jury trials mean that all facts will be heard and that the fairest decision will be rendered by the jury hearing all of the evidence.

The Loss of Judicial Control

Plea bargaining may signify a loss of judicial control of courtrooms, giving lawyers free reign to divert jurors from the facts with theories that portray their clients as supposed victims of an unfair criminal justice system (Champion 2005a). Most defendants are more than willing to ride through this loss of judicial control with a relatively lenient plea agreement, however. If a defendant is convicted through a trial, the punishment is almost invariably harsher than whatever had been contemplated in a plea bargain. Once a defendant has entered a guilty plea and a sentence has been imposed by the judge, it is difficult to withdraw the guilty plea. Despite the predictability of plea bargaining, there is always an elusive element. This is **judicial privilege,** which means that judges may accept or reject one or more plea bargain agreement terms and substitute more or less punitive sentences. Thus, although clients have been reassured by their counsel and the prosecutor that entering a plea of guilty to a specific charge will likely result in one type of sentence, another type of sentence may actually be imposed by the judge. Again, judges are not obligated to follow precisely every condition noted in plea agreements.

Defendant Ignorance and Plea Bargaining

Ignorance or mistake often lead to guilty pleas. Therefore, the plea agreement process may lack sufficient guarantees to ensure proper application of the law and sentencing options. Many defendants are ignorant of the law. Those with some knowledge of the law may lack the foresight to appreciate and understand the seriousness of the guilty plea they enter. Criminal convictions are serious and often result in a loss of one's job. Or naive defendants may enter into plea agreements with prosecutors not knowing that they have the right to litigate fully any charges against them. Their own attorneys often fail to apprise them of their various legal options. Relevant defense evidence is not presented. Opponents of plea bargaining single out this particular factor as most damaging to defendants. If the accused enters a guilty plea, crucial evidence that may have resulted in an acquittal if the case had gone to trial instead is often overlooked or deliberately ignored. Thus, opponents of plea bargaining argue, the true extent of one's case cannot be known unless it is subjected to a trial proceeding. But many defendants enter into plea agreements hoping that some of the evidence against them will never be heard. They see plea bargaining as a way of slipping through the system with minimal damage. Plea bargains often offer more benefits to the accused than would be forthcoming at a trial, where circumstances could be much worse.

Rejections of Guilty Pleas and Judicial Payback

Judges are more likely to be more severe with defendants who reject initial plea bargain agreements. Thus, one danger of plea bargaining is that if an offer to a defendant is made to plead guilty in exchange for what the prosecutor (and judge) believe is a reasonable punishment, refusal to accept that agreement and force the case to trial will sometimes disturb the judge. Upon conviction, the judge may exact some revenge by extending one's sentence by one or more years. Judicial intervention is minimized such that the ineffective-assistance-of-counsel issue cannot be adequately explored. When plea agreements are negotiated, there is little, if any, opportunity to ascertain whether one's defense counsel is representing the best interests of the client. Is defense counsel competent? With so many cases being plea bargained, and in fairly standard ways, there is no clear opportunity to evaluate defense competence.

The judge becomes an advocate intent on inducing a defendant to plead guilty, when due process presumes one innocent until proven guilty beyond a reasonable doubt. This particular factor is another sore point with plea bargaining opponents. They do not want judges to engage in a form of bribery by dangling attractive lenient sentences before defendants who would face much worse if they went to trial on the same charges. When plea bargaining is allowed, judges wield a great deal of power in the offers they make through judicial plea bargaining. There is a hint of coercion in plea bargaining, particularly implicit plea bargaining, where threats of greater punishments are implied if guilty pleas are not entered to less serious charges, which may cause some persons to plead guilty to crimes they did not commit. Thus, some innocent people may accept criminal convictions in order to avoid harmful or fatal punishments. Usually, these are cases where innocent defendants are swept into the criminal justice system through suspicious circumstances. Persons who cannot account for their whereabouts when crimes have occurred or appear to be involved may find themselves in the unenviable position of facing harsh punishments if convicted. Death rows throughout the United States have set free occasional convicts who were subsequently determined to be innocent through newly discovered evidence or confessions from the real perpetrators.

Circumventing Habitual Offender Statutes

Plea bargaining may circumvent **habitual offender statutes** or **three-strikes-and-you're-out policies,** where mandatory penalties are contemplated. The danger of plea bargaining here is that chronic or persistent offenders with multiple felony convictions can avoid mandatory punishments an unlimited number of times through plea bargaining. However, the purpose of mandatory penalties is to remove chronic and persistent offenders from society by incarcerating them either for life or substantial terms of years. Such punishments are thwarted through plea bargaining, however. Because of plea bargaining, therefore, there is an inconsistent application of mandatory penalties among jurisdictions (Vincent and Hofer 1994). Habitual offender statutes are frequently used as leverage for inducing guilty pleas from defendants. There is no apparent intent on the part of prosecutors to enforce such habitual offender statutes, however. Circumvention of sentencing guidelines is encouraged by plea bargaining (Stemen, Wilson, and Rengifo 2004). Sentencing guidelines are designed to establish fairness in sentencing. Whenever these guidelines are bypassed through plea bargaining, fairness is unevenly applied for those who do not plead guilty but rather, go to trial.

Sentencing Reductions for Those Undeserving of Sentencing Reductions

Sentences for many serious offenders are reduced when such sentences shouldn't be reduced (Kramer and Johnson 2004). Sex offenders and child sexual abusers find themselves given sentences that are often far too lenient, given the seriousness of their offending. Often, critical case information may be buried or overlooked in an attempt to get a plea bargain negotiated. Therefore, some very serious offenders may get lighter sentences, when in fact their punishments should be more severe. At the same time, such offenders may avoid helpful counseling and therapy that otherwise might occur through traditional trial convictions (Alexander 2004). Plea bargaining may reduce the sheer volume of criminal prosecutions. There is no reliable evidence, however, that the absolute number of prosecutions is abbreviated because of plea bargaining. We must remember that plea bargaining results from a prosecution. Thus, a decision by a prosecutor to prosecute someone for a crime sets the stage for offers and counteroffers from defense counsels and prosecutors, as plea bargain agreements are negotiated.

Concealing Heinous Aspects of Crimes Through Plea Bargaining

Prosecutors and others may be able to conceal more serious aspects of a crime from the sentencing judge by withholding certain information from a plea agreement. Some professionals object to this circumstance as ethically wrong. Justice somehow seems politicized by this process (Champion 2005b). Defense lawyers who have cultivated amicable relations with prosecutors over the years are more seasoned and better-prepared to negotiate desirable plea bargains for their clients. New lawyers performing public defender functions are at a disadvantage, since they are often unaware of how the system works in a particular jurisdiction. Where who you know gets you a better deal in the plea agreement process, this is a fairly clear indication that plea bargaining has been politicized.

Rubber-Stamping Plea Agreements

Judges tend to rubber-stamp plea bargain agreements without doing their jobs effectively. Judges are supposed to determine whether a factual basis exists for a defendant's plea of guilty. Judges must also determine whether guilty pleas are voluntary. Do defendants wish to relinquish critical constitutional rights, such as giving up the right to cross-examine accusers or give evidence in one's own behalf? Because of the glut of court cases in many jurisdictions today, judges are often relieved to merely approve agreements where guilty pleas have been entered. They often are lax when performing their oversight functions. Since plea agreements often result in more lenient treatment for offenders, they tend to acquire a cynical view of the criminal justice system. They may take subsequent chances by committing new crimes, expecting leniency in the future where it was extended in the past. They are not wrong in their appraisal of the criminal justice system, nor are they wrong in anticipating further leniency from prosecutors.

The Potential for Gender Bias in Plea Bargaining

It is claimed that women tend to benefit to a far greater degree from plea bargaining than men. Women tend to be granted probation more often than men, given the similarity of their prior records, instant offenses, and other salient factors. Because of this less than even-handed application of justice, therefore, the goals of deterrence, incapacitation, and rehabilitation are either undermined or defeated. Another form of discrimination in the use of plea bargaining applies to the poor and those in the lower socioeconomic statuses (McConville and Mirsky 2005). Courts are deluged with thousands of indigent defendants, often drawn into the criminal justice system through police sweeps in drug-infested sections of cities. Much street crime is perpetrated by those who are unemployed. Youthful offenders are drawn into the criminal justice system as well, especially minority youths (Champion 2007). Less-affluent defendants are less likely to avail themselves of jury trials, where private counsels are most effective.

Does Plea Bargaining Invalidate the Jury Process?

Some critics say that plea bargaining invalidates the jury system (McConville and Mirsky 2005). By bypassing a jury trial, defendants are dealt with more swiftly and without the benefit of jury trials. However, it is incumbent upon judges to advise defendants of their right to a trial by jury and whether they wish to voluntarily relinquish that right. In more than a few instances, it is disadvantageous to criminal defendants to air their cases before juries, since the details and circumstances of their crimes may offend more sensitive jurors. This, in turn, could lead to more serious criminal convictions with accompanying and commensurate sentencing consequences. Thus, for some offenders at least, jury trials are not desired and for good reason (Enriquez 2005). Plea bargaining encourages more proactive policing and arrests of indigents (McConville and Mirsky 2005). According to this line of thinking, police officers are interested in making increasing numbers of arrests that will result in convictions. Street people, indigents, drug users, and youthful offenders who loiter or act suspiciously are often arrested and charged with assorted offenses. Police officers know that there is a strong likelihood that many of those arrested will be offered plea bargains resulting in probation or charge reductions. Convictions result in greater approval of the actions of law enforcement officers, and thus a self-reinforcing cycle is set in motion with predictable consequences.

Hampering Efforts to Reform Sentencing

Sentencing reforms are hampered through plea bargaining. If 90 percent or more of all convictions are obtained through plea bargaining, it is more difficult for reformists to convince legislatures of the necessity for sentencing reform. The existence of going rates and other traditional plea bargaining features has become institutionalized nationally. There is no dramatic need to reform a system that seems to be accepted by criminals, prosecutors, defense counsels, and judges. However, plea-bargaining is blamed for some amount of sentencing disparity (Park 2005). One obvious disparity resulting from plea bargaining is the difference in sentencing severity between plea-bargained cases and convictions resulting from trials. Another type of disparity occurs that is more difficult to detect. Different attorneys continually network with various assistant state's attorneys or district attorneys to work out agreements for their diverse clientele. All plea bargains are individualized; therefore, there is an inherent inequality that exists. Only judges monitor plea agreements, and little effort is made by these judges to ensure that sentencing uniformity occurs according to the salient factors that should influence sentencing decisions (e.g., prior record or criminal history, instant offense, victim injuries, and other aggravating or mitigating factors) (Johnson 2004). Without any consistent monitoring mechanisms to govern plea bargaining in any particular jurisdiction, sentencing disparity must be assumed to occur. We do not know how much sentencing disparity exists resulting from plea bargaining.

Racial Discrimination and Plea Bargaining

More people of color are discriminated against through plea bargaining. This means that much racial and ethnic discrimination occurs (Clark 2004a). Racial and ethnic discrimination also exists at other stages of criminal justice processing, including imprisonment (Spohn and Keller 2005). Street crimes are given greater attention by police officers, and proactive policing discussed above targets street people most often. These persons are frequently ethnic and racial minorities. These persons, frequently indigent, must accept defense counsel who often lack the experience and expertise of seasoned private attorneys retained by more affluent criminal clients. Efforts are currently being made to upgrade legal services for indigents. But such efforts are sporadic and unevenly applied among jurisdictions. Also, there is no one to monitor the actions of prosecutors. Thus, a serious accountability problem exists. Who should oversee the credibility and quality of case screening and prioritizing? Prosecutors in many jurisdictions have virtually unbridled authority to drop or pursue a case, adjust charges, and make recommendations (Connell 2004). In short, prosecutors have too much decision-making power in charging decisions. Also, shifting greater decision-making power to prosecutors reduces justice system accountability as case decision making is shifted toward the front of system. Rights activists are concerned that due process protections for the accused are jeopardized and that victim participation is minimized under widespread plea bargaining.

The Bureaucratization of Negotiated Guilty Pleas

The perfunctory nature of plea bargaining has certain bureaucratic characteristics. If there is greater reliance on bureaucratization, then there is less individualized attention given to more important cases (Ferdinand 1992). The existing administrative structures of some jurisdictions, such as Pennsylvania, are frequently relied upon by prosecutors so as to ensure consistency in plea bargaining practices. A positive consequence of bureaucratization in plea bargaining is that extralegal factors, such as race, social class, and gender, are less important in negotiating guilty pleas. In **coconspirator** cases, it is more difficult for innocent defendants to separate themselves from guilty defendants (Champion 2005a). If the guilty defendant enters into a plea agreement with prosecutors and agrees to testify against an innocent party named as a coconspirator, the innocent coconspirator is tainted. Thus, if the case comes to trial for the codefendant who does not plead guilty, such circumstances work to the disadvantage of the innocent party.

Are Lawyers Vested with Too Much Authority in Plea Bargaining?

Some critics say that plea bargaining gives too much authority to lawyers. There is little or no weight given to **fact-finders** or juries. Essentially, this is a complaint that jurors are in a better position to determine guilt or innocence and evaluate evidence in contrast to a prosecutor–defense attorney plea agreement where all pertinent facts about the crime may not be disclosed and weighed properly. Plea bargaining is so pervasive that many defense attorneys have become complacent about it. If defense counsel must defend indigents, these attorneys are not paid at rates equivalent to private counsel. Thus, the financial incentives do not exist to work hard for indigent clients. Particularly where indigents are involved, defense counsel are often quick to conclude a case with a plea bargain (Champion 2005a). If cases do go to trial, there are questions about the competence of defense counsel required to represent indigents. Are they enthusiastic enough to present the best defense, or do they go through the motions of defending clients, taking the easiest path that will conclude proceedings?

WHY IS PLEA BARGAINING BANNED IN SOME JURISDICTIONS?

Plea bargaining has been banned in various U.S. jurisdictions, most notably in Alaska. When Alaska announced that it was banning plea bargaining on a statewide basis in 1975, other jurisdictions were apprehensive. Would such a ban mean a glut of trials involving petty offenders? Would the wheels of Alaskan justice come to a grinding halt as more cases were processed without informal plea agreements worked out in advance?

It is important to note that although plea bargaining in Alaska was officially banned, it did not disappear. What occurred is that plea bargaining gave prosecutors considerably greater charging powers. With greater power over charging decision making, prosecutors in Alaska were more careful to screen those cases destined for trials. One result was that there was actually a reduction in the number of criminal prosecutions, as many cases that once were plea bargained were simply dropped. A more significant consequence of the Alaska plea bargaining ban was to create greater charge bargaining. Prosecutors were vested with considerably more authority to decide which charges should be brought against defendants. Subsequent bans of plea bargaining by various jurisdictions, such as New Hampshire, have revealed a similar pattern, with a substantial increase in charge bargaining (Herzog 2004).

At the core of plea bargaining bans is the unfairness inherent in sentencing bargaining. Most plea agreements contemplate a particular punishment. Much of the punishment meted out through plea bargaining is more lenient than traditional punishments associated with trial convictions. Thus, the leniency of plea bargaining concerning sentences received by convicted offenders, often serious offenders, has been objectionable to more than a few citizens and lawmakers.

Reasons for Banning Plea Bargaining

1. Where plea bargaining has been banned, a greater amount of charge reduction bargaining occurs. This has shifted much of the decision-making power to prosecutors and away from judges. Some experts view this shift unfavorably.

2. Under a plea bargaining ban, there is greater likelihood of incarceration. This means that jail and prison overcrowding could be exacerbated by an absence of plea bargaining. On the one hand, those who favor strong get-tough anticrime measures will applaud the elimination of plea bargaining. On the other hand, jail and prison officials may not be pleased with the overcrowding that will likely result.

3. Under a plea bargaining ban, cases are more carefully screened by prosecutors. Thus, only the more serious cases for which strong evidence exists will move forward to criminal trials.

4. Selective bans against bargaining with certain offenses targeted (e.g., no deals with dope pushers) appear to work in selected jurisdictions. Thus, when offense-specific plea bargaining restrictions are implemented, prosecutors are prohibited from accepting reduced-charge guilty pleas from drug dealers. This doesn't necessarily mean that convicted drug dealers will be treated harshly, however. Current sentencing policies in certain jurisdictions are intended to incarcerate more offenders who commit certain types of offenses, such as drug dealing, for longer periods of time (Champion 2005b).

5. Even if plea bargaining is banned, judges and others find ways to get around it (Spohn 2004). It is virtually impossible to eliminate plea bargaining. Informal negotiations will always occur, no matter how stringent the controls or plea bargaining restrictions.

JUDICIAL INSTRUCTIONS FOR ACCEPTING GUILTY PLEAS AND RIGHTS WAIVERS

In most jurisdictions, judges are obligated to determine the factual bases for guilty pleas, encourage frank discussion of the facts of the case, and facilitate further consideration of sentencing alternatives. In federal district courts, for example, judges must observe all of the **Federal Rules of Criminal Procedure** relating to plea bargaining (Ulmer and Burchfield 2004). Specifically, this is 18 U.S.C., Rule 11 (U.S. Code, 2001). Rule 11 outlines with considerable precision whatever judges must do in the process of approving plea agreements. Under Rule 11, federal judges must make sure that defendants who enter guilty pleas to criminal charges understand the following:

1. The nature of the charge(s) to which the plea is offered.
2. The maximum possible penalty provided by law.
3. The mandatory minimum penalty as provided by law.
4. The effect of any special supervised release term and any special provisions for compensating victims.

5. That a defendant who does not have an attorney has a right to one; and if the defendant cannot afford an attorney, one will be appointed at state expense.

6. That the defendant has the right to plead not guilty and to withdraw a guilty plea at any time.

7. That the defendant has the right to a trial by jury and the right to the assistance of counsel at the trial.

8. That the defendant has the right to confront and cross-examine prosecution witnesses.

9. That the defendant has the right not to incriminate himself or herself.

10. That if the plea of guilty or *nolo contendere* is accepted, there will be no further trial of any kind; therefore, the plea is a waiver of the right to a trial.

11. That there is a factual basis for the plea.

12. That the plea is voluntarily given and that it is not the result of force, threats, or coercion apart from a plea agreement.

13. That the judge may accept or reject the plea agreement.

14. That the plea is accurate.

15. If the plea is the result of prior discussions between prosecutors and defendants or their attorney.

Items 11, 12, 13, and 14 are of great significance to defendants. These items are to determine whether the guilty plea entered by a defendant is voluntary. There must be a factual basis for the plea; the judge may accept or reject the plea agreement; and the plea agreement is an accurate summarization of the facts. These provisions seemingly protect defendants from overzealous prosecutors who threaten long sentences and drawn-out prosecutions if guilty pleas are not entered and suggested sentences are not accepted. This is the ideal scenario. It does not always happen this way in the real world.

Federal judges have no special litany for determining these and other facts about a defendant's guilty plea and the nature and terms of the plea agreement. The spirit of the law is that federal judges must ascertain these facts, in open court, by orally addressing the defendant. Each judge uses his or her own style for covering these important items. Thus, Rule 11 provides general guidelines for judges to follow. Past challenges from defendants about whether judges asked them about these items in precise ways have been unsuccessful. That is, federal judges are not compelled by Rule 11 to recite these questions precisely in the context of the rule.

If a federal judge is not satisfied with the evidence proffered by a U.S. attorney or his/her assistant, then the judge is not bound to accept the plea agreement. Judges can throw out charges against defendants if the evidence against them does not or would not support a subsequent conviction if the case proceeded to trial. A case in Tennessee provides a good example.

A man from Chattanooga, Tennessee, was charged with several felonies relating to copyright infringement governing the use of 16mm films and their possession by private film collectors. He had collected feature films as a hobby, but the Motion Picture Association of America (MPAA) and the Film Security Office under the direction of President Jack Valenti instituted a series of legal actions against private collectors to prevent them from trafficking in these motion pictures. The government's theory, at the urging of the MPAA, was that no motion picture had ever been sold to private individuals; therefore, all motion picture 16mm prints in the hands of film collectors must be stolen or obtained in nefarious ways. While there are several flaws in the government's theory about the critical elements of criminal copyright infringement, suffice it to say that the Chattanooga film collector was innocent of any criminal wrongdoing. He had purchased most of his 16mm prints of these motion pictures from film rental companies or from film reclamation services. Thus, he had legal title to these pictures. At the time, film collecting was regarded by the MPAA as jeopardizing the profits of major motion picture film companies. In reality, the small number of motion picture collectors and the sum of their monetary profits from trafficking in motion pictures was trivial. Subsequently, these motion pictures have been made available in DVD format, and any private citizen may now own just about any motion picture sold in this format.

In Chattanooga, Tennessee, however, the defendant was a fairly high-volume trader of motion pictures at the time. While he probably profited from motion picture film trades and sales, he never intended to defraud film companies of any revenue that they might obtain through film rentals or leases. In any event, the assistant U.S. attorney (AUSA) for the federal district court in Chattanooga brought several criminal copyright infringement charges against the film collector. The defendant was in his early fifties and had a heart condition. He was employed only on a part-time basis and supported himself from a portion of the revenue he realized from his film collecting.

The AUSA in Chattanooga approached the defendant with an offer—plead guilty to a **federal misdemeanor** and the AUSA would recommend a 3-year probationary term. The defendant, who was assigned a court-appointed attorney, declined any offer to plead guilty to any criminal charge relating to his film-collecting hobby. However, a persuasive public defender pointed out to the defendant that a 3-year probationary term wasn't bad compared with the 30 years and $200,000 fine associated with felony convictions on the criminal copyright infringement charges. Reluctantly, the defendant agreed to plead guilty.

On the day of the plea agreement hearing, however, the defendant stood before the federal district court judge and answered the different questions faithfully. When it came to the matter of whether the defendant wanted to plead guilty to this crime, even a federal misdemeanor, the defendant balked. "I never committed any crime, judge," he said. With a frustrated expression on his face, the judge asked the defendant's attorney if he wanted to confer with his client before proceeding. The defense counsel had a lengthy discussion with his client who later went back into court before the judge and entered the guilty plea. Here is where things get interesting.

The judge next asked the AUSA what evidence would have been submitted to show that the criminal elements existed and could have been proved beyond a reasonable doubt. The AUSA said that the evidence was summarized as a part of the plea agreement. The judge asked, "Is that all you have against this man?" The AUSA said, "Yes, your honor." At that point, the judge faced the defendant and said, "You are hereby freed, as I am dismissing all criminal charges against you." Then he turned to the AUSA and chastised him for bringing such a poorly prepared case before him. It was clear to the judge that the defendant had been cajoled into pleading guilty for fear of a harsher prosecution.

Unfortunately for many federal and state criminal defendants, not all judges are as judicious and meticulous in examining federal or state plea agreements and their contents (Johnson 2004). A majority of federal and state court judges "rubber-stamp" these plea agreements, since the court is backlogged with many serious cases to be plea bargained. Many judges give plea agreements only a cursory glance and overview before holding plea agreement hearings. Thus, often their actions relating to accepting plea agreements are perfunctory.

Can Judges Participate in Plea Negotiations Between Prosecutors and Defense Counsel? No and Yes

At the federal level, district court judges are prohibited from participating in plea agreement negotiations between defense counsels and prosecutors. The policy about judicial participation in plea bargaining negotiations varies among the states. However, most states follow the federal government and prohibit judicial involvement in these negotiations. The primary reason is that where judges are involved in these discussions, it places them in the position of configuring an agreement that they will most certainly approve later. This type of influence is considered unethical and inappropriate in most jurisdictions.

Only a few states, such as North Carolina, permit state court judges to participate in plea negotiations. Thus, defense counsels and prosecutors can confer with judges about what judges will accept or reject as plea agreement terms. Some opponents of judicial participation in plea bargain negotiations rightly note that the adversarial nature of the justice system is substantially removed through judicial intervention of any kind (Worden 1995).

Should Judges Be Excluded from Plea Bargaining Negotiations Between Prosecutors and Defense Counsels?

Some researchers believe that judges should be an integral part of the plea bargaining process. Judges can give both parties a clearer idea of what the sentence will be, the specific parameters of plea negotiations, and various correctional options. Essentially, judges can tell prosecutors and defense attorneys "This is the deal I will accept. Don't bring me anything more lenient than that."

Sometimes judicial concern focuses more on particular offenses, such as those involving drugs. Political sentiment and the judiciary in one jurisdiction, a county in the Midwest, established a policy of "no deals with drug pushers" (Church 1976). In that Midwest jurisdiction, reduced-charge plea bargaining for drug cases was all but eliminated, but trial rates soared. Court dockets were incredibly crowded. Judges were hard-pressed to resolve their court cases quickly. Interestingly, judges became concession-givers, a role abandoned in drug cases by the district attorney. Defense counsel shifted their attention to judges and negotiating with them instead of prosecutors. If defense counsel could not obtain probation for their clients charged with various drug offenses, then they would insist on a full-fledged trial, a time-consuming proceeding. Judges were compelled to make concessions, usually by granting probation or short jail terms for a majority of charged drug offenders.

Judicial participation in plea negotiations is sometimes suspect because of the implication that the defendant is guilty. Traditionally and consistent with due process, judges are supposed to assume a stance of neutrality and consider all defendants innocent until their guilt is proven in court beyond a reasonable doubt. Suppose a judge says that he/she will approve a particular guilty plea from Defendant X. Later Defendant X withdraws his guilty plea and goes to trial before the same judge. Can that judge continue to remain neutral and impartial in rulings on motions and other matters during Defendant X's trial? It seems somewhat contradictory for a judge to be an advocate during plea bargaining who encourages the defendant to admit his guilty, and then turn around in the defendant's trial and judge him fairly if he decides to reject the plea bargain agreement.

SENTENCING SYSTEMS AND PLEA BARGAINING

Plea bargaining has been modified in different jurisdictions depending upon the sentencing scheme adopted (Herzog 2004). One purpose of sentencing reform is to reduce sentencing disparities among judges, which are attributable to extralegal factors, such as one's race, age, ethnicity, gender, or socioeconomic status. Sentencing guidelines have been created in most jurisdictions to create sentencing uniformity, although no sentencing guideline scheme has completely eliminated the influence of extralegal factors in sentencing offenders (McManimon 2005b).

Sentencing Guidelines and Restrictions on Plea Bargaining

For federal courts, however, the U.S. sentencing guidelines have operated to limit the negotiating parameters of prosecutors and defense counsel (Levine 2005). Prior to the establishment of U.S. sentencing guidelines, federal prosecutors could tailor their plea agreements in ways that would maximize a defendant's acceptance of the plea agreement terms and encourage more guilty pleas. If a firearm was used in the commission of a robbery, for instance, the prosecutor could leave that fact out of the plea agreement. This omission would enable prosecutors to downgrade more serious felonies to less serious ones and offer defendants more lenient (and acceptable) punishments. Probation was used about 60 percent of the time in most federally plea-bargained cases prior to the establishment of sentencing guidelines.

When the federal sentencing guidelines were established, new rules were instituted requiring U.S. probation officers to include all relevant legal variables in **presentence investigation reports (PSIs).** Prosecutors were prohibited from omitting these relevant variables. Thus, if a federal defendant used a firearm during the commission of a felony (e.g., robbing a U.S. post office), this fact had to be reported and noted in subsequent plea agreements. Further, the use of probation under the new federal sentencing guidelines (October 1987) dramatically decreased to about 12 percent of all plea-bargained cases. Guidelines tables now exist that restrict the use of probation to only a limited number of minor federal offenses (Ulmer and Burchfield 2004). If federal defendants are recidivists, then the chances for probation as a sentence are eliminated. Thus, federal prosecutors have lost an important plea bargaining chip in the game of negotiating plea agreements with those charged with federal crimes. Furthermore, under new federal and state sentencing guidelines, penalties for specific types of offenses, such as drug trafficking, have greatly increased (Inciardi et al. 2004).

Other Systems and Plea Bargaining

If a particular offense carries with it a mandatory term, this means that judges must impose a specific sentence as required by law. Their hands are effectively tied. However, under **indeterminate sentencing** or **determinate sentencing** schemes absent any guidelines or other restrictions, judges and prosecutors may operate more or less freely in configuring plea bargain agreements with various defendants. There is considerable jurisdictional variation in this regard. In many jurisdictions without definite guidelines in place for offender sentencing, judges' sentencing practices are often influenced more by their work circumstances, their close relationships with courtroom prosecutors, and an absence of competing recommendations from probation (Worden 1995).

SUMMARY

Over 90 percent of all criminal convictions, both felonies and misdemeanors, are obtained through plea bargaining. Plea bargains or plea bargain agreements are preconviction agreements wherein defendants enter guilty pleas in exchange for some form of sentencing leniency from prosecutors and judges. It is difficult to imagine how the criminal justice system would operate smoothly without plea bargaining, inasmuch as criminal court dockets are notoriously clogged even with plea bargaining eliminating over 90 percent of all criminal trials.

Several advantages for criminal defendants are that plea bargaining generally results in a lesser punishment than one that might have been imposed had the case gone to trial. Plea bargaining thus results in shorter sentences, greater use of probation, and generally greater freedoms for defendants. Prosecutors are advantaged by plea bargaining, since they are spared having to prove their cases against criminal defendants in court beyond a reasonable doubt. The sheer volume of criminal cases is reduced. Prosecutors generate much higher conviction rates and improve their chances of re-election in those areas where their positions are contested by popular vote. Generally, plea bargaining works well for prosecutors who have weak cases and for defendants where evidence against them is strong. Under plea bargain agreements, some of the more serious aspects of one's crime(s) may never be disclosed, since the plea agreement may stipulate such omissions. Plea bargaining has been used to resolve criminal cases for several centuries. Furthermore, plea bargaining exists in many other countries. It is not a uniquely American phenomenon.

Not all state jurisdictions condone plea bargaining in the United States. In Alaska, for instance, plea bargaining has been banned. However, informal forms of plea bargaining continue to exist in Alaska despite the ban. Plea bargaining may occur at almost any stage in offender processing. Plea bargaining is typically attempted before a case comes to trial, in an effort to spare the state the expense of a lengthy trial. If plea bargaining efforts are not successful, plea bargaining may nevertheless occur during a trial as evidence is disclosed against the defendant, and even during jury deliberations. Some persons have labeled plea bargaining as coercive, since prosecutors sometimes overcharge defendants and then offer lenient sentencing options if defendants enter guilty pleas to lesser offenses. Generally, if there is a basis for one or more charges against a defendant, then plea bargaining is not coercive. It only becomes coercive if prosecutors engage in malicious prosecutions or pursue charges against criminal suspects where insufficient evidence exists to convict them. Whenever prosecutors make promises to defendants in order to induce guilty pleas from them, these promises must be kept. Otherwise, plea bargain agreements are invalidated. Judges oversee and approve all plea agreements between prosecutors, defendants, and defense counsels.

Four major types of plea bargaining have been identified. These include implicit plea bargaining, charge reduction plea bargaining, judicial plea bargaining, and sentence recommendation plea bargaining. Implicit plea bargaining is a subtle form of plea bargaining where both prosecutors and defense counsels are familiar with going rates for particular types of offenses. Negotiated guilty pleas generally are close to these going rates associated with particular offenses. An understanding is reached between prosecutors and defense attorneys and a plea agreement is configured that both sides can live with, with judicial approval.

Charge reduction bargaining arises when prosecutors stack multiple charges against defendants. Subsequently prosecutors offer to drop one or more of the serious charges in exchange for a guilty plea, usually to a lesser charge. Defendants see charge reduction bargaining as beneficial since they will not be prosecuted for other offenses they may have committed. Judicial plea bargaining occurs whenever judges offer defendants a particular sentence in exchange for a guilty plea. Often this type of plea bargaining occurs in misdemeanor cases, where judges may offer defendants fines in exchange for guilty pleas.

Sentence recommendation plea bargaining is initiated by prosecutors. Prosecutors make a recommended sentence known to defense counsels who advise their clients whether to accept it. The pros and cons of the sentence are evaluated, and defendants enter guilty pleas if the offered sentence recommendation is acceptable. Although prosecutors generally initiate sentence recommendation plea bargaining, judicial approval is necessary. Thus, some knowledge about what judges will or will not approve is quite useful when configuring sentences to recommend.

There are several arguments for and against plea bargaining. Arguments in favor of it include that the uncertainty is removed from the outcome of a criminal trial if one were held. It is difficult to anticipate what juries will decide, even if defendants are innocent of the charges against them (Gants 2005). More than a few innocent defendants have been convicted of crimes they have never committed. Also, plea bargaining reduces the sheer number of trials conducted and the delays such trials would cause. Plea bargaining also guarantees more convictions for prosecutors. Plea bargaining generally reduces the harshness of sentences and reduces the costs of criminal trials, since they are essentially avoided.

Arguments against plea bargaining, some of which are used by Alaska where it is banned, include that plea bargaining is self-incriminating. Defendants must admit to crimes they may or may not have committed in order to secure lenient treatment from prosecutors. In this respect, at least, plea bargaining has a coercive dimension. Although judges must approve all plea agreements, some degree of judicial control is relinquished as the interaction between the prosecution and defense becomes more important. Sometimes defendants are ignorant of the full implications of pleading guilty to certain charges. They literally relinquish all of their constitutional rights to a jury trial, to cross-examinations of witnesses against them, and they cannot give statements or testimony in their own behalf. Other rights are also waived voluntarily. In some instances, plea bargains are rejected by judges inasmuch as prosecutors have failed to provide sufficient evidence to support guilty pleas entered by less sophisticated defendants.

Another criticism is that plea bargaining circumvents habitual offender statutes that most often carry mandatory penalties. Habitual offender statutes are designed to remove chronic and dangerous offenders from the streets, but plea bargaining often bypasses these mandatory penalties that would result in an offender's incarceration. Also some heinous aspects of one's crime are not disclosed in plea agreements approved by judges. Thus, some offenders may escape harsher sanctions simply because judges are not aware of the full extent of their crimes and the harm they have caused victims. Plea agreements are often rubber-stamped with little or no effort by judges to ascertain whether a factual basis exists for the plea. Although judges must determine from defendants the voluntariness of their pleas and give close attention to the plea agreements they sign, there are simply too many plea agreements in many jurisdictions for judges to do a proper job in this respect.

Plea bargaining is said to invalidate the jury process, since trials are almost always avoided. But since greater leniency is extended to offenders through plea bargaining compared with what the penalty would be if the case were tried before a jury, most criminal defendants are satisfied with the results of plea agreements and their punishments. Plea bargaining also hampers attempts to reform different types of sentencing systems. If sentencing systems are designed to provide certainty of sentencing as a deterrent, these efforts are more than offset by plea bargaining, which undermines such efforts.

Another criticism of plea bargaining is that it may result in gender and/or racial bias in its application. Often, indigent defendants who cannot afford more competent counsel, are pressured into accepting plea agreements without fully understanding their consequences. Guilty pleas are also bureaucratized and streamlined, as both prosecutors and defense counsels seek quick solutions to otherwise lengthy trial proceedings. The matter of power in the hands of lawyers is also a criticism of plea bargaining. Some persons question whether attorneys should have such powers to determine one's fate.

In jurisdictions where plea bargaining has been banned, such as Alaska, authorities have cited several reasons for such a ban. These include that there is a greater likelihood that just deserts and justice will be served and that offenders will have to suffer some loss of liberty through incarceration. At the same time, however, others say that more charge-reduction bargaining occurs, where greater decision-making power shifts from the judge to prosecutors and attorneys (Connell 2004). In some jurisdictions, selective bans on plea bargaining have targeted particular offenses, such as capital murder or aggravated rape. Ultimately, however, even where plea bargaining has been banned outright, various courtroom actors have found ways to defeat the ban. In short, it is impossible to completely eradicate plea bargaining in any jurisdiction.

All plea agreements are supervised and approved by judges. In most jurisdictions, with exceptions such as North Carolina, judges are prohibited from participating in plea agreement proceedings and exerting undue influence on this process by declaring what they will or will not approve. Judges are obligated in all jurisdictions to determine the voluntariness of one's plea, whether one wishes to waive the right against self-incrimination, the right to cross-examine one's accuser, and other important due process rights. One of the more important functions of judges in overseeing the plea agreement process is to determine whether a factual basis for the guilty plea has been exhibited. It is incumbent upon prosecutors to demonstrate for judges what evidence would have been presented to show defendant guilt had the case gone to trial. Absent such incriminating evidence, the plea agreement fails, and more than few plea agreements have been rejected by judges and cases against defendants have been dismissed for lack of evidence.

KEY TERMS

Charge bargaining
Charge reduction bargaining
Coconspirator
Concession givers
Determinate sentencing
Differential discretion
Electronic monitoring
Fact-finders
Factual basis for the plea

Federal misdemeanor
Federal Rules of Criminal Procedure
Flat time
Going rate
Guilty plea
Habitual offender statutes
Home confinement
Implicit plea bargaining
Indeterminate sentencing

Intensive supervised probation
Judicial plea bargaining
Judicial privilege
Jury waiver system
Labeling theory
Negotiated guilty pleas
Nolle prosequi
Presentence investigation reports
(PSIs)

Selective chivalry
Self-incrimination
Sentence recommendation
bargaining
Three-strikes-and-you're-out
policies
Trial delays
Typicality hypothesis
United States sentencing guidelines

QUESTIONS FOR REVIEW

1. What is plea bargaining? Why is it controversial?

2. Name four types of plea bargaining and differentiate between each. Which one do you prefer and why?

3. What is the nature of judicial participation in plea bargaining for individual states and the federal government?

4. Should plea bargaining be banned? Why or why not?

5. What is meant by the going rate?

6. Briefly outline the history of plea bargaining in the United States.

7. In some jurisdictions, such as Alaska, plea bargaining has been banned. Does plea bargaining still go on in Alaska, even though it has been banned?

8. What is the significance of Federal Rule of Criminal Procedure 11 as it relates to plea bargaining?

9. What specific rights are waived by defendants who enter into plea bargain agreements?

10. How does the type of sentencing scheme influence plea bargaining?

SUGGESTED READINGS

1. George Fisher (2000). "Plea Bargaining's Triumph." *Yale Law School Journal* **109**:868–1086.

2. M. McConville and C. L. Mirsky (eds.) (2005). *Jury Trials and Plea Bargaining: A True History.* Oxford, UK: Hart.

3. S. Herzog (2004). "Plea Bargaining Practices: Less Covert, More Public Support?" *Crime and Delinquency* **50**:590–614.

4. Susan Rose-Ackerman (2002). "Corruption and the Criminal Law." *Forum on Crime and Society* **2**:3–21.

5. Yue Ma (2002). "Prosecutorial Discretion and Plea Bargaining in the United States, France, Germany, and Italy: A Comparative Perspective." *International Criminal Justice Review* **12**:22–52.

Chapter 9

Trial Process and Procedures

Chapter Objectives

As a result of reading this chapter, you will have accomplished the following objectives:

1. Understand the necessity for a speedy trial for a defendant.

2. Understand the difference between bench trials and jury trials.

3. Understand the trial process from indictment through to the judges' instructions to the jury.

4. Describe the different pretrial motions including motion to suppress, motion for dismissal of charges, motion for discovery, motion for continuance, motion for change of venue, and others.

5. Understand what opening arguments are for, and how the state presents its case.

6. Understand the right to cross-examination and re-cross-examination.

7. Understand the role of eyewitnesses and expert testimony.

8. Describe the process of defense presentation of its case and summation including closing arguments.

9. Understand jury deliberations and whether or not a jury must agree on a verdict.

10. Describe the jury verdict and its aftermath.

■ In Louisiana, Mark L. Stephens was on trial for armed robbery and aggravated assault. It was alleged that Stephens had entered a convenience store late at night and pistol-whipped and robbed a clerk. The case was weak and was based primarily on the testimony of three eyewitnesses and the clerk who identified Stephens in a police lineup later. Stephens had been released from prison on parole about 6 months prior to the robbery, and he had been serving a 10-year sentence for armed robbery and attempted murder. However, Stephens had two alibi witnesses who swore that he was with them all evening in a late-night poker game at the home of one of the witnesses. These witnesses were former offenders themselves, and thus their credibility as witnesses was suspect. When the trial was over, the jury deliberated for four days without reaching a decision. On the fifth day, they returned to the courtroom and advised that 11 of them believed that Stephens was guilty, while the 12th juror believed Stephens was innocent. The judge accepted the 11–1, nonunanimous jury decision and Stephens was convicted. He was subsequently sentenced to 20 years in prison.

In nearby Mississippi, Roland Abernathy was on trial for armed robbery and aggravated assault. Abernathy had allegedly robbed a convenience store late at night in Biloxi, and had shot and wounded the store clerk, making off with over $300 in cash. No one other than the clerk was in the store at the time, and thus the clerk's testimony was the only clear evidence against Abernathy, who had a prior record for three armed robberies. Like Stephens, Abernathy had two alibi witnesses who placed him over 100 miles away from Biloxi at the time of the robbery, claiming that he was drinking with friends at a bar until the early morning hours. The jury heard all of the testimony and when the case was concluded, they deliberated for over five days, failing to reach a verdict. They returned to court on the sixth day and advised the judge that they were not unanimous in reaching a verdict. Of the 12 jurors, 11 voted for guilty, while one juror voted for not guilty. The 11–1 vote was questioned by the judge, who asked the jurors if they believed that further deliberation would be helpful in arriving at a unanimous verdict. The jurors said that they were "hopelessly deadlocked" and would "never reach agreement." Therefore, the judge declared a mistrial.

Why was Stephens convicted of armed robbery in Louisiana in an 11–1 jury decision, while Abernathy was not convicted by the same 11–1 jury vote in Mississippi? Under state law, which has been upheld by the U.S. Supreme Court, nonunanimous jury verdicts are constitutional in Louisiana. Under state law in Mississippi, however, jury verdicts must be unanimous. Stephens picked the wrong state to commit his crime.

■ A black defendant, Horace Green, is charged with the murder in Marietta, Georgia, of a white child, Leslie Williams, 8, who was found in the woods nearby her home sexually assaulted and brutally murdered. A trial is scheduled in Marietta and a list of 75 prospective jurors is compiled. Notices are sent to all of these persons, who comprise the veniremen list. Of the original 75, 68 appear at the courthouse on the appointed date to be screened for jury service in Green's forthcoming trial. The white prosecutor as well as the black public defender representing Green question successive prospective jurors. Of the 68 prospective jurors, 14 are black, while the others are largely white. Many prospective jurors are summarily dismissed for cause, while each side uses peremptory challenges to remove certain persons for the final jury. The prosecutor successfully challenges 5 of the black prospective jurors for cause, where she is able to demonstrate their prejudice in the case or other factors that would otherwise disqualify them as jurors. She then uses 9 of her 12 peremptory challenges to strike the remaining 9 black prospective jurors. Green is finally tried by an all-white jury in the predominantly white community of Marietta. His attorney objects to the jury composition and requests that a new jury be impaneled. The judge denies the public defender's motion and the trial proceeds. Green is convicted and sentenced to death. In an appeal later, the U.S. Supreme Court sets aside Green's conviction and sentence of death, remanding the case to the Marietta trial court for a new trial. The Supreme Court declares that it is apparent that in this case, at least, the prosecution violated Green's constitutional right to a fair and impartial jury of his peers, in that all blacks were effectively struck from jury service, either with challenges for cause or peremptory challenges. That this event was something other than a chance occurrence was obvious. Furthermore, the Supreme Court did not accept the prosecution's explanation for striking all black prospective jurors for racially neutral reasons. Green would be given a new trial, this time without the obvious bias in jury selection, which typified his first trial.

INTRODUCTION

This chapter is about the trial process. Although, as described in previous chapters, the trial process is rare, most cases are processed through some type of plea agreement, there are many different types of trial systems. A trial could involve a judge (bench trial) or a jury of one's peers (jury trial). A jury trial begins with the selection of a 12-member jury. A bench trial is simply a trial by judge, and is usually conducted for defendants charged with petty offenses. In this type of trial the defendant has waived their right to a jury trial and the judge hears the evidence, and then decides on the case according to the rules of law. Those persons who are charged with felonies are guaranteed the right to a jury trial. In these cases, the jury will hear the case, decide guilt or innocence based on the facts presented, and then the judge would be responsible for handing out a sentence, if one was mandated. In many jurisdictions, voter registration lists are used to select persons from the community for possible jury service. These persons form the pool from which the jurors will be selected. The jury selection process is important in order to ensure the defendant a fair trial. That process will further be presented in this chapter.

Several constitutional amendments pertain to jury trials and one's right to a trial. The Sixth Amendment guarantees all persons the right to a trial by jury. The Seventh Amendment provides that the right of trial by jury shall be preserved. And finally, the Fourteenth Amendment provides that no state shall make or enforce any law that deprives citizens of their right to due process or from enjoying all privileges or immunities as citizens.

The chapter begins by examining one's right to a speedy trial. The idea of a speedy trial varies among the states and the federal government. Several important speedy trial cases will be presented. According to the federal government, a speedy trial occurs within a 100-day timeline. Probably the longest speedy trial period is in New Mexico, which sets forth a 180-day timeline for a trial. Some states have speedy trial provisions of 90 days. These different definitions of speedy trials will be examined.

Next, bench and jury trials will be distinguished. The process of selecting jurors is described in detail, commencing with the creation of a list of prospective jurors called a *venire* and following through with a **screening** process known as *voir dire*. Once jury members have been selected and the trial commences, judges still serve the function of observing rules of criminal procedure. These rules govern the conduct of trial proceedings. Other rules, such as rules of evidence, govern the nature of evidence that may be introduced or excluded.

Trial proceedings are also accompanied by several pretrial motions. Such motions will be described and explained. Both the prosecution and defense present opening statements. The government presents its case against the defendant, followed by the defense's case. Witnesses from both sides are called in these **adversarial proceedings.** Witnesses could include eyewitnesses, who give an interpretation of the events as they saw them and provide the degree to which the defendant may or may not have been involved, or expert witnesses, who are used by both sides to interpret the meaning of certain types of evidence. Witnesses are cross-examined by each side to determine their veracity and credibility. When the trial is concluded, the prosecution and defense present summations or closing arguments and the jury deliberates. Juries either reach unanimous verdicts or judgments, or fail to agree. The process of jury deliberation and voting will be described. Both the federal government and the states have different criteria that govern jury deliberations and voting, either for a defendant's guilt or acquittal. These different scenarios will be described. The chapter concludes with an examination of the aftermath of jury deliberations and verdicts, as well as the judge's role in sentencing.

THE SPEEDY TRIAL

Many options are available to defendants from the time they are arrested to the time they are arraigned and a trial date is set. In fact, there are many contingencies available to defendants even during the trial and after the conclusion of it.

A plea of **not guilty** by a defendant will obligate the presiding judge to set a trial date and eventually conduct a trial. Normally, this is the case unless some alternative plea is entered, or the prosecution elects to drop charges against the defendant, or if an agreement can be reached between the defendant and prosecutor whereby a formal trial can be avoided. This last contingency is usually referred to as a plea bargain agreement.

Federal courts are bound by law to observe the **Speedy Trial Act of 1974** and its subsequent 1979 and 1984 amendments. The purposes of the Speedy Trial Act are (1) to clarify the rights of defendants, (2) to ensure that (alleged) criminals are brought to justice promptly, and (3) to give effect to a citizen's Sixth Amendment right to a speedy trial (*Klopfer v. North Carolina*, 1967).

According to the provisions of this act, suspects must be charged with a criminal offense within 30 days following their arrest or receipt of a summons. Then the trial should commence not less than 30 days nor more than 70 days from the suspect's initial appearance. A 100-day federal provision exists, which is spread out as follows: 30 days from arrest to initial appearance; 10 days from initial appearance to an arraignment; and 60 days from the date of an arraignment to trial.

The leading case relating to a speedy trial is *Klopfer v. North Carolina* (1967). In Klopfer's case, he was charged with criminal trespass. Klopfer eventually went to court and his case resulted in a mistrial. Klopfer then tried to find out if the government intended to prosecute him again for the same crime, but government officials declined to make a commitment. Instead, they formally entered upon the court record a *"nolle prosequi* with leave," which meant that while they were permitting the defendant to be discharged, they were allowing themselves an opportunity to retry Klopfer at a later, unspecified date. This case eventually came before the U.S. Supreme Court who declared that the government violated Klopfer's Sixth and Fourteenth Amendment rights, and that it was unconstitutional to indefinitely postpone his trial without providing an adequate reason. The Supreme Court cited some of the reasons for their decision to endorse a speedy trial provision, which included the facts that (1) witness testimony would be more credible through an early trial; (2) the defendant's pretrial anxiety would be minimized; and (3) the defendant's ability to defend himself/herself and the fairness of the trial would not be jeopardized through extensive, adverse pretrial publicity.

Notwithstanding certain delays for a variety of reasons attributable to either the defense, prosecution, or both, the Speedy Trial Act of 1974 provides:

1. In a case where a plea of "not guilty" is entered, the trial shall commence within 70 days from the date when an information or indictment has been made public or from the date of the defendant's arraignment, whichever date last occurs.
2. Unless the defendant consents in writing to the contrary, the trial shall not commence less than 30 days from the date on which the defendant first appears through counsel or expressly waives counsel and elects to proceed *pro se* (on his own).

These provisions not only make it possible for a criminal defendant to enjoy the right to a speedy trial, but they also eliminate delays otherwise caused by crowded court dockets (*United States v. Nance*, 1982). Some courts have been notorious for their slowness in conducting trial proceedings. Federal judges have considerable power in deciding what evidence to admit and what evidence to exclude, for example. One judge may permit lengthy tape-recordings of conversations between an FBI agent and a defendant. These recordings may consume many hours. In another district court, however, the judge may deny the admission of such tape-recordings and insist that such materials be presented through more direct and brief testimony from witnesses. With the provisions of the Speedy Trial Act in force, all federal judges are obligated to comply with these provisions in spite of the "general congestion of

BOX 9.1 ON SPEEDY TRIALS

■ *Dickey v. Florida*

398 U.S. 30 (1970) Dickey was charged with various crimes in 1968 for crimes allegedly committed in 1960. He made motions to have an immediate trial in several different court appearances, but for various reasons, his trial was delayed until 1968. Between 1960 and 1968, some witnesses died, while others became unavailable for various reasons. Also, some relevant police records were destroyed or misplaced. Following his conviction, he appealed, arguing that his speedy trial rights had been violated. The U.S. Supreme Court overturned his conviction, saying that prompt inquiry is a fundamental right, and the charging authority has a duty to provide a prompt trial to ensure the availability of records, recollection of witnesses, and availability of testimony.

■ *Barker v. Wingo*

407 U.S. 514 (1972) Barker and another person were alleged to have shot an elderly couple in July 1958. They were arrested later and a grand jury indicted them in September 1958. Kentucky prosecutors sought 16 continuances to prolong the trial of Barker. Barker's companion, Manning, was subjected to five different trials, where a hung jury was found except in the fifth trial, where Manning was convicted. Then, Barker's trial was scheduled. During these five trials, Barker made no attempt to protest or to encourage a trial on his own behalf. After scheduling and postponing Barker's trial for various reasons, his trial was finally held in October 1963 when he was convicted. He appealed, alleging a violation of his right to a speedy trial. The U.S. Supreme Court heard the case and declared that since, from every apparent factor, Barker did not want a speedy trial, he was not entitled to one. The case significance is that if you want a speedy trial, you must assert your privilege to have one. Defendants must assert their desire to have a speedy trial in order for the speedy trial provision to be invoked and for amendment rights to be enforceable. In Barker's case, the U.S. Supreme Court said that Barker was not deprived of his due process right to a speedy trial, largely because the defendant did not desire one (at 2195).

■ *Strunk v. United States*

412 U.S. 434 (1973) Strunk was arrested for a crime and eventually tried ten months later. He was convicted and appealed, arguing that the ten-month delay was a violation of his speedy trial rights. The U.S. Supreme Court heard the case and noted several considerations in determining whether speedy trial rights of suspects have been violated. These considerations are: (1) whether there are overcrowded court dockets and understaffed prosecutor's offices; (2) whether there is substantial emotional

(continued)

BOX 9.1 (continued)

distress caused defendants because of long delays; and (3) whether an accused is released pending a trial and whether there is little or no immediate interest in having a trial.

■ *Dillingham v. United States*

423 U.S. 64, 96 S.Ct. 303 (1975) Dillingham was arrested for a crime. After a 22-month interval, an indictment was issued against Dillingham, and 12 months after that, Dillingham was brought to trial. Dillingham was convicted and appealed, arguing that the 22-month interval between his arrest and indictment violated his speedy trial rights under the Sixth Amendment. His conviction was overturned and the U.S. Supreme Court declared that invocation of the speedy trial provision thus need not await indictment, information, or other formal charge. Thus, the delay was unreasonable between arrest, indictment, and trial to satisfy Dillingham's speedy trial rights under the Sixth Amendment.

■ *Doggett v. United States*

505 U.S. 647, 112 S.Ct. 2686 (1992) Doggett was convicted of conspiracy to distribute cocaine in a U.S. district court. Because of various delays, mostly caused by the government, Doggett's trial was not held for 8 1/2 years. He appealed his conviction, contending that the 8 1/2-year delay before his case was tried violated his speedy trial rights under the Sixth Amendment. The U.S. Supreme Court overturned Doggett's conviction, concluding that an 8 1/2-year delay in one's trial, largely because of government causes, violates the Sixth Amendment rights of the accused.

■ *Fex v. Michigan*

507 U.S. 403, 113 S.Ct. 1085 (1993) Fex, a prisoner in Indiana, was brought to trial in Michigan 196 days following his trial request to Michigan officials and 177 days after the request was received by Michigan prosecutors. Fex was convicted and appealed, alleging that the 180-day speedy trial time period was violated, inasmuch as his trial commenced 196 days after his own request was submitted to Michigan to have a trial. The U.S. Supreme Court heard Fex's appeal and upheld his conviction, noting the detainer warrant phraseology that the statutory 180-day period did not begin until the Michigan prosecutor received his request. The U.S. Supreme Court said that if the warden in Indiana delayed the forwarding of a prisoner's request for a speedy trial, that this merely postponed the starting of the 180-day clock. Thus, the receipt of such a notice from a prisoner under a detainer warrant in another state by the state prosecutors triggers the 180-day clock to determine whether one's speedy trial rights are being observed.

the court's calendar" (Title 18, U.S.C., Sec. 3161 (h)(8)(C), 2007). Certainly one consequence of this provision is a more rapid trial proceeding.

The not less than thirty nor more than seventy days provision of the Speedy Trial Act applies to the period between one's initial appearance. Ordinarily, there is a ten-day interval between the initial appearance of a defendant and the defendant's arraignment. A federal trial date should be set within sixty days following one's arraignment. The time interval is designed to permit a defendant, together with defense counsel, adequate time to prepare a defense and to spare the defendant any undue delay in coming to trial. If the defendant wishes to consent to an earlier trial date, however, it is the defendant's right to do so under the act.

Many factors affect the seventy-day requirement, however. Defendants may discharge one attorney and appoint another. New attorneys will need sufficient time to examine the case and prepare for a defense of their clients (*United States v. Darby*, 1984). The defendant may be ill (*United States v. Savoca*, 1984), or an important witness for either the prosecution or defense must be called and require additional time to arrive (*United States v. Strong*, 1985). The judge may even request a psychiatric examination of a defendant if, in the judge's opinion, there is reason to believe the defendant is not competent to stand trial (*United States v. Howell*, 1983; *United States v. Crosby*, 1983).

Many local and state jurisdictions follow the federal provisions set forth in the Speedy Trial Act, although they are not bound to do so. For example, North Carolina has a 90-day limit from the time of arrest or arraignment to trial, while New Mexico has a 180-day limit. The "speedy trial" provision of the Sixth Amendment is construed differently from one jurisdiction to the next. Federal courts are bound by the Speedy Trial Act provisions, however.

BENCH TRIALS AND JURY TRIALS CONTRASTED

While the jury system first appeared in the United States in 1607 under a charter granted to the Virginia Company in Jamestown by James I, jury trials existed as early as the eleventh century in England. A criminal trial is an adversarial proceeding within a particular jurisdiction, where a judicial examination and determination of issues can be made, and where a criminal defendant's guilt or innocence can be decided impartially by either a judge or jury (Black 1990, 52). There were about 924,900 persons convicted of felonies in state courts in 2000, criminal trials accounted for only 5 percent of these, the remaining 95 percent were guilty pleas (Maguire and Pastore 2005).

In U.S. district courts there were 83,530 criminal cases concluded in 2003 (Maguire and Pastore 2005, 426). Federal district judges dismissed 7,957 of these cases (9.5 percent), while less than 1 percent of the defendants were acquitted either by the judge or the jury. There were 74,850 defendants convicted, or about 89 percent. Of these, 96.3 percent (72,110) entered guilty pleas through plea bargaining or by pleading *nolo contendere* or "no contest." In federal criminal trials for the 3,463 defendants whose cases actually went to trial and were not plea bargained, federal juries found 2,413 of these defendants guilty, while judges found 327 defendants guilty. Thus, nearly 80 percent of those who went to trial were convicted.

In both state and federal courts, therefore, trials are comparatively infrequent, inasmuch as plea bargaining is used most of the time to secure convictions. But in approximately 10 percent of all criminal cases, there are trials conducted. These are either: (1) bench trials or (2) jury trials.

Bench Trials

A **bench trial,** also known as a **trial by the court** or **trial by the judge,** is conducted either where petty offenses are involved and a jury is not permitted, or in cases where defendants waive their right to a jury trial. A judge presides, hears the evidence, and then decides the case, relying on rational principles of law.

Several popular television shows depict bench trials. Television programs such as *Judge Judy* and *Judge Joe Brown* are examples of bench trials. In cases heard by these courts, litigants or parties to the lawsuits have waived their right to a jury trial and have permitted the judge to decide their cases. In criminal courts, defendants often waive their right to a jury trial and permit the judge to decide their cases based on the evidence introduced.

One explanation for waiving one's right to a jury trial is that juries are sometimes more likely to convict persons for felonies than judges. If the crimes alleged are especially heinous or involve emotionally charged issues, defendants will often opt for a bench trial instead of a jury trial, because juries might be more persuaded by emotional appeals and arguments from prosecutors rather than the cold, hard facts of the case. In the early 1990s, for example, the Reverend Moon, known for his indoctrination of children known as "Moonies," was on trial for income tax evasion. Because of the sensationalism associated with his religion and the impact he had on thousands of teenage followers, his defense attorney requested a bench trial, where the judge would decide his guilt or innocence (Wettstein 1992). Other cases involving child abuse in cults have also been decided by judges rather than juries, reflecting the defense counsel's belief that judges can be more impartial when evaluating the factual evidence (Wettstein 1992). Research has also revealed that judges are more likely to impose shorter sentences as the result of a bench trial as opposed to a jury trial, although many other investigations do not support this view (Champion 2005b).

From a purely practical standpoint, bench trials are more efficient than jury trials. If the process of jury selection does not occur, judges can hear evidence and decide a case in less time, since jury deliberations are avoided. For instance, in New York City, a **Misdemeanor Trial Law** was enacted and took effect in 1985. The purpose of this law was to make it possible to reduce the incarcerative punishments for certain types of misdemeanors to six months or less, meaning that jury trials for defendants charged with these misdemeanor offenses could be avoided (Dynia 1987, 1990). Case backlogs were expedited and overall case processing time greatly decreased. Interestingly, sentencing patterns among judges remained the same both before and after the new law went into effect.

There are several criticisms of bench trials. When judges determine one's guilt or innocence, they may be influenced by extralegal factors, such as one's race, class, ethnicity, and/or gender. Judges are also influenced in their decision making by their own personal feelings about the types of charged offenses. For example, some judges impose more severe sentences upon convicted offenders who commit specific types of heinous offenses, such as child sexual abuse, compared with sentences they might impose for rape, aggravated assault, and murder convictions (Champion 2005b).

When judges decide cases on their own, their susceptibility to corruption is increased. Some judges become susceptible to bribery by influential defendants. In recent years, more than a few judges at the state and federal levels have been charged with corruption and accepting bribes to render decisions favorable to their constituency. **Bribery** is the giving or offering of anything to someone in a position of trust to induce that person to act dishonestly. In 1987, the FBI investigated 105 Pennsylvania judges because of allegations of judicial misconduct. The results of these FBI investigations led the Pennsylvania Supreme Court to temporarily suspend 15 of these judges for bribery. In another FBI investigation, Operation Greylord, a sting operation was conducted against several corrupt judges. Operation Greylord was commenced in 1978 in Cook County, Illinois. FBI agents tapped judges' telephones, recorded conversations, and initiated bogus bribery attempts to induce judges into acting dishonestly in deciding cases. Operation Greylord was successful over the next several years in obtaining convictions against over 60 judges for various criminal misconduct charges, including bribery (Bensinger 1988). Recommendations made by the American Bar Association following Operation Greylord included adopting new ethical requirements for judges and attorneys and the implementation of procedural safeguards to monitor judicial discretion.

Briefly summarizing, the major advantages of bench trials are that:

1. Case processing is expedited.
2. Cases are usually decided on the merits of the case rather than on emotionally charged appeals in the case of heinous offenses.
3. Appearances of defendants may be undesirable to jurors, but judges can usually be dissuaded from considering such extralegal factors.

4. In complex cases, judges are often in a better position to evaluate the sufficiency of evidence against the accused and make fairer judgments.

5. Judges are less persuaded by media attention given to high-profile cases where juries might be unduly influenced against defendants.

6. Bench trials are usually cheaper than jury trials, since they don't take as long to complete and require less defense attorney time.

Some of the major disadvantages of bench trials are that:

1. Judges may impose more severe punishments on certain defendants, depending upon the crimes they have committed.

2. Judges are more susceptible to corruption when left to their own decision making.

3. Defendants waive their right to a jury trial, where the defendant's situation, appearance, and emotional appeal may work to the defendant's benefit.

Jury Trials

Persons charged with felonies are guaranteed the right to a jury trial in the United States. This guarantee also applies to the states. The landmark case of *Duncan v. Louisiana* (1968) has specified an objective criterion that restricts the right to a jury trial only to those offenses other than petty crimes where the possible punishment of imprisonment of more than six months can be imposed. Other cases such as *Baldwin v. New York* (1970) and *Blanton v. City of North Las Vegas, Nev.* (1989) have upheld this standard.

In the last few decades, the number of trials by jury has increased for both major crimes as well as the lesser offenses or misdemeanors (Maguire and Pastore 2005). While trials by jury are increasing compared with their frequency in previous years, the trend is that criminal convictions are obtained increasingly through plea bargaining. And in at least one major city, the number of jury trials conducted for all felony arrests has dropped to about 2 percent (Vidmar 2000).

BOX 9.2 U.S. SUPREME COURT CASES ABOUT THE RIGHT TO JURY TRIALS

■ *Duncan v. Louisiana*

391 U.S. 145 (1968) States must provide jury trials for defendants charged with serious offenses. Duncan was convicted in a bench trial of simple battery in a Louisiana court. The crime was punishable as a misdemeanor, with two years' imprisonment and a fine of $300. In Duncan's case, he was sentenced to only 60 days and a fine of $150. He appealed, saying that he

demanded a jury trial and none was provided for him. The U.S. Supreme Court agreed with Duncan, saying that a crime with a potential punishment of two years is a *serious crime,* despite the sentence of 60 days imposed. Thus, for serious crimes, under the Sixth Amendment, Duncan is entitled to a jury trial.

■ *Baldwin v. New York*

399 U.S. 66 (1970) Baldwin was arrested and prosecuted for "jostling" (pickpocketing), a Class A misdemeanor punishable by a maximum term of imprisonment of one year in New York. New York law prescribed at the time that this was a petty offense and one not entitling a defendant to a jury trial. Baldwin asked for and was denied a jury trial. The U.S. Supreme Court heard Baldwin's appeal and declared that petty offenses carrying a one-year incarcerative term are *serious* in that jury trials are required if requested. Specifically, the wording of Baldwin attaches great significance to the months of imprisonment constituting *serious* time. The U.S. Supreme Court said that a potential sentence in excess of six-months' imprisonment is sufficiently severe by itself to take offense out of category of "petty" as respects right to jury trial (at 1886, 1891). The U.S. Supreme Court overturned Baldwin's conviction and sent the case back to the lower court for a jury trial for Baldwin.

■ *Blanton v. City of North Las Vegas, Nev.*

489 U.S. 538 (1989) Melvin Blanton was charged with DUI (driving while intoxicated). Blanton requested but was denied a jury trial by the North Las Vegas, Nevada Municipal Court. In Nevada, the maximum sentence for a DUI conviction was six months in jail, while the maximum fine was $1,000. Blanton's driver's license was suspended for 90 days and he was ordered to pay court costs and perform 48 hours of community service while dressed in attire identifying him as convicted of a DUI offense. Blanton appealed, contending that he was entitled to a jury trial because the offense, he alleged, was "serious" and not "petty." The U.S. Supreme Court considered his appeal and upheld his DUI bench trial conviction, saying that the most relevant criteria for determining the seriousness of an offense is the severity of the maximum authorized penalty fixed by the legislature. Thus, any offense carrying a maximum prison term of six months or less, as does Nevada's DUI law, is presumed to be petty unless it can be shown that any additional statutory penalties are so severe that they might distinguish the offense as "serious." A further proclamation by the U.S. Supreme Court was that the $1,000 fine did not approach an earlier standard of $5,000 established by Congress in its 1982 definition of "petty" offense, Title 18, U.S.C. Section 1. Thus, the *Blanton* case clearly affirms the earlier holding in *Baldwin* that a defendant is entitled to a jury trial only if the possible incarceration is beyond six months.

THE TRIAL PROCESS

Trial procedures vary greatly among jurisdictions, although the federal district court format is followed most frequently by judges in state and local trial courts. Figure 9.1 shows a diagram of a typical trial from the indictment stage through the judge's instructions to jury members.

Pretrial Motions

Before the start of court proceedings, attorneys for the government or the defense may make **pretrial motions.** Pretrial motions are **motions *in limine*,** and one purpose of such motions is to avoid potentially serious or embarrassing situations that may occur later during trial, such as the attempt by either side to introduce evidence that may be considered prejudicial, inflammatory, or irrelevant. In a brutal murder case, for example, it may be considered inflammatory for the prosecution to introduce photographs of a dismembered body or a mutilated corpse. The jury may be emotionally persuaded to interpret the photographs as conclusive evidence that the defendant committed the crime. Or the photographs may enhance sentencing severity, if additional and overwhelming evidence exists of the defendant's guilt.

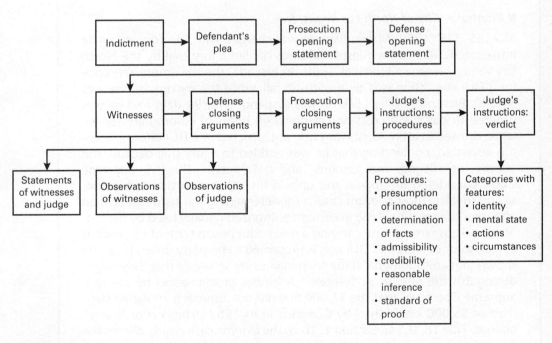

FIGURE 9.1
The Trial Process

In some instances, a defense attorney will make a **motion to suppress** certain evidence from being introduced because it was illegally seized by police at the time the defendant was arrested (Bell 1983). This is known as the **exclusionary rule,** and it provides that where evidence has been obtained in violation of the privileges guaranteed citizens by the U.S. Constitution, the evidence must be excluded at the trial (Black 1990, 564). Generally, any evidence seized by law enforcement officers as the result of an illegal search would be considered inadmissible in court later. Such evidence would fall within the exclusionary rule, and it would be excluded as evidence against the accused. The leading case in the adoption of the exclusionary rule is *Mapp v. Ohio* (1961). This case involved an illegal search of Ms. Dollree Mapp's premises by police officers in Cleveland, Ohio. Police were searching for a suspect in a bombing incident and believed he was hiding in Mapp's home. They entered her home without a warrant and proceeded to search it. They found nothing incriminating, but in their search, they discovered crude pencil sketches in an old trunk in Ms. Mapp's basement. They considered these drawings as obscene, and they charged Ms. Mapp with violating a Cleveland obscenity ordinance. She was subsequently convicted of possessing obscene materials.

Later, the U.S. Supreme Court overturned Ms. Mapp's conviction because of the illegal search, and they declared that the seizure of the "evidence" by police was unlawful and therefore inadmissible against Mapp. Without the evidence, there was no case against Mapp. The U.S. Supreme Court took that particular opportunity to chide the police officers who conducted the illegal search of Mapp's premises. They warned police officers that in future cases, such misconduct would not be tolerated. Thus, the exclusionary rule was subsequently interpreted by police officers as "tying their hands" and limiting their investigative powers, although the real reason for the rule was to prevent police misconduct relating to warrantless searches.

In another leading case involving narcotics sales, a Chinese suspect, Wong Sun, was arrested by police, charged, and convicted of violating federal narcotics laws (*Wong Sun v. United States*, 1963). Earlier, federal agents had acted on a tip and without a warrant, broke down the door of James Wah Toy's dwelling and arrested him. They searched his home for narcotics but found none. But Toy told police later under questioning that Johnny Yee was selling narcotics. Yee was arrested and narcotics were taken from his home. Yee, in turn, implicated Wong Sun who was also arrested. All of the subsequent action against Wong Sun stemmed from an original unlawful search of James Wah Toy's premises and illegally obtained statements from Toy when immediately arrested.

The U.S. Supreme Court overturned Wong Sun's conviction and declared that the statements implicating Wong Sun in narcotics sales were

fruits of the poisonous tree. The fruits of the poisonous tree doctrine provides that evidence derived from an illegal search or an illegal interrogation is inadmissible against a defendant because it has been tainted. If the tree is poison, then the fruit from the tree will also be poison. Similarly, if a search is illegal and evidence is seized, then the "fruits" of that search or the seized evidence will also be considered illegally seized. Such illegally seized evidence will be excluded later against the accused in court.

Often, a defense attorney will file **motions,** such as a **motion to dismiss,** which is a motion attacking the prosecutor's evidence as insufficient or to signify the absence of a key prosecution witness upon which a conviction depends. Such pretrial motions are ordinarily conducted outside of the presence of the jury. The judge rules on these motions and the trial proceeds. A summary of some of the more frequently used pretrial motions is presented below.

1. **Motion for dismissal of charges** (motion seeking to dismiss the case against an accused based on the failure of the prosecution to state a sufficient case to be prosecuted; alleges critical weaknesses in prosecution's case).

2. **Motion for discovery** (motion to obtain and examine certain documents and evidence collected by the prosecution and the list of the witnesses to be called).

3. **Motion for a bill of particulars** (motion to require the prosecutor to furnish a written statement of charges, outlining the crime(s) alleged, the time and place of crime, and other information).

4. **Motion for continuance** (motion seeks to delay trial proceedings, usually in order to interview additional witnesses and collect additional evidence).

5. **Motion for severance** (if more than one defendant is charged in a conspiracy or crime where several defendants are involved, attorneys for each client may wish to separate the cases so that each defendant can be tried independently in order to avoid any conflict of interest, where one defendant may incriminate other defendants).

6. **Motion for suppression of evidence** (motion seeks to exclude incriminating evidence against the accused, such as any evidence illegally seized from one's premises in violation of Fourth Amendment provisions against unreasonable searches and seizures; in the Denver, Colorado, federal trial of Timothy McVeigh and Terry Nichols, charged with the bombing of the Oklahoma City, Oklahoma, federal building in 1995, for example, several incriminating statements made by Nichols and a receipt for bomb materials with McVeigh's fingerprint on it were the subject of a motion to suppress by their defense attorney).

7. **Motion for determination of competency** (motion seeks to question whether the defendant is competent or sufficiently sane to stand trial; an examination by a psychiatrist might be requested before the trial proceeds).

8. **Motion for a change of venue** (the trial of Timothy McVeigh for the bombing of the Murrah Federal Building in Oklahoma City in 1995 was moved from Oklahoma City to Denver, Colorado, where it was believed that a more impartial jury could be selected, which would be less prejudiced toward McVeigh compared with an Oklahoma jury).

9. **Motion for intention to provide alibi** (motion seeks to demonstrate that the defendant did not commit the offense alleged since the defendant was elsewhere when the crime was committed).

10. **Motion for summary judgment** (motion requesting the judge to order a judgment for the defendant based on the insufficiency of evidence presented by the prosecution to sustain a conviction).

Opening Arguments

Unless both the prosecution and defense attorneys agree to waive their opening statements, the prosecutor makes an opening statement to the jury. Usually, this statement includes the state's theory about the case and why the defendant is guilty. Often, prosecutors will tell the jury what they intend to prove and attempt to persuade them to consider the importance of certain kinds of evidence to be presented later. This outline or summary of the nature of the case is to advise the jury of the facts to be relied upon and the issues involved (Black 1990, 1091).

The defense attorney is also permitted to make an opening statement. The defense is given considerable latitude by the court in addressing the jury. Basically, the defense's statement is intended to undermine the state's case against the defendant and to indicate that in the final analysis, the accused should be acquitted of all charges.

The State Presents Its Case

The prosecution begins its case by calling witnesses and presenting evidence that a crime has been committed and that the defendant committed it. Each witness is **sworn in** by a court officer. Being sworn in means that a witness is obliged under the law to be truthful in all subsequent testimony given. This stage is termed **direct examination**. Direct examination is the question–answer exchange between the prosecutor and the prosecutor's witnesses, or between the defense and the defense's witnesses.

The defense has the right to challenge any question asked a **witness** by the prosecution on direct examination. Usually, defense attorneys raise **objections** to certain questions. Or they may object to an answer given by a witness. The presiding judge rules on such objections and either sustains or grants them or overrules or denies them. The same option is available to defense attorneys whenever evidence is introduced by the prosecution. Objections by either side may be raised at any time, and the judge sustains or overrules these objections. When the defense presents witnesses, prosecutors may also raise objections for the same purposes. Sometimes following an adverse ruling on an objection by the prosecution or defense, the prosecutor or defense counsel will say the word, "exception." The judge will usually say, "Exception noted." This use of "exception" is outmoded in contemporary courtrooms, although some older attorneys continue to use this term. This is because whenever a motion is denied or sustained, this ends further dialogue about the motion. More than anything else, the term is intended to annoy the judge because it is entirely unnecessary. In essence, it is an insulting remark and is intended by either side to chide the judge for whatever ruling is made about the particular motion.

The **Federal Rules of Evidence** contain explicit guidelines for judges and attorneys to follow regarding which types of evidence are admissible and which evidence is inadmissible (Saltzburg and Redden 1994). These are very elaborate and technical rules. If they are not followed by any of the major participants in the trial proceeding, such rule violations could be the basis for overturning a "guilty" verdict on appeal to a higher court. The prosecution is also entitled to appeal a "not guilty" verdict on similar grounds. If certain evidentiary rules were violated, the verdict in favor of the defendant could be reversed on appeal. This scenario actually occurred in the cases of Stacey Koon and Laurence Powell, Los Angeles police officers who were convicted in a federal district court in the Rodney King beating. The federal judge was especially lenient in sentencing Koon and Powell, and the U.S. Attorney's Office appealed the lenient sentences to the Ninth Circuit Court of Appeals. The Ninth Circuit overruled the federal judge. Later, attorneys for Koon and Powell appealed the Ninth Circuit ruling to the U.S. Supreme Court, which rendered a mixed opinion in the matter. The point is that either side may appeal a judge's rulings or particular conduct to a higher court.

The Right of Cross-Examination

After the prosecution has questioned a witness, the defense has the right to ask that same witness questions. This is known as **cross-examination.** The right to cross-examine witnesses is not only a constitutional right, but it also illustrates the adversarial nature of the trial system. The defense attorney attempts to impeach the credibility of the prosecutor's witnesses or to undermine their veracity or truthfulness to the jury (Graham 1985). Sometimes, defense attorneys can use prosecution witnesses to their own advantage and elicit statements from them that are favorable to the defendant.

Re-Direct Examination

Once testimony has been given by a witness from either side, that witness may be cross-examined by the opposition. Once such cross-examination has been completed, additional questioning of the witness may be done by the side who called the witness initially. This questioning is called **re-direct examination.** The purpose of re-direct examination is to clarify certain issues that may be confusing to juries, or to cause the witness to elaborate on points the other side may have introduced, which appear to be incriminating. In contrast with the direct examination, the lawyer conducting the cross-examination is allowed to proceed in a leading fashion. Typically, the lawyer during cross-examination will use short, clear statements that cannot reasonably be denied and that ultimately support the lawyer's version of events. Questions during cross-examination do not seek to disclose new information. Rather, this is an opportunity for the attorney to direct the testimony in support of the position of the questioning party.

For instance, a witness may testify on behalf of the defense in a case where the defendant, Mr. X, a noted sports figure, claimed to have cut his hand *after* a murder had been committed in Denver, Colorado, where the unknown assailant had been injured on the hand. Some blood at the crime scene does not appear to be the victim's blood. In fact, investigators suspect that the blood is from the perpetrator, probably from a cut sustained to his hand from a knife wound during the murder. However, the time interval is such that the defendant claims to have cut his hand on the day following the murder when the unknown assailant's injuries occurred. It is claimed by the defendant, for instance, that he boarded an airplane on the evening of the terrible murder. Investigators have fixed the time of death of the deceased at about 10:00 p.m. At 11:30 p.m., it is known that the defendant boards an airplane and flies to New York. As a passenger on the airline, the defendant sits next to another passenger. The passenger and the defendant converse. The following day, the defendant is notified of the murder and is suspected of it. He flies back to Denver on another airline. He has a cut on his hand. The defendant claims that when he learned of the death of the victim the following day, he smashed his hand down on a table in his hotel room while holding a glass. The glass shattered and the pieces cut his fingers. While on the return flight to Denver, the defendant sits next to another passenger and they converse throughout the trip.

On the witness stand, the passenger who sat next to Mr. X on the first flight is called as a witness for the defendant. The witness is called to confirm that Mr. X did not have a cut hand or fingers later in the evening, after the murder had occurred. The witness is asked some questions by the defense counsel on direct examination.

Defense: "Did you sit next to Mr. X on Flight 161 to New York on the evening of February 26th?"

Witness: "Yes."

Defense: "Did you have a conversation with Mr. X during this flight?"

Witness: "Yes."

Defense: "Did you notice whether there were any cuts on Mr. X's hands while you were talking with him?"

Witness: "I didn't see any cuts on Mr. X's hands."

Defense: "Did you know Mr. X by reputation when you were sitting next to him?"

Witness: "Yes, I did."

Defense: "Did you make any special requests of Mr. X?"

Witness: "Yes, I asked him to autograph a pad of paper in my pocket."

Defense: "You asked Mr. X for his autograph?"

Witness: "Yes, I did."

Defense: "Did he sign something for you?"

Witness: "Yes, he signed the paper pad."

Defense: "Where exactly did he sign this pad, you know, did he sign it while holding it in his lap or did he write on some surface?"

Witness: "He wrote his autograph on the pull-out tray in front of my seat. He leaned over and signed my paper pad on my pull-out tray."

Defense: "The pull-out tray on *your* seat. OK. And therefore, this gave you a good opportunity to look closely at his hands?"

Witness: "Yes, it did."

Defense: "And you didn't see or notice any cuts on his hands or fingers?"

Witness: "No, I didn't."

Defense: "And the overhead lights were on when he gave you his autograph?"

Witness: "Yes, the lights were on."

Defense: "And you had a clear view of *both* of his hands?"

Witness: "Yes, he used one hand to hold the pad and the other to sign his name."

[The prosecutor takes over and cross-examines the witness.]

Prosecution: "Sir, could Mr. X have been sitting in such a way so as to hide his hands from you?"

Witness: "I don't think so. We talked a lot that evening, and he was quite animated, using his hands."

Prosecution: "But you cannot say for certain that there were *no* cuts on his hands when you were talking with him?"

Witness: "No, I can't say for certain."

Prosecution: "And so if there *were* cuts, it is possible that you just didn't happen to see them that evening."

Witness: "That's right. I didn't see any cuts when he gave me his autograph, but maybe I just didn't notice them."

[The defense *re-directs:*]

Defense: "Well, you say that you can't say for sure that there were no cuts on Mr. X's hands. Is that right?"

Witness: "Yes, that's right."

Defense: "But suppose there was a deep gash, or perhaps even several deep gashes on Mr. X's hands? If such gashes were there, they would probably be bloody. Perhaps you would notice, for instance, if Mr. X was wearing some sort of covering to protect such cuts if they were there?"

Witness: "I didn't see any bandages."

Defense: "But if there was a deep cut, and if it had been made a short time before Mr. X boarded the plane, then you would probably have noticed that, wouldn't you?"

Witness: "Sure, I probably would have noticed that. We were sitting side-by-side in adjacent seats. Lights were on overhead, and I could see both of his hands."

Defense: "And you saw no cuts?"

Witness: "No, I saw no cuts on his hands. I think I would have seen them if there had been cuts there."

Defense: "Was there any blood on the paper pad where he signed his autograph?"

Witness: "No. There was no blood on the paper pad. Just his autograph."

Now, suppose we have the second witness on the stand, the one who sat next to Mr. X on his return flight from New York back to Denver. The next witness, also called by the defense, is asked the following questions.

Defense: "Were you a passenger on Flight 215 from New York to Denver on the day of February 27th?"

Witness: "Yes, I was."

Defense: "And who did you sit next to while on the airplane, if anyone?"

Witness: "I sat next to Mr. X."

Defense: "Did you have a conversation with Mr. X while you flew from New York to Denver?"

Witness: "Yes, we talked with one another."

Defense: "Did you notice Mr. X's hands while you were talking to him?"

Witness: "Yes, I did."

Defense: "Was there anything unusual or extraordinary about them that you recall?"

Witness: "Yes, there was a big bandage on one of his fingers on his right hand. It looked like it was seeping with blood."

Defense: "You say the wound was seeping with blood?"

Witness: "That's the way it looked to me."

Defense: "Did Mr. X tell you how he received that wound?"

Witness: "Yes, he said he cut it on a glass in his hotel room."

Defense: "Did he say *when* he cut his hand?"

Witness: "Yes. He said he cut it this morning, after he received an upsetting telephone call."

The prosecution cross-examines the second witness:

Prosecution: "When you saw this wound, you don't know precisely *when* the wound was made, do you?"

Witness: "Mr. X says it happened that morning, a few hours before the flight to Denver."

Prosecution: "Yes, but you don't really know for sure *when* that cut was made, do you?"

Witness: "No, I don't."

Prosecution: "It could have been the night before, couldn't it, maybe even around 10:00 p.m. at night?"

Witness: "I suppose so."

Prosecution: "So you really don't know *when* the cut was made, and that it could perhaps have been made the night before, is that right?"

Witness: "That's right."

The defense re-directs:

Defense: "Did you actually *see* the cut on Mr. X's hand or just the bandage covering it?"

Witness: "I saw the cut. He changed the bandage once, just before we landed."

Defense: "When you saw the cut, how did it look to you?"

Witness: "What do you mean?"

Defense: "Did it look like an old cut or a new one?"

Witness: "It looked like a cut that was made fairly recently."

Defense: "If a cut like the one you saw had been made the night before you actually saw it, would it still be bleeding like that, as you have described?"

Witness: "I don't think so. It probably would have healed some. I don't know."

Defense: "And so you are saying that the cut looked entirely consistent with Mr. X's explanation that he had just cut his hand on some glass in his hotel room, is that it?"

Witness: "Yes, that's it."

As can be seen from the above exchange, each side, the defense and prosecution, attempt to use these two witnesses in ways that work to their particular advantage. The prosecution wants the jury to think that the cut occurred when Mr. X, believed to be the murderer, used a knife to kill the victim. The defense wants to show that there was no hand or finger cuts when Mr. X left Denver late on the evening of the murder, but that a cut *was* there when Mr. X was seen by others the following day. If it can be established that Mr. X's hand cut occurred the day following the murder, then it couldn't have been made when the murder was committed. The prosecution wants the jury to believe that the cut occurred during the murder, not afterward. Both the defense and prosecution are permitted to engage in re-direct examinations and **re-cross examinations** of each witness until they feel that they have adequately made their respective points. They are shaping and forming versions of events that make a case for or against Mr. X. We might even consider re-direct and re-cross-examinations as refinements of witness testimony, to know for sure, what the witness saw or did not see. The jury listens and decides which version seems most believable.

Re-Cross-Examination

While some persons consider re-cross-examination prolonging an otherwise long trial, each side is entitled to re-cross-examine witnesses and recall witnesses to the stand for further questioning. This tactic is particularly important whenever new evidence is revealed from other witnesses. Judges may abbreviate extensive cross-examinations and re-cross-examinations if they believe that attorneys are merely covering previous information disclosed in earlier testimony.

Impeaching Witnesses

Impeachment means to call into question the truthfulness or credibility of a witness. If either the prosecutor or defense attorney can demonstrate that a particular witness may be lying or is otherwise unreliable, then that witness's testimony is called into question. Jury members may not believe such witnesses and the evidentiary information they provide for or against defendants. Of course, defendants themselves are subject to impeachment if they testify.

There are several ways defense attorneys can impeach a witness. Attorneys can obtain inconsistent testimony from the witness or can get the witness to admit confusion over certain facts recalled. Or attorneys can introduce evidence of the untruthfulness of the witness based on previous information acquired through investigative sources. Perhaps a witness previously has been fired from a company because of embezzlement. Embezzlement is one form of dishonesty, and an inference may be made by jurors that if witnesses were dishonest in their employment, they may not be telling the truth on the witness stand even though they may be telling the truth in the present case. Of course, when the defense presents its witnesses, the prosecution has the same cross-examination rights and can make similar attempts to impeach the credibility of the witnesses called in the defendant's behalf.

Eyewitnesses and Expert Witnesses

There are many instances in criminal law where expert testimony is solicited (Penrod, Fulero, and Cutler 1995). Experts can testify and identify blood samples, firearms, and ballistics reports; comment on a defendant's state of mind or sanity; and provide opinions about any number of other pieces of evidence that would link the defendant to the crime. By the same token, defense attorneys can introduce expert testimony of their own to rebut or counter the testimony of the prosecution's experts.

Expert witnesses are used by either side to interpret the meaningfulness of evidence presented by either the prosecution or defense (Ross, Read, and Toglia 1994). Expert witnesses have extensive training and experience in matters of fact that may be introduced as evidence in a trial. Their opinions are given more weight than laypersons who do not have such training and experience. Complex issues or topics are clarified for jurors whenever expert testimony is presented (Penrod, Fulero, and Cutler 1995).

Being an expert witness involves certain hazards or risks, however. Some expert witnesses have reported that they were harassed by defendants or their attorneys outside of the courtroom. Particularly in the case of forensic psychiatrists who might testify as to a defendant's sanity or criminal motives, some expert witnesses have reported actually being physically assaulted or threatened with harm (Read, Yuille, and Tollestrup 1992). A majority of cases involving harassment involved criminal cases or where the insanity defense was raised.

Eyewitnesses are also of significant value to both prosecutors and defense attorneys (Davies et al. 1995). They can provide opinions and interpretations of events they actually experienced, and they can provide accounts of the defendant's involvement in the crime alleged. But some researchers have

BOX 9.3 CAREER SNAPSHOT

Braulio Gloria
Probation Officer, Webb County, Texas

Statistics: B.A. (political science), Texas A & M International University; Texas Department of Criminal Justice Probation Officer Training; Texas Department of Criminal Justice Residential Service Training

Background: I am presently employed as an Adult Probation Officer with Webb County, Texas. I have been a probation officer for about a year. Prior to this position I was a shift supervisor for a local halfway house or community residential treatment facility called the Webb County Court Residential Treatment Center (CRTC) for about 5 years.

I first became interested in the criminal justice field while employed at the CRTC. The CRTC was my basic training ground for my current profession because I had daily interactions with probationers who resided at this facility. The CRTC housed 45 male probationers with drug/alcohol dependencies. My job entailed monitoring the probationers via various techniques such as surveillance, searches, and drug screens. Within six months following my employment there, I decided to enroll at a local community college. Eventually I earned an A. A. in criminal justice. I continued my schooling at Texas A & M International University where I earned bachelor's and master's degrees in political science and sociology. Shortly thereafter I was hired as a probation officer and eventually came to be employed in my present position.

Work Experiences: I encountered several challenging situations while employed at the CRTC, but the most severe situations had to do with suicidal probationers. You really do not know what to expect when dealing with anyone who is suicidal, and working with a population that is alcohol/drug dependent only serves to heighten the tension of the situation. Furthermore, most probationers residing at the CRTC have gone through life full of obstacles preventing them from having a normal life. Some find suicide the only solution, as they see it, in overcoming their personal problems. On more than one occasion, I have received calls from ex-probationers whom I assumed were under the influence and threatening to kill themselves. In these situations I found myself trying to counsel them throughout most of the night. However, sometimes you do not get an opportunity to do even that. During one afternoon shift, a probationer slit one of his wrists while in his dormitory room. He did not notify any staff member that he was depressed or contemplating suicide, and none of us (the staff) saw any of the typical symptoms or warning signs of a suicide-prone person. Fortunately, the situation was quickly controlled and the probationer

(continued)

BOX 9.3 *(continued)*

received immediate medical attention and survived. He was given counseling as a part of his therapy and rehabilitation.

I believe that the worst situation I ever experienced at CRTC was when one employee became romantically involved with a probationer residing at the facility. The probationer was successfully released from the CRTC and the employee decided to resign and live with the released offender. About 1 1/2 years later, the ex-employee was murdered by the ex-probationer. The ex-probationer dismembered the woman's body and scattered it in different parts of the community. The ex-probationer was subsequently arrested and sealed his fate in jail by committing suicide. Although I have not painted a particularly pretty picture, these situations are rare, few and far between. Additionally, this line of work can be very rewarding. I am proud to call myself a probation officer because I know that I am helping to keep my community safe. Moreover, it is very rewarding when you actually get to see a probationer turn his/her life around to become a productive citizen.

Advice to Students: Prepare, prepare, prepare. Even though this may sound like a cliché, in this field, you need to get as much experience as possible. Also, do not be discouraged if you do not land the career you want immediately. You will soon learn that elite criminal justice agencies and court systems are hard to enter as a professional. You need to be persistent, and in order to have a competitive edge, you need to prepare. Lastly, continue to develop yourself by continuing your education.

explored the impact of eyewitness testimony on jury verdicts and have suggested strongly that any such testimony should be corroborated with additional supportive evidence in order to be more fully reliable (Champion, 2005b).

There has been some criticism and suspicion about the credibility and reliability of eyewitness testimony. Despite these doubts countless hundreds of persons every year are convicted on little more than the testimony of witnesses. This has become a problem for courts that they have yet to resolve in spite of research showing that juries overrate the reliability of witnesses (Loftus 1996).

A major problem faced by prosecutors is obtaining the cooperation of victims or witnesses to testify in court as to pertinent information they might have about a particular case. The courtroom is a frightful experience for many persons, and the thought of enduring questioning on the witness stand is not a desirable one. In an effort to allay fears of victim-witnesses, various victim-witness assistance programs have been initiated, particularly by prosecutors and courts in various jurisdictions.

Victim-witness assistance programs are services that are intended to explain court procedures to various witnesses and to notify them of court dates. Additionally, such programs permit victim-witnesses to feel more comfortable with the criminal justice system generally. One particularly important function performed by such programs is to assist witnesses in providing better and clearer evidence in criminal prosecutions, with the result that a greater number of convictions will be forthcoming where their testimony has been given (Finn and Lee 1985).

Children as Eyewitnesses

One area that has received much attention in recent years is the reliability of the testimony of child witnesses, especially in cases alleging child sexual abuse (Dent and Flin 1992; McGough 1994). The scientific study of child witnesses by psychologists in the United States began during the early 1900s, and some researchers have concluded that children are the most dangerous witnesses of all (McGough 1994). One reason for this view is that a child's memory of an especially traumatic event such as a rape or homicide is often distorted, and that their recall or true impression of what actually occurred is flawed in one respect or another (Dent and Flin 1992; Mason 1991).

A large number of child victims of sexual abuse are under age 12, and nearly a third are under age 6 (McGough 1994). By 1994, half of all states had adopted special hearsay exceptions when children are giving testimony about being abused, however. Of primary concern to the judge and other participants in the courtroom scene is the ability of children to distinguish between real and imagined events (Davies et al. 1995; Whitcomb et al. 1994).

In addition to the obvious trauma of being asked about emotionally disturbing events such as sexual molestation, the parents of sexually abused children are often reluctant to allow their children to testify in court. Some persons have suggested that children be permitted to testify in an isolated location away from the actual courtroom, and that their testimony should be monitored through closed-circuit television (Whitcomb et al. 1994). Under the Sixth Amendment, however, defendants are entitled to a face-to-face confrontation with their accusers (Ceci and Bruck 1995; Zaragoza 1995). Thus, at least for the present, it would seem that the utilization of closed-circuit television in cases such as child sexual abuse will need to be assessed further by the U.S. Supreme Court before it is approved on a national scale.

At the conclusion of the state's case against the defendant, the defense attorney may make a motion for a **directed verdict of acquittal.** A directed verdict of acquittal requests the judge to dismiss the case against the defendant because the prosecution has not proved the defendant's guilt beyond a reasonable doubt. Thus, the defense believes that their client has not been proved guilty and should be freed. No evidence exists to indicate the frequency with which such a verdict is requested, but such a motion is probably made often in many criminal cases. One reason is that it doesn't cost the defense anything to make such a motion. And on occasion, the motion may be granted. In most instances, if the case is being tried by a jury, the presiding judge is reluctant to grant such a motion. The jury is charged with the responsibility of determining one's guilt or innocence. Judges may grant such a motion, however, if they believe that the state has failed to present a compelling case of the defendant's guilt. If the case is a high-profile one, such as the trial of O. J. Simpson, the judge is even less likely to grant such a motion. Such a motion was made in Simpson's trial in early 1996 following the prosecution's case, but presiding Judge Lance Ito denied the motion.

The Defense and Summation

The defense attorney presents all relevant evidence and calls all witnesses who have relevant testimony favorable to the defendant. The prosecutor may object to the introduction of certain witnesses or to any kind of evidence the defense intends to introduce. Defendants may or may not choose to testify in their own behalf. Their right not to testify is guaranteed under the Fifth Amendment of the U.S. Constitution, and no defendants may be compelled to give testimony against themselves. Evidence from defendants themselves may be self-incriminating, and the Fifth Amendment provides for the right against self-incrimination. Of course, if a defendant does not testify, the jury may believe that the defendant has something to hide. It is difficult to make the jury understand that defendants are merely exercising their right not to testify under the Fifth Amendment, and that no inferences should be made by jurors if the defendant elects not to testify in his or her own behalf. It is the responsibility of the state, the prosecution, to prove the case against the defendant beyond a reasonable doubt. The defendant is entitled to a presumption of innocence until guilt is established according to the "beyond a reasonable doubt" standard. The judge is charged with the responsibility of instructing the jury in this regard and acquainting them with the Fifth Amendment protections extended to defendants under the law.

Some persons erroneously claim that if a jury finds a defendant not guilty and votes for acquittal, that this doesn't necessarily mean that the defendant is innocent. Thus, the status of being found "not guilty" is not the equivalent of the status of being acquitted of criminal charges. But this erroneous belief undermines the fundamental principles of the U.S. Constitution and the rights it conveys to all citizens, regardless of how guilty they may appear to the public or media. Therefore, if we presume correctly that a defendant is innocent until proved guilty in a court of law, beyond a reasonable doubt, then an acquittal causes the presumption of innocence to remain unchanged. For instance,

Fred Graham, a former attorney and expert commentator for *Court TV,* accepted a telephone call from an interested viewer following the O. J. Simpson trial. The caller posed the following question to Graham: "Mr. Graham, the fact that the jury found Simpson not guilty doesn't mean that Simpson is innocent, does it?" Graham answered, "That's right, it doesn't mean he is innocent." Graham was clearly wrong in his response to the anonymous caller. The presumption of innocence continues as a part of our right to due process throughout a trial and its conclusion, unless a guilty verdict is declared by the jury. In the eyes of the law, therefore, O. J. Simpson continues to be viewed as innocent of the crimes previously alleged.

Interestingly, two quite different books appeared in 1996 following the verdict in the murder trial of sports figure O. J. Simpson. A work by Ron Huff, Arye Rattner, and Edward Sagarin, *Convicted But Innocent: Wrongful Conviction and Public Policy,* and another work, *Guilty: The Collapse of Criminal Justice* by Harold J. Rothwax, both address fundamentally different views of jury voting. Jury decisions may result in convictions of innocent persons, while jury decisions may result in acquittals of guilty persons. Rothwax, a former judge, suggests that current laws and procedures handicap the police and prosecutors from apprehending and convicting criminals, and preventing the courts from resolving the primary question of whether the accused committed the crime. He explores various drastic changes in the laws so that the ends of justice might be served more effectively, through more frequent convictions and fewer reversals of convictions on technical grounds. The work by Huff and his colleagues examines various wrongful convictions, where innocent persons were convicted anyway, despite the fact that they were innocent. Presently, we acknowledge that our legal system is flawed, and it is likely that it will always be flawed.

Various interesting scenarios have been portrayed by motion pictures, where a guilty offender is convicted of murder but later his conviction is overturned because evidence is found implicating another offender of the murder. The other offender has murdered several persons, and so it is believed that he is fully capable of murdering one more person. The fact is that the second murderer has entered into an agreement with the first murderer. The agreement is that the second murderer wants his parents killed, and the first murderer (who really is a murderer) agrees to kill the second murderer's parents if the first murderer is freed. Therefore, a plot unfolds where evidence is suddenly discovered that leads to freeing the first murderer. While this convoluted plot seems peculiar, it is no more silly than imagining scenarios where guilty suspects are acquitted and innocent suspects are convicted. In many murder cases, only the real murderers know for sure. While these two books offer criticisms of the criminal justice system that allow for such events to occur, there is no foolproof way of preventing their occurrence, no matter what reforms are implemented.

Can Prosecutors Criticize Defendants for Not Testifying in Their Own Behalf?

The prosecution is forbidden from mentioning a defendant's refusal to testify to the jury (*Griffin v. California*, 1965). For instance, if the prosecutor were to say, "Ladies and gentlemen of the jury, if this defendant were innocent, he would get up here on the stand and say so," this statement would be improper, and the judge would order the statement stricken from the record. In fact, such an utterance by the prosecutor may cause the judge to declare a mistrial. Both prosecutors and defense attorneys alike are bound by legal ethics to comply with court rules when presenting a case or representing a client in the courtroom. But occasionally, some attorneys engage in unethical conduct, either deliberately or inadvertently. Sometimes, such conduct will result in the judge declaring a mistrial, and the case will have to proceed from the beginning in front of a new jury.

Ordinarily, judges will give the jury instructions when it is ready to deliberate and decide the case. These instructions include statements about the rights of the accused and whether any inferences, either positive or negative, may be drawn from an accused's right not to testify in his own behalf. The jury is instructed not to consider the fact that a defendant chose not to testify in his own behalf. One reason for this admonition is to remind the jury that it is the prosecutor's burden to show, beyond a reasonable doubt, that the accused is guilty of the crime(s) alleged. It is not the responsibility of the accused to prove himself *innocent* to the jury. While these admonitions may seem self-evident, more than a few jurors have been influenced by the refusal of defendants to testify. We cannot possibly know what impact this refusal to testify will have on jury decision making.

Each side is permitted a **summation** at the conclusion of all evidence presented. Ordinarily, defense attorneys present the final oral argument on behalf of their client. This argument is followed by the closing argument of the prosecuting attorney. Sometimes, with court consent, prosecutors may present a portion of their closing argument, followed by the closing argument of the defense, followed by the remainder of the prosecutor's closing argument. In short, the prosecutor gets in the final remarks to the jury. There is a very good reason for this order of summation. Since the burden of proving guilt beyond a reasonable doubt is so difficult, prosecutors are given the last word. It is assumed that if these prosecutorial remarks are the last words heard by the jury, besides the instructions they receive from presiding judges, then their subsequent deliberations will be tainted initially by these prosecutorial remarks. During jury deliberations, however, a critical examination of all evidence introduced will lead the jury to one conclusion or the other. If the prosecutor has failed to carry the burden of proof in the case, the jury will vote to acquit the defendant.

JURY DELIBERATIONS

After the prosecution and defense have presented their final arguments, the judge instructs the jury on the procedures it must follow in reaching a verdict, and the jury retires to the jury room to consider the evidence and arrive at a verdict. The judge's instructions to the jury often include a recitation of the charges against the defendant, a listing of the elements of the crime the prosecution must prove beyond a reasonable doubt, and a charge for jurors to carefully weigh and consider the evidence and testimony of witnesses.

Again, depending upon whether the case is in federal district court or in a state jurisdiction, the jury must either be unanimous or comply with the particular state rules governing jury verdicts. It will be recalled that federal juries must be unanimous. If a jury of twelve persons fails to agree, a mistrial will be declared by the federal judge. And if one jury member becomes ill, an eleven-member federal jury, with court approval, is acceptable and must render a unanimous verdict as well. In states such as Louisiana and Oregon, the particular state rules governing jury verdicts have approved 9–3 or 10–2 majority votes in order for verdicts of guilty to be rendered. In six-person juries, the jury must reach a unanimous decision, according to the U.S. Supreme Court (*Burch v. Louisiana*, 1979).

Jury deliberations and the decision-making process of arriving at particular verdicts have also been targeted for study by social scientists in recent years (Kerr 1994; Kerr and MacCoun 1985). The primary difficulty confronting those interested in studying jury deliberation processes is that such deliberations are conducted in secret. Some investigators have participated as actual jury members in their respective jurisdictions. And the insight gained through such experiences has been instrumental in preparing defense attorneys more adequately in presenting convincing cases to juries on behalf of their clients.

Jury deliberations have often been the subject of feature films and novels. The 1957 drama, *Twelve Angry Men*, starring Henry Fonda, epitomized the emotion and anger of jurors in a murder case. In that film, Fonda was the lone juror voting "not guilty" against the other eleven "guilty" votes. The remainder of the film described the jury's attempt to convince Fonda that he was wrong. As it turned out, Fonda convinced the other jurors that *they* were wrong, and the defendant was acquitted. And in a 1996 novel by author/lawyer John Grisham, *The Runaway Jury*, a detailed depiction of jury deliberations is presented, with an incredible amount of interplay among jurors and the ease with which jurors' opinions are changed by particularly dominant jury members.

Jury deliberations such as those occurring in *Twelve Angry Men* are not uncommon. Jurors who differ as to their estimation of the value of particular evidence attempt to persuade the other jurors to side with them. At the outset,

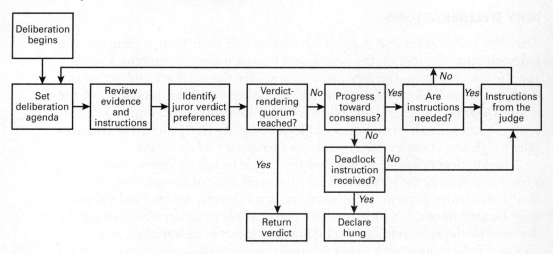

FIGURE 9.2
Jury Deliberations

jurors may take an informal ballot or vote to see where they stand for conviction or acquittal. More often than not, this initial ballot influences significantly the final verdict by presenting to all jury members the disposition or determination of the majority of jurors favoring guilt or acquittal.

Group pressure is often responsible for changing minority factions in a jury to aligning themselves with the majority opinion. And in jurisdictions where the majority-rule option is in effect, such as Oregon and Louisiana, agreement among jurors is achieved more rapidly than in those states where unanimity of opinion is required. Figure 9.2 shows the jury deliberation task.

When deliberations commence, juries may or may not establish a deliberation agenda. But ordinarily, discussions take place concerning the relevance and importance of particular pieces of evidence and witness testimony. If there is an initial vote and the jury is in disagreement as to the verdict, deliberations continue until a verdict is reached. If the jury simply cannot agree on a verdict, or if the required majority cannot be obtained in those jurisdictions providing for a majority vote for conviction, the judge will likely declare a mistrial.

Must Juries Agree on a Verdict?

Jury Voting in U.S. District Courts

In federal district courts, juries consist of twelve persons. The judge may or may not permit the selection of alternate jurors. **Alternate jurors** are used in the event that one or more of the regular jurors become ill during the proceedings. Also, during jury deliberations, if a juror cannot continue to serve, Title 18 U.S.C., Rule 23 (2006) provides that "if the court finds it necessary to excuse a juror for just cause after the jury has retired to consider its verdict, in the discretion of the court a valid verdict may be returned by the remaining 11 jurors" (Title 18, U.S.C., 2006). In federal courts, whether a 12- or 11-member jury hears a case, the decision reached for either guilt or acquittal must be unanimous. If one or more jurors disagree and persist in their disagreement with the other jurors, the judge declares a hung jury and a mistrial is declared. Mistrials are erroneous, invalid, or nugatory trials (Black 1990, 1002). This means that the entire case will have to be heard again before a new jury later. Mistrials also occur during the trial, especially if irregularities or errors occur to jeopardize a defendant's fair trial rights. Sometimes, inadmissible evidence may be admitted erroneously. A witness may make an utterance which may tend to substantial jury bias. Whenever such trial irregularities and other errors occur, the judge ordinarily grants a motion by either side for a mistrial (Hodge 1986; Institute for Court Management 1983).

Jury Voting in State Courts

At the local and state levels, however, the federal rule for jury agreement or unanimity does not always apply. Under existing U.S. Supreme Court guidelines, state juries may vary in size from a minimum of six persons to twelve persons. Actually, the U.S. Supreme Court has established the minimum number of jury members at six in the case of *Williams v. Florida* (1970). However, no such precedent has been established for upper limits of jury sizes. Thus, it is conceivable that a defendant may request a jury consisting of more than 12 persons, such as 25 or 50 jurors. But this would be very unusual. It would also pose severe logistical problems for courtrooms, where it would be difficult to find sufficient seating for all of these jurors. Furthermore, there would be considerable difficulty for all of these jurors to reach agreement about the guilt or innocence of criminal defendants.

Six-member juries must be unanimous in their verdict (*Burch v. Louisiana*, 1979). However, if juries consist of twelve persons, a majority verdict may be acceptable in certain states, unless unanimity is required under state or local laws. For instance, in the cases of *Apodaca v. Oregon* (1972) and *Johnson v. Louisiana* (1972), the respective defendants were convicted by a majority of jurors, but there was no unanimity of agreement. In most states, however, unanimous verdicts are required by statute.

An example of a legitimate nonunanimous verdict is the case of *Johnson v. Louisiana* (1972). In the *Johnson* case, Frank Johnson was arrested, tried, and convicted of armed robbery in 1968. The twelve-person jury convicted him by a 9–3 vote (the absolute minimum majority required under Louisiana law). In another case, unanimity of jury voting was not required either. This was the case of *Apodaca v. Oregon* (1972). In Apodaca's case, Robert Apodaca and several other defendants were convicted of assault with a deadly weapon. Apodaca was convicted by an 11–1 jury vote. In Oregon, the minimum vote required by a jury for conviction is 10–2. Their respective appeals were heard by the United States Supreme Court. The U.S. Supreme Court upheld both of their convictions and underscored the right of states to utilize the rule of a majority vote in their jury trials. Also in some states, such as Tennessee, the Tennessee State Legislature has copied the Federal Rules of Criminal Procedure and required their 12-member juries to be unanimous in their voting. There are some exceptions to nonunanimous jury voting, however. In capital cases where the death penalty may be imposed, the jury vote for conviction must always be unanimous.

Polling the Jurors

Judges will frequently poll jurors once they have rendered their verdict. **Polling jurors** simply refers to asking each juror to state in open court whether the verdict is a true reflection of his/her feelings and how he/she voted. It is unlikely that a jury will vote to acquit a defendant, where a particular juror will say to the judge that he or she did not agree with that vote. In those cases where juries must be unanimous in their decision to convict or acquit defendants, such an event is especially important. In situations such as Louisiana or Oregon where unanimous votes are not needed, polling individual jury members identifies the specific vote breakdown. However, in the event that one or more jurors disagree with the majority in a state or federal court where the jury vote must be unanimous, judges will send the juries back to deliberate more extensively, until unanimity of voting is reached. Otherwise, if the jury deliberates for an unusually long period and cannot agree on a verdict, a mistrial will be declared and a new trial may be scheduled. Scheduling a new trial is up to the prosecutor. Mistrials are sometimes based on unclear or insufficient evidence. If prosecutors believe that the issues to be resolved in particular criminal cases are so controversial that no jury will likely agree in the future, then no further prosecution against the defendant will be conducted.

The Selling of Jury Deliberations

During the 1980s and 1990s, increasing interest has been expressed in jury deliberations and the factual accounts of what transpires in jury rooms (Kerr 1994). Juries have become increasingly scrutinized bodies. Individual jury members have exploited their jury membership to their advantage for profit. This phenomenon is not peculiar to the United States. Other countries, such as Australia and Great Britain, have found that jurors in particularly high-profile cases have focused on the profit motive as a primary reason for their jury involvement (Findlay and Duff 1988).

In particularly sensational trials, jury members' opinions about jury deliberations are increasingly marketable products. Several jurors in the murder trial of O. J. Simpson were excused as jurors when it was learned by the judge that the jurors were planning to write books about their experience and actually negotiating with publishers for book contracts. One former juror had been keeping a journal about his experiences as a juror. Keeping such a journal of trial events was forbidden and regarded as juror misconduct. Another juror, a former airline attendant, was excused for a different reason. It was learned that she had been approached by representatives of *Playboy* magazine and had agreed to pose nude for a large sum of money when the trial was completed. Thus, she was exploiting her role as a juror in the high-profile trial. While posing nude for a men's magazine is not against the law, it raises serious questions about the juror's original motives for becoming a juror.

Whenever jurors in any trial consider the potential profits stemming from their roles as jurors, this raises doubts about their veracity or truthfulness when the *voir dire* was originally conducted. If they have hidden agendas, such as writing a book about their experiences, no laws prohibit subsequent expressions of their opinions and views. But it is juror misconduct to keep journals about their jury involvement and observations. If the prosecution or defense learns about such activities or behaviors, then these revelations become grounds to bar these jurors from further jury service.

In one New York City trial, for instance, a highly publicized event occurred in the Howard Beach community. The case involved a racial attack. During the trial, several jurors contacted the media in an attempt to sell their story and give their account of jury deliberations. Some news reporters believed that such conduct by jurors was acceptable and within the boundaries of free speech. The court and prosecution took a different view by condemning those jurors who sought to profit from their experiences as jurors. The jurors were excused (Kleinig 1989).

What if persons seek to become jurors for the purpose of advancing some political view or social cause? Ideally, juries are comprised of persons who will render fair decisions and consider and weigh all factual information presented by both sides during the trial. But if some jurors are sidetracked with collateral issues not directly relevant to the trial proceedings, this may impair their ability to render fair judgments about what they have seen and heard.

THE VERDICT AND ITS AFTERMATH

After deliberating, the jury returns to the courtroom and delivers its **verdict** to either the judge or an officer of the court. The defendant rises and faces the jury, while either the jury foreman or the judge reads the verdict aloud. If the verdict is "not guilty," the defendant is released. In some cases, acquitted defendants may be rearrested for other crimes that have occurred. Ordinarily, an acquittal effectively removes the defendant from the criminal justice system.

BOX 9.4 ON WRONGFUL CONVICTIONS

■ Kenneth Marsh, 50, from San Bernardino County, California, spent nearly 21 years in prison following his conviction for the second-degree murder of his girlfriend's son, 3-year-old Phillip Buell in 1983. Marsh claimed at the time that Buell had fallen from a couch and hit his head on the fireplace hearth. Prosecutors alleged that Marsh had beaten the boy. After many years and appeals, Marsh's case was newly investigated. It was discovered that Buell had been treated at a local hospital following his head injury and that doctors at the hospital treated him with the drug, Mannitol, which turned out to be a "substantial factor" in the boy's death. Philip Buell also had an undiagnosed blood disorder that was unknown to physicians at the time. Although he had been stabilized for a time at the local hospital, a physician administered Mannitol to the boy during his recovery, which only served to exacerbate his bleeding and swelling, thus leading to his death. An appellate court overturned Marsh's conviction and freed him. The appellate court ruled that the death of Buell appeared to be an accident, not a deliberate act on Marsh's part. Subsequently, the California State Compensation Board approved $750,000 for Marsh, which amounted to approximately $100 per day that Marsh spent in prison. Marsh says that "Nothing can make up for the time I spent in prison unless they gave me my 21 years back." San Bernardino County Prosecutor Michael Ramos personally apologized to Marsh. Marsh added that Ramos's apology "goes a long way." Marsh has since then filed a $50 million lawsuit in federal court against the doctors and hospital where Buell was treated, alleging malpractice. Lawyers for the hospital and doctors were seeking to have the lawsuit dismissed, since the allegations were "far-fetched."

■ Ray Krone, 48, was living in Phoenix, Arizona, in 1991 and worked for the U.S. Post Office. He played darts regularly at a Phoenix bar where Kim Ancona, a bartender, worked. Subsequently Ancona was killed under mysterious circumstances, and he was bitten in several places on his body. Ray Krone was called in for investigation and gave police an impression of his teeth for comparison with the bite marks on Ancona's body. Krone was convicted in 1992 of Ancona's murder and sentenced to death, largely on the basis of expert testimony from a forensic pathologist who testified that the bite marks on Ancona's body were made by Krone's teeth. Krone's 1992 conviction was overturned by an appellate court on procedural grounds in 1994, but a new trial resulted in a new conviction and sentence in 1996. This time, Krone was sentenced to life, because the judge said he wasn't sure that Krone was the killer.

In 2002, new DNA testing proved that Krone was definitely not Ancona's killer. Using the FBI database, DNA was matched with a man who was already in prison for another crime. The other man was charged with Ancona's murder and Krone was ordered released and his conviction was expunged. Krone subsequently received $3 million from Maricopa County for his wrongful conviction and imprisonment. Nevertheless, he filed a new lawsuit against Phoenix police who he claims did a shoddy job of investigating the murder and didn't look at other suspects closely enough. His lawsuit alleged that Phoenix authorities used altered and manufactured evidence, and that the forensics expert gave false testimony that he knew to be untrue. Krone also sued Arizona agencies for mental anguish and for the physical pain and suffering he had endured. Also, he was stabbed by another inmate while in prison, had his arm broken, and contracted hepatitis C. In 2006, Krone was living in Dover Township, Pennsylvania, near his family. He currently serves on the Commission on Safety and Abuse in America's Prisons and speaks out against the death penalty. He supports the use of DNA testing in capital cases. In 2005, Krone was on the television show, *Extreme Makeover*, where he received extensive dental treatment. During his trial and afterwards, he was dubbed the "snaggletooth killer" for his crooked smile. Now he has a straight row of pearly whites.

How much liability should states or the federal government absorb for wrongful convictions? Should there be limits on the amounts wrongfully convicted persons can recover from their governments following the discovery of new evidence showing their innocence? What do you think? [Sources: Adapted from the Associated Press, "$750K for Man Wrongfully Jailed," January 20, 2006; adapted from Beth DeFalco and the Associated Press, "City Approves $3 Million Settlement for Wrongfully Convicted Man," September 27, 2005.]

In the event that a "guilty" verdict is rendered by the jury, the defendant has the right to appeal the verdict. The defense attorney may again request the judge to issue a directed verdict of acquittal despite the jury's decision. The judge may, indeed, exercise this option. However, if the judge sets aside the jury verdict and declares the defendant acquitted, the prosecution may appeal that decision to a higher court.

If the judge does not grant the defense attorney's request, the defendant is sentenced. The appeals process may take many years. In all of the U.S. Supreme Court cases presented in this and previous chapters, the interval of time between the offense, the conviction, and the U.S. Supreme Court decision has been several years. Before a case gets before the U.S. Supreme Court, however, it must be reviewed by higher courts within the particular state jurisdiction where the original judgment was entered against the defendant. This appeals process consumes much time as well. Cases presented before the U.S. Supreme Court usually involve constitutional issues. Were a defendant's constitutional rights violated at any stage of the criminal proceeding? Were there procedural errors committed by different court participants, such as the judge, such that the original conviction might be set aside and a new trial ordered?

SUMMARY

A trial proceeding provides defendants with the opportunity to confront and cross-examine their accusers and to offer exculpatory evidence favoring a verdict of "not guilty." A trial is an adversarial proceeding, where the prosecution attempts to establish a defendant's guilt and the defense attempts to prove their clients innocent of any offenses alleged.

Trial procedures vary from one jurisdiction to the next. A bench trial could be held, where the judge oversees the proceedings and is responsible for hearing the facts of the case and making a judgment based on those facts. Bench trials are usually used for less serious and petty offenses in which the defendant has waived their right to a jury trial. Some advantages of a bench trial include expedited case processing, judges are less likely than juries to consider extralegal factors, judges are usually in a better position to decide the sufficiency of evidence in more complex cases, judges are less persuaded by media attention, and bench trials are usually cheaper than jury trials. Disadvantages, however, include that judges may impose more severe punishments on certain defendants, and a defendant waives their right to a jury trial where maybe their appearance, emotional appeal, and situation could have worked to their benefit in front of a jury. Those defendant's charged with felonies are guaranteed the right to a trial by jury. This guarantee also applies to the states, the case of *Duncan v. Louisiana* specified the right to trial by jury for those charged with offenses other than petty crimes for which the possible punishment imposed could be six months of imprisonment. Where a jury trial is conducted, the number of jurors ranges from six to twelve. At the federal level, a jury verdict must be unanimous. At the state and local levels, however, a unanimous verdict may or may not be required, depending upon the prevailing laws.

The trial process is varied in the different jurisdictions of the United States. There are many stages that characterize the trial process beginning with the indictment of a defendant through to the judge's instructions to the jury members. There are also a number of motions that may be made, and either granted, or denied. Pretrial motions are used to ensure that there are no surprises at trial. For instance, a motion to suppress is used in an attempt to exclude certain evidence from being introduced at trial, evidence that the defense believes has been obtained illegally. The exclusionary rule provides that evidence obtained in violation of certain privileges U.S. citizens enjoy must be excluded at trial. A motion to dismiss may be filed by the defense attorney, stating that they do not believe the prosecutor has sufficient evidence to proceed with a trial. A motion for discovery is usually by the defense, which will enable them to obtain and examine evidence collected by the prosecution as well as the witnesses they plan to call to testify. A motion for continuance is usually made to allow delay of the trial for the purposes of collecting more evidence or interviewing additional witnesses. A motion for determination of competency is made to question if the defendant is competent or sufficiently sane to stand trial. A motion for change of venue is a request to hold the trial elsewhere in the belief that in the current jurisdiction the ability of the defendant to have a fair trial would be difficult. These and many other motions are usually made before a trial begins in order to ensure that the defendant is given a fair trial by an impartial jury.

During the actual trial process itself many procedures are also followed. Each side is permitted to address the jury with an opening statement. Both the prosecution and the defense will make opening arguments where each side will give a preview of what they are going to prove or disprove throughout the trial. The prosecution will usually present their theory of the events and why the defendant is in fact guilty. The defense will try to undermine the state's case saying that the prosecution doesn't have enough evidence to prove the elements of the crime, and that when all is said and done, the jury will see that the defendant should be acquitted. Following opening statements, the prosecution will present its case by presenting evidence and bringing in witnesses that prove a crime has been committed and that the defendant is the one who committed it. There are federal rules of evidence that judges and the attorneys must follow regarding which types of evidence are admissible or inadmissible. Judges are responsible for determining the relevance of objections and evidence. The defense also has the right to question the prosecution's witnesses; this is known as cross-examination. This is where the defense will attempt to show that the witness is not a credible one. Once cross-examination is finished, the prosecution can then ask additional questions of their witness; this is called redirect examination. As the trial progresses and new evidence surfaces, prior witnesses can be called to the stand again, this is known as re-cross-examination.

Both sides usually call to the stand eyewitnesses and expert witnesses to give various testimony. Expert witnesses are used to give meaning to the evidence that is presented. Usually expert witnesses will have extensive training and experience in particular matters. This gives their testimony more influence that the testimony of laypersons. Eyewitnesses can also be of value to both the prosecution and defense. These witnesses provide opinions or interpretations of the events that transpired, and can account for the involvement, or lack of involvement of the defendant in the crimes alleged. After the prosecution has rested, the defense then presents its case, revealing evidence and witness testimony favorable to the defendant. The process continues until both sides are satisfied that the evidence before the jury has been adequately presented. The final procedure involves a summation by both sides. This time the defense presents its closing arguments first, and the prosecution has the last word to show that they have proven, beyond a reasonable doubt, that the defendant is in fact guilty of the crimes they have been charged with.

After summations, the judge will instruct the jury on the procedures to be followed in deliberations. The jury system first emerged in the United Stated around 1607; however, they existed in England as early as the eleventh century. Juries are made up of persons from a cross section of the community or region in which the crime has occurred. The selection of jury members involves questioning them concerning their possible biases or prejudices in the case before the court, whether biases are specific (knowing the defendant) or general (having certain ideas about crime and criminal offenders), a potential juror with either should be excluded from duty so that an impartial jury can be formed. Both prosecution and defense attorneys attempt to select jurors favorable to their particular interests. Jurors are excluded from jury duty for reasons of illness, their occupations, or if they do not meet requirements, and both prosecution and defense attorneys may challenge any juror for cause. Jurors may also be excluded by means of peremptory challenges, as the prosecutor and defense attorney attempt to construct the most favorable jury for their particular position. These peremptory challenges may not be used for purposes of discrimination, however.

The science of jury selection is popular. Many attorneys turn to consulting firms that specialize in the selection of jury members. However, the results of studies investigating particular jury member characteristics and their decision-making inclinations have been inconsistent and disappointing. No one has been able to predict with 100 percent certainty how particular jury members will vote in a given trial. Questions of ethics about scientifically selecting a jury have also been raised.

Jury deliberations are conducted following the presentation of witnesses and evidence from both the prosecution and defense, and a verdict is determined. Jury deliberations are done in secret, meaning that no one other than jury members are allowed in this process. Jurors may attempt to persuade each other to side with their decision. Research has shown that group pressure can cause those in the minority decision to align themselves with the majority. Depending on whether the case is a federal, state, or other trial, the verdict must either be unanimous, or in compliance with the jurisdiction's rules regarding verdicts. Federal juries must be unanimous. If the jury cannot agree on a verdict as local, state, or federal law requires, the presiding judge will declare a mistrial. This will require a new trial before a new jury. If a jury finds the defendant guilty of the crime alleged, the judge will sentence the convicted offender, either at the conclusion of the trial or in a separate subsequent proceeding.

After deliberations, the jury returns to the courtroom to give its verdict. The defendant must rise and face the jury, and the foreperson or the judge will read the verdict aloud. If a verdict of guilty is found, the defendant may appeal; appeals can take several years before they are exhausted depending on the seriousness and nature of the appeal. If found guilty, the judges is responsible for handing out a punishment to the defendant. Usually the defendant is remanded to custody and the sentence will be given at a sentencing hearing on a subsequent date.

KEY TERMS

Adversarial proceedings
Alternate jurors
Bench trial
Bribery
Cross-examination
Directed verdict of acquittal
Direct examination
Exclusionary rule
Expert witnesses
Eyewitnesses
Federal Rules of Evidence
Fruits of the poisonous tree doctrine
Jury deliberations
Misdemeanor Trial Law
Motion for a bill of particulars
Motion for a change of venue
Motion for continuance
Motion for determination of competency
Motion for discovery
Motion for dismissal of charges
Motion for intention to provide alibi
Motion for severance

Motion for summary judgment
Motion for suppression of evidence
Motions
Motions *in limine*
Motion to dismiss
Motion to suppress
Nolo contendere
Objections
Not guilty
Polling jurors
Pretrial motions
Re-cross-examination
Re-direct examination
Screening
Speedy Trial Act of 1974
Summation
Sworn in
Trial
Trial by the court
Trial by the judge
Verdict
Victim-witness assistance programs
Witnesses

QUESTIONS FOR REVIEW

1. What is a pretrial motion? What is it called? What are some examples of pretrial motions?

2. Differentiate between a "bench trial" and a "jury trial." Is there any evidence to indicate that a defendant is better off having a bench trial as opposed to a jury trial?

3. What is a trial? What are some of the functions of a trial proceeding?

4. Does a criminal defendant have to have a jury trial if he/she is charged with murder? Can the defendant waive his/her right to a jury trial? What constitutional amendment pertains to jury trials?

5. Identify three functions of juries. What U.S. Supreme Court decision pertained to setting lower limits for jury sizes? What was the limit established?

6. In a particular criminal case before a six-person jury, the jury brought back a verdict of guilty, but the vote was 5–1. Evaluate this verdict in view of what you have learned about jury size and unanimity of agreement among jurors.

7. On the basis of some of the research conducted about jury size, is a twelve-member jury more representative of community interests compared with a six-person jury? What are some differences between these jury sizes other than the number of jurors?

8. What are five "maxims" believed by many attorneys about juror characteristics and accompanying juror attitudes?

9. What is meant by the "fruit of the poisonous tree"? What does it have to do with evidence? Explain briefly.

10. What is the exclusionary rule?

11. How reliable is the testimony of a child witness? Cite some research that has investigated the competency of child witnesses.

12. What is the purpose of a victim-witness assistance program?

13. Who usually gets the last word and closing argument in a criminal case before a jury?

SUGGESTED READINGS

1. Raymond A. Atkins and Paul H. Rubin (2003). "Effects of Criminal Procedure on Crime Rates: Mapping Out the Consequences for the Exclusionary Rule." *Journal of Law and Economics* **46**:157–179.
2. Donald Dripps (2001). "The Case for the Contingent Exclusionary Rule." *American Criminal Law Review* **38**:1–146.

3. Alejo Freire et al. (2004). "Lineup Identification By Children: Effects of Clothing Bias." *Law and Human Behavior* **28:**339–354.
4. Jakub Gubanski (2004). "Comparative Criminal Justice: Special Investigation Techniques During the Criminal Trial: Disclosure Issues in Polish and American Legal Systems." *Crime, Law and Social Change: An Interdisciplinary Journal* **41:**15–32.
5. Douglas N. Husak (2004). "Guns and Drugs: Case Studies on the Principled Limits of the Criminal Sanction." *Law and Philosophy* **23:**437–493.
6. Thomas N. McInnis (2001). *The Christian Burial Case: An Introduction to Criminal and Judicial Procedure.* Westport, CT: Praeger Publishers.
7. Robert J. Ramsey (2003). *False Positives in the Criminal Justice Process: An Analysis of Factors Associated with Wrongful Conviction of the Innocent.* Ann Arbor, MI: University Microfilms, Inc.
8. Tim Valentine, Alan Pickering, and Stephen Darling (2003). "Characteristics of Eyewitness Identification That Predict the Outcome of Real Lineups." *Applied Cognitive Psychology* **17:**969–993.

Chapter 10

Sentencing and Appeals

Chapter Objectives

As a result of reading this chapter, you will have accomplished the following objectives:

1. Understand the functions and goals of sentencing, including punishment, incapacitation, crime control, rehabilitation and reintegration, and prevention and deterrence.

2. Describe different forms of sentencing, including indeterminate, determinate, guidelines-based or presumptive, and mandatory sentencing and their implications for criminal defendants.

3. Describe habitual offender or chronic offender statutes and their use in different jurisdictions.

4. Understand truth-in-sentencing provisions and how such provisions have evolved.

5. Understand sentencing disparities and how factors such as race/ethnicity, gender, socioeconomic status, and age affect one's sentence.

6. Describe the sentencing hearing and its various functions.

7. Describe presentence investigation reports, their contents and components, preparation, and usefulness in the sentencing process.

8. Understand victim impact statements, the circumstances under which such statements are appended to presentence investigation reports, and the usefulness of such statements in the sentencing process.

9. Describe various types of alternative sentencing, including shock probation and split sentencing and the implications of such sentencing practices for offenders.

10. Describe the death penalty and bifurcated trials, including the functions of such trial proceedings.

11. Understand the appeals process, who initiates appeals, various bases for appeals, including *habeas corpus* petitions, tort claims, and civil rights Section 1983 actions.

■ Jeffrey Morse, 30, of Schaumburg, a Chicago suburb, wants to be castrated. Why? He is a sex offender who cannot control his sexual impulses. He attacked a 12-year-old girl in 1996 and molested her sexually. He tried to attack an 11-year-old girl in 1997, but was unsuccessful. He tried to lure her to his car, where he planned to rape her. Morse was convicted of the 1996 sexual molestation charge, and he faced from 6 to 100 years in prison for the crime. His sentence was scheduled for February 1998. Morse's attorney, Paul B. Wharton, advised news sources that Morse planned to have himself castrated, since, as Wharton put it, "someone said that if the flagpole isn't flying, the compulsion to sing the *Star-Spangled Banner* is not the primary thought in the man's mind." Wharton said that a group of anonymous donors has contributed over $5,000 to cover the cost of the castration for Morse. Morse was permitted a one-day furlough from jail in order to have the castration. An anonymous group of doctors would perform the operation, Wharton said. Why would a sex offender such as Morse undergo castration? One explanation is that Morse believes that besides minimizing his sex drive, it will also have some weight in mitigating his potentially lengthy sentence. Morse hoped that his decision to have the castration surgery would persuade the judge to be lenient with him. This is not a compulsory order from the court. Rather, Morse himself initiated the idea, and believes that it is the best alternative in his case. In other jurisdictions, judges have attempted to impose castration of sex offenders in lieu of lengthy prison terms, but the U.S. Supreme Court has ruled that they cannot offer convicted offenders this alternative. It would violate their constitutional rights. Is it unconstitutional in any way for a convicted sex offender to want to be castrated? Should judges mitigate or downgrade the sentencing of such offenders who voluntarily undergo castration? What do you think? [Source: Adapted from the Associated Press, "Sex Offender Wants Castration," January 17, 1998.]

■ Calvin Burdine was convicted of murder in 1984. He was sentenced to death and placed on death row in Texas. A significant part of the case against Burdine was his confession to police, where he admitted stabbing to death his gay lover, W. T. Wise, at a trailer home they shared in the Houston, Texas, area during 1983. Subsequently, Burdine recanted his confession and denied killing Wise. In virtually all death penalty cases, there is an endless string of appeals on various issues. Although the federal government and various states have attempted to limit the number of appeals to which death row inmates are entitled, there are still a large number of death row inmates and other prisoners who manage to file many appeals to prolong their days in prison or on death row. Calvin Burdine is no exception. He has filed numerous appeals. However, his most recent appeal has caught the attention of a federal court. In fact, the fifth Circuit Court of Appeals has ruled that Burdine is entitled to a new trial on the murder charge because his attorney was asleep during some of the trial proceedings in which he was convicted. Burdine's attorney, Robert McGlasson, contended that Burdine's attorney, Joe Cannon, who is now dead, frequently slept at the 1984 trial, with his head drooping and sometimes resting on the table. The U.S. Supreme Court has long recognized that a trial is unfair if the accused is denied counsel at a critical stage of his trial, according to the fifth Circuit Court of Appeals. The fifth Circuit Court of Appeals heard Burdine's appeal *en banc*, which means that all 14 of the appellate judges sat in and voted in a 9–5 decision to recommend a new trial for Burdine. Burdine's attorney said, "We were obviously pleased. We believe common sense prevailed and the court agreed with the arguments we've made all along. Such an event runs counter to any sense of fairness and fair play." Peter Loge, director of the Campaign for Criminal Justice Reform at the Justice Project, noted, "The American people believe that anyone accused of a crime deserves a fair trial." It's up to Congress to fix a system that makes cases like Mr. Burdine's the norm." How many appeals should a convicted murderer be allowed? Why wasn't the issue of attorney incompetence brought up in an earlier appeal by Burdine? Should Burdine be allowed a new trial in Wise's death? What do you think? [Source: Adapted from April Castro and the Associated Press, "Texas Death Row Inmate Whose Lawyer Slept Could Get New Trial," August 15, 2001.]

INTRODUCTION

This chapter is about the sentencing process. Sentencing offenders is not as simple as it may appear. There are many types of sentencing schemes, and changes are being made in different jurisdictions annually as various forms of sentencing are established and practiced. Sentencing means to impose a penalty on an offender convicted of a crime. The chapter opens with a discussion of the functions and goals of sentencing. These functions and aims include punishment or just deserts, incapacitation and crime control, rehabilitation, reintegration, and prevention and deterrence. For each function and aim, issues are raised about whether the function or aim is realized as the result of a particular sentencing scheme used.

Several sentencing forms are examined in the next section. These include indeterminate sentencing, which is the most pervasive sentencing form in the United States. Indeterminate sentences are distinguished as those where parole boards can intervene and abbreviate the sentences inmates are serving. The advantages and disadvantages of indeterminate sentencing are presented. Among the criticisms of indeterminate sentencing are that extralegal factors such as age, race/ethnicity, gender, and socioeconomic status often influence early-release decisions, and thus, some inmates may serve longer or shorter terms depending on these factors. These charges of sentencing disparity are discussed.

Another sentencing form is determinate sentencing. Determinate sentencing is similar to indeterminate sentencing, except that one's early release from prison is determined by the accumulation of good-time credit and other noteworthy accomplishments. During the 1970s and 1980s, a major shift occurred from indeterminate to determinate sentencing. The implications of this sentencing shift are discussed.

A third sentencing form is presumptive or guidelines-based sentencing. Almost all states and the federal government have implemented sentencing guidelines to assist judges in determining proper sentences for convicted offenders, where extralegal factors are essentially excluded and have no bearing on sentencing decisions. However, even presumptive sentencing can be abused by judges and others, often through plea bargaining, and thus, justice may not be served in particular cases. In subsequent years, the U.S. Supreme Court has interpreted the federal sentencing guidelines primarily as suggested sentences, and that federal district court judges may apply other sentences if they wish. Thus, even under federal sentencing guidelines, individualization of sentencing has been allowed and condoned by the highest court in the land. The pros and cons of presumptive sentencing are discussed.

The fourth type of sentencing is mandatory sentencing. Often mandatory sentencing is imposed for specific offenses. Closely associated with mandatory sentencing are habitual offender statutes and certain conditions or circumstances under which certain crimes are committed. If offenders use a firearm when committing a crime, this may result in a mandatory sentence, which varies by jurisdiction. If a gun is used during a crime in Michigan, an additional 2-year mandatory term of incarceration is added to one's sentence for the crime itself. In Virginia, a 5-year mandatory prison term is imposed for the same scenario. Mandatory sentences are believed to be deterrents to criminals and may prevent them from using dangerous weapons where victims or innocent bystanders may be injured or killed. But this is speculative and has not been confirmed by social research.

Some states have evolved statutes that attempt to give a sentence some substance. Under indeterminate sentencing, for instance, offenders may often serve 20 to 30 percent of their time and are paroled. Citizen reaction to such abbreviated sentences is very negative. Seeking to placate citizens, legislatures have evolved truth-in-sentencing provisions, whereby offenders must serve most of their sentences instead of small portions of them (McManimon 2005a). Regardless of the form of sentencing used in any jurisdiction, the goals of these sentencing schemes can easily be defeated. Habitual offender statutes, for instance, where mandatory sentences apply, can be plea bargained away and pose no threat to criminals. Jail and prison overcrowding is out of control in many jurisdictions, and harsh sentencing policies cannot be enforced because there is no space to place convicted criminals. These issues will be examined and discussed.

For most serious crimes, a sentencing hearing is held following one's conviction. This hearing is to examine various aggravating and mitigating circumstances that exacerbate one's punishment or lessen it. Usually victims or their relatives speak out against convicted offenders during these hearings, while offenders' relatives and close friends speak out in their behalf. Judges ultimately decide the punishment, which often is codified according to the seriousness of the offense.

The next section examines presentence investigation reports, or documents that are usually prepared by probation officers. These reports contain a vast amount of information about the crime one has committed, their version of events, the police report, a victim impact statement, and the background of the defendant. Judges use presentence investigation reports in their sentencing decisions, although it is unknown how much credence such reports receive. These reports are also used later in parole decision making when parole boards are considering certain inmates for early release. The format and contents of presentence investigation reports are described and discussed. Other sentencing options are included and described, such as shock probation and split sentencing. Their implications for offenders are presented.

In death penalty cases, the U.S. Supreme Court has declared that such proceedings should be conducted in the form of bifurcated trials, where the trials consist of two stages. The first stage is to determine the guilt or innocence of the defendant. If the defendant is guilty, then the jury reconvenes and determines the sentence to be imposed. This sentence may be death or life imprisonment, or several other sentencing options.

All convictions may be appealed. The next section of this chapter examines the appeal process. Several important bases for appeals are described. These include *habeas corpus* petitions, which challenge the length, nature, and fact of confinement. Another basis for appeals may be through a tort claim. Finally, inmates may appeal on the basis that their civil rights were violated in some way. This civil rights litigation is through the Fourteenth Amendment and is called a Section 1983 action, since it is found in Title 42, Section 1983, of the U.S. Code. Each of these bases for appeal are described, and examples are provided illustrating their use by inmates.

Appealing a case to higher courts is also described. The U.S. Supreme Court may be petitioned through a writ of *certiorari*, and the appeals process is rather lengthy. It may be several years from the time an appeal is filed before it is eventually heard by the high court. Many cases are not heard at all and are dismissed because they lack merit or are frivolous. The appeals process is discussed and several implications for convicted offenders are indicated.

FUNCTIONS AND GOALS OF SENTENCING

Sentencing offenders serves the following functions and aims: (1) punishment/ "just deserts," (2) incapacitation/crime control, (3) rehabilitation, (4) reintegration, and (5) prevention/deterrence.

Punishment

Punishment is any sanction imposed following a criminal conviction. The primary function and aim of sentencing is to punish offenders for their crimes. Each crime carries minimum and maximum penalties. When judges or juries find defendants guilty of committing one or more crimes, sentences are imposed that presumably punish offenders (Gants 2005). Considerable variation exists regarding the application of penalties for each crime. Depending upon the circumstances and jurisdiction, judges can impose probation for a period of years, or they can subject convicted offenders to incarceration in either a jail or prison. How harshly or leniently convicted offenders are treated should depend on the crime's seriousness. Ideally, the more serious the crime, the harsher the penalties imposed. In reality, however, it doesn't always work this way. Investigators can always find examples of some rapists and robbers, even murderers, receiving probation instead of prison sentences. Accordingly, some burglars and thieves may receive lengthy sentences in jails or prisons.

Incapacitation/Crime Control

A second function of sentencing is **incapacitation.** A primary aim of sentencing is to incapacitate those convicted of crimes, particularly those who are persistent or chronic offenders. **Career criminals** who make their living from crime are frequently targeted by the criminal justice system to receive the harshest penalties. Special statutes have been written to make it possible to mete out stringent penalties for **chronic recidivists** or **chronic offenders.** It is believed by many state legislatures that if **persistent felony offenders** and chronic recidivists are removed from society for prolonged periods through longer sentences, then they cannot commit new crimes against society while confined in prison. Thus, the system takes these offenders out of circulation for a period of years. If such offenders are allowed to remain in their communities through some form of probation, then probation departments maintain surveillance over these clients by monitoring their whereabouts in different ways. Home confinement and electronic monitoring systems are used, together with regular face-to-face visits with probation officers. These forms of managing convicted offenders in their communities don't prevent them from committing new crimes in any absolute sense, but for many of these offenders, there exists some degree of crime control depending on the nature of these management methods.

Rehabilitation

One intended function of punishment is **rehabilitation.** A high degree of cynicism is prevalent among jurisdictions, however, concerning just how well corrections in any form actually rehabilitates convicted offenders. Some experts believe that rehabilitation never occurs, while others believe that for many offenders, particularly those incarcerated in prisons, rehabilitative programs have been successful in enabling them to turn their lives around and become law-abiding when they are eventually released back into society.

Most prisons include various vocational/technical/educational programs for offenders who wish to take advantage of these rehabilitative services. Individual and group counseling and other forms of social and psychological assistance are provided inmates. Some jails and prisons have rules and regulations requiring inmates to participate in certain programs, whether or not they wish to participate. Literacy programs have been established in jurisdictions, such as Virginia, where it is expected that illiterate inmates who are serving long prison terms must learn how to read and write as one condition for their early release. Some authorities question whether voluntary or mandatory participation in any particular prison program is directly responsible for one's rehabilitation over time.

Reintegration

A fourth function or aim of sentencing is **reintegration,** or assisting criminals to become readjusted so that they can fit into their communities and society. This aim is most closely associated with non-incarcerative sentences, including all forms of probation. When judges sentence offenders to probation, there are usually several conditions of probation attached. These conditions might include mandatory participation in counseling programs, job placement services, restitution programs, and other activities that will assist offenders in finding employment and becoming self-sufficient without having to return to crime. Particularly for first-offenders, community correctional programs are quite helpful in enabling them to become reintegrated in society. They may remain with their families and receive their social support. Further, these offenders will not have to be exposed to the criminogenic influence of incarceration.

Prevention/Deterrence

Sentencing is also symbolic, both to convicted offenders and to those who are contemplating committing crimes. When judges impose sentences, there is a tacit expectation that others will consider the harshness of these sentences and refrain from crime because of their fear of punishment. Thus, sentencing is designed as a form of **crime prevention** and/or **deterrence.** One direct intention of the **get-tough movement** is to mete out harsher penalties for offenders to set examples and deter others from crime. The death penalty is regarded by some persons as an effective deterrent for those who are contemplating capital offenses. No one wants to be executed. Theoretically, if the **death penalty** is the punishment for murder, then fewer murders will be committed. This view has been challenged by experts frequently, and most criminal justicians agree that the death penalty does not necessarily deter some persons from killing others (Robinson and Darley 2004). Also, longer prison terms for those who deal in drugs do not prevent drug dealers from carrying out their illicit activities. Nevertheless, in an ideal world, sentencing is supposed to act as a deterrent and prevent others from committing crime. Largely because of this aim, the sentencing systems of all jurisdictions throughout the United States have been changed to maximize sentencing effectiveness. As we will see in the next section, sentencing reform has yielded several important types of sentencing schemes to further the aim of crime deterrence and prevention. Unfortunately, all forms of sentencing have generated criticism from experts and the general public, with little agreement as to which sentencing scheme is best (Champion 2005b).

FORMS OF SENTENCING

Federal and state judges tend to believe that the toughest part of their jobs is imposing punishments on convicted offenders. There are so many types of offenders with varied backgrounds and criminal histories that the act of sentencing them is one of the most stressful and complex decisions made by these judges (Aas 2004). Assisting judges in their sentencing decision making are various legislatively enacted sentencing schemes. These sentencing schemes provide a rational structure within which to make sentencing decisions. Currently, there are four types of sentencing schemes used by various jurisdictions throughout the United States. These are: (1) indeterminate sentencing, (2) determinate sentencing, (3) presumptive or guidelines-based sentencing, and (4) mandatory sentencing.

Indeterminate Sentencing

Indeterminate sentencing is a sentence imposed by the judge that includes a minimum term of years and/or months and a maximum term, where the offender's early release from prison is determined by a **parole board.** Thus, the maximum term may or may not be served by any particular offender, depending upon their institutional behavior and other factors (Stemen 2004).

Indeterminate sentencing has its roots in early correctional history from the 1850s and 1860s. Influenced by penal reforms in Ireland, Scotland, and England, the United States was inclined to experiment with indeterminate sentencing as a means of providing incentives for inmates to behave well while confined. Provided that their institutional conduct was acceptable, once inmates had served the minimum portion of their sentences as imposed by judges, then they would become eligible for parole or early release or serving their full terms. Parole boards would decide whether to grant **early release** to these parole-eligible inmates. Their institutional conduct would be examined, together with the circumstances and seriousness of their conviction offenses, and the parole board would either grant or deny their parole. Those denied parole on one occasion may apply for it on subsequent occasions, usually at regular intervals such as once a year or every two years. Most paroling authorities in the United States today continue to make such decisions.

However, indeterminate sentencing has been criticized for its potential for discrimination on the basis of race, gender, and/or socioeconomic status (Champion 2005b). Both judges and parole boards have been accused of respectively abusing their sentencing and early-release discretionary authority by making decisions on factors other than legal ones. These **extralegal factors** are most often racially or ethnically based, or related to gender or socioeconomic differences. Convicted black offenders and other minorities more often receive longer sentences by judges or are denied early release by parole boards more frequently compared with white offenders who have a similar **criminal history.** Those with private counsel often are treated more leniently in sentencing compared with indigent convicted offenders who are represented by public defenders or **court-appointed counsel** (Weiss 2004). Since these factors should not be considered as significant in such decision making, substantial efforts have been made by different interests to reform state and federal sentencing policies and practices. In some instances, states and the federal government have abolished parole in favor of what they believe to be more equitable sentencing schemes. One noticeable shift among many states has been from indeterminate sentencing to determinate sentencing (Champion 2005b).

Determinate Sentencing

Determinate sentencing is a sentence imposed by the judge involving a fixed minimum term and a fixed maximum term, but where one's early release from prison is determined by the accumulation of **good-time credit,** which is deducted from one's maximum term. **Good-time** or good-time credit is a fixed number of days inmates may accumulate based upon the amount of time they serve. A substantial number of states provide that offenders may accumulate up to 30 days for every 30 days they serve. Thus, if an inmate serves one year, he/she may accumulate one year of good-time credit. This credit is deducted from the maximum sentence originally imposed by the judge. It is conceivable, therefore, that inmates sentenced to ten years under a determinate sentencing system may only serve five years, with the accumulated good time deducted from their maximum ten-year sentences. Thus, determinate sentencing is intended to produce greater certainty, proportionality, and rationality in punishment (Champion 2005b).

Determinate sentencing is believed by its proponents to correct the potential for discrimination according to extralegal factors by judges and parole boards. With determinate sentencing, inmates can calculate their own approximate early-release dates. Thus, there is greater release certainty with determinate sentencing compared with indeterminate sentencing. But inmates may jeopardize their good-time credit by misbehaving while confined. They may receive write-ups from correctional officers for fighting or possessing illegal contraband or drugs. Violations of other institutional rules will result in good-time being revoked or cancelled.

Determinate sentencing has received mixed criticisms. Several states, such as Delaware, Colorado, Iowa, Minnesota, North Carolina, and Washington, have used determinate sentencing to replace indeterminate sentencing. Some of these states, including Minnesota and Washington, have opted for additional sentencing changes after experimenting with determinate sentencing for several years. Despite the promise of significant reform in curing previous ills of discrimination in sentencing, determinate sentencing has not been as successful in this regard as originally projected. More than a few states have opted for yet another variety of sentencing designed to curb judicial sentencing discretion and the potential for its abuse. In the last few decades, guidelines-based or presumptive sentencing schemes have been proposed and implemented (Champion 2005b).

Presumptive or Guidelines-Based Sentencing

Presumptive sentencing or **guidelines-based sentencing** is the establishment of fixed punishments for each criminal offense, graduated according to offense severity and one's criminal history. Punishments for different offenses are ranged according to months. Punishment range midpoints are the presumptive number of months imposed according to a fixed table. Minnesota was one of the first states to implement **sentencing guidelines** (DeLone and Wilmot 2004; Kramer and Johnson 2004). Subsequently, many other states established their own guidelines, such as Florida, California, and North Carolina (Crow 2004). The federal government established sentencing guidelines as well, following the extensive work of the **United States Sentencing Commission.** The U.S. Sentencing Commission originated as the result of the Comprehensive Crime Control Act of 1984 and promulgated punishment guidelines for all federal crimes. These guidelines were implemented in 1987. Federal parole was abolished in 1992 and replaced with supervised release.

An example of guidelines-based or presumptive sentencing is the U.S. Sentencing Guidelines. These guidelines are shown in Table 10.1.

Across the top of the table are Criminal History categories. These range from I, where offenders have little or no criminal history, to VI, which reflects persons who have the most extensive and serious criminal histories. Down the left-hand side of the table are offense levels ranging from 1 to 43. There is an offense seriousness level for every federal crime. The more serious the crime, the larger the offense seriousness score. In the body of the table where the criminal history and offense seriousness scores intersect are ranges of months. These are guidelines used by judges when sentencing offenders. Judges must remain within these month ranges in most cases. The midpoint in each month

TABLE 10.1 U.S. SENTENCING GUIDELINES (MONTHS)

Offense Level	Criminal History Category					
	I 0 or 1	II 2 or 3	III 4, 5, 6	IV 7, 8, 9	V 10, 11, 12	VI 13 or more
1	0–1	0–2	0–3	0–4	0–5	0–6
2	0–2	0–3	0–4	0–5	0–6	1–7
3	0–3	0–4	0–5	0–6	2–8	3–9
4	0–4	0–5	0–6	2–8	4–10	6–12
5	0–5	0–6	1–7	4–10	6–12	9–15
6	0–6	1–7	2–8	6–12	9–15	12–18
7	1–7	2–8	4–10	8–14	12–18	15–21
8	2–8	4–10	6–12	10–16	15–21	18–24
9	4–10	6–12	8–14	12–18	18–24	21–27
10	6–12	8–14	10–16	15–21	21–27	24–30
11	8–14	10–16	12–18	18–24	24–30	27–33
12	10–16	12–18	15–21	21–27	27–33	30–37
13	12–18	15–21	18–24	24–30	30–37	33–41
14	15–21	18–24	21–27	27–33	33–41	37–46
15	18–24	21–27	24–30	30–37	37–46	41–51
16	21–27	24–30	27–33	33–41	41–51	46–57
17	24–30	27–33	30–37	37–46	46–57	51–63
18	27–33	30–37	33–41	41–51	51–63	57–71
19	30–37	33–41	37–46	46–57	57–71	63–78
20	33–41	37–46	41–51	51–63	63–78	70–87
21	37–46	41–51	46–57	57–71	70–87	77–96
22	41–51	46–57	51–63	63–78	77–96	84–105
23	46–57	51–63	57–71	70–87	84–105	92–115
24	51–63	57–71	63–78	77–96	92–115	100–125
25	57–71	63–78	70–87	84–105	100–125	110–137
26	63–78	70–87	78–97	92–115	110–137	120–150
27	70–87	78–97	87–108	100–125	120–150	130–162
28	78–97	87–108	97–121	110–137	130–162	140–175
29	87–108	97–121	108–135	121–151	140–175	151–188
30	97–121	108–135	121–151	135–168	151–188	168–210
31	108–135	121–151	135–168	151–188	168–210	188–235
32	121–151	135–168	151–188	168–210	188–235	210–262
33	135–168	151–188	168–210	188–235	210–262	235–293
34	151–188	168–210	188–235	210–262	235–293	262–327
35	168–210	188–235	210–262	235–293	262–327	292–365
36	188–235	210–262	235–293	262–327	292–365	324–405
37	210–262	235–293	262–327	292–365	324–405	360–life

TABLE 10.1   U.S. SENTENCING GUIDELINES (MONTHS)

| Offense Level | Criminal History Category | | | | | |
	I 0 or 1	II 2 or 3	III 4, 5, 6	IV 7, 8, 9	V 10, 11, 12	VI 13 or more
38	235–293	262–327	292–365	324–405	360–life	360–life
39	262–327	292–365	324–405	360–life	360–life	360–life
40	292–365	324–405	360–life	360–life	360–life	360–life
41	324–405	360–life	360–life	360–life	360–life	360–life
42	360–life	360–life	360–life	360–life	360–life	360–life
43	Life	Life	Life	Life	Life	Life

Source: U.S. Sentencing Commission. U.S. Sentencing Guidelines, Washington, DC: U.S. Government Printing Office, 1997.

range is considered the presumptive sentence judges must impose, unless certain factors dictate otherwise. For instance, if the month range is 40 to 50, the presumptive number of months is 45. If the range is 30 to 40 months, then 35 would be the presumptive number of months. Judges may move upward or downward within each range, depending upon whether there are aggravating or mitigating circumstances. They may impose sentences outside of any particular month range if they believe there are circumstances to justify such departures (Ulmer, 2004). They must provide in writing their rationale for such departures. Such was the case in *Koon v. United States* (1996). [See Box 10.1.]

A comprehensive study of various sentencing schemes was completed in 1995 (Austin et al. 1995). This study examined the nature of sentencing reform and evaluated the various sentencing schemes presently used. According to this report, by 1994, the federal government and 16 states had adopted presumptive sentencing schemes. Another five states had adopted determinate sentencing systems. The most promising of all sentencing schemes was presumptive sentencing. Presumptive sentencing is considered most promising because of its potential for minimizing sentencing disparities according to extralegal factors, minimizing incarceration rates, and reducing prison overcrowding. Similar conclusions have been reached by those investigating different dispositional schemes for juvenile offenders (Champion 2005b).

Many states have sentencing reform acts to change the ways convicted offenders are sentenced. The federal government passed the **Sentencing Reform Act of 1984,** which led to the creation of the U.S. Sentencing Commission and a revision of the entire federal criminal code. Also in Washington, the state's Sentencing Reform Act of 1981 established determinate sentencing for felonies. But various deficiencies in determinate sentencing laws have caused state officials to modify their existing sentencing policy with a

BOX 10.1 JUDGES MAY STRAY FROM PRESUMPTIVE SENTENCING GUIDELINES

■ *United States v. Granderson*

511 U.S. 39, 114 S.Ct. 1259 (1994). Granderson, a letter carrier for the U.S. Postal Service, was convicted of destruction of mail and sentenced to five years' probation, although the U.S. Sentencing Guidelines provided for a zero- to six-month incarcerative term. Subsequently, Granderson's probation was revoked when it was discovered that he possessed a controlled substance. U.S.C. Section 3565(a) of Title 18, the criminal code, provides that one-third of the original sentence should be imposed as a punishment when revoking a federal probation. Thus, relying on the five-year (60-month) probationary term, the judge sentenced Granderson to 20 months of imprisonment. Granderson appealed, contending that the U.S. Sentencing Guidelines govern incarcerative terms, not probationary sentences. A circuit court of appeals reversed this sentence and ordered Granderson released. Its logic was that the original sentence was the U.S. Sentencing Guidelines of zero to six months, not the original probationary sentence. Because Granderson had already served 11 months of imprisonment at the time of the appellate decision, his immediate release was ordered. The government appealed, and the U.S. Supreme Court heard the case. The U.S. Supreme Court upheld the circuit court of appeals, concluding that indeed, the U.S. Sentencing Guidelines governed this situation, not the probationary sentence imposed by the federal judge.

■ *Koon v. United States*

518 U.S. 81 (1996). Police officers Stacy C. Koon and Laurence M. Powell were convicted in federal court of violating constitutional rights of motorist, Rodney King, under color of law during arrest and sentenced to 30 months' imprisonment. U.S. district court trial judge used U.S. sentencing guidelines and justified a downward departure of 8 offense levels from "27" to "19" to arrive at a 30- to 37-month sentence. Government appealed, contending that downward departure of 8 offense levels from "27" was an abuse of judicial discretion and that the factors cited for the downward departure were not statutory. An original offense seriousness level of "27" would have meant imposing a sentence of 70 to 87 months. The Ninth circuit court of appeals rejected all of the trial court's reasons for the downward departure and Koon and Powell petitioned the Supreme Court. The Supreme Court upheld the circuit court of appeals in part and reversed it in part. Specifically, the Court said that the primary question to be answered on appeal is whether the trial judge abused his discretion by the downward departure in sentencing. The reasons given by the trial judge for the downward departure from an offense level of "27" to "19" were that: (1) the victim's misconduct provoked police use of force,

(2) Koon and Powell had been subjected to successive state and federal criminal prosecutions, (3) Koon and Powell posed a low risk of recidivism, (4) Koon and Powell would probably lose their jobs and be precluded from employment in law enforcement, and (5) that Koon and Powell would be unusually susceptible to abuse in prison. The Supreme Court concluded that a 5-level downward departure based on the victim's misconduct that provoked officer use of force was justified, because victim misconduct is an encouraged [by the U.S. Sentencing Commission] basis for a guideline departure. The Supreme Court said that the remaining 3-level departure was an abuse of judicial discretion. Federal district judges may not consider a convicted offender's career loss as a downward departure factor. Further, trial judges may not consider an offender's low likelihood of recidivism, because this factor is already incorporated into the Criminal History Category in the sentencing guideline table. Considering this factor to justify a downward departure, therefore, would be tantamount to counting the factor twice. The Supreme Court upheld the trial judge's reliance upon the offenders' susceptibility to prison abuse and the burdens of successive state and federal prosecutions, however. The Court remanded the case back to the district court where a new sentence could be determined. Thus, a new offense level must be chosen on the basis of the victim's own misconduct, which provoked the officers, and where offender susceptibility to prison abuse and the burden of successive state and federal prosecutions could be considered. The significance of this case for criminal justice is that specific factors are identified by the Supreme Court to guide federal judges in imposing sentences on police officers convicted of misconduct and violating citizen rights under color of law. Victim response that provokes police use of force, an officer's susceptibility to abuse in prison, and the burden of successive state and federal prosecutions are acceptable factors to be considered to justify downward departures in offense seriousness, while one's low recidivism potential and loss of employment opportunity in law enforcement are not legitimate factors to justify downward departures in offense seriousness.

■ *Melendez v. United States*

518 U.S. 120, 116 S.Ct. 2057 (1996). Melendez was convicted of conspiring to distribute cocaine, a crime carrying a statutory minimum sentence of 10 years' imprisonment. However, in a plea agreement with the government, Melendez agreed to furnish valuable information leading to the arrest and conviction of other drug dealers. The government described the assistance rendered by Melendez to the court and recommended a lesser sentence than that provided under the sentencing guidelines. Under the sentencing guidelines, Melendez's sentence would have been from 135 to 168 months, and the government moved the court to grant a downward departure from this higher range. However, the government

(continued)

BOX 10.1 *(continued)*

did *not* move to have the court reduce Melendez's sentence *below* the mandatory minimum of 120 months or 10 years. The federal district judge imposed the statutory minimum 10-year sentence and Melendez appealed, contending that the substantial assistance he rendered to the government and their implied promise of a downward departure should be honored. Melendez expected that his sentence would be less than the statutory 10-year minimum. The U.S. Supreme Court heard the case and affirmed the lower-court decision, holding that the district court lacked the authority to impose less than the minimum 10-year mandatory sentence where the government did not bring a motion requesting or authorizing such a departure below the 10-year minimum sentence based on substantial assistance from Melendez. Furthermore, the U.S. Supreme Court held that a motion by the government for departure from applicable guidelines based on substantial assistance does not authorize departure from statutory minimum sentences.

■ *Blakely v. Washington*

___U.S.___, 124 S.Ct. 2531 (2004). Pursuant to a plea bargain agreement in Washington, Ralph Blakely pleaded guilty to kidnapping his estranged wife and was convicted of second-degree kidnapping involving domestic violence and the use of a firearm. In his plea agreement, Blakely admitted to the kidnapping and to limited facts that supported a maximum sentence of 53 months under Washington's guidelines sentencing scheme. However, the judge rejected the prosecutor's recommended 49- to 53-month sentence and instead imposed an exceptional sentence of 90 months, 37 months longer than contemplated by the plea agreement. The judge justified his departure because of "deliberate cruelty" exhibited by Blakely, because the maximum sentence is up to 10 years, and because "deliberate cruelty" is an aggravating factor under Washington's Sentencing Reform Act. Blakely appealed, contending that this sentencing procedure denied him the right to have a jury determine all facts legally essential to his sentence. The Washington Supreme Court denied Blakely's appeal and the case was heard by the U.S. Supreme Court. The U.S. Supreme Court invalidated Blakely's 90-month sentence, holding that because the facts supporting Blakely's exceptional sentence were neither admitted in the plea agreement nor found by a jury, the sentence violated his Sixth Amendment right to a trial by jury. The U.S. Supreme Court elaborated, stating the trial judge could not have imposed the exceptional 90-month sentence solely on the basis of the facts admitted in the guilty plea. According to U.S. Supreme Court precedent, statutory maximum sentences are maximum sentences judges may impose solely on the basis of the facts reflected in a jury verdict or admitted by the defendant. The U.S. Supreme

Court further noted that this decision does not question Washington's sentencing guidelines scheme or its constitutionality. Rather, it reflects the scope of judicial discretion in sentencing under the circumstances of this case.

■ *Shepard v. United States*

___U.S.___, 125 S.Ct. 1254 (2005). Reginald Shepard pleaded guilty to and was convicted of being a felon in possession of a firearm. Under the U.S. sentencing guidelines, Shepard's sentence would be 30 to 37 months, but the government sought a 15-year mandatory minimum sentence under the Armed Career Criminal Act (ACCA) in view of the fact that Shepard had three prior convictions for burglary. The government claimed that Shepard's burglaries were "generic burglaries," as defined under the ACCA, which defines generic burglaries as those committed in a building or enclosed space, violent crimes. Shepard's burglary convictions occurred in Massachusetts, and Massachusetts has a broad range of burglary categories, which render them nongeneric burglaries. The government failed to show the district court evidence that Shepard's burglaries were generic burglaries according to the ACCA, and the court refused to impose the 15-year mandatory minimum sentence. The government appealed, and the First Circuit Court of Appeals reversed the district court. Shepard appealed to the U.S. Supreme Court who heard the case. The U.S. Supreme Court reversed the appellate court, holding that the government had failed to show that Shepard's burglaries were generic in the context of the ACCA, and furthermore, it would be improper for a sentencing court to look to police reports in making a "generic burglary" decision under the ACCA as the government had earlier requested.

■ *United States v. Booker*

___U.S.___, 125 S.Ct. 738 (2005). Booker and another defendant in an unrelated case, Fanfan, were convicted in separate jury trials in different federal district courts of cocaine distribution. In Booker's case, a 21-year, 10-month sentence was prescribed for his conviction offense by the U.S. Sentencing Guidelines. However, during the sentencing hearing, the judge found additional facts by a preponderance of the evidence to support a sentence of from 360 months to life and gave Booker a 30-year sentence. In Fanfan's case, a judge made a similar finding and imposed a harsher sentence, 16 years instead of the 6 years prescribed by the U.S. Sentencing Guidelines, on Fanfan. Both cases were appealed, Booker's to the seventh Circuit and Fanfan's to the First Circuit. Both circuit courts overturned these convictions, holding that any fact(s) that increase the penalty for a crime beyond the prescribed statutory maximum must be submitted to a jury and proved beyond a reasonable doubt. The government appealed both cases

(continued)

BOX 10.1 *(continued)*

and the U.S. Supreme Court heard them. The U.S. Supreme Court affirmed the circuit court decisions and vacated the enhanced sentences for both Booker and Fanfan. The U.S. Supreme Court held that the federal sentencing guidelnes are subject to Sixth Amendment jury trial requirements, and that if a judge authorizes a punishment on the finding of a fact, that fact, no matter how the judge labels it, must be found by a jury beyond a reasonable doubt.

more structured one, a sentencing system that will obligate sentenced offenders to make frugal use of institutional resources in becoming rehabilitated. Thus, with new sentencing guidelines, the Washington Sentencing Guidelines Commission expects to address the following issues: truth in sentencing, prosecution standards, sentencing standards and ranges, juvenile dispositions, and mentally ill offenders (Champion 2005b).

Perhaps the most immediate impact of newly implemented presumptive sentencing guidelines is the reduction of sentencing disparities, where similar offenders receive widely divergent sentences (Davis-Frenzel and Spohn 2004). In Minnesota, for example, a 22 percent decline in **sentencing disparity** was observed to occur in the year following the implementation of guidelines. A 60 percent reduction in sentencing inequality for the length-of-time-in-prison decision was also observed. But even presumptive sentencing guidelines can be circumvented by creative sentencing judges (Geoghagan 2004). One way of seemingly curbing such abuses of discretion is through mandatory sentences where judges must impose specific terms regardless of their own views and prejudices (Piquero and Davis 2004).

Mandatory Sentencing

Mandatory sentencing is the obligatory imposition of a specified period of years and/or months for specific types of offenses. Judges are bound to impose a **mandatory sentence** for certain types of conviction offenses. For instance, Michigan has a mandatory penalty of two years for using a gun during the commission of a felony. The use-a-gun-and-go-to-prison law in Michigan is added to whatever sentence is imposed when offenders are convicted. Thus, a bank robber might be sentenced in Michigan to twenty years, with an additional two years as a mandatory sentence for using a firearm when robbing the bank. When all or part of the offender's twenty-year term is served, a mandatory additional two years must be served by the offender for the weapons offense. The intent of this mandatory law is to discourage criminals from using weapons when they commit crimes. Weapons use reductions by criminals usually mean fewer serious injuries or deaths resulting from their crimes. The deterrent effect of Michigan's law and other states with similar laws is presently unknown.

Virginia Exile

One of the more recent gun control measures enacted by the states is Virginia's **Virginia Exile.** Virginia Exile, which went into effect on July 1, 1999, provides for a mandatory term of five years for anyone convicted of using a firearm during the commission of a felony. While this idea is not new in view of Michigan's two-year tack-on for essentially the same type of offense, the length of mandatory flat time is unique among other mandatory laws governing the use of firearms during commissions of felonies. Virginia Exile targets three crimes: (1) possession of a firearm by a convicted violent felon; (2) possession of a firearm on school property with the intent to use it, or displaying it in a threatening manner; and (3) possession of a firearm and drugs such as heroin and cocaine. The Virginia legislature has said that Virginia Exile gets straight to the point: a gun associated with drugs, felons, or school gets you five years in a Virginia prison. You will be going away—exiled—for a long time—no suspended sentence, no probation, and probably no bail. Virginia Exile is modeled after Richmond, Virginia's **Project Exile,** a highly effective federal, local, and state cooperative effort initiated by the U.S. Attorney's Office. Persons who are arrested by city police and charged with illegal possession or use of firearms have been prosecuted under federal laws that generally have provided stiffer penalties. Thus, this is a tough new effort designed to reduce gun violence throughout the state. Similar initiatives have been observed in other jurisdictions (Hemenway 2004).

The most important feature of mandatory sentencing is the obligation it places on judges to impose consistent sentences for a variety of convicted offenders, regardless of their gender, race or ethnicity, or socioeconomic status. Under these mandatory sentencing provisions, judges must impose specific sentences as authorized by their state legislatures. However, even mandatory sentencing policies may be circumvented. Prosecutors may choose to ignore those aspects of one's crime that carry mandatory penalties. Larger numbers of plea bargains are obtained if certain facts about one's crime are ignored. Armed robbery may be downgraded to simple robbery, for instance. The fact that a firearm was used in the offense is not mentioned. Even in the presentence investigation report prepared by probation officers, certain facts may be omitted. Thus, sentencing judges may never see the full set of circumstances involving the crime committed. If crimes with mandatory penalties are not included in the prosecutor's information or charges, and if these facts are also omitted in the plea bargain agreement, the judge imposes a sentence consistent with presumptive guidelines or determinate sentencing.

Such a scenario occurs too frequently throughout the United States, according to some critics. Many law-and-order proponents advocate greater truth in sentencing. If someone uses a gun when committing a crime, then this fact ought to be made known to the court. Further, if the convicted offender is a recidivist with prior felony convictions, this information ought to be made known to the court. All states have habitual offender statutes that apply to **habitual offenders** with lengthy criminal records. These persons are in jeopardy of being given a **life-without-parole-sentence** as a mandatory sentence for their conviction as habitual offenders.

HABITUAL OFFENDER STATUTES AND TRUTH IN SENTENCING

Habitual Offender Statutes

Chronic, persistent, and violent felony offenders pose the greatest risk to the public. These criminals commit new crimes frequently, and these crimes often result in serious victim injuries and/or deaths. There is also a broad class of chronic and persistent felony offenders who commit property crimes, such as larceny, vehicular theft, and burglary. All types of chronic recidivists have been targeted in recent decades for special and harsher treatment by the criminal justice system. Since the 1970s, virtually every jurisdiction throughout the United States has evolved habitual offender statutes (Champion 2005b). In some jurisdictions, these laws are called **persistent offender statutes.** Habitual offender or persistent offender statutes are laws that proscribe life sentences for those who are convicted of three or more felonies.

The intent of habitual offender statutes is to incapacitate those who persist in committing crimes. If these high-rate offenders are removed from society, then some crime prevention or crime control occurs. The primary problem is that there are so many persistent and chronic felony offenders that there isn't enough prison space to house them for extended terms. Furthermore, more than a few inmates convicted as habitual offenders have filed lawsuits challenging their lengthy prison sentences compared with the nonserious nature of their conviction offenses. These are usually *habeas corpus* actions, where relief is sought in the form of sentence reductions (Fletcher 2004). Also, some experts do not consider these statutes as particularly beneficial as deterrents or methods of crime control (Freedman 2001; Hack 2003).

Who Are Habitual Offenders?

A key problem confronted by all jurisdictions with habitual offender statutes is defining who are the habitual offenders. Do habitual offenders include all types of offenders, or is the definition limited to those committing only the most serious and violent types of felonies? This problem seems universal in nature.

England, for instance, has been vexed by the problem of habitual offender legislation and its inability to provide precise guidance about who qualifies as habitual offenders. Are habitual offenders only violent criminals who pose an immediate threat to society, or are they also the bumbling petty thieves and property offenders?

Florida has attempted to refine the habitual offender definition by establishing a limited number of categories and a guideline matrix (Champion 2005b). Thus, not every Florida felon with numerous convictions qualifies as habitual offender. Further, Florida law provides for gradations in offense seriousness and whether certain convicted offenders will be classified as habitual offenders.

A subsequent study of the application of Florida's habitual offender statute has generated an offender database consisting of 25,806 persons eligible for habitualization. Interestingly, only 18 percent or 4,783 persons from this database were actually prosecuted and convicted as habitual offenders (Florida Joint Legislative Management Committee 1992). This finding is consistent with the earlier work of Hunzeker (1985) who found that although every state has habitual offender statutes, relatively few inmates are serving sentences as habitual offenders. In fact, eight states have reported that 2 to 3 percent of the inmates were serving terms as habitual offenders. Nine states reported that less than 1 percent of their inmate populations were serving terms as habitual offenders.

The consensus is that while all states have habitual offender statutes, most states do not enforce these habitual offender statutes with any consistency (Champion 2005b). More often than not, prosecutors in most jurisdictions use habitual offender statutes as mechanisms of coercion to elicit guilty pleas from persistent offenders. Thus, prosecutors threaten to prosecute particular habitual criminals as habitual offenders unless they agree to plead guilty to other crimes. This sort of leverage is perfectly legal and is not considered coercive by the U.S. Supreme Court (*Bordenkircher v. Hayes*, 1978).

Narrowing the Habitual Offender Definition: Three-Strikes-and-You're-Out!

In recent years, the federal government and various states have enacted provisions to punish more serious felons with harsh punishments if they are convicted of three or more felonies. Such legislation is termed **three-strikes-and-you're-out.** Essentially, offenders convicted of three serious felonies are out in that they are sentenced to life terms in prison. The get-tough movement and general public seem supportive of legislation aimed at incapacitating persistent felony offenders (Ueckert 2005).

California is one of several jurisdictions where three-strikes-and-you're-out legislation has been passed. Under this new three-strikes legislation, it is mandated that felons found guilty of a third serious crime must be locked up for twenty-five years to life. However, the long-term effect of such legislation on California's correctional population is grim. California does not have suffi-cient prison space to accommodate all of these offenders presently, despite the fact that it has one of the nation's most vigorous prison construction programs in progress (Stephenson-Lang 2005).

A **cost-benefit analysis** of this new sentencing legislation has been con-ducted by the Rand Corporation under the direction of researcher Peter Greenwood and others (Greenwood et al. 1994). Greenwood investigated three-strikes legislation according to arrest rates, time served, prison popula-tions, and length of criminal careers. He found that if the new law were fully implemented as written, serious felonies committed by adults would decrease by 22 to 34 percent. A third of all felonies eliminated (by incarceration) would be violent crimes such as murder and rape. The reduction in these types of crime would cost the California public about $4.5 to $6.5 billion annually, largely attributable to the costs of incarceration. Greenwood has speculated that California may not be able to afford this crime reduction as the law is presently written.

A Felony Is a Felony Is a Felony . . .

Some attempt has been made by California and other states to limit the types of offenses that qualify under the habitual offender statute and three-strikes legislation. Distinctions have been made between those who commit **violent felonies** (rape, murder, aggravated assault, armed robbery), **serious felonies** (robbery, drug dealing), and **felony property offending** (larceny/theft, vehic-ular theft, burglary). In theory, at least, the most serious persistent felons will be given twenty-five years to life, while less serious felons will receive shorter sentences. But few states, including California, have found the three-strikes legislation to be effective in reducing violent crime (Ueckert 2005).

Furthermore, three-strikes legislation has sometimes resulted in greater racial and ethnic discrimination by targeting proportionately larger numbers of blacks and others for long mandatory sentences. In California, for instance, blacks are arrested at a rate 4.7 times greater than whites; blacks are incarcer-ated 7.8 times greater than whites; and blacks are incarcerated as habitual of-fenders at a rate that is 13 times greater than whites. California is not an isolated case, however. Disparities in mandatory sentencing laws according to race, gender, socioeconomic status, and ethnicity have been found to exist in other jurisdictions (Champion 2005b).

Use-a-Gun-and-Go-to-Prison Statutes

Not all mandatory penalties involve **life imprisonment** or life without parole. Some mandatory penalties are intended to downgrade the seriousness of vio-lent crimes whenever they are committed. One way of discouraging some violent offenders from using firearms when committing their crimes is to provide mandatory sentences of incarceration whenever firearms are used (Lightfoot and Umbreit 2004). Other types of mandatory penalties are associated with crimes such as repeat-offense driving-while-intoxicated cases.

Michigan has enacted a mandatory penalty for using a firearm during the commission of a felony. This penalty is a **flat term,** two-year sentence that must be served following whatever other sentence is imposed. Thus, if someone is convicted of armed robbery, a sentence of ten to twenty years might be imposed for the armed robbery charge, and then a separate sentence of two years will be added on to the original sentence. This second sentence must be served in its entirety. If the offender is parole-eligible after serving fifteen years of the ten- to twenty-year sentence, then the two-year sentence commences. No time off for good behavior will be extended to those serving these mandatory sentences. California enacted such a law over a decade before Michigan (Champion 2005b). Presently, most states have such mandatory sentencing provisions for firearms usage whenever felonies are committed.

Many of these mandatory sentences are primarily symbolic, in that they show the public that the legislature and other politicians are concerned about public safety and citizen fear of crime. Frequently, mandatory penalties are circumvented by defense counsel, prosecutors, and judges through plea bargaining, where the violations incurring mandatory penalties are carefully omitted from any reports or written documents. Many presentence investigation reports are doctored by probation officers at the request of prosecutors, so that judges will be more willing to impose variable sentences under indeterminate or determinate sentencing. If judges don't know whether particular defendants used a firearm when a felony was committed, then they cannot be compelled to impose mandatory penalties, even in Michigan. However, more than few jurisdictions have made it increasingly difficult for these mandatory sentencing provisions to be circumvented. The federal sentencing guidelines and changed roles of U.S. probation officers have greatly restricted the degree to which certain aspects of one's crime can be ignored (Champion 2005b).

Truth in Sentencing

The federal Crime Bill of 1994 provided in part for monies to states that changed their sentencing provisions in the direction of harsher sanctions. For instance, convicted offenders in 1994 North Dakota typically served about 35 to 40 percent of their maximum sentences. Offenders sentenced to 10 years, therefore, would usually serve about 3 1/2 to 4 years and then be paroled. Because of the incentive of federal money, North Dakota changed its sentencing policy in 1995 so that all convicted offenders would have to serve at least 85 percent of their maximum sentences before becoming parole-eligible. This type of sentencing reform is known as **truth in sentencing** (Ostrom,

Cheesman, and Jones 1999). The get-tough movement and general public have been alarmed over the fact that inmates in North Dakota and many other states have been serving only fractions of their maximum sentences.

While **truth-in-sentencing laws** have been enacted and the public's feelings have been assuaged to a degree, corrections has had to find more space for those offenders spending longer terms in prison. The direct result of truth-in-sentencing has been enormous prison population growth. Prison overcrowding is now a characteristic of all U.S. prisons. A significant contributing factor has been the **Crime Bill of 1994.** President Bill Clinton promoted this bill to provide for greater numbers of police officers on city streets as a means of preventing crime. Another provision of this bill was to maximize offender sentences so that convicted persons must serve between 80 and 90 percent of the maximum sentences before being granted early release or parole.

Originally, the intent of truth-in-sentencing provisions was to make sure that inmates would serve a large portion of their prison terms (McManimon 2005a). While this event has occurred in those jurisdictions where it has been mandated by state legislatures, other problems have been created. For instance, in 1994 North Dakota was one of six states without an overcrowding problem. Its state prison in Bismarck could house about 650 inmates. Shortly after enacting truth-in-sentencing laws, however, the North Dakota Penitentiary quickly became overcrowded and a new prison facility had to be built in Jamestown. In 1998, North Dakota officials were planning two additional **tiers** in the Jamestown prison facility as dramatic increases in the inmate population were projected. Thus, North Dakota taxpayers now face unprecedented tax increases to help defray some or all of the new prison construction. While the public may want greater truth-in-sentencing and longer prison terms for inmates, they may not want to pay the dollar cost of new prison construction in order for this policy to remain in place. North Dakota is not alone in dealing with prison overcrowding, however (Steiner and Wooldredge 2005).

Sentencing Disparities: Race/Ethnicity, Gender, and Socioeconomic Status

Sentencing disparity takes several different forms (Dobbs 2004). Disparities in sentencing may occur when different judges within any given jurisdiction impose vastly different sentences on offenders charged with similar crimes (McManimon 2005b). Judges may be inclined to be more lenient with female offenders compared with their male counterparts. Blacks and Hispanics may receive harsher sentences compared with whites when the same kinds of offenses are involved. Older offenders may receive less harsh sentences from judges compared with younger offenders, even when the same crimes have been committed (McManimon 2005b; Roy 2004).

Promoters of sentencing reforms have been quick to point out these sorts of deficiencies in our sentencing system. Many states are modifying their existing sentencing systems from an indeterminate to a determinate form. Such changes are almost always accompanied by reductions in sentencing disparities attributable to racial, ethnic, gender, or socioeconomic qualities. The influence of race, ethnicity, gender, and socioeconomic status on sentencing severity and sentencing disparities generally has been investigated extensively (Weidner, Frase, and Pardoe 2004).

Race and Ethnicity

Different jurisdictions report variations in sentencing attributable to race. A study of 183 defendants in Leon and Gadsden County Circuit Courts in Tallahassee and Quincy, Florida, revealed, for example, that black appellants who were sentenced in excess of the recommended maximum sentence were more likely to have the trial court's recommendation affirmed on appeal (Williams 1995a, 1995b). Thus, at least in these jurisdictions, appellate decision making is far from "routine" as otherwise reported by official sources.

An investigation of sentencing disparities among 685 white and black women in Alabama during the period 1929–1985, whites who killed interracially were the most likely to have light sentences (of 1 to 5 years) compared with blacks who killed interracially. Black women who killed interracially tended to receive moderate to heavy sentences (6 to 10 or 11 to 20 years) (Hanke 1995). Also, a sample of 755 defendants prosecuted for burglary and robbery was examined. In Tucson, being Hispanic made no difference on the type of adjudication received, the verdict, or sentence severity. However, in El Paso, Hispanic defendants were more likely to receive less-favorable pretrial release outcomes than white defendants, were more likely to be convicted in jury trials, and consistently received more severe sentences when they were found guilty at trial. Interviews with DAs and other officials in both cities indicated that these disparities may be partially attributable to differing language difficulties in the two jurisdictions, different mechanisms for providing attorneys to indigent defendants, and differences between established Hispanic Americans and less well-established Mexican American citizens and Mexican nationals (LaFree 1985).

Despite the increasing attention given to sentencing disparities and the sentencing reforms established to correct such disparate sentences, there is considerable evidence to indicate that racial and ethnic sentencing disparities are becoming more disproportionate rather than diminishing (Van Zyl Smit and Ashworth 2004). Blacks are overrepresented at virtually every processing stage in the criminal justice system, and they are increasingly included in incarcerated populations. Scholars report that such disproportionate representation of blacks is due to greater offending rates of blacks, and such reports are supported by the literature. However, at the root of such disproportionate representation of blacks and other minorities in the criminal justice system are poverty and un-employment. It has been recommended, for instance, that greater use of special circumstances should be exercised by judges when sentencing minority offenders. With more honest sentencing policies, less disproportionate sentencing should occur that is attributable to race or ethnicity (Williams and Holcomb 2004).

Sentencing disparities attributable to race differences are particularly noticeable in the South. It has been shown, for instance, that for 21,169 convicted felons in Georgia for the years 1973–1980, blacks tended to receive longer sentences compared with whites (Clayton 1983). As a matter of fact, blacks received sentences that were on the average 2.5 years longer than sentences for whites convicted for the same crimes. Similar disparities have been observed and are considered pervasive regarding capital cases (Sorenson and Wallace 1995).

Gender

Do women tend to receive more lenient sentences compared with men? A study of 1,027 male and female offenders in Minneapolis, Minnesota, who were convicted of theft, forgery, or drug law violations between 1972 and 1976 revealed that sex status does have a significant effect on sentencing severity in that women receive more lenient sentences compared with men who have committed similar offenses (Kruttschnitt 1984). Women not only received more lenient sentences, but they also received more lenient treatment related to pretrial release. And in a related study of 1,558 convicted males and 1,365 convicted females in Minneapolis between 1965 and 1980, it was found that women were more likely to receive pretrial release than men as well as less severe sentences for similar offenses (Kruttschnitt and Green 1984).

Other research has been largely supportive of the Minnesota study. For example, Daly and Bordt (1995) conducted an extensive statistical review of sentencing disparity literature to determine whether "sex effects" favoring women over men in sentencing exist. Over half of the fifty studies surveyed indicated that gender effects favoring women over men existed. Both older and more recent data sets reveal similar patterns, where females have received more lenient sentences compared with sentences for male offenders.

Investigations have also been made of the relation between gender and the application of the death penalty in capital cases. Both surveys of citizens and actual patterns of capital punishment use in selected states reveals that females convicted of capital crimes are far less likely to receive the death penalty compared with men convicted of a capital crime under similar circumstances (Vollum, Longmire, and Buffington-Vollum 2004). Further, citizens surveyed tended to favor more lenient treatment for females convicted of capital offenses (i.e., life-without-parole sentences as opposed to death sentences). One explanation for gender differentiation is the chivalry hypothesis, which is that decision makers or judges tend to treat female offenders with chivalry during sentencing, and further that judges will be inclined to dispense selective chivalry toward white females compared with other females or minorities of either gender (Kakar 2004). Data from 9,866 felony theft cases and 18,176 felony assault cases from California courts in 1988 show that females with no prior record were more likely to receive charge reductions compared with male offenders. Also, female offenders' chances for probation were increased greatly compared with a similar aggregate of male offenders (Champion 2005a).

As more states adopt reforms including presumptive and determinate sentencing systems, fewer sentencing disparities will be observed from one jurisdiction to the next. Also, judges seem to favor greater uniformity in their sentencing practices within the same jurisdictions. The adoption of consistent sentencing standards will gradually eliminate patterns of gender, ethnic, or racial discrimination in sentencing in future years.

Socioeconomic Status

One's socioeconomic status plays a significant part in explaining sentencing disparities. Offenders whose resources are limited cannot afford private counsel, and less-experienced public defenders are often appointed to defend them (Weiss 2004). Further, the sentencing guidelines in many states tend to overpenalize street crimes, which are most often committed by those with lower socioeconomic status (Wooldredge and Griffin 2004).

Evidence of sentencing disparities attributable to one's socioeconomic status is considerable. Studies of sentencing patterns in southeastern states have shown that there is an inverse relation between one's socioeconomic status and sentence length (D'Allessio and Stolzenberg 1993). When 2,760 convicted offenders were examined, those of lower socioeconomic status drew longer sentences than those of higher socioeconomic statuses. Thus, it was concluded that this extralegal factor was significant in explaining differential sentence lengths of offenders, controlling for one's criminal history and conviction offense (D'Allessio and Stolzenberg 1993). Other research has supported the idea that those with lower socioeconomic status are disenfranchised by the criminal justice system. However, the influence of socioeconomic status may adversely affect certain persons of higher socioeconomic statuses. A survey of white-collar offenders sentenced in seven U.S. district courts tended to receive imprisonment more often compared with comparable offenders of lower statuses, and furthermore, the sentences imposed on white-collar offenders were longer (Weisburd, Waring, and Wheeler 1990). The general consensus seems to be that lower socioeconomic status offenders will tend to receive harsher and longer sentences compared with offenders of higher socioeconomic statuses, although there are always exceptions.

THE SENTENCING HEARING

When offenders are convicted, they are sentenced by a judge to a term of years, either on probation or in jail or prison. In most felony cases, before offenders are sentenced, they must have a **sentencing hearing.** A sentencing hearing is a proceeding where evidence and testimony is presented both for and against the offender. The hearing furnishes the sentencing judge with additional information about the offender, the crime, and the victims. In the context of this additional information, judges can make an informed decision about the best sentence to impose. Oral testimony is given by anyone who has relevant information. Usually, testimony is given by the offender and those speaking on his behalf. Victims and their families also offer their opinions and tell how they were affected by the offender's actions. This oral testimony is considered by the judge in making the sentencing decision.

Weighing the Aggravating and Mitigating Circumstances

The sentencing hearing is also important because it permits the judge to consider **aggravating circumstances** and **mitigating circumstances.** Aggravating circumstances are those factors that tend to intensify the severity of the punishment. Aggravating factors include whether the crime involved death or serious bodily injury, whether the offender was out on bail or on probation at the time the crime was committed, whether the offender has a prior criminal record, whether there was more than one victim, whether the offender was the leader in the commission of the offense involving two or more offenders, whether the victim was treated with extreme cruelty by the offender, and whether a dangerous weapon was used by the offender when committing the crime (Fryling 2005).

Mitigating circumstances are those that tend to lessen the severity of punishment. Mitigating circumstances include whether the offender was cooperative with police and gave information about others who may have been involved in the crime, whether the offender did not cause serious bodily injury or death to a victim, whether the offender acted under duress or extreme provocation, whether there was any possible justification for the crime, whether the offender was mentally incapacitated or was suffering from some mental illness, whether the offender made restitution to the victim, whether the offender had no previous criminal record, or whether the offender committed the crime to provide necessities for himself or his family.

Judges consider these aggravating and mitigating circumstances, and it is determined whether the aggravating circumstances outweigh the mitigating ones. If this is the case, then judges can mete out harsher sentences. However, if the mitigating circumstances outweigh the aggravating ones, then judges can be more lenient with offenders in their sentencing decision (Fryling 2005).

When the jury or judge finds the defendant guilty, a sentence is not imposed immediately. Sentencing hearings are usually scheduled four to six weeks following the trial. Within the context of due process, defendants are presumed innocent of any crime until they are proven guilty beyond a reasonable doubt in court. When this event occurs, most judges wish to gather additional information about the convicted offender, the circumstances surrounding the commission of the crime, and the impact of the crime upon the victim(s). Probation officers are most frequently assigned the task of researching the background of each convicted offender in an effort to furnish judges with a fairly complete package of information. This information is compiled in a presentence investigation report or PSI. A **probation officer** needs time to gather all relevant information, and thus, this explains the lapse of time between conviction and sentencing. Probation officers interview the offender's employer, relatives, friends, church and school officials, and victims. The offender's criminal history is described as well. All of this information is summarized in the PSI report and submitted to the judge. Defendants are also given the opportunity to describe their involvement in the crime and to take responsibility for what they did.

THE PRESENTENCE INVESTIGATION REPORT (PSI): CONTENTS AND FUNCTIONS

A presentence investigation report or PSI report is a written summary of information obtained by probation officers concerning an investigation of the convicted offender's background and other relevant evidence about the nature of the crime's commission and implications of the crime for all relevant parties, including victims. A sample presentence investigation report form for Iowa is shown in Figure 10.1.

The Iowa PSI report is a fairly standardized document and is typical of those PSI reports prepared in other state jurisdictions. An inspection of this report shows that although it consists of 6 pages, considerable background information must be compiled. Notice that the following information is required: the names of the judge, prosecutor, and defense attorney (private or appointed); county, file number, date PSI ordered, due, and completed; docket or file number of case and location of court; name, address, telephone number, marital status, and dependents of defendant; whether home is rented or owned; how long defendant has lived at the address provided; occupation and income; Social Security number; employer and gross monthly income; education, military service record, if any, type of discharge, and general physical condition; prior criminal record; instant offense, seriousness, and offense classification;

PRESENTENCE INVESTIGATION

Date

August 10, 2006

Name and DOB

John Choi
November 20, 1972

PRESENT OFFENSE

Description of Offense

Attempted Sexual Assault. Offense date is November 3, 2005. This offense involves an incident in which a 29-year-old nude woman's body was discovered on a rural road. The body had been decapitated, and the woman's head and articles of bloody clothing were discovered on another road three miles away. It was discovered that the woman, in an intoxicated condition, had accompanied some men from a tavern who reportedly took the woman to their apartment, forced her to engage in sexual intercourse, then at least one of the men attacked the woman with a kitchen knife, cut her throat, then decapitated her. Four men were eventually charged in the offense, including the defendant, Mu Chou (life sentence), Bok Suk Kim (life sentence), and Raymond Phu (10 years). Mr. Choi admits that he resides at the apartment where the offense occurred, but denies any involvement in or knowledge of the offense until his arrest two weeks later. He was not released on bond. Rationale: "I never see girl, I don't know about it."

Offender's Version

The subject is a 34-year-old Chinese National male, first-offender, who is currently confined in the Briggs Unit facing a 10-year sentence in Deschutes County for one count of Attempted Sexual Assault. The subject states that on or about November 3, 2005 during an unknown time he allegedly committed the offense of Attempted Sexual Assault on a 29-year-old female, but he denies the Attempted Sexual Assault and any knowledge of the woman's murder or decapitation. He admits to occasional marijuana use at age 27; admits to three prior arrests resulting in a two-year probationary term for DWI. He states that he left the apartment for an unknown period of time, and when he returned, his friends and the woman were gone. He admits that there was blood on the floor and in the bedroom where the woman was allegedly raped by the other men.

Victim's Statement

Not applicable

PRIOR RECORD

Juvenile Record

No record of juvenile arrests

Adult Record

Three prior arrests for DWI; sentenced to two years probation; claims completed.

Pending Charges

One detainer warrant from U.S. Immigration "Hold"

FIGURE 10.1

Presentence Investigation Report Example from Iowa

Correctional Experience

Good jail report from Deschutes County Jail from jail authorities

Offender's Explanation of Record

Claims no contact with father, mother, or two siblings; claims single; residence unstable; education claims high school completed; employment claims "laborer"; home stability poor due to lack of contact with family; admits to experimental use of marijuana at age 27; current offense of Attempted Sexual Assaulting a 29-year-old female and allegedly cutting her head off, subject denies; speaks little English.

PERSONAL HISTORY

Academic/Vocational Skills

Subject states he completed 12 years of school in China. Subject worked as "laborer" but did not elaborate on what "laborer" did.

Employment

Worked as "laborer" at various jobs in different states; would not disclose which establishments employed him. No information is available on Choi about subject's past educational level or occupations in his native country of China. He has been in English classes in Indiana for about a year prior to Choi to Iowa. While in Iowa the subject worked in a few different jobs. He bussed tables in a restaurant, worked in a furniture factory, and did some janitorial work. He then moved to Des Moines where he worked for the ABC Packing Company as a meat cutter.

Financial Management

Has given no indication of ability to manage financial affairs.

Marital/Alternate Family Relationships

Has not seen family for many years.

Companions

Has no close associates presently. Admits to knowing other men who were convicted of woman's murder only because they were also Oriental and in the tavern when he was there. He admits to being drunk when he left tavern but denies any involvement in woman's murder.

Emotional Health

See attached Psychiatric Evaluation.

Physical Health

Transferred to mental health unit at Briggs for psychiatric and psychological evaluation. Subject was referred because he was mute, refused to eat, and exhibited unusual behavior. Subject appeared detached, withdrawn, in distress, and depressed. His blood pressure was low, he had lost much weight, and he appeared to be dehydrated. He would give no information to medical staff. He would sit in one place on his bunk for seven or eight hours at a time. At that time he stated that he was very nervous and scared. He had been making statements that he needed to stay in prison because he would not have anything on the outside now. He flooded his cell on one occasion and became quite unresponsive. His physical and mental condition deteriorated further. He lost 26 pounds of weight because he was not eating. He was transferred to the medical unit for acute care. When received, the subject was on Haldol C, 15 mgs. TID, and Cogentin, 2 mgs. BID. The subject may have been a suicide risk and was placed on suicide precaution status. The subject began to eat on the second day of his admission. The subject is being treated for a positive TB test with INH. The file reflects no other medical problems at this time.

Mental Ability

The subject is now 34 years old, frail looking, Chinese male who was dressed in a disheveled Department of Corrections white uniform. He looked undernourished. He was mute and had poor eye contact. He was able to answer one question by head movement at one time. His mood seemed depressed to euthymic. He had an inappropriate smile at some part of his evaluation. There was no indication that subject had delusions or hallucinations, although he reportedly has history of having fairly loose delusions and grandiose delusions in the past. The rest of his mental status examination was not tested because of his uncooperativeness and because he remained mute.

Chemical Usage

Subject admitted to using marijuana and drinking beer. Presently on prescribed medications as indicated.

Sexual Behavior

Convicted of Attempted Sexual Assault, subject denies. Has no close friends or acquaintances.

Military

None

Religion

Born into Buddhist faith; now is non-denominational.

Leisure Activities

None determined.

Residential History

Taipei, Taiwan	1972–1995
Lafayette, Indiana	1995–1996
Des Moines, Iowa	1996–present

SUMMARY AND CONCLUSIONS

Agent's Impressions

Choi is a Line Class I inmate, unassigned due to his mental health status. He needs recreational therapy. He does not attend any educational, vocational, or character development programs due to his mental status. He is not a gang member. Choi is receiving INH for TB prevention. Choi denies any mental health treatment in society and denies suicide attempts. Choi has been diagnosed with Schizoeffective Disorder, Bipolar Type Rule Out Bipolar Disorder, Mixed with Psychotic Features, Rule Out Schizophrenia, Chronic, Catatonic Type with Acute Exacerbation. Alcohol use in remission. Addicted to Cannabis, in remission due to incarceration. Interviews with Choi indicate that he is unwilling or unable to relate any new information to this officer about his present offense. Choi maintains he is not guilty and claimed he did not know any details about the present offense until he was arrested. Choi claims he does not know if he was ever physically or sexually assaulted and has never been married and has no children. Choi claims he cannot remember if he engaged in sex with prostitutes. Due to the subject's past probation for DWI, it appears he may need monitoring in the area of alcohol usage. He may also benefit from psychological counseling.

FIGURE 10.1

(continued)

Restitution Information

Not applicable

Recommendation

Recommend that Choi be confined in mental unit at Briggs until such time as his eating behavior is stabilized. Recommend Choi for psychological counseling. Statutory punishment of 10 years should be imposed. Choi must accept responsibility for his actions, since this officer interviewed two other persons convicted of the murder and they give consistent accounts of Choi's involvement in the female victim's murder and decapitation. Both subjects accused Choi of committing the decapitation and joking about it later. Other than mental problems contained in psychiatric evaluation, there are no outstanding mitigating circumstances that would cause this officer to recommend sentencing leniency or a shorter incarcerative term at this time.

1. Confinement is necessary to protect the public from further criminal activity.
2. The subject is in need of correctional treatment that can most effectively be provided through confinement.
3. Nonconfinement would unduly depreciate the seriousness of the instant offense.

Probation is not recommended.

_____

Phillip L. Marlowe, Probation Officer, Deschutes County

PSYCHIATRIC EVALUATION
IOWA DEPARTMENT OF CORRECTIONS

NAME: John Choi
IDOJ#:   47324568
DATE: July 15, 2006
EXAMINER: Jane Cummings, M.D.

SOURCE OF INFORMATION:

Patient and IDOC Records.

PERTINENT MEDICAL HISTORY:

The patient's chart indicates that he has tuberculosis Class II and he is currently taking medication for this. He has no allergies to medications.

PERTINENT PSYCHIATRIC AND LEGAL HISTORY:

Reports in patient's brown chart indicated that he has a history of psychiatric hospitalizations and was given the diagnoses of Psychotic Disorder, NOS, Alcohol Abuse, and Cannabis Abuse. During that hospitalization, he was given Ativan 1 mg po hs prn for his complaint of having difficulty with his sleeping. He was also treated with other psychotropic medications prior to his discharge. His final diagnosis was Schizophrenia, Chronic, Undifferentiated Type, Alcohol Abuse, and Cannabis Abuse. His previous records also indicated that he had experienced delusional thinking such as thinking that he has special powers and special knowledge of prediction of the future, and he had worldwide powerful activities. His mental status on his psychiatric hospitalization indicated that he made a statement that he went with too many gods in the war, saw them and talked to them, go with them anywhere and that they told him things about the CIA and the life of Americans and that the American religions were always at odds with his religion. Social History done at Briggs indicated that patient reported being arrested one time in Indianapolis, Indiana for not having any money for a bus ticket. He reportedly spent a week in jail and a friend paid the fine and got him out. He was also arrested once in Lafayette, Indiana for driving while intoxicated. He was released and was told to appear in court which he did not do and which led to his being arrested later for failure to appear. He reportedly paid a fine and as a result was discharged. The patient is reportedly serving a ten-year sentence for murder.

FAMILY HISTORY:

There is no available information about the patient's family or history of medical or psychiatric illness at this time.

SOCIAL HISTORY:

This information is obtained from the social history compiled during the patient's hospitalization at Briggs. The patient was reportedly born in Taipei, Taiwan and his family all reside in Taipei. He reportedly went to school there. He was not married. He came to the United States in 1995 as a refugee, is staying in Indiana for one year, and worked in a factory in Des Moines, Iowa for three years prior to his present incarceration. For additional Social History, please read Social History in the brown chart.

MENTAL STATUS EXAMINATION:

The patient is 34 years old, frail looking, Chinese male who was dressed in a disheveled white IDOC uniform. He looked undernourished. He was mute and he had poor eye contact. He was able to answer one question by head movement at one time. There were no indications that patient had delusions or hallucinations. The rest of his mental status examination was not tested because of his uncooperativeness and for him remaining mute.

SUMMARY OF POSITIVE FINDINGS AND TARGET SYMPTOMS:

This 34-year-old male reportedly came to the United States as a refugee in 1995 and has been living with friends in Des Moines prior to his incarceration. He reportedly is serving a 10-year sentence for murder. His records indicated that he has a history of delusions and hallucinations and was hospitalized at a mental hospital with a diagnosis of Undifferentiated Schizophrenia, Alcohol Abuse and Cannabis Abuse. He reportedly was observed to have unusual behavior at Briggs, remaining mute and not making eye contact with anyone and was observed looking at his wall while in his cell. He also started refusing to eat causing him to lose weight. The patient was transferred to the medical unit at Briggs electively mute and not eating although he started eating the next day. The patient at this time remains mute although he started to answer by moving his head. It is possible that this patient has a Schizoaffective Disorder and a possible Bipolar Disorder in addition to his history of Alcohol and Cannabis Abuse.

DIAGNOSIS:

Axis I: 295.70 Schizoaffective Disorder, Bipolar Type
              Rule Out Bipolar Disorder, Mixed with Psychotic Features 296.64
              Rule Out Schizophrenia, Chronic, Catatonic Type with Acute Exacerbation 295.24
              305.00 Alcohol Abuse, in remission due to incarceration
              305.20 Cannabis Abuse, in remission due to incarceration
Axis II: 799.90 Deferred
Axis III: Tuberculosis Class II
Axis IV: Severe (incarceration and no family support)
Axis V: Current GAF: 20   Highest GAF Past Year: 0

FIGURE 10.1
(continued)

PROGNOSIS:

Poor.

_____

Jane Cummings, MD

RECOMMENDATIONS:

It is recommended that Inmate Choi be kept in acute care until he is stabilized. He should do well on a dorm unit once he has achieved some remission.

PROGNOSIS:

Guarded.

_____   _____

Raul Ortega, ACP III   William G. Johnson, Ph.D.

Staff Psychologist   Supervising Psychologist

REASON FOR REFERRAL:

Inmate Choi was informed that the contents of this report would be shared with the appropriate treating personnel and the evaluation was completed following inmate's tacit consent.

This inmate is a thin, frail, 34-year-old Chinese male who understands English better than he can speak it. Records indicate that he has been hospitalized before. His travel card indicates that he is serving time for Rape. He allegedly cut off the victim's head. There is some question as to whether he might have been charged with the crime, and did not actually participate in the decapitation. This was a gang-rape situation. Inmate Choi has been electively mute since his admission to Briggs. He will look at this examiner, however, he makes no verbal response. Records indicate that he has experienced delusional thinking in the past. He has verbalized special powers, special knowledge, and has been able to predict the future. He has been diagnosed with Psychotic Disorder, NOS, Schizoaffective Disorder, Depressed, and Schizoaffective Disorder, Bipolar Type. There has also been some question as to whether or not he may be a catatonic schizophrenic.

MENTAL STATUS:

Inmate Choi cannot be interviewed or tested at this time because of his refusal to talk. He does not appear to be attending to hallucinations. He appears flat, withdrawn, depressed, detached, and medicated.

PSYCHOMETRICS:

Not applicable.

This is a real PSI and psychiatric evaluation of an offender who is currently incarcerated in another state. The names of the offender, accomplices, probation officers, and physicians were changed for reasons of confidentiality.

date of offense and arresting agency; days in custody following arrest; co-defendants if any; victim and victim address; defendant's version of crime (offender's **sentencing memorandum**); investigating officer's version of crime or **narrative;** other information including defendant's reputation, attitude, leisure-time activities, associates; comments by probation officer about sentencing alternatives, treatment proposals, community service; and mandatory attachments, including criminal information/complaint, law enforcement investigation report, and victim impact statement (if applicable).

Probation officers sometimes locate school officials and associates of the offender and interview them. Likewise, victims and their families are interviewed. Probation officers summarize this information and make their own recommendations to the judge. Judges consider the PSI report in making their sentencing decision. It is important to note that both the sentencing hearing testimony and the contents of the PSI report are considered by the judge. None of this information, even the recommendation of a sentence by the probation officer, binds the judge in any way. The judge has already presided at the trial where all relevant evidence was introduced. Judges know the facts of the case. Thus, they may contemplate a particular sentence. But before the actual sentence is imposed, judges have one final opportunity to consider any additional relevant information.

For instance, defendants do not have to testify in their own criminal trials. The sentencing hearing, therefore, gives them a chance to speak, to apologize, and to accept responsibility for what they have done. **Acceptance of responsibility** for one's crimes is considered important as the first step toward rehabilitation (Champion 2005b). Sometimes judges are persuaded to be more lenient in cases where convicted offenders admit the wrongfulness of their actions and express genuine regret for what happened. However, additional testimony from victims may persuade the judge to deal more harshly with offenders when it is learned how much the lives of others were adversely affected by the offender's crime (Champion 2005b).

Functions of PSI Reports

The functions of PSI reports are to (1) provide information for offender sentencing, (2) aid probation officers in determining the most appropriate treatment or rehabilitative programs for offenders in need of assistance, (3) assist prisons and jails in their efforts to classify offenders effectively, and (4) furnish parole boards with important offender background data to assist them in determining one's early release. Probation officers attempt to solicit the most accurate information about the offender and victims. The contents of PSI reports are disclosed not only to judges, but to prosecutors and defense counsel as well. This is to ensure that they are accurate reports. Disclosures of the contents of PSI reports are usually mandated by legislative provisions for both the states and federal government. Two important components of PSI reports are the offender's sentencing memorandum and victim impact statements (Champion 2005b).

The Offender's Sentencing Memorandum

A **defendant's sentencing memorandum** is a document prepared by the convicted offender that describes the crime, why it was committed, and the attitudes and feelings of the offender concerning his/her involvement. The memorandum also provides an opportunity for the offender to accept responsibility for the crime.

In recent years, the phrase *acceptance of responsibility* has become an increasingly important part of the sentencing process. The U.S. Sentencing Commission provided that acceptance of responsibility would enable sentencing judges to possibly mitigate one's sentence. Various states have added acceptance of responsibility to their sentencing provisions. Thus, offenders who make full admissions regarding their crimes and apologize for these crimes in open court during the sentencing hearing may incur some leniency from judges. It is insufficient to merely declare, "Your honor, I'm sorry for what I've done and I accept responsibility for my actions." Much depends on the circumstances and sincerity of the person making such an admission. Many convicted offenders learn to act contrite and make false statements about their acceptance of responsibility. Judicial discretion is accorded great weight here. If the judge is convinced that the offender has truly accepted responsibility for the crime, then the judge may decide to mitigate the harshness of the penalties imposed. Defense counsel are often key players in the sentencing process. They have one final opportunity to summarize the facts as they see them and to make a case for judicial leniency toward their client.

Victim Impact Statements and Victim Input

Another important part of the sentence mosaic is the victim impact statement (VIS). Victim impact statements are oral and/or written testimony concerning how the victims and their close relatives were affected by the offender's crime. The nature of victim impact is very important, since judges can learn much more than what was originally disclosed about the crime during the trial. Most jurisdictions in the United States permit victims and their relatives to provide written and/or oral evidence of how the offender's crime has affected them. VISs are also used in other countries, such as Canada (Phillips 1997).

The inclusion of VISs in sentencing hearings is not new. Many states have provided for victim involvement in the sentencing process in past years. Between 1980 and well into the 1990s, victim involvement in sentencing decisions has dramatically increased (Phillips 1997). In 1987 the admissibility of

VISs was prohibited by the U.S. Supreme Court in the case of *Booth v. Maryland*. However, by 1992, the U.S. Supreme Court changed its position to allow VISs in most criminal proceedings, including sentencing hearings (*Payne v. Tennessee*).

One reason for increased victim participation in sentencing decisions is that more than a few citizens regard the criminal justice system as far too lenient on offenders, particularly those who have committed violent felonies. Many factors enter into the judge's sentencing decision besides victim impact, however. Sometimes there are logistical constraints, such as chronic prison overcrowding, such that not all convicted felons who deserved to be imprisoned actually are imprisoned. California, for instance, places about 70 percent of its convicted felons on probation annually. This fact disturbs critics of the criminal justice system as well as the general public.

In an effort to make judges more accountable and impose sentences more in line with the seriousness of the offense, victims and their families have attempted to provide information that will cause judges to deal with offenders more harshly. Investigators have studied VISs and whether judicial sentencing practices have been influenced, either one way or another, in different jurisdictions. Little evidence exists today to show a direct correlation between how victims have been affected by one's crime and the severity of sentences imposed by judges (Phillips 1997). However, there is evidence that victim participation in sentencing has a cathartic effect. This means that victims and their families who participate in the sentencing hearing tend to be more satisfied with the sentences imposed by judges. It has been suggested that victim participation may not directly influence judicial sentencing decisions, but victims or their relatives may feel as though their input *was* somehow influential nevertheless.

Experiments have been conducted with mock juries in death penalty proceedings. At North Carolina State University, for example, 99 undergraduate students were asked to place themselves in the position of jurors in a hypothetical death penalty case. Other students acted as victims and gave testimony about a convicted offender who had murdered their relative. Later, the students were polled to determine whether the VISs were influential in any way concerning whether the death penalty would be applied. Significant numbers of students disclosed that the VISs were important in persuading them to vote for the death penalty, where the death penalty or life-without-parole penalties were options. While this experiment involved students reacting to an imaginary scenario, this does provide some evidence of how actual jurors might react to similar testimony from real victims in capital trials. Other researchers have arrived at similar conclusions (Jacoby and Bronson 2004; Unnever and Cullen 2004).

VISs may sometimes contain factual inaccuracies. Sometimes victims and their families may exaggerate the adverse effects of the offender's actions, particularly where property losses were involved. Some studies have revealed that

BOX 10.2 CASE LAW ON VICTIM IMPACT STATEMENTS

■ *Booth v. Maryland*

482 U.S. 496, 107 S.Ct. 2529 (1987). Booth was convicted of first-degree murder in a Baltimore, Maryland court. During his sentencing hearing, a victim-impact statement (VIS) was read so that his sentence might be enhanced or intensified. Following the sentence of death, Booth appealed, alleging that the VIS was a violation of his Eighth Amendment right against cruel and unusual punishment. The U.S. Supreme Court agreed and said that during sentencing phases of capital murder trials, the introduction of VISs is unconstitutional. Among its reasons cited for this opinion, the U.S. Supreme Court said that VISs creates an unacceptable risk that a jury may impose the death penalty in an arbitrary and capricious manner. At the time, therefore, VISs were considered unacceptable and inadmissible during the sentencing phase of one's trial. The U.S. Supreme Court's position about VISs changed in 1991 in the case of *Payne v. Tennessee*.

■ *Payne v. Tennessee*

501 U.S. 808, 111 S.Ct. 2597 (1991). Payne was convicted of a double murder. At the sentencing hearing, Payne introduced various witnesses on his behalf to avoid the death penalty. During the same hearing, the victims' relatives introduced their victim impact statement, pressing the jury to impose the death penalty on Payne. The death penalty was imposed and Payne appealed, contesting the introduction of damaging evidence and opinions expressed in the victim impact statement. The U.S. Supreme Court upheld Payne's death sentence, holding that victim impact statements do not violate an offender's Eighth Amendment rights. The significance of this case is that it supports and condones the use of victim impact statements against convicted offenders during sentencing hearings. Presently, VISs are considered admissible during the sentencing phase of one's trial.

female offenders are more favorably treated by victims compared with male offenders whenever VISs are provided (Booth 2004).

VISs have additional uses. Further into an offender's processing and imprisonment, VISs may be relied upon by parole boards in determining whether any particular offender should be granted early release. Any written VISs are maintained in an offender's file and used by parole board members whenever an inmate's early-release eligibility occurs. Further, some victims may participate in parole hearings and give additional oral testimony about why the offender should be denied parole (Myers et al. 2004). However, not all victims present oral testimony against their victimizers. In some cases, victims will speak in favor of one's early release during parole hearings. While these cases are exceptional, they do occur with some frequency (Booth 2004).

IMPOSING THE SENTENCE

When sentences are imposed by judges, they are guided by information provided in PSI reports, the offender's sentencing memorandum, probation officer recommendations, victim impact statements, and their own interpretation and consideration of the offender and the crime's seriousness. Depending upon the sentencing scheme used in each jurisdiction, judges may be bound to sentence offenders in a consistent way. That is, all convicted bank robbers in a given jurisdiction are supposed to receive a specified sentence as punishment, with consideration given to any present aggravating or mitigating circumstances. But judges are permitted latitude under almost every sentencing scheme (Fryling 2005). This is judicial discretion.

Each judge relies upon previous rulings in similar cases and attempts to be fair and impartial when meting out a specific sentence (Austin et al. 1995). Special consideration may be given to one's age in the case of elderly offenders. If an offender is mentally ill, retarded, or in some other way impaired, judges may take these impairments into account for virtually every type of special offender. Judicial sentencing decisions may be challenged, but appellate courts are inclined to assume that the original sentence imposed was the right one. It is difficult to overcome such a presumption on appeal.

SHOCK PROBATION AND SPLIT SENTENCING

Where judges are permitted great latitude in their sentencing discretion, they are inclined to impose probation for many first-offenders convicted of minor offenses or less serious felonies. Offenders sentenced to some form of probation are assigned by the judge to a probation department or some community corrections agency where their behavior will be supervised for a period of time (Champion 2005b).

One type of sentence designed to shock or scare convicted offenders, particularly those who have never served time in a prison or jail, is **shock probation, shock incarceration,** or **shock parole.** Shock probation and shock parole refer to planned sentences whereby judges order offenders imprisoned for statutory incarceration periods related to their conviction offenses. However, after 30, 60, 90, or 120 days of incarceration, these offenders are taken out of jail or prison and resentenced to probation or parole (Champion 2007). Ohio introduced shock probation for the first time in 1965. Since then, shock probation has spread to almost every U.S. jurisdiction.

The intent of shock probation is to literally shock or frighten convicted offenders through the incarceration experience (Champion 2005b). No one wants to be imprisoned. For those who have never been confined for either short or long terms, the experience of being behind bars for one or more months is sufficiently traumatic to deter them from further criminal activity. Early evidence suggests that the recidivism rates among shock probationers are relatively low compared with other probationers who have not been imprisoned for short periods (Vito 1984).

Split Sentencing

In several jurisdictions, judges may engage in **split sentencing.** Split sentencing, also known as **mixed sentencing, intermittent sentencing,** and **jail as a condition of probation,** are combination sentences imposed by judges, a portion of which includes incarceration and a portion of which includes probation. If an offender has committed more than one offense, then the judge may impose a separate sentence for each offense. One sentence may be one year in jail, while the other sentence for the second offense may be probation. Thus, this mixed sentence means that the offender will spend some time in jail as well as on probation.

Intermittent sentences involve offenders who are sentenced to partial confinement. These offenders may be sentenced to a jail on weekends, but they may be permitted freedom during the week to work at a job and support themselves and their families. Jail as a condition of probation is where the judge orders the offender to serve a specified term of months in a jail before being placed on probation (Vito 1984). The intent of these split sentencing options is to dramatize the seriousness of the offender's crime. Serving some time in jail or prison will make the point that crime is bad and should be avoided. Otherwise, imprisonment will result. This simplistic view underscores the fact that many shock probationers take this experience to heart and never reoffend. The effectiveness of shock probation varies among jurisdictions. Generally, however, shock probationers tend to have lower rates of recidivism compared with other types of offenders (Champion 2005b).

THE DEATH PENALTY AND BIFURCATED TRIALS

The most serious sentence criminal courts can impose is the death penalty. The death penalty is reserved only for those who have committed capital crimes, primarily murder. In recent years, the death penalty has been approved for use in cases where certain federal offenders have been convicted of large-scale drug dealing.

The death penalty is controversial. However, surveys during the 1990s reveal that about 75 percent of all U.S. citizens support its use as a suitable punishment for capital offenses. In 1997, Timothy McVeigh was convicted of bombing a federal building in Oklahoma City, Oklahoma, and he was given the

BOX 10.3 CAREER SNAPSHOT

Dennis R. Longmire
Sam Houston State University

Statistics: Ph.D. (criminal justice and criminology), University of Maryland, Institute for Criminal Justice and Criminology; M.A. (criminology), University of Maryland, Institute for Criminal Justice and Criminology; B.A. (sociology), Towson State College

Biographical Sketch: I began my career as a criminologist after concluding my formal education in 1979. I worked for a year as an assistant professor of criminal justice at California State University–Long Beach and then moved to Ohio State University where I worked as an assistant professor in the Department of Sociology. In 1984 I accepted the position of Assistant Dean of Graduate Studies at Sam Houston State University, where I also served as Associate Dean until 1993 when I left the administrative responsibilities behind to enjoy the life of a full professor. I am internationally recognized for my work in the death penalty abolition movement and serve as co-advisor to the Sam Houston State University's student group of Amnesty International. I am on the advisory boards of the Houston/Harris County Chapter of Murder Victim's Families for Reconciliation, the *Texas Death Row Journal,* and the Texas Coalition to Abolish the Death Penalty. During Texas's last legislative session, I provided expert resource testimony for committees in both the House and Senate. As a resident of Huntsville, Texas, I regularly hold a prayer vigil at the corner of 12th Street and Avenue I on the evening of each execution, and I was recently featured in the *Contemporary Justice Review*'s "Justice Profile" for my work in this area.

What Attracted Me to the Field and the Study of the Death Penalty: When I was taking a class in juvenile delinquency as an undergraduate student, I read about the Outward Bound Programs, which were designed to help delinquent youths develop patterns of inner strength that would give them necessary coping skills to avoid the temptations of crime and delinquency that seemed to be all too present in their (our) lives. At that time in my life, I knew that I wanted to do something aimed at prevention and reform rather than punishment and control. I naively thought that I would pursue a career in social work with a special focus on the needs of the youth and that I would be able to do this. I spent a brief time working with the juvenile probation system in Baltimore City and then as a correctional officer in a maximum security prison in Maryland (the infamous Paxtuent Institution). Both of these real-world experiences led me to the realization that there were serious problems with the systems of justice we had constructed to deal with juvenile and adult offenders, and that these systems needed to be reformed before we could even begin to reform the offenders. This realization led me to graduate studies at the University of Maryland where they had just instituted a new graduate program focusing on criminal justice and criminology.

Very early in my graduate studies, I came to a second realization about the systems of justice operating in the United States: They are driven more by who you are than by what you have done. Whether we talked about this in the context of arrest, prosecution, conviction, or delivery of sanction, conclusions were the same. At that time, the scholarship being written under the rubric of Marxist, critical, radical, humanist, or anarchist criminology seemed to offer the most accurate descriptions of the reality of how the systems of justice I had worked in actually operated and gave me a general frame of reference to draw from as I continued to struggle with questions about how these systems needed to be reformed. I was also introduced to the scholarship offered under the context of critical legal theory and quickly concluded that there was little hope that we could reform the entire system of justice at once, but that we could begin to make significant changes in different aspects of the system by focusing attention on specific areas of justice. The U.S. Supreme Court announced in its decision to re-authorize the death penalty in the collection of cases referred to as the *Gregg v. Georgia* in January 1976, and at that moment I realized that this was one area of reform that should be given priority over all others. While I could see that the biases in the systems of justice were endemic and that the entire system of law was, in my mind, in need of considerable reform, the most pressing issue seemed to be in the delivery of the ultimate sanction: the penalty of death. In my mind, there could be no real hope for justice as long as we continued to authorize the state to exercise this ultimate form of punishment knowing that everything leading up to it was influenced by the socioeconomic and political biases that were so much a part of the administration of law at that time in our history.

Unfortunately, as I understand the current statistics describing the way our justice systems work, little has changed since I began my career as a student of criminal/juvenile justice. Our juvenile and adult justice systems continue to target people of color and people with little economic or political status. Our laws continue to be enforced differentially depending on who you are rather than what you have done, and in many ways we have become even more calloused to these differences because of a false sense of equality that has been claimed following the civil rights movement. I continue to hope that we can reform the systems by calling attention to the inequities and biases that show themselves so obviously when we study the demographics of who is selected to receive the ultimate sanction.

Advice to Students: The basic things I try to teach everyone who comes into contact with me is to think critically and to focus your critical thoughts

(continued)

BOX 10.3 *(continued)*

toward the question of justice. Reflect on what this concept means to you and try to re-form your understanding of it on a daily basis. The field of criminal justice/criminology is driven by some fundamental belief in a principle called "justice," but relatively little time is spent reflecting on what this principle is and how it is reflected in the actions of lawmakers, law enforcers, and other administrators of justice working in the various agencies we refer to as criminal/juvenile justice agencies. Engage yourselves in the pursuit of justice rather than the enforcement of law and do not be afraid to ask questions about how or why the agencies operate the way they do.

death penalty for his role in this crime that killed 169 persons. Another participant in this bombing is Terry Nichols. In a separate federal trial, Nichols was convicted as a conspirator in the bombing and the federal prosecutor sought the death penalty in his case. However, the jury was unable to agree on which punishment should be imposed. The federal court sentenced Nichols to life without parole instead of death.

Furman v. Georgia (1972) and Gregg v. Georgia (1976)

The death penalty is used as the maximum punishment in about two-thirds of all states. The minimum age for executing persons in the United States is 18 (*Roper v. Simmons*, 2005). In 1972, the constitutionality of the death penalty in Georgia was challenged. Disproportionately large numbers of blacks were being executed compared with whites, often in cases involving rape or assault. In 1972 the U.S. Supreme Court declared in *Furman v. Georgia* that the death penalty as it was currently being applied in a discriminatory manner in Georgia was unconstitutional. All states temporarily suspended the death penalty until more information could be obtained from the U.S. Supreme Court about the procedural appropriateness of the death penalty and its application.

In 1976, the U.S. Supreme Court held in *Gregg v. Georgia* that the revised procedural application of the death penalty in Georgia was constitutional. States resumed the application of the death penalty shortly thereafter. Gary Gillmore, a Utah murderer, was executed by firing squad in 1979 and was the first person executed after the U.S. Supreme Court approved of Georgia's new method for imposing death penalties on those convicted of capital crimes (Merlo and Benekos 2004). The U.S. Supreme Court approved Georgia's legislative revision of the death penalty statute, which called for a **bifurcated trial** in all capital cases.

Bifurcated Trials

A bifurcated trial is a two-stage proceeding wherein the first stage consists of the main trial, where one's guilt or innocence is established; if an offender is found guilty of the crime, the jury meets in a second stage to consider the punishment and whether the death penalty should be imposed. Aggravating and mitigating factors are weighed by juries, and the death penalty will be recommended to the judge in those instances where the aggravating factors outweigh the mitigating ones (Kremling, 2004).

Bifurcated trials are presently commonplace in those states with death penalty provisions. Bifurcated trials permit juries to consider both aggravating and mitigating circumstances (Gants 2005; Levine and Petitt 2005). It is believed that the nature of bifurcated trials overcomes the criticisms of those who believe that the death penalty is applied in a discriminatory manner. One's race is not a factor in these two-stage proceedings. We have already examined the common set of statutory aggravating and mitigating circumstances that juries consider.

Another feature of bifurcated trials is that death penalties can no longer be automatically applied. It used to be the case on some felony murders or when police officers were killed during a crime that those convicted of such crimes would automatically be sentenced to death. The *Gregg* case was significant in causing these automatic death penalty statutes to be declared unconstitutional. The 1980 case of *Woodson v. North Carolina* held that automatic death penalties were unconstitutional anyway, even though the essence of this holding was conveyed in *Gregg* four years earlier. The main reason is that automatic death penalties do not permit juries to weigh any possible aggravating or mitigating circumstances.

APPEALS OF SENTENCES

The Purposes of an Appeal

Once defendants have been convicted of crimes, they are entitled to at least one appeal to a higher court. The primary purpose of an appeal is to correct a wrong that may have been committed. These wrongs may be mistakes by police, the prosecution, or the court. Errors may have occurred that influence the trial outcome. Appeals are intended to correct these mistakes and errors.

A secondary purpose of an **appeal** is to render judgment about one or more issues that will influence future cases. Thus, when an appellate court hears a case from a lower trial court, their decision becomes a precedent for subsequent similar cases. This is the doctrine of *stare decisis,* meaning that once a higher court has ruled a particular way on a particular issue, lower courts are bound to make rulings consistent with higher court holdings whenever similar cases are heard. However, trial court judges have some discretion in deciding whether certain subsequent cases resemble previous cases where appellate courts have ruled. Thus, trial court judges may decide that although a subsequent case is similar in various respects to previous cases already decided by higher courts, there may be sufficient differences in the cases so that trial judges decide that the higher court rulings do not apply.

Appeals of Sentences

All death sentences are automatically appealed (Champion 2005b). The appellate process for any case, capital or otherwise, begins by filing an appeal with the most immediate appellate court above the trial court level. When offenders are convicted in federal district courts, for instance, their appeals are directed to one of 13 different circuit courts of appeal. In California, for example, Stacy Koon and Laurence Powell were two police officers convicted in a federal district court of inflicting great bodily harm upon a motorist, Rodney King, under color of their police authority. Under the U.S. sentencing guidelines, these former officers were supposed to be sentenced to several years of prison. However, the federal district judge downgraded the seriousness of their offense and sentenced them to time served. The U.S. Attorney's Office in Los Angeles filed an appeal with the Ninth Circuit Court of Appeals, contending that the reasons cited by the federal judge for downgrading their offense were not appropriate. The Ninth Circuit reversed the trial judge and reinstated the original sentence called for under the U.S. Sentencing Guidelines. Koon and Powell appealed, this time to the U.S. Supreme Court, since this is the court of last resort above the circuit courts of appeal.

In capital cases originating in state courts, state remedies must be pursued on appeal before the federal system is accessed. For instance, a person convicted of murder in Tennessee and sentenced to death must direct his/her appeal first to the court of criminal appeals. If there is an unfavorable ruling by that appellate court, then the offender can direct an appeal to the Tennessee Supreme Court. If the ruling by this court is unfavorable for the offender, then a direct appeal may be made to the U.S. Supreme Court for relief.

Appellants and Appellees

Appellants are persons who initiate appeals. **Appellees** are those who prevailed in the trial court and argue against reversing the decision of the lower court. Those convicted of capital crimes and sentenced to death are appellants. In most instances, the state is the appellee. Cases are given names to fit the two parties. Thus, we have *Furman v. Georgia*, *Gregg v. Georgia*, *Woodson v. North Carolina*, or *Payne v. Tennessee*. In each of these cases, the appellant is mentioned first and the appellee second. There are many grounds on which to base appeals (Unnever and Cullen 2004). Further, appeals in most death penalty cases cause these cases to drag out over a period of 10 to 15 years before the appellants are eventually executed (Harmon 2004).

Bases for Appeals

Appeals may be directed to appellate courts on diverse grounds. Appellants may raise questions before appellate courts about how they were originally arrested and processed. They may challenge the admissibility of certain evidence used to convict them. They may claim incompetence or ineffective assistance of counsel (Albonetti and Barron 2004). They challenge the sentence imposed by the judge. Almost every one of these challenges about what happened at different points in their processing as criminal defendants can be included within the scope of a *habeas corpus* petition.

Habeas Corpus *Petitions*

Habeas corpus means literally produce the body. A *habeas corpus* petition challenges three things: (1) the fact of confinement, (2) the length of confinement, and/or (3) the nature of confinement. The fact of confinement involves every event that led to the present circumstances of the appellant (Belbot et al. 2004). If the appellant is on death row resulting from a capital offense conviction, then any aspect of the justice process leading to the offender's placement on death row is a potential *habeas corpus* target (Westervelt and Cook 2004).

For example, the fact of confinement was challenged in the case of *Preiser v. Rodriguez* (1973). Rodriguez was a state prisoner who was deprived of good-time credits by the New York Department of Correctional Services because of disciplinary proceedings. Rodriguez filed a *habeas corpus* petition. The lower court dismissed the petition, saying that it was not relevant for challenging the fact and duration of one's confinement. However, the U.S. Supreme Court overturned the lower court decision, holding that when state prisoners are challenging the very fact or duration of their physical confinement, and the relief sought is a determination that they are entitled to immediate release from that imprisonment, the sole federal remedy is a writ of *habeas corpus*.

The length of confinement has been challenged numerous times by prisoners who feel that their sentences are too long and disproportionately harsh in relation to the crimes they have committed. In the case of *Hutto v. Davis* (1982), for instance, Roger Davis was a Virginia inmate who had been sentenced to 40 years in prison and a $20,000 fine for a conviction for marijuana possession with intent to distribute. Davis sought *habeas corpus* relief, contending that the 40-year sentence was disproportionate to the crime, and thus, it was cruel and unusual punishment. Ultimately, after considerable hearing and rehearing through the appellate process, the U.S. Supreme Court decided the matter by upholding Virginia authority to mandate sentences for crimes as they see fit without labeling such sentences as cruel and unusual. In Davis's case, the 40-year sentence was legislatively mandated, and thus, the U.S. Supreme Court believed that it would be improper to interfere with state legislative sanctions. Davis's sentence was therefore upheld.

The **conditions of confinement** of jails or prisons are frequent grounds for *habeas corpus* relief. Prisoners who are ordered confined in jails rather than prisons for long periods may object to the lack of facilities and amenities in jails that would ordinarily be found in prisons. If prisoners had a choice, they would almost always wish to be confined in a prison, where there is a broad array of facilities and services for long-term inmates. Most jails are designed for inmates serving short sentences of less than a year. Thus, no attempt is made by most of these jails to furnish their inmates with weight rooms and saunas, a general store, outdoor or indoor recreational facilities, or other amenities.

In the case of *Youngberg v. Romeo* (1982), Romeo was a mentally retarded individual with a history of violence. Subsequently he was involuntarily committed to a state mental hospital, where he sustained numerous physical injuries at the hands of others. A *habeas corpus* action was filed by his mother on his behalf, alleging that her son is entitled to safe conditions of confinement, freedom from bodily restraints, and training or rehabilitation. The U.S. Supreme Court heard the case and declared that Romeo is entitled to conditions of reasonable care and safety, reasonably nonrestrictive confinement conditions, and such training as may be required by these interests. The judge gave an improper jury instruction in Romeo's subsequent civil proceeding when he advised the jury to consider the standard of cruel and unusual punishment as set forth in the Eighth Amendment.

Another conditions-of-confinement case was *Hutto v. Finney* (1978). In 1970, the Arkansas prison system was declared unconstitutional on various grounds through a *habeas corpus* petition filed by inmates. The U.S. Supreme Court ruled that the conditions of confinement were cruel and unusual, violative of the Eighth Amendment. Subsequently, a check by federal officials revealed that the reforms to be implemented had not been completed. The Court issued additional orders for prison official compliance. These orders included (1) limiting the number of prisoners who could reasonably be confined in one cell, (2) discontinuing particular types of nonnutritious meals, (3) maximizing the days of **solitary confinement** or **isolation** as punishment to 30, and (4) obligating the state to pay for attorneys' fees and expenses. Hutto, the Arkansas commissioner of corrections, appealed, contending that the 30-day confinement standard was too lenient and that the court had wrongfully assigned attorneys' fees to the state. The U.S. Supreme Court heard the case and upheld the lower court. The 30-day punitive limitation on solitary confinement was upheld as well as the assessment of attorneys' fees against the state.

Habeas corpus relief is also sought for a myriad of problems arising from the time offenders are arrested all the way through to their sentencing dispositions. For instance, in the case of *Frazier v. Cupp* (1969), Frazier was convicted of murder in Oregon. Prior to his conviction, Frazier was indicted together with his cousin, Rawls, who entered a guilty plea to the same murder. Some question arose about whether Rawls would actually testify against Frazier, and whether the prosecutor ought to rely on such testimony. The prosecutor made statements in his opening remarks to the jury about what they could expect to hear from Rawls. This and other statements by the prosecutor were regarded as prejudicial to Frazier, especially a prosecutorial reference to a confession made by Rawls implicating Frazier. Also, when Frazier was being questioned by police, he made a passing reference to "I had better get a lawyer," but he continued to answer questions. His appeal to the U.S. Supreme Court through a writ of *habeas corpus* was that his Miranda rights had not been observed when questioned by police and that there was prosecutorial misconduct and that his due process rights had been violated. The U.S. Supreme Court upheld his conviction and rejected his claims. The prosecutor's comments were harmless errors and Frazier had been advised of his Miranda rights and had simply failed to exercise them.

Sometimes, offender/petitioners allege that the sentencing judge acted inappropriately by making prejudicial remarks in front of the jury. In the case of *Arave v. Creech* (1993), for instance, Creech was convicted of the murder of another inmate while confined in the Idaho Penitentiary. At his trial and sentencing, the judge sentenced him to death and based his decision, in part, on aggravating circumstances. He used the phrase, utter disregard and the cold-blooded pitiless slayer. Creech appealed the sentence, contending that the phrase *utter disregard* was facially invalid. The U.S. Supreme Court upheld Creech's conviction, holding that the phrase *utter disregard* does not violate any constitutional provisions.

Also, inmates will file *habeas corpus* petitions where they believe prosecutors acted in bad faith or engaged in improper conduct, such as suppressing exculpatory evidence. In one case (*Arizona v. Washington*, (1978), for instance, George Washington was convicted of murder, but an Arizona court granted Washington a new trial because the prosecution had withheld exculpatory evidence during discovery. At the beginning of the second trial, defense counsel made various remarks in his opening statement concerning hidden information from the first trial. The prosecutor moved for a mistrial, which was granted. Washington was subsequently convicted in a third trial. However, later as an inmate, Washington filed a *habeas corpus* petition seeking to have his conviction overturned because of the trial judge's decision to declare a **mistrial** in the second trial. Washington contended that the judge's decision to declare a mistrial was erroneous and that this led to his being placed in double jeopardy by a third trial. The U.S. Supreme Court rejected Washington's arguments, holding that the mistrial was properly declared by the judge. Thus, no previous trial had been concluded with an acquittal where Washington was again being tried for the same offense.

Another reason for seeking *habeas corpus* relief is for ineffective assistance of counsel. If convicted offenders believe that they were not properly represented by counsel since they were convicted, they may allege that their counsel was ineffective. Most of these types of petitions are denied by the U.S. Supreme Court. In the case of *Darden v. Wainwright* (1986), Willie Darden was a convicted murderer under sentence of death. He filed a *habeas corpus* petition challenging the exclusion of a juror from his earlier trial, allegedly improper remarks made by the prosecutor during his summation to the jury, and ineffective assistance of counsel. One prospective juror had been excused by the judge when the juror declared a moral and religious opposition to the death penalty, which was one option in Darden's case. Prosecutorial remarks regarded by Darden as improper were references made to Darden's furlough program at the time he committed murder, and that the prosecutor referred to him as an animal. The third allegation involved a one-half hour preparation by Darden's attorney between the trial's guilt phase and the trial's penalty phase. Darden did not believe this time interval gave his attorney sufficient time to prepare an adequate mitigation statement. The U.S. Supreme Court rejected all of Darden's arguments. The U.S. Supreme Court held that jurors may be excused from death penalty cases where their religious views or moral feelings would render them unable to vote for a death penalty if warranted. Further, the emotional rhetoric from the prosecutor was insufficient to deprive Darden of a fair trial. Finally, evidence showed that the defense counsel spent considerable preparatory time for both the trial and mitigation statement during the penalty phase.

Additional reasons for *habeas corpus* actions include allegations that the judge gave the jury improper instructions (*Cabana v. Bullock*, 1986); failure of the court to provide counsel to the offender or to determine whether a guilty plea was indeed voluntary (*Carter v. People of State of Illinois*, 1946); failure of one's counsel to inform the offender of possible sentence enhancements because a firearm was used during the commission of a felony (*Custis v. United States*, 1994); the search by police was conducted without a **warrant** where the circumstances required the issuance of one before the search would be lawful (*Gerstein v. Pugh*, 1975); and that cyanide gas is a cruel and unusual punishment (*Gomez v. United States District Court*, 1992).

Over the years, inmates have frequently abused the writ of *habeas corpus* by submitting numerous petitions with frivolous claims. The U.S. Supreme Court has limited such filings in recent years so that inmates and others cannot continue to abuse such petitions. Currently, the use of *habeas corpus* has been severely limited so that inmates must set forth all arguable issues encompassed by *habeas corpus* and not use a separate *habeas corpus* action per issue (*Delo v. Stokes*, 1990). For instance, Winford Stokes was convicted of capital murder

BOX 10.4 WRONGFUL CONVICTIONS IN DEATH PENALTY CASES

One of the most devastating things that can happen in the criminal justice system is to wrongfully convict a defendant of a capital crime (Mullendore 2005). It is unknown how many innocent persons are presently housed on death rows throughout the United States. Depending upon the statistics or organizations consulted, such as Amnesty International or the American Civil Liberties Union, the estimates vary. While it is quite likely that most persons on death rows are guilty of their crimes and have been convicted by solid, direct evidence showing their actual involvement and participation, a few death row inmates were convicted on the basis of circumstantial evidence and/or perjured testimony (Dykstra and Mullendore 2005). Two cases where it was proved that persons were innocent of a capital crime but were convicted of one anyway involve Joseph Burrows and Ronald Jones.

■ **Joseph Burrows**

On November 8, 1988, an 88-year-old retired farmer, William Dulan, was found murdered in Iroquois County, Illinois. A few hours later, a cocaine addict, Gayle Potter, attempted to cash a $4,050 check in Dulan's name at the Iroquois Farmer's State Bank. She was promptly arrested and charged with murder. Almost immediately Potter implicated two other persons: Ralph Frye, a retarded acquaintance, and Joseph Burrows, who Potter said was the triggerman who shot Dulan. Both Frye and Burrows were arrested by Illinois authorities and questioned. Burrows had an alibi. At the time of Dulan's murder, Burrows was in the company of four other persons 60 miles away from the crime scene. After a lengthy interrogation, however, Frye corroborated Potter's version of events and stated that Burrows was the triggerman. The police recovered the murder weapon, a firearm belonging to Potter. Potter also had a gash on her head, which was attributed to a struggle with Dulan. Her blood was found at the crime scene. No physical evidence could be found, however, which linked Burrows to the crime in any way. No evidence linked Frye to the crime either, although he subsequently admitted to being an accomplice under intensive police questioning. Despite his denials of any involvement in the crime or knowledge of it, Burrows was convicted of capital murder and sentenced to death. Because of their cooperation in the case and identifying Burrows, Potter and Frye both received prison sentences.

Burrows was actually tried twice. The first trial ended in a hung jury, where agreement about his guilt or innocence could not be reached. He was convicted in a second trial, however. Two years later, Frye spoke with a reporter with the *Champaign-Urbana News-Gazette,* and he disclosed that he had lied about being involved in Dulan's murder as well as implicating Burrows. Frye, with an IQ of 76, stated that Potter had put him up

(continued)

BOX 10.4 *(continued)*

to lying. He also claimed that police had intimidated him into giving a confession about his role in the crime. When the reporter's story ran in the newspaper, several appellate attorneys became involved and sought a new trial for Burrows. In the meantime, a letter written by Potter to one of her friends asking him to lie for her in the Dulan case was discovered by Burrows's attorneys, Kathleen Zelner and Michael Hemstreet. When Potter was confronted with the letter, she admitted she had lied and falsely implicated Burrows. Armed with this evidence, Burrows's attorneys launched a successful appeal, which resulted in the state overturning Burrows's murder conviction over strong prosecutor objections. Reluctantly, Illinois authorities released Burrows from prison. Burrows now works for a landscaping company in the Champaign-Urbana area.

■ Ronald Jones

On March 10, 1985, a 28-year-old mother of three was raped and murdered in South Chicago. Although the crime remained unsolved for over 6 months, investigators chased down various leads. One involved a homeless alcoholic who was loitering in the area where the murder had occurred. The man was Ronald Jones, 34. Jones was picked up by police officers and interrogated at length by detectives. Eventually Jones confessed to the crime, admitting that he had ejaculated during the rape. During Jones's trial, Jones recanted his confession, claiming that the detectives had beat it out of him. He claimed that one detective used a blackjack to hit him about the head, while the other punched him repeatedly in his stomach. The confession also included that the woman was a prostitute, although she had no prior record of prostitution. No physical evidence linked Jones to the crime, and the semen specimens retrieved from the woman's body and clothes were alleged to be insufficient in quantity to test. Jones was convicted of capital murder and sentenced to death in 1989. In 1994, an appellate public defender, Richard Cunningham, approached the trial judge, John Morrissey, and requested a DNA test of the semen specimen collected at the crime scene. The request was refused. Subsequently a higher court overruled Morrissey and a DNA test was conducted. The DNA results showed positively that Jones was not the semen donor, since his DNA didn't match the semen on the victim or victim's clothing. Despite this conclusive evidence of Jones's innocence, the state's attorneys were stubborn and refused to abandon the case. Jones continued to be confined for the next five years, while his attorneys sought a new trial. Eventually on May 17, 1999, Jones was released from prison after a new trial date for Jones was set. The state decided to back off and not pursue the case further. [Source: Center on Wrongful Convictions, Chicago, IL, February 14, 2003.]

and sentenced to death. Following several *habeas corpus* petitions where Stokes raised several issues on appeal, he was granted a stay of execution and Missouri prosecutors sought an appeal to the U.S. Supreme Court. The U.S. Supreme Court heard the state's appeal, and reversed a U.S. district judge's granting of a stay of execution in Stokes's case. It was determined that Stokes had raised four *habeas corpus* petitions earlier, and that he could have raised the present issue as a part of one of his earlier petitions. Thus, the U.S. Supreme Court said, it was abuse of judicial discretion for the federal judge to grant a stay of execution to Stokes when he filed his fourth petition. Thus, the application from the state to vacate the stay of execution is granted.

Furthermore, state prisoners must first exhaust all of their state appellate remedies before seeking relief directly from the U.S. Supreme Court. In the case of *Duckworth v. Serrano*, 454 U.S. 1 [1981]), a prisoner, Serrano, sought to challenge his conviction through a *habeas corpus* petition. He alleged that he was denied effective assistance of counsel at his trial, and thus his due process rights had been violated. Serrano had not sought relief in state courts first, however. The U.S. Supreme Court took significant notice of the fact that Serrano commenced his petition with the court of appeals in the Seventh Circuit, a federal appellate body, rather than in an Indiana state court. The U.S. Supreme Court dismissed his *habeas corpus* petition because he had failed to exhaust all state remedies. The significance of this case is that any petitioner who has been convicted of a state crime must first exhaust all state remedies before attempting to file petitions in federal courts. This is considered a landmark case because it obligates prisoners to direct their *habeas corpus* petitions first to state courts, before they pursue federal remedies. This decision is no doubt calculated to reduce crowded federal court dockets.

This was underscored in the case of *McCleskey v. Zant* (1991). This case limits access to the federal courts since all *habeas corpus* claims must be raised in the initial petition. McCleskey was charged with and convicted of murder and armed robbery. A cell mate of McCleskey's, Evans, was called to testify against him. Evans said that McCleskey boasted about the killing and admitted it. McCleskey was convicted and sentenced to death. He appealed, claiming that the cell mate-induced conversations were made without the assistance of his counsel. The U.S. Supreme Court rejected his claim, stating that it could have been made in an earlier appeal proceeding. The fact that McCleskey was making it in a subsequent proceeding nullified the claim. Thus, in order for such claims to be considered, they must be made in a timely way and at the right time, shortly after they occur; not after several appeals have been unsuccessfully lodged with state and federal courts.

New technological developments concerning identification of suspects through DNA testing or **DNA fingerprinting** and other forensic achievements have caused more than a few inmates to be released from prison after they have been determined to be innocent of the crimes for which they were originally convicted (Warden 2004). In order to obtain their release from prison or get new trials, inmates must file *habeas corpus* petitions. But the courts have been reluctant to cause old cases to be reopened, except under the most compelling of circumstances. This is consistent with the general policy change by the U.S. Supreme Court to make it more difficult in recent years for inmates to pursue *habeas corpus* writs without limit (Federman 2004).

Both the number of *habeas corpus* petitions filed by prisoners and the proportion of prisoners filing *habeas corpus* actions are declining steadily. Even in capital cases, *habeas corpus* appeals have declined. This is because of the greater restrictions imposed on such appeals by the U.S. Supreme Court and Congress. This trend is also observed in various states, including California (Atherton 2004).

Writs of Certiorari

A writ of *certiorari* is issued by a higher court directing a lower court to prepare the record of a case directing a lower court to prepare the record of a case and send it to the higher court for review. It is also a means of accessing the U.S. Supreme Court in order for a case to be heard. Writs of *certiorari*, especially from those on **death row,** must contain compelling arguments in order for the U.S. Supreme Court to grant them. Most writs of *certiorari* from those sentenced to death are denied. Of those petitions that are heard by the U.S. Supreme Court, only a handful each year result in the death penalty being overturned. Usually, the U.S. Supreme Court may order a new trial if a particularly strong argument is presented showing a flagrant constitutional rights violation.

The Lengthy Process of Appeals

Appeals of any kind, especially death penalty appeals, consume a great deal of time. On the average, it takes about 10 or 11 years for inmates to be executed. In some instances, the appeals process has dragged out over a 15-year period (Maguire and Pastore 2005). One reason for the lengthy appeals process is that prisoners have been allowed to file new petitions with either state or federal courts, under a variety of theories. While *habeas corpus* is the most frequently used type of appeal, there is almost no limit to the number of issues that may be raised by inmates and their counsel that could result in their convictions and/or sentences being overturned.

If an offender's case is reviewed by the U.S. Supreme Court and the Court rules in their favor, often the case is reargued in a new trial. When second or third trials occur, the results are almost always the same as the first trial. However, some evidence exists to show that sentencing judges may abuse their sentencing discretion and punish these offenders with harsher penalties than earlier prescribed. But the U.S. Supreme Court has usually condoned harsher sentences by judges, especially where judges have provided a logical written rationale for the enhanced or harsher sentence. Increased sentences have survived constitutional challenges as violations of double jeopardy, equal protection, and due process without limiting a trial judge's wide sentencing discretion (Wilmot 2002).

Initiating Appeals

Appeals are launched by appellants, or those who lose in the trial court. Most frequently, appellants are convicted offenders. They must first file a **notice of appeal.** A notice of appeal is a written statement of the appellant's intent to file an appeal with a higher court. Such notices are required within a fixed period of time following an offender's conviction.

A copy of the court record or complete transcript of proceedings is forwarded to the appellate court for review. Also, a **brief** is filed with the appellate court, outlining the principal arguments for the appeal. These arguments may pertain to particular judicial rulings, which are believed to be incorrect. Appellants are required to list the issues that are the substance of the appeal. If the appellant believes that 30 mistakes were committed by the trial judge, or if the prosecutor was believed to have made prejudicial remarks to the jury where such remarks are prohibited, or if the police did not advise the offender of his Miranda rights when arrested, all of these mistakes or errors should be listed in the brief or legal argument. These errors or mistakes are considered appealable issues. An offender's first appeal should contain all of these issues, since it is unlikely that courts will consider further appeals concerning omitted issues.

Appellants, or those who succeed in the trial court (usually the prosecution) may file briefs as well, noting why they believe there were no procedural irregularities or errors committed by different actors in the system. Thus, the groundwork is provided for **argument** later before the appellate court.

Most states and the federal government have criminal appellate courts, where offenders direct their appeals. These appellate courts frequently consist of three-judge panels who will hear the legal arguments and decide whether the trial court was in error. Rulings by appellate courts that overturn a lower trial court are rare, however. One reason is that appellate courts assume that whatever transpired during the offender's trial was correct, and that the criminal conviction was valid. This is a difficult presumption for appellants to overcome. They must often present overwhelming evidence of prosecutorial misconduct or judicial indiscretion in order to convince an appellate court to reverse or set aside their conviction. And if a conviction is reversed, this decision does not absolve the offender of any criminal liability. A new trial may be ordered, or a sentencing decision may be modified to be consistent with a higher court ruling.

Presenting the case for the appellant is the defense attorney in most criminal cases, while the district attorney or state prosecutor (the U.S. Attorney or Assistant U.S. Attorney in federal courts) will give the government's position in the matter to be argued. This dispute process is **oral argument.** Once the appellate court has heard the oral argument from both sides and has consulted the trial transcript, it will render an **opinion.** An opinion is a written decision about the issue(s) argued, and a holding as to which side, the appellant or appellee, prevails. If the appellate court holds in favor of the appellant, and if the appellant is a convicted offender, then the case is **reversed and remanded** back to the trial court with instructions for modifying the original decision. Whenever the ruling favors the government, the appellate court is said to **affirm** the holding or judgment against the appellant/offender. When the case against the offender is affirmed by an appellate court, the offender may direct an appeal to the next higher appellate court. In state courts, this higher appellate court is the state supreme court or court of last resort within the state judicial system. If the state supreme court affirms the conviction, the offender may direct an appeal to the U.S. Supreme Court.

In some opinions by appellate courts, not all of the appellate judges agree about the decision rendered. The minority view is sometimes summarized in a **dissenting opinion.** Legal historians value dissenting opinions, because they believe that appellate court policy change can be predicted over time. This is especially true if those rendering dissenting opinions are younger judges on appellate panels. However, the fact is that these minority or dissenting opinions have no impact on the appeal outcome. The majority opinion, however, is the governing opinion in the case and is the more important one. Appellate judges who write the majority opinion also outline the legal rationale for their opinion. These opinions are more or less lengthy.

The Discretionary Powers of Appellate Courts

Appellate courts may or may not decide to hear appeals from lower courts. Their powers in this regard are discretionary. They may choose which cases to review as well as decide which cases not to review.

Usually, only a small proportion of cases is reviewed by appellate courts at the state and federal levels annually. For instance, the U.S. Supreme Court receives thousands of appeals from convicted offenders annually. However, only a small fraction, less than 100 cases, are heard each year where written opinions are provided. Most appeals from convicted offenders are denied. The U.S. Supreme Court is also a discretionary body, where their cases to be heard are carefully chosen. Furthermore, the Rule of Four applies, where at least four or more justices must agree to hear the case. And even if the U.S. Supreme Court consents to hear a case, the sheer volume of scheduled cases may be such that the case may not be heard. This is because the U.S. Supreme Court's time is quite limited. More than a few scheduled cases are not heard each year, because the Court has run out of time. And these cases are not carried over to the next term of the Court. Rather, appellants must refile their appeals with the Court the following term.

Appeals by Indigents

Indigent defendants who are sentenced to death are entitled to counsel on their first nondiscretionary appeals (Harmon 2001). However, more than a few inmates on death rows have filed numerous subsequent appeals, almost always at taxpayer expense, where public defenders have been appointed to assist them. However, as we have seen, the U.S. Supreme Court has limited the number of appeals indigents may file as well as their right to publicly appointed counsel each and every time they launch a new appeal.

Wrongful Convictions and Pardons

The American criminal justice system is not perfect. While no conclusive data are available to dispute the matter one way or another, more than a few innocent persons are sometimes convicted of serious crimes (Gould 2004). This same phenomenon occurs in other countries as well, such as Canada (Denov and Campbell 2005). There are many reasons for **wrongful convictions** (Burrow 2004). Sometimes there is extensive **circumstantial evidence,** which implicates the defendant and makes him/her appear to be guilty (Burnett 2005). A defendant may have the motive, means, and opportunity to commit particular crimes, but he/she may be unable to account for his/her whereabouts when the crime was committed. Sometimes the simple fact of not being able to explain satisfactorily where you were at a particular time, coupled with other incriminating factors, may make you appear guilty in the eyes of jurors who hear and decide the case.

Some aggressive prosecutors may threaten or intimidate certain defendants with the possibility of charging them with crimes that carry stringent penalties, such as long sentences of incarceration, and even the death penalty. While it is wrong and unethical to engage in such prosecutorial misconduct, some prosecutors threaten and overwhelm certain defendants with very serious charges that have little or no basis in fact. A gray area exists within which prosecutors have great latitude in their charging decisions. Most skillful prosecutors can present only incriminating or inculpatory information to grand juries about criminal suspects and withhold exculpatory information that might exonerate the suspect. Indictments against almost anyone can be obtained, depending upon the prosecutor's wishes (Leo 2005).

But as we have seen, indictments do not mean someone is guilty of a crime. Rather, indictments are simply findings by grand juries that probable cause exists to believe that a crime was committed and a particular suspect named by the prosecutor may have committed the crime. These one-sided proceedings, where defendants and their attorneys are barred from presenting their side or giving exculpatory evidence, frequently overwhelm those indicted for various crimes. Most citizens who read a newspaper article reading, "Federal Grand Jury Indicts James Jones for Six Counts of Burglary," or "The Craig County Grand Jury Indicts Elmer Gantry for Sexual Assault" likely conclude that James Jones or Elmer Gantry are probably guilty of these crimes based on the powerful innuendo of an indictment. But proving the facts alleged in an indictment in court beyond a reasonable doubt may be difficult, particularly if these cases lack direct evidence against particular suspects or are at best circumstantial.

For many suspects, their cases never come to trial. The plea bargaining process circumvents most trials in over 90 percent of all criminal cases. After being overwhelmed by very serious charges, defendants and their attorneys may be approached by "generous" prosecutors who wish to save the government the time and expense of a protracted trial. A compromise is offered, such as a lesser charge. If the defendant pleads guilty to a lesser charge, then probation may be offered instead of jail or prison time that might be imposed if a jury trial were held and the suspect were convicted. Many defense attorneys urge their clients to accept these "generous" offers from prosecutors, especially if these clients have prior criminal records or appear guilty because of the circumstantial evidence the state has compiled. Thus, many defendants relinquish their right to a jury trial as well as other important constitutional rights in an effort to avoid potentially serious punishments if a trial were held and they were convicted.

Then there are cases where innocent defendants go to trial anyway and are convicted, simply because they look guilty to the jury and the state has overwhelmed the jury with extensive circumstantial evidence. These innocent convicted persons spend a great deal of time seeking appeals of their cases by higher courts. But these innocent persons must overcome a powerful presumption that the trial court was correct when the case was originally decided. This is an extremely difficult presumption to overcome, especially if there is little or no hard evidence to substantiate one's claim of innocence.

In recent years there has been greater media attention focused upon very serious cases, particularly death penalty cases, where technology has advanced to the point of conclusively demonstrating one's innocence (Davis 2005). Evidence in most serious criminal cases is carefully preserved for many years following the crime in anticipation of the appeals that will follow. In 1975, for instance, an alleged black rapist with Type A negative blood might have been convicted of a rape because the semen recovered from the rape victim was consistent with Type A negative blood and testimony from the rape victim was that her black attacker "looked like" the alleged rapist apprehended by police. Type A negative blood is a relatively rare blood type, but it is not so rare that others don't have it. Unfortunately for the black defendant, he did not have an alibi or could not substantiate his whereabouts when the rape took place.

During the 1990s, however, DNA typing was increasingly used as evidence against suspects (*Technology Review* 2005). But its use also led authorities to exclude certain persons as suspects. By 2005 many of those serving lengthy prison sentences or who were on death rows throughout the United States were demanding re-examinations of blood evidence that was originally used to convict them (Burnett 2005). In the case of the 1975 convicted black rapist with Type A negative blood, it may turn out that there is not a DNA match for that offender. In fact, increasing numbers of law enforcement agencies and correctional institutions are collecting blood specimens from suspects or convicted offenders and typing these specimens according to unique DNA patterns. As it might turn out on re-examination, not only was the black defendant wrongfully convicted in 1975, but another convicted rapist presently serving time for another crime is a perfect DNA match for the other rape. Often, a confrontation of the actual perpetrator with DNA evidence may elicit a confession. While prosecutors are reluctant to admitting their mistakes, appellate courts have been persuaded with such DNA evidence and wrongful convictions have been overturned (Boller 2005).

The president of the United States or a state governor may **pardon** certain persons who have been found to be wrongfully convicted of crimes. Pardons are unconditional releases from prison. Pardons are intended to overcome a governmental mistake or right wrongs. They are not extensively invoked, but when they *are* invoked, they frequently have the weight of restoring a person to his/her citizen status prior to being convicted of a crime. Persons may be pardoned from death row if they are subsequently found to be innocent of the crimes for which they were originally convicted. The government may or may not compensate such persons for the time they were incarcerated until pardoned. For instance, North Carolina compensates wrongfully convicted persons $20,000 per year spent in incarceration, while some jurisdictions have no compensation policies.

In 2005, only 37 percent of all wrongfully convicted persons received compensation from various states for the months or years these innocent persons spent in prison. Only 20 states had mechanisms in place and institutional pathways for seeking compensation for wrongful imprisonment or conviction (Scheck and Neufeld 2002). Not all of these states had uniform reimbursement provisions. For instance, Ohio capped awards to wrongfully convicted offenders in 2005 at $25,000 per year of incarceration, while the federal government capped such awards at $100,000 per year (Innocence Project 2005). Also by 2005, 119 persons had been set free from death rows throughout the United States and classified as actually innocent of their original convictions. They were granted full pardons on the basis of evidence showing their innocence conclusively; they had all charges against them dropped by the prosecution; and/or they were acquitted of all charges that originally placed them on death row (Death Penalty Information Center 2005).

BOX 10.5 WRONGFULLY CONVICTED MAN GETS PARDONED

■ **Raleigh, North Carolina and Darryl Hunt**

It happened in August 1984. Deborah Sykes, 25, a copyeditor for the *Winston-Salem Sentinel* newspaper, was raped and murdered as she was walking to work. She was stabbed 16 times. At about the same time of Sykes's rape, another rape had occurred in the general area, and a suspect, Willard E. Brown, was apprehended and charged with that rape. Brown was erroneously believed by police to be incarcerated at the time when Sykes was raped and murdered. But he wasn't in prison. He was free. In the meantime, police and prosecutors focused upon Darryl Hunt, a 19-year-old black man who was identified by an eyewitness and was unable to satisfactorily account for his whereabouts when Sykes was raped and murdered. Hunt was convicted on the basis of flimsy circumstantial evidence, but his case was overturned on an appeal. He was tried again and convicted, sentenced to life imprisonment for a crime he did not commit.

Interestingly when DNA testing was being used in courts increasingly, Hunt's DNA was compared in 1994 and again in 1995 with the semen evidence from Sykes's crime scene. The DNA didn't match in either comparison. Despite this mismatch, the appellate courts refused to grant Hunt a new trial. Prosecutors in the case adapted the explanation of how the crime occurred to fit the changed circumstances of the newly discovered DNA evidence, claiming with a new theory that Hunt was a participant in the sexual assault and murder and guilty despite whatever the DNA tests disclosed.

In April 2004, a DNA test was performed on Willard Brown, who was being held in a county jail in North Carolina on minor drug and trespassing charges. Brown was believed by Hunt's defense counsel to be the likely perpetrator of the rape-murder of Sykes, especially when it was discovered that Brown was not incarcerated at the time Sykes was murdered. When confronted by the DNA evidence, Brown confessed to killing Sykes. He declared that he acted alone. Brown was charged with murder, rape, kidnapping, and robbery in the Sykes case. In February 2004 Hunt was pardoned by North Carolina governor Mike Easley for the crime Brown had committed. He had spent 18 years in prison because of a wrongful conviction.

The prosecutors in the Sykes case had a different view of the DNA evidence. They continued to insist that despite Brown's confession and assertion that he acted alone, Hunt was nevertheless an accomplice and equally guilty. This sentiment was also shared by Sykes's family members who also rejected the DNA evidence exonerating Hunt. Hunt was entitled to receive $20,000 per year from North Carolina for the years he was wrongfully incarcerated. Hunt said, "I'm not looking for an apology from the DA (prosecutor). What they need to do is apologize to Mrs. Sykes's family." Prosecutors had refused to reinvestigate Sykes's attack even after the DNA results had been disclosed in 1994 and 1995. In the meantime, Hunt, now 39, said he has spent his time since his release speaking out against capital punishment and is starting a new career, which he hopes will help others. Hunt commenced studying at Winston-Salem State University and eventually wants to work with children and former inmates. He said that the state settlement money will help him pay for his education and the house he and his wife, April, hope to buy. [Source: Adapted from William L. Holmes, Associated Press, "Man Falsely Convicted Gets Pardon," April 14, 2004.]

SUMMARY

When offenders are convicted of crimes, they are sentenced, either to probation or incarceration. The length of probation or incarceration, and the nature and requirements of these sentencing alternatives vary according to different jurisdictions. But the goals and functions of sentencing are more or less universal, regardless of jurisdiction. The goals and functions of sentencing are punishment, incapacitation, crime control, rehabilitation, reintegration, crime prevention, and deterrence.

Punishment is a primary sentencing objective. Persons who have violated the law and been convicted of one or more crimes must be held accountable for these acts in some way. Punishment, usually proportional to the seriousness and nature of the offense, is a suitable measure to be taken against convicted offenders. Punishments are generally restrictive, in that convicted persons are limited in their freedom to move about in their communities. They suffer losses such as the right to vote or to possess firearms. Other types of punishments may be imposed. For the most serious offenses, such as capital murder, the death penalty may be imposed as a punishment in those jurisdictions with death penalty statutes. Less serious punishments include incarceration in a jail or prison for specified periods, or placement on probation or parole. Fines and restitution orders may also be imposed.

Incapacitation as a goal of sentencing seeks to remove offenders from society, at least temporarily, so that such offenders cannot commit new crimes against citizens. Prisons and jails in many jurisdictions have been increasingly used to warehouse offenders, to remove them from public view, and to place them in circumstances where they pose no threats to others. This is a form of crime control, since incapacitated persons are not in a position to reoffend. Persons who are career criminals or chronic recidivists and who make their livelihood from crime are especially targeted for incarceration, and for lengthy periods. However, these persons often revert to their criminal ways once released, and recidivism rates among such persons are quite high.

Although rehabilitation is a sentencing goal, many persons believe that no type of sentencing or punishment is truly rehabilitative. Although vocational, technical, educational, and other useful programs are offered to persons convicted of crimes and incarcerated or placed under community supervision of some form, high recidivism rates among offenders suggest that only about a third of all convicted persons actually benefit from these programs. For those with addictions or who suffer from psychological problems, individual or group counseling and other treatment programs and therapies exist to assist them. But the benefits of these programs are limited to a small proportion of those willing to utilize these resources effectively. Thus, cynicism often characterizes the public view toward rehabilitation as a correctional goal.

Reintegration seeks to maintain a convicted person's connection with their communities, families, and work. Probation is used as a punishment to foster reintegration, and parole permits incarcerated persons to be released short of serving their full sentences in order to live law-abiding lives through the assistance of parole officers and others. Sentencing also attempts to send the message that violating the law will have adverse consequences for criminals, and that they will be caught and convicted for their crimes. The severity of their punishment seeks to deter them and others from repeating these acts in the future. But the deterrent effects of sentencing are questionable. It is unknown to what extent sentencing, even tough sentences imposed, actually function to prevent crime and deter those punished from committing new crimes when they are eventually released.

Several types of sentencing are being used as methods for determining appropriate punishments for offenders. All of these sentencing schemes have been criticized for different reasons, largely because they seem ineffective at accomplishing their various goals and functions. No sentencing system seems to work perfectly in any jurisdiction, and thus considerable experimentation with different sentencing variations has been observed.

Four basic types of sentencing schemes have been described. These include indeterminate sentencing, determinate sentencing, presumptive or guidelines-based sentencing, and mandatory sentencing. Indeterminate sentencing has been used for over two centuries. This sentencing form specifies a minimum and maximum sentence, with one's early release from incarceration being determined by a paroling authority or equivalent body. Determinate sentencing is similar to indeterminate sentencing, but early releases of inmates are governed by an accumulation of good-time credits, or days off one's maximum sentence for so many days served. A shift from indeterminate to determinate sentencing occurred during the 1970s. It was believed that parole board discretion was not entirely objective and ineffective. But removing discretionary power over one's early release has raised concerns among citizens and legislators that some inmates may be released automatically when it is believed that they should remain incarcerated for longer periods. There are no easy solutions to these particular sentencing conflicts and problems (Levine 2005).

Presumptive or guidelines-based sentencing has been used for several decades, both by the federal government and different states. Each crime is given a seriousness score, and one's criminal history or prior record and other factors are combined to determine an approximate range of months to be served. The middle number of months of any specified range is the presumptive sentence, and aggravating or mitigating factors can increase or decrease the number of months of incarceration imposed within the recommended range. But the U.S. Supreme Court has declared that at least for the federal government, the sentencing guidelines it created in 1987 are merely recommended sentencing ranges judges must follow. The intended function of sentencing guidelines is to create greater fairness in sentencing, where extralegal factors such as gender, socioeconomic status, race, and/or ethnicity are not serious considerations. The implementation of sentencing guidelines was originally intended to limit or remove sentencing disparities among different judges according to these and other extralegal variables. However, despite the establishment of guidelines, sentencing disparities continue to exist in all jurisdictions.

Mandatory sentences mean that offenders must serve flat time, or full sentences of incarceration without any time deducted from their sentence maximums for good behavior, however significant that behavior may be. Habitual offender statutes or chronic offender provisions seek to impose mandatory sentences on offenders who have been convicted of three or more felonies. California's three-strikes-and-you're-out law was intended to impose life sentences on persistent dangerous felons. Virginia Exile and its five-year mandatory minimum sentence and Michigan's two-year mandatory flat time provision were both passed by legislatures and intended to extend the time of one's incarceration by these respective years to discourage felons from using firearms when committing crimes. It is believed that these mandatory penalties associated with the use of firearms during the commission of a felony will decrease the incidence of deaths of innocent bystanders and others if deadly weapons use carries mandatory incarcerative penalties. The effectiveness of these measures has been questioned, since deaths of persons from firearms use during crimes have not diminished significantly since such mandatory sentencing laws have gone into effect.

Many states have truth-in-sentencing provisions, where legislatures have acted to provide that convicted persons should serve most of their sentences instead of smaller portions of them. Violations of federal criminal laws require that convicted federal offenders must serve at least 85 percent of their sentences before becoming eligible for early release. Many states have emulated the federal government by passing similar legislation. However, truth-in-sentencing laws have done little to deter violent crime, and in many jurisdictions, mandatory sentencing provisions and truth-in-sentencing laws have either been ignored or circumvented through plea bargaining and other sentencing options (Champion 2005a).

Persons who are convicted of serious crimes are subjected to sentencing hearings. These are proceedings where both sides may present evidence and witnesses favoring harsher or more lenient punishments. Aggravating and mitigating circumstances are presented by the prosecutor and defense counsel respectively in an effort to influence the judge in his/her sentencing decision making. Also relevant to these proceedings is the presentence investigation report (PSI), which is often prepared by a probation officer. PSIs contain a depiction of the crime committed, the police report, the offender's version of events, background information about the offender, psychiatric reports, a victim impact statement, and other vital information useful to judges and others in making decisions about offenders. Offenders have an opportunity to accept responsibility in such reports in an effort to create a favorable impression on judges and secure some leniency in the sentences imposed. Later, parole boards may refer to PSIs in their early-release decision making for inmates who have served varying amounts of prison time. When all information has been presented at these sentencing hearings, the judge imposes a sentence on the offender, who subsequently is supervised in different ways by corrections departments. Some offenders are given shock probation or split sentences. They may be placed in prison or jail for up to 120 days and then brought back before the court to be resentenced to probation. It is believed that the shock of incarceration for some persons at least is sufficiently traumatic to discourage them from committing new crimes. Split sentences involve mixed sentences of probation and confinement, usually in a jail, for short time intervals. Several split sentencing variations have been described.

The death penalty is a special punishment that has evolved its own court protocol over the years. It is incumbent upon criminal courts today to provide bifurcated trials for those facing the death penalty as a possible punishment for capital murder and other crimes, such as terrorist acts or large-scale drug trafficking. A bifurcated trial is a two-part proceeding. The first part is the trial phase, where guilt or innocence of the defendant is determined. If the jury finds the defendant guilty, it must deliberate in a second stage or phase to determine and recommend a punishment, either death, life without the possibility of parole, or life imprisonment. All death sentences are automatically appealed. Most appeals of these sentences are unsuccessful.

The appeals process for any criminal conviction is a lengthy and tedious process. If an offender is convicted, one or more appeals may be launched to the next higher court above the trial court. States have their own court hierarchy, and convicted offenders are expected to follow it when filing appeals. Sometimes offenders may file appeals in federal district courts, under certain circumstances. Ordinarily, state prisoners must exhaust all of their state court appeals remedies before approaching federal courts with their appeals.

The bases for appeals vary, although several types of appeals have been described. Convicted persons may file *habeas corpus* petitions, wherein they challenge the fact, length, and nature of their confinement. They may also file tort claims, if they feel they have suffered losses or damages as the result of government officer negligence, deliberate or otherwise. A third avenue of appeals is a civil rights, Section 1983 petition, which alleges one or more violations of one's rights under the Fourteenth Amendment. Title 42, Section 1983, of the U.S. Code contains equal protection guarantees as well as due process provisions. If convicted persons believe their civil rights have been violated in any way, this avenue is available to them (Houston, Steffel and McKenzie 2005). Generally, most appeals from convicted offenders are unsuccessful. A small portion of appeals each year is heard by the U.S. Supreme Court, especially where issues of constitutional significance are involved. U.S. Supreme Court appeals are initiated by writs of *certiorari*. Many death row inmates file appeals seeking to have their death penalty sentences overturned or set aside. Most of the time, petitioners, including death row inmates, fail to convince the high court that their claims are justified. Most trial court decisions and declarations are affirmed by higher courts. Indigent convicted offenders may file appeals as well, and these appeals are paid for by the government.

Subsequent free appeals for indigents and others are severely limited or restricted. Therefore, an offender's initial appeal must consolidate all known claims to be made against the government or others in order that all arguable issues may be decided. Some inmates file numerous petitions, many of which are deemed frivolous by the courts. Sometimes these persons are barred from filing further appeals based on their previous filing records and the frivolity of their claims.

KEY TERMS

Acceptance of responsibility
Affirm
Aggravating circumstances
Appeal
Appellants
Appellees
Argument
Bifurcated trial
Brief
Career criminals
Chronic offenders
Chronic recidivists
Circumstantial evidence
Conditions of confinement
Cost-benefit analysis
Court-appointed counsel
Crime Bill of 1994
Crime prevention
Criminal history
Death penalty
Death row
Defendant's sentencing memorandum
Deterrence
Dissenting opinion
DNA fingerprinting
Early release
Extralegal factors
Felony property offending
Flat term
Get-tough movement
Good-time
Good-time credit

Guidelines-based sentencing
Habeas corpus
Habitual offenders
Incapacitation
Intermittent sentencing
Isolation
Jail as a condition of probation
Life imprisonment
Life-without-parole sentence
Mandatory sentence
Mandatory sentencing
Mistrial
Mitigating circumstances
Mixed sentencing
Narrative
Notice of approval
Opinion
Oral argument
Pardon
Parole board
Persistent felony offenders
Persistent offender statutes
Presumptive sentencing
Probation officer
Project Exile
Punishment
Rehabilitation
Reintegration
Reversed and remanded
Sentencing disparity
Sentencing hearing
Sentencing memorandum
Sentencing Reform Act of 1984

Serious felonies
Shock incarceration
Shock parole
Shock probation
Solitary confinement
Split sentencing
Stare decisis
Three-strikes-and-you're-out

Tiers
Truth in sentencing
Truth-in-sentencing laws
United States sentencing commission
Violent felonies
Virginia Exile
Warrant
Wrongful convictions

QUESTIONS FOR REVIEW

1. What is a *habeas corpus* petition? What are three types of issues challenged by such petitions?

2. What is a writ of *certiorari*? Under what circumstances might this type of writ be used?

3. What are some trends regarding the use of *habeas corpus* petitions by jail and prison inmates? What factors seem to account for such trends?

4. What are four general functions or aims of sentencing?

5. How does indeterminate sentencing differ from determinate sentencing?

6. What constraints are imposed on judges by presumptive or guidelines-based and mandatory sentencing schemes?

7. What is a habitual offender statute? Do most states have such statutes? Are these statutes used frequently by these states? Why or why not? Explain.

8. Differentiate between shock probation and split sentencing. What are three types of split sentences?

9. What is a use-a-gun-and-go-to-prison statute?

10. What is a sentencing hearing? What are the major functions of such hearings?

11. What is a presentence investigation report? Who prepares it and how is it used to determine an offender's punishment?

12. What is a bifurcated trial? Under what circumstances is it used? What are two significant cases relating to bifurcated trials?

13. What is meant by truth-in-sentencing? How is truth-in-sentencing achieved?

14. What are victim impact statements? Where are such statements found and what purposes do they serve in the sentencing process?

15. Why is the appeals process for death sentences so lengthy?

SUGGESTED READINGS

1. Pauline K. Brennan (2006). "Sentencing Female Misdemeanants: An Examination of the Direct and Indirect Effects of Race/Ethnicity." *Justice Quarterly* **23**:60–94.

2. Myriam S. Denov and Kathryn M. Campbell (2005). "Criminal Injustice: Understanding the Causes, Effects, and Responses to Wrongful Conviction in Canada." *Journal of Contemporary Criminal Justice* **21**:234–249.

3. R. S. Frase (2005). "Sentencing Guidelines in Minnesota, 1978–2003." In M. Tonry (ed.), *Crime and Justice: A Review of Research, Vol. 32.* Chicago: University of Chicago Press.

4. David Holleran and Cassia Spohn (2004). "On the Use of the Total Incarceration Variable in Sentencing Research." *Criminology* **42**:211–240.

5. Tomislav V. Kovandzic, John J. Sloan, III, and Lynne M. Vieraitis (2002). "Unintended Consequences of Politically Popular Sentencing Policy: The Homicide Promoting Effects of 'Three Strikes' in the U.S. Cities (1980–1999)." *Criminology and Public Policy* **3**:399–424.

6. Richard A. Leo (2005). "Rethinking the Study of Miscarriages of Justice: Developing a Criminology of Wrongful Conviction." *Journal of Contemporary Criminal Justice* **21**:201–223.

7. Nancy Merritt, Terry Fain, and Susan Turner (2006). "Oregon's Get-Tough Sentencing Reform: A Lesson in Justice System Adaptation." *Criminology and Public Policy* **1**:5–36.

8. Sara Steen, Rodney L. Engen, and Randy R. Gainey (2005). "Images of Danger and Culpability: Racial Stereotyping, Case Processing, and Criminal Sentencing." *Criminology* **43**:435–468.

9. Robert L. Young (2004). "Guilty Until Proven Innocent: Conviction Orientation, Racial Attitudes, and Support for Capital Punishment." *Deviant Behavior* **25**:151–167.

Chapter 11

Juvenile Courts, Juvenile Rights, and Processing

Getty Images, Inc.

Chapter Objectives

As the result of reading this chapter, you will have accomplished the following objectives:

1. Understand the basic components of the juvenile justice system and how juveniles are processed differently from adult offenders.

2. Distinguish between delinquents and status offenders and the reasons for making such distinctions.

3. Understand the jurisdiction of juvenile courts and the influence of *parens patriae* on court actions.

4. Describe the influence of due process upon juvenile offender processing, including an examination of the legal rights of juveniles.

5. Examine the role of juvenile court prosecutors and the changing nature of juvenile court proceedings as defense counsels are increasingly used in most jurisdictions.

6. Understand the waiver, transfer, and certification processes, how these procedures move juveniles to criminal court jurisdiction, and the implications of these decisions for juvenile offenders.

7. Describe several key cases in the evolution of juvenile rights and how these rights have affected how juveniles are processed.

8. Understand blended sentencing statutes and how these statutory provisions have changed the nature of juvenile sentencing and rehabilitation.

9. Describe several important trends in juvenile justice that have significance for how juveniles are processed by juvenile courts.

■ At United South Middle School in Laredo, Texas, a 12-year-old boy was ordered detained in a juvenile detention center for 10 days following threats he made at school. The youth allegedly pointed a gun at the head of another student, Jerry Garcia, and he made terroristic threats against two other students. The parents of the threatened students filed complaints with the police and with the school district. An investigation followed. A juvenile referee heard the case and decided that it was in the best interests of the child to close the hearing to the general public. Webb County (TX) juvenile referee Antonio Figueroa made a statement. He said, "I weighed the interest of the child and the interest of the public, and that is what I decided," in reference to the closed hearing. Also kept out of the courtroom was the mother of one of the threatened students, Rebecca Schunior. Schunior said that she had previously called the juvenile center and was told that she could not attend the proceeding or enter the premises. Webb County officials have not decided whether to take further action in the incident besides the 10-day detention. But during the detention period, the youth will be tutored from 8:30 a.m. until 3:30 p.m. Along with his tutoring, the boy will attend counseling sessions and will follow a boot camp–like schedule, which includes waking up at 4:45 a.m. every morning, marching, and other activities. Case management officer Pat Campos said, "Because the boy is only 12, it can be that we can get to him in time. If the psychologist provides him adequate help, then he may be able to help him in time." Is 10 days in a juvenile detention center adequate punishment for a 12-year-old who wields a gun at another student and threatens the lives of other students? Would you want your children to go to school with this 12-year-old? [Source: Adapted from Diana de la Garza, Robert Garcia, and the Associated Press, "Boy Gets 10 Days Inside 10 Minutes," May 3, 2001.]

■ It happened in New Haven, Connecticut. A 13-year-old girl who was in the seventh grade in a middle school and had an otherwise unblemished juvenile record was suddenly thrust into the national spotlight over truancy. For unknown reasons, the girl suddenly refused to attend her seventh-grade classes. School officials reported her truancy to a juvenile court judge, who ordered her to attend her classes. She continued to absent herself from the classroom against the judge's orders and suddenly found herself in contempt of court. Authorities were sent to pick her up and take her to juvenile detention. When she arrived at the Connecticut juvenile detention center in New Haven, a matron at the center ordered her to strip. The girl didn't know what to do. She said, "The lady told me I had to take off my clothes so that they could look for scars so that I can't go home and say that they did it and my parents can sue. I was embarrassed. I don't like having to take my clothes off in front of anyone." The following day, the girl was moved to another center for the remainder of her detention and ordered to strip again. Connecticut officials were interviewed about the incident. Apparently it is juvenile detention center policy to strip-search all juveniles to check for drugs or weapons, as well as for signs of abuse requiring treatment. The girl strip-searched shot back, "I can see it if I was there for carrying a weapon, but for not going to school?" Strip searches are among the most invasive procedures, and considerable opinion and case law says it should be used judiciously, even with adults. In June 2001, for example, New York City settled a class-action suit filed by thousands of adults who had been strip-searched upon arrest for low-level crimes in the city. Connecticut officials say that some adult prisoners are exempt from strip searches. Adults held in jail prior to arraignment on misdemeanor or motor vehicle charges are not searched unless there is the reasonable belief that they are concealing contraband. Most places in Connecticut do not ordinarily strip-search children. In New York, chronic runaways and truants are not placed in detention, much less strip-searched. In New Jersey, strip searches are not routine in facilities that hold children who have committed low-level crimes. But Connecticut is different. All juveniles who are placed in detention, including runaways, truants, and those held in contempt of court are subject to being strip-searched upon entering detention. According to William H. Carbone, executive director of court support services for the state's judicial branch, it is really for the overall security of the detainees. Carbone said that these searches are to protect children from themselves. He added, "A chronic runaway may have a razor blade taped to his foot or have barbiturates under his arm." Opponents of strip searches involving juveniles say that strip searches don't make sense in most cases. Jeanne Milstein, a child advocate, says that strip searches make sense if you are dealing with violent juvenile offenders or those accused of serious crimes. But only 12 percent of all juveniles taken into custody fit this scenario, she said. Anthony Wallace, an attorney representing the 13-year-old girl filing a lawsuit against Connecticut, said, "Why should the state force these children to bend over and show them their private parts because they didn't go to school or committed some low-level crime?" Should status offenders be submitted to strip searches whenever they are taken into custody for the purpose of being held in detention? Which types of juveniles should qualify for strip searches? What do you think? [Source: Adapted from Matthew Purdy and the New York Times News Service, July 19, 2001.]

INTRODUCTION

This chapter examines the juvenile justice system, which is interconnected in various ways with the criminal justice system. Many of the adults who are processed by the criminal justice system began their careers of crime in their early years as juveniles. An overview of the juvenile justice system is presented. The first section begins with a distinction between juvenile delinquents and status offenders. This distinction is important because juvenile delinquents are those who have committed or are alleged to have committed offenses that would be crimes if adults committed them. In contrast, status offenders commit acts that would not be crimes if adults committed them. For many decades, the juvenile justice system has not differentiated between these types of offenders, despite the fact that delinquents are considerably more serious than status offenders and pose greater risks to society. Described is the establishment of the Juvenile Justice and Delinquency Prevention Act of 1974, which did much to change how status offenders are presently treated. In subsequent years, most juvenile courts have divested themselves of their jurisdiction over status offenders, preferring to focus their resources on more serious delinquent offenders. The changes brought about by this act will be described.

Next, the chapter focuses upon the jurisdiction of the juvenile court. Jurisdiction refers to the power of courts to hear particular kinds of cases. A brief history of the juvenile court is presented, and several important contrasts between juvenile and criminal courts are illustrated. The juvenile justice process begins with a referral, which may be made by a parent, guardian, school official, police officer, or neighbor. Over 2 million juveniles annually are referred to the juvenile justice system, although only about half of these are processed eventually by the system in more formal ways. About half of all juveniles who enter the juvenile justice system are there as the result of petitions. Petitions allege that juveniles have committed different acts that juvenile courts must adjudicate.

The process of screening juveniles, intake, is described. Beyond intake, juvenile court prosecutors perform chores relating to juveniles that are quite similar to the tasks performed by criminal court prosecutors. They must decide which cases to pursue and which ones not to pursue. About half a million juveniles or more appear before juvenile court judges annually, and their cases are adjudicated. An adjudication is a juvenile court judicial decision that the facts alleged against the juvenile, either by petition or other means, are true or not true. If judges decide that the facts are true and that the juvenile committed one or more delinquent acts, one of several different kinds of dispositions is imposed. These dispositions are nominal, conditional, and custodial. These dispositions roughly equate respectively with verbal warnings, probation, or incarceration in a secure facility. The adjudicatory process is described, as well as the different types of dispositions imposed on juveniles by juvenile court judges.

Juveniles have the right to due process, which vests them with many of the same rights as adults charged with crimes. All juveniles are entitled to counsel. If the juvenile or the juvenile's family/guardian is indigent, then an attorney will be appointed to represent the juvenile. Cases against juveniles may be plea bargained in much the same way that adult cases are plea bargained. Thus, many juvenile cases are never brought before the juvenile court judge for a formal adjudicatory hearing. At least eleven states make provisions for jury trials for juveniles if they request them. Jury trials for juveniles are not a matter of right, but rather, certain states extend the jury trial privilege to certain juveniles depending on their age, offense seriousness, and other important and relevant criteria.

About 1 percent of all juveniles referred to the juvenile court each year are transferred, waived, or certified to the jurisdiction of criminal courts where the juveniles are treated as adults. Transfers, waivers, or certifications make it possible for criminal courts to impose harsher sanctions against juveniles, such as the death penalty or life imprisonment. Such sanctions are beyond the jurisdiction of juvenile courts. The waiver process is described, and various positive and adverse implications for juveniles are discussed.

There are four major types of waiver actions. These include judicial waivers, prosecutorial waivers, statutory exclusion or legislative or automatic waivers, and demand waivers. Each of these types of waivers is defined and discussed. All juveniles who are transferred to criminal court jurisdiction are entitled to a hearing before they are waived. The implications of such hearings are described.

The next section discusses the legal rights of juveniles, and several important U.S. Supreme Court cases involving juvenile rights are presented. Their implications for juvenile court treatment are discussed. Several rights conveyed to juveniles by the U.S. Supreme Court include the right to an attorney, the right to a notice of charges, the right to cross-examine one's accuser, the right to give testimony in one's own behalf, the right against self-incrimination, and the right to the beyond a reasonable doubt standard where one's liberty is in jeopardy. Also, juveniles have the right against double jeopardy, which may occur when a juvenile is adjudicated delinquent by the juvenile court and a criminal court subsequently finds him/her guilty of the same charge. This is considered double jeopardy and is thus unconstitutional. Juveniles do not have the right to a jury trial, however, unless provided for by state statutes or by judicial decree. Most juvenile court judges do not allow jury trials for juveniles, inasmuch as this procedure would delay juvenile court processing of youthful offenders considerably.

In recent decades, most states have evolved blended sentencing statutes. The next section of this chapter examines several types of blended sentencing statutes whereby either juvenile court judges or criminal court judges may hear and decide juvenile cases and impose either juvenile sanctions, criminal sentences, or both, depending upon the jurisdiction. The advantages and disadvantages of blended sentencing statutes will be described. The chapter concludes with an examination of several important trends in juvenile justice, and a discussion of the favorable and unfavorable implications of these trends for affected juveniles.

DELINQUENCY, JUVENILE DELINQUENTS, AND STATUS OFFENDERS

Juvenile Delinquents

Juveniles

Juvenile court jurisdiction is dependent upon established legislative definitions of who **juveniles** are and the offenses they commit. There is considerable variation among the states as to which juvenile offenders are within the purview of juvenile courts. The federal government has no **juvenile court.** Rather, federal cases involving juveniles infrequently are heard in federal district courts, but adjudicated juveniles are housed in state or local facilities if the sentences involve incarceration. Ordinarily, upper and lower age limits are prescribed. However, these age limits are far from uniform among jurisdictions. The common law or **English common law** standard sets the minimum age of juveniles at 7, although no state is obligated to recognize this common-law definition. In fact, some states have no lower age limits that would otherwise function to limit juvenile court jurisdiction.

Some states with the lowest maximum age for juvenile court jurisdiction include Connecticut, New York, and North Carolina. The lowest maximum age for juvenile court jurisdiction is 15 in these states. Other states having a low maximum age of 16 for juvenile court jurisdiction are Georgia, Illinois, Louisiana, Massachusetts, Michigan, Missouri, South Carolina, and Texas. All other states and the federal government use age 18 as the minimum age for criminal court jurisdiction (Champion 2007).

In most jurisdictions, youths under the age of 7 are often placed in the care of community agencies, such as departments of human services or social welfare. These children frequently have little or no responsible parental supervision or control. In many cases, the parents themselves may have psychological problems or suffer from alcohol or drug dependencies. Youths from such families may be abused and/or neglected, and in need of supervision and other forms of care or treatment. Under common law in those states where common law applies, children under the age of 7 are presumed incapable of formulating criminal intent. If a 6-year-old child kills someone, for instance, deliberately or accidentally, he/she will likely be treated rather than punished.

Juvenile Delinquency

Juvenile delinquency is the violation of a criminal law of the United States by a person prior to his eighteenth birthday, which would have been a crime if committed by an adult (18 U.S.C., Sec. 5031, 1997). Generally, juvenile delinquency is the violation of any state or local law or ordinance by anyone who has not yet become an adult. Any act committed by a juvenile that would be a crime if an adult committed it is a delinquent act. A **juvenile delinquent** is anyone who has committed juvenile delinquency.

Status Offenders

Status offenders are those who commit offenses that would not be crimes if adults committed them. Typical status offenses are runaway behavior, truancy, and curfew violation. Adults may run away from home, be truant from their classes, and stay out late at night without violating the law. However, juveniles are required to observe these laws that pertain specifically to them (Urban 2005).

Runaways

In 2004, there were approximately 250,000 **runaways** reported to police (Bureau of Justice Statistics 2005). This is less than 1 percent of all offenses charged that year. Over half of these runaways are 15 to 17 years of age. Runaways consist of those youths who leave their homes, without permission or their parents' knowledge, and who remain away from home for prolonged periods ranging from several days to several years. Many run-aways are eventually picked up by police in different jurisdictions and returned to their homes. Others return of their own free will and choice.

Truants and Curfew Violators

Truants are those who absent themselves from school without either school or parental permission. **Curfew violators** are those youths who remain on city streets after specified evening hours when they are prohibited from loitering or not being in the company of a parent or guardian. In 2004, there were 125,000 youths charged with curfew violation in the United States (Bureau of Justice Statistics 2005).

Juvenile and Criminal Court Interest in Status Offenders

Juvenile courts are interested in status offenders who habitually appear before juvenile court judges. Repeated juvenile court appearances may be symptomatic of subsequent adult criminality. The chronicity of juvenile offending seems to be influenced by the amount of contact youths have with juvenile courts. Greater contact with juvenile courts is believed by some experts to **stigmatize** youths and cause them either to be labeled or acquire **stigmas** as delinquents or deviants. Therefore, diversion of certain types of juvenile offenders from the juvenile justice system has been advocated and recommended to minimize stigmatization (McLean, Cocozza, and Skowyra 2004).

One way of removing status offenders from juvenile courts and their stigmatizing effects is to deprive juvenile court judges of jurisdiction over status offenders (Blackmore, Brown, and Krisberg 1988). Another way of minimizing status offender stigmatization is to remove them from custodial institutions where they are housed for various terms, such as industrial schools. These methods are known as **divestiture of jurisdiction** and **deinstitutionalization of status offenders (DSO)** or simply **deinstitutionalization.**

Divesting Juvenile Courts of Their Jurisdiction over Status Offenders

Under divestiture, juvenile courts cannot detain, petition, adjudicate, or place youths on probation or in institutions for committing *any* status offense. In lieu of juvenile court intervention, various community agencies and social services are used to care for and place status offenders.

Deinstitutionalization of Status Offenders (DSO)

There is a prevalent belief that institutionalizing status offenders in juvenile industrial schools (e.g., prisons for juveniles) will harden them, thus increasing their likelihood of committing future, more serious offenses. Therefore, in the late 1960s, a movement began to remove status offenders from juvenile penal institutions such as industrial schools. In 1974 the U.S. Congress passed enabling legislation to accomplish this objective on a national basis.

The **Juvenile Justice and Delinquency Prevention Act of 1974 (JJDPA)** (and modified in 1984) was established in response to a national concern about growing juvenile delinquency and youth crime. This act authorized the establishment of the **Office of Juvenile Justice and Delinquency Prevention (OJJDP),** which has been extremely helpful and influential in matters of disseminating information about juvenile offending and prevention and as a general data source. The JJDPA provides for a state relations and assistance division. The JJDPA has also been modified extensively since its inception in 1974.

The State Relations and Assistance Division

This division addresses directly the matter of removing juveniles, especially status offenders, from secure institutions (facilities similar to adult prisons), jails, and lockups. The second division, Research and Program Development, examines how juvenile courts process juvenile offenders.

Changes and Modifications in the JJDPA

Congress modified the act in 1977 by declaring the juveniles should be separated by both sight and sound from adult offenders in detention and correctional facilities. Also in 1977, states were given five years to comply with the DSO mandate. Congress prohibited states in 1980 from detaining juveniles in jails and lockups. Congress also directed that states should examine their secure confinement policies relating to minority juveniles and to determine reasons and justification for the disproportionately high rate of minority confinement (Mukoro 2005). In 1992, Congress directed that any participating state would have up to 25 percent of its formula grant money withheld to the extent that the state was not in compliance with each of the JJDPA mandates. Thus, it is clear that state compliance with these provisions of the JJDPA was encouraged and obtained by providing grants-in-aid to various jurisdictions wishing to improve their juvenile justice systems and facilities (Rodriguez 2004).

THE JURISDICTION OF JUVENILE COURTS

The Age Jurisdiction of Juvenile Courts

Upper age limits for juveniles have been established in all U.S. jurisdictions (either under 16, under 17, or under 18 years of age). However, presently there is no uniformity concerning applicable lower age limits. Technically, juvenile courts have jurisdiction over 3-year-old murderers. However, no juvenile court will adjudicate a 3-year-old delinquent and place the child in an industrial school. The type of jurisdictional control over such children by juvenile courts is more care and treatment-oriented. This treatment and care may include placement of children or infants in foster homes or under the supervision of community service or human welfare agencies who can meet their needs. Neglected, unmanageable, abused, or other **children in need of supervision (CHINS)** are placed in the custody of these various agencies, at the discretion of juvenile judges. Generally, juvenile courts have broad discretionary powers over most persons under the age of 18.

The Treatment and Punishment Functions of Juvenile Courts

Not all juveniles who appear before juvenile court judges are delinquents. Many youths in juvenile court have not violated any criminal laws (Feld 2003). Rather, their status as juveniles means that they are within juvenile court control. Several circumstances make these youths susceptible to juvenile court jurisdiction. These circumstances may be the quality of their adult supervision, if any. Other circumstances may be that they run away from home, are truant from school, or loiter on certain city streets during evening hours. Runaways, truants, or **loiterers** are considered status offenders, since their actions would not be criminal ones if committed by adults.

Physically, psychologically, or sexually abused children are within the jurisdictional control of juvenile courts. Many of these juvenile courts are instead called family courts. However, the majority of youthful offenders who appear before juvenile courts are juvenile delinquents. However, in more than a few jurisdictions, a delinquent act is whatever juvenile courts say it is. Thus, juvenile courts have broad discretionary powers over all types of juveniles. Much of this state authority originated under the early English doctrine of *parens patriae*.

Parens Patriae

Parens Patriae

Parens patriae originated with the king of England during the twelfth century. It literally means the father of the country. Applied to juvenile matters, *parens patriae* means that the king is in charge of, makes decisions about, or has responsibility for all matters involving juvenile conduct. Within the scope of early English common law, parental authority was primary in the early upbringing of children. However, as children advanced to age 7 and beyond, they acquired some measure of responsibility for their own actions. Accountability to parents was shifted gradually to accountability to the state, whenever youths

7 years of age or older violated the law. In the name of the king, chancellors in various districts adjudicated matters involving juveniles and the offenses they committed. Juveniles had no legal rights or standing in any court. They were the sole responsibility of the king or his agents. Their future often depended largely upon decisions made by **chancellors.** In effect, children were wards of the court, and the court was vested with the responsibility to safeguard their welfare.

Since children could become wards of the court and subject to their control, a key concern for many chancellors was for the future welfare of these children. The welfare interests of chancellors and their actions led to numerous rehabilitative and/or treatment measures. Some of these measures included placement of children in foster homes or their assignment to various work tasks for local merchants. Parental influence in these child placement decisions was minimal.

Modern Applications of *Parens Patriae*

Parens patriae in the 1990s is pervasive in all juvenile court jurisdictions. The pervasiveness of this doctrine is exhibited by the wide range of dispositional options available to juvenile court judges and others involved in earlier stages of offender processing in the juvenile justice system. Most of these dispositional options are either nominal or conditional, meaning that the confinement of any juvenile for most offenses is regarded as a last resort.

The strong treatment or rehabilitative orientation inherent in *parens patriae* is not acceptable to some juvenile justice experts. Contemporary juvenile court jurisprudence stresses individual accountability for one's actions (Champion 2007). Consistent with a growing trend in the criminal justice system toward just deserts and justice, a similar trend is being observed throughout the juvenile justice system (Champion and Mays 1991). This get-tough movement is geared toward providing law violators with swifter, harsher, and more certain justice and punishment than the previously dominant rehabilitative philosophy of American courts.

The *parens patriae* doctrine has been influenced greatly by the changing rights of juveniles. Since the mid-1960s, juveniles have acquired greater constitutional rights commensurate with those enjoyed by adults in criminal courts. Some professionals believe that as juveniles are vested with greater numbers of constitutional rights, a gradual transformation of the juvenile court is occurring toward one of greater **criminalization** (Feld 2000, 2001). Interestingly, as juveniles obtain a greater range of constitutional rights, they become more immune to the influence of *parens patriae*. Quite simply, juvenile judges are gradually losing much of their former, almost absolute, autonomy over juveniles and their life chances.

VARIATIONS IN CRIMINAL AND JUVENILE COURT PROCESSING

Some of the major differences between juvenile and criminal courts are indicated below.

1. Juvenile courts are civil proceedings exclusively designed for juveniles, whereas criminal courts are proceedings designed to try adults charged with crimes. The civil-criminal distinction is important because a civil adjudication of a case does not result in a criminal record.

2. Informality characterizes juvenile court proceedings, whereas criminal proceedings are formal. Juvenile court judges frequently address juveniles directly and casually. Formal criminal or evidentiary procedures are not followed rigorously, and hearsay from various sources is considered together with factual evidence.

3. In thirty-nine states, juveniles are not entitled to a trial by jury, unless the juvenile court judge approves. In those jurisdictions that do not provide jury trials for juveniles in special circumstances, judicial approval of a jury trial for juveniles is required.

4. Juvenile court and criminal court proceedings are adversarial.

5. All criminal courts are courts of record, whereas transcripts of most juvenile proceedings are made only if the judge decides. However, some juvenile court judges may have the resources and/or interest to provide for such transcriptions, particularly if serious offenses against certain juveniles have been alleged.

6. The **standard of proof** used for determining one's guilt in criminal proceedings is beyond a reasonable doubt. This same standard is applicable in juvenile courts where violations of criminal laws are alleged and incarceration in a juvenile facility is a possible punishment. However, the less rigorous civil standard of preponderance of evidence is used in most other juvenile court matters where one's loss of liberty is not at issue.

7. Criminal courts have the full range of penalties, including death and life-without-parole options. Juvenile courts have limited jurisdiction, and they can only dispose juveniles to terms that terminate when they reach adulthood.

JUVENILE COURT HISTORY

A Brief History of Juvenile Courts in the United States

Juvenile courts are primarily an American creation. The first juvenile court was established in Illinois in 1899 under the **Illinois Juvenile Court Act.** This does not mean that other states were unconcerned about juveniles at the time, or that other events had not occurred pertaining to youths, their conduct, and their welfare. In fact, numerous agencies and organizations had been established earlier in other jurisdictions, particularly during the latter half of the 1800s.

Reformatories

The first public **reformatory** for juveniles was the New York House of Refuge. It was established in New York City in 1825 by the Society for the Prevention of Pauperism (Champion 2005b). This house of refuge had several goals relating to juveniles, including providing food, clothing, and lodging for all poor, abused, or orphaned youths. However, the **Society for the Prevention of Pauperism** was comprised, in part, of many benefactors, philanthropists, and religionists, and these individuals sought to instill within the youths they serviced a commitment to hard work, strict discipline, and intensive study. These houses were established in various parts of New York and staffed largely by volunteers who knew little or nothing about individual counseling, group therapy techniques, or other useful interventions that might assist youths in surviving city hazards. Because the organization of these houses was decentralized, there were few, if any, external controls that could regulate the quality of care provided.

Child Savers

While houses of refuge operated to provide services for misplaced youths, other random efforts led to the creation of child-saving programs. **Child savers** referred to no one in particular, because anyone who wished to be of assistance in helping children and intervening in their lives for constructive purposes could define themselves as child savers. No one knows what child-saving meant, but many persons were involved in providing food, shelter, and other forms of care for needy children.

Community-Based Private Agencies

Jane Addams established and operated **Hull House** in Chicago, Illinois, in 1889. This was a settlement home used largely by children from immigrant families in the Chicago area. Many adults worked long hours, and many youths were otherwise unsupervised and wandered about their neighborhoods looking for something to do. Using money from various charities and philanthropists, Addams supplied many children with creative activities to alleviate their boredom and monotony. Addams integrated these activities with moral, ethical, and religious teachings. In her own way, she was hoping to deter these youths from lives of crime with her constructive activities and teaching.

Truancy Statutes

Truancy laws were passed by the Massachusetts state legislature in 1852, where the first compulsory school attendance statutes were established. By 1918, all jurisdictions had truancy statutes. Juveniles who did not attend school were subject to being taken into custody. State homes were used to place such youths, where it could be demonstrated that they had little, if any, adult supervision at home.

The Lack of Juvenile Court Uniformity

Much variation exists among juvenile court organization and operation in the United States (Champion 2007). Even great variations in juvenile court operations and functions are found within the same state. Some jurisdictions have courts that adjudicate juvenile offenders as well as decide child custody. Thus, while it is true that all jurisdictions presently have juvenile courts, these courts are not always called juvenile courts.

Specialized Juvenile Courts

Most early juvenile court proceedings were different from criminal courts. These proceedings often involved a juvenile charged with some offense; a petitioner claiming the juvenile should be declared delinquent, or dependent, or neglected; and a judge who would decide things. Juveniles had no rights, no attorneys, and were not permitted to call witnesses or testify in their own behalf. Juvenile court judges made decisions about juveniles according to what the judges believed to be in the best interests of the children. Thus, much individualized justice was dispensed by juvenile court judges.

The Closed and Arbitrary Nature of Juvenile Court Proceedings

Early juvenile court proceedings were closed to the general public in order to protect the identities of the youthful accused. Mere allegations, together with uncorroborated statements and pronouncements from probation officers and others, were sufficient for juvenile court judges to declare any juvenile either delinquent or not delinquent. Penalties imposed ranged from verbal reprimands and warnings to incarceration in a state reform school or industrial school.

The Bureaucratization and Criminalization of Juvenile Courts

Generally, juvenile courts are viewed as **due process courts** rather than **traditional courts** (Feld 2003). Due process juvenile courts involve more formal case dispositions, a greater rate of intake dismissals, and greater importance attached to offense characteristics and seriousness. Traditional courts are characterized as less formal, with greater use made of secure confinement. Both defense and prosecuting attorneys play more important roles in due process juvenile courts compared with traditional ones (Guevara and Herz 2004).

Public Defenders for Juveniles

Greater procedural formality in the juvenile justice system has been observed relating to the appointment of public defenders for juvenile indigents. Formerly, defense counsels for juveniles often were the juvenile's probation officer or a social caseworker with a vested interest in the case. It is not entirely clear how these officers and workers were able to separate their law enforcement and defense functions to avoid allegations of conflicts of interest. Little public interest was exhibited in the quality of defense of juvenile cases.

In recent years, juvenile court proceedings have become increasingly formalized (Champion 2004). Further, public access to these proceedings in most jurisdictions is increasing. Thus, the presence of defense counsel, an adversarial scenario, a trial-like atmosphere where witnesses testify for and against juvenile defendants, and adherence to Rules of Procedure for Juvenile Courts are clear indicators of greater formalization, bureaucratization, and criminalization. Also with greater formalization, less disparity in dispositional decision making has occurred relating to one's gender, ethnic identity, or race (Charish 2004; Rosay and Myrstol 2004).

THE JUVENILE JUSTICE PROCESS

Referrals and Petitions

Referrals

Many juvenile encounters with the juvenile justice system are prompted by referrals from police officers (Champion 2007). Referrals are notifications made to juvenile court authorities that a juvenile requires the court's attention. Referrals may be made by anyone, such as concerned parents, school principals, teachers, neighbors, and others. However, over 90 percent of all referrals to juvenile court are made by law enforcement officers. Some researchers have suggested that disparities in juvenile offender processing begin at this stage and continue throughout the entire juvenile justice system, where factors such as race, ethnicity, gender, and socioeconomic status intervene to affect juveniles in different ways (Ketchum and Embrick 2004). Arrest and being taken into custody is the first of three major processing points that indicate different degrees of entry into the juvenile justice system for juveniles. The other entry points include probation disposition and court disposition. Each of these entry points involves the exercise of discretion from various actors in the juvenile justice system.

Petitions

A petition is a legal document filed by interested parties alleging that a juvenile is delinquent, a status offender, or in need of adult supervision. The petition requests that the juvenile court decide whether the allegations are true and determine an appropriate penalty or disposition. When a petition is filed against a particular juvenile, the juvenile is subjected to an intake hearing or simply, intake.

Intake

Intake varies in formality among jurisdictions (Worling 1995). Intake is a screening procedure conducted by a court officer or a probation officer, where one or several courses of action are recommended. Some jurisdictions conduct **intake hearings,** where comments and opinions are solicited from significant others such as the police, parents, neighbors, or victims. These proceedings are important, regardless of their degree of formality.

An **intake officer** is either a court-appointed official who hears complaints against juveniles and attempts early resolutions of them, or is more often a juvenile probation officer who performs intake as a special assignment. In many small jurisdictions, juvenile probation officers may perform diverse functions, including intake screenings, enforcement of truancy statutes, and juvenile placements. Intake officers consider youths' attitudes, demeanor, age, offense seriousness, and a host of other factors. If the offenses alleged are serious, what evidence exists against the offender? Should the offender be referred to certain community social service agencies, receive psychological counseling, receive vocational counseling and guidance, acquire educational or technical training and skills, be issued a verbal reprimand, be placed on some type of diversionary status, or be returned to parental custody? Interviews with parents and neighbors may be conducted as a part of an intake officer's information gathering. In most jurisdictions, intake normally results in one of five actions, depending, in part, upon the discretion of intake officers:

1. dismissal of the case, with or without a verbal or written reprimand;
2. remand youths to the custody of their parents;
3. remand youths to the custody of their parents, with provisions for or referrals to counseling or special services;
4. divert youths to an alternative dispute resolution program, if one exists in the jurisdiction;
5. refer youths to the juvenile prosecutor for further action and possible filing of a delinquency petition.

Juvenile Court Prosecutors and Decision Making

Like their criminal court counterparts, juvenile court prosecutors have broad discretionary powers. They may dismiss cases against certain juveniles. They may screen cases by diverting some of the most serious ones to criminal court through waiver, transfer, or certification. A **prosecutorial waiver** is used for this purpose. Some cases are diverted out of the juvenile justice system for informal processing (Feld 2000). Prosecutors may also file petitions or act on the petitions filed by others. These documents assert that juveniles fall within the categories of dependent or neglected, status offender, or delinquent, and the reasons for such assertions are usually provided (Champion 2007). Filing a petition formally places the juvenile before the juvenile court judge in many jurisdictions.

ADJUDICATORY PROCEEDINGS

Most of the physical trappings of criminal courts are present in juvenile courts, including the judge's bench, tables for the prosecution and defense, and a witness stand. Juvenile court judges have almost absolute discretion in how their courts are conducted. Juvenile defendants may or may not be granted a trial by jury, if one is requested. Few states permit jury trials for juveniles in juvenile courts, according to legislative mandates. After hearing the evidence presented by both sides in any juvenile proceeding, the judge decides or **adjudicates** the matter in an **adjudication hearing.** An **adjudication** is a judgment or action on the petition filed with the court by others. If the petition alleges delinquency on the part of certain juveniles, the judge determines whether the juveniles are delinquent or not delinquent. If the petition alleges that the juveniles involved are dependent, neglected, or otherwise in need of care by agencies or others, the judge decides the matter. If the adjudicatory proceeding fails to support the facts alleged in the petition filed with the court, the case is dismissed and the youth is freed. If the adjudicatory proceeding supports the allegations, then the judge must sentence the juvenile or order a particular disposition (A. Harris 2004).

Dispositions

Twelve dispositions are available to juvenile court judges, if the facts alleged in petitions are upheld. These dispositions may be grouped into (1) nominal, (2) conditional, or (3) custodial options.

Nominal Dispositions

Nominal dispositions are the least punitive of the three major courses of action available to juvenile court judges. These are usually verbal warnings or reprimands. Release to the custody of parents or legal guardians completes the juvenile court action.

Conditional Dispositions

All **conditional dispositions** are probationary options. Youths are placed on probation and required to comply with certain conditions during the probationary period. Conditional options or dispositions usually provide for an act or acts on the part of juveniles to be fulfilled as conditions of the sentence imposed. If juveniles have been adjudicated as delinquent and if the delinquency involved damage to a victim's property or bodily harm, restitution to victims may be required to pay for the property or medical bills (Wood 2004). Various kinds of community service are performed by juveniles, such as cutting courthouse lawns, cleaning up city parks, and cleaning debris from city highways or public areas. Group or individual therapy may be required of certain juveniles who exhibit psychological or social maladjustment. If some juveniles are alcohol- or drug-dependent, they may be required to participate in various recovery programs.

Custodial Dispositions

Custodial dispositions are either **nonsecure custody** or **confinement** or **secure custody** or **confinement.** Nonsecure custody consists of placing certain juveniles into a **foster home, group home,** or **camp, ranch,** or schools. These are temporary measures often designed to make more permanent arrangements for juvenile placement later. Juveniles have freedom of movement, and they can generally participate in school and other youthful activities. For juveniles, secure custody is often the last resort considered by most juvenile court judges. There is a general reluctance among judges to incarcerate youths because of adverse labeling effects. Furthermore, there are increasing numbers of alternatives to incarceration within communities. Judges are increasingly apprised of these programs and are assigning more youths to them in lieu of industrial school placements (Kupchik 2004).

Changing Juvenile Court Practices

Minimizing the Confidentiality of Juvenile Court Records and Proceedings

In 1995, 22 states had provisions for open hearings in juvenile or family court proceedings. Only 11 states did not provide for the release of the names of those juveniles charged with serious offenses. Only six states did not permit court record releases to interested parties. In fact, all states currently make available juvenile court records to any party showing a legitimate interest. In such cases, information is ordinarily obtained through a court order. Finger-printing and photographing of juveniles is conducted routinely in most states. Half the states require registration of all juvenile offenders when they enter new jurisdictions. Also, most states presently have state repositories of juvenile records and other relevant information about juvenile offending. Seventeen states prohibited sealing or expunging juvenile court records after certain dates, such as one's age of majority or adulthood (Champion 2007). Therefore, juveniles today are considerably more likely to have their offenses known to the public in one form or another.

The protections previously enjoyed by juveniles are rapidly disappearing. The greater formality of juvenile proceedings as well as their openness to others may restrict the discretion of juvenile court judges, although this limitation is not particularly an undesirable one. This is because juvenile court judge decision making has often been individualized, and individualized decision making is inherently discriminatory. With more open proceedings, less individualization is evident, thus making due process a greater priority for juvenile court judges. Theoretically, at least, more open proceedings are fairer proceedings. Table 11.1 summarizes some of the current developments regarding confidentiality provisions relating to serious and violent juvenile offenders for 2005.

The Prosecution Decision in 2000

The juvenile justice system has been slow in its **case processing** of juvenile offenders. In fact, delays in filing charges against juveniles and the eventual adjudicatory hearing are chronic in many jurisdictions. Juveniles arrested for various types of offenses may wait a year or longer in some jurisdictions before their cases are heard by juvenile court judges. Juvenile court prosecutors may delay filing charges against particular juveniles for a variety of reasons. The most obvious reasons for delays—court **case backlogs,** crowded court dockets, insufficient prosecutorial staff, too much paperwork—are not always valid reasons. In many instances, the actors themselves are at fault. In short, prosecutors and judges may simply be plodding along at a slow pace, because of their own personal dispositions and work habits. It has been illustrated that in many jurisdictions where prosecutors and judges have aggressively tackled their caseload problems and forced functionaries to work faster, juvenile caseload processing has been greatly accelerated. Thus, the time between a juvenile's arrest and disposition has been greatly shortened because of individual decision making and not because of any organizational constraints or overwork (Champion 2007).

TABLE 11.1 SUMMARY OF CONFIDENTIALITY PROVISIONS RELATING TO SERIOUS AND VIOLENT JUVENILE OFFENDERS, 2005 (continued)

State	Open Hearing	Release of Name	Release of Court Record[a]	Statewide Repository	Finger-printing	Photo-graphing	Offender Registration	Seal/ Expunge Records Prohibited
Totals:	30	42	48	44	47	46	39	25
Alabama	•	•	•	•	•	•	•	•
Alaska		•	•		•	•	•	
Arizona	•	•	•	•	•	•	•	•
Arkansas	•	•	•	•	•	•	•	
California		•	•	•	•	•	•	•
Colorado	•		•	•	•	•	•	•
Connecticut		•	•	•	•	•	•	
Delaware	•	•	•		•	•	•	
Dist. of Columbia		•	•	•	•	•	•	
Florida	•	•	•	•	•	•	•	•
Georgia	•	•	•	•	•	•	•	
Hawaii		•	•	•	•	•	•	
Idaho	•	•	•	•	•	•	•	
Illinois	•	•	•	•	•	•	•	•
Indiana	•	•	•	•	•	•	•	
Iowa	•	•	•	•	•	•		
Kansas	•	•	•	•	•	•	•	•
Kentucky	•	•	•	•	•	•	•	
Louisiana	•	•	•	•	•	•	•	•
Maine	•	•	•	•	•	•	•	

Maryland
Massachusetts
Michigan
Minnesota
Mississippi
Missouri
Montana
Nebraska
Nevada
New Hampshire
New Jersey
New Mexico
New York
North Carolina
North Dakota
Ohio
Oklahoma
Oregon
Pennsylvania
Rhode Island
South Carolina
South Dakota
Tennessee
Texas

(continued)

TABLE 11.1 SUMMARY OF CONFIDENTIALITY PROVISIONS RELATING TO SERIOUS AND VIOLENT JUVENILE OFFENDERS, 2005 (continued)

State	Open Hearing	Release of Name	Release of Court Record[a]	Statewide Repository	Finger-printing	Photo-graphing	Offender Registration	Seal/Expunge Records Prohibited
Utah	•	•	•	•	•	•	•	•
Vermont								
Virginia	•	•	•	•	•	•	•	•
Washington	•	•			•	•	•	•
West Virginia		•			•	•		•
Wisconsin	•	•	•	•			•	
Wyoming			•	•	•	•	•	•

Legend: • indicates the provision(s) allowed by each state as of the end of the 1997 legislative session.

[a] In this category • indicates a provision for juvenile court records to be specifically released to at least one of the following parties: the public, the victims(s), the school(s), the prosecutor, law enforcement, or social agency; however, all states allow records to be released to any party who can show a legitimate interest, typically by court order.

Source: Patricia Torbet and Linda Szymanski, *State Legislative Responses to Violent Juvenile Crime: 1996–1997 Update.* Washington, DC.: U.S. Department of Justice, 1998:10. Updated 2005 by author.

However, in 30 states in 2005, juvenile court prosecutors were at liberty to file charges against juvenile offenders whenever they decided. No binding legislative provisions were applicable to these actors to force them to act promptly and bring a youth's case before the juvenile court. In the meantime, 20 states have established time limits that cannot be exceeded between the time of a juvenile's court referral and the filing of charges by prosecutors.

Defense Counsels as Advocates for Juveniles

Attorneys for Juveniles as a Matter of Right

Juveniles are entitled to attorneys at all stages of juvenile proceedings. Despite this safeguard, attorney representation for juveniles in juvenile courts in most jurisdictions is less than 75 percent. In several states, only 50 percent of all adjudicated juveniles are represented by counsel (Johnson 2002).

Defense Counsel and Ensuring Due Process Rights for Juveniles

The manifest function of defense attorneys in juvenile courts is to ensure that **due process** is fulfilled by all participants. Defense attorneys are the primary advocates of fairness for juveniles who are charged with crimes or other types of offenses (Rodriguez and Armstrong 2004). Minors, particularly very young youths, are more susceptible to the persuasiveness of adults.

Are Attorneys Being Used More Frequently by Juvenile Defendants?

Yes. At least a survey of five states during the 1980–1989 period (California, Montana, Nebraska, North Dakota, and Pennsylvania) found that attorney use by juvenile offenders increased systematically across these years (Champion 1992). Attorney use varies by jurisdiction, however. In the late 1980s, about 90 percent of all California juvenile cases involved either private or publicly appointed defense counsel. However, in states such as Nebraska and North Dakota, attorney use by juveniles occurred in about 60 percent of the cases.

Do Defense Counsel for Juveniles Make a Difference in Their Case Dispositions?

Having an attorney to represent you generally makes a difference in the case disposition. But not all dispositions are favorable for juveniles. The presence of attorneys may heighten juvenile court formality. Earlier in the processing of juveniles, attorney presence may cause intake officers to take sterner measures with juveniles who ordinarily would be dismissed from the system. More than a few intake officers, for instance, are intimidated by attorneys, if present. If an intake officer would be inclined to divert a particular case from the juvenile justice system because of his/her judgment that the youth will probably not

BOX 11.1 TEENS CAN RAISE INSANITY DEFENSE FOR SERIOUS CRIMES

Christopher Tindall, 16, is a Logan County, Ohio youth who had previously served two years in a state correctional facility for youths for raping a 14-year-old girl. Subsequently Tindall was released from custody and was placed in a group home, where he was able to freely roam about his community. One evening, December 23, 2005, Tindall sneaked out of the group home and broke into the home of 72-year-old Joan Green, who lived two doors away. Following the discovery of her dead body the next day, police linked Tindall to the crime. She had been robbed, raped, and murdered. Furthermore, there was evidence that Tindall mutilated Green's corpse after she was dead. Tindall subsequently confessed and was charged with aggravated murder, rape, aggravated burglary, breaking and entering, and abuse of a corpse. He could face trial as an adult if waived to criminal court. If so, he could be sentenced to life imprisonment.

Tindall's attorney immediately filed a motion to declare Tindall insane. The defense counsel, Daniel J. LaRoche, says that Tindall suffers from a mental illness or a disability. The victim's family, including her son, Steve Green, says that he's not worried that Tindall could end up in a mental institution for his crimes rather than a prison if convicted. Green said, "I don't think he's insane and I don't think anyone else thinks he's insane. He's just trying anything he can." In fact, when Tindall was being transferred to a state facility after being confined in a local county jail cell for several days, sheriff's deputies discovered two metal strips, which had been taken from the above ceiling tiles. They were secreted away underneath Tindall's bed and had been sharpened. It is uncertain what Tindall planned to do with the metal strips, although they could have been used as lethal weapons. According to Colonel Keith LeVan of the Logan County Sheriff's Office, "It was just time for him to go." He is now in the custody of the Ohio Department of Youth Services and under constant surveillance.

Prosecutor Gerald Heaton said that he had expected an insanity plea to be entered in Tindall's case. He said the court would order psychiatric examinations, although he believes that Tindall is fully competent and knows exactly what he did as well as the possible consequences of his actions.

Should the insanity plea be allowed in juvenile cases? What sort of punishment is most appropriate for Tindall, who had previously been adjudicated delinquent in the rape of a 14-year-old? Should this factor aggravate his subsequent crimes? What do you think? [Source: Adapted from Holly Zachariah and the *Columbus Dispatch*, "Teenager's Attorneys Enter Insanity Plea in Slaying Woman Before Christmas," February 24, 2006.]

reoffend, this diversion decision may not be selected if an attorney is present to represent the juvenile's interests. The intake officer may feel that the prosecutor of juvenile court judge should decide the case. However, in an otherwise attorney-free environment, the intake officer would act differently. Thus, an attorney's presence or absence may cause intake officers to react differently and make decisions that are better or worse for juveniles charged with delinquency or status offenses.

Defense Counsel as Guardians Ad Litem

Defense counsel perform additional responsibilities as they attempt to ensure that the best interests of their clients are served in ways that will protect children from parents who abuse them (Kupchik 2004; Ward 2004). A **guardian** *ad litem* are special guardians appointed by the court in which a particular litigation is pending to represent a youth, ward, or unborn person in that particular litigation (Williams, Rodeheaver, and Guerrero 2004). Most juvenile court jurisdictions have guardian *ad litem* programs, where interested persons serve in this capacity. In some cases, defense counsel for youths perform the dual role of defense counsel and the youth's guardian *ad litem*. Guardians *ad litem* are supposed to work in ways that will benefit those they represent, and such guardians provide legal protection from others. Defense counsel working as guardians *ad litem* may act to further the child's best interests, despite a child's contrary requests or demands.

Juvenile Offender Plea Bargaining and the Role of Defense Counsel

Many juveniles plea bargain with juvenile court prosecutors (Helms et al. 2004). Plea bargaining is an invaluable tool with which to eliminate case backlogs that might occur in some of the larger juvenile courts. Most frequently sought by defense counsel are charge reductions against their clients by prosecutors. Defense counsel are interested in reducing the stigma of a serious, negative juvenile court profile of their youthful clients by seeking reduced charges from prosecutors (Burruss and Kempf-Leonard 2002). Prosecutors benefit because plea agreements would increase case processing time.

Jury Trials for Juveniles

In 1997 the National Center for Juvenile Justice investigated various state jurisdictions to determine their present status concerning jury trials and other formal procedures for juveniles. The categories created by this investigation included the following: (1) states providing no right to a jury trial for juvenile delinquents under any circumstances, (2) states providing a right to a jury trial

BOX 11.2 MOST YOUTHS GET PROBATION FOR THEIR DELINQUENT ACTS

■ In Columbus, Ohio, 11-year-old Javon VanCleaf and 13-year-old Kareem VanCleaf kicked out the supports of a porch, causing it to collapse. The porch fell on a 12-year-old boy, Dwayne Gordon, killing him instantly. The boys were taken into custody by police and held for an adjudicatory hearing in juvenile court. They were charged with criminal mischief and involuntary manslaughter. Subsequently a juvenile court judge placed the boys in a rehabilitative program and ordered them monitored by the county children's services. The involuntary manslaughter charge was dismissed. The boys were ordered to serve one year of probation under supervision.

■ Twin sisters, Hanaa and Namaa Babieh, 16, Newark, Ohio, posted death threats against various high school classmates on a website. Subsequently their identity was determined by investigators and they were taken into custody by police who charged them with delinquency and disorderly conduct. They were also charged with inducing panic among those threatened by their Web postings. Judge Robert Hoover heard their case. They claimed that their postings or death threats were only a prank. The judge thought otherwise. He told them, "You frightened, you scared many, many people. You scared parents, students, faculty, and staff." He adjudicated the girls on the disorderly conduct charge and disposed the girls to probation for 120 days as well as 20 hours of community service. He also ordered them to pay a $100 fine from their own money. Finally, he ordered them to write a 500-word essay about building character based on positive values. The charges of inducing panic were dismissed as a part of a plea agreement.

■ It happened in Hamilton County, Ohio. Four Westwood teens were charged with aggravated robbery in the theft of bicycles from several 11- and 12-year-olds. The four teenage robbers, ages 14 and 15, approached the younger children and put hands in their shirts, claiming to have weapons and demanding the youths' bikes. No weapons were ever found. However, witnesses were able to give the police sufficient identifying information to locate the teen robbers and arrest them. The teens were kept in a youth detention facility for the entire summer while awaiting their delinquency adjudication on the robbery charges. The judge told them, "Did you have a nice summer? No? Freedom is a precious thing. It can be taken away from you, by your own actions. Very quickly and substantially." The judge ordered the teens to juvenile court in shackles. Judge Thomas Lipps of the Hamilton County Juvenile Court ordered the offenders placed on probation for one year, under intensive supervision. They were off the streets for at least five weeks of the summer, and the time they served is something the judge hopes they never will forget. The judge said that he hoped that this disposition would send a strong message to other teens. One of the teen robbers' mothers said, "I wondered for a minute because of the justice system with juveniles, you know, but he (the judge) came through and he was good and he was fair. He did make them serve some time and let them think about things." Calls to the parents of the teen victims were not returned.

■ A 14-year-old hacker, unnamed by the juvenile court for purposes of confidentiality, was ordered to serve three years on probation by a federal court. The case occurred in Seattle, Washington, where the youth had released a computer worm against Microsoft software. The "Blaster Worm" was released by the youth in August 2003 and caused thousands of computers in the Seattle area and elsewhere to crash. The federal district court judge ordered the youth to perform 300 hours of community service to the homeless and less fortunate members of the community. He also required the youth to submit to mental health counseling. The costs to Microsoft and computer users were estimated in the millions of dollars.

■ Two 13-year-old girls from Marietta, Georgia, were caught serving tainted cake to their classmates at school. They laced a cake with glue, hot sauce, and modeling clay, although no toxic ingredients were subsequently detected. Authorities learned of the incident and had the cake examined after several students became ill from eating cake portions. The girls were arrested by police and initially charged with attempted murder. But a juvenile court judge later reduced the charges from felonies to misdemeanors after it became clear that the girls did not intend to poison their classmates. They were adjudicated delinquent on the charge of disrupting a public school and disposed to nine and twelve months of probation, respectively. Their identities were not released to the press because of confidentiality privileges involving juveniles in Georgia. The girls have been allowed to return to classes, but at different schools.

■ A 17-year-old youth was driving his car down a city street in Castle Rock, Colorado, while text-messaging a friend with his cell phone. While doing so, he ran down and killed a bicyclist. The high school senior was arrested and charged with vehicular manslaughter and careless driving causing death, crimes that carried up to five years in prison. The cyclist, 63-year-old Jim R. Price, was a retired geologist who died two days following being struck by the car. The juvenile court judge hearing the case allowed the youth to address the court, where he accepted responsibility for his actions. "If I hadn't been on my cell phone that day, Mr. Price would still be alive. There are no words to explain to them (the Price family) how sorry I am," the youth said. The Price family accepted that the teen is genuinely remorseful for his actions and asked the judge to spare him a jail sentence.

(continued)

BOX 11.2 (continued)

The judge was moved and imposed a 9-day jail sentence on the youth, together with 300 hours of community service aimed at persuading other teens to pay attention to their driving. Additionally, the youth will serve 98 days of house arrest and may not operate a motor vehicle or own a cell phone during that time interval. Douglas County Court judge Michelle Marker said, "Nothing I'm going to do is going to make him any more sorry than he is," but she added that he had to atone for his actions and that others should see the consequences of his carelessness.

Are all of these cases deserving of the light sentences meted out by the judges in each situation? Obviously, some acts committed by these youths were more serious than others. Should more youths be locked up for committing serious offenses? What do you think? [Sources: Adapted from the Associated Press, "Two Boys Sentenced to Probation in Fatal Porch Collapse," March 3, 2005; adapted from the Associated Press, "Twins Sentenced for Threats Posted on Web Site," January 22, 2006; adapted from Bill Price, Liz Foreman, and *9News,* "Westwood Teens Sentenced for Bike Thefts," September 22, 2003; adapted from *Seattle Post-Intelligencer,* "14-Year-Old Hacker Sentenced to Probation," February 12, 2005; adapted from the Associated Press, "Girls Sentenced to Nine Months Probation in Cake Case," February 9, 2005; adapted from the Associated Press, "Texting Teen Who Killed Cyclist is Sentenced to Jail, Probation," February 9, 2006.]

for juvenile delinquents under any circumstances, (3) states not providing a jury trial for juvenile delinquents except under specified circumstances, (4) states providing the right to a jury trial for juvenile delinquents under specified circumstances, and (5) states with statutes allowing juvenile delinquents with a right to jury trial to waive that right.

States Not Providing Jury Trials for Juvenile Delinquents Under Any Circumstances:

Alabama, Arizona, Arkansas, California, District of Columbia, Georgia, Hawaii, Indiana, Kentucky, Louisiana, Maryland, Mississippi, Nevada, New Jersey, North Dakota, Ohio, Oregon, Pennsylvania, South Carolina, Tennessee, Utah, Vermont, and Washington

States Providing Jury Trials for Juveniles Under Any Circumstance:

Alaska, Massachusetts, Michigan, and West Virginia

States Not Providing Jury Trials for Juvenile Delinquents Except Under Specified Circumstances:

Colorado (all hearings, including adjudicatory hearings shall be heard without a jury; juvenile not entitled to a trial by jury when petition alleges a delinquent act that is a class 2 or class 3 misdemeanor, a petty offense, a violation of a municipal or county ordinance, or a violation of a court order if, prior to the trial and with the approval of the court, the district attorney has waived in writing the right to seek a commitment to the department of human services or a sentence to the county jail); District of Columbia (probation revocation hearings heard without a jury); Florida (adjudicatory hearings heard without a jury); Louisiana (adjudication hearings heard without a jury); Maine (adjudicatory hearing heard without a jury); Montana (hearing on whether juvenile should be transferred to adult criminal court heard without a jury; probation revocation proceeding heard without a jury); Nebraska (adjudicatory hearing heard without a jury); New Mexico (probation revocation proceedings heard without a jury); North Carolina (adjudicatory hearing heard without a jury); Texas (detention hearing heard without a jury; hearing to consider transfer of child for criminal proceedings and hearing to consider waiver of jurisdiction held without a jury; disposition hearing heard without a jury, unless child in jeopardy of a determinate sentence; hearing to modify a disposition heard without a jury, unless child in jeopardy of a sentence for a determinate term); Wisconsin (no right to a jury trial in a waiver hearing); Wyoming (probation revocation hearing heard without a jury; [14–6–237]: transfer hearing heard without a jury).

States Where Juvenile Delinquent Has a Right to a Jury Trial Under Specified Circumstances:

Arkansas (if amount of restitution ordered by the court exceeds $10,000, juvenile has right to jury trial on all issues of liability and damages); Colorado (no right to a jury trial unless otherwise provided by this title; juvenile may demand a jury trial, unless the petition alleges a delinquent act that is a class 2 or class 3 misdemeanor, a petty offense, a violation of a municipal or county ordinance, or a violation of a court order if, prior to the trial and with the approval of the court, the district attorney has waived in writing the right to seek a commitment to the department of human services or a sentence to the county jail; any juvenile alleged to be an aggravated juvenile offender (defined in statute) has the right to a jury trial); Idaho (any juvenile age 14 to 18 alleged to have committed a violent offense defined in statute or a controlled substance offense has the right to a jury trial); Illinois (any habitual juvenile offender defined in statute has the right to a jury trial); Kansas (any juvenile alleged to have committed an act that would be a felony if committed by an adult has the right to a jury trial); Minnesota (child who is prosecuted as an extended jurisdiction juvenile has the right to a jury trial on the issue of guilt); Montana (any juvenile who contests the offenses alleged in the petition has the right to a jury trial); New Mexico (jury trial on issues of alleged delinquent acts may be demanded when the offenses alleged would be triable by a jury if committed by an adult); Oklahoma (child has the right to a jury trial in an adjudicatory hearing); Rhode Island (child has the right to a jury trial when the court finds the child is subject to certification to adult court); Texas (child has the right to a jury trial at adjudicatory hearing; child has the right to a jury trial at disposition hearing only if the child is in jeopardy of a determinate sentence; child has the right to a jury trial at a hearing to modify the disposition only if the child is in jeopardy of a determinate sentence on the issues of the violation of the court's orders and the sentence); Virginia (if the juvenile indicted, the juvenile has the right to a jury trial; if found guilty of capital murder, the court fixes the sentence with intervention of a jury; where the appeal is taken by the child on a finding that he or she is delinquent and the alleged delinquent act would be a felony if done by an adult, the child is entitled to a jury); Wyoming (juvenile has right to a jury trial at an adjudicatory hearing).

States Providing Right to a Jury Trial for Juvenile Delinquents Where Juvenile Delinquents Can Waive Their Right to a Jury Trial:

Colorado (unless a jury is demanded, it shall be deemed waived); Illinois (the minor can demand in open court and with advice of counsel, a trial by the court without a jury); Massachusetts (the child can file written waiver and consent to be tried by the court without a jury; this waiver cannot be received unless the child is represented by counsel or has filed, through his parent or guardian, a written waiver of counsel); Montana (in the absence of a demand, a jury trial is waived); Oklahoma (the child has right to waive jury trial); Texas (the trial shall be by jury unless jury is waived); Wyoming (failure of party to demand a jury no later than 10 days after the party is advised of his right, is a waiver of this right). [Sources: Linda A. Szymanski, *Juvenile's Right to a Jury Trial in a Delinquency Hearing (1996 Update).* Pittsburgh: National Center for Juvenile Justice, 1997; updated by author 2005.]

TRANSFERS, WAIVERS, AND CERTIFICATIONS

A **transfer** means changing the jurisdiction over certain juvenile offenders to another jurisdiction, usually from juvenile court jurisdiction to criminal court jurisdiction. A transfer is also known as a **waiver,** referring to a change of jurisdiction from the authority of juvenile court judges to criminal court judges. Prosecutors or juvenile court judges decide that in some cases, juveniles should be waived or transferred to the jurisdiction of criminal courts (Bishop et al. 2004).

In Utah, juveniles are waived or transferred to criminal courts through a process known as **certification** (Listwan and Miethe 2004). A certification is a formal procedure whereby the state declares the juvenile to be an adult for the purpose of a criminal prosecution in a criminal court (Sridharan et al. 2004). The results of certifications are the same as for waivers or transfers. Thus, certifications, waivers, and transfers result in juvenile offenders being subject to the jurisdiction of criminal courts where they can be prosecuted as though they were adult offenders. A 13-year-old murderer, for instance, might be transferred to criminal court for a criminal prosecution on the murder charge (Merlo and Benekos 2004).

The Rationale for Transfers, Waivers, or Certifications

The basic rationale underlying the use of waivers is that the most serious juvenile offenders will be transferred to the jurisdiction of criminal courts where the harshest punishments, including capital punishment, may be imposed as sanctions (Jordan 2004b). A listing of reasons for the use of transfers, waivers, or certifications include the following:

1. To make it possible for harsher punishments to be imposed.
2. To provide just-deserts and proportionately severe punishments on those juveniles who deserve such punishments by their more violent actions.
3. To foster fairness in administering punishments according to one's serious offending.
4. To hold serious or violent offenders more accountable for what they have done.
5. To show other juveniles who contemplate committing serious offenses that the system works and that harsh punishments can be expected if serious offenses are committed.
6. To provide a deterrent to decrease juvenile violence.
7. To overcome the traditional leniency of juvenile courts and provide more realistic sanctions.
8. To make youths realize the seriousness of their offending and induce remorse and acceptance of responsibility.

The Characteristics of Transferred Juveniles

In 2004, there were 13,200 youths who were transferred to criminal court. Most juveniles transferred were male, with only 625 females (4.7 percent) being waived (Bureau of Justice Statistics 2005). About 7,200 (54 percent) of all transferred juveniles were black or other minority, despite the fact that white juveniles comprised about 66 percent of all cases referred to juvenile court.

Furthermore, those charged with person offenses and waived to criminal court made up only 41 percent of those transferred (Johnson, Banister, and Alm 2004). About 44 percent of those charged with property or public order offenses were waived to criminal courts, while about 14 percent of those waived were charged with drug offenses (Bureau of Justice Statistics 2005).

Youngest Ages at Which Juveniles Can Be Transferred to Criminal Court

In 1987, all federal districts and 15 states indicated no specified age for transferring juveniles to criminal courts for processing. One state, Vermont, specified age 10 as the minimum age at which a juvenile could be waived. Montana established age 12 as the earliest age for a juvenile waiver. Fourteen states used age 14 as the youngest transfer age, while seven states and the District of Columbia set the minimum transfer age at 15, and seven states used the minimum transfer age of 16. During the 1990s, however, more states moved to have their juvenile age ranges lowered for transfers or waivers. Table 11.2 shows the various states that have modified or enacted changes in their transfer provisions for juveniles during the 1992–1995 period.

Inspecting Table 11.2, under **judicial waiver** modifications, eleven states lowered the age limit at which juveniles can be transferred to criminal court. One example of a significant age modification is Missouri, where the minimum age for juvenile transfers was lowered from 14 to 12 for any felony. In the case of Texas, the minimum transfer age was lowered from 15 to 10. Virginia lowered the transfer age from 15 to 14. Table 11.2 also shows that other modifications were made to get tough toward juvenile offenders. Ten states added crimes to the list of those qualifying youths for transfer to criminal courts. In six states, the age of criminal accountability was lowered, while 24 states authorized additional crimes to be included that would automatically direct that the criminal court would have jurisdiction rather than the juvenile court.

Types of Waivers

Four types of waiver actions include (1) prosecutorial waivers, (2) judicial/discretionary waivers, (3) demand waivers, and (4) legislative or automatic waivers.

Prosecutorial Waivers

Prosecutorial waivers are also known as **direct file** or concurrent jurisdiction. Thus, under direct file, the prosecutor has the sole authority to decide whether a particular juvenile case will be heard in criminal court or juvenile court. In Florida, one of the states where prosecutors have concurrent jurisdiction,

TABLE 11.2   STATES MODIFYING OR ENACTING TRANSFER PROVISIONS, 1996–2005

Type of Transfer Provision	Action Taken (Number of States)	States Making Changes	Examples
Discretionary Waiver	Added crimes (7 states)	DE, KY, LA, MT, NV, RI, WA	Kentucky: 1996 provision permits the juvenile court to transfer a juvenile to criminal court if 14 years old and charged with a felony with a firearm.
	Lowered age limit (4 states)	CO, DE, HI, VA	Hawaii: 1997 provision adds language that allows waiver of a minor at any age (previously 16) if charged with first- or second-degree murder (or attempts) and there is no evidence that the person is committable to an institution for the mentally defective or mentally ill.
	Added or modified prior record provisions (4 states)	FL, HI, IN, KY	Florida: 1997 legislation requires that if the juvenile is 14 at the time of a fourth felony, and certain conditions apply, the State's attorney must ask the court to transfer him or her and certify the child as an adult or must provide written reasons for not making such a request.
Presumptive Waiver	Enacted provisions (2 states)	KS, UT	Kansas: 1996 legislation shifts the burden of proof to the child to rebut the pressumption that the child is an adult.
Direct File	Enacted or modified (8 states)	AR, AZ, CO, FL, GA, MA, MT, OK	Colorado: 1996 legislation adds vehicular homicide, vehicular assault, and felonious arson to direct file statute.
Statutory Exclusion	Enacted provision (2 states)	AZ, MA	Arizona: 1997 legislation establishes exclusion for 15- to 17-year-olds charged with certain violent felonies.
	Added crimes (12 states)	AL, AK, DE, GA, IL, IN, OK, OR, SC, SD, UT, WA	Georgia: 1997 legislation adds crime of battery if victim is a teacher or other school personnel to list of designated felonies.

(continued)

TABLE 11.2   STATES MODIFYING OR ENACTING TRANSFER PROVISIONS, 1996–2005 (continued)

Type of Transfer Provision	Action Taken (Number of States)	States Making Changes	Examples
	Lowered age limit (1 state)	DE	Delaware: 1996 legislation lowers from 16 to 15 the age for which the offense of possession of a firearm during the commission of a felony is automatically prosecuted in criminal court.
	Added lesser-included offense (1 state)	IN	Indiana: 1997 legislation lists exclusion offenses, including any offenses, that may be joined with the listed offenses.

Source: Patricia Torbet and Linda Szymanski, *State Legislative Response to Violent Juvenile Crime: 1996–1997 Update.* Washington, DC.: U.S. Department of Justice, 1998:5. Updated 2005 by author.

prosecutors may file extremely serious charges (e.g., murder, rape, aggravated assault, robbery) against youths in criminal courts and present cases to grand juries for indictment action. Or prosecutors may decide to file the same cases in the juvenile court.

Judicial or Discretionary Waivers

The largest numbers of waivers from juvenile to criminal court annually come about as the result of direct judicial action. Judicial waivers give the juvenile court judge the authority to decide whether to waive jurisdiction and transfer the case to criminal court. Known also as **discretionary waivers,** judicial waivers typically involve a juvenile court judge's consideration of various criteria, including the juvenile's age, current offense, criminal history, and amenability to rehabilitation. This particular type of transfer is invoked following a motion by the prosecutor (Champion 2004).

Legislative or Automatic Waivers

Legislative waivers or **automatic waivers** are statutorily prescribed actions that provide for a specified list of crimes to be excluded from the jurisdiction of juvenile courts, where offending juveniles are within a specified age range, and where the resulting action gives criminal courts immediate jurisdiction over these juveniles. By the mid-1980s, 36 states excluded certain types of offenses from juvenile court jurisdiction. These excluded offenses were either very minor or very serious, ranging from traffic or fishing violations to rape or murder. Also, many state jurisdictions have made provisions for automatic transfers of juveniles to criminal court. Among those states with automatic transfer provisions are Washington, New York, and Illinois (Steiner, Hemmens, and Bell 2004).

Automatic or legislative waivers are also known as **statutory exclusion** or **mandatory transfer.** Statutory exclusion generally refers to provisions that automatically exclude certain juvenile offenders from the juvenile court's original jurisdiction (Champion 2007). An example of statutory exclusion is to simply lower the upper age of original juvenile court jurisdiction from 18 to 17 or 16. States with statutory exclusion make provisions for the statutory exclusion of offenders of particular ages and who are alleged to have committed certain types of serious offenses. For instance, a state may prohibit juvenile courts from hearing any case involving a 15-year-old murderer. The age and offense are combined to create the statutory exclusion.

Demand Waivers

Under certain conditions and in selected jurisdictions, juveniles may submit motions for **demand waiver** actions. Demand waiver actions are requests or motions filed by juveniles and their attorneys to have their cases transferred from juvenile courts to criminal courts. If a juvenile's case is heard in a criminal court, the juvenile is entitled to the full range of rights available to adults charged with crimes.

Other Waiver Variations

Thirteen states, including the District of Columbia, have established **presumptive waiver** provisions, which require that certain offenders should be waived unless they can prove that they are suited for juvenile rehabilitation (Champion 2007). Essentially, a juvenile is considered waived to criminal court unless he/she can prove to be suitable candidates for rehabilitation. This rebuttable presumptive waiver, where the burden of proving one's rehabilitation potential rests with the juvenile and his/her attorney rather than the prosecutor, is used especially in those instances where juveniles have a history of frequent offending or where they have committed serious or violent offenses. It is difficult for any defense attorney to overcome this presumption if the juvenile client has committed an especially serious offense and has a prior record of violent offending.

Once an Adult/Always an Adult

The **once an adult/always an adult** provision is perhaps the most serious and long-lasting for affected juvenile offenders. This provision means that once juveniles at any age have been waived to the criminal court for processing, or once juveniles have been convicted and sentenced for one or more crimes by a criminal court, they are forever after considered adults for the purpose of criminal prosecutions.

Waiver and Reverse Waiver Hearings

All juveniles who are waived to criminal court for processing are entitled to a hearing on the waiver if they request one (Champion 2007). A **waiver hearing** is a formal proceeding designed to determine whether the waiver action taken by the judge or prosecutor is the correct action, and that the juvenile should be transferred to criminal court. Waiver hearings are normally conducted before the juvenile court judge. These hearings are to some extent evidentiary, since a case must be made for why criminal courts should have jurisdiction in any specific instance.

Reverse Waiver Hearings

For those jurisdictions with automatic or legislative waiver provisions, waiver actions may be contested through the use of **reverse waiver hearings.** Reverse waiver hearings are conducted before criminal court judges to determine whether to send the juvenile's case back to juvenile court. Reverse waiver hearings in those jurisdictions with automatic transfer provisions are also conducted in the presence of judges (Champion 2007).

Implications of Waiver Hearings for Juveniles

The Case for Having One's Case Decided in Juvenile Court

Among the positive benefits of having one's case heard in juvenile court are the following:

1. Juvenile court proceedings are civil, not criminal; thus, juveniles do not acquire criminal records.
2. Juveniles are less likely to receive sentences of incarceration.
3. Compared with criminal court judges, juvenile court judges have considerably more discretion in influencing a youth's life chances prior to or at the time of adjudication.
4. Juvenile courts are traditionally more lenient than criminal courts.
5. There is considerably more public sympathy extended to those who are processed in the juvenile justice system, despite the general public advocacy for a greater get-tough policy.
6. Compared with criminal courts, juvenile courts do not have as elaborate an information-exchange apparatus to determine whether certain

juveniles have been adjudicated delinquent by juvenile courts in other jurisdictions.

7. Life imprisonment and the death penalty lie beyond the jurisdiction of juvenile court judges, and they cannot impose these harsh sentences.

The Case Against Having One's Case Decided in Juvenile Court

Juvenile courts are not perfect, however, and they may be disadvantageous to many youthful offenders (Ward 2004). Some of their major limitations are the following:

1. Juvenile court judges have the power to administer lengthy sentences of incarceration, not only for serious and dangerous offenders, but for status offenders as well.

2. In most states, juvenile courts are not required to provide juveniles with a trial by jury.

3. Because of their wide discretion in handling juveniles, judges may underpenalize a large number of those appearing before them on various charges.

4. Juveniles do not enjoy the same range of constitutional rights as adults in criminal courts.

CRIMINAL COURT PROCESSING OF JUVENILE OFFENDERS

The Case for and Against Having One's Case Tried in Criminal Court

When juveniles are transferred, waived, or certified to criminal court, then all rules and constitutional guarantees attach for them as well as for adults. The primary benefits for juveniles of being processed in criminal courts are as follows. Positively, depending upon the seriousness of the offenses alleged, a jury trial may be a matter of right. Adversely, periods of lengthy incarceration in minimum, medium, and maximum security facilities with adults becomes a real possibility. Also negatively, criminal courts in a majority of state jurisdictions may impose the death penalty in capital cases. A sensitive subject with most citizens is whether juveniles should receive the death penalty if convicted of capital crimes (Horton 2005). In recent years, the U.S. Supreme Court has addressed this issue specifically and ruled that in those states where the death penalty is imposed, the death penalty may be imposed as a punishment on any juvenile who was age 18 or older at the time the capital offense was committed *Roper v. Simmons* (2005). Positively, one's youthfulness works to the benefit of the defense. Jury sympathy is often evoked for a youth who has committed a horrible crime, since it can be shown that one's home life, sexual or physical abuse, and other factors are to blame for one's present plight. Therefore, a jury often favors leniency for young offenders.

JUVENILE RIGHTS AND STANDARDS OF PROOF

During the mid-1960s and for the next 30 years, significant achievements were made in the area of juvenile rights. Although the *parens patriae* philosophy continues to be somewhat influential in juvenile proceedings, the U.S. Supreme Court has vested youths with certain constitutional rights. These rights do not encompass all of the rights extended to adults who are charged with crimes. But those rights conveyed to juveniles thus far have had far-reaching implications for how juveniles are processed. In the following section, several landmark cases involving juvenile rights will be described.

Landmark Cases in Juvenile Rights

Regardless of the causes, several significant changes have been made in the juvenile justice system and how youths are processed in recent decades. Each of the cases presented below represents attempts by juveniles to either secure rights ordinarily extended to adults.

Kent v. United States (1966)

Morris A. Kent, Jr., a 14-year-old in the District of Columbia, was apprehended in 1959 as the result of several housebreakings and attempted purse snatchings. He was placed on probation in the custody of his mother. In 1961, an intruder entered the apartment of a woman, took her wallet, and raped her. Fingerprints at the crime scene were later identified as those of Morris Kent, who was fingerprinted when apprehended for housebreaking in 1959. On September 5, 1961, Kent, 16, was taken into custody by police, interrogated for seven hours, and admitted the offense as well as volunteering information about other housebreakings, robberies, and rapes. Kent was summarily waived to criminal court by the juvenile court judge without a hearing on the waiver, which his attorney had demanded. Kent was later found guilty of six counts of housebreaking by a federal jury, although the jury found him not guilty by reason of insanity on the rape charge. Because of District of Columbia law, it was mandatory that Kent be transferred to a mental institution until such time as his sanity is restored. On each of the housebreaking counts, Kent's sentence was 5 to 15 years, or a total of 30 to 90 years in prison. His mental institution commitment would be counted as time served against the 30- to 90-year sentence. The U.S. Supreme Court reversed Kent's conviction on appeal. The Court held that Kent's rights to due process and to the effective assistance of counsel were violated when he was denied a formal hearing on the waiver and his attorneys' motions were ignored. Because of the *Kent* decision, waiver hearings are now considered critical stages requiring an attorney's advice and presence.

In re Gault (1967)

In re Gault (1967) is perhaps the most significant of all juvenile rights cases. It is certainly the most ambitious in terms of the rights sought by Gault. The U.S. Supreme Court granted the following rights for all juveniles as the result of the *Gault* decision: (1) the right to a notice of charges, (2) the right to counsel, (3) the right to confront and cross-examine witnesses, and (4) the right to invoke the privilege against self-incrimination.

The facts are that Gerald Francis Gault, a 15-year-old, and a friend, Ronald Lewis, were taken into custody by the Sheriff of Gila County, Arizona, in the morning of June 8, 1964. A verbal complaint had been filed by a neighbor of Gault, Mrs. Cook, alleging that Gault had called her and made lewd and indecent remarks. Gault was picked up while his mother and father were at work. They did not learn of their son's whereabouts until later that evening. Gault was being held at the Children's Detention Home. Gault's parents proceeded to the home and were advised that a petition had been filed against Gault and a hearing was scheduled in juvenile court the following day. No factual basis was provided for the petition, and Gault's parents were not provided with a copy of it in advance of the hearing. When the hearing was held, only Gault, his mother and older brother, probation officers Flagg and Henderson, and the juvenile court judge were present. The original complainant, Mrs. Cook, was not there. No one was sworn at the hearing, no transcript was made of it, and no memorandum of the substance of the proceedings was prepared. The testimony consisted largely of allegations by Officer Flagg about Gault's behavior and prior juvenile record. Gault was adjudicated delinquent by the judge and ordered to serve a six-year term in the Arizona State Industrial School (a juvenile prison). After exhausting their appeals in Arizona state courts, the Gaults appealed to the U.S. Supreme Court. Needless to say, the Court was appalled that Gault's case had been handled in such a cavalier and unconstitutional manner. They reversed the Arizona Supreme Court, holding that Gault did, indeed, have the right to an attorney, the right to confront his accuser (Mrs. Cook) and to cross-examine her, the right against self-incrimination, and the right to have notice of the charges filed against him. Perhaps Justice Black summed up the current juvenile court situation in the United States when he said, "This holding strikes a well-nigh fatal blow to much that is *unique* [emphasis mine] about the juvenile courts in this Nation."

In re Winship (1970)

Winship was a less complex case compared with *Gault*. But it established an important precedent in juvenile courts relating to the standard of proof used in established defendant guilt. The facts are that Samuel Winship was a 12-year-old charged with larceny in New York City. He purportedly entered a locker and stole $112 from a woman's pocketbook. Under Section 712 of the New York Family Court Act, a juvenile delinquent was defined as a person over seven and less than sixteen years of age who does any act, which, if done by an adult, would constitute a crime. While the juvenile court judge in the case acknowledged that the proof to be presented by the prosecution might be insufficient to establish the guilt of Winship beyond a reasonable doubt, he did adjudicate Winship delinquent and ordered him placed in a training school for 18 months. The U.S. Supreme Court heard Winship's case and reversed the New York Family Court ruling on the basis that an 18-month loss of liberty was substantial enough to warrant a stronger standard of proof such as beyond a reasonable doubt. Since this standard of proof was not used in Winship's case, he was unjustly adjudicated.

McKeiver v. Pennsylvania (1971)

The *McKeiver v. Pennsylvania* case is important because the U.S. Supreme Court held that juveniles are not entitled to a jury trial as a matter of right. The facts are that in May 1968, Joseph McKeiver, age 16, was charged with robbery, larceny, and receiving stolen goods. While he was represented by counsel at his adjudicatory hearing and requested a trial by jury, the judge denied his request. McKeiver was adjudicated delinquent. On appeal to the U.S. Supreme Court, McKeiver's adjudication was upheld. The U.S. Supreme Court said that it is the juvenile court judge's decision whether to grant jury trials to juveniles. By 2005 only twelve states legislatively mandated jury trials for juveniles in juvenile courts if they so requested such trials, depending upon the seriousness of the offense(s) alleged.

Breed v. Jones (1975)

This case raised the significant constitutional issue of double jeopardy. The U.S. Supreme Court concluded that after a juvenile has been adjudicated as delinquent on specific charges, those same charges may not be alleged against those juveniles subsequently in criminal courts through transfers or waivers. The facts of the case are that on February 8, 1971 in Los Angeles, California, Gary Steven Jones, was 17 years old, was armed with a deadly weapon, and allegedly committed robbery. Jones was subsequently apprehended and a petition was filed against him. He was adjudicated delinquent. The judge then transferred Jones through a judicial waiver to a criminal court where he could be tried as an adult. In a later criminal trial, Jones was convicted of robbery and committed for an indeterminate period to the California Youth Authority. The California Supreme Court upheld the conviction. When Jones appealed the decision in 1971, the U.S. Supreme Court reversed the robbery conviction. Jones's conviction in criminal court was overturned on the basis that it was a violation of his right against double jeopardy. Jones had already been adjudicated on the same charge in juvenile court. Juveniles cannot be adjudicated on a given charge in juvenile court and then sent to criminal court to face conviction on the same charge.

BOX 11.3 CAREER SNAPSHOT

Herbert C. Covey
Vice-Chair, Colorado State Juvenile Parole Board

Statistics: B.A., Sociology, Colorado State University; M.A., Sociology, University of Nebraska at Omaha; Ph.D., Sociology, University of Colorado at Boulder

Background: I serve as the vice-chair of the State Juvenile Parole Board and a part-time instructor at the University of Colorado teaching a class on Juvenile Delinquency. My main occupation is being a field administrator with the Colorado Department of Human Services. I provide management support to nine counties' departments of social services and five agencies working with aging populations. My serving on the board is a part-time activity.

Before I joined the board, I had a conversation with an office mate regarding his service on the board and how I could not imagine how he could do it given the responsibility and stress of making such important life-altering decisions. I recall stating, "I don't know how you do it." Two years later, I replaced him and have served over ten years on the board. It has been one of the richest experiences I have had in my life.

I was asked to serve on the board because Colorado law required my employer, the Department of Human Services, to have a representative. In addition, I had coauthored a book on youth street gangs and was teaching Juvenile Delinquency. To become a member of the board, the candidate must apply, be appointed by the governor, be approved by the Senate Judiciary Committee, and then confirmed by the full Senate. I remember my confirmation hearing as being more interesting than stressful. The committee essentially wanted to know how I would respond to pressure from juvenile corrections to parole youths that I felt were not ready. In other words, would I succumb to pressure to parole youths for

(continued)

BOX 11.3 *(continued)*

the purpose of freeing up beds in state facilities. For me, the answer was an obvious "no," community safety should come first. A second set of questions focused on my values relative to parole. I stated that after safety, the best interests of the youth and family should be considered. I also added that the sentiments of the victims have to be considered. Too often after trial, victims are excluded from the judicial process. Finally, I indicated that it was better to send out youth with transitional services, than to simply let them burn time and turn them lose to the community.

I was attracted to the board because I view parole hearings as being an important rite-of-passage for youth and their families. I wanted to be part of that important passage. For many youth, the parole hearing is similar to a graduation ceremony for their return to the community. For others, it is a wake-up call when they are denied parole and returned to facilities to work on their issues. Finally, I believe that if someone needed to take the responsibility of making parole decisions, it might as well be me because I deeply care about youth, families, victims, and communities.

Work Experiences: There are many pros and a few cons to serving on the board. One pro is that I have served on many committees, work groups, and boards none of which comes close to offering the kinds of rich experiences I have had serving on the Juvenile Parole Board. It has been my ticket to the "reality of it all." Over the course of about one hour, I get to delve into the human experience in ways not available to most other people. In my 10 years of service, I can honesty say that I have just about seen and heard it all. In saying this, I realize that my next hearing will offer new experiences and little about it will be routine. It can be very humbling at times. A second pro is that although little can occur in a one-hour hearing to turn a youth's life around, sometimes I get a sense that a youth may have been influenced in a positive direction. By being tough, supportive, honest, emphatic, holding the youth accountable, and otherwise appropriately addressing each case, I believe I am playing an important role in the system.

I cannot really think of many cons to serving on the board. If anything, I consider it a privilege to serve the citizens of Colorado. It does take a considerable amount of personal time preparing for hearings. I believe sometimes it is very difficult to not dwell on specific hearings and what life courses youth have taken. I find myself being haunted by some of human tragedies that are sometimes summarized over the course of a hearing for the victims as well as the families and offenders. There are also many success stories to counterbalance the negative.

As to the basic question of predicting how well youth do on parole, one must take into account that a one-hour parole hearing is not likely to tell a board member enough about the youth to be 100 percent sure how well the individual will do on parole. The old adage, "you can't judge a book by its cover," is also true for youth. Board members learn that they cannot stereotype youth and predict with 100 percent accuracy how they will behave on parole. Each parole candidate has to be considered on a case-by-case basis.

This is not to suggest that it is total guesswork. I learned early that prior behavior is a good predictor of future behavior. If a youth has a lengthy history of serious offending and started at an early age, then the risk of re-offending increases. Property offenders are more likely to re-offend than violent offenders. If a youth does well in rehabilitation programs, shows victim empathy, has a positive attitude, has positive peers in the community, has bonded with positive adult role models, takes accountability for actions, has developed tools to keep from relapsing, and has good support systems, the chances for success on parole are better. If the youth returns to the same crime-infested neighborhood, begins associating with negative peers, and other systems such as school and family have not changed, then the chances are higher the youth will not succeed on parole.

I have many positive memories of parolees and parole hearings. For instance, one sex offender attempted to re-offend within two weeks of being paroled. Because all the family members had been trained by a Multi-Systemic Therapist, he was caught early in his offense cycle and never re-offended. In another hearing, I witnessed a mother of a physical assault victim heal her anger by seeing the offending youth show genuine remorse for what he had done and had changed for the better. Without that hearing, she would have never healed her anger. Once, we revoked parole of a drug-using youth because he was not complying with parole and we thought he was a danger to himself. He reeked of drugs and had an enabling and argumentative mother. After she called us every name in the book, the revoked youth attempted suicide two weeks later. After much work by youth corrections and an insightful client manager, I later paroled a dramatically changed youth who successfully completed parole and finished college. I'd like to think the board played a role in turning this youth around.

Advice to Students: As a board member, I come into contact with many professionals working with youth offenders. I believe the common characteristics of those who are successful are that they really care about helping youth, have the ability to accept failure and success with grace, are forthright with youth and families, and get to know their cases in detail. They never become friends with their clients but are sources of authority and direction. I also offer that being able to work as a member of a multidisciplinary team is important. Many of today's delinquent youth have multiple and confounding issues, such as mental health and substance abuse, and this requires teamwork to address. If you do not have these qualities, along

(continued)

> ## BOX 11.3 (continued)
>
> with dedication, then you need to find something else to do with your life. If you possess these qualities and want a meaningful career, this is a great area to pursue.
>
> My advice to students interested in parole and aftercare services, or parole boards, is to contact people working in these areas and conduct informational interviews on how they developed their careers. Students should ask them what they like and dislike about their jobs and why they do what they do. How do they deal with parole successes and failures? What do they believe works and does not work for what types of youth? Many professionals are willing to share their thoughts and help students.
>
> I am convinced that considerable time and resources in the juvenile justice system are wasted by well-intentioned people who apply ineffective treatments to youth based on the feelings and emotions rather than evidence-based practice. Students will do well to become familiar with what research evidence shows works rather than the latest fad or what their feelings suggest. Evidence of effectiveness should drive treatment decisions, not program marketing or false assumptions about effectiveness. While our interventions may not always work for all youth, we want to at least ensure that our efforts are not making them worse.

Schall v. Martin (1984).   In this case, the U.S. Supreme Court issued juveniles a minor setback regarding the state's right to hold them in preventive detention pending a subsequent adjudication. The Court said that the preventive detention of juveniles by states is constitutional, if judges perceive these youths to pose a danger to the community or an otherwise serious risk if released short of an adjudicatory hearing. This decision was significant, in part, because many experts advocated the separation of juveniles and adults in jails, those facilities most often used for preventive detention. Also, the preventive detention of adults was not ordinarily practiced at that time. [Since then, the preventive detention of adults who are deemed to pose societal risks has been upheld by the U.S. Supreme Court (*United States v. Salerno*, 1987).]

The facts are that 14-year-old Gregory Martin was arrested at 11:30 p.m. on December 13, 1977 in New York City. He was charged with first-degree robbery, second-degree assault, and criminal possession of a weapon. Martin lied to police at the time, giving a false name and address. Between the time of his arrest and December 29 when a fact-finding hearing was held, Martin was detained (a total of 15 days). His confinement was based largely on the false information he had supplied to police and the seriousness of the charges pending against him. Subsequently, he was adjudicated a delinquent and placed on two years' probation. Later, his attorney filed an appeal, contesting his preventive detention as violative of the Due Process Clause of the Fourteenth Amendment. The U.S. Supreme Court eventually heard the case and upheld the detention as constitutional (Rodriguez 2004). Table 11.3 summarizes some of the major rights available to juveniles and compares these rights with selected rights enjoyed by adults in criminal proceedings.

BLENDED SENTENCING STATUTES AND THE GET-TOUGH MOVEMENT

The most significant change in waiver patterns throughout the United States is that between 1992 and 1996, all but ten states had adopted or modified laws making it easier to prosecute juveniles as adults in criminal courts (Champion 2007). Some of the reasons suggested for this tougher stance toward juvenile offending are that (1) juvenile rehabilitation has not been particularly effective at deterring juveniles from further offending, and (2) that the juvenile justice system is simply not punitive enough to impose the nature and types of punishments deserved by an increasingly violent juvenile offender population (Leiber, Fox, and Johnson 2004).

The major ways of making juveniles more amenable to criminal court punishment are to (1) lower the age at which they can be processed by criminal courts as adults, (2) expand the number of crimes that qualify juvenile offenders as adults for criminal court action, and (3) lower the age at which juveniles can be transferred to criminal courts for various offenses.

Blended Sentencing Statutes

Aaron Kupchik (2004) observes that in recent years, many states have legislatively redefined the juvenile court's purpose and role by diminishing the role of rehabilitation and heightening the importance of public safety, punishment, and accountability in the juvenile justice system. One of the most dramatic changes in the dispositional/sentencing options available to juvenile court judges is **blended sentencing.** Blended sentencing refers to the imposition of juvenile and/or adult correctional sanctions to cases involving serious and violent juvenile offenders who have been adjudicated in juvenile court or convicted in criminal court. Blended sentencing options are usually based on age or on a combination of age and offense (Champion 2007).

There are five basic models of blended sentencing. These include (1) juvenile–exclusive blend, (2) juvenile–inclusive blend, (3) juvenile–contiguous, (4) criminal–exclusive blend, and (5) criminal–inclusive blend.

The **juvenile–exclusive blend** involves a disposition by the juvenile court judge, which is either a disposition to the juvenile correctional system or to the adult correctional system, but not both. Thus, a judge might order a juvenile adjudicated delinquent for aggravated assault to serve three years in a ju-

TABLE 11.3   COMPARISON OF JUVENILE AND ADULT RIGHTS RELATING TO DELINQUENCY AND CRIME[a]

Right	Adults	Juveniles
1. "Beyond a Reasonable Doubt" standard used in court	Yes	Yes
2. Right against double jeopardy	Yes	Yes
3. Right to assistance of counsel	Yes	Yes
4. Right to notice of charges	Yes	Yes
5. Right to a transcript of court proceedings	Yes	No
6. Right against self-incrimination	Yes	Yes
7. Right to trial by jury	Yes	No in most states
8. Right to defense counsel in court proceedings	Yes	No
9. Right to due process	Yes	No*
10. Right to bail	Yes	No, with exceptions
11. Right to cross-examine witnesses	Yes	Yes
12. Right of confrontation	Yes	Yes
13. Standards relating to searches and seizures:		
a. "Probable cause" and warrants required for searches and seizures	Yes, with exceptions	No
b. "Reasonable suspicion" required for searches and seizures without warrant	No	Yes
14. Right to hearing prior to transfer to criminal court or to a reverse waiver hearing in states with automatic transfer provisions	N/A	Yes
15. Right to a speedy trial	Yes	No
16. Right to *habeas corpus* relief in correctional settings	Yes	No
17. Right to rehabilitation	No	No
18. Criminal evidentiary standards	Yes	Yes
19. Right to hearing for parole or probation revocation	Yes	No
20. Bifurcated trial, death penalty cases	Yes	Yes
21. Right to discovery	Yes	Limited
22. Fingerprinting, photographing at booking	Yes	No, with exceptions
23. Right to appeal	Yes	Limited
24. Waivers of rights:		
a. Adults	Knowingly, intelligently	
b. Juveniles		Totality of circumstances
25. Right to hearing for parole or probation revocation	Yes	No, with exceptions
26. "Equal protection" clause of Fourteenth Amendment applicable	Yes	No, with exceptions

TABLE 11.3   COMPARISON OF JUVENILE AND ADULT RIGHTS RELATING TO DELINQUENCY AND CRIME[a]

Right	Adults	Juveniles
27. Right to court-appointed attorney if indigent	Yes	No, with exceptions
28. Transcript required of criminal/delinquency trial proceedings	Yes	No, with exceptions
29. Pretrial detention permitted	Yes	Yes
30. Plea bargaining	Yes, with exceptions	No, with exceptions
31. Burden of proof borne by prosecution	Yes	No, with exceptions**
32. Public access to trials	Yes	Limited
33. Conviction/adjudication results in criminal record	Yes	No

[a] Compiled by the authors

*Minimal, not full, due process safeguards assured

**Burden of proof is borne by prosecutor in 23 state juvenile courts, while the rest make no provision or mention of who bears the burden of proof

venile industrial school; or the judge may order the adjudicated delinquent to serve three years in a prison for adults. The judge cannot impose *both* types of punishment under this model, however. In 1996, only one state, New Mexico, provided such a sentencing option for its juvenile court judges.

The **juvenile–inclusive blend** involves a disposition by the juvenile court judge, which is both a juvenile correctional sanction and an adult correctional sanction. In cases such as this, suppose the judge had adjudicated a 15-year-old juvenile delinquent on a charge of vehicular theft. The judge might impose a disposition of two years in a juvenile industrial school or reform school. Further, the judge might impose a sentence of three additional years in an adult penitentiary. However, the second sentence to the adult prison would typically be suspended, unless the juvenile violated one or more conditions of his/her original disposition and any conditions accompanying the disposition. Usually, this suspension period would run until the youth reaches age 18 or 21. If the offender were to commit a new offense or violate one or more program conditions, he/she would immediately be placed in the adult prison to serve the second sentence originally imposed.

The **juvenile–contiguous blend** involves a disposition by a juvenile court judge that may extend beyond the jurisdictional age limit of the offender. When the age limit of the juvenile court jurisdiction is reached, various procedures may be invoked to transfer the case to the jurisdiction of adult corrections. States with this juvenile–contiguous blend include Colorado,

Massachusetts, Rhode Island, South Carolina, and Texas. In Texas, for example, a 15-year-old youth who has been adjudicated delinquent on a murder charge can be given an incarcerative term of from one to thirty years. At the time of the disposition in juvenile court, the youth is sent to the Texas Youth Commission and incarcerated in one of its facilities (similar to reform or industrial schools). By the time the youth reaches age 17 1/2, the juvenile court must hold a transfer hearing to determine whether the youth should be sent to the Texas Department of Corrections. At this hearing, the youth may present evidence in his/her favor to show why he/she has become rehabilitated and no longer should be confined. However, evidence of institutional misconduct may be presented by the prosecutor to show why the youth should be incarcerated for more years in a Texas prison. This hearing functions as an incentive for the youth to behave and try to improve his/her behavior while confined in the juvenile facility.

The **criminal–exclusive blend** involves a decision by a criminal court judge to impose either a juvenile court sanction or a criminal court sanction, but not both. For example, a criminal court judge may hear the case of a 15-year-old youth who has been transferred to criminal court on a rape charge. The youth is convicted in a jury trial in criminal court. At this point, the judge has two options: The judge can sentence the offender to a prison term in an adult correctional facility, or the judge can impose an incarcerative sentence for the youth to serve in a juvenile facility. The judge may believe that the 15-year-old would be better off in a juvenile industrial school rather than an adult prison. The judge may impose a sentence of adult incarceration, but he/she may be inclined to place the youth in a facility where there are other youths in the offender's age range.

The **criminal–inclusive blend** involves a decision by the criminal court judge to impose both a juvenile penalty and a criminal sentence simultaneously. Again, as in the juvenile court–inclusive blend model, the latter criminal sentence may be suspended depending upon the good conduct of the juvenile during the juvenile punishment phase. For example, suppose a 12-year-old boy has been convicted of attempted murder. The boy participated in a drive-by shooting and is a gang member. The criminal court judge sentences the youth to a term of six years in a juvenile facility, such as an industrial school. At the same time, the judge imposes a sentence of twenty years on the youth to be spent in an adult correctional facility, following the five-year sentence in the juvenile facility. However, the adult portion of the sentence may be suspended, depending upon whether the juvenile behaves or misbehaves during his six-year industrial school incarceration. There is an additional twist to this blend. If the juvenile violates one or more conditions of his confinement in the juvenile facility, the judge has the power to revoke that sentence and invoke the sentence of incarceration in an adult facility. With good behavior, the youth can be free of the system following the period of juvenile confinement; the adult portion of the sentence is suspended if the youth deserves such leniency. Arkansas has the revocation power and ability to place youths in adult correctional facilities (Champion 2007).

TEEN COURTS

Increasing numbers of jurisdictions are using **teen courts** as an alternative to juvenile court for determining one's guilt and punishment. Teen courts are informal jury proceedings, where jurors consist of teenagers who hear and decide minor cases. First-offender cases, where status offenses or misdemeanors have been committed, are given priority in a different type of court setting involving one's peers as judges. Judges may divert minor cases to these teen courts. Adults function only as presiding judges, and these persons are often retired judges or lawyers who perform such services voluntarily and in their spare time. The focus of teen courts is upon therapeutic jurisprudence, with a strong emphasis upon rehabilitation (Reed 2004). One objective of such courts is to teach empathy to offenders. Victims are encouraged to take an active role in these courts. Youths become actively involved as advisory juries (Peterson 2005).

Teen courts are also known as youth courts, peer courts, and student courts (Preston and Roots 2004). In 1997 there were 78 active teen courts. By 2005 there were 1,019 youth court programs operating in juvenile justice systems, schools, and community-based organizations throughout the United States, with an anticipated 2,000 youth courts being established over the next few years (Peterson 2005). The American Probation and Parole Association has recognized the significance and contributions of teen courts by establishing September as National Youth Court Month to highlight the activities of youth courts and their contributions to the youth justice system (*APPA Perspectives* 2004a, 8).

The Use of Teen Courts

Among the first cities to establish teen courts were Seattle, Washington, and Denver, Colorado (Rasmussen 2004). Subsequently, teen courts have been established in many other jurisdictions, including Odessa, Texas. In Odessa, for instance, juveniles are referred to teen courts for class C misdemeanors and minor traffic violations. Defendants range in age from 10 to 16. Traffic citation cases result in teen court referrals by municipal judges, who give youths the option of paying their fines or having their cases heard by the teen court. If youths select the teen court for adjudication, then they do not acquire a juvenile record. The teen court listens to all evidence and decides the matter (Peterson 2005).

Teen court dispositions are always related closely to community service as well as jury service (Karp 2001, 2004). Thus, juveniles who are found guilty by teen courts may, in fact, serve on such juries in the future, as one of their conditional punishments (Rasmussen 2004). Or they may be required to perform up to 22 hours of community service, such as working at the animal shelter, library, or nursing home; picking up trash in parks or ball fields; or working with various community agencies. The teen court program in Odessa has been very successful. Prior to using teen courts, the recidivism rate for all juvenile offenders in the city was between 50 and 60 percent. However, teen court adjudications all but eliminated this recidivism figure. Interestingly, juveniles who are tried by the teen court often develop an interest in the legal system. Teen courts place a high priority on educating young people about their responsibilities of being individuals, family members, and citizens (Roberts 2003). As a part of one's diversion, conditional options such as restitution, fines, or community service may be imposed in those cases where property damage was incurred as the result of the juvenile's behavior (Chapman 2005). Juvenile court judges must exercise considerable discretion and impose dispositions that best meet the juvenile's needs and circumstances.

Constructive dispositions are the objective of teen courts in Kentucky. In September, October, and November 1992, teen jurors in a Kentucky teen court heard case details in nine different cases (Williamson, Chalk, and Knepper 1993). Referrals to teen court were made from the regular juvenile court, a division of the state's district court. If juveniles are found guilty by the teen court, then the court imposes constructive dispositions involving community service hours. It should be noted that these teen courts do not determine one's guilt or innocence—rather, they convene and recommend appropriate dispositions. Teenagers act as prosecutors, defense attorneys, clerks, bailiffs, jury forepersons, and jurors as they carry out roles similar to their counterparts in criminal courts. The Kentucky teen court variety is interesting because accused and judged teens are themselves recruited subsequently to serve as teen jurors. Thus, all defendants are assigned to jury duty following their teen court appearances. When this study was conducted, no youth had been returned to the teen court for noncompliance. Perhaps seeing how the process works from the other side, as jurors, made these teenagers understand the seriousness of what they had done themselves as victimizers in the past. One example of a teen court is the Anchorage, Alaska Youth Court.

The Anchorage Youth Court

By 2005, there were over 1,000 teen courts established in most states (Peterson, 2005). These courts are not always known as teen courts. In Anchorage, Alaska, for instance, a teen court program was established in 1989 and exists today as the **Anchorage Youth Court.** Subsequently 14 other youth courts have been established in various Alaska cities and modeled after the Anchorage Youth Court (AYC) (Anchorage Youth Court 2005). Funding for youth courts in Alaska varies. AYC receives a third of its funds from federal block grants, United Way, and program fees; a third from fundraising and donations; and a third from the Anchorage Assembly. The AYC targets first-time offenders and makes extensive use of volunteers from the community. The protocol of the AYC is outlined below.

At the intake stage, a decision is made whether to recommend a youth for AYC. Not all youths are eligible. Youths with extensive juvenile records or who are charged with extremely serious felonious offenses are usually prohibited from participating in AYC. For low-risk, first-time juveniles, however, they may be offered the opportunity to enter "no contest" pleas and attend AYC for sentencing. A no-contest plea means that the youth admits to the offense and avoids formal adjudication by a juvenile court judge. An appointment date is scheduled for the youth's subsequent appearance before the AYC for sentencing. The AYC utilizes volunteers from grades 7 to 12 who serve in different capacities. Thus, youths who volunteer may serve as prosecutors, defense counsels, judges, clerks, bailiffs, and jurors for youths who have committed misdemeanors and minor felonies. There are three AYC juvenile judges who hear each case and impose a punishment or sentence. Offenders and their parents are given a detailed list of instructions about when to appear, where, and how to behave while the AYC progresses. These instructions pertain to a courtroom dress code, courtroom decorum, courtroom attendance, and client contact. Also covered in detail is a list of consequences for not following AYC courtroom guidelines. If youths scheduled for AYC fail to appear, such nonappearances will be taken into account at a subsequent rescheduled sentencing hearing. The conduct of all participants, including judges, is also governed. An ethics committee has sanctioning power over all court officers who fail to appear for AYC duty. All AYC sessions are tape-recorded. Thus, the AYC is like a court of record in the event a dispute arises later over what was said or if any evidence presented is questioned.

The following sentencing options are available to impose on any defendant: (1) AYC classes, including anger management class, defensive driving class, property and theft crimes class, skills for life class, "Start Smart" and "Stay Smart" classes, victim impact class, and weapons safety class; (2) apology letter to family; (3) apology letter to victim; (4) community work service; (5) diversity awareness; (6) drug/alcohol assessment; (7) essay; (8) fire prevention program; (9) jail tour; (10) juvenile anti–shoplifting program; parent–adolescent mediation; restitution; and victim–offender mediation.

A no-contest script is presented to the defendant, the prosecutor, defense counsel, and the judges. The AYC no-contest script outlines the entire protocol for the AYC proceeding. The defendant is advised that one or more persons have been appointed to defend him/her. Prosecutors are named. Although AYC uses three-judge panels, sometimes two-judge panels are permitted, with defendant approval. The charging document is read, outlining all charges against the defendant as well as the defendant's admissions to all offenses alleged. The defendant is asked whether the facts outlined in the charging document are true and enters a no-contest plea.

The prosecution and defense both have an opportunity to examine the case, the facts, and circumstances, and make a recommendation to the AYC judges. Both prosecutors and defense counsels are provided with prep lists outlining their specific duties and options. These prep lists are quite specific, and defense counsels go over them with their clients to make sure all procedures are understood fully. Both sides also have access to the list of sentencing options noted earlier in this section. This listing is detailed also, and it describes the nature of each sentencing option. In the process of considering the case, both sides examine the Anchorage Youth Court Sentencing Matrix, which includes a listing of both aggravating and mitigating factors. Every youth processed by AYC performs a certain number of community work service hours (CWSs) determined by the seriousness of the offense and the presence or absence of aggravating and mitigating circumstances. It is not unusual for the defense and prosecution to disagree about which aggravating or mitigating factors should be counted or how much community work service hours should be performed. Both sides can recommend that the defendant should write an essay of a specified length, make restitution, attend one or more classes as needed, and engage in other activities.

A juvenile probation officer may prepare the equivalent of a predispositional report for any particular juvenile and make a recommendation. A probation officer's recommendation may be given considerable weight, or it may be discounted. All of this information is considered by the judges, who ultimately decide the nature and amount of punishment to impose. One or more victims are likely involved. Their opinions are solicited in written form. Also, information about the crime and damage or injuries to the victim(s) is solicited. Thus, victims have an opportunity to verbalize how the crime committed by the defendant affected them. An open-ended form is attached to the letter, and it is recommended that the material be returned to the AYC at the victim's earliest opportunity. Victims may indicate how the crime affected them, whether financial losses were sustained, and whether any other comments should be considered by AYC judges. This information is delivered to the AYC for their consideration.

Both the prosecution and defense make oral arguments that essentially reflect what their written recommendations to the court contain. Similar to criminal court plea bargain agreements, prosecutors must outline the factual basis for the crime admitted by the defendant. In short, they must show the AYC judges what they would have presented as evidence of defendant guilt. Defendants are permitted to address the AYC judges on their own behalf. This is their right, and they may or may not choose to exercise it. It is important to note that like criminal defendants, youthful offenders may take this opportunity to accept responsibility for their crime(s), to show remorse, and to perhaps argue for leniency. However, AYC judges admonish them that their words are the last thing these judges will hear before they deliberate and determine the sentence. As an integral part of the defense prep document, defense counsels can advise their clients that they may want to tell judges that they are sorry, what they've done to make things right, how they are going to win back the trust of the people they have harmed, and what they will do differently if they are in a similar situation in the future.

AYC judges retire to their chambers where they deliberate and eventually produce a sentencing document. The sentencing document is a unanimous decision by the judges, outlining the sentencing order and the reasons for it. The aggravating and mitigating factors considered by the judges are listed, and a rationale is given for why these factors were considered important. At that time, they must advise the defendant that he/she has the right to a reconsideration of the sentence by filing a written appeal within five working days. They are then asked to consult with their attorneys and determine whether the sentence is accepted or whether they will file an appeal. In a limited number of cases, judges may revise their original sentencing recommendations, but even these reconsidered sentences may be appealed. In most cases, however, defendants agree to the AYC judicial sentencing terms. The effectiveness of the AYC is measured by its low rate of recidivism. For the AYC, a recidivism rate of 11 percent has been exhibited by those processed. This means that there is nearly a 90 percent success rate, and that most sentenced offenders will not commit future crimes. A majority of youth or teen courts in the United States have reported similar success results, which attests to their growing popularity.

Blue Earth County Teen Court

A contrast to the AYC is the Blue Earth County Teen Court, in Makato, Minnesota (Blue Earth County 2005). According to Blue Earth County Teen Court (BECTC) officials, teen court is an alternative to the district court that handles very serious juvenile offenses. The BECTC is a collaborative effort that involves Blue Earth County officials and citizens. Juveniles are held accountable for their actions by a jury of their peers, and the rights of victims, if any, are respected. BECTC is also an opportunity for teens and adult volunteers to have an active, positive role in the juvenile justice system. The overall goal is to reduce the number of juvenile offenders who offend in Blue Earth County. Targeted are juveniles who commit petty offenses and choose to appear in the BECTC rather than in district court. These youths may have already participated in the Blue Earth County Youth Diversion Program as a result of a prior offense.

The goals of the BECTC are to (1) hold juvenile petty offenders accountable in a timely manner, (2) respect and maintain victims' rights, (3) reduce the number of petty offenses and less serious cases in district court, (4) educate all participants about the court system and other agencies involved in the teen court process, and (5) promote an awareness of the importance of community civic participation.

A teen jury asks juveniles questions about the offenses they committed. Victims will also have the opportunity to be heard and present any pertinent information. All juveniles appearing in the BECTC have already admitted their guilt. The BECTC jury will decide the consequences for the juvenile's behaviors. Since these are largely petty offenses, juveniles are not entitled to representation by public defenders or any other attorneys. Examples of petty offenses heard by the BECTC include shoplifting, alcohol offenses, smoking, curfew violations, and criminal damage to property or vandalism. Some possible consequences as punishments include community service hours, restitution to victims, fines, completion of offense-related educational programming, and service on teen court juries in the future. BECTC officials believe that it is quite useful for former offenders to sit in judgment of subsequent offenders, since this gives them insights into their own prior conduct.

There is a dress code for juveniles who appear before the BECTC jury. No shorts, tank tops, hats or caps, or inappropriate T-shirts are permitted. Jeans are okay if they are neat and clean. All BECTC clients pay a $25 fine. They qualify for the BECTC by being under age 18. They must admit guilt to the petty offense(s) alleged. The BECTC does not determine one's guilt or innocence. It decides the punishments and consequences of one's actions. Youths who admit their guilt will automatically be placed on probation for six months. If they successfully complete the terms of the probation program, then the charges against them will be dropped or dismissed. While on probation, they must (1) perform community service, (2) pay a fine, (3) apologize to the victim(s), (4) see a counselor, (5) write an essay, (6) attend other teen groups/sessions, and (7) serve on the teen court at a later date.

If some youths fail to complete the terms of their probation successfully, then they will be referred back to the district court for processing. They must appear before a judge for violating the BECTC's rules. There is the possibility that more serious consequences will be imposed on such juveniles by presiding judges.

It is important to note that the BECTC is totally voluntary. Youths who do not wish to participate in it can have their cases heard in the district court. There are obvious benefits to youths for keeping their cases away from district courts, however. The principal benefit is that they will not acquire a juvenile record if they complete the terms of their program successfully. This is a strong incentive to remain law-abiding and conform to all rules imposed by the BECTC.

Teen Court Variations

Several variations of teen courts have been described (Champion 2007). Four courtroom models of teen courts include (1) adult judge, (2) youth judge, (3) peer jury, and (4) tribunal.

Adult Judge Teen Court Model

Adult judge teen courts use adult judges to preside over all actions. The judge is responsible for managing all courtroom dynamics. Generally a youth volunteer acting as the prosecutor presents each case against a juvenile to a jury comprised of one's peers. This is similar to a prosecutor in the adult system presenting a case against a defendant in a grand jury action. A juvenile defense counsel offers mitigating evidence, if any, that the jury may consider. The jury is permitted to ask the youthful defendant any question in an effort to determine why the offense was committed and any circumstances surrounding its occurrence. Subsequently, the jury deliberates and determines the most fitting punishment. This is a recommendation only. The suitability of the recommended punishment, which is most often some form of community service and/or victim compensation or restitution, is decided by the judge. About half of all teen courts in the United States use the adult judge model.

Youth Judge Model

The youth judge variation of teen courts uses a juvenile judge instead of an adult judge. Youths are used as prosecutors and defense counsel as well. This teen court variation functions much like the adult judge teen court model. Again, a sentence is recommended by a jury, and the appropriateness of the sentence is determined by the juvenile judge. About a third of all teen courts use this model.

This model is used by the Elko, (Nevada) Teen Court (ETC). The ETC uses teens as judges, prosecutors, and defense counsels. The proceedings are conducted in real trial courtrooms. The procedures emulate adult proceedings as much as possible. The average teen court hearing lasts about 20 to 30 minutes. During the ETC proceedings, the jury is sworn in by a court clerk. The court clerk states to the jury the charge and the plea of guilty entered by the youthful defendant. The prosecutor summarizes the police report, or facts in the case, for the jury. The defense counsel calls one or more witnesses, including the defendant. The defendant's parents may also be called. The prosecutor can cross-examine witnesses. Both the prosecutor and defense counsel make closing arguments to the jury who then receives jury instructions from the judge and retires to reach a verdict. The verdict is returned. The objective of this proceeding is to heighten offender accountability, not deal with the guilt or innocence of the defendant. The teen jury determines the consequences of the juvenile's actions. The jury can require juvenile detention center tours, community service, educational classes, apology letters, and written reports (Elko Teen Court, 2005).

Peer Jury Model

In the peer jury model, an adult judge presides, while a jury hears the case against the defendant. There are no youth prosecutors or defense counsels present. After hearing the case, which is usually determined through jury questioning of the defendant directly, the jury deliberates and decides the sentence, which the judge must approve. This model is used by the Blue Earth County Teen Court example in Minnesota.

Tribunal Model

Under the tribunal model, one or more youths act as judges, while other youths are designated as prosecutors and defense counsels. The prosecution and defense present their side of the case against the youthful defendant to the judges who subsequently deliberate and return with a sentence. All sentences may be appealed. Again, the sentences usually involve restitution or some form of victim compensation, community service, or a combination of punishments depending upon the circumstances. This tribunal model is the one featured in the Anchorage Youth Court example.

Each of these models is summarized below:

	Judge	Youth Attorneys	Jury/Role of Jury
Adult Judge Model =	Adult	Yes	Recommend sentence
Youth Judge Model =	Youth	Yes	Recommend sentence
Peer Jury Model =	Adult	No	Questions defendant, recommends sentence
Tribunal =	Youths (1–3)	Yes	No jury present

The Successfulness of Teen Courts

The growing popularity of teen courts as alternatives to formal juvenile court actions attests to their successfulness in sanctioning first-time low-risk youthful offenders (Patrick et al. 2004). Being judged by one's peers seems to be an effective method of imposing sanctions. Youths who function as judges, prosecutors, and defense counsels usually receive a certain number of hours of training to perform these important roles (Carrington and Schulenberg 2004). In New York, for instance, an average of 16 to 20 hours of training is required of youth court juvenile officials (Champion 2007). In some instances, written tests are administered following one's training. These are the equivalent of bar exams for youths, to ensure that they understand some basic or fundamental legal principles.

Several national youth court guidelines have been articulated. These guidelines have been developed for (1) program planning and community mobilization, (2) program staffing and funding, (3) legal issues, (4) identified respondent population and referral process, (5) volunteer recruitment and sentencing options, (6) volunteer training, (7) youth court operations and case management, and (8) program evaluation.

Recidivism rates of teen courts have not been studied consistently throughout all jurisdictions. However, available information suggests that the recidivism rates among youthful defendants who have gone through the teen court process are very low, less than 20 percent. One positive consequence that is reported in many jurisdictions is that processed youth emerge with a greater appreciation for the law, a greater understanding of it, and a greater respect for authority figures. They appear to be more law-abiding compared with youths adjudicated in more traditional ways through juvenile courts (Champion 2007). A majority of states have adopted teen court models of one type or another, and many are in the process of considering legislation to establish them (Chapman 2005).

States vary in terms of the eligibility age limits and types of offenses that youth courts may consider. Mostly first-offense, low-level misdemeanors or status offenses are included. More serious offenses are usually passed along to the juvenile court beyond the intake stage. The accountability of participating youths is heightened considerably inasmuch as youths must admit guilt before participating in teen courts (Champion 2007). Furthermore, they must waive their confidentiality rights in most jurisdictions.

BOX 11.4   SHOULD MORE YOUTHS BE TREATED LIKE ADULTS?

■ It happened in Inverness, Florida. Charlotte Coadic walked into her garage one day to find someone stealing a six-pack of beer from her refrigerator. She called police and subsequently they apprehended 17-year-old Adam Bollenback. It seems that Bollenback has a long juvenile record with police. Bollenback was charged with petty theft, burglary, and escape, which means that the crimes are punishable by up to 15 years in prison. With Bollenback's former juvenile record, the judge could enhance the sentence up to 30 years in prison. Bollenback was charged as an adult, and circuit court judge Ric A. Howard sentenced him to 10 years in prison

(continued)

BOX 11.4 (continued)

for the six-pack beer theft. "I want to break your spirit," the judge advised Bollenback. Some citizens were outraged by such a stringent sentence imposed for such a minor offense where no one was harmed.

■ It happened in Henderson, Nevada. Jake Reeder, 15, fatally shot his best friend and was charged as an adult with murder. The circumstances were such that Reeder and another friend were playing with a firearm, which they didn't think was loaded. They pointed it at another friend, Dustin Osborn, 14, while playing "FBI" and after smoking marijuana, and a bullet discharged, fatally falling Osborn. Subsequently, defense counsels for Reeder succeeded in reversing the decision of the court to try Reeder as an adult. The juvenile court regained jurisdiction over the case. Provided that Reeder pleaded guilty to involuntary manslaughter, the juvenile court imposed probation. Part of the time would be served at the Spring Mountain Youth Camp or a state juvenile facility near Las Vegas. Reeder's attorney protested Reeder's placement in a youth camp, claiming that such a place is not appropriate for a 15-year-old boy.

■ It happened in Marion County, Indiana. A 15-year-old boy, Dennis Sloan, was speeding in an automobile when he was suddenly pursued by police. Sloan was fleeing police in a stolen van at speeds upwards of 105 mph. Another police cruiser attempted to block the youth, but the van crossed railroad tracks and became airborne, where it crashed into the police cruiser, killing a police officer, Craig Herbert. The youth was transferred to criminal court where he would be tried as an adult. Sloan was charged with resisting law enforcement, reckless homicide, failure to stop at an accident resulting in death, and auto theft. He has a prior record in juvenile court for fleeing law enforcement and arrests for auto theft and criminal mischief. Sloan will likely be sentenced to a long prison term based on the seriousness of the charges and his prior record as a juvenile.

■ In Westmoreland County, Pennsylvania, 15-year-old Robert M. Laskowski and another teen, 15-year-old Ian Bishop, bludgeoned to death Bishop's older brother, Adam, in the family home. Authorities said that Adam Bishop had been struck at least 15 times in the head with a hammer and was moved to various parts of the house before he was left to die in a bathtub. While Laskowski did not appear to strike Adam Bishop, he nevertheless participated in the murder. The two boys then decided they would kill Bishop's parents. But they were discovered before they had a chance to pull off the other murders. Both youths will be tried as adults and face charges of first-degree murder in the death of Adam Bishop. Witnesses say that the two boys planned these murders several weeks in advance, and thus premeditation was quite evident. They could face life imprisonment if convicted.

■ It happened in Oskaloosa, Iowa. Ross Allen Baxter, 16, was living in a home with his grandparents, who operated a daycare center for young children. One day while alone with the children, Baxter sexually molested several of them. This behavior occurred on more than one occasion, until authorities learned of the incidents through reports from the childrens' parents. Baxter was arrested by police and charged with three counts of sexual child molestation. Furthermore, it was decided that he would be tried as an adult in criminal court. The juvenile court judge declared that "the two years he would have served in the juvenile system would not be enough time for thorough treatment and rehabilitative therapy." In the criminal justice system, Baxter faces serious time, as much as 20 years, for his sexual acts. His bond was set at $32,500.

Should all youths who commit serious offenses be tried as adults? Where should states draw the line regarding the minimum age at which a juvenile can be transferred to adult court? Which court is best for trying serious juvenile cases? What do you think?

[Sources: Adapted from Carrie Johnson and the *St. Petersburg Times,* "Teenager's 10-Year Sentence Creates an Uproar," September 1, 2002; adapted from Molly Ball and the *Las Vegas Sun,* "Teen in Murder Case Won't Be Tried as an Adult," May 4, 2004; adapted from Tom Spalding and Vic Ryckaert and the *Indianapolis Star,* "Teen to Be Tried as Adult," August 13, 2005; adapted from Rick Cholodofsky and the *Tribune-Review,* "Judge: Juvenile Will Be Tried as an Adult in Bishop Slaying," December 13, 2002; adapted from Sue Salisbury and the *Oskaloosa Herald,* "Baxter To Be Tried as Adult on Third Charge," March 3, 2006.]

TRENDS AND IMPLICATIONS FOR JUVENILE OFFENDERS

A Summary of Juvenile Justice Trends

The trends discussed in this section pertain to (1) the legal rights of juveniles; (2) law enforcement; (3) the prosecution of juveniles and juvenile courts; (4) diversion, probation, and intermediate punishments; and (5) juvenile corrections and aftercare.

1. The juvenile justice system will experience greater reforms in the area of juvenile rights commensurate with those enjoyed by adult offenders.
2. Attaining constitutional rights commensurate with adult offenders. Currently, there are no speedy trial provisions for juvenile offenders.
3. Greater accountability and responsibility expected from juvenile offenders.

4. The deinstitutionalization of status offenses. As we have seen, there is a general trend toward DSO as a means of diverting less serious offenders from the jurisdiction of juvenile courts.

5. Greater attention to preventing short-term detention of juveniles with adult offenders after arrest.

6. Greater use of transfers and waivers to adult criminal courts.

7. The juvenile court will become increasingly adversarial, in many respects paralleling the adult system.

8. Greater formality of juvenile courts (Guevara and Herz 2004).

9. The increased use of transfers of juveniles to criminal courts will continue, especially for serious offenses including rape, robbery, and murder.

10. Greater concern for juvenile rights.

11. More stringent standards relating to the admissibility of evidence in juvenile proceedings.

12. Greater use of plea bargaining.

13. Greater use of diversion.

14. Greater innovations in juvenile offender management, including electronic monitoring and/or home confinement (Rodriguez, 2004).

15. Greater emphasis on victim restitution and community service.

SUMMARY

The juvenile justice system is a civil entity that parallels closely the criminal justice system, particularly in how juveniles are processed. Juvenile courts have jurisdiction over all juveniles who commit delinquency, or acts that would be crimes if adults committed them. Juveniles are any persons who have not reached the age of their majority or adulthood. Juvenile delinquents are distinguished from status offenders, who commit acts that would not be crimes if adults committed them. Status offenders may be runaways, truants, curfew violators, or those who engage in underage drinking. In more than a few jurisdictions, social welfare agencies and human services have gradually been granted jurisdiction over status offenders because of the nature of their offending.

The juvenile justice process has been influenced largely by the doctrine of *parens patriae*, which originated in England during the 1500s. The king of England utilized chancellors in different shires or English counties to make decisions in his behalf relating to all juveniles who committed various offenses. These decisions were most often influenced by what would be in the child's best interests. Today juvenile courts make decisions according to these same criteria, although bureaucratization and extended legal rights for juveniles have caused these courts to focus on due process and less on one's best interests. Nevertheless, these courts continue to perpetuate the *parens patriae* doctrine informally, and this practice, the traditional approach to juvenile justice, is largely individualized. Many juvenile courts regard their functions as largely treatment centered rather than punishment centered.

In 1974 the Juvenile Justice and Delinquency Prevention Act was passed, which sought to deinstitutionalize status offenders. At the time, it was customary for juvenile courts to institutionalize both delinquents and status offenders, and some states continue to do so. But most states have effectively removed status offenders from institutions where they were formerly housed together with qualitatively more serious delinquent offenders. Many juvenile courts have divested themselves of their jurisdiction over status offenders as well, thus giving greater jurisdictional power to social services and social welfare agencies who often supervise those charged with status offenses.

Some similarities and differences between juvenile courts and criminal courts have been described. As previously noted, juvenile courts are civil, while criminal courts process adults who are charged with committing felonies and misdemeanors. The consequences of a conviction in criminal court result in a criminal record, whereas civil consequences from juvenile court adjudications are largely noncriminal and are expunged from one's record upon attaining adulthood. All criminal courts are courts of record and juvenile courts are not. Both types of courts are adversarial, and both use the "beyond a reasonable doubt" standard of proof. Juvenile courts use this standard only when a juvenile is in jeopardy of losing his/her liberty or may be confined for any period of time. Criminal courts have a broader range of punishments, including life without the possibility of parole and the death penalty, which are beyond the scope of a juvenile court's jurisdiction. In most states, jury trials for juveniles are not permitted except with judicial approval. Juvenile courts are generally less formal proceedings compared with criminal courts, although in recent years, this difference has rapidly diminished.

Juvenile court history is relatively brief. The first juvenile court in the United States was established in 1899 in Illinois under the Juvenile Court Act. By the 1940s, all states had juvenile courts. Prior to 1899, juveniles were subject to a wide variety of sanctions by different bodies, such as children's tribunals. Many juveniles whose parents worked for long hours in factories to earn a living wandered city streets during daytime hours. Some of these juveniles were institutionalized for short periods as a punishment for vagrancy or begging. Child savers emerged, largely from the middle and upper classes, and these persons often established shelters or temporary homes where idle juveniles could be accommodated safely and removed from the dangers of the streets. During the late 1800s many persons and agencies became concerned and involved with child welfare matters, and the gradual progression to a full-fledged juvenile court was realized.

The juvenile justice process usually commences with a referral from a parent, the police, a guardian, a school official, or a neighbor, and one or more delinquent acts or status offenses are alleged. Juveniles are taken into custody and screened by intake officers, who often are juvenile probation officers. More serious cases are sent to juvenile court prosecutors, where further decision making about them occurs. Intake officers also have some limited discretionary powers and may defer actions against harmless youthful offenders who seem remorseful and unlikely to reoffend. About half of all juvenile cases are petitioned, where formal documents are filed with juvenile courts. Most petitioned cases result in adjudicatory proceedings before a juvenile court judge who listens and decides each case. If the facts alleged against the juvenile are true, juvenile court judges declare juveniles delinquent or status offenders and impose one of several types of dispositions as punishments. Dispositions are like sentences for adults, in that they involve nominal or verbal warnings, conditional punishments such as probation, or custodial sanctions, including incarceration in a juvenile facility for various lengths of time. Relatively few juveniles are actually incarcerated, and the terms of their incarceration are short compared with time served by convicted adults who are incarcerated.

The juvenile justice process has become increasingly legalistic, particularly since the 1960s, when the U.S. Supreme Court commenced hearing juvenile cases and extending various rights to juveniles. Presently a majority of juveniles processed by the juvenile justice system are represented by counsel, and attorney representation is increasing. Defense counsels for juveniles attempt to ensure that their due process rights are respected. Many juvenile cases are plea bargained similar to criminal cases. Defense counsels perform many of the same functions for juveniles as they do for adults, including representing them in adjudicatory proceedings. In those states where jury trials for juveniles are permitted, defense counsels are advocates for juveniles in every respect, seeking their acquittal of charges against them.

Approximately 1 percent of all juveniles referred to the juvenile justice system each year are transferred, waived, or certified as adults and processed by criminal courts. These transferred juveniles are not always the most serious offenders, despite the fact that the intent of transfers or waivers is to make it possible for criminal courts to impose more serious punishments, which are beyond the jurisdiction of juvenile courts. States vary in the youngest ages at which juveniles may be transferred to criminal court to be processed as though they were adults. Different types of waivers include judicial waivers, where judges on their own waive particular juveniles to the jurisdiction of criminal courts; prosecutorial waivers or concurrent jurisdiction or direct file, where prosecutors decide whether to prosecute juveniles in criminal or juvenile courts; and legislative or automatic waivers, also known as statutory exclusion, where juveniles are automatically waived to the jurisdiction of criminal courts for processing as adults. Viewed from the perspective of statutory exclusion, juvenile courts are prohibited by statute from hearing particular kinds of cases against juveniles. However, all juveniles are entitled to hearings on waiver actions. For those subject to legislative or automatic waivers, these juveniles may obtain hearings to have their cases placed back into juvenile courts for adjudication. These types of actions are known as reverse waiver hearings. Some juveniles may also initiate transfer proceedings through demand waiver actions. Thus, they ask juvenile courts to transfer jurisdiction over them to criminal courts.

The implications of transfers are several and diverse. Not all transferred juveniles are the most serious offenders. About 60 percent of all transferred juveniles are persistent or chronic property offenders or drug users. About 40 percent are violent offenders who are supposedly the most vulnerable to being transferred or waived. About 50 percent of all juvenile cases transferred to criminal court result in dismissals or the charges are downgraded, and probation is usually imposed through plea bargaining. Even where the remaining cases come to trial, the result for nearly another 40 percent of these offenders is probation. Only 12 percent or fewer juveniles ever serve time as the result of transfers and subsequent convictions in criminal courts. Thus, the transfer process does not necessarily achieve its manifest goals, and this general failure of the waiver process is repeated annually with uncanny similarity.

Several landmark cases involving juveniles have been decided by the U.S. Supreme Court and have vested all juveniles with most due process rights afforded adults. In *Kent v. United States* (1966), it was declared that all juveniles are entitled to a hearing before they are transferred to criminal court. *In re Gault* (1967) resulted in a juvenile's right to an attorney, the right to confront and cross-examine one's accuser and to give testimony in one's own behalf, the right against self-incrimination, and the right to a notice of charges against the juvenile. *In re Winship* (1970) established the "beyond a reasonable doubt" criminal court standard to prove one's guilt in juvenile court where any juvenile is in danger of losing his/her liberty through secure confinement in a juvenile institution. For cases not involving a possible loss of liberty, the civil standard of the preponderance of evidence continues to be used and governs determinations of whether juveniles have committed certain acts alleged by others in adjudicatory proceedings.

In *McKeiver v. Pennsylvania* (1971), it was decided that juveniles are not entitled to a jury trial in juvenile court as a matter of right. Today juvenile courts provide jury trials for juveniles under special circumstances as a matter of right in 11 states, and juvenile court judges have the discretion to approve jury trials in other jurisdictions if juveniles request one. In *Breed v. Jones* (1975), it was decided that juveniles cannot be simultaneously adjudicated in juvenile court on a charge and convicted of that same charge in criminal court without violating one's right against double jeopardy. In *Schall v. Martin* (1984) it was decided that juveniles may be held in preventive detention for different periods of time, pending their identification and risk posed if released.

Since the early 1990s increasing numbers of states have designed blended sentencing statutes that authorize either juvenile court or criminal court judges to impose either juvenile sanctions or criminal penalties or both on juvenile offenders. These blended sentencing statutes afford juveniles the full range of constitutional rights, including a trial by jury. But the transfer process is bypassed. Blended sentencing statutes include the juvenile–inclusive blend, the juvenile–exclusive blend, the juvenile–contiguous blend, the criminal–inclusive blend, and the criminal–exclusive blend. Inclusive blends for both juvenile and criminal courts authorize judges to impose both juvenile and criminal punishments. Exclusive blends for both juvenile and criminal courts authorize these same judges to impose either juvenile punishments or criminal punishments but not both. The juvenile–contiguous blend is unique in that a sentence of lengthy duration is imposed on a juvenile, but a board convenes six months before the juvenile becomes an adult and decides whether the remaining portion of the lengthy sentence should be continued. Prior institutional conduct of the juvenile is reviewed in making this decision. In fact, all blended sentencing statutes permit reviews of one's prior institutional conduct and thus function as incentives for juveniles to participate in self-help, educational, vocational, or other type of rehabilitative programs to improve themselves. Not everyone agrees that blended sentencing statutes are necessarily the best solutions for punishing juvenile offenders, however.

Several trends in juvenile justice include greater reforms in juvenile justice processing; greater emphasis on due process issues; greater accountability among juveniles in terms of sanctions imposed; greater use of waivers and transfers for more serious juvenile offenders; increasingly adversarial juvenile court proceedings; more stringent evidentiary standards; less use of secure confinement; greater use of plea bargaining; greater use of diversion and probation; greater use of innovations in offender supervision, including electronic monitoring, home confinement, and intensive supervised probation with conditions; and greater emphasis upon victim compensation, restitution, and restorative justice as sanctioning options.

KEY TERMS

Adjudicates
Adjudication
Adjudication hearing
Anchorage Youth Court
Automatic waivers
Blended sentencing
Camp, ranch
Case backlog
Case processing
Certification
Chancellors
Child savers
Children in need of supervision (CHINS)
Conditional dispositions
Confinement
Criminal–exclusive blend
Criminal–inclusive blend
Criminalization
Curfew violators
Custodial dispositions
Deinstitutionalization
Deinstitutionalization of status offenders (DSO)
Demand waiver
Direct file

Discretionary waivers
Divestiture of jurisdiction
Due process
Due process courts
English common law
Foster home
Group home
Guardian *ad litem*
Hull House
Illinois Juvenile Court Act
Intake
Intake hearings
Intake officer
Jane Addams
Judicial waiver
Juvenile court
Juvenile court jurisdiction
Juvenile delinquency
Juvenile delinquent
Juvenile Justice and Delinquency Prevention Act of 1974 (JJDPA)
Juvenile–contiguous blend
Juvenile–exclusive blend
Juvenile–inclusive blend
Juveniles
Legislative waivers

Loiterers
Mandatory transfer
Nominal dispositions
Nonsecure custody
Office of Juvenile Justice and
Delinquency Prevention (OJJDP)
Once an adult/always an adult
Parens patriae
Presumptive waiver
Prosecutorial waiver
Reformatory
Reverse waiver hearings
Runaways
Secure custody

Society for the Prevention of
Pauperism
Standard of proof
Status offenders
Statutory exclusion
Stigmas
Stigmatize
Teen courts
Traditional courts
Transfer
Truants
Waiver
Waiver hearing

▰▰▰ QUESTIONS FOR REVIEW ▰▰▰

1. Distinguish between a juvenile delinquent and a status offender. What has the federal government done to keep status offenders out of jails?

2. What is the jurisdiction of juvenile courts?

3. What is the doctrine of *parens patriae*? Why is it significant when investigating the actions of juvenile courts today? In what ways does *parens patriae* influence judicial decision making?

4. What is a referral? Who can make referrals? What are their purposes?

5. Identify four types of waivers. Which types of waivers are made by judges? Which types of waivers are made by legislatures?

6. Can juveniles contest waivers? How can these waiver actions be reversed? Describe several methods to accomplish this task.

7. What is a blended sentencing statute? How does it relate to the get-tough movement?

8. Identify three major rights cases involving juveniles. What are the major rights conveyed in the cases you have identified?

9. What are several important trends relating to juveniles and juvenile court processing of juveniles?

10. What is meant by DSO? What was the enabling legislation leading to DSO on the federal level?

11. What are some general differences between criminal courts and juvenile courts?

12. Under what circumstances can juveniles have jury trials in juvenile courts?

SUGGESTED READINGS

1. Alex Escarcega (2004). "Working Collaboratively: Addressing the Needs of Federally Sentenced Juvenile Offenders." *Corrections Today* **66**:20–22.
2. Barry C. Feld (2003). "The Politics of Race and Juvenile Justice: The 'Due Process Revolution' and the Conservative Reaction." *Justice Quarterly* **20**:765–800.
3. James Gondles (2004). "Kids are Kids, Not Adults." *Corrections Today* **66**:6–7.
4. Heather Hammer, David Finkelor, and Andrea J. Sedlak (2002). *Runaway/Throwaway Children: National Estimates and Characteristics.* Washington, DC: Office of Juvenile Justice and Delinquency Prevention.
5. Daniel P. Mears (2002). "Sentencing Guidelines and the Transformation of Juvenile Justice in the 21st Century." *Journal of Contemporary Criminal Justice* **18**:6–19.
6. Gerard A. Rainville and Steven K. Smith (2003). *Juvenile Felony Defendants in Criminal Courts.* Washington, DC: U.S. Department of Justice.
7. Lynn S. Urban, Jenna L. St. Cyr, and Scott H. Decker (2003). "Goal Conflict in the Juvenile Court: The Evolution of Sentencing Practices in the United States." *Journal of Contemporary Criminal Justice* **19**:454–479.
8. J.L. Viljoen, J. Klaver, and R. Roesch (2005). "Legal Decisions of Preadolescent and Adolescent Defendants: Predictors of Confessions, Pleas, Communications with Attorneys, and Appeals." *Law and Human Behavior* **29**:253–277.

Chapter 12

Courts, Media, and the Litigation Explosion

Chapter Objectives

As a result of reading this chapter, you will have accomplished the following objectives:

1. Understand how the media have been instrumental in shaping our perceptions of justice, and that the courts and the media are at odds with each other because of competing interests.

2. Describe the history of media and the courts from before the 1800s up until today and the idea of cameras in courtrooms.

3. Describe the current status of the access granted to media by the courts in the various jurisdictions throughout the United States.

4. Describe pretrial publicity and the effect it has on trials.

5. Understand the types of information that potential jurors consider to be prejudicial including case-specific and general pretrial publicity.

6. Describe the different ways in which pretrial publicity can be minimized including gag orders, jury instructions, change of venues, and jury sequestration.

7. Understand the litigation explosion and the reasons why America has become more litigious including the emergence of industrial capitalism, changing legal doctrines, and the transformation of scholarly legal thought.

8. Describe the different arguments for tort reform such as the fact that the number of tort cases has dramatically increased, and the belief that juries are unable to handle tort cases because they are usually sympathetic to the plaintiff and hand out excessive awards.

■ In June 2002, a New Jersey jury awarded $1,466,980 to Costello, who claims he was subjected to sexual harassment based on the perception that he was gay, and was wrongfully terminated when he initiated legal claims for the discriminatory treatment. The jury award was for pain and suffering. [*Costello v. Bell Atlantic-New Jersey, Inc.*, JVR No. 803831, 2002, WL 32158040, Hudson Co.]

■ A West Virginia convenience store worker was awarded $2,699,000 in punitive damages after she injured her back opening a pickle jar. The injured worker also received $130,066 in compensation and $170,000 for emotional distress. A state supreme court justice, Spike Maynard, said, "I know an excessive punitive damages award when I see one, and I see one here." Nevertheless, the woman's award was upheld. [Source: Adapted from "A Jarring Experience," *Power of Attorneys*, 2004.]

■ Mancini, a female police lieutenant, received a New Jersey jury award of $1.5 million for being subjected to offensive cartoons, magazines, and comments, and who had been demoted in retaliation for filing a sex discrimination suit. [*Mancini v. Township of Teaneck, et al.*, JVR No. 801654, 2000 WL 33125820, Hudson Co.]

■ Eighty-two-year-old Heyman was awarded $2 million from Corporate Express by a jury for age discrimination and wrongful termination in retaliation for lodging complaints. [JVR No. 803302, 2002 WL 1901323, Hudson Co.]

■ In the mid-1990s a blind man was given the gift of a seeing-eye dog. When the man went to a shopping mall in Bradenton, Florida, his seeing-eye dog allegedly stepped on the foot of a woman, who became distressed. When she learned that the blind man had no money, she filed a lawsuit against Southeastern Guide Dogs, Inc. for "loss of earning capacity and mental pain and suffering" resulting from the dog stepping on her foot. The case was "Susan Faith and Reverend Ian Faith, Plaintiffs, v. Southeastern Guide Dogs, Inc., Defendant." Kimberly Marlow, Southeastern Guide Dogs, Inc.'s development director, said that the nonprofit group had to gather extensive documents in preparation for the trial. But the case never made it to court. After being ridiculed in newspapers and on television, the plaintiffs dropped the suit. In fact, the plaintiff's law firm donated $1,000 to Southeastern Guide Dogs. [Source: Adapted from Robert Trigaux and the *St. Petersburg Times*, St. Petersburg, FL, 2005.]

■ Two Chicago men, Vadim Levin and Alex Sheyngis, bought copies of a special issue of *Penthouse* magazine for $8.99 per copy. The *Penthouse* issue was believed to contain nude photographs of tennis star Anna Kournikova. When these men looked at the photographs, they discovered that another woman had been photographed nude, not Anna Kournikova as they originally believed. They were "distressed" over this discovery and immediately wanted their money back. Additionally, they filed a class action suit against *Penthouse* magazine, seeking damages for the deceived customers and attorneys' fees. Earlier *Penthouse* magazine had hyped the issue, leading customers to believe that Anna Kournikova had been photographed by a jewelry salesman on a Florida beach. In fact, the pictures were of another naked woman unrelated to Kournikova. There were 1.2 million copies of the issue printed. An unspecified sum of money was sought from *Penthouse*. Subsequently *Penthouse* settled out of court with both women, issued apologies, and destroyed what remained of the few copies of the magazine that were unsold. Critics of the burgeoning class-action law practice say lawsuits like these routinely offer chump change for the plaintiffs but in many cases provide million-dollar bounties for their lawyers. [Source: Adapted from "Angry Anna Fans Sue Penthouse for $8.99." *Power of Attorneys*, 2004.]

INTRODUCTION

These awards and many others like them every year are given to plaintiffs by juries in civil cases. They seem exorbitant or out of proportion compared with the harm done in the case. The United States society is characterized as being too litigious, so much so that doctors, coaches, teachers, and even ministers have a fear of being sued. It is the reason insurance premiums in some professions are excessive, the reason why some cities have to cut funding to public services, and why the average citizen when wanting to have something as simple as a garage sale has to put up a sign saying that they are not responsible for accidents.

Do these things happen everyday? Should we be fearful of litigation against us? Or is the media blowing these things out of proportion by focusing on what constitutes an infinitesimal number of cases? According to the American system of justice, this media coverage of trials is supposedly irrelevant and should not be viewed by jurors. Jurors take an oath that they will remain impartial and objective. They are obliged to refrain from listening to, reading about, or watching anything related to the trial. In reality, however, many jurors keep in close touch with trial events and media coverage of them. And most people, including jurors, are affected by what they see and hear. We are in the midst of an era of media news frenzy, and in diverse ways almost everyone is influenced by the media and its news reports and characterizations.

Since the early 1900s, the courts have had an antagonistic relationship with the media. Increasing numbers of courtrooms are permitting limited or extensive television coverage. Such permissiveness is consistent with the public's right to know, about public access to the courts, and about the freedom of speech. However, the media has almost always sought to dramatize court events in different ways so as to stimulate listeners, readers, and viewers. *Court TV* and *CNN Headline News* shows have pioneered creative and innovative court reporting through the use of experts and panels of experts who debate, criticize, and overanalyze information bits from trial testimony and events. No court actor has escaped the intensive scrutiny of television cameras or the opinions, reactions, and interpretations of events through the eyes and ears of courtroom observers. Hourly reporting of who has testified, what the judge thought or seemed to think about the testimony, juror reactions, and other courtroom banter has riveted millions of television viewers. If the courtroom news has not been sufficiently dramatic, these shows will often create their own news by giving less newsworthy events fictitious spins for audience consumption. Conjectures from guests and "what ifs" from news commentators or legal experts and analysts are often passed off as factual information, when in fact it may simply be their opinion.

Today the public seems discontent with simple news reporting. Generally, judicial decisions are reported only when they seem newsworthy. When television producers or newspaper reporters determine that a judge has imposed a lenient sentence, or that a jury has failed to convict a guilty-appearing defendant, or if an unusually large monetary award is made in a civil case by a jury, these outcomes are reported on the evening news or in daily newspapers. The selection of the news events to report is not particularly random. Rather, the news selection process is carefully calculated to yield the greatest public impact. The more sensational the news and how it is reported, the greater the interest and viewership.

The police and prosecutors often have a symbiotic relationship with the media. In exchange for confidential information from the police or district attorney's offices, reporters will slant their stories in ways favorable to police conclusions and prosecutorial theorizing about the crime, how it was committed, and who probably committed it. Seldom is equal time allocated to defendants so that they can give their version of events or their side of the story. The courts have increasingly relied upon media technology to assist in processing cases. In many jurisdictions, initial appearances and arraignments are held by means of closed-circuit television. The defendant remains at the jail and enters a plea before the judge across town in the courthouse through closed-circuit television monitoring systems. Jurisdictions have adopted this alternative to minimize security problems and the costs of transporting defendants to and from their jails for short court appearances.

This chapter examines two important issues that shape our perceptions about the American court system. The first issue is the nature of the interplay between the courts and the media. This interplay has prompted much public discourse, especially as the direct result of several high-profile trials during the 1990s. The O. J. Simpson trial focused national attention both on court protocol and the various personalities involved in the trial. All relevant actors were scrutinized, including the judge, the prosecution and defense counsel, jury members, and witnesses. All persons watching the courtroom drama were active participants who critiqued the actions of the witnesses, attorneys, and the judge.

The second issue is our definition of justice as portrayed by the media. Has the legitimacy of the court system been undermined because our ideals of justice are inconsistent with courtroom reality delivered by the media into our homes through radio or television? Have the courts been effective and acted responsibly in their use of media technology? How has the media shaped our perceptions of the "litigation explosion"? We have witnessed seemingly outlandish jury judgments in civil cases extended to persons who have filed lawsuits that appear frivolous. We have seen an array of courtroom tactics used successfully by plaintiff's attorneys against big businesses and corporate giants. The mentality of juries and the racial and ethnic composition of jurors have been analyzed extensively by the media, and we are inclined to view the average juror in a criminal or civil case in disparaging ways. Jurors are perceived as both pawns of the legal system and as self-styled vigilantes with their own political and social agendas. The buzzword of the 1990s was jury nullification, where juries disregard the facts in favor of some alternative and contrary verdict that satisfies political ends rather than legal ones.

This chapter is organized as follows. First, a brief history is provided of the media and its uneasy association with the American justice system. Technological change has modified greatly the nature of courtroom intrusion by the media. Newspapers, radio, and television innovations have been significant in influencing what happens in courtrooms throughout the nation. Increasingly clear is the fact that the behaviors of courtroom actors have undergone a metamorphosis of sorts as courtrooms have been subjected to greater public scrutiny. The implications of these behavioral changes for the justice process are explored.

Several highly visible trials are described, together with the nature of media attention given to each. The media has been instrumental in promoting a defendant's guilt or innocence, depending on the specific case. Accordingly, jurors have been responsive to particular types of media coverage, such that it is questionable whether justice has been served in certain cases. Indeed, some jury verdicts have been reversed by the U.S. Supreme Court because of the undue influence of media trial coverage. Often, media coverage has been passed off and labeled as the **court of public opinion.** The media has magnified the popularity of this term over time, and many citizens accept media opinion as factually based and give considerable credence to it.

Next, pretrial publicity is described. Pretrial publicity is almost always prejudicial for the defense or prosecution. Sensationalized coverage of both spectacular and heinous crimes has created an emotionally charged milieu for more than a few defendants. In certain cases, defense counsels have sought to change the site of a trial because of extensive adverse pretrial publicity. The trials of Timothy McVeigh and Terry Nichols were changed from Oklahoma City, Oklahoma to Denver, Colorado because it was believed that the amount of pretrial publicity indicated that they could not receive a fair trial in Oklahoma. This section will also explore the factors that determine whether the prejudice generated by pretrial publicity is sufficient to jeopardize one's right to a fair and impartial trial. Several ways for minimizing the prejudicial effects of pretrial publicity are described.

Besides criminal trials, many civil trials have generated a considerable amount of publicity and media coverage. Often these trials involve **tort actions,** where monetary damages are sought instead of convictions. Tort actions may highlight negligence, wrongful death, or product liability. The **litigation explosion** is also depicted, where the volume of civil cases has burgeoned in recent decades. The media has labeled our society as litigious, emphasizing quite appropriately the increasing interest of persons in seeking monetary awards from their employers or from large corporations. The bases of these increasing numbers of lawsuits may be sexual harassment, product liability, or wrongful death. Many lawsuits are labeled by judges as frivolous and dismissed. Others are decided in civil courtrooms by juries. Again, the media is present and pervasive to assess and interpret what is going on and why. The chapter concludes with a discussion of tort reforms.

TRIALS AND THE COURT OF PUBLIC OPINION

The media has been instrumental in shaping our perceptions of justice. The media and the courts are often at odds because of their competing interests. The courts operate in a methodical fashion, following specific criminal or civil protocols that may at times frustrate the observer. A great deal of time is consumed over seemingly trivial details of events, although we are reminded by the experts on television talk shows that the most trivial details have profound importance in shaping trial outcomes. Verdicts are rendered only after juries have given careful review to factual details, expert witness testimony, and an intricate inspection of all relevant evidence. While the case proceeds at a snail's pace, the media has its story to tell. The most innocuous details of a case are given great weight. Thus, an otherwise boring media story is converted into an exciting one by creative media spins. The viability of a network television show is critically dependent upon the nature of sensational coverage given to the most mundane courtroom events.

There has been considerable debate about the role and influence of the media and the courts. The O. J. Simpson case brought all the arguments for and against media access to the courts into the public discourse. For instance, before the O. J. Simpson murder case, the presiding judge, Lance Ito, was initially reluctant to permit television cameras in his courtroom. Judge Ito believed that the presence of television cameras would undermine the justice process and cause viewers to misunderstand the proceedings. He also believed that tabloidization of the judicial process would occur. In retrospect, Judge Ito was right, although he permitted television cameras to cover most aspects of the trial anyway.

Judge Ito's reservations about the intrusion of television cameras and media representatives into his courtroom were well-founded and grounded in scientific research. Several scholars and legal experts have provided compelling arguments both for and against television cameras in courtrooms (Hoskins, Ruth, and Ruback 2004). While these arguments are inconclusive and inconsistent, the general sentiment is that television coverage of courtroom drama does influence what goes on in the courtroom. There is extensive debate about whether this influence jeopardizes one's right to a fair trial, however. Media representatives emphasize that their interest in covering courtroom events is based on the public's right to be present inside courtrooms as public events.

Thus, a judge's refusal to allow the media into courtrooms is perceived as a violation of the First Amendment. Technological change and the advent of television and closed-circuit broadcasting has done much to change the definition of public access to courtroom activities, however. In order to understand how the definition of public courtroom access has changed, we must first examine the early vestiges of courtroom coverage by the media.

HISTORY OF MEDIA AND THE COURTS

Court reaction to media intrusion has gradually changed with changing media technology. In the 1800s, trial outcomes or happenings were relayed by word-of-mouth. This information dissemination shifted from word-of-mouth to the printed page with the advent of newspapers. By the 1850s, trial events and court decisions were transmitted throughout the country by use of the telegraph. Those eager to hear the results would often gather at the local telegraph office and wait for the trial results to be announced. The most widely acknowledged example of this process was the murder trial of Harry Thaw. He had killed millionaire Stanford White over the affections of a very young Evelyn Nesbit also known as the "girl in the red velvet swing."

Soon courtroom photographers and newsreel cameras were common occurrences in the most high-profile cases. The Tennessee trial of teacher John Scopes, known as the "monkey trial," was the first to be broadcast over the radio. Attorneys Clarence Darrow and William Jennings Bryan were well aware of the impact of the media presence and structured their trial tactics not only for the benefit of the jury but also for the benefit of the larger national audience. In fact, compared with today's standards, the media seemed to intrude on court proceedings by making requests similar to those from a movie director to an actor rather than to court officers. For instance, media representatives have often made requests for the attorneys and judges to position themselves so that their cameras could get better picture angles.

The problems created by the media during the murder trial of Bartolomeo Vanzetti and Nicola Sacco in 1921, and during the trial of Richard Loeb and Nathan Leopold Jr. in 1924 prompted the American Bar Association to review the issue of news reporting and the courts. It took another "trial of the century" to force the courts to come to terms with the impact of the media on court proceedings.

The trial involved Bruno Hauptmann, a German immigrant. Hauptmann was accused of kidnaping and murdering the baby of Charles Lindberg. The trial started with over 700 representatives of the media, with 120 being cameramen. The trial was chaos. Witnesses were barraged by reporters and blinded by flashbulbs reminiscent of an opening at a Hollywood movie premiere. Hauptmann appealed his conviction, alleging that the extensive media coverage prevented him from receiving a fair trial. He lost his appeal, but the

BOX 12.1 THE FIRST TRIAL OF THE CENTURY

■ The Girl in the Red Velvet Swing

Stanford White was one of the brightest stars in New York society at the turn of the century. As an architect he was a visionary. Many of the new millionaires of the Industrial Revolution flocked to White to have him design their mansions. His talent was recognized by officials of the city and he was hired to design the New York Public Library and Madison Square Garden. White's appetite for design was only matched with his desire for young women. He had several apartments throughout Manhattan where young girls were often accompanied by White. At the turn of the century, the newest sensation in New York was 16-year-old Evelyn Nesbit. Nesbit had arrived in New York from Pittsburgh with her mother, a widowed seamstress. Evelyn was slim and beautiful and soon found work as an artist's model and later landed a role in a Broadway musical. She was an instant sensation. Soon many admirers were waiting for her after the show. One of the hopeful suitors was Stanford White.

In 1901, White convinced Nesbit to have lunch with him. This was the beginning of an affair that would last for five years. Nesbit was raped by White while she was intoxicated with champagne drunk at White's apartment during one of their meetings. She did not seem to be fazed by this development and continued their relationship. Nesbit eventually fell in love with White and made frequent visits to his apartment where he encouraged her to swing on his red velvet swing—preferably naked.

Evelyn's mother knew a long-term financially secure future with White was not possible. White was married with children. Therefore, she encouraged her daughter to see other men. One of the men who met her mother's expectations was Harry Thaw who stood to inherit $40 million from the Pittsburgh Railroad fortune. Thaw courted Evelyn with antics like sending her roses individually wrapped in $50 bills. Thaw and Stanford White had more in common than an interest in Evelyn. Earlier White had blackballed Thaw from many of New York's social clubs. Thaw deeply resented this. During the courtship of Nesbit and Thaw, she told Thaw how White had taken advantage of her by getting her drunk and raping her. Upon hearing this Thaw became furious. A short time later during a trip to Europe, he tied her up and beat her with a whip until she was covered with welts. Six months later she married him because she believed he was the only rich man who would propose to her.

On June 25, 1906 Stanford White sat on the rooftop Madison Square Garden theater enjoying a production when Harry Thaw walked up and shot him three times, proclaiming "I did it because he ruined my wife." At the trial, Nesbit testified about White's sexual behavior in an effort to "save a husband I didn't love from the chair." Thaw's mother

(continued)

BOX 12.1 *(continued)*

went to considerable effort to demonstrate her son's insanity. She even went to the extreme of testifying that the entire Thaw family was crazy. The initial jury could not reach a verdict and the second jury found Thaw not guilty by reason of insanity. For what reasons does the media seem to present us with a new "trial of the century" every decade? Do you feel if this offense were to happen today the nation would be transfixed on the case? Are these types of cases good measures of how the criminal justice system operates? [Source: Adapted from "Stanford White and Evelyn Nesbit," *People Weekly,* February 12, 45:79–80, 2006.]

trial prompted the American Bar Association to review their position on camera access to court proceedings. They ultimately ruled in 1937 that photographing and broadcasting court proceedings should be prohibited. Most states adopted the position of the American Bar Association and forbid photographing and broadcasting trials and trial participants. In 1952, the American Bar Association extended the media ban to include television coverage of court proceedings.

Texas was one of the states that ignored the recommendation of the American Bar Association and allowed cameras into the courtroom at the discretion of the judge. In 1962, Texas provided the case that served as the basis for denying cameras into the courtroom. Billie Sol Estes, a friend of President Lyndon B. Johnson, was charged with swindling persons out of large sums of cash. The trial judge decided to allow television cameras into the courtroom, but they were restricted to the back of the courtroom in a specially constructed booth. Like Hauptmann thirty years earlier, Estes argued that the media coverage deprived him of a fair trial. The Texas Court of Appeals declared that his due process rights had not been violated, and Estes appealed to the United States Supreme Court. In a 5–4 decision, the U.S. Supreme Court reversed Estes's conviction. In the decision of the majority, the Court held that although no prejudice was actually shown, the circumstances of the case were suspect. Furthermore, Justice Clark believed that the presence of the cameras in the courtroom had a harmful effect on all of those involved in the trial. In its decision, the U.S. Supreme Court did not address the issue of whether the First Amendment extended to the media to broadcast from the courtroom (*Estes v. Texas*, 1965).

After the *Estes* decision, states continued to experiment with media coverage. Judges were generally given the discretion to allow cameras. For the next 12 years, courts individually struggled with the decision to allow cameras. In 1977, the Florida Supreme Court approved a one-year pilot study that allowed the electronic media to cover all of cases in Florida state courts without the consent of the participants. The crucial case that emerged during this year involved a 15-year-old boy who was charged with murdering an elderly neighbor while he and some friends burglarized the victim's house. The circumstances of the offense were not unusual. What attracted the media to the trial was the unusual defense of involuntary television intoxication, which was offered by the boy and his attorneys. The defense alleged that Zamora (the boy) did not know what he was doing because of the massive amounts of crime and violence he had watched on television. The local media broadcast segments of the trial on the nightly news and the worldwide audience was estimated at several million viewers. At the conclusion of the trial, Judge Paul Baker submitted a report including his observations about the effect of the media on the trial. He believed that the equipment did not produce any distracting noises or light flashes. In contrast, during the Estes trial, the camera and lighting equipment created various distractions. In the years between these cases, media and camera technology had changed significantly, and ultimately it became less intrusive in the courtroom and seemed to have little impact on the courtroom actors.

Judge Baker spoke with jurors about their reactions to the presence of the media. The jurors believed that the presence of the cameras caused only slight distractions. Yet the actions of the media did not hinder or distract the jurors from following the testimony, arguments of counsel, and judicial instructions. The judge also found no support for the assertion that judges would alter the way that they conduct business with the presence of the cameras.

Considering this information as well as the evidence from other cases, in 1979 the Florida Supreme Court permanently allowed cameras in the courts with the approval of the presiding judge. The new provisions were put to the test with the Ted Bundy murder trial. Ted Bundy defended himself and appeared to enjoy playing to the cameras. However, the trial judge believed that the rules in place were effective and the cameras did not hamper the court process. The court acknowledged that publicity could undermine a defendant's right to a fair trial. However, this risk did not allow for an absolute ban on news reporting and the broadcasting of trials. Essentially, the U.S. Supreme Court left the decision up to the individual states whether to allow the media into their courtrooms.

CURRENT STATUS OF MEDIA ACCESS TO THE COURTS

As of 2006, only three states did not allow cameras into their different courtrooms. Table 12.1 shows states that permit cameras in certain courtrooms, and under particular conditions. Most states have allowed cameras in their courtrooms on either an experimental or permanent basis. States that have allowed cameras in the courtroom have developed guidelines for their usage. In most states, the consent of the presiding judge is required. Many states require a

TABLE 12.1   CURRENT STATUS OF THE USE OF MEDIA IN U.S. COURTROOMS*

States that allow the most coverage; presiding judge has broad discretion:

California, Colorado, Florida, Georgia, Idaho, Kentucky, Michigan, Montana, Nevada, New Hampshire, New Mexico, North Dakota, South Carolina, Tennessee, Vermont, Virginia, Washington, West Virginia, Wisconsin, Wyoming

States with restrictions prohibiting coverage of important types of cases, or prohibiting coverage of all or large categories of witnesses who object to coverage of their testimony:

Alaska, Arizona, Connecticut, Hawaii, Iowa, Kansas, Massachusetts, Missouri, North Carolina, New Jersey, Ohio, Oregon, Rhode Island, Texas, Virginia

States that allow appellate coverage only, or that have such restricting trial coverage rules essentially preventing coverage:

Alabama, Arkansas, Delaware, Illinois, Indiana, Louisiana, Maine, Maryland, Minnesota, Mississippi, Nebraska, New York, Oklahoma, Pennsylvania, South Dakota, Utah

States that prohibit trial and appellate coverage entirely:

District of Columbia

*Compiled by the authors.

written application submitted in advance of the trial. Furthermore, in some states, if the defendant objects, cameras will not be permitted to record the trial proceedings.

Most states do not allow television coverage of cases involving juveniles, and coverage is limited where victims of sex crimes are involved or where cases involve trade secrets of business organizations. Fewer states limit coverage of jurors and the *voir dire* process. And all states ban the coverage of pretrial conferences or sidebars between the judge, prosecutor, and defense counsel in court. States have also developed guidelines that regulate media equipment and personnel. Courts specify which types of cameras are allowed and limit the movement and number of media personnel in the court.

PRETRIAL PUBLICITY

One of the primary concerns of those who study the relationship between the court and the media is the effect of **pretrial publicity.** Within this area there are two different issues. The first is that the extensive pretrial publicity will make it difficult if not impossible to locate jurors who have not heard of the cases and developed some preconceived notions about the defendant's guilt or innocence. The second is that the jurors, as the result of the pretrial publicity,

BOX 12.2 TELEVISION IN THE COURTROOM?

■ **Court TV** was able to cover the trial of an incestuous cult leader and much of the Scott Peterson murder trial. But in 2005 *Court TV* was in court itself seeking admission into New York criminal courts under the First Amendment. New York courts have consistently refused to allow televised coverage of their criminal trials since 1952, when a state law banning cameras in courtrooms was passed. *Court TV* alleges that New York courts should allow cameras in the courtroom, since to ban them would infringe a basic First Amendment right of citizens to see justice in action literally. In 2005, a total of 43 states approved the use of cameras in courtrooms to televise proceedings. Those states where it is banned, including New York, oppose cameras on grounds having to do with undue influence of court officers. New York officials say that admitting cameras into criminal proceedings would have a negative effect on those proceedings, causing lawyers, judges, and witnesses to be intimidated and act unnaturally. These claims have never been proven in the states where cameras have been used to cover trials.

Court TV and other broadcasting organizations say that televised court proceedings would give the public a valuable education on the workings of the justice system. That would have been especially useful during the volatile legal proceedings like those surrounding the shooting death of Amadou Diallo by New York City police officers. The educational benefit could be even greater in the nation's highest court. However, the U.S. Supreme Court has typically been opposed to televising their work, just as Congress at one time balked at having cameras cover their proceedings. But today, programs such as those on C-Span have given millions of Americans a better understanding of how their laws are made. The public also deserves to see how the courts carry out and interpret the law. Sometimes, however, what the public sees isn't especially what the courts want them to see. Lawyers, judges, and others may act in ways that cast unfavorable images of themselves and hold them up to public ridicule. The New York governor, the New York State Bar Association, American Civil Liberties Union, and other organizations favor cameras in the courtroom and support legislation to make that happen in New York and the other states where cameras are presently banned.

Should all courts allow cameras in the courtroom? Shouldn't all persons be allowed to see their appointed and elected officials, including the U.S. Supreme Court, in action first-hand? What harm would cameras cause, if any? What do you think? [Source: Adapted from the Associated Press, "Allow Cameras in New York Courts and the U.S. Supreme Court," April 18, 2005.]

will recognize that their decision will be scrutinized by friends, family, neighbors, and the larger community. This pressure will ultimately influence them to vote on the basis of how their own lives will be affected rather than the actual facts of the case. In the *Estes* decision, this was probably the issue that concerned the U.S. Supreme Court the most. The Court wrote that the potential impact of television on the jurors is perhaps of the greatest significance. They are the nerve center of the fact-finding process. And we must remember that realistically it is only the notorious trial that will be broadcast, because of the necessity of the paid sponsorship. The conscious or unconscious effect that this may have on the juror's judgment cannot be evaluated, but experience indicates that it is not only possible but probable that it will have a direct bearing on his vote as to guilt or innocence. Where pretrial publicity of all kinds has created intense public feeling that is aggravated by the telecasting or picturing of the trial, the televised jurors cannot help but feel the pressure of knowing that friends or neighbors have their eyes upon them. If the community is hostile to an accused, then a televised juror, realizing he must return to neighbors who saw the trial themselves, may well be led "not to hold the balance nice, clear and true between the State and the accused." [*Estes v. Texas*, 1965:545.]

Some persons have argued that juror concerns over the impact of their decisions should not allow for their identity to be concealed. In fact juror anonymity should only be allowed in the rarest of cases. In fact jurors in high-profile cases should be regarded as citizen-soldiers in the quest for justice.

It may be that the concern over pretrial publicity placed in the context of day-to-day operations of the court should not be a concern. Daily, the courts process thousands of cases, usually in empty courtrooms. Some persons might assert that rather than having a problem with pretrial publicity, the larger problem facing the court is public apathy. When somebody wanders into a courtroom merely to watch the proceedings, the courtroom actors take notice. They assume that the observer must be a defendant, and when this is not the case, they wonder why this person doesn't have anything better to do than watch courtroom proceedings. Researchers have estimated that only 7 percent of felony arrests are covered by the press (Champion 2005b).

The concern over pretrial publicity only occurs when there is a high-profile case. The common assumption is that pretrial publicity almost always favors the prosecution and therefore limits the defendant's ability to receive a fair and impartial trial. Researchers have disclosed that most courtroom actors do not believe that pretrial publicity does not significantly affect juror behavior. Judges believe that the *voir dire* process is an effective method for removing jurors who have been prejudiced by the media. Prosecutors acknowledge that pretrial publicity usually works in their favor. Simon and Eimermann (1971), for example, found that 65 percent of those exposed to pretrial publicity had pro-prosecution attitudes compared to 45 percent of those not exposed to pretrial

BOX 12.3 PRETRIAL PUBLICITY

■ **Sheppard v. Maxwell**

384 U.S. 333, 86 S.Ct. 1507 (1966). Sheppard claimed that someone un-known to him entered his home in Bay Village, Ohio, and hit him on the head. When he awakened, he saw his wife had been injured and was sit-ting in a chair, bleeding and not moving. Early in the case, police sus-pected Sheppard of killing his wife and diverting attention from himself to so-called unknown assailants. The police made known their views to the media, which dramatized the event, as Sheppard was a well-respected physician in the community. Front-page headlines in the local newspapers created a media frenzy, with Sheppard at its center. During his subsequent trial, Sheppard was subjected to considerable media attention, and cam-eras and other media agents and apparatuses were admitted into the courtroom to witness the proceedings. This action by the court further in-tensified the media frenzy. In this milieu, Sheppard was convicted of mur-der. He appealed, and the U.S. Supreme Court overturned his murder conviction, holding that the failure of the state trial judge to protect Shep-pard from inherently prejudicial publicity, which saturated the community, and to control disruptive influences in court had deprived Sheppard of a fair trial consistent with due process.

■ **Dobbert v. Florida**

432 U.S. 282, 97 S.Ct. 2290 (1977). Dobbert was convicted of first-degree murder, second-degree murder, child torture, and child abuse and sen-tenced to death. He appealed, alleging that changes in the jury decision to recommend mercy instead of the death penalty without review by a trial judge had jeopardized his chances of receiving a life sentence. Further, he claimed that there was no death penalty "in effect" in Florida at the time he was convicted, because an earlier death-penalty statute had been held to be invalid when *Furman v. Georgia* (1972) had been decided. Dobbert also claimed that excessive pretrial publicity denied him the right to a fair trial. The U.S. Supreme Court rejected all of his arguments, saying that changes in the death-penalty statute were simply procedural, and thus there was no rights violation. Further, new statutes provided convicted of-fenders with *more* procedural safeguards rather than fewer of them. Dob-bert's equal-protection rights under the Fourteenth Amendment were not violated either, because the new statute did not deny him such protection. Finally, the pretrial publicity, in view of the "totality of circumstances," was insufficient to conclude that he was denied a fair trial. The U.S. Supreme Court upheld his conviction and sentence.

(continued)

BOX 12.3 *(continued)*

■ **Mu'Min v. Virginia**

500 U.S. 415, 111 S.Ct. 1899 (1991). Mu'Min was charged with and convicted of a murder while he was out on a prison work detail (where he was serving a term on another charge). There was considerable news publicity surrounding the killing, and when the case came to trial, Mu'Min's attorney made a motion for the judge during *voir dire* to ask whether any specific jurors had any knowledge of the pretrial publicity and if so, what effect it would have on their ability to hear and decide the case fairly. The judge denied the motion, and Mu'Min was subsequently convicted. He appealed, alleging that his right to an impartial jury as provided by the Sixth Amendment had been violated. The U.S. Supreme Court upheld his conviction, holding that the refusal of the judge to question jurors about specific contents of news reports to which they had been exposed had not violated Mu'Min's Sixth or Fourteenth Amendment rights to due process.

---

publicity. As prosecutors contend, whether defense attorneys can overcome this bias depends on the type of information prospective jurors are exposed to prior to the trial. Defense attorneys are most inclined to believe that pretrial publicity adversely affects their clients. However, it is believed that pretrial publicity is an insignificant problem. Surveys of the public reveal that while pretrial publicity may affect juror attitudes about the case, they still believe that despite this information, they could render objective and impartial judgments and base their decisions on the facts presented at trial.

WHAT TYPES OF INFORMATION DO POTENTIAL JURORS CONSIDER PREJUDICIAL?

Researchers have identified two ways that jurors are affected by prejudicial information. The first is **case-specific pretrial publicity** (Greene 1990). This is information about a specific case where jurors must make a determination of one's guilt or innocence. An example of case-specific pretrial publicity might come from the Rodney King state and federal cases. Most Americans were repeatedly exposed to the videotape showing police officers beating King as he lay on the ground. Jurors asked to serve in that case were probably exposed to that videotape numerous times prior to the trial. Their perceptions of the event were only relevant to this individual case.

The second type of pretrial publicity is **general pretrial publicity.** This includes information about crime, criminals, and the criminal justice system that is constantly in the media and shapes our perceptions when we are asked to serve as jurors. For example, most of us have probably developed an opinion about the insanity defense based on several cases and stories about the insanity defense presented to us in the media. Jurors with these vague perceptions may have already formed an opinion about whether they might accept insanity as a valid defense before hearing any relevant evidence or testimony about one's sanity in an actual trial. Many jurors may still believe that if they find the defendant guilty but mentally ill, he will escape punishment or receive a light sentence.

Research has revealed that when jurors were exposed to pretrial publicity revealing a confession or a prior lengthy criminal record of a particular defendant, they were more likely to believe that the defendant was guilty. Furthermore, when information was released prior to the trial about the defendant failing a lie detector test, jurors were more likely to infer guilt from this event.

Uncovering the effects of general pretrial publicity is more difficult. The best research comes from conducting experiments with mock juries. Greene and Loftus (1984) compared three groups of mock jurors. The first group read newspaper stories about a defendant who was mistakenly identified and convicted of rape. The second group was asked to read stories about how the testimony of an eyewitness led to the conviction of a mass murderer. The final group was exposed to no pretrial publicity and acted as the control group. All three groups were then asked to make a decision about guilt or innocence for the cases involving an alleged armed robbery and murder. The prosecution's case consisted primarily of the testimony of an eyewitness. The first group had a significantly higher acquittal rate than either of the other two groups. From this evidence, we might infer that the story about the miscarriage of justice influenced the jurors and made them more skeptical of law enforcement and increased the probability of acquittal.

Research has also indicated that the entertainment media influences individual's perceptions of criminality and the criminal justice system. Jurors may expect the courtroom to be an exciting and dramatic place if they have watched crime dramas such as *L.A. Law*, *Law and Order*, *Judge Judy*, or *Perry Mason*. These shows do not accurately portray what happens in real courtrooms. Court proceedings are typically routine and bland. There are no riveting revelations or courtroom confessions. Jurors are more likely to struggle to find ways to overcome boredom.

HOW TO MINIMIZE THE EFFECTS OF PRETRIAL PUBLICITY

Trial judges can minimize the effects of pretrial publicity by various methods. The most radical and least-used approach is to issue a **gag order.** This is the most controversial approach because it raises serious First Amendment questions. Gag orders usually require that the media cannot publish or broadcast any prejudicial information about a case. Sometimes gag orders are extended to include the attorneys involved in the case. When a gag order includes attorneys, they are under court order not to talk about the case; this means that they are prohibited from giving television interviews or appearing on talk shows while the trial is in progress.

BOX 12.4 CAREER SNAPSHOT

Nancy Degollado-Lopez
United States Pretrial Services Officer Laredo, Texas

Statistics: B.A. (criminal justice), M.A. (sociology), Texas A & M International University.

Work History and Experience: Law enforcement has always been a male-dominated field, especially from a female's point of view. Never did I imagine myself following a career in law enforcement. Even though law enforcement is still a male-dominated field, women are slowly gaining momentum. My college education began with a course in business, plus several other majors even before enrolling in a criminal justice course. This is where I found myself, sitting in a criminal justice course among a majority of male students, which later became the norm. Then I changed my major and earned a bachelor's degree in criminal justice.

After graduating from college, my first career opportunity was not in the criminal justice field, but rather in a school setting. I was a social caseworker at a local alternative education school focused on assisting juvenile delinquents and at-risk youths. This somehow correlated with criminal justice due to the constant interventions with law enforcement agencies.

Shortly afterwards, a position became available with the adult probation department. I applied, and due to having experience in this field from an internship, I was hired. In April 1999 I officially began my career in the criminal justice field, as an adult probation officer. I was assigned to a specialized unit that focused on probationers convicted of domestic violence offenses. My duties were not only to supervise the probationers on my caseload, but also to verify that they were attending an 18-week domestic violence counseling program. I was in this specialized domestic violence unit for approximately two years before being transferred to a court residential treatment center. At this facility, I supervised probationers who were sentenced, under special conditions, to a drug treatment facility in lieu of incarceration. My position as a probation officer at the drug treatment center was short-lived due to an opportunity to apply for a federal position with the U.S. Pretrial Services.

Ecstatic to say the least, I was hired into the federal criminal justice field as a U.S. Pretrial Services Officer in September 2001 and continue in this position to the present day. It was not until I began working here that I truly discovered what my former chief meant when he said, "This is a very fast-paced job." I have to say that even though he is now retired, he was not exaggerating. Needless to say, I truly enjoy what I am doing and know that I made the right decision to follow my interest with a career in law enforcement.

Advice to Students: Love who you are and what you do to succeed in life. There are many challenges and obstacles that we face, but they only make us stronger and better at what we do.

Another possible remedy to minimize pretrial publicity is to grant a **change of venue.** A change of venue would shift the trial from one location to another. The objective is that jurors selected from the new trial location have not been exposed to the same degree of pretrial publicity as the potential jurors in the original jurisdiction. This remedy is rarely used because it is quite costly. All the people who have been called to testify have to travel great distances to the new jurisdiction. Family and friends of the victim and the accused have to travel to the new jurisdiction as well, and this hardship increases their emotional and financial stability. Granting continuances is another method judges use to lessen the effect of pretrial publicity. Most high-profile cases only capture the public's and media attention for a brief period. It is a short time before something new has attracted media attention. Similar to our fleeting attention, memories also fade with time. This allows judges to grant short trial delays in the hope of selecting a jury who has forgotten the media stories about a particular case.

Another method used to minimize pretrial publicity is the use of **judicial instructions.** During the O. J. Simpson trial, Judge Ito gave the jury detailed judicial instructions about what they could and could not do. The question is, do jurors abide by the judge's wishes and follow these judicial instructions? This is one area where much research points to the same conclusion. Judicial warnings do relatively little or nothing to change juror behavior. In fact, judicial warnings seem to make matters worse.

Many attorneys and judges believe that they can eliminate jurors who have been affected by pretrial publicity through **jury selection.** They assume that an intensive *voir dire* will unmask those prospective jurors who have been unduly influenced by the media. In cases where the publicity has reached most of the potential jurors, lawyers may have to permit some jurors to be seated who have been exposed to stories about the case, although they argue that such media information can be disregarded and an impartial verdict can be rendered. While their intentions may be honorable, research does not support their assertion. Jurors exposed to pretrial publicity and who argue that such publicity will not influence their ability to evaluate the facts are much more likely to convict defendants than those who have not been exposed to any pretrial publicity.

Legal scholars have suggested that juries can police themselves during jury deliberations. The belief is that once juries are in the jury room, anyone who begins to depart from the judicial instructions and introduces information that was not presented during trial will be censured by the other members of the jury. The evidence on the jury's ability to police itself has been inconsistent. Some evidence has shown that when jury members who have particular biases join with others with similar biases, this makes the group's determination stronger such that it has a more profound impact on the decision rather than the opinions of any particular juror. When reinforced, individual biases of the group are difficult for juries to overcome. Therefore, it seems that jury deliberations strengthen rather than weaken juror biases.

Overall, these investigations of juror conduct indicate that eliminating biased jurors during *voir dire* is ineffective. The jury is unable to eliminate bias during its deliberations, and judicial instructions simply go unheeded. The most effective option available to judges is granting a continuance until the media fascination with the case has disappeared and people forget case details.

THE LITIGATION EXPLOSION

Like many children, Denise Richie was afraid of monsters and demons. However, Denise Richie's demons were real. For five years until she ran away from home, she was sexually abused by her father. As a result of the abuse at the hands of her father, she spiraled downwards into depression, emotional distress, and several subsequent suicide attempts. Finally, when she was able to pull herself together, she brought criminal charges against her father who was convicted and sent to jail for the sexual abuse. For Denise the legal battle was not over. At the urging of her attorneys, she filed a lawsuit against her mother. Was the lawsuit against her mother because, for a year, she had turned a blind eye to the abuse of her daughter and two other family members? In a word, no. Denise had sued the Richie household because of an insurance policy covering negligence. Detractors argue that Denise did not sue to garnish wages from her father's paycheck. Instead, she went for the "deep pockets" of the insurance company. And she argued that her mother was negligent in her failure to respond to her suspicions regarding her husband's sexual abuse. A jury agreed and awarded $1 million against Mr. Richie in punitive damages and $1.4 million against Mrs. Richie in a negligence lawsuit ultimately paid by the insurance company. The Richie family seems to have overcome their differences

BOX 12.5 JOURNALISM V. THE COURTS: A COMPROMISE

Journalists, judges, and legal experts have debated the limitations and merits of allowing cameras in the courts. At the heart of the matter is a conflict between the First and Sixth Amendments. Judges and lawyers argue that often the press limits a defendant's Sixth Amendment right for a fair trial. However, journalists argue that free press and free speech protections are equally as important under the First Amendment.

The press has argued that journalists should have more access to court proceedings. "The presumption of openness should be the first presumption," says Paul Masters, Freedom Forum First Amendment ombudsman. "When we increase the amount of secrecy, we increase the amount of suspicion and erode confidence in the system," Masters adds.

Legal scholars and lawyers believe that camera access to the courtroom may serve to erode public confidence in legal system. Peter Arenella, professor of UCLA Law School, believes that this occurs when the public acting as the thirteenth juror sees the testimony and other coverage, often reaching a different verdict from the jury. Ira Reiner, former Los Angeles district attorney and NBC commentator, believed that some coverage would shed light on courtroom weaknesses. Reiner has declared, "Live TV . . . revealed the single greatest weakness in the court system: inadequate judicial management of criminal trials."

Ten recommendations have been developed by the judges, journalists, legal scholars, and lawyers attending the conference.

1. Encourage and establish continuing interdisciplinary educational opportunities and dialogue for judges, journalists, and lawyers to foster an understanding of each other's roles through journalism schools, law schools, and the National Judicial College.

2. Assume accuracy in all court proceedings and records and place the burden of proof for closure on the entity seeking secrecy. Privacy issues may overcome the presumption in appropriate cases.

3. Refrain from imposing gag orders on the news media or attorneys. The court should seek other remedies in lieu of gag orders except in extraordinary cases.

4. Establish and or support bench bar media committees that will meet regularly in every community to address issues of mutual concern.

5. Establish guidelines for trial-press management in high-profile cases. Court officials should confer and consult with media representatives to avoid unanticipated problems and understand each other's legal constraints.

6. Adopt professional standards for journalists that are nonbinding and encourage industry-administered certification.

(continued)

BOX 12.5 *(continued)*

7. Assume that cameras should be allowed in the courtroom, including the federal system, and that such access should be limited or excluded for only the strongest of reasons.

8. Encourage judges to explain, on the record, the reasons for their rulings.

9. Develop a national model to determine when it may be appropriate to compel reporters to testify or produce notes and tapes, with the understanding that the media cannot serve as an arm of law enforcement.

10. Encourage media organizations to develop an ombudsman system to hear recommendations from the courts and public wherever feasible. [Source: Adapted from Steve Geiman, "Journalism v. Courts," *The Quill,* July–August 1996:46–48.]

because at the same time Denise was in court suing her mother, she was also in criminal court urging the judge to be lenient so that her father could keep his job and support her mother and younger brother.

Another example involves Texas attorney Joe Jamails. Jamails likes civil litigation. In his office he proudly displays the $3 billion bank deposit slip that was his part of the $10.5 billion award to Pennzoil against Texaco. He often urges companies to settle their case rather than to face him in court and suffer the same fate as Texaco. Tort cases have spread the wealth to other attorneys in the Houston area. In fact five of the highest-paid trial attorneys in the United States reside in the Beaumont suburb of Houston, Texas. In 1994 these attorneys collectively made a total of $188 million. They specialize in product liability cases, primarily breast implants and asbestos. There is no end in sight for such litigation and the enormous financial awards that follow. Jamails is estimated to be worth $600 million, and many other attorneys are looking forward to working out similar settlements with tobacco companies.

Within the last decade there has been a concerted effort to limit tort litigation. The impetus for this movement has been fueled by allegations that the tort system is careening out of control. The arguments for reform revolve around two central themes. First, there has been a dramatic increase in the number of tort cases. Second, juries are handing out excessive awards. A public opinion poll conducted for the Aetna Life and Casualty Insurance Company revealed that 59 percent of the American population believed that the number of lawsuits has been growing faster than the population. Sixty-eight percent of Americans polled believe that more people originate lawsuits than they should, and that many of these lawsuits are frivolous. Over half of the

Americans polled believe that the sizes of awards have risen faster than inflation. And 45 percent of the Americans polled are convinced that the size of jury awards in personal injury cases has been excessive (Taylor, Kagay, and Leichenko 1987).

Referendums to reform the tort system and the litigation explosion extend back in time for many decades. For instance, it has been argued that the current trend in litigation will force the collapse of the court system. This sentiment was echoed in the popular press. *Newsweek* magazine (2003) revealed that Americans from all walks of life are being buried under an avalanche of lawsuits. Doctors are being sued by patients. Lawyers are being sued by clients. Teachers are being sued by students. Merchants, manufacturers, and all levels of government, even cities themselves are being sued by all sorts of persons. The fear of being sued is ubiquitous and no profession is insulated from it.

Even Chief Justice Burger has warned that one reason our courts have become overburdened is that Americans are increasingly turning to the courts for relief from a range of personal distresses and anxieties. Remedies for personal wrongs were once considered the responsibilities of institutions other than the courts. But now damages for personal wrongs are boldly asserted as legal entitlements. The courts have been expected to fill the void created by the decline of church, family, and neighborhood unity (Burger 1982).

BOX 12.6 ON PIRATE'S BOOTY AND JACK ASSES

Meredith Berkman filed a $50 million lawsuit against *Pirate's Booty*, a snack food. *Pirate's Booty* is basically flavored puffed rice, containing 147 calories and 8.5 grams of fat, while the label says it contains 120 calories and 2.5 grams of fat, according to a Good Housekeeping Institute inspection and analysis of the product. Berkman alleges in her anti-fat lawsuit that based on the stated amounts of calories and fat, she consumed too much *Pirate's Booty* and gained considerable weight, for which she now has various health problems and has had to rigorously diet and exercise to lose the gained weight. Following Berkman's lawsuit, the manufacturer of *Pirate's Booty*, Robert's American Gourmet Foods, a subsidiary of Keystone Foods, blamed the problem on the manufacturing process and immediately recalled the product from store shelves. Berkman went on to allege that because of this "false advertising," many consumers ruined their diets and had to spend more time at the gym because they ate mislabeled *Pirate's Booty*. Berkman claims she has suffered from extreme emotional distress and weight gain, mental anguish, outrage, and indignation.

Jack Ass, a Montana resident, has sued media giant, Viacom, contending that their MTV show, *Jackass*, plagiarized his name, infringed on his trademark

(continued)

BOX 12.6 *(continued)*

and copyright of his name, and defamed his good character. Jack Ass, whose earlier name was Bob Craft, had his name changed to "Jack Ass" in 1997 in order to raise awareness about the dangers of drunken driving. Subsequently, MTV aired *Jackass,* which premiered in 2000 and features a group of guys performing ludicrous and sometimes dangerous stunts. It was made into a movie in 2002. In his suit against Viacom, Jack Ass claims the organization is liable for injury to his reputation that he has built and defamation of the character, which he has tried so hard to create. He is seeking $10 million in damages. He claims that Viacom committed "trademark and copyright infringement on his legal name and on a cartoon character, called Andi Ass, who he created to help spread his message."

How should courts respond to frivolous lawsuits such as these? Should such suits be allowed to be filed? What limitations, if any, should be set in place to protect the courts from frivolous lawsuits? Should filers of such suits be held liable for wasting valuable court time? What do you think? [Sources: Adapted from the Associated Press, "A Little Too Much Booty," June 1, 2006; adapted from CNN, "'Jackass' Sued By Real Jack Ass," March 5, 2006.

TORTS

The emergence and development of **torts** and tort law in America can be attributed to three diverse but ultimately related phenomena. These are: (1) the emergence of industrial capitalism, (2) changing legal doctrine and legislative intervention, and (3) a transformation of scholarly legal thought. In the following section, a brief description of each of these phenomena is provided.

Industrial Capitalism

Prior to industrial capitalism, interaction and transactions among strangers was governed by contract law. Upon entering into a contract, each individual had a responsibility to uphold their obligation or the contract would be declared null and void. This form of law was well suited for governing obligations that occurred between a small number of people. However, the emergence of industrial capitalism greatly reduced face-to-face interaction between producers and consumers. Consumers were inundated with an unprecedented array of products created by an ever-increasing number of manufacturers. Furthermore, because production became more efficient through mechanization, producers were able to sell larger numbers of products to consumers. Capitalism also increased stranger interaction because it increased urbanization. Richard Abel explains why this is problematic when he says that the frequency of interaction among strangers is significant because strangers, unlike acquaintances or intimates, have less incentive to exercise care not to injure one another inadvertently and find it more difficult to resolve differences that arise when such injury occurs (Abel 1990). Industrialization also has the dubious distinction of being directly related to increasing the number of personal injuries. Machines of the Industrial Revolution have had a marvelous capacity for smashing the human body. Increasing the number of accidents is a natural result of increasing the number of persons working with and around dangerous machinery. Because contract law was not developed to deal with these new forms of personal injury, an increasing number of injured persons began to demand some alternative legal solution (Abel 1990).

Changing Legal Doctrine and Legislative Intervention

Initial tort claims brought against organizations in the emerging Industrial Revolution were usually unsuccessful. This was because legal doctrines were generally more supportive of industry than of individuals. Also, the courts were hesitant to support claims that could possibly cause irreparable harm to fledgling industries. Friedman says about this process that lawsuits and damage might injure the health of precarious enterprise. The machines were the basis for economic growth, for national wealth, and for the greater good of society (Friedman 1985, 468).

Doctrines that have guided American legal decisions had their origins in common law. According to Friedman, this occurred because England had experienced initial forms of the Industrial Revolution prior to those occurring in America. The initial doctrines that guided legal decisions regarding tort law were the doctrine of contributory negligence, the fellow servant rule, and the doctrine of assumptive risk.

The **doctrine of contributory negligence** essentially held that the defendant was not negligent if the plaintiff was in any degree responsible for his/her own injury. This doctrine was initially developed in England in 1809, and was transplanted in American law to deal with railroad cases. The courts believed that if a person crossing the tracks had any degree of negligence in relation to his/her injury, the railroad could not be held liable.

The **doctrine of assumptive risk** was equally as problematic for plaintiffs. This doctrine generally held that a person could not recover any damages if he/she willingly placed himself/herself in danger. Initially, this doctrine does not seem restrictive but in reality, it offered no satisfactory remedy for persons who knowingly worked in hazardous occupations.

The first two new legal doctrines that began to chip away at existing legal rules were the doctrine of last clear chance and *res ipsa loquitur* (Friedman 1985). The **doctrine of last clear chance** was developed in England in the case of *Davies v. Mann* (1842). This doctrine allowed some degree of negligence on the part of plaintiffs while holding defendants responsible for their actions if they had the slightest chance of avoiding the injury. In the *Davies* case, Mann failed to hobble his donkey and it wandered into the path of Davies's approaching wagon, which smashed into the donkey and killed it. It is clear that Mann contributed to the death of his own animal because he failed to control it, but the court ruled that Davies was also negligent because he had the "last clear chance" to avoid hitting the animal but failed to do so. The **doctrine of res ipsa loquitur** or "the thing speaks for itself" originated in *Byrne v. Boadle* (1863). This case is important because it shifted the burden of responsibility from the plaintiff to the defendant where negligence was alleged and damages were sought.

Developing simultaneously with the notion of assumptive risk was the **fellow servant rule.** The fellow servant rule was the largest obstacle that faced injured plaintiffs. However, as the number of industrial accidents increased, so did the number of injured parties bringing suit against organizations rather than specific individuals. The courts began to realize that the plight of the injured worker could not be ignored. This rule held that a servant or employee could not sue his master or employer for injuries caused by the negligence of another employee (Friedman 1985, 472). The doctrine essentially left no recourse for employees who were injured in the workplace. They had the option of bringing a lawsuit against the fellow employee who caused the injury. However, this was often a futile effort because the negligent employee was equally as impoverished as the employee bringing suit.

In the 1840s and throughout the 1860s, these doctrines were relatively unchallenged. However, by the 1890s labor had obtained a collective voice and there was diverse judicial opinion concerning personal injury cases. Furthermore, political and legislative intervention began to erode previously existing legal doctrines. One of the original legal rules that limited the fellow servant rule was the **vice principal doctrine.** This doctrine has been described by Friedman (1985) who says that an employee could sue his employer in tort if the careless fellow servant who caused the injury was a supervisor or a boss, more properly compared to an employer than a fellow servant.

Employer immunity for tort law has also been limited by federal and state legislatures. As early as the 1850s, statutes were established that outlined safety regulations for railroads. These regulations forced railroads to ring bells prior to passing through railroad crossings, and railroads were also responsible for any fires caused by their locomotives and had to compensate ranchers for any cattle that were killed by their trains.

The Influence of Legal Scholars

Originating and continuing through the middle of the eighteenth century, prominent legal scholars began to rethink the role and purposes of law. Prior to this period, law was believed to have naturalistic and religious origins. These religious foundations seemed less applicable to a world that was experiencing radical social transformations caused by the Industrial Revolution. Consequently, only a few legal scholars believed that order and law had to be based on these new principles. White (1999) explains this process when he indicates that in general, post–Civil War intellectuals were interested in restoring a sense of order and unity that had characterized eighteenth-century thought, but they rejected efforts to derive order and unity from "mythologic" religious principles. A particular interest of the intellectuals in the quarter of century after the war was the conceptualization and the transformation of data into theories of universal applicability.

The two leading proponents of this legal reconceptualization were Nicholas St. John Green and Oliver Wendel Holmes, Jr. These scholars rejected the notion that law was static and bound by religious or naturalistic rules. Rather, they believed that law should be evolutionary. Holmes and Green were convinced that life was in constant flux and that laws and the legal system must adapt in order to address these social changes. It is precisely because contract law and the writ system were unable to adequately address the changing social structure that Holmes and Green advocated the expansion of tort law.

More recent expansions of tort law, specifically enterprise liability, were profoundly influenced by twentieth-century legal scholars. In fact, Priest (1985) has rejected the argument that tort expansion was significantly influenced by industrialization, urbanization, mechanization, and expanding intervention of the federal government. Instead, Priest believes that the current form of tort law classified as enterprise liability was the handiwork of three legal scholars: Flemming James, Friedrich Kessler, and William Prosser. The literary and oratory confluence of James's notion of "risk distribution," Kessler's conviction that contract law was inadequate for monopolized capitalism, and Prosser's synthesis of contract and tort law gave rise to the current conception of enterprise liability. Presently, many legal scholars, businesses, and interest groups believe that tort law has expanded too far and is in need of substantial legislative reform.

ARGUMENTS FOR TORT REFORM

Advocates of **tort reform** argue for its necessity because (1) in the last few years the number of tort cases has increased dramatically, and this event can be attributed to the increased litigiousness of American society; and (2) juries are incompetent to handle tort cases because they are sympathetic to plaintiffs and consistently dole out large awards. In the following section each of these arguments will be examined.

A Dramatic Increase in the Number of Tort Cases

Until the mid-1960s, most courts never kept records concerning the number and types of cases that they decided. Consequently, gathering statistics for a longitudinal study of American litigiousness is extremely difficult. Within the last two decades a handful of agencies have emerged that compile statistics on litigation rates. These include the National Center for State Courts, the Administrative Office of the U.S. Courts, and the Rand Corporation's Institute for Civil Justice. When investigations are conducted to determine whether we have experienced a litigation explosion, researchers at the Institute for Civil Justice have found that, overall, tort filings in state courts have increased between 2.3 percent and 3.9 percent annually. Federal courts experienced a similar annual increase of 4 percent. Galenter's analysis of tort filings in federal district courts between 1975 and 1984 has shown that these courts had a 46 percent increase during that nine-year period. This percentage may be misleading because the absolute percent increase of tort cases in this nine-year period was only 8.2 percent. During this same time interval, federal government suits against individuals for overpayments comprised 31.6 percent of the entire federal caseload (Galenter 1986).

More recent statistics reveal that civil cases may be decreasing. In 2001, there were 11,908 civil cases in the 75 largest counties, which represents a 47 percent decline from the 22,451 cases in the same counties in 1992. Federally, from 1985 to 2003, tort cases decreased 79 percent (Cohen 2004).

It should be noted that statistics reveal as much as they conceal. The above analyses would suggest that tort litigation has increased from 1979 to 1984, and then decreased from 1985 to 2003. However, several interesting results are disclosed when we control for the actual type of tort filing. For example, it may be that the number of people injured by unsafe products has increased, thus causing the rise in the litigation rate. Perhaps large toxic torts, where a large number of claims are processed in a short time period, have caused the litigation rate to be exaggerated. And perhaps this increased rate is an anomaly of the federal system and should not be used as evidence of a litigation explosion, since federal courts handle only 5 percent of all tort cases. Also, if we disaggregate the statistics across the years from 1985 to 2003, we find that cases were actually increasing until about 1990 and then began to decline but spiked again around the year 2000. Several other factors have been given for the recent decline. For instance, the federal system increased its use of alternative dispute resolution, steering a number of cases away from the

BOX 12.7 ARE JURY AWARDS OUT OF CONTROL?

■ Betty Bullock, Newport Beach, California

A $28 billion award was given by a jury to Betty Bullock, 64, of Newport Beach, California. A lawsuit was filed against Philip Morris, Inc. for fraud and negligence. Bullock alleged that Philip Morris had failed to warn her about the possible cancer-causing ingredients of the cigarettes they marketed, and that over the years, Bullock contracted lung and liver cancer as the result of the cigarettes she smoked. [Source: Adapted from Henry Weinstein and the *Los Angeles Times,* October 5, 2002.]

■ The largest award in aviation history was given to James Cassoutt, his wife, Cindy, and a passenger, Judy Kealey, who were flying in a Cessna 185 airplane that crashed in 1989. The verdict included $400 million in punitive damages and $80 million in compensatory damages. The plaintiffs claimed that the crash was caused by a defective seat latching mechanism. The suit claimed that the pilot's seat suddenly slid back as he was attempting to land the plane and caused the nose to pitch up because he had the control yoke in his grasp. The single-engine Cessna 185 then crashed and burned in a small clearing amid thick woods 75 yards from the runway at Coastal Airport, a small Pensacola landing strip. Cessna's lawyers claimed that the seat did not slip, and they denied that the locking mechanisms were defective. They blamed the crash on pilot error, since James Cassoutt had little experience or instruction on flying the Cessna 185. Cindy Cassoutt suffered third-degree burns over half of her body. Her husband and Kealey were burned less seriously, but Kealy also suffered a broken back. [Source: Adapted from the Associated Press, "Cessna Fined $480M," August 17, 2001.]

■ There were almost twice as many $1 million awards in 2002 as in 2001 by juries in Michigan, according to a survey. Juries in Michigan awarded a record $101 million to various plaintiffs. The largest was a $22.5 million verdict against McLaren Regional Medical Center in Genesee Circuit Court, one of two medical malpractice verdicts. Other big verdicts included a $13 million wrongful death verdict against Garden City with a construction company that it hired to make water main and streetscape improvements. Also $12 million was awarded in a verdict against a Wayne County car dealership that allowed a prospective buyer to use its vehicle without first transferring the title. The prospective buyer's negligent driving killed a teenager. [Source: Adapted from David Shepardson and *The Detroit News,* "Jury Awards Set Record in 2002," January 14, 2003.]

(continued)

BOX 12.7 *(continued)*

■ When Scott Peterson's trial occurred in San Mateo County in 2004, news teams from across the country converged on the Redwood City courthouse where the trial was held. Only a limited amount of sidewalk space was available to accommodate these numerous news teams, and San Mateo County officials determined that television stations must pay a monthly rental fee of $8,500 for sidewalk space. It was estimated that during the Peterson trial, television stations would each pay $51,000 to reserve a coveted spot next to the courthouse. County officials indicated that the trial, which was estimated to last six months, would cost $255,000 to the county just for providing services to the media. An additional indoor media center was to be made available at a cost of $582 per month for space in a large room with audio feeds from the trial. With 20 outlets available to interested media networks and publications, the operating costs to the county would be defrayed. The county officials declared also that if not enough media outlets agreed to pay the required fees, the audio feed room would be closed and the county will discontinue sidewalk services provided to television outlets, such as generators, portable toilets, and security. [Source: Adapted from the Associated Press, "Media Fees for Peterson Trial Coverage Reduced," February 10, 2004.]

courts. Another reason may be that it has become increasingly complex and costly to take a civil case to trial (Cohen 2004).

Juries Delivering Excessive Awards

When arguing about whether juries deliver excessive awards, both proponents and opponents of tort reform seem to have the relevant statistics to support their respective positions. This does not mean that one group's statistics are wrong, but rather, they may be the result of applying incorrect statistical techniques. When analyzing data that are extremely skewed (e.g., jury awards), it is inappropriate to use the mean or arithmetic average because a few large cases can severely skew the results. Therefore, it is more appropriate to use the median, or the midpoint of the data, when analyzing jury awards and trends. Using data from San Francisco and Cook County, Illinois, the Institute for Civil Justice has conducted a study of jury awards. Between 1960 and 1979 the median jury award for all tort cases was approximately $30,000. However, in 1979 the awards in Cook County decreased dramatically, while in San Francisco the awards increased dramatically.

The awards declined in Cook County because of a shift to comparative negligence, which may have increased attorney propensity to bring cases involving smaller damage amounts to trial. Conversely, the awards in San Francisco increased because a mandatory arbitration program eliminated most of the smaller cases from reaching courts. When the median tort awards are disaggregated, the median award for auto claims ranges between $5,000 and $40,000. Meanwhile, in product liability cases, the juries award between $180,000 and $200,000 per case. This represents an increase from $70,000 to $150,000 since 1960. When arithmetic means are used as indicators of the average tort award, the picture is quite different. In 1960, for instance, the average award for all tort cases ranged from $50,000 to $75,000. By 1984 this number had increased to between $250,000 and $300,000. When the average award is disaggregated, the data reveal that malpractice awards average about $1.2 million. Average awards for San Francisco automobile accidents and personal injury awards were $150,000 and $250,000, respectively.

More recent statistics reveal that federally, from 1985 to 2003 the number of tort trials in U.S. district courts has declined, and median awards for plaintiff winners in 2003 were around $200,000 (Cohen 2004). Also in the 75 largest counties in the United States, the median award decreased from $65,000 in 1992 to around $37,000 in 2001, yet approximately $4 billion in damages were awarded to plaintiffs in 2001 (Cohen 2004).

Proponents of tort reform have utilized mean awards to support their position that juries are delivering excessive awards and that legislative limits should be placed on the amount of these awards, especially in malpractice suits. In this regard, they have been relatively successful because as of 2003, 24 states had passed legislation that limited maximum awards courts would approve. Furthermore, state legislatures have become convinced that tort law is out of control and is in need of reform. In fact, by 2005 about two-thirds of states had passed some form of legislation limiting the amount of awards against the state. There is little doubt that these reforms have significantly altered the tort system. But scholars are beginning to ask whether these reforms are a benefit to citizens or to businesses.

Who Benefits from Tort Reform?

If reform measures were supportive of citizen's interests, we might assume that when reform measures were passed, insurance availability would increase and insurance premiums would decrease. Research has revealed several instances where reform measures have had no appreciable impact on the availability or affordability of insurance. For example, Florida, Minnesota, Washington, Wisconsin, and Ontario, Canada have passed legislative reform measures. Despite these reforms, all locations have experienced increased insurance premiums, and many locations are unable to locate any insurance carriers. In fact, allegations by manufacturers and the medical community that reform was necessary because their rates were too high have no basis in fact. Abel (1990) has said that

BOX 12.8 MEDICAL MALPRACTICE LAWSUITS AND JURY AWARDS

■ It happened in Cody, Wyoming. Chad Ooten, a Cody resident, underwent surgery for a back injury in 2000. But Dr. Stephen Emery removed the wrong cervical disc from Ooten's spine, requiring three follow-up surgeries. Ooten filed a lawsuit against the doctor and hospital where the surgery was originally performed, alleging medical malpractice. A jury awarded Ooten a total of $1 million for economic and noneconomic damages, and his wife was given $175,000. Wyoming Medical Society president Dr. Robert Monger of Cheyenne criticized the verdict. He says that it will increase the state's medical malpractice insurance considerably and make the state's doctor shortage even worse than it presently is. The plaintiff's attorney, Todd Hambrick, said that the insurance industry is to blame for failing to agree to settle on such claims when the doctor clearly is at fault.

■ It happened in Madison, Wisconsin. Jessica Greenfield, 33, underwent surgery in 2000 for acid reflux. However, the surgery went awry and left her stomach and intestines unable to function properly. No subsequent surgery has been successful to remedy the problem. Following the original surgery, Greenfield has had to receive nutrition through a feeding tube. Ms. Greenfield filed suit against the surgeon and hospital, alleging negligence in performing the surgery. She alleged substantial pain and suffering and lost wages. Additionally, her son joined the lawsuit with one of his own, alleging loss of companionship with his mother. The jury awarded $4.13 million to Ms. Greenfield for economic damages, lost wages, and medical expenses, as well as $4.25 million for pain and suffering. An award of $82,000 was made to her son for loss of companionship with his mother. Wisconsin recently removed caps on damages awarded by juries for medical malpractice suits.

■ Janice Bird, a daughter of Nita Bird, was at the Los Angeles County Hospital one evening where her mother was undergoing outpatient surgery. Janice was soon joined by one of her sisters. However, something went wrong with the surgical procedure, and hospital personnel rushed Mrs. Bird to the emergency surgery room. Janice Bird and her sister happened to be standing in the hallway when hospital personnel rushed their mother by on a gurney. Janice Bird and her sister claim that her mother was bright blue and that her head was almost touching the floor. This caused them so much emotional distress, they claim, that they decided to sue the hospital for several million dollars. The daughters sued, not for malpractice, but for the emotional distress to them, not their mother.

■ Stephen Roel got drunk at the Las Vegas Hilton and Mandalay Hotel and Casino. While intoxicated, he claimed to gamble away over $1 million.

When he sobered up, he sued the casino and hotel for damages, claiming that they permitted him to gamble despite his drunken condition. He had established a $50,000 credit line with the casino and had played there for 15 years. In exchange for his gambling, the casino always permitted him to stay free at the hotel, and they paid for his roundtrip flights to Las Vegas, meals, and other incidentals. However, the casino allowed him to go over his limit on that particular evening. In the days following his loss, he sobered up and sued the casino for unspecified damages in excess of $2 million, alleging negligence and other improper behaviors on the part of casino staff. Hotel authorities wanted to know that if he had won $1 million in his drunken state, would he have given it back?

Should states and the federal government put limits on monetary awards for lawsuits against physicians, hospitals, and others? If so, what should be these limits? What do you think? [Sources: Adapted from the Associated Press, "Jury Awards $1.2 Million for Botched Surgery, Largest Award in Years," May 25, 2006; adapted from the Associated Press, "Jury Awards $8.4 Million in Medical Malpractice Case," March 13, 2006; adapted from the Associated Press, "Birds of a Feather Sue Together," May 12, 2006; adapted from the Associated Press, "A Million Dollar Gamble," March 1, 2005.]

product, occupier, and general liability costs or insurance premiums plus damage payments have totaled less than 0.2 percent of sales; in the manufacturing sector where these costs were highest (e.g., rubber and plastic manufacture), they constituted only 0.58 percent; even among hospitals, these costs were only 2.35 percent of gross income.

The research that focuses on the efficacy of jurors would contradict the notions of jurors portrayed by tort reformers. These reforms allege that juries are sympathetic to plaintiffs simply because they deliver large cash awards. However, research focusing on jury behavior finds the opposite is true. Some jurors are extremely careful and often frugal when deciding cash awards. Sometimes jurors make very precise calculations of medical expenses, repair bills, and other costs when determining awards in order to ensure that the plaintiffs got no more than they were entitled to receive. Furthermore, such careful accounting, particularly in the case of tragic dimensions, contrasts sharply with the common view of juries as overgenerous and free spending.

Legislators are convinced that litigation has increased at a dramatic rate and reform measures (e.g., alternative dispute resolution) might control this problem. Increased litigation rates would indeed be a problem if an increasing number of litigants were bringing frivolous cases while the injury rate remained the same. However, research has revealed the contrary. Abel summarizes research reporting that among those who suffered major permanent partial disability as a result of medical malpractice, less than 17 percent filed claims, and only 6.5 percent received any payment (Abel 1990, 785–788). Regarding workplace injury claims, only 37 percent of the injured workers made worker's compensation claims. These results indicate that contrary to the perception of a litigious public, the majority of persons who have a legitimate injury fail to make a claim. These results seem to indicate that tort reform measures are not intended to help the average citizen. In each of the examples cited, the reform measures have limited the recourse of injured individuals and benefitted insurance companies, businesses, and interest groups.

SUMMARY

This chapter has examined some of the major issues that are facing the American court system. The first is the relationship between the courts and the media. The media and the courts have had a relationship dating back to the 1800s. The media have always had a desire to report about certain cases that involve celebrities or are bizarre or unique in some respect. The courts, on the other hand, operate in a more methodical manner, following specific criminal or civil rules of procedure that at times can be very boring. A large amount of trial time is spent on the facts of the case, and specific detail of the events that occurred. Verdicts are rendered only after juries have carefully reviewed all the facts presented in trial, and expert and witness testimony. While this attention to detail and legal procedures may drag out for an extended period of time, the media wants to tell the story now. The media may focus on the most trivial aspects of a trial that are not even relevant legally, like the defendant's demeanor, the defendant's appearance or clothing, or missteps that the prosecution has made. Therefore, a boring, drawn-out trial is converted into an exciting media story. The coverage of the trial may even be sensationalized in order to obtain greater viewership. When the ratings of a network are dependent upon the nature of sensational coverage given, the most mundane courtroom events will be blown out of proportion.

During the 1900s there have been many "trials of the century," including the trial of Stanford White, Bruno Hauptmann, Sacco and Vanzetti, John and Lorena Bobbit, and O. J. Simpson. In each of these cases the media and the courts have battled to balance the power of the media with the objectives of justice. In most cases the court has had to determine whether the defendant can have a fair trial because of pretrial publicity generated by the media. Several methods are used to limit pretrial publicity from gag orders to sequestration of the jury. However, with technological advances and the idea of cameras in the courtrooms, there has been some contention about balancing the fact that trials are public with affording the defendant a fair trial by an impartial jury. For instance, in the 1800s, verdicts were relayed by word-of-mouth. This changed with the advent of newspapers, where verdicts were given on printed page. By the 1850s, the telegraph was used to transmit trial events and court decisions. Soon courtroom photographers and newsreel cameras became the plague of the most high-profile cases. The Scopes trial was the first to be broadcast over the radio. Attorneys became aware of the impact the media presence could have and used trial tactics that were not only intended for the jury but for the larger national audience. Media representatives have even made requests for the attorneys and judges to position themselves so that their cameras could get better picture angles. It was during the Hauptmann trial that the court realized the media was not going to go away. Soon the American Bar Association would rule that photographing and broadcasting court proceedings should be prohibited. Most states adopted the position of the American Bar Association and forbid photographing and broadcasting trials and trial participants. In 1952, the American Bar Association extended the media ban to include television coverage of court proceedings. Today, most states allow cameras in their courtrooms but have developed guidelines for their usage. In most states, the consent of the presiding judge is a requirement, and many states require a written application submitted in advance of the trial. Finally, in some states, if the defendant objects to cameras in the courtroom, they will not be permitted.

The primary concern of the relationship between the court and the media is the effect of pretrial publicity. Two different issues emerge here—the first is that pretrial publicity will make the process of finding jurors who have not heard of the case very difficult; the second is that because of the pretrial publicity, the jurors will realize their decision could be analyzed by the community, and this will influence them to vote on how their lives will be affected in the aftermath rather than on the facts of the case. A concern is that the effect of pretrial publicity on a juror's decision cannot be known. It should be mentioned, however, that the majority of cases are not subject to media scrutiny and usually it is only the high-profile cases that get coverage. Some research has shown that most courtroom actors say pretrial publicity does not significantly affect juror behavior because they believe that the *voir dire* process is effective at removing those jurors who have been prejudiced by the media.

There are two basic ways in which jurors can be affected by pretrial publicity. The first is case-specific, which is information about a specific case, and the second is general pretrial publicity, which includes information about crime, criminals, and the criminal justice system that may shape the perceptions of those asked to serve as jurors. This pretrial publicity can be minimized in several ways. The least used method is probably for the judge to issue a gag order. Gag orders usually say that the media cannot publish or broadcast any prejudicial information about a case, which borders on fundamentally free speech issues. Another method would be to grant a change of venue, which would change the location of the trial. The idea being that jurors from the new location have not had the same exposure to pretrial publicity as the jurors in the original jurisdiction. Change of venue is, however, rarely used because of the cost involved. Granting continuances can be another method for the judge to minimize pretrial publicity; most cases only get media attention for short periods. In this way, a judge can implement short trial delays in the hope that the jury will have forgotten the media attention for a case. The use of judicial instructions can also minimize the effect of pretrial publicity. Using this method, the judge gives the jury detailed instructions about what they can and cannot do. Lastly, the most common form of eliminating pretrial publicity is through jury selection. This process should reveal those prospective jurors who are no longer impartial because of media publicity. Legal scholars believe that juries also police themselves, and anyone who tries to depart from judicial instructions or uses information that was not presented at trial will be criticized by the other jury members.

Another issue facing the courts is the perception that juries are out of control and awarding excessive damage awards in civil cases. The evidence suggests that this is more myth than reality. The amount of litigation spikes up and down from year to year but appears to actually be on the decline as of 2003. Whether because of the greater time and monetary resources needed to take a case to trial or the increase in the use of alternative dispute resolution, caseloads do not appear to be overwhelming, and the awards juries are handing out also seem to be declining, although they vary depending on the type of tort. Furthermore, excessive jury awards have been reduced on appeal in more than a few instances. One side believes that due to the emergence of industrial capitalism, changing legal doctrine and legislative intervention, and a transformation of scholarly legal thought about torts and litigation have inevitably increased. The other side believes that if we delve into the statistics, litigation is actually on the decline. The increased use by the federal system of alternative dispute resolution and the complexity and costliness of taking a civil case to trial have been a couple of reasons proffered for the steering of a number of cases away from the courts.

Several states have, however, started implementing legislation placing caps on monetary damages especially where medical malpractice is concerned. Whether this is because state legislators believe awards given by juries in these cases are out of control, or that medical insurance premiums have skyrocketed, is not known. The media, however, does seem to be still perpetuating a myth that the litigiousness of U.S. society is excessive. One fact that does remain is that doctors, teachers, and state and city officials will continue to be the aim of litigation due to the very nature of the jobs that they hold, and that disputes will arise from human interaction.

KEY TERMS

Case-specific pretrial publicity
Change of venue
Court of public opinion
Doctrine of assumptive risk
Doctrine of contributory negligence
Doctrine of last clear chance
Doctrine of *res ipsa loquitur*
Fellow servant doctrine
Gag order

General pretrial publicity
Judicial instructions
Jury selection
Litigation explosion
Pretrial publicity
Tort actions
Tort reform
Torts
Vice principal doctrine

QUESTIONS FOR REVIEW

1. What is meant by "trials of the century"? What is the relation between the court and the media in so-called trials of the century?

2. How much pretrial publicity is necessary for a change of venue?

3. What are some of the advantages and disadvantages of allowing the media into courtrooms?

4. What are some opposing views regarding frivolous lawsuits and excessive jury awards? Should defendants be allowed millions of dollars in damages for minor injuries or mental suffering? Why or why not?

5. What is tort reform? Who benefits from tort reform?

6. What is a change in venue?

7. What types of circumstances suggest that pretrial publicity is unfavorable to defendants?

8. What is the litigation explosion? Why do you believe that it has occurred?

9. What is a gag order? Why do judges impose gag orders on jurors and other participants in legal actions?

10. Do media representatives have a constitutional right to enter and record what is going on in U.S. courtrooms? What are your opinions on this issue?

SUGGESTED READINGS

1. Janet Cotterill (2002). *Language in the Legal Process.* New York: Palgrave Macmillan.
2. Steve Kroll-Smith (2004). "Toxic Torts and Environmental Justice." *Law and Policy* **26:**177–307.
3. *Newsweek* (2003). "Civil Wars." *Newsweek*, December 15, 43.
4. Joanne Terrell and Karen M. Staller (2003). "Buckshot's Case: Social Work and Death Penalty Mitigation in Alabama." *Qualitative Social Work Research and Practice* **2:**7–23.
5. Neil Vidmar (2002). "Case Studies of Pre- and Midtrial Prejudice in Criminal and Civil Litigation." *Law and Human Behavior* **26:**73–105.

Glossary

ABA Model Code of Professional Responsibility American Bar Association standards of behavior, which are voluntary and intended as self-regulating for lawyer conduct in the courtroom and between lawyers and clients.

Acceptance of responsibility A genuine admission or acknowledgment of wrongdoing. In federal presentence investigation reports, for example, convicted offenders may write an explanation and apology for the crime(s) they committed. A provision that may be considered in deciding whether leniency should be extended to offenders during the sentencing phase of their processing.

Accused Person alleged to have committed a crime; the defendant in any criminal action.

Acquittal Any judgment by the court, considering a jury verdict or a judicial determination of the factual basis for criminal charges, where the defendant is declared not guilty of the offenses alleged.

Action, actions at law A court proceeding; either civil, to enforce a right, or criminal, to punish an offender. Court litigation where opposing parties litigate an issue involving an alleged wrongdoing; may be for the protection of a right or for the prevention of a wrong.

Actus reus One component of a crime; any overt act that accompanies the intent to commit a crime (e.g., pulling out a pistol in front of a convenience store clerk while robbing the store is an *actus reus* or overt act); drawing plans of a bank floor layout while conspiring to rob the bank would be an overt act in furtherance of the criminal conspiracy.

Addams, Jane (circa 1860–1910) Founded Hull House in the 1890s in Chicago, a shelter for runaways and others who were in need of housing, food, and clothing.

Adjudicates To judge, decide a case, conclude a matter.

Adjudication Legal resolution of a dispute; when a juvenile is declared delinquent or a status offender, the matter has been resolved; when an offender has been convicted or acquitted, the matter at issue (guilt or innocence) has been concluded by either a judge or jury.

Adjudication hearing Formal proceeding involving a prosecuting attorney and a defense attorney where evidence is presented and a juvenile's status or condition is determined by the juvenile court judge.

Administrative law The body of laws, rules, orders, and regulations created by an administrative agency.

Administrative Office of United States Courts   Organization that hires federal probation officers to supervise federal offenders. Also supervises pretrial divertees; probation officers prepare presentence investigation reports about offenders at the request of a district judge.

Admissible   An evidentiary term designating testimony or physical evidence that may be presented to the finders of fact (juries or judges) in criminal proceedings. Restrictions and conditions are usually articulated in federal and state rules of evidence.

Admission   A confession; a concession as to the truthfulness of one or more facts, usually associated with a crime that has been committed. May also apply to tort actions.

Admit   A plea of guilty, an acknowledgment of culpability, accuracy of the facts alleged in either an adult or juvenile proceeding.

Adversarial proceedings   Opponent-driven court litigation, where one side opposes the other; prosecution seeks to convict or find defendants guilty, while defense counsel seeks to defend their clients and seek their acquittal.

Adversary system   Legal system involving a contest between two opposing parties under a judge who is an impartial arbiter.

Affiant   Person who makes an affidavit.

Affidavit   A statement in writing given under oath before someone who is authorized to administer an oath.

Affirm   To uphold the opinion or decision of a lower trial court; usually an action by an appellate court.

Affirmation   In courts, an oath, declaration in place of an oath for persons whose religious beliefs prohibit oaths, to tell the truth and nothing but the truth when giving testimony.

Affirmative defenses   Responses to a criminal charge where the defendant bears the burden of proof (e.g., automatism, intoxication, coercion, duress, mistake). Goes beyond simple denial of facts and gives new facts in favor of the defendant, if facts in the original complaint are true.

Affirmative registration   Action on the part of women to actively seek to be included on juries, which were formerly comprised exclusively of men.

Age of majority   Chronological date when one reaches adulthood, usually either 18 or 21; when juveniles are no longer under the jurisdiction of the juvenile courts, but rather the criminal courts; also age of consent.

Aggravating circumstances   Events about crime that may intensify the severity of punishment, including bodily injury, death of victim, or the brutality of the act.

Alford Plea   A *nolo contendere* plea whereby defendants plead "no contest" to the factual scenario as outlined in the charges; originated with the case of *North Carolina v. Alford* (1970) whereby a defendant did not wish to admit guilt, but entered a *nolo contendere* plea, admitting to certain facts as specified by the prosecution.

Alibi   Defense to a criminal allegation that places an accused individual at some other place than the crime scene at the time the crime occurred.

Allegation   Assertion or claim made by a party to a legal action.

Allege   To aver, assert, claim; usually a prosecutor will allege certain facts in developing a case against a criminal defendant.

Allocution   Right of convicted offenders to address the court personally prior to the imposition of sentences.

Alternate jurors   Jurors who have been selected to replace any of the regular jurors who may become ill and cannot attend the full trial proceeding; these jurors have been vested with the same tasks as regular jurors who will hear and decide cases.

Alternative dispute resolution (ADR)   Procedure whereby a criminal case is redefined as a civil one and the case is decided by an impartial arbiter, where both parties agree to amicable settlement. Usually reserved for minor offenses.

Amendment   A modification, addition, deletion.

American Bar Association (ABA)   National organization of U.S. lawyers headquartered in Chicago, Illinois.

Amicus curiae   A friend of the court. Persons may initiate petitions on behalf of others, perhaps for someone who is in prison. Such *amicus* briefs are designed to present legal arguments or facts on behalf of someone else. Person allowed to appear in court or file a brief even though the person has no right to participate in the litigation otherwise.

Answer   A written response in relation to a filed complaint prepared by a litigant or defendant.

Appeal, appeal proceedings   Any request by the defense or prosecution directed to a higher court to contest a decision or judgment by a lower court.

Appearance   Act of coming into a court and submitting to the authority of that court.

Appellant   Person who initiates an appeal.

Appellate court   A court hearing appeals emanating from lower courts. These courts typically do not try criminal cases.

Appellate jurisdiction   Authority to rehear cases from lower courts and alter, uphold, or overturn lower court decisions.

Appellate review   A comprehensive rehearing of a case in a court other than the one in which it was previously tried.

Appellee   Party who prevailed in lower court, who argues on appeal against reversing the lower court's decision.

Argument   Any rationale provided by the defense or prosecution to support their position in court; any oral persuasion attempted before a jury.

Arraignment   Official proceeding in which defendant is formally confronted by criminal charges and enters a plea; trial date is established.

Arrest   Taking persons into custody and restrain them until they can be brought before court to answer the charges against them.

Arrestee   Person who has been arrested by police for suspicion of committing a crime.

Assembly-line justice   Term applied to overworked, inadequately staffed court that is unsympathetic and unfair to criminal defendants.

Assigned counsel system   Program wherein indigent clients charged with crimes may have defense attorneys appointed for them; these defense attorneys may be private attorneys who agree to be rotated to perform such services for a low rate of reimbursement from the city, county, or state.

Assistant state's attorneys   Prosecutors who serve under other prosecutors in local or state jurisdictions; government prosecutors.

Assistant U.S. attorneys (AUSAs)   Government prosecutors who are subordinate to the U.S. attorney who heads the prosecutor's office for each federal district.

Attorney–client confidentiality and privilege   Relation between a counsel and his/her client wherein any information exchanged between parties will not be disclosed to others, such as prosecutors; attorneys are protected from disclosing information about the clients they represent because of this privilege.

Attorney competence   Standards for determining whether clients are fairly and intelligently represented by their lawyers when they are charged with crimes.

Attorney general   Senior U.S. prosecutor in each federal district court. A cabinet member who heads the Justice Department.

Attorney, lawyer, counsel   Anyone trained in the law who has received a law degree from a recognized university and who is authorized to practice law in a given jurisdiction.

Automatic waivers   Jurisdictional laws that provide for automatic waivers of juveniles to criminal court for processing; legislatively prescribed directive to transfer juveniles of specified ages who have committed especially serious offenses to jurisdiction of criminal courts.

Automatism   A set of actions taken during a state of unconsciousness.

Backdooring hearsay evidence   Action by prosecutor where prosecutor comments about or mentions information that is otherwise inadmissible in court; remarks made in front of a jury for their emotional and persuasive effects, which are otherwise barred because of the inadmissibility of evidence.

Backlog   Number of impending cases that exceeds the court's capacity that cannot be acted upon because the court is occupied in acting upon other cases.

Bail   Surety provided by defendants or others to guarantee their subsequent appearance in court to face criminal charges. Available to anyone entitled to it (not everyone is entitled to bail); is denied when suspects are considered dangerous or likely to flee. *See also* preventive detention and *United States v. Salerno* in list of cases.

Bail bond   A written guarantee, often accompanied by money or other securities, that the person charged with an offense will remain within the court's jurisdiction to face trial at a time in the future.

Bail bond companies   Any organization established for the purpose of posting bail for criminal suspects.

Bail bondsperson, bail bondsman   Person who is in the business of posting bail for criminal suspects. Usually charges a percentage of whatever bail has been set.

Bail recovery agent   One who seeks to take into custody a fugitive or someone who has jumped bail by fleeing the jurisdiction before trial; also a person who seeks to recover the amount of bail from a fugitive from justice.

Bail Reform Act   Original act passed in 1966 to assure that bail practices would be revised to ensure that all persons, regardless of their financial status, shall not needlessly be detained to answer criminal charges.

Bail Reform Act of 1984   Revision of original 1966 Bail Reform Act where changes in bail practices were implemented to assure that all persons, regardless of their financial status, shall not needlessly be detained to answer criminal charges; gave judges and magistrates greater autonomy to decide conditions under which bail would be granted or denied. Does not mean that all persons are entitled to bail regardless of their alleged offense.

Bail revocation   Judicial decision to deny a previously granted bail for a defendant.

Bail system   Practice of releasing defendants after they place a financial guarantee with the court to ensure their subsequent trial appearance. Usually defendants may place the entire amount with the court or pay a premium to the bondsman.

Bailiff   Court officer who maintains order in the court while it is in session. Bailiff oversees jury during a trial proceeding, sometimes has custody of prisoners while they are in the courtroom. Also known as messengers.

Bar   Aggregate denoting all attorneys admitted to practice law in every jurisdiction.

Bench trial   Tribunal where guilt or innocence of defendant is determined by the judge rather than a jury.

Bench warrant   Document issued by judge and not requested by the police demanding that a specified person be brought before the court without undue or unnecessary delay.

Best evidence rule   In the course of presenting evidence in court, this edict states that if factual information or tangible documents are offered as proof, the original information or documents are preferred; if such original information or documents are unavailable, then a reasonable facsimile is the next most preferred item (e.g., a photocopy of an unavailable automobile title would be the best evidence, in the event that the original automobile title was destroyed or missing).

Beyond a reasonable doubt   Standard used in criminal courts to establish guilt of criminal defendant.

Bifurcated trial   Tribunal in capital cases where jury is asked to make two decisions. First decision is to determine guilt or innocence of defendant; if guilty, jury meets to decide punishment, which may include the death penalty.

Bill of Rights   First ten amendments to the U.S. Constitution setting forth certain freedoms and guarantees to U.S. citizens.

Bind over   Following a finding of probable cause that a crime has been committed and the defendant has committed it, a court action to cause the defendant to be tried on the charges later in a criminal court.

Blaming   A step in the dispute process whereby the victim singles out someone as a potential target for legal action.

Blaming the victim   The stereotypical practice of charging the socially and psychologically handicapped with the lack of motivation. An attitude or belief that the adverse conditions and negative characteristics of a group, often of minorities, are the group's own fault.

Blended sentencing   Any type of sentencing procedure where either a criminal or juvenile court judge can impose both juvenile and/or adult incarcerative penalties.

Blue-ribbon jury   A jury considered by either side, prosecution or defense, to be ideal because of its perceived likelihood of rendering a verdict favorable to that side; jurors often are selected because of their higher educational level and intellectual skills.

Bona fide   "In good faith." Without the attempt to defraud or deceive.

Bond   Written document indicating that defendants or sureties assure the presence of these defendants at a criminal proceeding; if not, then the bond will be forfeited.

Booking   Process of making written report of arrest, including name and address of arrested persons, the alleged crimes, arresting officers, place and time of arrest, physical description of suspect, photographs, sometimes called "mug shots," and fingerprints.

Bounties, bounty hunters   Monetary rewards offered for capture of persons who escape prosecution from a given jurisdiction. Often, such persons have posted a bond with a bonding company and the bonding company hires a bounty hunter (person who earns living by apprehending these persons) to track them down so that monies deposited with the courts by the bonding company can be recovered.

Brady materials   Exculpatory materials must be disclosed through discovery to defense counsel by the prosecution when the defendant is to be tried for a crime. *See Brady v. Maryland* (1963).

Brady violation   Violation of discovery rules when prosecutor fails to turn over exculpatory materials acquired during a criminal investigation to defense counsel. Violation occurs whenever three conditions are met: (1) the evidence at issue must be favorable to the accused, either because it is exculpatory, or because it is impeaching; (2) the evidence must have been suppressed by the state, either willfully or inadvertently; and (3) prejudice must have ensued.

Bribery   Crime of offering, giving, requesting, soliciting, receiving something of value to influence a decision of a public official.

Brief   A document filed by a party to a lawsuit to convince the court of the merits of that party's case.

Burden of proof   The requirement to introduce evidence to prove an alleged fact or set of facts.

Bureaucracy   Organizational model that vests individuals with authority and spheres of competence in a predetermined hierarchy with abstract rules and selection by test.

Camp, ranch   Any of several types of similar correctional confinement facilities for adults or juveniles, usually located in rural areas.

Canons of Professional Ethics   Part of ABA Model Code of Professional Responsibility formulated in 1908; nine canons pertain to representing clients in a competent way; improving the legal system; avoiding the appearance of impropriety; and observing client confidences.

Capacity   Mental state of being legally responsible; having the mental acuity to know the difference between right and wrong and to realize and appreciate the nature and consequences of particular actions.

Capias   "That you take." A general term for various court orders requiring that some named person be taken into custody.

Capital punishment   Imposition of the death penalty for the most serious crimes. May be administered by electrocution, lethal injection, gas, hanging, or shooting.

Career criminals   Those offenders who make their living through crime. Usually offenses occur over the lifetime of the offender.

Case   Incident investigated by law enforcement officers. A single charging document under the jurisdiction of a court. A single defendant.

Case backlogs   Crowded court dockets in either juvenile court or criminal court; a massive buildup of cases, where judges cannot hear all cases in a timely fashion.

Case law   Legal opinions having the status of law as enunciated by the courts (e.g., U.S. Supreme Court decisions become case law and governing cases when identical or very similar cases are subsequently heard in lower courts).

Case processing   The speed with which cases are heard in either criminal or juvenile court.

Case-specific pretrial publicity   Direct familiarity with actual events that transpired in particular cases where persons are to serve as jurors; example is the Rodney King case, where millions of viewers watched the privately recorded videotape of the Rodney King beating by police on national television newscasts.

Cash bail bond   Cash payment for situations in which charges are not serious and the scheduled bail is low. Defendants obtain release by paying in cash the full amount, which is recoverable after the required court appearances are made.

Centralization   Limited distribution of power among a few top staff members of an organization.

Certification (juvenile)   *See* waiver.

Certiorari, **writ of**   A writ issued by a higher court directing a lower court to prepare the record of a case and send it to the higher court for review; a means of accessing the U.S. Supreme Court in order for a case to be heard.

Challenge   *See* peremptory challenge.

Challenges for cause   In jury selection, the method used by either the prosecution or defense attorneys to strike or remove prospective jurors from the available jury pool because of prejudices they might have, either toward the defendant or prosecution. Prospective jurors may also be excused from jury duty because of being law enforcement officers, relatives of law enforcement officers, court officers, or relatives of court officers. Any obvious bias for or against a defendant may result in the exclusion of the biased prospective juror.

Challenges of jurors   Questions raised of jurors by the judge, prosecutor, and/or defense attorney relating to their qualifications as impartial finders of fact; a determination of juror bias one way or another for or against the defendant.

Chambers   Usually a judge's office in a courthouse.

Chancellors   King's agents used to settle disputes between neighbors in his behalf, such as property boundary issues, trespass allegations, and child misconduct. Early equivalent of the chancellor with similar duties and responsibilities was the justice of the peace, dating back to about 1200 A.D.

Chancery court   Tribunal of equity rooted in early English common law where civil disputes are resolved. Also responsible for juvenile matters and adjudicating family matters such as divorce. Has jurisdiction over contract disputes, property boundary claims, and exchanges of goods disputes.

Change of venue   A change in the place of trial, usually from one county or district to another. Changes of venue are often conducted to avoid prejudicial trial proceedings, where it is believed that a fair trial cannot be obtained in the specific jurisdiction where the crime was alleged to have been committed.

Charge   A formal allegation filed against some defendant in which one or more crimes are alleged.

Charge reduction bargaining, charge bargaining   Negotiation process between prosecutors and defense attorneys involving dismissal of one or more charges against defendants in exchange for a guilty plea to remaining charges, or in which the prosecutor downgrades the charges in return for a plea of guilty.

Chief justice   The presiding or principal judge of a court, possessing nominal authority over the other judges (e.g., the chief justice of the U.S. Supreme Court).

Child savers   Groups who promoted rights of minors during the nineteenth century and helped create a separate juvenile court. Their motives have been questioned by modern writers who see their efforts as a form of social control and class conflict.

Children in need of supervision (CHINS)   Typically unruly or incorrigible children who cannot be supervised well by their parents. Also includes children from homes where parents are seldom present. State agencies exist to find housing for such children.

Chronic offenders   Habitual offenders; repeat offenders; persistent offenders; youths who commit frequent delinquent acts.

Chronic recidivists   Persons who continue to commit new crimes after being convicted of former offenses.

Circuit courts   Originally, courts that were held by judges who followed a circular path, hearing cases periodically in various communities. The term now refers to courts with several counties or districts within their jurisdiction. In the federal court organization, there are 13 federal circuit courts of appeal, having jurisdiction over U.S. district courts within specified states.

Circuit riders Judges who rode from jurisdiction to jurisdiction in remote locations of states or federal territories to hold trials on a regular basis, such as once a month or once every six months.

Circumstantial evidence Material provided by a witness from which a jury must infer a fact.

Citation, citation to appear Any document issued by a law enforcement or court officer directing one to present oneself in court on a specific date and time.

Cite, citation Any legal reference in which a point of law is made. In law enforcement, a summons.

Civil action Any lawsuit brought to enforce private rights and to remedy violations thereof.

Civil law All state and federal law pertaining to noncriminal activities, also referred to as municipal law. Laws pertain to private rights and remedies. A body of formal rules established by any society for its self-regulation.

Civil liability In tort law, the basis for a cause of action to recover damages.

Claiming The process in a dispute where a grievance is expressed and a cause of action is cited.

Class action, class action suit Any lawsuit on behalf of a segment of the population with specific characteristics, namely that they are victims of whatever wrongs are alleged. The class of persons may persist over time and change, but the action is for all current and future members of the class.

Coconspirator Another party besides the defendant who is alleged to have committed the same crime in concert with the defendant.

Code A systematic collection of laws.

Code of ethics Regulations formulated by major professional societies that outline the specific problems and issues that are frequently encountered in the types of research carried out within a particular profession. Serves as a guide to ethical research practices.

Codefendants Two or more defendants charged with the same crime and tried in the same judicial proceeding.

Coercion Affirmative defense similar to duress, wherein defendants allege that they were made or forced to commit an illegal act.

Common law Authority based on court decrees and judgments that recognize, affirm, and enforce certain usages and customs of the people. Laws determined by judges in accordance with their rulings.

Community service An alternative sanction requiring offenders to work in the community at such tasks as cleaning public parks or working with handicapped children in lieu of an incarcerative sentence. Restitution involves paying back a victim through money received from one's work.

Community service orders Judicially imposed restitution for those convicted of committing crimes; some form of work must be performed to satisfy restitution requirements.

Complaint   Written statement of essential facts constituting the offense alleged, made under oath before a magistrate or other qualified judicial officer.

Comprehensive Crime Control Act of 1984   Significant act that authorized establishment of U.S. Sentencing Commission, instituted sentencing guidelines, provided for abolition of federal parole, and devised new guidelines and goals of federal corrections.

Concession givers   Judges who make plea agreement offers to criminal defendants, wherein the defendants will plead guilty to a criminal charge in exchange for judicial leniency in sentencing.

Conclusive evidence   Any compelling evidence that is so strong that it cannot be disputed or discounted. Proof establishing guilt beyond a reasonable doubt.

Concurrent jurisdiction   Situation in which offender may be held accountable in several different jurisdictions simultaneously. Courts in the same jurisdiction.

Concurring opinion   A judge's written opinion agreeing with the result in the case, but disagreeing with the reasoning of the majority opinion.

Conditional dispositions   Decisions by juvenile court judge authorizing payment of fines, community service, restitution, or some other penalty after an adjudication of delinquency has been made.

Conditions of confinement   The nature of jail or prison incarceration; refers to heat and humidity, cleanliness of one's cell and surroundings, and general treatment; often is basis for legal action filed as *habeas corpus* petitions.

Confidentiality   Any privileged communication between a client and an attorney.

Confidentiality privilege   Right between defendant and his/her attorney where certain information cannot be disclosed to prosecutors or others because of the attorney–client relation; for juveniles, records have been maintained under secure circumstances with limited access, and only then accessed by those in authority with a clear law enforcement purpose.

Conflict stage   Either a pretrial or alternative dispute resolution phase where a plaintiff and a defendant confront one another and an accusation is made; a confrontation where the victim faces an alleged victimizer or defendant; may involve a third-party arbiter.

Consent decree   A formal agreement involving the child, parents, and the juvenile court in which the youth is placed under the court's supervision without an official finding of delinquency.

Constitutional law   An area of study in law schools involving the U.S. Constitution and its amendments. An investigation and discussion of the principles articulated by the U.S. Supreme Court and its interpretations of the law in different legal contexts.

Constitutional rights   Rights guaranteed to all U.S. citizens by the U.S. Constitution and its amendments.

Contempt of court   Disobeying orders from judges in their courtrooms. Failing to observe the proper decorum of legal proceedings. Crossing the line of proper conduct, either as a defense attorney or prosecutor (e.g., failing to give testimony when compelled to do so).

Contract system   Providing counsel to indigent offenders by having an attorney under contract to the county to handle some or all of these types of cases.

Conviction   State of being judged guilty of a crime in a court, either by the judge or jury.

Corroboration   Evidence that strengthens the evidence already given.

Cost-benefit analysis   Method of analyzing the costs associated with particular policies and determining whether the benefits or value derived from those policies are justified on the basis of the results.

Court   Public judiciary body that applies the law to controversies and oversees the administration of justice.

Court administrator   Any individual who controls the operations of the court in a particular jurisdiction. May be in charge of scheduling, juries, judicial assignment.

Court-appointed counsel   Attorneys who are appointed to represent indigent defendants.

Court calendar   Docket; the schedule of events for any judicial official.

Court clerk   Court officer who may file pleadings, motions, or judgments, issue process, and may keep general records of court proceedings.

Court of last resort   The last court that may hear a case. In the United States the Supreme Court is the court of last resort for many kinds of cases.

Court of limited jurisdiction   *See* trial court of limited jurisdiction.

Court of public opinion   Informal reactions to legal cases by unofficial pollsters and media broadcasters who cover high-profile cases on television and in the newspapers; independent reactions to court events by persons who may have only a passing interest in cases.

Court order   Any judicial proclamation or directive authorizing an officer to act on behalf of the court.

Court reporter   Court official who keeps a written word-for-word and/or tape-recorded record of court proceedings. *See also* transcript.

Courtroom work group   The phrase denoting all parties in the adversary process who work together cooperatively to settle cases with the least amount of effort and conflict.

Courts of general jurisdiction   Any court having the power to hear diverse types of cases, both civil and criminal.

Courts of last resort   Either state or federal supreme courts that function as the final stage for appeals from lower courts; the ultimate court of last resort is the U.S. Supreme Court.

Courts of record   Any legal proceedings where a written record is kept of court matters and dialogue.

Crime   Act or omission prohibited by law, by one who is held accountable by that law. Consists of legality, *actus reus*, *mens rea*, consensus, harm, causation, and prescribed punishment.

Crime Bill of 1994   Legislation supported by President Bill Clinton designed to increase crime prevention measures and put more police officers on city streets; also established truth-in-sentencing laws to maximize the amount of time inmates must serve in relation to their maximum sentences.

Crime prevention   Any overt activity conducted by individuals or groups to deter persons from committing crimes. May include "target hardening" by making businesses and residences more difficult to burglarize; neighborhood watch programs, in which neighborhood residents monitor streets during evening hours for suspicious persons or automobiles and equipping homes and businesses with devices to detect crime.

Criminal courts   Tribunals handling criminal cases. May also handle civil cases, and are then called criminal courts only in reference to the criminal cases that they handle.

Criminal–exclusive blend   Form of sentencing by a criminal court judge where either juvenile or adult sentences of incarceration can be imposed, but not both.

Criminal history   One's prior convictions, indictments, and arrests.

Criminal information   A written accusation made by a public prosecutor against a person for some criminal offense, usually restricted to minor crimes or misdemeanors, without an indictment.

Criminal–inclusive blend   Form of sentencing by a criminal court judge where both juvenile and adult sentences can be imposed simultaneously.

Criminal law   Body of law that defines criminal offenses and prescribes punishments (substantive law) and that delineates criminal procedure (procedural law).

Criminal trial   An adversarial proceeding within a particular jurisdiction, in which a judicial determination of issues can be made, and in which a defendant's guilt or innocence can be decided impartially.

Criminalization   Transformation of civil proceedings into criminal proceedings; the juvenile court has undergone a transformation toward greater criminalization as juveniles have acquired almost the same number of legal rights as adults.

Critical legal studies   Movement involving an examination of the entire legal system; recognizes that law is subjective rather than objective.

Cross-examination   Questioning of one side's witnesses by the other side's attorney, either the prosecution or defense.

Culpable, culpability   State of mind of persons who have committed an act that makes them liable for prosecution for that act.

Curfew violators   Persons under the legal age of adulthood who roam city streets beyond times when they are supposed to be in their homes; a type of status offender.

Custodial dispositions   Outcomes by juvenile judge following adjudication of juvenile as delinquent. Includes nonsecure custody (in a foster home, community agency, farm, camp) or secure custody (in a detention center, industrial, reform school).

Damages   Monetary sums awarded to prevailing litigants in civil actions.

De facto   "In fact," as a matter of fact.

De jure   "In law," as a matter of law.

De minimus   Minimal.

De novo   Anew, afresh, as if there had been no earlier decision.

Death penalty   *See* capital punishment.

Death row   Arrangement of prison cells where inmates who have been sentenced to death are housed.

Decriminalization, decriminalize   Legislative action whereby an act or omission, formerly criminal, is made noncriminal and without punitive sanctions.

Defendant   Person against whom a criminal proceeding is pending.

Defendant dispositions   Any one of several adjudication and dispositional options available to a judge at various places during a criminal proceeding, ranging from dismissal of the case to long-term imprisonment.

Defendant's sentencing memorandum   Version of events leading to conviction offense in the words of the convicted offender. Memorandum may be submitted together with victim impact statement.

Defense   A response by defendants in criminal law or civil cases. May consist only of a denial of the factual allegations of the prosecution (in a criminal case) or of the plaintiff (in a civil case). If defense offers new factual allegations in an effort to negate the charges, this is called an affirmative defense.

Defense attorney, counsel   A lawyer who represents a client accused of a crime.

Defense of property   Affirmative defense to justify illegal conduct, wherein defendants claim that they broke one or more laws to safeguard their property or possessions or the property or possessions of others.

Defenses to criminal charges   Includes claims based upon personal, special, and procedural considerations that defendants should not be held accountable for their actions, even though they may have acted in violation of the criminal laws.

Defense strategy   Approach taken by defense counsel for defending his/her client; usually involves a particular defense to criminal charges.

Deferred prosecution   Temporary halting of a prosecution against a defendant while he/she is subjected to a program with particular requirements for a short period. *See also* diversion.

Deinstitutionalization   Providing programs in community-based settings instead of institutional ones.

Deinstitutionalization of status offenses (DSO)   Movement to remove nondelinquent juveniles from secure facilities by eliminating status offenses from the delinquency category and removing juveniles from or precluding their confinement in juvenile correction facilities. Process of removing status offenses from jurisdiction of juvenile court.

Demand waiver   Request by juveniles to have their cases transferred from juvenile courts to criminal courts.

Demonstrative evidence   Material related to a crime that is apparent to the senses, in contrast to material presented by the testimony of other persons.

Deponent   Person who gives testimony through a deposition. If someone cannot physically attend a trial and give testimony under oath, then a deposition is taken and read into the court record.

Derivative evidence   Information obtained as the result of previously discovered evidence (e.g., residue from an automobile tire may suggest that a crime was committed in a part of the city where such residue is found and police discover subsequent "derivative" evidence by investigating that area).

Determinate sentencing   Sanctioning scheme in which court sentences offender to incarceration for fixed period, and which must be served in full and without parole intervention, less any good time earned in prison.

Deterrence, general or specific   Actions that are designed to prevent crime before it occurs by threatening severe criminal penalties or sanctions. May include safety measures to discourage potential lawbreakers such as elaborate security systems, electronic monitoring, and greater police officer visibility; influencing by fear, where fear is of apprehension and punishment.

Differential discretion   View that sentencing disparities are more likely to occur during informal charge reduction bargaining than in the final sentencing process following trial and the sentencing hearing.

Direct evidence   Evidence offered by an eyewitness who testifies to what was seen or heard.

Direct examination   Questioning by attorney of one's own (prosecution or defense) witness during a trial.

Direct file   Prosecutorial waiver of jurisdiction to a criminal court; an action taken against a juvenile who has committed an especially serious offense, where that juvenile's case is transferred to criminal court for the purpose of a criminal prosecution.

Directed verdict of acquittal   Order by court declaring that the prosecution has failed to produce sufficient evidence to show defendant guilty beyond a reasonable doubt.

Discovery   Procedure where prosecution shares information with defense attorney and defendant. Specific types of information are made available to defendant before trial, including results of any tests conducted, psychiatric reports, transcripts or tape-recorded statements made by the defendant. Also known as "Brady materials" after a specific court case.

Discretionary waivers   Transfers of juveniles to criminal courts by judges, at their discretion or in their judgment; also known as judicial waivers.

Disposition   Action by criminal or juvenile justice court or agency signifying that a portion of the justice process is completed and jurisdiction is relinquished or transferred to another agency or signifying that a decision has been reached on one aspect of a case and a different aspect comes under consideration, requiring a different kind of decision.

Disposition hearing   Hearing in juvenile court, conducted after an adjudicatory hearing and a finding of delinquency, status offender, dependent/neglected, to determine the most appropriate punishment/placement/treatment for the juvenile.

Disputants   Opposing sides in a civil action or case.

Dispute resolution   Civil action intended to resolve conflicts between two parties, usually a complainant and a defendant.

Dispute stage   Public revelation of a dispute by filing of a legal action.

Dissenting opinion   Any judicial opinion disavowing or attacking the decision of a collegial court.

District attorneys   City, county, and state prosecutors who are charged with bringing offenders to justice and enforcing the laws of the state.

District court   Trial courts at the state or federal level with general and original jurisdiction. Boundaries of their venue do not conform to standard political unit boundaries, but generally include several states or counties.

Diversion   Removing a case from the criminal justice system, while a defendant is required to comply with various conditions (e.g., attending a school for drunk drivers, undergoing counseling, performing community service). May result in expungement of record. Conditional removal of the prosecution of a case prior to its adjudication, usually as the result of an arrangement between the prosecutor and judge.

Diversion programs   One of several programs preceding formal court adjudication of charges against defendants; defendants participate in therapeutic, educational, and other helping programs. *See also* diversion.

Divestiture of jurisdiction   Juvenile court relinquishment of control over certain types of juveniles, such as status offenders.

DNA fingerprinting   Deoxyribonucleic acid (DNA) is an essential component of all living matter, which carries hereditary patterning. Suspects can be detected according to their unique DNA patterning, as each person has a different DNA pattern. Similar to fingerprint identification, in which no two persons have identical fingerprints.

Docket   A court record of the cases scheduled to appear before the court.

Doctrine of assumptive risk   Theory holding that plaintiffs who engage in dangerous enterprises must accept some or all of the responsibility when accidents happen to them.

Doctrine of contributory negligence   Theory holding that a plaintiff by his/her own actions has brought about injuries for which he/she seeks relief from a defendant.

Doctrine of last clear chance   Theory holding that when an accident occurs, the responsibility lies largely with the party who has the last clear chance to avoid the accident; example is a person standing on a railroad track who is subsequently struck by the train; the person is more in the position of avoiding the train than the train is of avoiding the person, even if the train engineer sees the person on the tracks before striking him/her.

Doctrine of *res lipsa loquitur* "The thing speaks for itself"; blame in a legal action lies on the part of the defendant, since the instrument(s) bringing about the injury to a plaintiff was within the control of the defendant.

Document Any written paper, official or unofficial, having potential evidentiary importance.

Documentary evidence Any written evidence.

Double jeopardy Subjecting persons to prosecution more than once in the same jurisdiction for the same offense, usually without new or vital evidence. Prohibited by the Fifth Amendment.

Dual court system A system consisting of a separate judicial structure for each state in addition to a national structure. Each case is tried in a court of the same jurisdiction as that of the law or laws broken.

Due process Basic constitutional right to a fair trial, presumption of innocence until guilt is proven beyond a reasonable doubt, the opportunity to be heard, to be aware of a matter that is pending, to make an informed choice whether to acquiesce or contest, and to provide the reasons for such a choice before a judicial official. Actual due process rights include timely notice of a hearing or trial that informs the accused of charges, the opportunity to confront one's accusers and to present evidence on one's own behalf before an impartial jury or judge, the presumption of innocence under which guilt must be proved by legally obtained evidence and the verdict must be supported by the evidence presented, the right of accused persons to be warned of their constitutional rights at the earliest stage of the criminal process, protection against self-incrimination, assistance of counsel at every critical stage of the criminal process, and the guarantee that individuals will not be tried more than once for the same offense.

Due process courts Juvenile courts where the emphasis is upon punishment and offender control rather than individualized treatments and assistance.

Due process of law A right guaranteed by the Fifth, Sixth, and Fourteenth Amendments of the U.S. Constitution, and generally understood to mean the due course of legal proceedings according to the rules and forms that have been established for the protection of private rights. *See also* due process.

Duress Affirmative defense used by defendants to show lack of criminal intent, alleging force, psychological or physical, from others as stimulus for otherwise criminal conduct.

Early release *See* parole board.

Electronic monitoring The use of electronic devices (usually anklets or wristlets) which emit electronic signals to monitor offenders, probationers, and parolees. The purpose of their use is to monitor an offender's presence in a given environment where the offender is required to remain or to verify the offender's whereabouts.

Element of the offense   Any conduct, circumstance, condition, or state of mind which in combination with other conduct, circumstances, conditions, states of mind constitutes an unlawful act.

En banc   "In the bench." Refers to a session of the court, usually an appellate court, where all of the judges assigned to the court participate.

English common law   *See* common law.

Entrapment   Activity by law enforcement officers that suggests, encourages, or aids others in the commission of crimes, which would ordinarily not have occurred without officer intervention. Defense used by defendants to show otherwise criminal act would not have occurred without police intervention, assistance, and/or encouragement.

Equal protection   Clause of Fourteenth Amendment of U.S. Constitution guaranteeing to all citizens equal protection of the law, without regard to race, color, gender, class, origin, or religion.

Equity   The concept that the relationships between men, women, and society should be just and fair and in accordance with contemporary morality.

Error in fact   Any error made in a court of law that may or may not affect a judicial decision or judgment.

Error in law   Any error made by the court that may affect the case outcome (e.g., permitting the prosecution to show numerous bloody photographs of a crime scene to inflame the jury and enhance a defendant's likelihood of being convicted and sentenced harshly). *See also* reversible error, harmless error.

Ethical code   Canons of professional responsibility articulated by professional associations such as the American Bar Association.

Evarts Act   Introduced in 1891 and sponsored by New Jersey lawyer William M. Evarts, this act created circuit courts of appeal to hear appeals emanating from the U.S. district courts.

Evidence   All materials or means admissible in a court of law to produce in the minds of the court or jury a belief concerning the matter at issue.

Evidence, corroborating   Any collateral evidence that enhances the value of other evidence.

Evidence-driven jury   Jury that decides to consider all evidence presented as relevant rather than selected evidence based on juror interest or preferences.

Evidentiary   Pertaining to the rules of evidence or the evidence in a particular case.

Ex parte   A hearing or examination in the presence of only one party in the case.

Ex post facto **laws**   Laws making criminal any act committed before they were passed or laws that retroactively increase the penalty for a crime. Such laws are unconstitutional.

Ex rel   Latin term used in case citations to designate parties for whom others are acting.

Examination, direct and cross   *See* direct examination and cross-examination.

Exception   An objection to a ruling, comments made by the judge or attorneys.

Excessive bail   Any bail amount that so grossly exceeds the proportionality of the seriousness of the offense so as to be prohibited by the Eighth Amendment.

Exclusionary rule   Rule providing that where evidence has been obtained in violation of the privileges guaranteed by the U.S. Constitution, such evidence may be excluded at the trial.

Exclusive jurisdiction   Specific jurisdiction over particular kinds of cases. The U.S. Supreme Court has authority to hear matters involving the diplomats of other countries who otherwise enjoy great immunity from most other courts. Family court may have exclusive jurisdiction to hear child custody cases.

Exculpate, exculpatory   Tending to exonerate a person of allegations of wrongdoing.

Exculpatory evidence   Any information that exonerates a person of allegations of wrongdoing; any information that reflects favorably upon the accused and shows that they are innocent of the crimes with which they are charged.

Expert testimony   Any oral evidence presented in court by someone who is considered proficient and learned in a given field where such evidence is relevant. Testimony provided by an expert witness.

Expert witnesses   Witnesses who have expertise or special knowledge in a relevant field pertaining to the case at trial. Witness who is qualified under the Federal Rules of Evidence to offer an opinion about the authenticity or accuracy of reports, who has special knowledge relevant to the proceeding. Sometimes called "hired guns."

Expunge, expungement   Deletion of one's arrest record from official sources. In most jurisdictions, juvenile delinquency records are expunged when one reaches the age of majority or adulthood.

Expungement orders   Juvenile court orders to seal juvenile records.

Extenuating circumstances   Conditions under which offenders might be excused from culpability in criminal conduct.

Extralegal factors   Any element of a nonlegal nature. In determining whether law enforcement officers are influenced by particular factors when encountering juveniles on the streets, extralegal factors might include juvenile attitude, politeness, appearance, dress. Legal factors might include age, specific prohibited acts observed by the officers.

Eyewitnesses   Persons who testify in court as to what they saw when the crime was committed.

Facsimile   A copy of an original object or document.

Fact   A true statement. An actual event.

Fact-finders   Juries who hear cases, criminal or otherwise.

Factual basis for the plea   Evidence presented to the judge by the prosecutor that would have been used if a plea-bargained case had gone to trial; evidence of one's guilt beyond a reasonable doubt to substantiate a plea bargain agreement.

Factual question   A question designed to elicit objective information from respondents regarding their background, environments, and habits.

Failure to appear   When defendants fail to present themselves for trial or some other formal proceeding, such as arraignment or a preliminary hearing/examination.

Federal district courts   Basic trial courts for the federal government that try all criminal cases and have extensive jurisdiction. District judges are appointed by the president of the United States with the advice, counsel, and approval of the Senate. Cases from these courts are appealed to particular circuit courts of appeal.

Federal misdemeanor   Any federal crime where the maximum punishment is less than one year in prison or jail.

Federal Rules of Criminal Procedure   Contained in Title 18 of the U.S. Code, all protocols and regulations that must be followed during offender processing, from arrest to conviction.

Federal Rules of Evidence   Official rules governing the introduction of certain types of evidence in U.S. district courts.

Fellow servant doctrine   Theory holding employer responsible for actions of employees.

Felony   Crime punishable by incarceration, usually in a state or federal prison, for periods of one year or longer.

Felony property offending   Any crime punishable by more than one year in prison or jail and causes property loss or damage (e.g., burglary, larceny/theft, vehicular theft).

Feminist legal studies   View that women use a different type of logic than men when interpreting the law, favoring less litigation and more mediation.

Filing   The commencement of criminal proceedings by entering a charging document into a court's official record.

Financial/community service model   Restitution model for juveniles that stresses the offender's financial accountability and community service to pay for damages.

Finding   A holding or ruling by the court or judge.

Finding of fact   Court's determination of the facts presented as evidence in a case, affirmed by one party and denied by the other.

Fine   Financial penalties imposed at time of sentencing convicted offenders. Most criminal statutes contain provisions for the imposition of monetary penalties as sentencing options.

Flat term   A specific, definite term for a conviction, not necessarily known in advance of sentencing.

Flat time   Actual amount of time required to be served by a convicted offender while incarcerated.

Foster home   Dwelling including family where child is placed, usually where such child is from an abusive household or without parents or legal guardians; foster home parents are responsible for proper upbringing of child for a period of time.

Frivolous lawsuits   Legal actions commenced by one or more parties where there is little hope of a successful outcome; often groundless legal actions without sufficient bases.

Fruits of the poisonous tree   A U.S. Supreme Court decision in *Wong Sun v. United States* (1963) holding that evidence that is spawned or directly derived from an illegal search or an illegal interrogation is generally inadmissible against a defendant because of its original taint.

Fugitive recovery agent   One who seeks to return to a jurisdiction a person who has been charged with a crime and has jumped bail or fled the jurisdiction before trial.

Fundamental fairness   Legal doctrine supporting the idea that so long as a state's conduct maintains the basic elements of fairness, the Constitution has not been violated.

Gag order   Official declaration by the judge in a trial proceeding that all parties in the action, including the jurors, must refrain from discussing the case with the media.

General jurisdiction   Power of a court to hear a wide range of cases, both civil and criminal.

General pretrial publicity   Information about a legal case involving general details, including suspects, how the crime was committed, names of victims and alleged perpetrators, covered by the news media.

General sessions courts   Tribunals in particular states with limited jurisdiction to hear misdemeanor cases and some low-level felony cases.

General trial courts   Any one of several types of courts, either civil or criminal, with diverse jurisdiction to conduct jury trials and decide cases.

Geographic jurisdiction   The power to hear particular kinds of cases depending upon the legally defined boundaries of cities, counties, or states.

Get-tough movement   General orientation toward criminals and juvenile delinquents that favors the maximum penalties and punishments for crime and delinquency; any action toward toughening of strengthening sentencing provisions or dispositions involving adults or juveniles.

Going rate   Local view of the appropriate sentence or punishment for a particular offense, the defendant's prior record, and other factors; used in implicit plea bargaining.

Good time, good-time credit   An amount of time deducted from the period of incarceration of a convicted offender, calculated as so many days per month on the basis of good behavior while incarcerated. Credits earned by prisoners for good behavior. Introduced in early 1800s by British penal authorities, including Alexander Maconochie and Sir Walter Crofton.

Grand jury   Investigative bodies whose numbers vary among states. Duties include determining probable cause regarding commission of a crime and returning formal charges against suspects. *See also* true bill and no true bill.

Grievance, grievance procedure   Formalized arrangements, usually involving a neutral hearing board, whereby institutionalized individuals have the opportunity to register complaints about the conditions of their confinement.

Group home Facilities for juveniles that provide limited supervision and support. Juveniles live in homelike environment with other juveniles and participate in therapeutic programs and counseling. Considered nonsecure custodial. *See also* foster home.

Guardian *ad litem* A court-appointed attorney who protects the interests of children in cases involving their welfare and who works with the children during the litigation period.

Guidelines-based sentencing *See* sentencing guidelines.

Guilty plea A defendant's formal affirmation of guilt in court to charges contained in a complaint, information, indictment claiming that they committed the offenses listed.

Habeas corpus Writ meaning "produce the body"; used by prisoners to challenge the nature and length of their confinement.

***Habeas corpus* petition** Writ filed, usually by inmates, challenging the legitimacy of their confinement and the nature of their confinement. Document commands authorities to show cause why an inmate should be confined in either a prison or jail. Also includes challenges of the nature of confinement. A written order by the court to any person, including a law enforcement officer, directing that person to bring the named individual before the court so that it can determine if there is adequate cause for continued detention.

Habitual offenders Persons who have been convicted of two or more felonies and may be sentenced under the habitual offender statute for an aggravated or longer prison term.

Habitual offender statutes Statutes vary among states. Generally provide life imprisonment as a mandatory sentence for chronic offenders who have been convicted of three or more serious felonies within a specific time period.

Harmful errors Errors made by judges that may be prejudicial to a defendant's case. May lead to reversals of convictions against defendants and to new trials.

Harmless error doctrine Errors of a minor or trivial nature and not deemed sufficient to harm the rights of parties in a legal action. Cases are not reversed on the basis of harmless errors.

Hearing Any formal proceeding in which the court hears evidence from prosecutors and defense and resolves a dispute or issue.

Hearing, probable cause A proceeding in which arguments, evidence, or witnesses are presented and in which it is determined whether there is sufficient cause to hold the accused for trial or whether the case should be dismissed.

Hearsay evidence Evidence that is not firsthand but is based on an account given by another.

Hearsay rule Courtroom precedent that hearsay cannot be used in court. Rather than accepting testimony on hearsay, the trial process asks that persons who were the original source of the hearsay information be brought into court to be questioned and cross-examined. Exceptions to the hearsay rule may occur when persons with direct knowledge are either dead or otherwise unable to testify.

Hierarchical jurisdiction   Distinction between courts at different levels, where one court is superior to another and has the power to hear appeals from lower-court decisions.

Holding   The legal principle drawn from a judicial decision. Whatever a court, usually an appellate court, decides when cases are appealed from lower courts. When an appellate court "holds" a particular decision, this may be to uphold the original conviction, set it aside, overturn in part, and uphold in part.

Home confinement   Housing of offenders in their own homes with or without electronic monitoring devices. Reduces prison overcrowding and prisoner costs. Sometimes an intermediate punishment involving the use of offender residences for mandatory incarceration during evening hours after a curfew and on weekends. Also called "house arrest."

Hung jury   Jury that cannot agree on a verdict.

Illinois Juvenile Court Act   Legislation establishing first juvenile court in United States in 1899.

Impartial arbiters   Persons such as judges, attorneys, or prominent citizens who are called upon to be objective and neutral third parties in disputes between perpetrators and their victims under conditions of restorative justice or alternative dispute resolution.

Impeachment   Proceeding for the removal of a political officer, such as a governor, president, or judge.

Implicit plea bargaining   Occurs when defendant pleads guilty with the expectation of receiving a more lenient sentence. *See also* plea bargaining.

In camera   In a judge's chambers.

In delicto   Fault, as to a crime or happening; a finding that one is at fault in causing an accident or committing a crime.

In flagrante delicto   Caught in the act. The fact that the perpetrator of a crime was caught during the crime's commission is direct evidence of guilt.

In forma pauperis   "In the manner of a pauper." Refers to waiver of filing costs and other fees associated with judicial proceedings in order to allow indigent persons to proceed with their case.

In loco parentis   "In the place of the parents." Refers to someone other than a parent acting on behalf of a juvenile in any juvenile proceeding.

In re   "In the matter of." Refers to cases being filed for juveniles who must have an adult act on their behalf when filing motions or appeals.

In toto   Completely, entirely.

Inadmissible   Evidentiary term used to describe something that cannot be used as evidence during a trial.

Incapacitation, isolation   Philosophy of corrections espousing loss of freedom proportional to seriousness of offense. Belief that the function of punishment is to separate offenders from other society members and prevent them from committing additional criminal acts.

Inculpatory evidence   Any information that places the defendant in an unfavorable light and increases the likelihood of his/her guilt.

Incumbents   Political officers who are currently in power, but who are seeking to be re-elected or reappointed.

Indeterminate sentencing   Sentencing scheme in which a period is set by judges between the earliest date for a parole decision and the latest date for completion of the sentence. In holding that the time necessary for treatment cannot be set exactly, the indeterminate sentence is closely associated with rehabilitation.

Indictment   A charge or written accusation found and presented by a grand jury that a particular defendant probably committed a crime.

Indigent defendants   Poor persons; anyone who cannot afford legal services or representation.

Ineffective assistance of counsel   Standard for determining whether client is defended in a competent way; guidelines for determining counsel's effectiveness articulated in case of *Strickland v. Washington* (1984), and include (1) whether counsel's behavior undermined the adversarial process to the degree that the trial outcome is unreliable; and (2) the counsel's conduct was unreasonable to the degree that the jury's verdict would have been different otherwise.

Information   Written accusation made by a public prosecutor against a person for some criminal offense, without an indictment. Usually restricted to minor crimes or misdemeanors. Sometimes called criminal information.

Initial appearance   Formal proceeding during which the judge advises the defendant of the charges, including a recitation of the defendant's rights and a bail decision.

Insanity   Degree of mental illness that negates the legal capacity or responsibility of the affected person.

Insanity defense   Defense that seeks to exonerate accused persons by showing that they were insane at the time they were believed to have committed a crime.

Insanity plea   A plea entered as a defense to a crime. The defendant admits guilt but assigns responsibility for the criminal act to the condition of insanity presumably existing when the crime was committed.

Intake   Review of a case by a court (juvenile or criminal) official. Screening of cases includes weeding out weak cases. In juvenile cases, intake involves the reception of a juvenile against whom complaints have been made. Decision to proceed or dismiss the case is made at this stage.

Intake hearings   Proceedings, usually presided over by an intake officer, where determinations are made about whether certain juveniles should undergo further processing by the juvenile justice system; a screening mechanism for juvenile offenders.

Intake officer   Process of screening juveniles who have been charged with offenses. Officer who conducts screening of juveniles. Dispositions include release to parents pending further juvenile court action, dismissal of charges against juvenile, detention, treatment by some community agency.

Intake screening   A critical phase where a determination is made by a juvenile probation officer or other official whether to release juveniles to their parent's custody, detain juveniles in formal detention facilities for a later court appearance, or release them to parents pending a later court appearance.

Intensive supervised probation   Varies from standard probation and includes more face-to-face visits between probation officers and probationers under community supervision.

Intent   A state of mind, the *mens rea*, in which a person seeks to accomplish a given result, such as a crime, through a given course of action.

Inter alia   "Among other things."

Interim judges   Temporary judge who is appointed following the death, resignation, or retirement of another judge, usually to complete the original judge's term; after the interim judge serves, a new judge is appointed or elected according to the rules of judicial selection in the particular jurisdiction.

Interlocutory appeal   An appeal during a trial proceeding in which the judgment of the trial court is suspended pending the successfulness of an appeal.

Intermittent sentencing   Imposed punishment where offender must serve a portion of sentence in jail, perhaps on weekends or specific evenings. Considered similar to probation with limited incarceration. *See also* split sentencing.

Intoxication   The state of being incapable of performing certain tasks legally, such as operating motor vehicles or boats. Can be induced through consumption of alcoholic beverages, inhaling toxic fumes from petroleum products, or consumption of drug substances. May also be a defense to criminal conduct, although the courts often rule that it is voluntary.

Ipso facto   "By the mere fact." By the fact itself (e.g., "We can assume, *ipso facto*, that if the defendant was observed beating another person in a bar by ten witnesses, then he is likely guilty of the beating inflicted on the victim.").

Isolation   A sentencing philosophy seeking to remove the offender from other offenders when confined by placing prisoner in a cell with no communication with others. Also known as solitary confinement, which originated in the Walnut Street Jail in Philadelphia, Pennsylvania in the late 1700s. Another usage of this term is to segregate offenders from society through incarceration.

Jail as a condition of probation   Sentence in which judge imposes limited jail time to be served before commencement of probation. *See also* split sentencing.

Jencks materials   Discoverable materials available from either the prosecutor or defense counsel prior to trial. *See Jencks v. United States* (1957).

Judge   A political officer who has been elected or appointed to preside over a court of law, whose position has been created by statute or by constitution and whose decisions in criminal and juvenile cases may only be reviewed by a judge or a higher court and may not be reviewed *de novo*.

Judgment   Final determination of a case. A proclamation stating one's guilt or innocence in relation to criminal offenses alleged. In tort law, a finding in favor of or against the plaintiff. The amount of monetary damages awarded in civil cases.

Judicial activism   U.S. Supreme Court's use of its power to accomplish social goals.

Judicial appointments   Selections of judges by political figures, such as governors or presidents.

Judicial conduct commission   Investigative body created in California in 1960, comprised of other judges, attorneys, and prominent citizens; task was to investigate allegations of judicial misconduct, incompetence, and unfairness.

Judicial instructions   Specific admonitions to jurors, prosecutors, and defense counsels to do or refrain from doing different things.

Judicial misconduct   Depature of a judge from accepted modes of conduct becoming a judicial official; forms of misconduct are accepting bribes in exchange for money or services; making biased decisions favoring one side or the other during a trial; engaging in behaviors (e.g., drunkenness, driving while intoxicated, perjury) while serving on the bench.

Judicial plea bargaining   Recommended sentence by judge who offers a specific sentence and/or fine in exchange for a guilty plea. *See also* plea bargaining.

Judicial powers   Court jurisdiction to act in certain cases and decide punishments.

Judicial privilege   Power of judges to change plea bargain agreements and substitute their own punishments; the power to override prosecutors and defense counsel concerning the agreed upon terms of plea agreements.

Judicial process   The sequence of procedures designed to resolve disputes or conclude a criminal case.

Judicial review   The authority of a court to limit the power of the executive and legislative branches of government by deciding whether their acts defy rights established by the state and federal constitutions.

Judicial waiver   Decision by juvenile judge to waive juvenile to jurisdiction of criminal court.

Judiciary Act of 1789   A congressional act that provided for three levels of courts: (1) thirteen federal district courts, each presided over by a district judge; (2) three higher circuit courts of appeal, each comprising two justices of the Supreme Court and one district judge; and (3) a Supreme Court, consisting of a chief justice and five associate justices.

Jumping bail   Act by defendant of leaving jurisdiction where trial is to be held. Attempt by defendant to avoid prosecution on criminal charges.

Jurisdiction   The power of a court to hear and determine a particular type of case. Also refers to territory within which court may exercise authority such as a city, county, or state.

Juror misconduct   Any impropriety by a juror; acceptance of illegal gratuities in exchange for a favorable vote for or against the defendant; sleeping during the trial; reading newspaper accounts, listening or watching newscasters voice their opinions about the case, and then relating this information to other jurors in attempt to persuade them one way or another for or against the defendant.

Jury   *See* petit jury.

Jury deliberations   Discussion among jury members concerning the weight and sufficiency of witness testimony and other evidence presented by both the prosecution and defense. An attempt to arrive at a verdict.

Jury misconduct   Any impropriety exhibited by one or more jurors, such as sleeping during a trial; attempting to bias other jurors for or against a particular defendant by illegal means; or accepting bribes or gratuities from persons interested in the case.

Jury nullification   Jury refuses to accept the validity of evidence at trial and acquits or convicts for a lesser offense (e.g., although all of the elements for murder are proved, a jury may acquit defendants who killed their spouses allegedly as an act of mercy killing).

Jury panel   A list of jurors summoned to serve on possible jury duty at a particular court. From the jury panel, the petit jury is selected.

Jury poll   A poll conducted by a judicial officer or by the clerk of the court after a jury has stated its verdict but before that verdict has been entered into the record of the court, asking each juror individually whether the stated verdict is his or her own verdict.

Jury pool   Aggregate of persons from which a jury is selected; use of voter registration lists, driver's licenses, home ownership records, and other public documents are used to create such pools; also known as a *venire* or venireman list.

Jury selection   The process whereby a jury is impaneled for either a civil or criminal trial proceeding.

Jury sequestration   The process of isolating a jury from the public during a trial; the objective is to minimize the influence of media publicity and exposure, which might otherwise influence juror opinions about the guilt or innocence of the defendant.

Jury size   Traditional twelve-member jury at federal level and many state and local levels; may vary between six-member jury and twelve-member jury at state and local level.

Jury trial   Proceeding by which guilt or innocence of defendant is determined by jury instead of by the judge.

Jury waiver system   Occurs when defendants waive their constitutional right to a jury trial and enter into a plea bargain agreement with the prosecutor.

Juvenile—contiguous blend   Form of blended sentencing by a juvenile court judge where the judge can impose a disposition beyond the normal jurisdictional range for juvenile offenders; for example, a judge may impose a 30-year term on a 14-year-old offender, but the juvenile is entitled to a hearing when he/she reaches the age of majority to determine whether the remainder of the sentence shall be served.

Juvenile court   Formal adjudicatory hearing to determine whether one is a juvenile delinquent, a status offender, or in need of supervision.

Juvenile court jurisdiction   Power of juvenile courts to hear cases involving persons under the legal age of adulthood.

Juvenile–exclusive blend   Blended sentencing form where a juvenile court judge can impose either adult or juvenile incarceration as a disposition and sentence but not both.

Juvenile–inclusive blend   Form of blended sentencing where a juvenile court judge can impose *both* adult and juvenile incarceration simultaneously.

Juvenile court   A term for any court with original jurisdiction over persons statutorily defined as juveniles and alleged to be delinquents, status offenders, or dependents.

Juvenile delinquency   The violation of criminal laws by juveniles. Any illegal behavior or activity committed by persons who are within a particular age range and subjects them to the jurisdiction of a juvenile court or its equivalent.

Juvenile delinquent   Any minor who commits an offense that would be a crime if committed by an adult.

Juvenile Justice and Delinquency Prevention Act of 1974   Act passed by Congress in 1974 and amended numerous times, including 1984, encouraging states to deal differently with their juvenile offenders. Promotes community-based treatment programs and discourages incarceration of juveniles in detention centers, industrial schools, or reform schools.

Juvenile justice system, process   The system through which juveniles are processed, sentenced, and corrected after arrests for juvenile delinquency.

Juveniles   Persons who have not as yet achieved their eighteenth birthday or the age of majority.

Kales plan   The 1914 version of Missouri plan, in which a committee of experts creates a list of qualified persons for judgeships and makes recommendations to governor. *See also* Missouri plan.

Labeling theory, labeling   Theory attributed to Edwin Lemert that persons acquire self-definitions that are deviant or criminal. Persons perceive themselves as deviant or criminal through labels applied to them by others, thus the more people are involved in the criminal justice system, the more they acquire self-definitions consistent with the criminal label.

Landmark decision   Decision handed down by U.S. Supreme Court that becomes the law of the land and serves as a precedent for subsequent similar legal issues in lower courts.

Law   The body of rules of specific conduct, prescribed by existing, legitimate authority in a particular jurisdiction and at a particular point in time.

Law in action   Procedural law.

Law in books   Substantive law.

Legal realism   View that law and society are constantly evolving and that law should be the means to a social end rather than an end in itself.

Legislative waivers   Provisions that compels juvenile court to remand certain youths to criminal courts because of specific offenses that have been committed or alleged.

Lex non scripta   "The unwritten law" or common law. Law not written down in some codified form.

Lex talionis   The law of retaliation or retribution. A form of revenge dating back to the Apostle Paul and used up until the Middle Ages.

Libel   A tort of defamation through published writing or pictures critical of others.

Lie detector   An apparatus that records one's blood pressure and various other sensory responses and records one's reactions by means of a moving pencil and paper. Designed to determine whether one is telling the truth during an interrogation. Also known as polygraphs. Results of tests are not admissible in court.

Life imprisonment   Any sentence involving lengthy incarceration, presumably for the life expectancy of the convicted offender; however, life imprisonment in the United States averages about seven years.

Life-without-parole sentence   Penalty imposed as maximum punishment in states that do not have death penalty; provides for permanent incarceration of offenders in prisons, without parole eligibility; early release may be attained through accumulation of good-time credits.

Limited jurisdiction   Court is restricted to handling certain types of cases such as probate matters or juvenile offenses. Also known as special jurisdiction.

Litigation   Civil prosecution in which proceedings are maintained against wrongdoers, as opposed to criminal proceedings.

Litigation explosion   Sudden increase in inmate suits against administrators and officers in prisons and jails during late 1960s and continuing through 1980s. Suits usually challenge nature and length of confinement or torts allegedly committed by administration, usually seek monetary or other forms of relief.

Loiterers   Persons who stand around idly, hanging around. Often used as a provocation by police officers to stop and question citizens who appear suspicious, to describe vagrants, persons who are in public places with no visible means of support.

Magistrate   A judge who handles cases in pretrial stages. Usually presides over misdemeanor cases. An officer of the lower courts.

Magistrate courts   Courts of special jurisdiction, usually urban.

Mala fides   Bad faith.

Mala in se **crimes**   Illegal acts that are inherently wrong or intrinsically evil (e.g., murder, rape, or arson).

Mala prohibita **crimes**   Illegal acts that have been codified or reduced to writing. Offenses defined by legislatures as crimes. Many state and federal criminal statutes are *mala prohibita*.

Malfeasance   Misconduct by public officials. Engaging in acts that are prohibited while serving in public office.

Malicious prosecution   Prosecutorial action against someone without probable cause or reasonable suspicion.

Mandamus   *See* writ of *mandamus*.

Mandatory sentencing, mandatory sentence   Sentencing where court is required to impose an incarcerative sentence of a specified length, without the option for probation, suspended sentence, or immediate parole eligibility.

Mandatory transfer   Automatic waiver of certain juveniles to criminal court on the basis of (1) their age and (2) the seriousness of their offense; for example, a 17-year-old in Illinois who allegedly committed homicide would be subject to mandatory transfer to criminal court for the purpose of a criminal prosecution.

Material witness   Any witness who has relevant testimony about a crime.

Mediation   Informal conflict resolution through the intervention of a trained negotiator who seeks a mutually agreeable resolution between disputing parties.

Mens rea   Intent to commit a crime. Guilty mind.

Merit selection   Reform plan in which judges are nominated by a committee and appointed by the governor for a given period. When the term expires, the voters are asked to signify their approval or disapproval of the judge for a succeeding term. If judge is disapproved, the committee nominates a successor for the governor's appointment.

Miranda warning, rights   Warning given to suspects by police officers advising suspects of their legal rights to counsel, to refuse to answer questions, to avoid self-incrimination, and other privileges. Named after landmark case of *Miranda v. Arizona* (1966).

Misdemeanor   Crime punishable by fines and/or imprisonment, usually in a city or county jail, for periods of less than one year.

Misdemeanor Trial Law   Action by New York City passed in 1985 permitting low-level misdemeanor cases involving incarceration of six months or less to be disposed of by bench trials rather than jury trials; a time-saving strategy for more rapid criminal case processing.

Missouri plan   Method of selecting judges in which merit system for appointments is used. Believed to reduce political influence in the selection of judges.

Mistake   Affirmative defense that alleges an act was not criminal because the person charged did not know the act was a prohibited one.

Mistake of fact   Unconscious ignorance of a fact or the belief in the existence of something that does not exist.

Mistake of law   An erroneous opinion of legal principles applied to a given set of facts. A judge may rule on a given court issue and the ruling may be wrong because the judge misunderstands the meaning of the law and how it should be applied.

Mistrial   A trial that cannot stand, is invalid. Judges may call a mistrial for reasons such as errors on the part of prosecutors or defense counsel, the death of a juror or counsel, or a hung jury.

Mitigating circumstances   Factors about a crime that may lessen the severity of sentence imposed by the judge. Cooperating with police to apprehend others involved, youthfulness or old age of defendant, mental instability, and having no prior record are considered mitigating circumstances.

Mittimus   An order by the court to an officer to bring someone named in the order directly to jail.

Mixed sentencing   Two or more separate sentences imposed after offenders have been convicted of two or more crimes in the same adjudication proceeding. *See also* split sentencing.

Modus operandi   The characteristic method a person uses in the performance of repeated criminal acts.

Motion for a bill of particulars   An action before the court asking that the details of the state's case against a defendant be made known to the defense. *See also* discovery.

Motion for a change of venue   Action requested by either the prosecutor or defense counsel seeking to change the trial site to a different jurisdiction or geographical location, possibly because of extensive pretrial publicity and the belief that prospective jurors might be biased one way or another toward the defendant.

Motion for continuance   An action before the court asking that the trial or hearing or proceeding be postponed to a later date.

Motion for determination of competency   Action requested by defense counsel where the court is asked to order a psychiatric examination of the defendant to determine whether the defendant is competent to stand trial for a crime.

Motion for discovery   Action initiated by either prosecutor or defense counsel entitling either side to certain discoverable evidence, such as police reports and defendant interviews, and any other relevant evidentiary items that might be useful as the basis for case arguments at trial later.

Motion for dismissal of charges   Action requested by defense counsel to have charges against the defendant dismissed because of an insufficiency of evidence presented by the prosecutor.

Motion for intent to provide alibi   Defense-initiated motion to indicate the intention to use an alibi witness or witnesses, evidence, or some type of rationale to show cause for why defendant was not at the scene of the crime(s) alleged and for which the defendant is being tried.

Motion for severance   Action requested by either the prosecutor or defense counsel to have separate trial proceedings for different persons charged with the same offense and who are accused of acting in concert with one another to effect a crime.

Motion for summary judgment   Request granted by judges who have read the plaintiff's version and defendant's version of events, and a decision is reached holding for the defendant.

Motion for suppression of evidence   Action initiated by prosecutor or defense counsel asking the judge to bar the admission of certain evidence from the trial proceeding.

Motion to dismiss   An action before the court requesting that the judge refuse to hear a suit. Usually granted when inmates who file petitions fail to state a claim upon which relief can be granted.

Motion to suppress   An action before the court to cause testimony or tangible evidence from being introduced either for or against the accused.

Motions   Oral or written requests to a judge asking the court to make a specific ruling, finding, decision, or order. May be presented at any appropriate point from an arrest until the end of a trial.

Motions *in limine*   A pretrial motion, generally to obtain judicial approval to admit certain items into evidence that might otherwise be considered prejudicial or inflammatory.

Municipal courts   Courts of special jurisdiction whose jurisdiction follows the political boundaries of a municipality or city.

Naming   Identifying a party in a legal action as the target of that action.

Narrative   A portion of a presentence investigation report prepared by a probation officer or private agency, which provides a description of offense and offender. Culminates in and justifies a recommendation for a specific sentence to be imposed on the offender by judges.

Necessity   A condition that compels someone to act because of perceived needs. An affirmative defense (e.g., when someone's automobile breaks down during a snowstorm and an unoccupied cabin is nearby, breaking into the cabin to save oneself from freezing to death is acting out of "necessity" and would be a defense to breaking and entering charges later).

Negligence   Liability accruing to prison or correctional program administrators and probation or parole officers as the result of a failure to perform a duty owed clients or inmates or the improper or inadequate performance of that duty. May include negligent entrustment, negligent training, negligent assignment, negligent retention, or negligent supervision (e.g., providing probation or parole officers with revolvers and not providing them with firearms training).

Negotiated guilty pleas   Pleas of guilty entered in exchange for some form of sentencing leniency during plea bargaining.

New trial   Tribunal *de novo*. After a hung jury or a case is set aside or overturned by a higher court, a new trial is held to determine one's guilt or innocence.

New York House of Refuge   Established in New York City in 1825 by the Society for the Prevention of Pauperism; school that managed largely status offenders; compulsory education provided; strict prison-like regimen was considered detrimental to youthful clientele.

No bill   *See* no true bill.

No true bill   Grand jury decision that insufficient evidence exists to establish probable cause that a crime was committed and a specific person committed it.

Nolle prosequi   An entry made by the prosecutor on the record in a case and announced in court to indicate that the specified charges will not be prosecuted. In effect, the charges are thereby dismissed.

Nolo contendere   Plea of "no contest" to charges. Defendant does not dispute facts, although issue may be taken with the legality or constitutionality of the law allegedly violated. Treated as a guilty plea. Also known as "Alford plea" from leading case of *North Carolina v. Alford* (1970).

Nominal dispositions   Juvenile court outcome in which juvenile is warned or verbally reprimanded, but returned to custody of parents.

Nonpartisan elections   Voting process in which candidates who are not endorsed by political parties are presented to the voters for selection.

Nonsecure custody, confinement   A facility that emphasizes the care and treatment of youths without the need to place constraints to ensure public protection.

Nonsuit   A judgment in favor of a defendant because of the failure of the plaintiff to state a case upon which relief can be granted.

Notice   An official document advising someone of a proceeding that usually requires their attendance.

Notice of appeal   Filing a formal document with the court advising the court that the sentence is to be appealed to a higher court or appellate court.

Nullen crimen, nulla poena, sine lege   "There is no crime, there is no punishment, without law."

Objections   Actions by either the prosecutor or defense requesting that certain questions not be asked of witnesses or that certain evidence should or should not be admitted.

Office of Juvenile Justice and Delinquency Prevention (OJJDP)   Established by Congress under the Juvenile Justice and Delinquency Prevention Act of 1974; designed to remove status offenders from jurisdiction of juvenile courts and dispose of their cases less formally.

Once an adult/always an adult   Provision that once a juvenile has been transferred to criminal court to be prosecuted as an adult, regardless of the criminal court outcome, the juvenile can never be subject to the jurisdiction of juvenile courts in the future; in short, the juvenile, once transferred, will always be treated as an adult if future crimes are committed, even though the youth is still not of adult age.

Open court   Any court where spectators may gather.

Opening statement   Remarks made by prosecution and defense attorneys to the jury at the commencement of trial proceedings. Usually these statements set forth what each side intends to show by evidence to be presented.

Operation Greylord   FBI undercover investigation of corruption among judges in Cook County (Chicago), Illinois in 1978; results of investigation disclosed numerous instances of judicial corruption.

Opinion   The official announcement of a court's decision and the reasons for that decision. In research methods, the verbal expression of an attitude.

Opinion of the court Opinion summarizing the views of the majority of judges participating in a judicial decision; a ruling or holding by a court official.

Oral argument Verbal presentation made to an appellate court by the prosecution or the defense in order to persuade the court to affirm, reverse, or modify a lower court decision.

Order Any written declaration or proclamation by a judge authorizing officials to act.

Original jurisdiction First authority over a case or cause, as opposed to appellate jurisdiction.

Overrule To reverse or annul by subsequent action (e.g., judges may overrule objections from prosecutors and defense attorneys in court, nullifying these objections; lower court decisions may be overruled by higher courts when the case is appealed).

Parens patriae "Parent of the country." Refers to doctrine that the state oversees the welfare of youth, originally established by the king of England and administered through chancellors.

Parole board, paroling authority Body of persons either appointed by governors or others or elected, which determines whether those currently incarcerated in prisons should be granted parole or early release.

Parole evidence Oral testimony given in court.

Particularity Requirement that a search warrant must state precisely where the search is to take place and what items are to be seized.

Parties to offenses All people associated with the crime, either before or after it was committed, whether they actually committed the crime or assisted in some way in its planning; may include those who assist criminals in eluding capture.

Partisan election An election in which candidates endorsed by political parties are presented to the voters for selection.

Per curiam "By the court." Phrase used to distinguish an opinion rendered by the whole court as opposed to an opinion expressed by a single judge.

Per diem "By the day." The cost per day, for example, the daily cost of housing inmates.

Per se "By itself." In itself (e.g., the death penalty is not unconstitutional *per se*, but a particular method of administering the death penalty may be unconstitutional in some states).

Percentage bail A publicly managed bail service arrangement that allows defendants to deposit a percentage (about 10 percent) of the amount of bail with the court clerk.

Peremptory challenge Rejection of a juror by either the prosecution or the defense in which no reason needs to be provided for excusing the juror from jury duty. Each side has a limited number of these challenges. The more serious the offense, the more peremptory challenges are given each side.

Perjury Lying under oath in court.

Persistent felony offenders   Habitual offenders who commit felonies with a high recidivism rate.

Persistent offender statutes   Any law prohibiting someone from being a habitual offender or someone who has been convicted of several serious crimes.

Petit jury   The trier of fact in a criminal case. The jury of one's peers called to hear the evidence and decide the defendant's guilt or innocence. Varies in size among states.

Petition   A document filed in juvenile court alleging that a juvenile is a delinquent, a status offender, or a dependent and asking that the court assume jurisdiction over the juvenile or that the juvenile transferred to a criminal court to be prosecuted as an adult.

Petition not sustained   Finding by juvenile court at an adjudicatory hearing that there is insufficient evidence to sustain an allegation that a juvenile is a delinquent, status offender, or dependent.

Petitioner   Person who brings a petition before the court.

Petty offenses   Minor infractions or crimes, misdemeanors. Usually punishable by fines or short terms of imprisonment.

Philadelphia Experiment   Study conducted involving setting bail guidelines in Philadelphia, Pennsylvania during 1981–1982 and the use of release on one's own recognizance (ROR); experiment led to greater equity in bail decision making for persons of different socioeconomic statuses.

Pickpocketing   The theft of money or valuables directly from the garments of the victim.

Plea   Answer to charges by defendant. Pleas vary among jurisdictions. Not guilty, guilty, *nolo contendere*, not guilty by reason of insanity, and guilty but mentally ill are possible pleas.

Plea, guilty   A defendant's formal answer in court to the charges in a complaint, information, or an indictment where the defendant states that the charges are true and that he or she has committed the offense(s) as charged.

Plea, initial   The first plea entered in response to a given charge entered in a court record by or for a defendant.

Plea, not guilty   A defendant's formal answer in court to the charges in a complaint or information or indictment, in which the defendant states that he or she has not committed the offense(s) as charged.

Plea agreement hearing   Meeting presided over by a trial judge to determine the accuracy of a guilty plea and acceptability of general conditions of a plea bargain agreement between the prosecution and defense attorneys.

Plea bargain agreement   Formal agreement between prosecutor and defense counsel wherein the defendant enters a guilty plea to one or more criminal charges in exchange for some form of sentencing leniency.

Plea bargaining   A preconviction deal-making process between the state and the accused in which the defendant exchanges a plea of guilty or *nolo contendere* for a reduction in charges, a promise of sentencing leniency, or some other concession from full, maximum implementation of the conviction and sentencing authority of the court. Includes implicit plea bargaining, charge reduction bargaining, sentence recommendation bargaining, and judicial plea bargaining.

Plea bargains Formal agreements between the prosecutors and defense concerning the defendant offering a guilty plea in exchange for some form of sentencing leniency.

Plea negotiation *See* plea bargaining.

Plea *nolo contendere* *See nolo contendere.*

Plead To respond to a criminal charge.

Polling jurors A direct method of asking each juror to state whether he or she has voted in a particular way.

Polygraph test *See* lie detector.

Postconviction relief Term applied to various mechanisms whereby offenders may challenge their conviction after other appeal attempts have been exhausted.

Postconviction remedies Various means convicted persons have of seeking redress for their incarceration or conviction.

Pound's model Plan of court organization with three tiers: supreme court, major trial court, and minor trial court.

Power of attorney Authority given to another to act in one's place.

Precedent Principle that the way a case was decided previously should serve as a guide for how a similar case currently under consideration ought to be decided.

Pre-conflict stage Perception by individuals or groups that they are involved in a conflict situation where a legal resolution is sought.

Prejudicial error Wrongful procedure that affects the rights of parties substantially and thus may result in the reversal of a case.

Preliminary examination *See* preliminary hearing.

Preliminary hearing, preliminary examination Hearing by magistrate or other judicial officer to determine if person charged with a crime should be held for trial. Proceeding to establish probable cause. Does not determine guilt or innocence.

Preplea conference A discussion in which all parties participate openly to determine ways of bringing about an agreement on a sentence in return for a plea of guilty.

Preponderance of evidence Civil standard whereby the weight of the exculpatory or inculpatory information is in favor of or against the defendant; the greater the weight of information favoring the defendant, the greater the likelihood of a finding in favor of the defendant.

Presentence investigation report, presentence report (PSI) Report filed by probation or parole officer appointed by the court containing background information, socioeconomic data, and demographic data relative to defendant. Facts in the case are included. Used to influence the sentence imposed by the judge and by the parole board considering an inmate for early release.

Presentment   An accusation, initiated by the grand jury on its own authority, from their own knowledge or observation, which functions as an instruction for the preparation of an indictment.

Presiding judge   The title of the judicial officer formally designated for some period as the chief judicial officer of the court.

Presumption of innocence   Premise that a defendant is innocent unless proven guilty beyond a reasonable doubt. Fundamental to the adversary system.

Presumption of validity   In constitutional law, a premise that a statute is valid until it is demonstrated otherwise.

Presumptive sentencing, presumptive sentences   Statutory sentencing method that specifies normal sentences of particular lengths with limited judicial leeway to shorten or lengthen the term of the sentence.

Presumptive waiver   Type of judicial waiver where burden of proof shifts from the state to the juvenile to contest whether youth is transferred to criminal court.

Pretrial conference   A meeting between opposing parties in a lawsuit or criminal trial, for purposes of stipulating things that are agreed upon and thus narrowing the trial to the things that are in dispute, disclosing the required information about witnesses and evidence, making motions, and generally organizing the presentation of motions, witnesses, and evidence.

Pretrial diversion   *See* diversion.

Pretrial motions   *See* motions *in limine.*

Pretrial publicity   Any media attention given to a case before it is tried in court.

***Prima facie* case**   A case for which there is as much evidence as would warrant the conviction of defendants if properly proved in court. A case that meets the evidentiary requirements for a grand jury indictment.

Pro bono   Literally "for the good," in legal terms, legal services provided at no cost to the defendant (e.g., indigent clients receive assistance from defense attorneys on a *pro bono* basis).

Pro forma   According to form or a matter of policy or procedure; following specific rules.

Pro se   Acting as one's own defense attorney in criminal proceedings. Representing oneself.

Probable cause   Reasonable suspicion or belief that a crime has been committed and that a particular person committed it.

Probation officer   Professional who supervises probationers.

Procedural law   Rules that specify how statutes should be applied against those who violate the law. Procedures whereby the substantive laws may be implemented.

Process   A summons requiring the appearance of someone in court.

Process of law   Procedural law.

Project Exile   Local, state, and federal cooperative effort providing for a five-year mandatory extension of one's sentence for using a firearm during the commission of a felony. Deemed a deterrent to the use of firearms in serious crimes, particularly involving convicted violent felons, persons who possess firearms on school property, and those who use both drugs and firearms.

Proof beyond a reasonable doubt   Standard of proof to convict in criminal case.

Property bond   Setting bail in the form of land, houses, stocks, or other tangible property. In the event the defendant absconds prior to trial, the bond becomes the property of the court.

Prosecuting attorney   *See* prosecutor.

Prosecution   Carrying forth of criminal proceedings against a person, culminating in a trial or other final disposition such as a plea of guilty in lieu of trial.

Prosecution agency, prosecutorial agency   Any local, state, or federal body charged with carrying forth actions against criminals. State legal representatives, such as district attorneys or U.S. attorneys and their assistants, who seek to convict persons charged with crimes.

Prosecutor   Court official who commences civil and criminal proceedings against defendants. Represents state or government interest, prosecuting defendants on behalf of state or government.

Prosecutorial bluffing   Attempt by prosecution to bluff the defendant into believing the case is much stronger than it really is. Used to elicit a guilty plea from a defendant to avoid a lengthy trial where the proof of a defendant's guilt may be difficult to establish.

Prosecutorial discretion   The decision-making power of prosecutors based upon the wide range of choices available to them in the handling of criminal defendants, the scheduling of cases for trial, and the acceptance of bargained pleas. The most important form of prosecutorial discretion lies in the power to charge or not to charge a person with an offense.

Prosecutorial information   A criminal charge against someone filed by the prosecutor.

Prosecutorial misconduct   Any deliberate action that violates ethical codes or standards governing the role of prosecutors; usually the action is intended to injure defendants and illegally or unethically strengthen the case of prosecutors.

Prosecutorial waiver   Authority of prosecutors in juvenile cases to have those cases transferred to the jurisdiction of criminal court.

Proximate cause   The factor that is closest to actually causing an event, such as the death of a victim.

Public defender agency   Any local, state, or federal organization, public or private, established to provide a defense to indigent clients or those who otherwise cannot afford to pay for their own defense against criminal charges. Because everyone is entitled to counsel, whether or not counsel can be afforded, such services exist to meet the needs of those without funds to hire their own private counsel.

Public defender system   Means whereby attorneys are appointed by the court to represent indigent defendants.

Punishment   Any sanction imposed for committing a crime; usually a sentence imposed for being convicted of either a felony or misdemeanor.

Quash   To vacate a sentence or annul a motion.

Real evidence   Physical evidence such as a weapon, records, fingerprints, or stolen property.

Reasonable doubt   Standard used by jurors to decide if the prosecution has provided sufficient evidence for conviction. Jurors vote for acquittal if they have reasonable doubt that the accused committed the crime.

Reasonable suspicion   Warranted suspicion (short of probable cause) that a person may be engaged in criminal conduct.

Rebutting testimony, evidence   Any questioning or presentation of evidence designed to offset, outweigh, or overwhelm evidence presented by the other side or question the veracity or truthfulness of witnesses.

Recall election   Special election called to remove a politician or judge from his/her office.

Recognizance   Personal responsibility to return to court on a given date and at a given time.

Re-cross-examination   Opposing counsel further examines an opposing witness who has already testified.

Recusal   Act of judges excusing themselves from proceedings, especially where they have an apparent conflict of interest in the case being tried.

Re-direct examination   Questioning of a witness following the adversary's questioning under cross-examination.

Referral   Any citation of a juvenile to juvenile court by a law enforcement officer, interested citizen, family member, or school official; usually based upon law violations, delinquency, or unruly conduct.

Reformatory   Detention facility designed to change criminal behavior or reform it.

Refreshing one's memory, reminding   During testimony, witnesses may have their memories refreshed by rereading some document or looking at pictures to enable them to recall with greater clarity something that happened some time ago.

Rehabilitation, rehabilitative ideal   Correcting criminal behavior through educational and other means, usually associated with prisons.

Reintegration   Punishment philosophy that promotes programs that lead offenders back into their communities. Reintegrative programs include furloughs, work release, and halfway houses.

Release on own recognizance (ROR)   Arrangement where a defendant is able to be set free temporarily to await a later trial without having to post a bail bond; persons released on ROR are usually well known or have strong ties to the community and have not been charged with serious crimes.

Remand   To send back (e.g., the U.S. Supreme Court may remand a case back to the lower trial court where the case was originally tried).

Remedy Any declared solution to a dispute between parties (e.g., if someone is found guilty of slashing another's automobile tires, the remedy may be to cause the convicted offender to compensate the victim with money for the full value of the destroyed tires).

Reparations Damages assigned to be paid by a defendant found liable in a civil action; may include restitution to victims; usually follows trial showing liability or culpability of defendant in lawsuit filed by plaintiff who is seeking damages.

Res judicata "Things judged." Refers to matters already decided in court, not subject to relitigation.

Respondeat superior Doctrine under which liability is imposed upon an employer for the acts of his employees that are committed in the course and scope of their employment.

Respondent A person asked to respond in a lawsuit or writ.

Responsible Legally accountable for one's actions and obligations.

Restitution Stipulation by the court that offenders must compensate victims for their financial losses resulting from crime. Compensation to the victim for psychological, physical, or financial loss. May be imposed as a part of an incarcerative sentence.

Restorative justice Mediation between victims and offenders whereby offenders accept responsibility for their actions and agree to reimburse victims for their losses; may involve community service and other penalties agreeable to both parties in a form of arbitration with a neutral third party acting as arbiter.

Reverse waiver hearing Formal proceeding, usually conducted by a criminal court judge, to determine whether a transferred juvenile should be sent back to be tried for his/her crimes in juvenile court rather than criminal court.

Reversed and remanded Decision by the appellate court to set aside or overturn the verdict of a lower trial court with instructions to the trial court to rehear the case with suggested modifications.

Reversible errors Mistakes committed by judges during a trial that may result in reversal of convictions against defendants.

Review The procedure whereby a higher court examines one or more issues emanating from a lower court on an appeal by the prosecution or defense.

Right of allocution Right of a defendant to speak before the sentence is pronounced.

Rights of defendant Constitutional guarantees to all persons charged with crimes. Includes representation by counsel at various critical stages, such as being charged with crimes, preliminary hearings, arraignments, trial, and appeals.

Right to counsel Right to be represented by an attorney at critical stages of the criminal justice system. Indigent defendants have the right to counsel provided by the state.

ROR *See* release on own recognizance.

Rule of Four   U.S. Supreme Court rule whereby the Court grants *certiorari* only on the agreement of at least four justices.

Rule of law   Describes willingness of persons to accept and order their behavior according to rules and procedures that are prescribed by political and social institutions.

Rules of Civil Procedure   Rules governing civil cases where compensatory damages are sought. Rules governing courts of equity.

Rules of Criminal Procedure   Rules legislatively established by which a criminal case is conducted. Law enforcement officers, prosecutors, and judges use rules of criminal procedure in discretionary actions against suspects and defendants.

Runaways   Juveniles who abscond from their homes or residences without parental permission; often these youths seek a free life in another city away from parental control; a type of status offender.

Scientific jury selection   Applying the scientific method to select jurors who it is believed will render favorable decisions for or against defendants.

Screening   Process of jury selection by attempting to remove biased jurors and select only the most competent and objective ones.

Screening cases   Procedure used by prosecutor to define which cases have prosecutive merit and which ones do not. Some screening bureaus are made up of police and lawyers with trial experience.

Seal   To close from public inspection any record of an arrest, judgment, or adjudication, either criminal or juvenile.

Secure custody, confinement   Incarceration of juvenile offender in a facility that restricts movement in the community. Similar to an adult penal facility involving total incarceration.

Selective chivalry   View that judges tend to favor white females in their sentencing decisions compared with females of other races or ethnicities or males.

Self-defense   Affirmative defense in which defendants explain otherwise criminal conduct by showing necessity to defend themselves against aggressive victims.

Self-incrimination   The act of exposing oneself to prosecution by answering questions that may demonstrate involvement in illegal behavior. Coerced self-incrimination is not allowed under the Fifth Amendment. In any criminal proceeding, the prosecution must prove the charges by means of evidence other than the testimony of the accused.

Self-representation   *See pro se.*

Sentence   Penalty imposed upon a convicted person for a crime. May include incarceration, fine, both, or some other alternative. *See also* mandatory sentencing, presumptive sentencing, indeterminate sentencing, determinate sentencing.

Sentence bargaining   Any negotiation between prosecutors and defense attorneys for the prosecutor's recommendation of a reduced sentence in exchange for a guilty plea to a lesser charge from a defendant.

Sentence disparity   *See* sentencing disparity.

Sentence hearing *See* sentencing hearing.

Sentence recommendation bargaining Negotiation in which the prosecutor proposes a sentence in exchange for a guilty plea. *See also* plea bargaining.

Sentencing Process of imposing a punishment on a convicted person following a criminal conviction.

Sentencing disparity Inconsistency in sentencing of convicted offenders, in which those committing similar crimes under similar circumstances are given widely disparate sentences by the same judge. Usually based on gender, race, ethnic, or socioeconomic factors.

Sentencing guidelines Instruments developed by the federal government and various states to assist judges in assessing fair and consistent lengths of incarceration for various crimes and past criminal histories. Referred to as presumptive sentencing in some jurisdictions.

Sentencing hearing Optional hearing held in many jurisdictions in which defendants and victims can hear contents of presentence investigation reports prepared by probation officers. Defendants and/or victims may respond to the report orally, in writing, or both. This hearing precedes the sentence imposed by the judge.

Sentencing memorandum Court decision that furnishes ruling or finding and orders to be implemented relative to convicted offenders. Does not necessarily include reasons or rationale for the sentence imposed.

Sentencing Reform Act of 1984 Act that provided federal judges and others with considerable discretionary powers to provide alternative sentencing and other provisions in their sentencing of various offenders.

Sequester, sequestration The insulation of jurors from the outside world so that their decision making cannot be influenced or affected by extralegal factors.

Sequestered jury A jury that is isolated from the public during the course of a trial and throughout the deliberation process.

Serious felonies Any crime punishable by more than a year in prison or jail that causes substantial property loss or fraud; may include some crimes against persons, such as robbery.

Service of process The act of serving a summons on someone notifying them to be in court at a particular time.

Severance Separation of related cases so that they can be tried separately in different courts.

Sexual predator laws Somewhat ambiguous laws enacted in various states to identify and control previously convicted sex offenders; may include listing such persons in public announcements or bulletins, or some other form of community notification.

Shadow juries Persons who resemble actual jurors and are used by both prosecutors and defense counsels to test their ideas prior to trials; shadow juries emulate actual jurors in criminal cases in terms of their background characteristics and attitudes.

Shock incarceration   *See* shock probation.

Shock parole   *See* shock probation.

Shock probation   Sentencing offenders to prison or jail for a brief period, primarily to give them a taste or "shock" of prison or jail life, and then releasing them into the custody of a probation or parole officer through a resentencing project.

Sides   Opposing parties in an adversarial relation, usually in the courtroom; prosecutors and defense counsel are considered "sides" in the adversarial system of U.S. justice.

Social change   Process whereby ideas and/or practices are modified either actively or passively or naturally.

Social control   Informal and formal methods of getting members of society to conform to norms, folkways, and mores.

Society for the Prevention of Pauperism   Philanthropic society that established first public reformatory in New York in 1825, the New York House of Refuge.

Sociological jurisprudence   View that holds that part of law should be devoted to making or shaping public policy and social rules.

Solitary confinement   *See* isolation.

Speedy trial   Defined by federal law and applicable to federal district courts, where a defendant must be tried within 100 days of an arrest. Every state has speedy trial provisions that are within reasonable ranges of the federal standard. Originally designed to comply with the Sixth Amendment of the U.S. Constitution. The longest state speedy trial provision is in New Mexico, which is 180 days.

Speedy Trial Act of 1974 (amended 1979, 1984)   Compliance with Sixth Amendment provision for a citizen to be brought to trial without undue delay 30 to 70 days from date of formal specification of charges, usually in arraignment proceeding.

Spirit of the law   Efforts by police officers to exhibit leniency where law violations are observed. Usually first-offenders may receive leniency because of extenuating circumstances.

Split sentencing   Procedure whereby a judge imposes a sentence of incarceration for a fixed period, followed by a probationary period of a fixed duration. Similar to shock probation.

Spontaneous declaration   An excited utterance, such as confessing to a crime during emotional stress at the crime scene.

Standard of proof   Norms used by courts to determine validity of claims or allegations of wrongdoing against offenders; civil standards of proof are "clear and convincing evidence" and "preponderance of evidence," while criminal standard is "beyond a reasonable doubt."

Standing   A doctrine mandating that courts may not recognize a party to a suit unless that person has a personal stake or direct interest in the outcome of the suit.

Stare decisis   Legal precedent. Principle whereby lower courts issue rulings consistent with those of higher courts, where the same types of cases and facts are at issue. The principle of leaving undisturbed a settled point of law or particular precedent.

State bar associations   Professional organizations of lawyers bound to observe the laws of the various states where they reside; state affiliate organizations in relation to national American Bar Association.

State's attorneys   Government prosecutors.

Status offenders   Juveniles who have committed an offense that would not be considered a crime if committed by an adult (e.g., a curfew violation would not be criminal action if committed by an adult, but such an act is a status offense if engaged in by a juvenile).

Status offense   Any act committed by a juvenile that would not be a crime if committed by an adult.

Statute of limitations   Period of time after which a crime that has been committed cannot be prosecuted. No statute of limitations exists for capital crimes.

Statutes   Laws passed by legislatures. Statutory definitions of criminal offenses are embodied in penal codes.

Statutory exclusion   Provisions that automatically exclude certain juveniles and offenses from the jurisdiction of the juvenile courts; for example, murder, aggravated rape, armed robbery.

Statutory law   Authority based on enactments of state legislatures. Laws passed by legislatures.

Stigmas   The result of the process of being labeled as a delinquent or unruly child by others.

Stigmatization   Social process whereby offenders acquire undesirable characteristics as the result of imprisonment or court appearances. Undesirable criminal or delinquent labels are assigned to those who are processed through the criminal and juvenile justice systems.

Stigmatize   The process of labeling someone as a delinquent or a criminal on the basis of their exhibited behavior.

Strike for cause   *See* challenge for cause.

Subject matter jurisdiction   Term applied when certain judges have exclusive jurisdiction over particular crimes.

Subornation of perjury   The crime of procuring someone to lie under oath.

Subpoena   Document issued by a judge ordering a named person to appear in court at a particular time to either answer to charges or to testify in a case.

Substantive criminal law   Legislated rule that governs behaviors that are required or prohibited. Usually enacted by legislatures. Such law also specifies punishments accompanying such law violations.

Substantive due process   Refers to the practice of having substantive law conform to the principles of fairness set forth in the U.S. Constitution.

Substantive law   Body of law that creates, discovers, and defines the rights and obligations of each person in society. Prescribes behavior, whereas procedural law prescribes how harmful behavior is handled.

Summary judgment   Any granted motion following the presentation of a case against a defendant in a civil court. Any argument countering the plaintiff's presented evidence. Usually the result of failing to state a claim upon which relief can be granted.

Summary justice   Trial held by a court of limited jurisdiction, without benefit of a jury trial.

Summation   Conclusionary remarks made by the prosecutor and defense counsel at the end of a trial before the jury.

Summons   Same form as a warrant, except it commands a defendant to appear before the magistrate at a particular time and place.

Superior courts   The courts of record or trial courts.

Supreme Court   The federal court of last resort as specified by the U.S. Constitution; at the state level, any court of last resort in most kinds of cases.

Suppression hearing   Session held before a judge who presides at one's trial. Purpose of the session is to determine which evidentiary documents and/or statements will be permitted later at trial. Motions are heard from both the defense and prosecution to keep out or put in particular evidence, and the judge decides which evidence can and cannot be introduced at trial.

Supra   "Above." In U.S. Supreme Court written opinions, references are made to earlier statements (e.g., in the case of *Doe, supra,* the matter was concluded in a particular way).

Surety bond   A sum of money or property that is posted or guaranteed by a party to ensure the future court appearance of another person. *See also* bail bond.

Surrebuttal   Introducing witnesses during a criminal trial in order to disprove damaging testimony by other witnesses.

Sustain   To uphold (e.g., the conviction was sustained by a higher appellate court).

Sustained petitions   Adjudication resulting in a finding that the facts alleged in a petition are true; a finding that the juvenile committed the offenses alleged, which resulted in an adjudication and disposition.

Sworn in   The process whereby persons who offer testimony in court swear to tell the truth and nothing but the truth, usually by oath upon the Bible.

Teen court   Proceeding conducted by youths who try other youths for nonserious misdemeanors such as shoplifting or mischief; punishments are nonincarcerative and usually involve restitution of some form of victim compensation of community service; an adult supervises the proceeding and the decisions by youths and juries of youths are valid and enforceable.

Texas model   Also known as the "traditional" model of state court organization. Two "supreme" courts, one for civil appeals, one for criminal appeals. Has five tiers of district, county, and municipal courts.

Three-strikes-and-you're-out   Legislation designed to prevent offenders from becoming recidivists; provides that persons who commit three or more serious felonies are in jeopardy of being incarcerated for life terms.

Three-strikes-and-you're-out policies   A crime prevention and control strategy that proposes to incarcerate those offenders who commit and are convicted of three or more serious or violent offenses; usual penalty is life imprisonment or the life-without-parole option. Intent is to incarcerate high-rate offenders to reduce crime in society. *See also* habitual offender statutes.

Tiers   Different floor levels in prisons and jails where inmates are housed; usually, different tiers house different types of offenders according to their conviction offenses and offense seriousness.

Tort actions   Any legal proceeding where a plaintiff is seeking damages from a defendant for a civil wrong.

Tort reform   Any action taken by an individual or group to revise existing rules governing tort actions in courts, including limiting monetary awards for prevailing in lawsuits.

Torts   Private or civil wrongs or injuries, other than breach of contract, for which the court will provide a remedy in the form of an action for damages. A violation of a duty imposed by law. Existence of a legal duty to plaintiff, breach of that duty, and damage as a result of that breach.

Totality of circumstances   Exception to exclusionary rule, whereby officers may make warrantless searches of property and seizures of illegal contraband on the basis of the entire set of suspicious circumstances; sometimes applied to bail decision making, where the entire set of circumstances is considered for persons considered bail-eligible.

Traditional courts   Juvenile proceedings characterized by individualized treatments and proscriptions for assistance; the opposite of due process courts.

Transcript   A written record of a trial or hearing.

Transfer   Proceeding to determine whether juveniles should be certified as adults for purposes of being subjected to jurisdiction of adult criminal courts where more severe penalties may be imposed. Also known as "certification" or "waiver."

Transfers   Proceedings where the jurisdiction over juvenile offenders shifts from the juvenile court to criminal court.

Trial   An adversarial proceeding within a particular jurisdiction, in which a judicial examination and determination of issues can be made, and in which a criminal defendant's guilt or innocence can be decided impartially by either a judge or jury. *See also* bench trial, jury trial.

Trial by the court   *See* bench trial.

Trial by the judge   *See* bench trial.

Trial court   Court where guilt or innocence of defendant is established; may be criminal or civil, depending on the nature of the charge; criminal courts try defendants charged with crimes; civil courts seek to resolve disputes between plaintiffs, who seek damages, against named defendants who claim they should not be held liable.

Trial court of general jurisdiction   Criminal court that has jurisdiction over all offenses, including felonies, and may in some states also hear appeals from lower courts.

Trial court of limited jurisdiction   Criminal court where trial jurisdiction either includes no felonies or is limited to some category of felony. Such courts have jurisdiction over misdemeanor cases, probable-cause hearings in felony cases, and sometimes, felony trials that may result in penalties below a specific limit.

Trial delays   Any one of several legitimate reasons that may contribute to delaying or prolonging the occasion that a trial commences; may be due to crowded court dockets; requests from the defense or prosecution for more time in case preparation; or the health of different courtroom actors, such as the prosecutor, defense counsel, or defendant.

Trial *de novo*   A new judicial hearing or proceeding. A new adversarial proceeding occurring as though there had never been a first trial or proceeding, usually granted to defendants where egregious wrongs or misconduct occurred to nullify former adjudicatory proceedings.

Trial judge   *See* judge.

Trial jury   *See* petit jury.

Trial sufficiency   Presence of sufficient legal elements to ensure successful prosecution of a case. When prosecutor's decision to prosecute a case is customarily based on trial sufficiency, only cases that seem certain to result in conviction at trial are accepted for prosecution. Use of plea bargaining is minimal. Good police work and court capacity are required.

Tribunal   A court. A place where judges sit. A judicial weighing of information leading to a decision about a case.

Truants   Juveniles who absent themselves from school during school hours and without excuse of parental or school consent; a type of status offender.

True bill   Grand jury decision that sufficient evidence exists that a crime has been committed and that a specific suspect committed it. A charge of an alleged crime. An indictment.

Truth in sentencing   Policy of imposing a sentence, most of which must be served in prison or jail; maximizing one's incarceration under the law.

Truth-in-sentencing laws   Any legislation intended to maximize one's sentence and time served for committing a crime; intent is to compel offenders to serve at least 80 or 90 percent of their maximum sentences before they become eligible for parole or early release.

Typicality hypothesis   View that judges give women greater consideration than men during sentencing, but only when their criminal charges are consistent with stereotypes of female offenders.

Ultra vires   Beyond the scope of one's prescribed authority.

United States attorneys Officials responsible for the prosecution of crimes that violate the laws of the United States. Appointed by the president and assigned to a U.S. district court jurisdiction.

United States Attorney's Office Chief prosecuting body affiliated with each U.S. district court in the federal court system.

United States Circuit Courts of Appeal Appellate courts from which U.S. district court decisions are appealed; cases appealed from the U.S. Circuit Courts of Appeal are appealed directly to the U.S. Supreme Court; there are 13 circuit courts of appeal.

United States Code, United States Code Annotated Comprehensive compendium of federal laws and statutes, including landmark cases and discussions of law applications. Annotated version contains paragraphs of contemporary cases summarizing court decisions applying specific statutes.

United States Courts of Appeal The federal circuit courts of appellate jurisdiction. As of 1996, there were 13 circuit courts of appeal zoned throughout the United States and its territories.

United States District Courts The basic trial courts for federal civil and criminal actions.

United States magistrates Judges who fulfill the pretrial judicial obligations of the federal courts. Formerly, United States commissioners.

U.S. Sentencing Commission Body of persons originating from Sentencing Reform Act of 1984 and promulgated sentencing guidelines for all federal crimes.

U.S. sentencing guidelines Rules implemented by federal courts in November 1987 obligating federal judges to impose presumptive sentences on all convicted offenders. Guidelines are based upon offense seriousness and offender characteristics. Judges may depart from guidelines only by justifying their departures in writing.

U.S. Supreme Court Court of last resort; final and highest court that decides particular issues, usually issues with constitutional significance.

Vacate To annul, set aside, or rescind.

Vacated sentence Any sentence that has been declared nullified by action of a court.

***Venire*, veniremen list, veniremen** List of prospective jurors made up from registered voters, vehicle driver's licenses, tax assessors' records. Persons must reside within the particular jurisdiction where the jury trial is held. Persons who are potential jurors in a given jurisdiction.

Venue Area over which a judge exercises authority to act in an official capacity. Place where a trial is held.

Venue, change of Relocation of a trial from one site to another, usually because of some pretrial publicity making it possible that a jury might be biased and that a fair trial will be difficult to obtain.

Verdict Decision by judge or jury concerning the guilt or innocence of a defendant.

Verdict-driven jury   Jury that decides guilt or innocence first without considering adequately the relevant evidence in the case; jurors are polled initially to see to what extent they agree or disagree among themselves; if most or all of the jurors vote the same way, then they conclude their deliberations without further consideration of the evidence.

Verdict, guilty   In criminal proceedings, the decision made by a jury in a jury trial, or by a judicial officer in a bench trial, that defendants are guilty of the offense(s) for which they have been tried.

Verdict, not guilty   In criminal proceedings, the decision made by a jury in a jury trial, or by the judge in a bench trial, that defendants are not guilty of the offense(s) for which they have been tried.

Verstehen   Understanding. The notion that social scientists can understand human behavior through empathy.

Vicarious liability   Doctrine under which liability is imposed upon an employer for the acts of employees that are committed in the course and scope of their employment.

Vice principal doctrine   Theory holding that someone may be sued by another if he/she is a supervisor or boss, and not necessarily the owner of an organization.

Victim   Person who has either suffered death or serious physical or mental suffering, or loss of property resulting from actual or attempted criminal actions committed by others.

Victim compensation   Any financial restitution payable to victims by either the state or convicted offenders.

Victim compensation programs   Any plans for assisting crime victims in making social, emotional, and economic adjustments.

Victim impact statement   Information or version of events filed voluntarily by the victim of a crime, appended to the presentence investigation report as a supplement for judicial consideration in sentencing the offender. Describes injuries to victims resulting from convicted offender's actions.

Victim–offender mediation model   Meeting between criminal and person suffering loss or injury from criminal whereby third-party arbiter, such as a judge, attorney, or other neutral party decides what is best for all parties. All parties must agree to decision of third-party arbiter. Used for both juvenile and adult offenders.

Victim–offender reconciliation   Any agreement between the victim and the perpetrator concerning a satisfactory arrangement for compensation for injuries or financial losses sustained.

Victim–Offender Reconciliation Project (VORP)   Form of alternative dispute resolution, whereby a civil resolution is made by mutual consent between the victim and an offender; objectives are to provide restitution to victims, hold offender accountable for crime committed, and to reduce recidivism.

Victim/reparations model   Restitution model for juveniles in which juveniles compensate their victims directly for their offenses.

Victim-witness assistance programs   Plans available to prospective witnesses to explain court procedures and inform them of court dates, and to assist witnesses in providing better testimony in court.

Victims of Crime Act of 1984   Also known as the Comprehensive Crime Control Act of 1984, includes sanctions against offenders such as victim compensation, community service, and/or restitution.

Violent felonies   Any crime that is punishable by more than one year in a prison or jail and causes serious bodily injury or death (e.g., rape, aggravated assault, murder, armed robbery).

Virginia Exile   Program that targets three types of crimes: (1) possession of a firearm by a convicted felon; (2) possession of a firearm on school property with the intent to use it, or displaying it in a threatening manner; and (3) possession of a firearm and drugs such as cocaine or heroin.

Virginia Plan   Scheme deriving from England's royal court system, projecting superior and inferior courts; also called "Randolph Plan."

Voir dire   "To speak the truth." Interrogation process whereby prospective jurors are questioned by either the judge or by the prosecution or defense attorneys to determine their biases and prejudices.

Voluntariness   Willingness of defendant to enter a plea or make an agreement in a plea bargain proceeding. Judges must determine the voluntariness of the plea to determine that it was not coerced.

Waiver, waiver of jurisdiction   Made by motion, the transfer of jurisdiction over a juvenile to a criminal court where the juvenile is subject to adult criminal penalties. Includes judicial, prosecutorial, and legislative waivers. Also known as "certification" or "transfer."

Waiver hearing   Motion by prosecutor to transfer juvenile charged with various offenses to a criminal or adult court for prosecution, making it possible to sustain adult criminal penalties.

Warrant   A written order directing a suspect's arrest and issued by an official with the authority to issue the warrant. Commands suspect to be arrested and brought before the nearest magistrate.

Warrant, arrest   Document issued by a judge that directs a law enforcement officer to arrest a person who has been accused of an offense.

Warrant, bench   Document issued by a judge directing that a person who has failed to obey an order or notice to appear be brought before the court without undue delay.

Warrant, search   Any document issued by a judicial official, based upon probable cause, directing law enforcement officers to conduct an inspection of an individual, automobile, or building with the intent of locating particular contraband or incriminating evidence as set forth in the document.

With prejudice   To dismiss charges, but those same charges cannot be brought again later against the same defendant.

Without prejudice   To dismiss charges, but those same charges can be brought again later against the same defendant.

Without undue delay or unnecessary delay   Standard used to determine whether suspect has been brought in a timely manner before a magistrate or other judicial authority after arrested. Definition of undue delay varies among jurisdictions. Circumstances of arrest, availability of judge, and time of arrest are factors that determine reasonableness of delay.

Witnesses   Persons who have relevant information about the commission of a crime; any person who has seen or heard inculpatory or exculpatory evidence that may incriminate or exonerate a defendant.

Writ   A document issued by a judicial officer ordering or forbidding the performance of a specific act.

Writ of *certiorari*   An order of a superior court requesting that the record of an inferior court (or administrative body) be brought forward for review or inspection. Literally, "to be more fully informed."

Writ of error   A writ issued by an appellate court for the purpose of correcting an error revealed in the record of a lower court proceeding.

Writ of *habeas corpus*   See *habeas corpus.*

Writ of *mandamus*   An order of a superior court commanding that a lower court, administrative body, or executive body perform a specific function. Commonly used to restore rights and privileges lost to a defendant through illegal means.

Writ of prohibition   An appellate court order that prevents a lower court from exercising its jurisdiction in a particular case.

Wrongful convictions   Adjudications of guilt by either a judge or jury and where the convicted offender is actually innocent of the charges alleged.

References

Aas, K. F. (2004). "Sentencing Transparency in the Information Age." *Journal of Scandinavian Studies in Criminology and Crime Prevention* 5:48–61.

Abel, Richard (1990). "A Critique of Torts." *UCLA Law Review* 37: 785–831.

Adler, Stephen J. (1995). *The Jury: Disorder in the Court.* New York: Doubleday.

Abrams, Stan (1995). "False Memory Syndrome vs. Total Repression." *Journal of Psychiatry and Law* 23:283–293.

Ajzenstadt, Mimi, and Odeda Steinberg (2001). "Never Mind the Law: Legal Discourse and Rape Reform in Israel." *Affilia* 16:337–259.

Albonetti, Celesta A., and Chana Barron (2004). "On the Way to Settled Law: An Examination of Law Making and Law Finding in Federal Appellate Decisions." Unpublished paper presented at the annual meeting of the American Society of Criminology, November (Nashville, TN).

Alfini, James J. (1981). "Mississippi Judicial Selection: Election, Appointment, and Bar Anointment." In *Courts and Judges*, James A. Cramer (ed.). Beverly Hills, CA: Sage.

Alexander, R. (2004). "The United States Supreme Court and the Civil Commitment of Sex Offenders." *The Prison Journal* 84:33–54.

Ambos, Kai (2003). "International Criminal Procedure: 'Adversarial,' 'Inquisitorial,' or Mixed?" *International Criminal Law Review* 3:1–27.

Anchorage Youth Court (2005). "Youth Courts Strive for Sustainability." *Gavel* 16:1–4.

APPA Perspectives (2004a). "APPA Resolves Support for Youth Courts." *APPA Perspectives* 28:8.

APPA Perspectives (2004b). "Project Safe Neighborhoods: Incorporating and Training Probation and Parole Professionals to Reduce Gun Crime." *APPA Perspectives* 28:9.

Arpey, Andrew W. (2003). *The William Freeman Murder Trial: Insanity, Politics and Race.* Syracuse, NY: Syracuse University Press.

Arrigo, Bruce A., and Mark C. Bardwell (2000). "Law, Psychology, and Competency to Stand Trial: Problems with and Implications for High-Profile Cases." *Criminal Justice Policy Review* 11:16–43.

Asch, Solomon E. (1966). "Effect of Group Pressure Upon the Modification and Distortion of Judgments." *Group Dynamics* 14:189–199.

Associated Press (1998). "Judge Who Drank after Trial Quits." *Minot (N.D.) Daily News*, April 8, 1998:A2.

Associated Press (2005). "Location of Body Key to Case, Peterson's Attorney Says." *Contra Costa Times*, June 5, 2005.

Atherton, Matthew (2004). "Study of Hispanic Outcomes in U.S. Federal Courts." Unpublished paper presented at the annual meeting of the American Society of Criminology meeting, November (Nashville, TN).

Atkins, Holly (2005). "Evaluation of a Large Urban Drug Court." Unpublished paper presented at the annual meeting of the Academy of Criminal Justice Sciences, March (Chicago).

Auerhahn, Kathleen (2004). "Homicide Sentencing and the Behavior of Law." Unpublished paper presented at the annual meeting of the American Society of Criminology, November (Nashville, TN).

Austin, James et al. (1995). *National Assessment of Structured Sentencing.* Washington, DC: U.S. Bureau of Justice Statistics.

Ball, Jeremy D. (2005). "Does Race Matter? Assessing Racial and Ethnic Bias." Unpublished paper presented at the annual meeting of the Academy of Criminal Justice Sciences, March (Chicago).

Barrile, Leo G., and Neal Slone (2005). "Punishing Environmental Criminals: Extra Legal Factors and the Sentencing Guidelines." Unpublished paper presented at the annual meeting of the Academy of Criminal Justice Sciences, March (Chicago).

Beechen, Paul D. (1974). "Can Judicial Elections Express the People's Choice?" *Judicature* **57**:242–256.

Beger, Randall R. (2003). "The Worst of Both Worlds: School Security and the Disappearing Fourth Amendment Rights of Students." *Criminal Justice Review* **28**:336–354.

Belbot, Barbara et al. (2004). "Legal Issues in Corrections." *Prison Journal* **84**:287–410.

Bell, Bernard P. (1983). "Closure of Pretrial Suppression Hearings: Resolving the Fair Trial/Free Press Conflict." *Fordham Law Review* **51**:1297–1316.

Bensinger, Gad J. (1988). "Operation Greylord and Its Aftermath." *International Journal of Comparative and Applied Criminal Justice* **12**:111–118.

Birzer, M. L., and R. Tannehill (2003). "Criminal Justice Practitioners' Perceptions of Themselves, Each Other, and Selected Criminal Justice Practices." *Journal of Crime and Justice* **26**:77–100.

Bishop, Donna M. et al. (2004). "Prosecutorial Charging Decisions in Transfer Cases." Unpublished paper presented at the annual meeting of the American Society of Criminology, November (Nashville, TN).

Black, Henry Campbell (1990). *Black's Law Dictionary.* St. Paul, MN: West Publishing Company.

Blackmore, John, Marci Brown, and Barry Krisberg (1988). *Juvenile Justice Reform: The Bellwether States.* Ann Arbor, MI: University of Michigan.

Blackwell, Kevin R. (2004). "Is There a Penalty for Going to Trial in Federal Court?" Unpublished paper presented at the annual meeting of the American Society of Criminology, November (Nashville, TN).

Blankenship, Michael B., Jerry B. Sparger, and W. Richard Janikowski (1994). "Accountability v. Independence: Myths of Judicial Selection." *Criminal Justice Policy Review* **6**:69–79.

Blue Earth County (2005). *Blue Earth County Teen Court.* Mankato, MN: Blue Earth County Teen Court.

Boari, Nicola, and Gianluca Fiorentini (2001). "An Economic Analysis of Plea Bargaining: The Incentives of the Parties in a Mixed Penal System." *International Review of Law and Economics* **21**:213–231.

Boller, Kelley G. (2005). "Wrongful Convictions: Theoretical Explanations for the Differing Perceptions of Criminal Justice Actors." Unpublished paper presented at the annual meeting of the Academy of Criminal Justice Sciences, March (Chicago).

Booth, Tracey (2004). "Homicide, Family Victims and Sentencing: Continuing the Debate about Victim Impact Statements." *Current Issues in Criminal Justice* **15**:253–257.

Boyle, Robert, Donna R. Newman, and Sam A. Schmidt (2003). "Center for Professional Values and Practice Symposium: Criminal Defense in the Age of Terrorism." *New York Law School Law Review* **48**:3–384.

Bradfield, A., and D. E. McQuiston (2004). "When Does Evidence of Eyewitness Confidence Inflation Affect Judgments in a Criminal Trial?" *Law and Human Behavior* **28**:369–387.

Braithwaite, John (2002). *Restorative Justice and Responsive Regulation*. Oxford, UK: Oxford University Press.

Breckenridge, S. P. (1906). "Legislative Control of Women's Work." *Journal of Political Economy* **15**:115–120.

Brocke, Michaela et al. (2004). "Attitudes Toward the Severity of Punishment: A Conjoint Analytic Approach." *Psychology, Crime and the Law* **10**:205–219.

Bullock, Jennifer Leslie (2002). "Involuntary Treatment of Defendants Found Incompetent to Stand Trial." *Journal of Forensic Psychology Practice* **2**:1–34.

Bureau of Justice Statistics (2005). *Annual Reports*. Washington, DC: U.S. Department of Justice, Bureau of Justice Statistics.

Burger, Warren (1982). "Isn't There a Better Way?" *American Bar Association Journal* **68**:274–275.

Burnett, Cathleen (2005). "Restorative Justice and Wrongful Capital Convictions." *Journal of Contemporary Criminal Justice* **21**:272–289.

Burrow, John D. (2004). "The Death of Innocence: Factual and Procedural Errors That Result in Wrongful Convictions." Unpublished paper presented at the annual meeting of the American Society of Criminology, November (Nashville, TN).

Burruss, George W., and Kimberly Kempf-Leonard (2002). "The Questionable Advantage of Defense Counsel in Juvenile Court." *Justice Quarterly* **19**:37–67.

Carey, Bryan A. (2001). "Should American Courts Listen to What Foreign Courts Hear? The Confrontation and Hearsay Problems of Prior Testimony Taken Abroad in Criminal Proceedings." *American Journal of Criminal Law* **29**:29–58.

Carr, Patrick J., Kim A. Logio, and Shana Maier (2003). "Keep Me Informed: What Matters for Victims as They Navigate the Juvenile Criminal Justice System in Philadelphia." *International Review of Victimology* **10**:117–136.

Carrington, Peter J., and Jennifer L. Schulenberg (eds.) (2004). "The Youth Criminal Justice Act." *Canadian Journal of Criminology and Criminal Justice* **46**: 219–389.

Carter, Linda E. (2001). "The Sporting Approach to Harmless Error in Criminal Cases: The Supreme Court's 'No Harm, No Foul' Debacle in *Neder v. United States*. " *American Journal of Criminal Law* **28**:229–246.

Ceci, Stephen J., and Maggie Bruck (1995). *Jeopardy in the Courtroom: A Scientific Analysis of Children's Testimony*. Washington, DC: American Psychological Association.

Chambers, Rex L. (1989). "Comparative Performance of Women in Law School." *Excelsior Law Review* **22**:196–222.

Champion, Dean J. (1992). *The Use of Attorneys in Juvenile Courts Five States: A Trend Analysis, 1980–1989*. Pittsburgh, PA: National Center for Juvenile Justice.

Champion, Dean J. (2004). "Juvenile Felons and Waivers, 1990–1999: Bursting the 'Get Tough' Bubble." Unpublished paper presented at the annual meeting of the American Society of Criminology, November (Nashville, TN).

Champion, Dean J. (2005a). "Plea Bargaining in Texas 2000–2001: A View from Prosecutors." Unpublished paper presented at the annual meeting of the Academy of Criminal Justice Sciences, March (Chicago).

Champion, Dean J. (2005b). *Probation, Parole, and Community Corrections* (5th ed.). Upper Saddle River, NJ: Prentice-Hall.

Champion, Dean John (2007). *The Juvenile Justice System: Delinquency, Processing and the Law* (5th ed.). Upper Saddle River, NJ: Prentice Hall/Pearson.

Champion, Dean J., and G. Larry Mays (1991). *Juvenile Transfer Hearings: Some Trends and Implications for Juvenile Justice.* New York: Praeger.

Chapman, Yvonne K. (2005). "Teen Courts and Restorative Justice." Unpublished paper presented at the annual meeting of the Academy of Criminal Justice Sciences, Chicago (March).

Charish, Courtney L. (2004). "Gender Effects on Juvenile Justice System Processing." Unpublished paper presented at the annual meeting of the American Society of Criminology, November (Nashville, TN).

Church, Thomas (1976). "Plea Bargains, Concessions and the Courts: Analysis of a Quasi-Experiment." *Law and Society Review* **10:**377–401.

Clark, James D. (2004a). "Racial, Ethnic, and Citizenship Disparity in Sentencing Under Federal Sentencing Guidelines: A Comparison of Two Judicial Districts." Unpublished paper presented at the annual meeting of the American Society of Criminology, November (Nashville, TN).

Clark, John W. III (2004b). "The Utility of Jury Consultants in the Twenty-First Century." Unpublished paper presented at the annual meeting of the American Society of Criminology, November (Nashville, TN).

Clark, M. Wesley (2005). "Enforcing Criminal Law on Native American Lands." *FBI Law Enforcement Bulletin* **74:**22–31.

Clarke, Stevens H., Ernest Valente Jr., and Robyn R. Mace (1992). *Mediation of Interpersonal Disputes: An Evaluation of North Carolina's Programs.* Chapel Hill, NC: Institute of Government, University of North Carolina at Chapel Hill, Mediation Network of North Carolina.

Clayton, Obie Jr. (1983). "Reconsideration of the Effects of Race in Criminal Sentencing." *Criminal Justice Review* **8:**15–20.

Cohen, Thomas H. (2004). "The Impact of Bench Trial Convictions on Sentencing." Unpublished paper presented at the annual meeting of the American Society of Criminology, November (Nashville, TN).

Connell, Nadine M. (2004). "The Power of the Prosecutor: Understanding Prosecutorial Discretion in a Social Network Analysis Framework." Unpublished paper presented at the annual meeting of the American Society of Criminology, November (Nashville, TN).

Cook, A., J. Arndt, and J. D. Lieberman (2004). "Firing Back at the Backfire Effect: The Influence of Mortality Salience and Nullification Beliefs on Reactions to Inadmissible Evidence." *Law and Human Behavior* **28:**389–410.

Coomber, Ross, Michael Oliver, and Craig Morris (2003). "Using Cannibis Therapeutically in the United Kingdom: A Qualitative Analysis." *Journal of Drug Issues* **33:**325–356.

Correctional Association of New York (1993). *Court Case Processing in New York: Problems and Solutions.* New York: Correctional Association of New York.

Cossins, Anne (2003). "Saints, Sluts, and Sexual Assault: Rethinking the Relationship Between Sex, Race, and Gender." *Social and Legal Studies* **12:**77–103.

Crow, Matthew S. (2004). "The Impact of Sentencing Guidelines Policy Reform: Florida's 1994 Sentencing Guidelines." Unpublished paper presented at the annual meeting of the American Society of Criminology, November (Nashville, TN).

Cummingham, Scott (2005). "Perspectives on Prosecutors, Community Prosecution, and Collective Bargaining Issues." Unpublished paper presented at the annual meeting of the Academy of Criminal Justice Sciences, March (Chicago).

Cunningham, Mark D., and Mark P. Vigen (1999). "Without Appointed Counsel in Capital Postconviction Proceedings: The Self-Representation Competency of Mississippi Death Row Inmates." *Criminal Justice and Behavior* 26:293–321.

Dabney, Dean, Sue Carter Collins, and Volkan Topalli (2004). "Statutory Provisions and Legal Precedents in the Area of Bail Bondsmen and Bail Recovery Agents: Assessing a Fringe Element of the Criminal Justice System." Unpublished paper presented at the annual meeting of the American Society of Criminology, November (Nashville, TN).

D'Allessio, Stewart J., and Lisa Stolzenberg (1993). "Socioeconomic Status and the Sentencing of the Traditional Offender." *Journal of Criminal Justice* 21:61–77.

Daly, Kathleen, and Rebecca L. Bordt (1995). "Sex Effects and Sentencing: An Analysis of the Statistical Literature." *Justice Quarterly* 12:141–175.

Davies, Graham M. et al. (1995). "Seminar: A New Look at Eyewitness Testimony: Papers presented at the BAFS Joint Seminar on 12 October 1994." *Medicine Science and the Law* 35: 95–149.

Davis, Jacqueline (2005). "Texas Landmark Cases: An Analysis and Comparison of *Ruiz v. Estelle* and *Morales v. Turman.* " Unpublished paper presented at the annual meeting of the Academy of Criminal Justice Sciences, March (Chicago).

Davis-Frenzel, Erika, and Cassia Spohn (2004). "Questioning the Measurement of the Dependent Variable Used in Sex Disparity Research." Unpublished paper presented at the annual meeting of the American Society of Criminology, November (Nashville, TN).

Death Penalty Information Center (2005). *Innocence and the Crisis in the American Death Penalty.* Washington, DC: Death Penalty Information Center.

DeLone, Miriam A., and Keith A. Wilmot (2004). "Minnesota Sentencing Guidelines Revisited: Does Race Matter for Native American Offenders?" Unpublished paper presented at the annual meeting of the American Society of Criminology, November (Nashville, TN).

Demuth, Stephen (2003). "Racial and Ethnic Differences in Pretrial Release Decisions and Outcomes: A Comparison of Hispanic, Black, and White Felony Arrestees." *Criminology* 41:873–907.

Denov, Myriam S., and Kathryn M. Campbell (2005). "Understanding the Causes, Effects, and Responses to Wrongful Conviction in Canada." *Journal of Contemporary Criminal Justice* 21:224–249.

Dent, Helen, and Rhona Flin (eds.) (1992). *Children as Witnesses.* Chichester, UK: Wiley.

Deukmedjian, John Edward (2003). "Reshaping Organizational Objectives in Canada's National Police Force: The Development of the RCMP Alternative Dispute Resolution." *Policing and Society* 13:331–348.

DiCristina, Bruce (2004). "Durkheim's Theory of Homicide and the Confusion of the Empirical Literature." *Theoretical Criminology* **8**:57–91.

Dobbs, Rhonda R. (2004). "Determinancy and Equal Treatment: The Case of Florida." Unpublished paper presented at the annual meeting of the American Society of Criminology meeting, November (Nashville, TN).

Dubois, Philip L. (1990). "Voter Responses to Court Reform: Merit Judicial Selection on the Ballot." *Judicature* **73**:238–247.

Dykstra, Nicole M., and Kristine Mullendore (2005). "Innocence Project's Influence on Convicted Death Row Inmates and Social Implications." Unpublished paper presented at the annual meeting of the Academy of Criminal Justice Association, March (Chicago).

Dynia, Paul A. (1987). *Misdemeanor Trial Law Study: Final Report.* New York: New York City Criminal Justice Agency.

Dynia, Paul A. (1990). *Misdemeanor Trial Law: Is It Working?* New York: New York City Criminal Justice Agency.

Elko Teen Court (2005). *Elko, Nevada Teen Court.* Elko, NV: Elko Teen Court.

Enriquez, Roger (2005). "Courts and Juries." Unpublished paper presented at the annual meeting of the Academy of Criminal Justice Sciences, March (Chicago).

Enriquez, Roger, and John W. Clark (2005). "The Relationship Between Personality and Jury Selection: An Exploratory Study of Jurors in Bexar County, Texas." Unpublished paper presented at the annual meeting of the Academy of Criminal Justice Sciences, March (Chicago).

Erez, Edna, and Peter R. Ibarra (2004). "Making Your Home a Shelter: The Electronic Monitoring of Domestic Violence Cases." Unpublished paper presented at the American Society of Criminology, November (Nashville, TN).

Fearn, Noelle (2004). "The Main and Conditioning Effects of Community Characteristics on Sentencing: A Multilevel Analysis." Unpublished paper presented at the annual meeting of the American Society of Criminology, November (Nashville, TN).

Federman, C. (2004). "Who Has the Body? The Paths to Habeas Corpus Reform." *The Prison Journal* **84**:317–339.

Feld, Barry C. (2000). *Cases and Materials on Juvenile Justice Administration.* St. Paul, MN: West Group.

Feld, Barry C. (2001). "Race, Youth Violence, and the Changing Jurisprudence of Waiver." *Behavioral Sciences and the Law* **19**:3–22.

Feld, Barry C. (2003). "The Constitutional Tension Between *Apprendi* and *McKeiver*: Sentence Enhancements Based on Delinquency Convictions and the Quality of Justice in Juvenile Courts." *Wake Forest Law Review* **38**:1111–1224.

Felstiner, William, Richard Abel, and Austin Sarat (1980). "The Emergence of Disputes: Naming, Blaming, and Claiming." *Law and Society Review* **15**: 631–634.

Ferdinand, Theodore (1992). *Boston's Lower Criminal Courts, 1814–1850.* Newark, DE: University of Delaware Press.

Finn, Peter, and B. Lee (1985). "Collaboration with Victim-Witness Assistance Programs: Payoffs and Concerns for Prosecutors." *Prosecutor* **18**: 27–36.

Findlay, Mark, and Peter Duff (eds.) (1988). *The Jury Under Attack.* Sydney, Australia: Butterworths.

Fischer, Gloria J. (1997). "Gender Effects on Individual Verdicts and on Mock Jury Verdicts in a Simulated Acquaintance Rape Trial." *Sex Roles: A Journal of Research* **36**:491–502.

Fisher, George (2000). "Plea Bargaining's Triumph." *Yale Law Journal* **109**:868–1086.

Fisher, Jim (1999). *The Ghosts of Hopewell: Setting the Record Straight in the Lindbergh Case.* Carbondale, IL: Southern Illinois University Press.

Fletcher, George P. (2004). "Black Hole in Guantanamo Bay." *Journal of International Criminal Justice* **2**:121–132.

Florida Joint Legislative Management Committee (1992). *An Empirical Examination of the Application of Florida's Habitual Offender Statute.* Tallhassee, FL: Florida Joint Legislative Management Committee Economic and Demographic Research Division.

Foley, M. A. (ed.) (2003). *The Supreme Court, the Constitution, and the Death Penalty.* Westport, CT: Praeger.

Forst, Brian (2004). "Minimizing Errors of Justice: The Role of the Prosecutor." Unpublished paper presented at the annual meeting of the American Society of Criminology, November (Nashville, TN).

Freedman, Eric M. (2001). *Habeas Corpus: Rethinking the Great Writ of Liberty.* New York: New York University Press.

Friedman, Lawrence (1985). *History of American Law 2/e.* New York: Simon and Schuster.

Fryling, Tina M. (2005). "Mitigating and Aggravating Factors in Death Penalty Cases: A Review of State Law." Unpublished paper presented at the annual meeting of the Academy of Criminal Justice Sciences, March (Chicago).

Galenter, Marc (1986). "The Day After the Litigation Explosion." *Maryland Law Review* **46**:3–39.

Gallinetti, J., J. Redpath, and J. Sloth-Nielsen (2004). "Race, Class and Restorative Justice in South Africa: Achilles Heel, Glass Ceiling, or Crowning Glory?" *South African Journal of Criminal Justice* **17**:17–40.

Gants, Earl III (2005). "Why Do You People Always Think About Race? Historically African-Americans and Courts." Unpublished paper presented at the annual meeting of the Academy of Criminal Justice Sciences, March (Chicago).

Geoghagan, Angel D. (2004). "Race and Gender Disparities in Criminal Justice Treatment." Unpublished paper presented at the annual meeting of the American Society of Criminology, November (Nashville, TN).

Gerwitz, Marian (1987). *Court-Ordered Releases—November 1983.* New York: New York City Criminal Justice Agency.

Gilbertson, D. Lee (2005). "Gangs in the Law." *Journal of Gang Research* **13**:1–16.

Glick, Henry R., and Craig F. Emmert (1987). "Selection Systems and Judicial Characteristics: The Recruitment of State Supreme Court Judges." *Judicature* **70**:228–235.

Goldkamp, John S., and Michael R. Gottfredson (1984). *Judicial Guidelines for Bail: The Philadelphia Experiment.* Washington, DC: U.S. Government Printing Office.

Goldman, Sheldon et al. (2003). "George W. Bush Remaking the Judiciary: Like Father Like Son?" *Judicature* **86**:282–309.

Goodman, John C., and Philip Porter (2002). "Is the Criminal Justice System Just?" *International Review of Law and Economics* **22**:25–39.

Gottlieb, Barbara (1984). *Public Danger As a Factor in Pretrial Release: Summaries of State Danger Laws.* Washington, DC: Toborg.

Gould, Jon B. (2004). "A First Try: The Innocence Commission for Virginia." Unpublished paper presented at the annual meeting of the American Society of Criminology, November (Nashville, TN).

Graham, Michael H. (1985). *Witness Intimidation: The Law's Response.* Westport, CT: Quorum.

Greene, J. (1990). "Media Effects on Jurors." *Law and Human Behavior* **14:**439–450.

Greene, J., and Loftus, C. (1984). What's News in the News? The Influence of Well-Publicized News Events on Psychological Research and Courtroom Trials." *Basic and Applied Social Psychology* **5:**123–135.

Greenstein, Marla N., and Kate Sampson (2004). *A National Symposium on Sentencing: Report and Policy Guide.* Des Moines, IA: American Judicature Society.

Greenstein, Steven C. (1994). *The Impact of Restrictions on Post-Indictment Plea Bargaining in Bronx County: The Processing of Indictments Already Pending.* Albany, NY: New York State Division of Criminal Justice.

Greenwood, Peter W. et al. (1994). *Three Strikes and You're Out: Estimated Benefits and Costs of California's New Mandatory Sentencing Law.* Santa Monica, CA: Rand.

Gubanski, Jakub (2004). "Comparative Criminal Justice: Special Investigation Techniques During the Criminal Trial: Disclosure Issues in Polish and American Legal Systems." *Crime, Law, and Social Change: An Interdisciplinary Journal* **41:**15–32.

Guevara, Lori, and Denise C. Herz (2004). "Race, Gender, and Juvenile Justice: Differences in Dispositional Outcomes." Unpublished paper presented at the annual meeting of the American Society of Criminology, November (Nashville, TN).

Hack, Peter (2003). "The Roads Less Traveled: Post-Conviction Relief Alternatives and the Antiterrorism and Effective Death Penalty Act of 1996." *American Journal of Criminal Law* **30:**171–223.

Hanke, Penelope J. (1995). "Sentencing Disparities by Race of Offender and Victim: Women Homicide Offenders in Alabama, 1929–1985." *Sociological Spectrum* **15:**277–297.

Harmon, Talia Roitberg (2000). *Overturned Convictions in Capital Cases.* Ann Arbor, MI: University Microfilms International.

Harmon, Talia Roitberg (2001). "Guilty Until Proven Innocent: An Analysis of Post-*Furman* Capital Errors." *Criminal Justice Policy Review* **12:**113–139.

Harmon, Talia Roitberg (2004). "Close Calls: Exonerations in Capital Cases in the Post-*Furman* Era." Unpublished paper presented at the annual meeting of the American Society of Criminology, November (Nashville, TN).

Harris, Alexes (2004). "The Institutional Careers of Juvenile Delinquents: Offending and Processing Patterns of a Sample of Violent and Chronic Offenders." Unpublished paper presented at the annual meeting of the American Society of Criminology, November (Nashville, TN).

Harris, M. (2004). "From Australian Courts to Aboriginal Courts in Australia: Bridging the Gap?" *Current Issues in Criminal Justice: Journal of the Institute of Criminology* **16:**26–41.

Harris, Victoria, and Christos Dagadakis (2004). "Length of Incarceration: Was There Parity for Mentally Ill Offenders?" *International Journal of Law and Psychiatry* **27**:387–393.

Hayes, Hennessey D. (2004). "Effectiveness of Restorative Justice." Unpublished paper presented at the annual meeting of the American Society of Criminology, November (Nashville, TN).

Haynes, Andrew (2000). "The Struggle Against Corruption: A Comparative Analysis." *Journal of Financial Crime* **8**:123–135.

Helms, Michael et al. (2004). "Waiver of Counsel among Young Offenders: Variability Between the Juvenile and Criminal Justice Systems." Unpublished paper presented at the annual meeting of the American Society of Criminology, November (Nashville, TN).

Hemenway, David (2004). *Private Guns, Public Health*. Ann Arbor, MI: University of Michigan Press.

Hermida, Julian (2005). "Comparative Analysis of the Theory of Offense in Common Law and Civil Law Criminal Justice Systems." Unpublished paper presented at the annual meeting of the Academy of Criminal Justice Sciences, March (Chicago).

Herzog, Sergio (2003). "The Relationship Between Public Perceptions of Crime Seriousness and Support for Plea Bargaining in Israel: A Factorial-Survey Approach." *Journal of Criminal Law and Criminology* **94**:103–131.

Herzog, Sergio (2004). "Plea Bargaining Practices: Less Covert, More Public Support?" *Crime and Delinquency* **50**:590–614.

Hewitt, William E. (1995). *Court Interpretation: Model Guides for Policy and Practice in the State Courts*. Williamsburg, VA: National Center for State Courts.

Hodge, John L. (1986). "Deadlocked Jury Mistrials, Lesser Included Offenses, and Double Jeopardy: A Proposal to Strengthen the Manifest Necessity Requirement." *Criminal Justice Journal* **9**: 9–44.

Hollander, Jocelyn A. (2004). " 'I Can Take Care of Myself': The Impact of Self-Defense Training on Women's Lives." *Violence Against Women* **10**:205–235.

Holmes, Malcolm D. et al. (1992). "Plea Bargaining Policy and State District Court Caseloads: An Interrupted Time Series Analysis." *Law and Society Review* **26**:139–159.

Holmes, Oliver Wendell (1897). *Courts and the Law*. New York: Knopf.

Horton, Candace L. (2005). "America's Stance." Unpublished paper presented at the annual meeting of the Academy of Criminal Justice Sciences, March (Chicago).

Hoskins, Stacy N., Gretchen R. Ruth, and R. Barry Ruback (2004). "Courtroom Workgroups: A Quantitative Description and Analysis of Their Effect on Sentencing." Unpublished paper presented at the annual meeting of the American Society of Criminology, November (Nashville, TN).

Houston, James (2005). "Examining Punishments: Can America Maintain a Civil Society Within Her Criminal Justice System?" Unpublished paper presented at the annual meeting of the Academy of Criminal Justice Sciences, March (Chicago).

Houston, James, Jeff Steffel, and Douglas McKenzie (2005). "1983 Lawsuits: Can Improvement Come Out of Trouble?" Unpublished paper presented at the annual meeting of the Academy of Criminal Justice Sciences, March (Chicago).

Hunzeker, Donna (1985). "Habitual Offender Statutes." *Corrections Compendium* **10**:1–15.

Illinois Supreme Court (1993). *Final Report.* Chicago: Illinois Supreme Court Special Commission on the Administration of Justice.

Inciardi, James A. et al. (2004). "Sentencing Drug Offenders." *Criminology and Public Policy* **3**:397–492.

Innocence Project (2005). *An Act Concerning Claims for Wrongful Conviction and Imprisonment: Model Legislation 2005 State Legislative Sessions.* Washington, DC: Innocence Project.

Institute for Court Management (1983). *Evaluation of Telephone Conferencing in Civil and Criminal Court Cases.* Denver: Prepared for the National Institute of Justice and the National Science Foundation; American Bar Association Action Commission to Reduce Court Costs and Delay.

Jacoby, Joseph E., and Eric F. Bronson (2004). "More Executions, Less News, Little Public Knowledge: News Coverage and Public Awareness of Executions in the U.S., 1977–2003." Unpublished paper presented at the annual meeting of the American Society of Criminology, November (Nashville, TN).

Jaffe, P. G., and C. V. Crooks (2004). "Partner Violence and Child Custody Cases: A Cross-National Comparison of Legal Reforms and Issues." *Violence Against Women* **10**:917–934.

Johnson, Brian D. (2004). "Judges on Trial: The Impact of Judge Characteristics Across Modes of Conviction." Unpublished paper presented at the annual meeting of the American Society of Criminology, November (Nashville, TN).

Johnson, Deborah L., Debra Bannister, and Michelle Alm (2004). "The Violent Youth Offender and Juvenile Transfer to the Adult Criminal Court." Unpublished paper presented at the annual meeting of the American Society of Criminology, November (Nashville, TN).

Johnson, Matthew B. (2002). "Juvenile Miranda Case Law in New Jersey, from Carlo, 1966, to JDH, 2001: The Relevance of Recording All Custodial Questioning." *Journal of Psychiatry and Law* **30**:3–57.

Jones, Marilyn J. (2003). "Jamaica: Marijuana Decriminalization Conundrum." *Canadian Journal of Law and Society* **18**:91–114.

Jordan, C. E. (2004a). "Intimate Partner Violence and the Justice System: An Examination of the Interface." *Journal of Interpersonal Violence* **19**:1412–1434.

Jordan, Kareem L. (2004b). "Youth in Adult Court: Examining the Predictors of Juvenile Decertification." Unpublished paper presented at the annual meeting of the American Society of Criminology, November (Nashville, TN).

Jordan, Kareem L., and David L. Meyers (2003). "Attorneys, Psychiatrists, and Psychologists: Predictors of Attitudes Toward the Insanity Defense." *Criminal Justice Studies* **16**:77–86.

Kakar, Suman (2004). "Causes of Disproportionate Minority Representation: A Pilot Study." Unpublished paper presented at the annual meeting of the American Society of Criminology, November (Nashville, TN).

Kales, A. H. (1914). *Unpopular Government in the United States.* Chicago: University of Chicago Press.

Kalven, Harry Jr., and Hans Ziesel (1966). *The American Jury.* Chicago: University of Chicago.

Karp, D. R., G. Bazemore, and J. D. Cheshire (2004). "The Role and Attitudes of Restorative Board Members: A Case Study of Volunteers in Community Justice." *Crime and Delinquency* **50**:487–515.

Karp, David R. (2001). "Harm and Repair: Observing Restorative Justice in Vermont." *Justice Quarterly* **18:**727–757.

Karp, David R. (2004). "Teen Courts." *APPA Perspectives* **28:**18–20.

Katz, Charles M., and Cassia Spohn (1995). "The Effect of Race and Gender on Bail Outcomes: A Test of An Interactive Model." *American Journal of Criminal Justice* **19:**161–184.

Kaufman, Whitley (2004). "Is There a 'Right' to Self-Defense?" *Criminal Justice Ethics* **23:**20–32.

Keil, K. Douglas et al. (1994). "Election, Selection, and Retention." *Judicature* **77:** 290–321.

Keller, Elizabeth M. (2005). "Security and Prosecution Issues." Unpublished paper presented at the annual meeting of the Academy of Criminal Justice Sciences, March (Chicago).

Keller, Elizabeth M., and Cassia Spohn (2005). "Focal Concerns in Federal Sentencing Decisions." Unpublished paper presented at the annual meeting of the Academy of Criminal Justice Sciences, March (Chicago).

Kellough, Gail, and Scot Wortley (2002). "Remand for Plea: Bail Decisions and Plea Bargaining as Commensurate Decisions." *The British Journal of Criminology* **42:**186–210.

Kerr, Norbert L. (1994). "The Effects of Pretrial Publicity on Jurors." *Judicature* **78:**120–127.

Kerr, Norbert L., and Robert J. MacCoun (1985). "The Effects of Jury Size and Polling Method on the Process and Product of Jury Deliberation." *Journal of Personality and Social Psychology* **48:**349–363.

Ketchum, Paul Robert, and David Geronimo Embrick (2004). "Where Are All the White Kids? An Analysis of the Effects of Race in Juvenile Court." Unpublished paper presented at the annual meeting of the American Society of Criminology, November (Nashville, TN).

Kirschner, Stuart M., and Gary J. Galperin (2001). "Psychiatric Defenses in New York County: Pleas and Results." *Journal of the American Academy of Psychiatry and the Law* **29:**194–201.

Klein, Richard, and Robert Spangenberg (1993). *The Indigent Defense Crisis.* Washington, DC: Section of Criminal Justice, American Bar Association.

Kleinig, John (ed.) (1989). "Ethics in Context: The Selling of Jury Deliberations." *Criminal Justice Ethics* **8:**26–34.

Knab, Karen M. (ed.) (1977). *Courts of Limited Jurisdiction: A National Survey.* Washington, DC: U.S. National Institute of Law Enforcement and Criminal Justice.

Kramer, J. H., and J. T. Ulmer (1996). "Sentencing Disparities and Guidelines Departures." *Justice Quarterly* **13:**401–426.

Kramer, John H., and Brian D. Johnson (2004). "Guideline Revisions and Courtroom Actor Decision-Making: Assessing the Influence of Legislative Changes in Pennsylvania, 1991–2000." Unpublished paper presented at the annual meeting of the American Society of Criminology, November (Nashville, TN).

Kremling, Janine (2004). "An Empirical Analysis of the Role of Mitigation on Capital Sentencing in North Carolina Before and After *McKoy v. North Carolina* (1990)." Unpublished paper presented at the annual meeting of the American Society of Criminology, November (Nashville, TN).

Kruttschnitt, Candace (1984). "Sex and Criminal Court Dispositions." *Journal of Research in Crime and Delinquency,* **21:**213–232.

Kruttschnitt, Candace. and Donald E. Green (1984). "The Sex-Sanctioning Issue: Is It History?" *American Sociological Review* **49**:541–551.

Kuckes, N. (2004). "The Useful, Dangerous Fiction of Grand Jury Independence." *American Criminal Law Review* **41**:1–66.

Kupchik, Aaron (2004). "The Negotiated Balance of Care and Control in the Juvenile Court." Unpublished paper presented at the annual meeting of the American Society of Criminology, November (Nashville, TN).

Lafferty, Elaine (1994). "Now, a Jury of His Peers." *Time*, Nov 14.

LaFree, Gary D. (1985). "Official Reactions to Hispanic Defendants in the Southwest." *Journal of Research in Crime and Delinquency* **22**:213–237.

Lee-Tao, Nicole, and Brandon R. Kooi (2005). "Community Prosecution: Problematic Issues and Implications." Unpublished paper presented at the annual meeting of the Academy of Criminal Justice Sciences, March (Chicago).

Leiber, Michael J., Kristan Fox, and Joe Johnson (2004). "Race, Gender, and Juvenile Justice: Differences in Disposition Outcomes." Unpublished paper presented at the annual meeting of the American Society of Criminology, November (Nashville, TN).

Lemley, Ellen C. (2004). "Restorative and Perceived Fairness: A Gateway Variable." Unpublished paper presented at the annual meeting of the American Society of Criminology, November (Nashville, TN).

Leo, Richard A. (1994). "Police Interrogation and Social Control." *Social and Legal Studies* **3**:93–120.

Leo, Richard A. (2005). "Rethinking the Study of Miscarriages of Justice: Developing a Criminology of Wrongful Conviction." *Journal of Contemporary Criminal Justice* **21**:201–223.

Levenson, J. S. (2004). "Reliability of Sexually Violent Predator Civil Commitment Criteria in Florida." *Law and Human Behavior* **28**:357–368.

Levin, Martin H. (1988). "The Jury in a Criminal Case: Obstacles to Impartiality." *Criminal Law Bulletin* **24**:492–520.

Levine, James P. (2005). "Race, American Courts and Their Quest for Equal Protection." Unpublished paper presented at the annual meeting of the Academy of Criminal Justice Sciences, March (Chicago).

Levine, James P., and J. Petitt (2005). "The Impact of Excluding Convicted Felons from Jury Service on the Racial Composition of Juries." Unpublished paper presented at the annual meeting of the Academy of Criminal Justice Sciences, March (Chicago).

Lightfoot, E., and Mark Umbreit (2004). "An Analysis of State Statutory Provisions for Victim-Offender Mediation." *Criminal Justice Policy Review* **15**:418–436.

Listwan, Shelley Johnson, and Terance D. Miethe (2004). "Adult Certification and Juvenile Justice: A Comparative Analysis of Differential Treatment." Unpublished paper presented at the annual meeting of the American Society of Criminology, November (Nashville, TN).

Litwack, Thomas R. (2003). "The Competency of Criminal Defendants to Refuse, for Delusional Reasons, a Visible Insanity Defense Recommended by Counsel." *Behavioral Sciences and the Law* **21**:135–156.

Llewellyn, Karl (1931). "Some Realism about Realism: Responding to Dean Pound." *Harvard Law Review* **44**:1222–1235.

Lo, T. Wing, and Robert J. Harris (2004). "Community Service Orders in Hong Kong, England, and Wales: Twins or Cousins?" *International Journal of Offender Therapy and Comparative Criminology* **48**:373–388.

Lobo-Antunes, M. J. (2004). "Racial and Gender Discrimination in Federal Court Pretrial Processing." Unpublished paper presented at the annual meeting of the American Society of Criminology, November (Nashville, TN).

Loftus, Elizabeth F. (1996). *Eyewitness Testimony*. Cambridge, MA: Harvard University Press.

Lovrich, Nicholas P. Jr., and Charles H. Sheldon (1994). "Is Voting for State Judges a Flight or Fancy or a Reflection of Policy and Value Preferences?" *Justice System Journal* **16**:57–71.

Lutz, R. (1990). *Community Service Orders and Restitution*. Washington, DC: U.S. Government Printing Office.

Ma, Yue (2002). "Prosecutorial Discretion and Plea Bargaining in the United States, France, Germany, and Italy: A Comparative Analysis." *International Criminal Justice Review* **12**:23–52.

Maahs, Jeff (2005). "Evaluation of a Large Urban Drug Court." Unpublished paper presented at the annual meeting of the Academy of Criminal Justice Sciences, March (Chicago).

Mackay, Robert E., and Susan R. Moody (1996). "Diversion of Neighbourhood Disputes in Community Mediation." *Howard Journal of Criminal Justice* **35**:299–313.

Maguire, Kathleen, and Ann L. Pastore (2005). *Sourcebook of Criminal Justice Statistics 2004*. Albany, NY: The Hindelang Criminal Justice Research Center.

Martin, Jamie S., and Jennifer Roberts (2005). "To Die or Not To Die: Factors Influencing Death Sentences." Unpublished paper presented at the annual meeting of the Academy of Criminal Justice Sciences, March (Chicago).

Mason, Mary Ann (1991). "A Judicial Dilemma: Expert Witness Testimony in Child Sex Abuse Cases." *Journal of Psychiatry and Law* **19**:185–219.

Matthews, Roger, Catherine Pease, and Ken Pease (2001). "Repeated Bank Robbery: Theme and Variations." In *Repeat Victimization*, Graham Farrell and Ken Pease (eds.). Monsey, NY: Criminal Justice Press.

Maxwell, Christopher D., Steven B. Dow, and Sheila Royo Maxwell (2004). "The Impact of Defense Counsel on the Processing and Disposition of Felony Court Cases." Unpublished paper presented at the annual meeting of the American Society of Criminology, November (Nashville, TN).

Maxwell, Gabrielle, and Allison Morris (2002). "Restorative Justice and Reconviction." *Contemporary Justice Review* **5**:133–146.

McCart, Samuel W. (1964). *Trial by Jury: A Complete Guide to the Jury System*. New York: Chilton Books.

McCold, Paul (2003). "An Experiment in Police-Based Restorative Justice: The Bethlehem Pennsylvania Project." *Police Practice and Research* **4**:379–390.

McConville, Mike, and Chester Mirsky (2005). *Jury Trials and Plea Bargaining: A True History*. Oxford, UK: Hart.

McDonald, William F. (1985). *Plea Bargaining: Critical Issues and Common Practices*. Washington, DC: U.S. National Institute of Justice by the Institute of Criminal Law and Procedure, Georgetown University.

McGough, Lucy S. (1994). *Fragile Voices in the American Legal System*. New Haven, CT: Yale University Press.

McKimmie, B. M. et al. (2004). "Jurors' Responses to Expert Witness Testimony: The Effects of Gender Stereotypes." *Group Processes and Intergroup Relations* **7**:131–143.

McLean, Sarah J., Joseph Cocozza, and Kathy Skowyra (2004). "Understanding the Diversity of Juvenile Diversion Programs." Unpublished paper presented at the annual meeting of the American Society of Criminology, November (Nashville, TN).

McManimon, Patrick F. (2005a). "Effects of Truth-in-Sentencing on Inmate Conduct: The Good-Time Myth." Unpublished paper presented at the annual meeting of the Academy of Criminal Justice Sciences, March (Chicago).

McManimon, Patrick F. (2005b). "The Role of Sentencing Policy in the Corrections System." Unpublished paper presented at the annual meeting of the Academy of Criminal Justice Sciences, March (Chicago).

McSherry, B. (2004). "Criminal Responsibility: Fleeting States of Mental Impairment, and the Power of Self-Control." *International Journal of Law and Psychiatry* **27**:445–457.

Menkel-Meadow, Carrie (1986). "The Comparative Sociology of Women Lawyers." *Osgood Law Journal* **24**:897–918.

Merlo, Alida V., and Peter J. Benekos (2004). "The Constitution and the Death Penalty for Juveniles: Assessing Standards of Decency." Unpublished paper presented at the annual meeting of the American Society of Criminology, November (Nashville, TN).

Minor, Kevin I., James B. Wells, and Brandi Jones (2004). "Staff Perceptions of the Work Environment in Juvenile Group Home Settings: A Study of Social Climate." *Journal of Offender Rehabilitation* **38**:17–30.

Mitchell, Edward W. (2003). *Self-Made Madness: Rethinking Illness and Criminal Responsibility.* Aldershot, UK: Ashgate.

Morgan, Thomas D. (1983). *Legal Ethics.* Chicago: Harcourt Brace Jovanovich Legal and Professional Publications, Inc.

Morrill, Calvin, and Cindy McKee (1993). "Institutional Isomorphism and Informal Social Control: Evidence from a Community Mediation Center." *Social Problems* **40**:445–463.

Mukoro, Saliba D. (2005). "Disproportionate Minority Confinement: What Way Forward?" Unpublished paper presented at the annual meeting of the Academy of Criminal Justice Sciences, March (Chicago).

Mulford, Carrie Fried et al. (2004). "Legal Issues Affecting Mentally Disordered and Developmentally Delayed Youth in the Justice System." *International Journal of Forensic Mental Health* **3**:3–22.

Mullendore, Kristine (2005). "Legal Issues and Court Practices." Unpublished paper presented at the annual meeting of the Academy of Criminal Justice Sciences, March (Chicago).

Myers, Bryan et al. (2004). "Victim Impact Statements and Mock Juror Sentencing: The Impact of Dehumanizing Language on a Death Qualified Sample." *American Journal of Forensic Psychology* **22**:39–55.

Myers, Laura B., and Sue Titus Reid (1995). "The Importance of County Context in the Measurement of Sentence Disparity." *Journal of Criminal Justice* **23**: 223–241.

Nadeau, Sarah, Melissa W. Burek, and Marian R. Williams (2005). "Quit Mocking Me: An Examination of Racial Composition of Juries on Non-Capital Felony Case Outcomes." Unpublished paper presented at the annual meeting of the Academy of Criminal Justice Sciences, March (Chicago).

Nader, Laura (1979). "Disputing within the Force of the Law." *Yale Law Journal* **88**:998–1043.

Nader, Laura, and Harry F. Todd (eds.) (1978). "Introduction." In *The Disputing Process: Law in Ten Societies*, Laura Nader and Harry F. Todd (eds.). New York: Columbia University Press.

National Association of Pretrial Services Agencies (1995). *Performance Standards and Goals for Pretrial Release and Diversion.* Frankfort, KY: National Association of Pretrial Services Agencies.

Newsweek (2003). "Lawsuits Out of Control in Major Cities." Editorial, *Newsweek*, November 3, 2003:61.

New York Times (2006). "Annual Salaries of Federal Judges." January 1, 2006, 1.13.

Nicholson, Marlene Arnold, and Bradley Scott Weiss (1986). "Funding Judicial Campaigns in the Circuit Court of Cook County." *Judicature* **70**:17–25.

Nunn, Samuel (2003). "Seeking Tools for the War on Terror: A Critical Assessment of Emerging Technologies in Law Enforcement." *Policing* **26**:454–473.

O'Rourke, W. (1972). *The Harrisburg 7 and the New Catholic Left.* New York: Thomas Y. Crowell.

Ostrom, Brian J., Fred Cheesman, and Ann M. Jones (1999). *Truth-in-Sentencing in Virginia: Evaluating the Process and Impact of Sentencing Reform.* Washington, DC: National Center for State Courts.

O'Sullivan, Julie R. (2001). *Federal White Collar Crime: Cases and Materials.* St. Paul, MN: West Group.

Palermo, George B. (2004). "Tattooing and Tattooed Criminals." *Journal of Forensic Psychology Practice* **4**:1–25.

Palumbo, Dennis J., Michael Musheno, and Michael Hallett (1994). "The Political Construction of Alternative Dispute Resolution and Alternatives to Incarceration." *Evaluation and Program Planning* **17**:197–203.

Park, Mirang (2005). "Racial Disparity in Drug Sentencing: Focusing on Hispanic." Unpublished paper presented at the annual meeting of the Academy of Criminal Justice Sciences, March (Chicago).

Patrick, Steven et al. (2004). "Control Group Study of Juvenile Diversion Programs." *Social Science Journal* **41**:129–135.

Penrod, Steven D., Solomon M. Fulero, and Brian L. Cutler (1995). "Expert Psychological Testimony on Eyewitness Reliability Before and After Daubert: The State of the Law and Science." *Behavioral Sciences and the Law* **13**: 229–259.

Peters, Roger H. et al. (2004). "Co-Occurring Disorders and the Criminal Justice System." *Behavioral Sciences and the Law* **22**:427–610.

Peterson, Scott (2005). *The Growth of Teen Courts in the United States.* Washington, DC: Office of Juvenile Justice and Delinquency Prevention.

Phillips, Amy K. (1997). "Thou Shalt Not Kill Any Nice People: The Problem of Victim Impact Statements in Capital Sentencing." *American Criminal Law Review* **35**:93–118.

Pickles, James (1987). *Straight from the Bench.* London, UK: Dent and Sons.

Pinello, Daniel R. (1995). *The Impact of Judicial Selection Method on State Supreme Court Policy: Innovation, Reaction, and Atrophy.* Westport, CT: Greenwood Press.

Piquero, N. L., and J. L. Davis (2004). "Extralegal Factors and the Sentencing of Organizational Defendants: An Examination of the Federal Sentencing Guidelines." *Journal of Criminal Justice* **32**:643–654.

Pohlman, H. L. (1995). *Constitutional Debate in Action: Criminal Justice*. New York: HarperCollins College Publishers.

Posey, Amy J., and Lisa M. Dahl (2002). "Beyond Pretrial Publicity: Legal and Ethical Issues Associated with Change of Venue Surveys." *Law and Human Behavior* **26:**107–125.

Pound, Roscoe (1912). "The Scope and Purpose of Sociological Jurisprudence." *Journal of Political Economy* **25:**489–500.

Prentice, Melissa A. (2001). "Prosecuting Mothers Who Maim and Kill: The Profile of Munchausen Syndrome by Proxy Litigation in the Late 1990s." *American Journal of Criminal Law* **28:**373–412.

President's Commission on Law Enforcement (1967). *President's Commission on Law Enforcement and the Administration of Justice*. Washington, DC: U.S. Government Printing Office.

Presser, Lis, Cynthia Hamilton, and Emily Gaarder (2004). "Power Dynamics of Victim-Offender Mediation." Unpublished paper presented at the annual meeting of the American Society of Criminology, November (Nashville, TN).

Preston, Frederick W., and Roger I. Roots (eds.) (2004). "When Laws Backfire: Unintended Impacts of Public Policy." *American Behavioral Scientist* **47:** 1371–1466.

Priest, George (1985). "The Invention of Enterprise Liability: A Critical History of the Intellectual Foundations of Modern Tort Law." *Journal of Legal Studies* **14:**461–527.

Proulx, Craig (2003). *Reclaiming Aboriginal Justice, Identity, and Community*. Saskatoon, CAN: Purich Publishing.

Rasmussen, A. (2004). "Teen Court Referral, Sentencing, and Subsequent Recidivism: Two Proportional Hazards Models and a Little Speculation." *Crime and Delinquency* **50:**615–635.

Read, J. Don, John C. Yuille, and Patricia Tollestrup (1992). "Recollections of a Robbery: Effects of Arousal and Alcohol Upon Recall and Person Identification." *Law and Human Behavior* **16:**425–446.

Reed, Gary (2004). "Therapeutic Communities in Restorative Justice." Unpublished paper presented at the annual meeting of the American Society of Criminology, November (Nashville, TN).

Reed, Judith (2004). *Teen Courts*. Albuquerque, NM: Youth Development and Diagnostic Center.

Roberts, Albert R. (ed.) (2003). *Critical Issues in Crime and Justice* (2d ed.). Thousand Oaks, CA: Sage.

Roberts, Julian V., and Edna Erez (2004). "Communication in Sentencing: Exploring the Expressive Function of Victim Impact Statements." *International Review of Victimology* **10:**223–244.

Roberts, Melinda, Jacinta M. Gau, and David C. Brody (2004). "Eligible Jurors' Knowledge, Information Sources, and Attitudes About the Jury System." Unpublished paper presented at the annual meeting of the American Society of Criminology, November (Nashville, TN).

Robinson, Paul H., and J. M. Darley (2004). "Does Criminal Law Deter? A Behavioral Science Investigation." *Oxford Journal of Legal Studies* **24:**173–205.

Rockwell, P., and A. E. Hubbard (2004). "The Effect of Attorneys' Nonverbal Communication on Perceived Credibility." *Polygraph* **33:**102–114.

Rodriguez, Nancy (2004). "Examining the Influence of Community Racial/Ethnic Composition in Juvenile Detention Decisions: The Mediating Role of Community Characteristics in Juvenile Court." Unpublished paper presented at the annual meeting of the American Society of Criminology, November (Nashville, TN).

Rodriguez, Nancy, and Gaylene S. Armstrong (2004). "The Relationship Between Offense Type and Attorney Presence in Juvenile Court Disposition Decisions." Unpublished paper presented at the annual meeting of the American Society of Criminology, November (Nashville, TN).

Rogers, Patrick, Sharon Cotliar, and Steve Erwin (2000). "Judgment Day." *People*, November 6, 2000:87–91.

Rojek, Dean G., James E. Coverdill, and Stuart W. Fors (2003). "The Effect of Victim Impact Panels on DUI Rearrest Rates: A Five-Year Follow-up." *Criminology* **41**:1319–1340.

Rosay, Andre B., and Brad A. Myrstol (2004). "Gender Effects in the Alaska Juvenile Justice System." Unpublished paper presented at the annual meeting of the American Society of Criminology, November (Nashville, TN).

Rose-Ackerman, Susan (2002). "Corruption and the Criminal Law." *Forum on Crime and Society* **2**:3–21.

Ross, David Frank, J. Don Read, and Michael P. Toglia (1994). *Adult Eyewitness Testimony: Current Trends and Developments.* Cambridge: Cambridge University Press.

Rottman, David B., Carol R. Flango, Melissa Cantrell, Randall Hansen, and Neil LaFountain (2000). *State Court Organization, 1998.* Washington, DC: Bureau of Justice Statistics.

Roy, Dina (2004). "Age Disparity in Criminal Court Sentencing." Unpublished paper presented at the annual meeting of the American Society of Criminology, November (Nashville, TN).

Roy, Sudipto, and Michael Brown (1992). "Victim-Offender Reconciliation Project for Adults and Juveniles: A Comparative Study in Elkhart County, Indiana." Unpublished paper presented at the annual meetings of the American Society of Criminology, November (San Francisco, CA).

Ruback, R. Barry (2002). *Restitution in Pennsylvania: A Multimethod Investigation.* Erie, PA: Pennsylvania Commission on Crime and Delinquency.

Sabelli, Martin, and Stacey Leyton (2000). "Train Wrecks and Freeway Crashes: An Argument for Fairness and Against Self-Representation in the Criminal Justice System." *Journal of Criminal Law and Criminology* **91**:161–235.

Sacks, Stanley, and Frank S. Pearson (2003). "Co-Occurring Substance Use and Mental Disorders in Offenders: Approaches, Findings, and Recommendations." *Federal Probation* **67**:32–39.

Saltzburg, Stephen A., and Kenneth R. Redeen (1994). *Federal Rules of Evidence Manual.* Charlottesville, VA: Michie.

Schauffler, Richard Y., Robert C. LaFountain, Neal B. Kauder, and Shauna M. Strickland (2004). *Examining the Work of State Courts, 2004.* Washington, DC: Bureau of Justice Statistics.

Scheb, John M. II (1988). "State Appellate Judges' Attitudes toward Judicial Merit Selection and Retention: Results of a National Survey." *Judicature* **62**:170–174.

Scheck, Barry, and Peter Neufeld (2002). "Toward the Formation of Innocence Commissions in America." *Judicature* **86**:98–105.

Schiff, Mara F., and Gordon Bazemore (2004). "Why Restorative Justice Works: Building and Testing Intervention Theories." Unpublished paper presented at the annual meeting of the American Society of Criminology, November (Nashville, TN).

Schmid, Karl H. (2002). "Journalist's Privilege in Criminal Proceedings: An Analysis of United States Courts of Appeals' Decisions from 1973–1999." *American Criminal Law Review* **39**:1441–1499.

Schmidt, Melinda G., Dickon N. Reppucci, and Jennifer L. Woolard (2003). "Effectiveness of Participation as a Defendant: The Attorney-Juvenile Client Relationship." *Behavioral Sciences and the Law* **21**:175–198.

Schoenfeld, Heather (2005). "Violated Trust: Conceptualizing Prosecutorial Misconduct." *Journal of Contemporary Criminal Justice* **21**:250–271.

Schram, Pamela J., Barbara A. Koons-Witt, and Merry Morash (2004). "Management Strategies When Working with Female Prisoners." *Women and Criminal Justice* **15**:25–50.

Schulman, William L. (2005). "Videotaping the Process: Technology in America's Jails and Courtrooms." Unpublished paper presented at the annual meeting of the Academy of Criminal Justice Sciences, March (2005).

Sheehy, Elizabeth (2004). "Advancing Social Inclusion: The Implications for Criminal Law and Policy." *Canadian Journal of Criminology and Criminal Justice* **46**:73–95.

Simon, R., and Eimermann, E. (1971). "The Jury Finds Not Guilty: Another Look at Media Influence on the Jury." *Journalism Quarterly* **48**:343–344.

Smith, A. (2004). *Law, Social Science, and the Criminal Courts.* Durham, NC: Carolina Academic Press.

Smith, Steven K., and Carol J. DeFrances (1996). *Indigent Defense.* Washington, DC: U.S. Department of Justice.

Sorensen, Jonathan R., and Donald H. Wallace (1995). "Arbitrariness and Discrimination in Missouri Capital Cases: An Assessment Using the Barnett Scale." *Journal of Crime and Justice* **18**:21–57.

Spangenberg, Robert L. (1990). *Overview of the Fulton County, Georgia Indigent Defense System.* West Newton, MA: Georgia Indigent Defense Council.

Spangenberg, Robert L. et al. (1999). *Indigent Defense and Technology: A Progress Report.* Washington, DC: Bureau of Justice Assistance.

Spohn, Cassia C. (2002). *How Do Judges Decide? The Search for Fairness and Justice in Punishment.* Thousand Oaks, CA: Sage.

Spohn, Cassia (2004). "Sentencing Decisions in Three U.S. District Courts: Testing the Assumption of Uniformity in the Federal Sentencing Process." Unpublished paper presented at the annual meeting of the American Society of Criminology, November (Nashville, TN).

Spohn, Cassia C., and Elizabeth Keller (2005). "U.S. Attorneys and the Federal Sentencing Process: A Test of Inter-Prosecutor Disparity." Unpublished paper presented at the annual meeting of the American Society of Criminology, November (Toronto, CAN).

Sridharan, S. et al. (2004). "Juvenile Transfer." *Criminology and Public Policy* **3**:599–649.

Stacey, Lynn R., and P. E. Dayton (1988). *Jury Deliberations and Judicial Opinions.* Washington, DC: U.S. Department of Justice.

Stalans, Loretta J. et al. (2004). "Identifying Three Types of Violent Offenders and Predicting Violent Recidivism While on Probation: A Classification Tree Analysis." *Law and Human Behavior* **28**:253–271.

Stalmaster, Irvin (1931). *What Price Jury Trials?* New York: Penguin.

Stanley, Steve (2004). " 'What Works'? Revisiting the Evidence in England and Wales." *Journal of Community and Criminal Justice* **51**:7–20.

Steelman, David C., and Samuel D. Conti (1987). *Representation of Indigent Criminal Defendants in the Courts of Hamilton County, Ohio*. North Andover, MA: National Center for State Courts.

Steiner, Benjamin, Craig Hemmens, and Valerie Bell (2004). "Legislative Waiver Reconsidered: An Examination of General Deterrence." Unpublished paper presented at the annual meeting of the American Society of Criminology, November (Nashville, TN).

Steiner, Benjamin, and John Wooldredge (2005). "Assessing the Relative Effects of Sentencing Policies and Institutional Resources on Crowding in State-Operated Prisons." Unpublished paper presented at the annual meeting of the Academy of Criminal Justice Sciences, March (Chicago).

Stemen, Donald (2004). "Policies of Imprisonment: The Adoption of Determinate Sentencing and Sentencing Guidelines in the United States, 1975–2002." Unpublished paper presented at the annual meeting of the American Society of Criminology, November (Nashville, TN).

Stemen, Donald, James A. Wilson, and Andres Rengifo (2004). "Of Fragmentation and Ferment: The Impact of Sentencing Policies on State-Level Incarceration Rates and Admissions to Prison, 1970–2002." Unpublished paper presented at the annual meeting of the American Society of Criminology, November (Nashville, TN).

Stephenson-Lang, Juli (2005). "Tipping the Scales of Justice: The Importance of Proportionality in a Balanced Sentencing Scheme." Unpublished paper presented at the annual meeting of the Academy of Criminal Justice Sciences, March (Chicago).

Stith, Kate, and Jose A. Cabranes (1998). *Fear of Judging Sentencing Guidelines in Federal Court*. Chicago: University of Chicago Press.

Strang, Heather (2004). "Effectiveness in Restorative Justice: First Doing No Harm." Unpublished paper presented at the annual meeting of the American Society of Criminology, November (Nashville, TN).

Suggs, David, and Bruce Sales (1981). "Juror Self-Disclosure in the Voir Dire: A Social Science Analysis." *Indiana Law Journal* 56:245–271.

Swain, F. W. (1985). *Of God and His Conscience: Judicial Selection in Louisiana*. Baton Rouge, LA: Louisiana State Legislature.

Swedlow, Kathy (2004). "Pleading Guilty v. Being Guilty: A Case for Broader Access to Post-Conviction DNA Testing." Unpublished paper presented at the annual meeting of the American Society of Criminology, November (Nashville, TN).

Tague, Peter W. (1999). "Representing Indigents in Serious Criminal Cases in England's Crown Court: The Advocates' Performance and Incentives." *American Criminal Law Review* 36:171–222.

Tappan, Christy (2005). "The New Face of Prosecution: Structural Characteristics and Outcomes Associated with Community Prosecution." Unpublished paper presented at the annual meeting of the Academy of Criminal Justice Sciences, March (Chicago).

Taylor, Humphrey, Michael Kagay and Stuart Leichenko (1987). *Public Attitudes Toward the Civil Justice System and Tort Law Reform*. New York: Louis Harris and Associates for Aetna Life and Casualty Insurance Company.

Technology Review (2005). "The DNA Defense." *Technology Review* **108**:20.

Teske, Raymond H. C. Jr., and C. Zhang (2005). "Disposition of Defendants Charged with Felony-Level Violation of Protective Orders in Harris

County, Texas." Unpublished paper presented at the annual meeting of the Academy of Criminal Justice Sciences, March (Chicago).

Thomas, Wayne (1976). *Bail Reform in America*. Berkeley: University of California Press.

Thomas, Wayne (1977). *National Evaluation Program: Pretrial Release Programs.* Washington, DC: Law Enforcement Assistance Administration.

Thompson, R. Alan (2005). "Results of the 2004 Mississippi Crime Poll." Unpublished paper presented at the annual meeting of the Academy of Criminal Justice Sciences, March (Chicago).

Tifft, Larry (2004). "A Critique of Restorative Justice Evaluation Research." Unpublished paper presented at the annual meeting of the Academy of Criminal Justice Sciences, November (Nashville, TN).

Tishler, C. L. et al. (2004). "Is Domestic Violence Relevant? An Exploratory Analysis of Couples Referred for Mediation in Family Court." *Journal of Interpersonal Violence* **19**:1042–1062.

Tomasi, Timothy B., and Jess A. Velona (1987). "All the President's Men: A Study of Ronald Reagan's Appointments to the U.S. Courts of Appeals." *Columbia Law Review* **87**:766–793.

Tonry, Michael (2004). *Punishment and Politics: Evidence and Emulation in the Making of English Crime Control Policy*. Cullompton, Devon, UK: Willan Publishing.

Tshehla, B. (2004). "The Restorative Justice Bug Bites the South African Criminal Justice System." *South African Journal of Criminal Justice* **17**:1–16.

Ueckert, Edwin (2005). "The Issue of Civil Commitment of Habitual Violent Offenders." Unpublished paper presented at the annual meeting of the Academy of Criminal Justice Sciences, March (Chicago).

Ulmer, Jeffery T. (2004). "Differences in Guideline Departures and Sentencing among Seven Federal District Courts." Unpublished paper presented at the annual meeting of the American Society of Criminology, November (Nashville, TN).

Ulmer, Jeffery T., and Keri B. Burchfield (2004). "Charge Manipulation and Relevant Conduct in Federal Criminal Case Processing." Unpublished paper presented at the annual meeting of the American Society of Criminology, November (Nashville, TN).

Ulrich, Thomas E. (2002). "Pretrial Diversion in the Federal Court System." *Federal Probation* **66**:30–37.

Umbreit, Mark S. (1994). "Victim Empowerment through Mediation." *APPA Perspectives* **18**:25–28.

U.S. Advisory Commission on Intergovernmental Relations (1971). *For a More Perfect Union—Court Reform*. Washington, DC: U.S. Government Printing Office.

U.S. Department of Justice (2005). *Justice Statistics*. Washington, DC: U.S. Department of Justice, Bureau of Justice Statistics.

U.S. General Accounting Office (1999). *Caseloads of Prosecutors and Defense Counsel*. Washington, DC: U.S. General Accounting Office.

U.S. Sentencing Commission (2003). *Downward Departures from the Federal Sentencing Guidelines*. Washington, DC: U.S. Sentencing Commission.

Unnever, James D., and Francis T. Cullen (2004). "Readdressing the Racial Divide in Support for Capital Punishment." Unpublished paper presented at the annual meeting of the American Society of Criminology, November (Nashville, TN).

Urban, Lynn S. (2005). "The Effect of a Curfew Check Program on Juvenile Opportunities for Delinquent Activity." Unpublished paper presented at the annual meeting of the Academy of Criminal Justice Sciences, Chicago (March).

Vago, Steven (2006). *Law and Society* (6th ed.). Upper Saddle River, NJ: Prentice Hall.

van Koppen, Peter J., and Steven D. Penrod (2003). *Adversarial Versus Inquisitorial Justice: Psychological Perspectives on Criminal Justice Systems.* New York: Kluwer.

Van Zyl Smit, D., and A. Ashworth (2004). "Disproportionate Sentences as Human Rights Violations." *Modern Law Review* **67**:541–560.

Vaughn, Michael S., Volkan Topalli, and Sarah Pierre (2004). "Legal Issues Involving Show-Ups, Line-Ups, and Photographic Identification." Unpublished paper presented at the annual meeting of the American Society of Criminology, November (Nashville, TN).

Veneziano, Carol (2005a). "An Evaluation of a Rural Drug Court Program." Unpublished paper presented at the annual meeting of the Academy of Criminal Justice Sciences, March (Chicago).

Veneziano, Carol (2005b). "Evaluating Drug Courts." Unpublished paper presented at the annual meeting of the Academy of Criminal Justice Sciences, March (Chicago).

Vidmar, Neil (2000). "Juries and Expert Evidence." *Brooklyn Law Review* **66**: 1121–1180.

Villanova Law Review (1982). "Judicial Selection in Pennsylvania: A Proposal." *Villanova Law Review* **27**:1163–1178.

Vincent, Barbara S., and Paul J. Hofer (1994). *The Consequences of Mandatory Minimum Prison Terms: A Summary of Recent Findings.* Washington, DC: U.S. Government Printing Office.

Vito, Gennaro F. (1984). "Developments in Shock Probation: A Review of Research Findings." *Federal Probation* **48**:22–27.

Volcansek, Mary L., Maria Eisabetta DeFranciscis, and Jacqueline Lucienne Lafron (1996). *Judicial Misconduct: A Cross-National Comparison.* Gainesville, FL: University Press of Florida.

Vollum, S., Dennis R. Longmire, and J. Buffington-Vollum (2004). "Confidence in the Death Penalty and Support for Its Use: Exploring the Value-Expressive Dimension of Death Penalty Attitudes." *Justice Quarterly* **21**:521–546.

Wanamaker, John L. (1978). "Computers and Scientific Jury Selection: A Calculated Risk." *Journal of Urban Law* **55**:345–370.

Ward, Geoff (2004). "Custody Against Care in the Concept of Accountability: Shifting Policies and Stubborn Priorities in Juvenile Court Organizations." Unpublished paper presented at the annual meeting of the American Society of Criminology, November (Nashville, TN).

Warden, Rob (2004). "DNA and Justice." *Newsfeed.* Evanston, IL: Northwestern University, May 3, 2004.

Weidner, R. R., R. Frase, and I. Pardoe (2004). "Explaining Sentence Severity in Large Urban Counties: A Multilevel Analysis of Contextual and Case-Level Factors." *The Prison Journal* **84**:184–207.

Weinberg, S., N. Gordon, and B. Williams (2005). *Harmful Error: Investigating America's Local Prosecutors.* Washington, DC: Center for Public Integrity.

Weisburd, David, Elin Waring, and Stanton Wheeler (1990). "Class, Status, and the Punishment of White-Collar Criminals." *Law and Social Inquiry* **15**:223–243.

Weiss, Michael Scott (2004). "Public Defenders' Pragmatic Motivations: A Qualitative and Inductive Study." Unpublished paper presented at the annual meeting of the American Society of Criminology, November (Nashville, TN).

Wely, Theodore (1904). *Hygiene of Occupation.* New York: Jena.

Westervelt, Saundra D., and Kimberly J. Cook (2004). "Life After Death: Life Histories of Innocents Released from Death Row." Unpublished paper presented at the annual meeting of the American Society of Criminology, November (Nashville, TN).

Wettstein, Robert M. (ed.) (1992). "Cults and the Law." *Behavioral Sciences and the Law* **10**:1–140.

Whitcomb, Debra et al. (1994). *The Child Victim as a Witness.* Washington, DC: U.S. Office of Juvenile Justice and Delinquency Prevention.

White, E.W. (1999). *History of Law in American Society.* New York: Cakewalk Books.

White, Welsh S. (2002). "Curbing Prosecutorial Misconduct in Capital Cases: Imposing Prohibitions on Improper Penalty Trial Arguments." *American Criminal Law Review* **39**:1147–1185.

Williams, James J., Daniel G. Rodeheaver, and Felicia Guerrero (2004). "Processing Offenders in Texas Juvenile Courts: Trends and Patterns." Unpublished paper presented at the annual meeting of the American Society of Criminology, November (Nashville, TN).

Williams, Jimmy J. (1995a). "Race of Appellant, Sentencing Guidelines, and Decisionmaking in Criminal Appeals: A Research Note." *Journal of Criminal Justice* **23**:83–91.

Williams, Jimmy J. (1995b). "Type of Counsel and the Outcome of Criminal Appeals: A Research Note." *American Journal of Criminal Justice* **19**:275–285.

Williams, M. R., and J. E. Holcomb (2004). "The Interactive Effects of Victim Race and Gender on Death Penalty Disparity Findings." *Homicide Studies* **8**:350–376.

Williams, L. Susan, Delores E. Craig-Moreland, and A. Elizabeth Cauble (2004). "Chivalry Revisited: The Case of Girls in Rural Areas." Unpublished paper presented at the annual meeting of the American Society of Criminology, November (Nashville, TN).

Williamson, Deborah, Michelle Chalk, and Paul Knepper (1993). "Teen Court: Juvenile Justice for the 21st Century?" *Federal Probation* **57**:54–58.

Wilmot, Keith Alan (2002). *Prosecutorial Discretion and Real Offense Sentencing Under the Federal Sentencing Guidelines: An Analysis of Relevant Conduct.* Ann Arbor, MI: University Microfilms International.

Wilmot, Keith Alan, and Cassia C. Spohn (2004). "Prosecutorial Discretion and Real-Offense Sentencing: An Analysis of Relevant Conduct Under the Federal Sentencing Guidelines." *Criminal Justice Policy Review* **15**:324–343.

Winston, Norma A., and William E. Winston (1980). "The Use of Sociological Techniques in the Jury Selection Process." *National Journal of Criminal Defense* **6**:79–97.

Wood, William R. (2004). "Defining Success in Juvenile Restorative Justice: A Community Based Approach in Clark County, WA." Unpublished paper presented at the annual meeting of the American Society of Criminology, November (Nashville, TN).

Wooldredge, John, and Tim Griffin (2004). "Neighborhood Level Disparities in Court Dispositions Before and After the Implementation of Sentencing Guidelines in Ohio." Unpublished paper presented at the annual meeting of the American Society of Criminology, November (Nashville, TN).

Worden, Alissa Pollitz (1995). "The Judge's Role in Plea Bargaining: An Analysis of Judges' Agreement with Prosecutor's Sentencing Recommendations." *Justice Quarterly* **12:**257–278.

Worling, James R. (1995). "Adolescent Sex Offenders Against Females: Differences Based on the Age of Their Victims." *International Journal of Offender Therapy and Comparative Criminology* **39:**276–293.

Xenos, Nicholas (ed.) (2003). "Restorative Justice." *Polity* 36:1–90.

Zalman, Marvin (2004). "The Adversary Jury Trial and Wrongful Conviction." Unpublished paper presented at the annual meeting of the American Society of Criminology, November (Nashville, TN).

Zaragoza, Maria S. (1995). *Memory and Testimony in the Child Witness.* Thousand Oaks, CA: Sage.

Cases Cited Index

Name Index

Subject Index

655

General pretrial publicity,
548–549
General sessions courts, 37
General trial courts, 56
Gennessee County Sheriff's
Department, 285
Geographic jurisdiction, 37–38
defined, 37
Get-tough movement,
404–405, 475
Gilmore, Gary, 48, 440
Ginsburg, Ruth Bader, 185
Gloria, Braulio (career
snapshot), 377–378
Going rates and plea
bargaining, 305, 318
Goldman, Ronald, 13, 141
Good faith exception, 185
Good-time, 406
Good-time credit, 406–407
defined, 406
determinate sentencing,
406–407
Graham, Fred, 381
Grand juries, 78–79, 86, 217,
276–277
actions, 277
history, 217
overwhelming with
inculpatory evidence, 86
Green, Nicholas St. John, 559
Grievance stage, 9
Group homes, 482
Guardians ad litem, 489
Guidelines-based sentencing,
407–414
defined, 407
Guilty but mentally ill (GMI),
277
Guilty plea acceptance form,
328
Guilty pleas, 279, 306

H

Habeas corpus petitions, 118,
246, 416, 443–450
defined, 443
functions, 443
numbers filed, 450
Habitual offender statutes, 316,
336–337, 415–419

defined, 416
offenders profiled, 416–417
Harmful errors, 203
defined, 203
Harmless error, 92
Harmless error doctrine, 93,
131
defined, 93
Harrisburg Seven, 229
Hauptmann, Bruno Richard,
540, 542
Hierarchical jurisdiction, 38
defined, 38
Hill, Anita, 184
Hinckley, John, 143
Holmes, Jr., Oliver Wendell,
20, 559
Home confinement, 333
Hull House, 477

I

Ignorance, 146–147
Illinois Bar Association, 202
Illinois Juvenile Court Act of
1899, 476–477
Impartial arbiters, 284–285
defined, 284
Impeaching witnesses,
375–376
Impeachment, 206–207,
375–376
defined, 206, 375–376
Implicit plea bargaining,
317–324
Inadmissible evidence, 91–92
Incapacitation, 403
sentencing, 403
Inculpatory evidence, 73, 75
Incumbent judges, 182
Indeterminate sentencing, 347,
405–406
defined, 405
extralegal factors, 406
Indian General Crimes
Act, 92
Indictments, 78–79, 276–277,
454
incriminating nature of, 454
Indigent defendants, 109–110,
453, 487
juveniles, 487

Ineffective assistance of
counsel, 112–121, 138,
449
defined, 118–121, 449
reasonableness standard,
126, 449
Informations, 79, 276
Initial appearance, 266–267
defined, 266
Innocence Project, 455
Intake, 480
Intake hearings, 480
Intake officer, 480
functions, 480
Intensive supervised probation,
333
Interim judges, 182
Intermediate courts of appeal,
58
Intermittent sentencing, 437
Interviewing witnesses,
76–77
Intoxication, 143
Investigative grand juries,
277
Isolation as cruel and unusual
punishment, 444
Ito, Judge Lance, 539

J

Jail as a condition of probation,
437
Jamails, Joe, 554–555
James, Flemming, 559
Jencks materials, 139
Johnson, Lyndon B., 542
Judges, 159–207
court delays, 204
criticisms, 203–205
disparate sentencing,
204–205
federal selection methods,
184–198
gender bias, 163, 168,
330–331
incompetence, 203–204
politicalization of judicial
selection, 163–165
rejecting guilty pleas in plea
bargaining, 336
qualifications, 159–165